A Historical and Legal Study of Sovereignty in the Canadian North

NORTHERN LIGHTS SERIES

COPUBLISHED WITH THE ARCTIC INSTITUTE OF NORTH AMERICA
ISSN 1701-0004 (PRINT) ISSN 1925-2943 (ONLINE)

This series takes up the geographical region of the North (circumpolar regions within the zone of discontinuous permafrost) and publishes works from all areas of northern scholarship, including natural sciences, social sciences, earth sciences, and the humanities.

No. 1 · **Nunavik: Inuit-Controlled Education in Arctic Quebec** Ann Vick-Westgate · Copublished with the Katutjiniq Regional Development Council

No. 2 · **Many Faces of Gender: Roles and Relationships through Time in Northern Indigenous Communities** Edited by Lisa Frink, Rita S. Shepard, and Gregory A. Reinhardt · Copublished with University Press of Colorado

No. 3 · **New Owners in their Own Land: Minerals and Inuit Land Claims** Robert McPherson

No. 4 · **War North of 80: The Last German Arctic Weather Station of World War II** Wilhelm Dege, translated and edited by William Barr · Copublished with University Press of Colorado

No. 5 · **Writing Geographical Exploration: Thomas James and the Northwest Passage 1631–33** Wayne K.D. Davies

No. 6 · **As Long as This Land Shall Last: A History of Treaty 8 and Treaty 11, 1870–1939** René Fumoleau

No. 7 · **Breaking Ice: Renewable Resource and Ocean Management in the Canadian North** Edited by Fikret Berkes, Rob Huebert, Helen Fast, Micheline Manseau, and Alan Diduck

No. 8 · **Alliance and Conflict: The World System of the Inupiaq Eskimos** Ernest S. Burch · Copublished with the University of Nebraska Press

No. 9 · **Tanana and Chandalar: The Alaska Field Journals of Robert A. McKennan** Edited by Craig Mishler and William E. Simeone · Copublished with University of Alaska Press

No. 10 · **Resurrecting Dr. Moss: The Life and Letters of a Royal Navy Surgeon, Edward Lawton Moss, MD, RN, 1837–1880** Paul C. Appleton, edited by William Barr

No. 11 · **Lands that Hold One Spellbound: A Story of East Greenland** Spencer Apollonio

No. 12 · **Biocultural Diversity and Indigenous Ways of Knowing: Human Ecology in the Arctic** Karim-Aly S. Kassam

No. 13 · **Arctic Scientist, Gulag Survivor: The Biography of Mikhail Mikhailovich Ermolaev, 1905–1991** A.M. Ermolaev and V.D. Dibner, translated and edited by William Barr

No. 14 · **The Reindeer Botanist: Alf Erling Porsild, 1901–1977** Wendy Dathan

No. 15 · **The Fast-Changing Arctic: Rethinking Arctic Security for a Warmer World** Edited by Barry Scott Zellen

No. 16 · **Shipwreck at Cape Flora: The Expeditions of Benjamin Leigh Smith, England's Forgotten Arctic Explorer** P.J. Capelotti

No. 17 · **A Historical and Legal Study of Sovereignty in the Canadian North: Terrestrial Sovereignty, 1870–1939** Gordon W. Smith, edited by P. Whitney Lackenbauer

A Historical and Legal Study of Sovereignty in the Canadian North

Terrestrial Sovereignty, 1870–1939

Gordon W. Smith
Edited by P. Whitney Lackenbauer

Northern Lights Series
ISSN 1701-0004 (Print) ISSN 1925-2943 (Online)

University of Calgary Press
2500 University Drive NW
Calgary, Alberta
Canada T2N 1N4
www.uofcpress.com

LIBRARY AND ARCHIVES CANADA CATALOGUING IN PUBLICATION

Smith, Gordon W., 1918-2000, author
A historical and legal study of sovereignty in the Canadian north : terrestrial sovereignty, 1870–1939 / Gordon W. Smith ; edited by P. Whitney Lackenbauer.

(Northern lights series, 1701-0004 ; no. 17)

Co-published by the Arctic Institute of North America.
Includes bibliographical references and index.
Issued in print and electronic formats.
ISBN 978-1-55238-720-7 (pbk.) —ISBN 978-1-55238-774-0 (open access pdf).—
ISBN 978-1-55238-776-4 (epub).—ISBN 978-1-55238-775-7 (pdf).—
ISBN 978-1-55238-777-1 (mobi)

1. Canada, Northern—International status—History. 2. Jurisdiction, Territorial—Canada, Northern—History. 3. Sovereignty—History. 4. Canada, Northern—History. 5. Canada—Foreign relations—1867-1918. 6. Canada—Foreign relations—1918-1945. I. Lackenbauer, P. Whitney, editor II. Arctic Institute of North America, issuing body III. Title. IV. Series: Northern lights series ; no. 17

FC3956.S58 2014 971.9 C2014-902964-0
C2014-902965-9

The University of Calgary Press acknowledges the support of the Government of Alberta through the Alberta Media Fund for our publications. We acknowledge the financial support of the Government of Canada through the Canada Book Fund for our publishing activities. We acknowledge the financial support of the Canada Council for the Arts for our publishing program.

Canadä

Canada Council for the Arts Conseil des Arts du Canada

Printed and bound in Canada by Marquis
This book is printed on FSC Silva Enviro paper
Cover design, page design, and typesetting by Melina Cusano

Contents

Foreword: Gordon W. Smith

Tom W. Smith and Nell Smith

Gordon Ward Smith is our uncle and we are the trustees of his life's work, A Historical and Legal Study of Sovereignty in the Canadian North and Related Law of the Sea Problems.

We, like him, love Canada and wish to act only in Canada's best interest. By making this work available to scholars and policy makers, we honour and acknowledge his legacy, represented by this comprehensive body of scrupulous research and unfailing historical accuracy that only a historian of Gordon's calibre could have produced.

Who was this man who devoted most of his life to his craft, literally until his last breath? What motivated him to work diligently on his own for many years, without compensation?

For answers we need to go back to his birth and early years.

Gordon was the middle child and second son born on 22 June 1918 to Sedalia, Alberta, homesteaders Tom Whiting Smith and Elizabeth Ward Smith. His parents had arrived in Canada from England to homestead and develop a farm in east central Alberta where they raised cattle and grew grain. His father became well known in the district for his skills with steam engines, while his mother supplemented the family income with the meagre earnings of a one-room-school teacher during the 1920s and the Depression of the 1930s. Gordon and his siblings were among the dozen or so children who were educated solely by his mother from Grades 1 through 9. During the week they lived in a small home built by their father next to the school. The children were called upon to help their mother keep the home and school heated and maintained, returning to the farm on weekends to help their father do farm chores. The Smith children lived frugally and worked hard but also had fun with their schoolmates, who were like an extended family. They met the challenge of tough economic times, coming up with their own fun and games, swimming in local sloughs and dams, and wearing homemade costumes in the annual school play that entertained the whole community.

Under his mother's tutelage, Gordon excelled in school, while she took pains to refrain from showing him any favouritism. As a young boy, Gordon was enthralled with Arctic exploration and read many books about British explorers that had been sent to him by his English relatives. While many of his classmates quit school after Grade 9, Gordon continued his education in Consort, where he boarded with the high school principal, R. Ross Annett, a First World War veteran and prolific short story writer about family life on a Depression-era farm. Annett mentored Gordon and taught him to write in a simple and direct style. Despite almost dying of a burst appendix in Grade 12 and missing most of the school year, Gordon managed to graduate with first class honours. Following in his mother's and his mentor's footsteps, he went on to become a teacher himself, graduating from the Calgary Normal School with a Teaching Certificate in 1936. He taught in several rural Alberta schools before becoming principal of a two-room school at Esther, Alberta.

At the outbreak of the Second World War, Gordon itched to join the war effort but was disappointed when he was rejected because of poor eyesight. Circumventing the system, Gordon decided to attend the University of Alberta and join the Canadian Officers Training Program instead. Then, in 1944, upon earning his Bachelor of Arts degree with a history major, he was finally able to join the armed forces and was serving as a lieutenant at a prisoner of war camp in Lethbridge, Alberta, when the war ended.

During his student years at the U of A, Gordon had his only experience exploring the North in person when, in 1943, he took a summer job working on the wartime Canol Project in the Northwest Territories.

As a military veteran, Gordon was fortunate to qualify for veterans' education funding. He returned to the U of A and earned his Master's degree in history in 1948. His appetite fully whetted for higher learning, he continued his studies at Columbia University in New York, where John Bartlet Brebner, author of the *North Atlantic Triangle* (1945), was Gordon's thesis supervisor. Through Brebner, he gained access to the Explorers Club, to meet people such as Vilhjalmur Stefansson, and to use Stefansson's own library. In 1952 he obtained his PhD degree in British History with his thesis "The Historical and Legal Background of Canada's Arctic Claims." This is still considered a definitive work on the subject.

Gordon's passion to study and document the history of Canada's Arctic claims, both terrestrial and maritime, never abated and consumed the remaining years of his life.

His first job upon graduation, however, was at Collège militaire royale de St. Jean (CMR) in the province of Quebec, where he was employed as a history professor from 1953 to 1962. Among his students at CMR were noted historians Jack Granatstein and Desmond Morton and national archivist Ian Wilson. He joined in extra-curricular activities, becoming the boxing team coach, building on a skill he had honed while boxing in the granary with his father and brother. He also indulged in his love of opera, which he had developed while a PhD student in New York, where he frequently attended the Metropolitan Opera.

After leaving CMR, Gordon worked from 1962 to 1964 on contract to the Arctic Institute of North America. Then, not quite done with teaching, he followed his interest in the history and culture of other countries by working on contract with the Canadian International Development Agency as a professor at the University of Trinidad and Tobago (1964–66) and the University of Malawi (1966–68), teaching courses in all areas of world history, an accomplishment that he felt proud to have achieved.

When Gordon returned to Canada in 1968, he also returned to the pioneer work he had done in the study of polar regions, a study that crossed national and disciplinary boundaries.

This began with a surprising event: the 1969 crossing of the Northwest Passage by the American icebreaking tanker SS *Manhattan*. This was done without seeking prior permission from the Canadian government and caused nationwide controversy. It prompted the Department of External Affairs in Ottawa to contract Gordon to research *Arctic Sovereignty and Related Problems of Maritime Law* and resulted in a nine-volume internal report in 1973.

With this report, Gordon knew that he had barely touched the surface of the massive records that had been produced by the departments of National Defence, External Affairs, Fisheries and Oceans, and Indian Affairs and Northern Development. Also relevant were files from the British Government, the Hudson's Bay Company, the Royal Canadian Mounted Police, the Law Library of the University of Ottawa, the National Library, Library of Parliament, Supreme Court Library, and records in the National Archives, to all of which he gained privileged access over the course of many years.

In addition to his research in Ottawa he did research in New York, Montreal, London, Oxford, Moscow, Oslo, and Washington, DC.

Pleading his case for further funding to complete his initial study, Gordon was granted intermittent contracts by the Department of Indian Affairs and Northern Development until 1981. After that time, Gordon was granted no further contracts. Even then, he knew his work was not yet done.

Driven to complete the manuscript he had started, he soldiered onward on his own, living on Canada Pension Plan funds and his own savings until he died in 2000 at age eighty-two. To facilitate his continued research and writing, he was tenacious in maintaining his privileged access to the records of many government departments and, because of security, had office space in several of them as well as a cubicle in the National Archives of Canada.

Gordon was a man of routine in all areas of his life and lived very frugally. He maintained a five-day work week that started early every morning and extended well into evening each day. He followed a regime of consulting the paper records in the offices of the varied government departments that he had access to by commuting from his Ottawa apartment on foot or by bus, as he never owned or operated a vehicle. A productive, satisfying day would result in one handwritten page of text and two pages of footnotes, as he was adamant on being 100 percent accurate in his research, fully verifying each entry from all the sources available to him. His day would end close to or after midnight.

In addition to his devotion to work, Gordon had a variety of interests. He enjoyed entertaining friends with dinner parties that he would execute with a great deal of planning and preparation. While he did not own a television, he enjoyed listening to the radio (he was a fan of CBC's Clyde Gilmour) and his collection of opera and music of many kinds. For many years he was a patron of the Ottawa Film Society. Baseball was another huge interest – he followed professional teams, especially the Montreal Expos, and could quote historical statistics that many others had long forgotten. He kept in touch with his roots with a subscription to the weekly *Consort Enterprise* from Alberta. He granted himself two holidays each year: two weeks for rest and relaxation in North Bay, Ontario, and the period between Christmas and New Year's Day, listening to music and reading his extensive collection of Agatha Christie mysteries. On a number of occasions he joined our family for Christmas, to celebrate the holiday with his nephew and niece-in-law and his grand-nieces and nephew.

In this scheduled, painstaking way, the written history of Canada's sovereignty in the North continued to grow bit by bit over the next thirty years. Gordon's goal was to complete his study up to the signing of the 1982 Convention on the Law of the Sea, including the historical and legal aspects of Canada's sovereignty claim over the lands and waters of the Arctic. Sadly, this was never to be completed before he died. There was always more information to consult, verify, and update. He set himself an almost impossible task in the days before computers, electronic databases, the Internet, and search engines became everyday tools that would have facilitated his research. He did this background study of incalculable value completely on his own. The undertaking is equivalent to a Royal Commission, an idea that had been considered and that would have warranted several additional experts plus support staff at a great deal of expense to Canada.

Throughout the arduous task Gordon assigned himself, he gained the respect and friendship of other experts in the field, in particular Dr. Donat Pharand and Léonard Legault. These two valued colleagues have become part of an Advisory Group we created to ensure Gordon's manuscript would be made accessible to government and scholars who would benefit from his meticulous and massive research. Dr. Pharand, aided by Mr. Legault, has been instrumental in examining and providing expert comments on concerns raised by Foreign Affairs on confidential aspects of the manuscript. Another key member of the Advisory Group was Tom's brother Bill. He undertook the major tasks of arranging and coordinating the archiving of Gordon's material, having the manuscript typed from the thousands of pages of handwritten notes, and extensive liaison with the Department of Foreign Affairs and other government entities. A fourth key member of the Advisory Group is Gordon's long-time friend since her childhood, Jeannette Tramhel. Jeannette was entrusted with managing all of Gordon's collection stored in his apartment during the archiving and typing operation as well as authoring a memorial tribute to Gordon in *The Canadian Yearbook of International Law* 2001. We continue to value her expertise and advice on all aspects of this project.

Professionally, Gordon had an extensive network of contacts, was a member of The Arctic Circle, the American Historical Society, the Canadian Institute of International Affairs, and Friends of the National Archives. Among others, he made presentations to The Arctic Circle in Ottawa and the Royal Commission on Aboriginal Peoples.

In the words of his friend and colleague, Dr. Donat Pharand, "Gordon W. Smith will be remembered as a man of exceptional qualities, both as a person and as a scholar."

Selected Publications by Gordon W. Smith

Governmental Publications

Territorial Sovereignty in the Canadian North: A Historical Outline of the Problem. Northern Co-ordination and Research Centre, Department of Northern Affairs and National Resources, Ottawa, Ontario, Canada (July 1963), NCRC-63-7.

The Permanent Joint Board on Defense and the North during World War II. Department of Indian Affairs and Northern Development (undated). Classified as "secret."

The Alaska Boundary Dispute. Department of Indian Affairs and Northern Development, Ottawa (1970).

Ice Islands in Arctic Waters. Department of Indian Affairs and Northern Development, Ottawa (1980). Classified as "secret."

Icebreakers and Icebreaking in Canadian Arctic Waters: The Canadian Coast Guard. Ottawa (1990).

Other Publications

"Sovereignty in the North: The Canadian Aspect of an International Problem," in R. St. J. Macdonald (ed.), *The Arctic Frontier.* University of Toronto Press, 1966.

"A Historical Summary of Maritime Exploration in the Canadian Arctic and Its Relevance in Connection with Subsequent and Recent Sovereignty Issues." Prepared for publication in the Proceedings of the International Commission of Maritime History, meeting in conjunction with the Thirteenth Congress of the International Committee for Historical Sciences in Moscow, August 1970.

"The Transfer of Arctic Territories from Great Britain to Canada in 1880, and some Related Matters, as seen in Official Correspondence," *Arctic: Journal of the Arctic Institute of North America* 14, no. 1 (1961).

"Canada's Arctic Archipelago: 100 Years of Canadian Jurisdiction. Part I. The Transfer." *North/Nord Magazine* (published by the Department of Indian and Northern Affairs) 27, no. 1 (Spring 1980).

"Canada's Arctic Archipelago: 100 Years of Canadian Jurisdiction. Part II. Making the North Canadian." *North/Nord* 27, no. 2 (Summer 1980).

"A Bit of Bernier." *North/Nord* 29, no. 2 (Summer 1982).

"The Falkland Islands Dispute: A Resume of its Background," 13 *Revue Général de Droit* 541 (1982).

Tom W. Smith and Nell Smith

Editor's Note

P. Whitney Lackenbauer

"Canada's Arctic is central to our national identity as a northern nation. It is part of our history. And it represents the tremendous potential of our future." Prime Minister Stephen Harper's message, delivered in July 2007, also suggested that "Canada has a choice when it comes to defending our sovereignty in the Arctic; either we use it or we lose it."[1] This statement reflects a context of tremendous uncertainty in the circumpolar world, with the ice cap shrinking in breadth and depth, permafrost melting, and indigenous flora and fauna changing. Questions abound about what these changes will mean for northern peoples, for transportation routes, for international boundaries, and for sovereignty, stability, and security in the circumpolar world. The prime minister, in his campaign speeches and announcements of major initiatives delivered in northern communities, has often repeated the message of "use it or lose it."[2] The line of argument is predicated on the idea that a more activist approach is necessary to defend Canada's national interests. Is Canada's sovereignty "on thinning ice"? As debate swirls around these questions, due to an allegedly impending "perfect storm" coalescing around climate change, a so-called "race" for arctic resources, and increased militarism in the Arctic,[3] Canadians should remember that scholars and policy makers have been grappling with these questions for decades. The Arctic is indeed part of our history, as the prime minister noted, and a robust understanding of sovereignty questions, policy, and practices should inform current scholarship and decision making.

As Gordon W. Smith's literary executors note in the Foreword, this dedicated scholar devoted most of his working life to the study of Arctic sovereignty issues. This massive study, which he completed in 1973, is not a typical narrative history written for a general audience. Rather, it is like a near-definitive sourcebook for its time, based upon decades of exhaustive research carefully accounted in meticulous detail and extensive direct quotations. The fact that he never published the manuscript in his lifetime is more a testament to his perfectionism and his continuous search for new information than evidentiary shortcomings. We hope that publishing Dr. Smith's main research findings, as he wrote them but with extensive editing to redact his material to manageable length, will establish his important place in the historiographical and policy landscape on Arctic sovereignty issues. Furthermore, we anticipate that making his writings available to students, scholars, and policy makers will serve as a strong basis for subsequent research into the development of Canada's sovereignty position through to the late 1940s.

A brief overview of the process that led to this book is warranted. In the year that followed Dr. Smith's death, his executors undertook to preserve the original manuscript of *A Historical and Legal Study of Sovereignty in the Canadian North and Related Law of the Sea Problems* in as proximate a manner as Dr. Smith would have ordered himself. It was compiled in accordance with his original outline and typed exactly as it was written. In 2008, the Department of Foreign Affairs and International Trade asked Professor Armand de Mestral, Jean Monnet Chair in the Law of International Economic Integration in the Faculty of Law at McGill University, and myself, an associate professor of Canadian history at St. Jerome's University at the University of Waterloo, to assess the value of Smith's work and the extent to which its sources remained classified, with an eye to the possibility of making it available to the public. We concur with an earlier academic and legal assessment that his source base for his writings on terrestrial sovereignty issues through to the late 1940s is now almost entirely in the public domain.

Dr. Smith's broad research "manuscript" is organized in two parts, with Part A dedicated to terrestrial sovereignty issues. Volume 1 of his work focuses on the early history of Canadian sovereignty in the North. It begins with the transfers of the northern territories to Canada in 1870 and 1880, their early organization and administration, their division into provisional districts by the Order in Council of 1895, and the boundary corrections that were necessary to organize and delimit these territories. The next section documents other activities by the Canadian government during this early period, such as expeditions in the former Hudson Bay Company lands, the early expeditions of Lieutenant Gordon to Hudson Bay and Strait, and other government expeditions to northern waters such as those by Wakeham, Low, Bernier, and Stefansson. The following six sections examine causes for Canadian concern over the status of the Northern Territories, namely, the Bering Sea fur seals dispute, the Yukon gold rush, the Alaska boundary dispute, foreign whalers, and explorers in the North during the period from about 1870 through 1918. Another section explains the sector principle and the background of Canada's sector claim, followed by the question of Danish sovereignty over Greenland and its relation to Canadian interests. The remaining two sections in the first volume look at Vilhjalmur Stefansson and his various plans for northern enterprises after the First World War, with special emphasis on the reindeer and muskox projects in the north.

Volumes 2 and 3 of Part A are concerned with the period between the First and Second World Wars. Critical events are described, such as the Ellesmere Island affair (1919–21), the Wrangel Island affair in the early 1920s, and the Krüger expedition (1930). Smith documented significant government activities in the North, such as the Eastern Arctic Patrol, the Royal Canadian Mounted Police, and other Canadian Government expeditions, surveys, investigations and patrols in the region. Sections also examine the question of sovereignty over the Sverdrup Islands, the activities of American explorers in the Canadian North from 1918 to 1939, and the Eastern Greenland case as it relates to Canada.

Subsequent volumes on terrestrial and maritime sovereignty deal with the period during and after the Second World War, and may be edited for publication in due course.

Overview of this Book

As Gordon Smith notes in the essay that we have included as the introduction to this book, explorers, fur traders, whalers, and missionaries were the only non-Aboriginal people active in the Arctic prior to the 1870s. The Hudson's Bay Company represented the only formal administration of any kind. In the first chapter, Smith describes and analyzes the two great transfers of 1870 and 1880, which made Canada responsible for half a continent. The territories of the Hudson's Bay Company, comprising Rupert's Land and the Northwest Territory, were surrendered to Great Britain in 1869, and Canada accepted them from Great Britain in 1870. All other British territories or territorial rights in the Arctic, involving approximately or ostensibly the archipelago, were handed over in 1880. In his careful analysis, Smith notes that in each case one form of British sovereignty was substituted for another, thus making the transfers binding upon British subjects, but not necessarily upon foreign states. Fortunately for Canada, no foreign state raised questions about the transfers.

Within a decade, the fledgling dominion had assumed responsibility for the northern half of North America, with the exception of Newfoundland, Alaska, and Greenland. With national attention dedicated to the settlement of the Prairie West, however, little to nothing was done regarding remote northern areas – and particularly the Arctic Archipelago – between 1880 and 1895. With no population or resource development pressures, the extension of "order and good government" to this region could wait for the future. In chapter 2, Smith explains the logic of Canadian inaction – and notes the modest expeditions and activities that did take place during this era.

Chapter 3 describes Canadian provisions for the organization and administration of its northernmost territories from 1895 to 1918. A Dominion order-in-council created the four provisional districts of Ungava, Yukon, Mackenzie, and Franklin – the latter of "indefinite extent" but including the archipelago. Subsequent measures were devised to demonstrate that these regions were under the effective control of the Canadian government, and to set new provincial boundaries that reduced the size of the Northwest Territories – but did not relinquish control over offshore islands to provincial jurisdictions.

The next series of chapters examines the activities of foreign states and nationals which contributed to Canada's growing concern over the status of its northern territories before 1914. Chapter 4 charts whaling disputes and questions related to the Klondike Gold Rush that complicated Canadian-American relations and generated sovereignty questions. The uninhibited and sometimes lawless behaviour of American whalers in Hudson Bay and in the Beaufort Sea provoked only a desultory and indecisive response at first, but eventually it provided one of the main reasons for a measure of carefully planned action calculated to preserve Canadian sovereignty in the North – particularly when news reached Ottawa that accused the whalers of debauching Inuit in both areas. Smith also shows how the rush to the Klondike, beginning in 1896, forced the Canadian government to grapple with the immense problem of maintaining law and order among hordes of foreign gold hunters. The North West Mounted Police and "a few capable and conscientious public servants" played a critical role in ensuring that "the difficult period of chaos and confusion was remarkably short," Smith explains, "and internally the Yukon was soon quiet and stable."

Determining the Yukon-Alaska boundary was less clear-cut. Chapter 5 provides a sober, sharply analytical, and comprehensive interpretation of the Alaska boundary dispute. The settlement of the dispute by arbitration in 1903 in favour of the United States did little to allay Canadian anxiety about American expansionist tendencies and the willingness of Great Britain to place Canadian interests over broader strategic ones. With a careful attentiveness to historical context and the legal arguments at play, Smith concludes that the heart of Canada's grievance actually related to Britain's concessions to Russia in the treaty of 1825, not American activities since 1867.

Chapter 6 charts the activities of foreign explorers in the Canadian North from 1878 to the end of the First World War. Their motives varied: searching for clues to the fate of the Franklin expedition, conducting scientific research, discovering unknown coasts and claiming islands for their home country, and completing the first transit of the Northwest Passage. These activities also generated sovereignty concerns. Norwegian explorer Otto Sverdrup discovered his namesake islands (comprising Axel Heiberg and the Ringnes Islands) during his 1898–1902 expedition and claimed them for Norway. His countryman Roald Amundsen took a ship through the Northwest Passage for the first time in 1903–6, exploring the unknown coastline of Victoria Island on the way. In his repeated attempts to reach the North Pole, American explorer Robert Peary used Ellesmere Island as his base. When he planted the American flag at or near the pole in 1909, he claimed "the entire region and adjacent" for the United States. On the whole, Smith leaves the strong impression that the Canadian authorities had some reason for concern over the situation in the Arctic territories over which they had recently assumed responsibility.

Chapter 7 documents Canadian government expeditions into northern waters from 1895 to the end of the First World War. This gradual "program of action," Smith explains, was "rather limited but nonetheless designed to solidify and consolidate Canadian sovereignty over the territories in question." The North West Mounted Police were sent to the Yukon, the Beaufort Sea region, and Hudson Bay, to "show the flag" and maintain law and order as an expression of sovereignty. Government expeditions commanded by William Wakeham in 1897, Albert Peter Low in 1903–4, Major John D. Moodie of the Mounted Police in 1904–5, and Joseph-Elzéar Bernier in 1906–7, 1908–9, and 1910–11, patrolled the waters of Hudson Bay and the eastern Arctic islands. Under government instructions they took note of all activities at the places visited, imposed licences upon Scottish and American whalers, collected customs duties upon goods brought into the region, conducted scientific research, and generally impressed upon both Inuit and *qallunaat* (non-Inuit) that they were expected to obey Canadian laws.

Wakeham, Low, and Bernier performed ceremonies of possession at various places, culminating with Bernier's proclamation on 1 July 1909 that Canada claimed the entire archipelago: "all islands and territory within the degrees 141 and 60 west longitude." This proclamation was in line with the sector principle enunciated by Senator Poirier in 1907 – the subject of chapter 8. Although the sector principle was not adopted officially at the time, Smith argues that it later became official in virtually every respect – except that it was never incorporated in a statute. Because Canada did not face outright resistance to these measures, Smith concluded that "during the decade or so before World War I it could fairly be said that the Far North, or at least the part of it frequented by white men, was being brought under Canadian jurisdiction."

During the war and immediately afterwards there was a general lapse of activity in the North, no doubt attributable to the exigencies of the war effort. A conspicuous exception was the Canadian Arctic Expedition under Vilhjalmur Stefansson, which operated in the western Arctic from 1913 to 1918. Stefansson took possession of several islands he discovered for Canada, as he was directed to do. After the war, he captivated North American audiences with his proclamations that the Arctic was destined to become a great "polar Mediterranean" because it offered the shortest air routes between the largest cities in the world. He also articulated various plans for northern enterprise, including the introduction of reindeer herds into the North American Arctic and the domestication of muskox. Both projects faced serious criticism at the time and after, and Stefansson's dreams were never realized – however much appeal they may have held in the 1920s. Smith notes that the principal figures dealing with pressing sovereignty issues were the same people involved in development plans, indirectly linking the two issues.

Government activity in the North resumed on a larger scale after the First World War. The immediate reason for the resumption of activity was Danish explorer Knud Rasmussen's apparently flat denial of Canadian sovereignty over Ellesmere Island, and the Danish government's apparent endorsement of his stance. When the Canadian government requested that Danish authorities restrain the killing of muskoxen by Greenland Inuit on Ellesmere Island, Rasmussen wrote that the only authority on the island was that which he exercised from his station at Thule, and that he needed no assistance whatever from the Canadian government. Stefansson, in an early articulation of a "use it or lose it doctrine," urged that if Canada did not occupy the northern islands of the archipelago she might lose them. Stefansson sought to organize an expedition for this purpose, but according to his own account the Canadian Cabinet split on the issue of whether he or Shackleton should lead it. In the end, the expedition did not materialize. "Fear about what Denmark might do in the archipelago was gradually replaced by concern over what Canada herself ought to do," Smith observed, leading the government to institute regular patrol voyages and establish RCMP posts to exercise its sovereignty. The government "made a very big issue out of what had turned out to be a very small one, and then had mishandled it by overreacting to presumed threats posed by Stefansson, Danes, and Americans," Smith concluded. "Regarding Stefansson in particular, senior officials in the civil service had been determined that they would not follow his lead, yet in some respects they had done so, naïvely if only temporarily, and had, as they saw it afterwards, been led down the garden path."

Stefansson's grand plans to colonize Wrangel Island, north of Siberia, reflected a similar pattern. The Canadian government, at first willing to support the initiative (but not willing to pay for it), retracted its support after one expedition met with disaster and the Russians forcibly removed a second. By 1925, the government reversed its initial stance that "Wrangel Island is part of the property of this country" when the Minister of the Interior declared that "we have no interest in Wrangel Island." Fortunately, the international damage to Canada was minimal. Russia made no attempt to retaliate for Canada's bad manners in the Wrangel Island affair, staying on her own side of the North Pole after it promulgated its own sector decree in 1926. Stefansson's reputation, however, was tainted by the disaster.

While the Canadian government took action to solidify its northern claims, other countries were losing interest. Denmark evidently let the issue of Ellesmere Island drop, and, at least tacitly, accepted Canadian sovereignty there. Lingering questions about Norwegian claims to the Sverdrup Islands, stemming from Sverdrup's 1898–1902 expedition, came to the surface after Norway inquired about the basis of Canada's rights to the island in 1924. Although this became tangled up with concerns about American interests in the Canadian Arctic Islands, Norway formally recognized Canadian sovereignty over the Sverdrup Islands in 1930. Later that year the Canadian government paid Sverdrup $67,000 for all his original maps, notes, diaries, and other documents relating to his expedition.

In March 1933, V. Kenneth Johnston argued in an article published in the *Canadian Historical Review* that foreign claims in the archipelago had disappeared and that Canada's own claim had been established. If any doubts remained, Gordon Smith argues in chapter 13, they were removed the following month by the Permanent Court of International Justice decision in the *Eastern Greenland Case* between Norway and Denmark. International law already indicated lessened requirements for sovereignty over remote, inaccessible, thinly settled or even uninhabited territories, and the *East Greenland* decision reinforced the trend. Smith noted that the analogy between Denmark's and Canada's Arctic territories was imperfect but strong, and he found it difficult to imagine how any international adjudication after 1933 could have denied recognition to Canada's title to the archipelago if it had been formally challenged in law.

Canada remained wary about the United States' interests in the North American Arctic, given the power asymmetry between the two countries. American newspapermen and international lawyers persisted in asking embarrassing questions about various aspects of Canada's Arctic sovereignty in the North. Although there was little official appetite in Washington to challenge Canadian claims to land territory, Smith notes that Ottawa officials still perceived "vague and ill-defined" possibilities of conflict with the United States. In the interwar years, the key controversies surrounded the American explorer Donald B. MacMillan. When he failed to secure the necessary permits before entering the archipelago to conduct scientific experiments in 1925, Canadian authorities submitted an official protest to the American government. MacMillan acquiesced and complied with licensing requirements during his expeditions of 1926, 1927, and 1928. "In sum, it would appear that during the 1920s and early 1930s the Canadian Government gradually succeeded in imposing its wishes and its regulations upon American explorers who wanted to conduct their operations on and among the Canadian arctic islands," Smith concluded. The tempo of American Arctic exploration activity declined in the 1930s, pushing to the back burner any lingering suspicions about whether the United States accepted of all of Canada's Arctic claims. It would take the Second World War to "put Canadian-American relations respecting the North, and accompanying problems, on a completely different footing."

The final chapter documents how Canada reconstituted ship patrols of the eastern Arctic in the old tradition of Low and Bernier, now on an annual basis, in 1922. Smith provides an invaluable summary of the Eastern Arctic Patrol expeditions through the interwar years, as well as Royal Canadian Mounted Police's legal activities during this era. The government expanded the Mounted Police permanent presence along the Arctic coast and on the Arctic islands, although in many situations they had no one but themselves to police. As Smith documents, their main activity was mounting long patrols around the islands of the high Arctic, showing the flag to demonstrate a Canadian presence.

From a strict international legal reading, Smith's verdict that Canada's terrestrial sovereignty position was secure by the end of the 1930s is reassuring. During and after the Second World War, however, Canadian officials again grappled with perceived sovereignty concerns when the Americans renewed their interests in the Canadian North for continental security reasons. While Canada's sovereignty over the islands of the Arctic Archipelago remained unchallenged, the status of the waters between the islands (the Northwest Passage) and within the Canadian "sector" more generally remained more contentious.

Research on the periods covered by Dr. Smith has grown substantially since he compiled his research. Rather than trying to integrate additional secondary sources into references throughout the text, I have appended a list of further readings that provides readers with a sampling of scholarship on subjects covered in this book that has appeared in the past three decades. Furthermore, careful readers will note that Dr. Smith gleaned most of his material from Canadian and British sources. As historians Janice Cavell and Jeff Noakes (both of whom had access to Smith's work as government researchers) demonstrate in their book *Acts of Occupation*, supplementing his research with evidence from other archives yields rich results. Accordingly, I hope that researchers view Dr. Smith's valuable work as a foundation for future study rather than a "definitive" account of the themes and events that he narrated and analyzed.

In general, I have retained the original language that Dr. Smith used in his writings. Nevertheless, the text has been extensively edited for spelling, grammar, and style (although I have left much of the passive voice that marked Smith's writings), and I have cut and removed sections to improve flow and to reduce repetition across chapters. Furthermore, I have updated his 1973 discussion of the 1895 Colonial Boundaries Act in light of his subsequent article in the magazine *Nord* (which historian Shelagh Grant kindly brought to my attention), and substantively reworked his draft sections on the Royal Canadian Mounted Police and miscellaneous scientific expeditions in chapter 15. Dr. Smith generally referenced individuals by their last name (sometimes with initials), and I have endeavoured to include full names where possible.

The author's writing style and turns of phrase reflect the era in which he researched and wrote. For example, his original manuscripts included the terms "Indian" and "Eskimo," which were still in common usage when he drafted the chapters. I have replaced these with "First Nations," "Inuit," and "Aboriginal peoples" in light of current norms. Some readers may be surprised that the manuscript does not examine Inuit use/governance as it relates to Canada's "international" sovereignty position. This is also a reflection of the time period in which Dr. Smith conducted his research, and readers are encouraged to engage other scholarly literature to learn more about this issue.

In preparing this manuscript for publication, I owe special thanks to several organizations and people. The ArcticNet project on the Emerging Arctic Security Environment and a St. Jerome's University faculty research grant supported research assistance and travel to Ottawa to verify sources, and Federation for the Humanities and Social Sciences' Awards to Scholarly Publications Program and St. Jerome's University Aid to Scholarly Publishing grants facilitated publication. Publication support came from research assistants Thirstan Falconer, Kristopher Kinsinger, Mark Sweeney, and Sheau Vong assisted with formatting, endnotes, and the bibliography. Peter Kikkert and Daniel Heidt helped to verify that various sources were unclassified and in the public domain. Janice Cavell, Shelagh Grant, and Ted McDorman suggested improvements (and additional sources), as did two helpful peer reviewers. Jennifer Arthur-Lackenbauer prepared maps and offered editorial suggestions, and Adam Lajeunnesse prepared the index. Finally, and foremost, thanks to Tom and Nell Smith for their patience and their dedication to seeing Gordon W. Smith's lifelong commitment to understanding Canada's Arctic sovereignty through to publication.

Introduction: Terrestrial Sovereignty before 1870

The question of sovereignty in the polar regions has fascinated international lawyers and bedevilled statesmen for years. The main reason is obvious enough: the unique physical, climatic, and demographic characteristics of the polar regions seem to forbid the application of normal rules of international law and to defy the creation of others. The issues involved are thus basically legal, but they are also political and diplomatic. Some are now of only historic and academic interest, while others are still significant. Until fairly recent times the major concern was with sovereignty over land territory, but, in the Arctic at least, this matter appears now to be essentially settled, and other questions involving territorial waters, ice islands, undersurface navigation of submarines, and airspace have come to the fore. In the Antarctic, the land issue has not been permanently resolved, but the interested states have by treaty put this and other problems "on ice" for a period of at least thirty-four years. The following pages attempt to summarize the Canadian aspect of the historic issues.

Some Legal and Historical Background

International law recognizes a number of basic modes of acquiring territory. Oppenheim's classification, perhaps the best known, includes five: cession, occupation, accretion, subjugation, and prescription.[1] In addition, the supplementary doctrines of continuity, contiguity, the hinterland, and the watershed have sometimes been invoked in support of territorial claims, and under certain circumstances may have weight. Papal grants, important in earlier times, have fallen into disuse; but discovery, although rather unlikely now on this planet, has been considered even by modern authorities to give an "inchoate" or temporary title, which must be perfected subsequently by other means. There is also that curious principle or theory of sectors, which has been put forward

Editor's Note: This introduction is extracted from Smith's chapter "Sovereignty in the North: The Canadian Aspect of an International Problem," in *The Arctic Frontier*, ed. R. St. J. Macdonald (Toronto: University of Toronto Press, 1966), which he completed in fall 1963 based upon a paper delivered at the annual meeting of the Canadian Political Science Association in Quebec City on 8 June 1963.

specifically for the polar regions. Without going into detail, it would appear that of the foregoing, the ones most likely to be invoked in Canada's case, validly or otherwise, are cession, occupation, prescription, contiguity, discovery, and the sector principle.

One well-known authority on the subject says that acquisitions of new territory were based mainly upon papal grants up to the sixteenth century, upon priority of discovery for the next two hundred years, and thereafter upon effective possession. He adds that effective possession was first advocated in theory and later required in fact.[2] His division may be too categorical. Another authority suggests that effective possession has always been important,[3] and, as just noted, discovery may still give at least an inchoate title. Also, although effective possession was laid down as a requirement at the Berlin Conference on Africa in 1884–85 for the acquisition of new territories in that continent,[4] a series of later legal settlements would seem to have modified the requirement, at least where such modification has been warranted by the circumstances. These observations provide an outline of the legal framework in which the history of the sovereignty problem may be discussed, in relation to Canada's Arctic territories.

Rights of sovereignty in any territory are likely to be based to a large extent upon the record of human activity therein. In the case of the Canadian Northland this record may be broadly divided into three phases, of which only two are of particular relevance here. Up to about 1500 AD, the only peoples to enter the region were First Nations and Inuit, and, to a lesser extent, Norsemen. During the middle period, from approximately 1500 to the third quarter of the nineteenth century, Aboriginal people were joined by white explorers, fur traders, whalers, and missionaries, and a number of territorial claims were made. With the transfers of 1870 and 1880, Canada assumed full responsibility for these territories, and in the period following undertook to bring them under her jurisdiction. For the purpose of this essay the first period may be disregarded. Although the First Nations and Inuit may have been monarchs of all they surveyed in ancient times, the white man pushed aside their "sovereignty" upon his arrival.[5] The Norsemen, whose wanderings in what is now Canada are still only vaguely known, established no permanent settlements,[6] and in modern times neither Norwegian nor Danish claims in the Canadian Arctic attempted to derive any benefit from their voyages.

With the Columbian discovery of America a new phase begins. The first post-Columbian explorer to land on the northeastern coast was evidently John Cabot, in 1497, and the first to land in the archipelago was Martin Frobisher, in 1576. During the three hundred years after Frobisher, the main geographical outlines of the North, both continental and insular, were gradually filled in, except for those of the more remote islands north of Lancaster Sound. For almost the whole period, exploration was concentrated mainly upon the goal of a northwest passage, and proceeded in a series of waves, each stopping before being succeeded by another. During the first years after the initial discoveries, in the time of the Cabots and their contemporaries, a vague familiarity with the coasts of Newfoundland, Labrador, and south Greenland was acquired. Frobisher and his immediate successors Davis, Hudson, Baffin, and others, collectively penetrated into Davis Strait, Baffin Bay, Hudson Strait, and Hudson Bay. After the founding of the Hudson's Bay Company in 1670, fur traders pushed on to the northwestern extremity of Hudson Bay by water and across the northwestern interior overland to the Arctic and Pacific Oceans. After a lapse following the great expeditions of Alexander Mackenzie, exploration began again in 1818, and during the next thirty years the Rosses, Parry, Franklin, Richardson, Back, Beechey, Simpson, and Rae practically finished tracing the Arctic coast and also became acquainted with the lands adjacent to some of the principal water passages. Later, the search for the lost Franklin expedition and repeated efforts to reach the rumoured open polar sea and the North Pole greatly extended knowledge of the region. By the time of the transfers the larger islands were all known, with the exception of those discovered afterwards by Sverdrup and Stefansson.

It was common practice for explorers to claim the lands they discovered on behalf of their monarchs. Thus, John Cabot was authorized by Henry VII of England to "conquer, occupy, and possess" lands unknown to other Christians,[7] and Martin Frobisher claimed "Meta Incognita" in Frobisher Bay for Queen Elizabeth at his first arrival, ordering his crew to bring him "whatsoever thing they could first finde, whether it were living or dead, stocke or stone, in token of Christian possession."[8] The pattern established by the early explorers was generally followed thereafter, even into the twentieth century, and thus claims to territory were numerous indeed. Attempts were often made to fortify rights of discovery by symbolic acts of appropriation, such as the raising of flags, the erection of crosses or cairns, the reading of proclamations, and the depositing of records. Whether symbolic acts of appropriation helped greatly in establishing title to land has often been questioned by authorities on international law, but the practice was universal. The authors of a detailed study on the subject have concluded that they were by no means without value, and in earlier times were considered to enhance mere rights of discovery.[9] Obviously discoveries and annexations were not all of equal force; an official annexation of newly discovered land at the direction and on behalf of a monarch or government would carry more weight than the unauthorized and unsupported claim of a private explorer. Obviously, too, a state would be likely to magnify the value of its own claims and pay as little heed as possible to those of others.

It is conspicuous that in what is now the Canadian Arctic, practically all the expeditions, discoveries, and claims prior to about the mid-nineteenth century were British. The most important exceptions were French voyages in Hudson Bay prior to the conquest, especially at the time of Pierre Le Moyne d'Iberville. There was also the expedition of the Dane Jens Munk to Hudson Bay in 1619, during which he claimed "New Denmark" for his monarch Christian IV.[10] However, nothing was done to follow up his claim. Some of the British claims were also ineffective, such as Frobisher's to south Greenland in 1578[11] and Cook's to the Alaskan territory around Cook Inlet in 1778.[12] Others were invalid, such as Simpson's at Point Barrow in 1837[13] and Moore's to small islands nearby in 1850.[14] These territories had been placed outside Britain's orbit by the British-Russian treaty of 1825, which established the 141st meridian as the common frontier.[15] After 1850, foreign explorers, mostly American, aided in the Franklin search and undertook independently to reach the supposed open polar sea and the North Pole. Their interests were generally non-political, however, and they made few outright claims to land. An exception, perhaps, was Hall's raising of the American flag in Frobisher Bay in 1861, which, judging from his narrative, may have been intended to show American possession.[16] On the whole, the activities of the predominantly British explorers were of considerable importance, because they provided the main basis for the assumption by the British government in the 1870s that Britain had certain territorial rights in the archipelago which could be transferred to Canada.

The Hudson's Bay Company was the principal authority in the regions north of Canada for two hundred years following the granting of its charter by Charles II in 1670. There is no doubt that the charter was intended to make the Governor and Company "true and absolute lords and proprietors" of Rupert's Land. It specified their authority over certain matters, such as land, trade, lawmaking, immigration, and settlement, and its wording indicates the Crown's intention that they should be sovereign in all respects whatsoever, excepting only the obligation of allegiance to the Crown itself. Unfortunately, although the charter attempted to define the territories it granted, the state of geographical knowledge at the time did not permit this to be done with precision. This circumstance, along with doubts as to the charter's validity, exposed the company to continual attack, from the French colony to the south until 1763, from other fur interests based on Montreal until 1821, and from the two Canadas, separate or united, until Confederation.

Rivalry with the French colony began with the founding of the company, and continued intermittently for almost a hundred years. During the Wars of the League of Augsburg and the Spanish Succession, the French dominated Hudson Bay and captured the company's posts, but these advantages were lost when France renounced all claims to the Hudson Bay region in the Treaty of Utrecht in 1713.[17] Troubles continued, however, partly because of the still unsettled boundary between Rupert's Land and the French colony, and also because of the French attempt, led by the Verendryes, to move into the region southwest of Hudson Bay. The surrender of New France in 1763 ended for all time the French threat to Rupert's Land.[18] Almost immediately another challenge appeared, in the form of English-speaking interlopers from Scotland and New England, who established themselves in Montreal and employed experienced French-Canadian voyageurs in an energetic prosecution of the western fur trade. During the first two decades of the nineteenth century the Hudson's Bay Company waged a life-and-death struggle against the Montreal interests, now consolidated into the North-West Company, and triumphed when the strife was ended in 1821 by an amalgamation that really constituted a victory for the older company. A further triumph for the Hudson's Bay Company was the reaffirmation of its rights in Rupert's Land by a statute of the British Parliament in 1821.[19] From 1821 to 1870 the company was at the pinnacle of its power and prestige, but during the same period it came increasingly under attack from the Canadas. Understandably they resented the colossus that claimed dominion over most of the territories into which they might otherwise expect to expand, and they were determined to bring its charter monopoly to an end.

The company defended its position with considerable tenacity. For support it still relied principally upon the Imperial authority which had granted its charter, and it is true that during the long history of controversy over the charter this support was seldom denied. As an eminent Canadian historian has put it:

> Few documents have been challenged by such powerful interests or recognized at one time or another for two centuries, by such an array of official evidence – by order-in-council, by act of parliament, by royal commission, by the opinion of law

FIGURE 0-1. B.F. LLOYD & CO *MAP OF CANADA AND ARCTIC REGIONS OF NORTH AMERICA*, C. 1826.

> officers of the crown, by treaty, and by select parliamentary committee.[20]

Finally, however, the Imperial authorities, even though still disposed to uphold the charter's validity, could hardly avoid coming to the conclusion that it was necessary for the company to surrender at least its control of the land. In coming to this decision they were influenced by pressure from Canada, by the evident need to promote settlement in the fertile parts of the Hudson's Bay Company territories, and by fears that American immigrants might turn these parts into another Oregon. In these circumstances the company's rule was brought to an end.

The claims of explorers, and the long proprietorship of the Hudson's Bay Company, provide the principal elements in any historical consideration of how Canada became heir to these northern territories. Other activities prior to the transfers, principally of whalers and missionaries, may be more briefly noted. The first whalers in the region appear to have been Dutchmen, who moved into Davis Strait from the waters east of Greenland in the early 1700s, after the Spitsbergen whaling industry had begun to decline. Later in the century they were joined by Englishmen and Scotsmen. They all appear to have gone no further than south Greenland coastal waters and Davis Strait until Ross and Parry showed the way into Baffin Bay and Lancaster Sound in 1818 and 1819. American whalers entered the scene towards the mid-nineteenth century, concentrating their activities on the west side of Davis Strait south of Cumberland Gulf, and in Hudson Strait and the northern part of Hudson Bay. Later the English whalers retired from the area, and the Americans abandoned Davis Strait to the Scots, devoting their own attention to Hudson Bay. Unlike the Scots, the Americans adopted the habit of wintering in the whaling grounds, and so they provisioned their ships for two years. Later the Scots developed "land stations" on Baffin Island, operated by a few whites with native help. After the 1870s, whaling in both Davis Strait and Hudson Bay went into decline. In the meantime other American whalers were pushing through Bering Strait into the western Arctic, but they did not reach Canadian waters until 1889, when they first arrived at Herschel Island.[21]

1

The Transfers of Arctic Territories from Great Britain to Canada, 1870–80

Canada's official responsibility for what is now familiarly called "the Canadian Arctic" or "the Canadian North" began with the transfers of northern territories in 1870 and 1880.[1] Confederation in 1867 had united only the small province of Canada, comprising Canada East and Canada West in the St. Lawrence River Valley, with the still smaller Atlantic provinces of Nova Scotia and New Brunswick. The neighbouring island colonies of Prince Edward Island and Newfoundland had refused, at least for the time being, to join. In the middle of the continent, just north of the 49th parallel, was Lord Selkirk's Red River Colony, and on the west coast was the recently enlarged British Columbia, each of them a separate entity. Apart from Alaska and Greenland, which were American and Danish respectively, the rest of North America north of the Canadian-American boundary and the 49th parallel fell mostly within the huge domains of the Hudson's Bay Company (HBC). There were also the Arctic islands beyond the mainland, which were vaguely looked upon as British, although their real status was uncertain.

By the transfer of 1870, the vast empire of the Hudson's Bay Company was formally handed over to Canada. This brought to an end exactly two hundred years of company proprietorship under the royal charter of 1670. The text of the charter shows clearly that the original intention was to make the governor and company "true and absolute Lordes and Proprietors" of Rupert's Land in all respects whatsoever, excepting only the obligation of loyalty and allegiance to the Crown itself. Some of the more important of their exclusive rights and privileges, for example with regard to trade, land, exploitation of natural resources, lawmaking, administration of justice, immigration, settlement, and defence, were specified in considerable detail. The charter also attempted to define and delimit the territories it granted, but unfortunately the state of geographical knowledge at the time did not permit this to be done with exactitude.[2] This circumstance, along with doubts and disputes about the validity of the charter, exposed the company to a succession of serious challenges, from the French colony to the south until 1763, from rival fur interests based on Montreal until the amalgamation with the North West Company in 1821, and from the two Canadas, separately or together, until Confederation. The company defended itself against these assaults with determination and a good deal of success, relying for support mainly upon the Imperial authority that had granted the charter; and it is true that throughout the long period of recurring controversy this support was seldom denied. Ultimately, however, the Imperial authorities were driven to

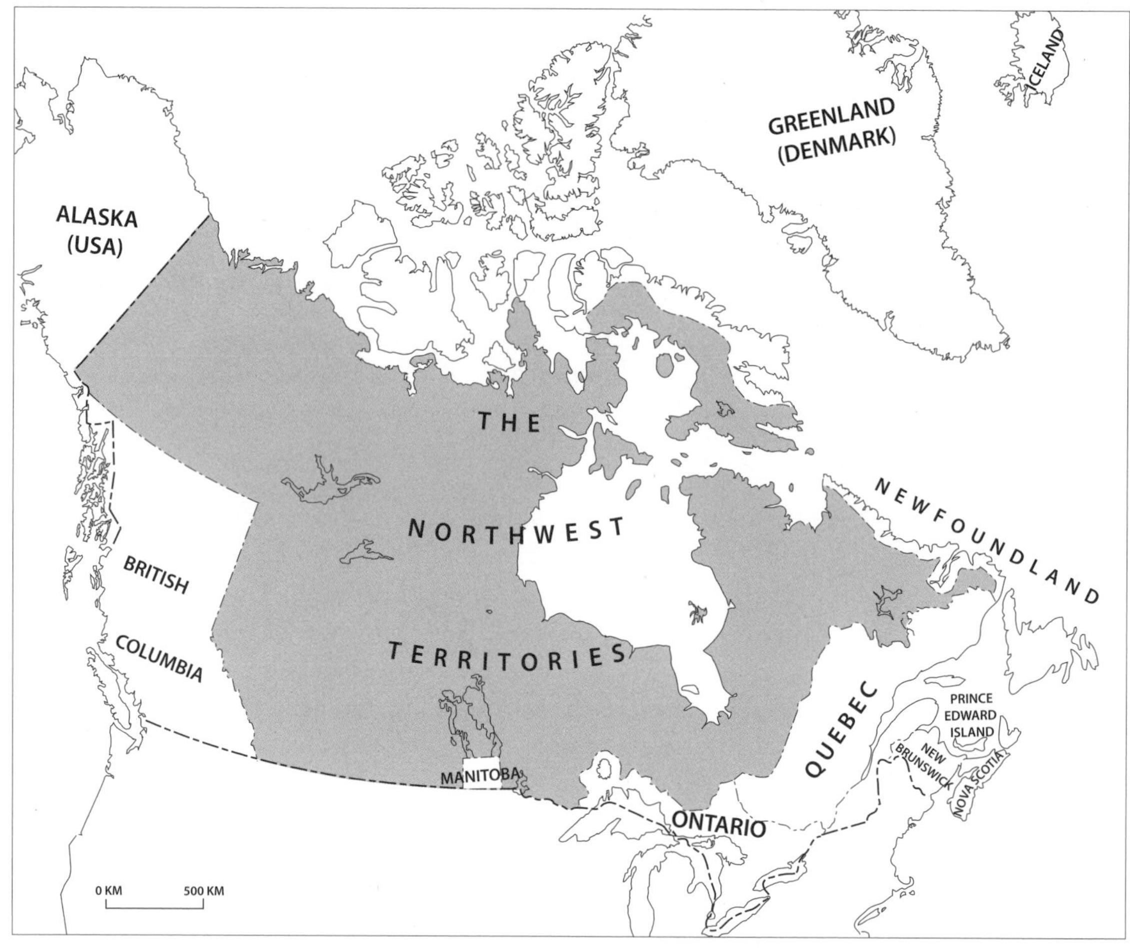

FIGURE 1-1: THE 1870 TRANSFER FOR RUPERT'S LAND TO CANADA. *NATIONAL ATLAS OF CANADA.*

the conclusion that the company must surrender at least its control of the land, and in these circumstances the proprietorship of the company was brought to a close. While the surrender was being arranged, the Canadian officials showed extreme unwillingness to recognize the company's title, but the Imperial authorities insisted that since the company had been lord-proprietor for two hundred years it would have to be treated as such for the purpose of the transfer. Thus, whatever flaws or loopholes there may have been in the charter, its validity was upheld by Imperial authority until the end.

The transfer itself was actually accomplished in two stages: the company's surrender of its territories to Great Britain in 1869, and Canada's acceptance of them from Great Britain in 1870.[3] The addition of the company's territories to Canada had been anticipated by the insertion of a clause (no. 146) for this purpose in the British North America (BNA) Act of 1867,[4] and by the passing of the Rupert's Land Act of 1868.[5] The Canadian Parliament passed addresses on two occasions formally requesting the transfer,[6] the deed of surrender turning over the company's territories to Great Britain was signed in November 1869,[7] and an Imperial order in council of 23 June 1870 finally admitted the HBC territories into the new Dominion.[8] A Canadian statute of 12 May 1870 had already made provision for the creation therefrom of the new province of Manitoba.[9] It is noticeable, however, that none of these documents attempted any further clarification of the outer limits of the lands that had been transferred.

The company itself had come to adopt the seemingly obvious implication in the charter that Rupert's Land comprised all territories draining into Hudson Bay and Strait, a view firmly stated by Governor Simpson before a Select Committee of the British House of Commons in 1857.[10] Beyond that was the North-Western or Indian Territory, which the company had held under licence, and which had been considered to include all remaining British continental territories west of Hudson Bay except British Columbia. After 1870, the title "North-West Territories" was generally applied to what was left of former Rupert's Land plus the old North-Western Territory, these being the lands that had been subject to the transfer. Canada's right to administer the North-West Territories as such was not thereafter seriously questioned, especially after the BNA Act of 1871 had been passed.[11] There did remain, however, certain lingering doubts about the validity of the charter as a basis for the transfer, and also about the limits (especially northern) of the lands that had been under the rule of the company, since it could hardly be said that these questions had ever been decisively settled.

* * *

These uncertainties, and particularly the status of the islands north of the mainland, were shortly to become sources of considerable concern. Two apparently innocent requests for concessions of Arctic territory in 1874 – one by a British subject and the other by an American – seem to have set in motion the tangled succession of developments outlined below. These led to the transfer of all remaining British North American Arctic territories to Canada in 1880, but as it turned out, this was not the end of the matter, and there followed years of doubt and confusion over the status of these northern regions.

On 3 January 1874, A. W. Harvey, then at South Kensington, London, wrote a letter to the Under Secretary of State for the Colonies which began with the following question: "Can you inform me whether the land known as Cumberland on the West of Davis Straits belongs to Great Britain and if it does – is it under the Government of the Dominion of Canada?" He added that he would like to know because he had been carrying on fisheries there for the past two years and expected to erect some temporary buildings.[12] On 15 January he wrote a second letter saying that he was leaving London in a short time and therefore would be glad to have the information he had asked for.[13]

The following day, Assistant Under Secretary for the Colonies Sir H. T. Holland, replying for Colonial Secretary Lord Kimberley, informed Harvey[14] rather vaguely that a reference to the Hudson's Bay Company had revealed[15] that the land in question had not been part of the company's territory prior to the transfer of 1869–70, nor did it appear to have been part of Canada before Confederation. Lord Kimberley suggested that Harvey ask the Board of Admiralty whether the land had ever been taken possession of on behalf of the Crown.

About a month later, on 10 February, Lieutenant William A. Mintzer of the US Navy Corps of Engineers wrote a letter to George Crump, Acting British Consul at Philadelphia, applying through him to the British government for a tract of land twenty miles square in Cumberland Gulf, for the purpose of carrying on a mining industry.[16] The application was forwarded by Crump to Foreign Secretary Lord Granville[17] and passed on by his department to Lord Carnarvon, who had just taken office as Colonial Minister with the new Disraeli administration in early 1874.[18]

The applications evidently aroused some discussion among British government officials, as the following brief excerpts from Colonial Office files reveal. One, written to Sir H. T. Holland on 22 April, ends: "If this territory does not belong to Canada as seems probable might it not be annexed with advantage to obviate possible future inconvenience?"[19] Another, dated 25 April, suggests:

> It would be desirable to ascertain the views of the Dominion Govt I think before the FO give any answer. We must remember that if this Yankee adventurer is informed by the British FO that the place indicated is not a portion of H. M. dominions he would no doubt think himself entitled to hoist the "Stars and Stripes" which might produce no end of complications.[20]

On 30 April, Lord Carnarvon enclosed Mintzer's application in a secret dispatch to Governor General Lord Dufferin of Canada, for confidential communication to his ministers, and raised the question whether "the territories adjacent to those of the Dominions on the N. American Continent, which have been taken possession of in the name of this Country but not hitherto annexed to any Colony or any of them should now be formally annexed to the Dominion of Canada." Carnarvon added that the British government would of course reserve for future consideration the course that should be taken but would not be disposed to authorize settlement in any unoccupied British territory near Canada, unless the Canadian authorities were prepared to assume the responsibility of maintaining law and order.[21]

Enclosed also was a report by Hydrographer of the Admiralty Frederick Evans,[22] dated 20 April, which had been prepared in response to a request from the Colonial Office for information,[23] particularly as to whether the territory referred to by Lieutenant Mintzer had ever been taken possession of on behalf of the Crown. The report gave a brief geographical and historical description of the territory in question, but admitted, "Our knowledge of the geography and resources of this region is very imperfect." Evans did note, however, that the coast some distance north of Cumberland Gulf had been visited in 1818 by Captain Ross of the British Navy, who had taken possession "in the usual form" at Agnes Monument, 70° 30' N. 68° W.

On 26 August, Lord Carnarvon sent another secret dispatch to Lord Dufferin containing copies of the correspondence his department had had with Harvey and saying, "I should be glad to receive an expression of the opinion of yourself and of your Ministers in regard to this application as well as on the similar one referred to in my despatch above mentioned."[24] During the interval that had elapsed since his first letter was written, Harvey had moved to St. John's, Newfoundland, and had renewed his application, asking for a square mile of land for buildings and mining as well as fishing rights, but he had received a rather discouraging response. On 25 August, Under Secretary for the Colonies R.G.W. Herbert had replied to him, saying that Lord Carnarvon felt obliged to consult the Governor General of

Canada regarding the matter, but was not very hopeful that the desired concessions could be granted.[25]

On 4 November, Dufferin sent a reply, also secret, to Carnarvon's dispatches of 30 April and 26 August, which indicated that the latter's proposition had been favourably received by the Canadian authorities.[26] Enclosed was a copy of an approved order in council, dated 10 October, which stated that "the Government of Canada is desirous of including within the boundaries of the Dominion the Territories referred to, with the islands adjacent."[27]

Several important features would appear to emerge from the correspondence thus far – the feeling in official circles in both Great Britain and Canada that there were still British territories north of the Dominion that had not yet been annexed to any colony, the willingness of the British Government to turn these territories over to Canada, the willingness of the Canadian Government to accept them, and the doubts of both governments as to what their boundaries might be.

Carnarvon's next dispatch,[28] dated 6 January 1875, included a rather barren report by the Hydrographer of the Admiralty[29] and a lengthier, more informative one done by his own department,[30] both having been submitted during the preceding December. From the evidence of the latter, he wrote:

> It appears that the boundaries of the Dominion towards the North, North East and North West are at present entirely undefined and that it is impossible to say what British territories on the North American Continent are not already annexed to Canada under the Order in Council of the 23rd of June 1870, which incorporated the whole of the territories of the Hudson's Bay Company, as well as the North Western territory in the Dominion.

Later in his communication, he requested the advice of the Canadian ministers respecting the form of the proposed annexation, and suggested that an act of the British Parliament might be suitable. He also asked that the Canadian ministers specify the territorial limits of the lands to be annexed. This point had been discussed in his own department's minutes, which, after referring to the 141st meridian separating British and American territory in the west, continued:

> To the East the British Territories might perhaps be defined to be bounded by the Atlantic Ocean, Davis Straits, Baffin Bay, Smith Sound and Kennedy Channel. But even this definition wld' exclude the extreme North West of Greenland, which is marked in some maps as British territory, from having been discovered probably by British subjects. To the North, to use the words of the Hudson's Bay Co. in 1750, the boundaries might perhaps be, 'the utmost limits of the lands towards the North Pole'.

This would appear to be the first time, in this correspondence at least, that these easterly and northerly limits were mentioned. In view of subsequent developments respecting the definition of Canada's arctic boundaries, the suggestion assumes a certain importance.

After some delay, which prompted a further letter from Lord Carnarvon on 27 March asking for a response to the above communication,[31] Lord Dufferin sent his reply[32] on 1

May. Enclosed was a copy of a Canadian order in council,[33] which agreed that the northern boundary of Canada had never been defined and that it was impossible to say what British territory had not already been annexed to Canada. Then, after stating its approval of the boundaries proposed, the order recommended:

> To avoid all doubt it would be desirable that an Act of the Imperial Parliament should be passed defining the Boundaries East and North as follows
>
> 'Bounded on the East by the Atlantic Ocean, and passing towards the North by Davis Straits, Baffins Bay, Smiths Straits and Kennedy Channel including such portions of the North West Coast of Greenland as may belong to Great Britain by right of discovery or otherwise.
>
> On the North by the utmost northerly limits of the continent of America including the islands appertaining thereto'.

The order in council concluded with a request that no action be taken until after the next session of the Parliament of Canada, because acquisition of the new territories would "entail a charge upon the revenue," and should therefore have the sanction of the Canadian Parliament.

Lord Carnarvon replied[34] on 1 June, acknowledging receipt of the above and agreeing to comply with the request for delay. However, the requisite action was not taken by the Canadian Parliament during its next session, and official correspondence on the subject seems also to have lapsed until August of the following year. Canadian Minister of Justice Edward Blake, at this time in England, sent a note to Lord Carnarvon[35] with an extract from the *New York Times* enclosed, the latter announcing the organization of an expedition under Lieutenant Mintzer to mine graphite and mica in Cumberland Sound. The report indicated that the project was to be under the auspices of the American government. The Colonial Office replied to Blake[36] on 22 August, acknowledging his letter and asking if the Canadian authorities had taken or intended to take any further action in accordance with their order in council of 30 April 1875. Blake in his answer had to admit that he did not know of any action taken, nor was he able to tell the intentions of the Canadian government, but he would submit the matter for discussion upon his return home.[37]

Three weeks later, Lord Carnarvon sent a copy of the correspondence with Blake to Lord Dufferin, adding, "In view of the probable annexation within a short time of this and other northern territories to Canada, H. M. Govt do not propose to take any action in reference to this expedition unless expressly asked to [do] so by the Dominion Govt."[38] A further communication from Lord Carnarvon[39] enclosed an extract taken by the *London Times* of 27 October from the *New York Times*, announcing the return of Mintzer's expedition from Cumberland Sound with approximately fifteen tons of mica estimated to be worth five to twelve dollars a pound.[40]

After another lengthy interval, Carnarvon wrote to Dufferin on 23 October 1877,[41] sending him nineteen charts of the North American Arctic which had been provided by the Admiralty in response to a Canadian request of 29 August preceding. Another letter from Carnarvon, bearing the same date, appears to demonstrate the minister's growing irritation at the lack of progress in bringing the project to a conclusion.

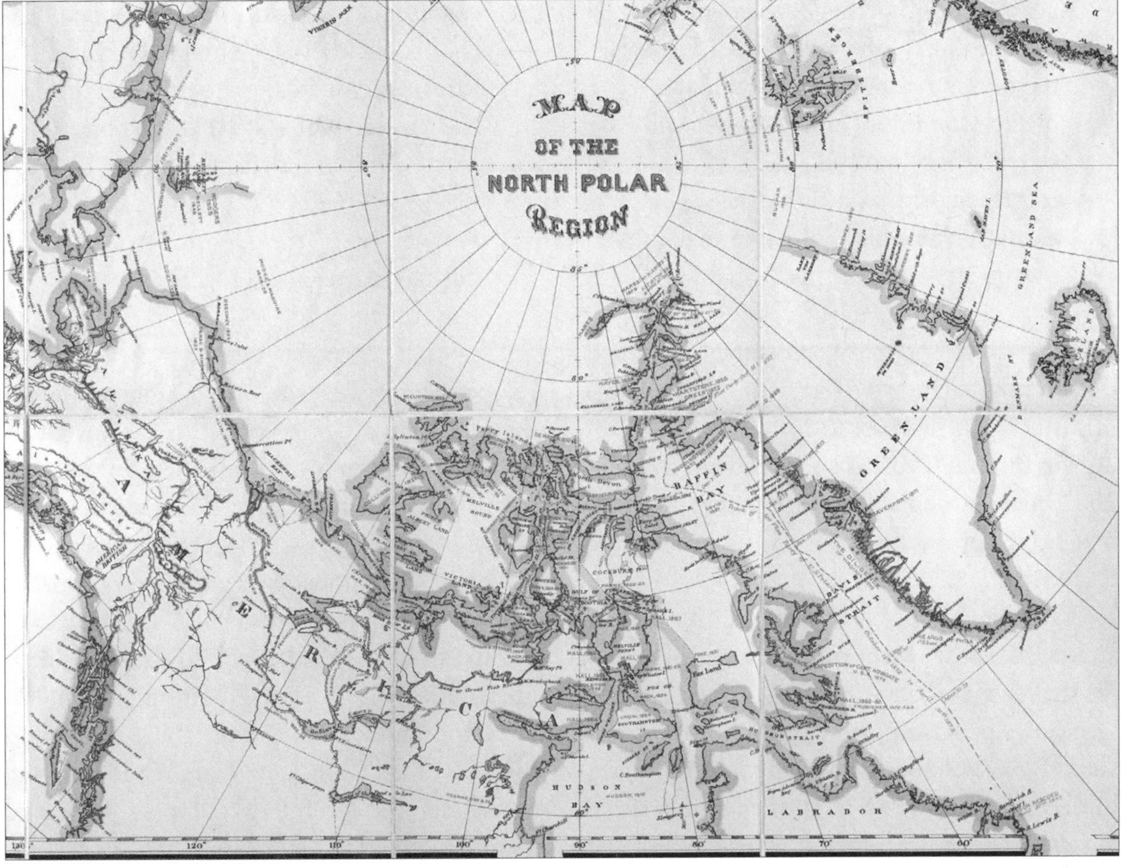

FIGURE 1-2: CHARLES FRANCIS HALL, "MAP OF THE NORTH POLAR REGION, 1879." *NARRATIVE OF THE SECOND ARCTIC EXPEDITION MADE BY CHARLES F. HALL HIS VOYAGE TO REPULSE BAY, SLEDGE JOURNEYS TO THE STRAITS OF FURY AND HECLA AND TO KING WILLIAM'S LAND AND RESIDENCE AMONG THE ESKIMOS DURING THE YEARS 1864-'69* (NEW YORK: THE GRAPHIC CO., 1879).

With reference to my Despatch, No. 297 of this days date, I have the honor to request that you will recall the attention of your Ministers to the correspondence noted in the margin....

From reports which have appeared in the Newspapers I have observed that the attention of the citizens of the United States has from time to time been drawn to these territories and that private expeditions have been sent out to explore certain portions of them, and I need hardly point out to you that should it be the wish of the Canadian people that they should be included in the Dominion great difficulty in effecting this may easily arise unless steps are speedily taken to place the title of Canada to these territories upon a clear and unmistakable footing.

I have therefore to request that you will move your Ministers to

> again take into their consideration the question of the inclusion of these territories within the boundaries of the Dominion, and that you will state to them that I shall be glad to be informed, with as little further delay as may be possible, of the steps which they propose to take in the matter.[42]

Dufferin's reply,[43] dated 1 December, informed Carnarvon that he had referred the matter to his ministers, who had passed an order in council[44] on the subject, a copy of which was enclosed. The order in council observed that nothing had been done subsequent to the earlier one of 30 April 1875, because "there did not seem at that time any pressing necessity for taking action," and then went on to recommend that "as the reasons for coming to a definite conclusion now appear urgent" resolutions should be submitted at the next Parliament authorizing the acceptance of the territories in question. No explanation was offered as to why, in the committee's view, the "reasons for coming to a definite conclusion" were so much more urgent in November 1877 than in April 1875.

A letter of 22 February 1878,[45] from W. R. Malcolm of the Colonial Office to the law officers of the Crown, raised the question as to whether an Imperial act would be the most desirable method of making the transfer.[46] After noting that an Imperial act had been suggested, Malcolm continued:

> I am desired to enclose copies of opinions delivered by the Law Officers of the Crown dated respectively the 8th of November 1866 and the 8th of May 1871 and I am to state that as it would appear to be lawful for Her Majesty to annex territory by Letters Patent to a Colony having representative Institutions provided the assent of the Colonial Legislature is signified thereto it seems to the Secretary of State that the object in view might be effected by Letters Patent followed by Legislation in the Parliament of the Dominion without having recourse to the Imperial Parliament.

In accordance with the proposal embodied in the Canadian order in council of 29 November 1877, the transfer was brought up in the next session of Parliament, and the outcome was a joint address to the Queen from the Senate and House of Commons, passed on 3 May 1878.[47] The resolutions were moved in the House of Commons by the Hon. David Mills, Minister of the Interior, and supported strongly by members from both sides of the House, including Prime Minister Mackenzie and Leader of the Opposition Sir John A. Macdonald. One lone member, the Hon. Peter Mitchell of Northumberland, New Brunswick, voiced strong opposition, maintaining that the acquisition would be both expensive and useless.[48]

The address stated in a resumé that doubts existed regarding the northern boundaries of Canada, that these doubts should be removed as soon as possible, that the British government had offered to transfer the territories in question to Canada, that the offer had been accepted, and consequently, to remove all doubts, it was desirable that "an Act of the Parliament of the United Kingdom of Great Britain and Ireland should be passed defining the North-Easterly, Northerly, and North-Westerly Boundaries of Canada, as follows...." The description of the desired boundaries following this passage was essentially similar to that contained in the order in council of 30 April 1875, except that it made no direct reference to possible British territories in northwestern Greenland and did establish a specific western boundary along the 141st meridian.

The question of whether an Imperial act was necessary to accomplish the transfer was again raised in Sir Michael Hicks-Beach's letter of 17 July 1878 to Lord Dufferin (Sir Michael having replaced Lord Carnarvon at the Colonial Office on 4 February).[49] After acknowledging receipt of the joint address of 3 May, and referring to the request for an Imperial act, Sir Michael continued:

> I have been in communication with the Law Officers of the Crown on this subject[50] and I am advised that it is competent for Her Majesty to annex all such territories to the Dominion by an Order in Council, but that if it is desired after the annexation has taken place to erect the territories thus newly annexed into Provinces and to provide that such Provinces shall be represented in the Dominion Parliament recourse must be had to an Imperial Act; since, as I am advised, the Crown is not competent to change the legislative scheme established by the British North America Act 1867 (30 and 31 Vict: c.3).
>
> I therefore propose to defer tendering to Her Majesty any advice upon the subject of the address of the Senate and House of Commons until I am informed whether it will meet the views of your Govt that Letters Patent be passed for annexing these territories to the Dominion leaving the question of Imperial legislation for future consideration if it should be thought desirable to erect any such territories not now belonging to the Dominion into Provinces.

Lord Dufferin's reply,[51] dated 8 October, enclosed a memorandum prepared by Minister of Justice Rodolphe Laflamme[52] and an order in council[53] concurring in it. These documents indicate that the Hicks-Beach proposal had been received rather doubtfully by the Canadian authorities, who clearly were by no means convinced of its soundness. The main points of disagreement were set forward very ably by the Minister of Justice in his memorandum.

Briefly reviewing the circumstances leading up to the situation, he noted that the joint address of 3 May 1878 had requested an Imperial act to make the transfer, while the law officers now advised that an Imperial order in council would be sufficient. He then pointed out that a principal reason for requesting Imperial legislation had been that Lord Carnarvon himself had suggested it in his dispatch of 6 January 1875. Apart from this, however, the Canadian government still doubted than an order in council would have validity and continued to regard an Imperial act as preferable. In their belief, the only power for extending the limits of Canada was given by section 146 of the BNA Act of 1867, where specific provision was made for the annexation to Canada by order in council of Newfoundland, Prince Edward Island, British Columbia, Rupert's Land, and the North-Western Territory. The two northern territories had been duly annexed in 1870 under the terms of section 146;[54] if they in fact included the territories under discussion nothing further needed to be done, but if they did not then resort to further Imperial legislation would be advisable, since the powers given by section 146 might be exhausted in this area. For this reason, and because the boundaries of Rupert's Land and the North-Western Territory were "unknown," it had been thought better to "avoid all doubt in the matter" and obtain an Imperial act.

So far as the other issue was concerned, respecting the law officers' belief that an Imperial act would be necessary if it were desired after the transfer to create provinces from the new territories, the Canadian authorities were much less troubled. The memorandum simply drew attention to the BNA Act of 1871,[55] which had granted the Canadian Parliament the right both to administer territories forming part of the Dominion but not included in any province and to create new provinces therefrom. The minister surmised that "the attention of the Law Officer of the Crown was probably not directed to this Statute."

In spite of Hicks-Beach's lack of enthusiasm for an act of Parliament to bring about the transfer, the Colonial Office proceeded to draw up a bill for this purpose and sent a draft copy[56] of it to the Secretary of the Admiralty on 18 January 1879. The accompanying letter[57] asked for any observations the Admiralty might have on the matter, and particularly any suggestions that would help to define more accurately Canada's new boundaries. It recognized, however, that it was asking for the virtually impossible since the northern boundary was "utterly unknown," and it was "with the view of meeting this difficulty that the N. and N. E. boundaries [had been] left so vague." The key passage in the draft, which appears the more significant both because it gave open expression to official uncertainties and because the bill was never enacted into law, began as follows: "The Dominion of Canada shall include all British Territory (if any) which is not already admitted to the Union nor part of the Colony of Newfoundland and which is situate within the following boundaries…." The description of boundaries that followed was almost identical with that given in the Canadian joint address of 3 May 1878. Even allowing for the vagueness admitted in the letter, it is evident that this description was considerably more precise than the one that ultimately replaced it in the document finally adopted.

The reply from the Admiralty[58] enclosed a commentary on the draft bill, with a proposed amendment, which had been prepared by Admiralty Hydrographer Frederick Evans,[59] and in which the Lords of the Admiralty concurred. Evans expressed doubts whether Britain should presume to claim all territory up to the northernmost extent of the archipelago, noting that British explorers had reached no further than the entrance to Smith Sound (about 78°30' N) prior to 1852, while Americans between that date and 1873 had penetrated beyond the 82nd parallel. However, the British arctic expedition of 1875–76 had then gone some distance beyond the most northerly point reached by the Americans. His amendment, to replace the draft bill's definition of boundaries, ran as follows:

> On the East the Atlantic Ocean, which boundary shall extend towards the North by Davis Straits, Baffin's Bay and Smith's Sound as far as the parallel of 78° 30' of North Latitude, including all the islands in and adjacent thereto, which belong to Her Majesty by right of discovery or otherwise. Thence on the North the boundary shall be the parallel of 78° 30' North Latitude, to include the entire continent to the Arctic Ocean, and also the islands in the same Westward to the one hundred and forty first Meridian West of Greenwich; and thence on that Meridian Southerly till it meets on the N.N.W.

> part of the continent of America the United States territory of Alaska.

Thus, if the hydrographer's statement had been adopted, no mention would have been made of the most northerly territories, and the British claim would have stopped at 78°30' N.

During the next few days there was an interesting exchange of comments among Colonial Office officials,[60] including a tartly worded suggestion from Hicks-Beach to the effect that members of his department should not propose Imperial legislation without his sanction.[61] Ernest Edward Blake of the department expressed grave doubts about the wisdom of attempting as precise a delimitation of northern and northeastern boundaries as the hydrographer proposed, and stated his preference for leaving them indefinite.[62] This idea was put forward still more specifically by Under Secretary Herbert in a memorandum to the minister commenting on the latter's desire to avoid a bill:

> I see the objection to legislation very clearly: on the other hand I fear that without it there will be no means of establishing the right of Canada to territories which are believed to be British but the boundaries of which have never been authoritatively defined.
>
> If a Bill is found to be unavoidable, perhaps it might take the less assailable form of a measure "to declare that all territories and places in North America now belonging to the Crown, but not hitherto specially included within the boundaries of the Dominion, shall be so included."[63]

Sir Michael agreed with this suggestion, remarking that such a form would be best whether the case were dealt with by a bill or an order in council.[64]

The memorandum of the preceding year by the Canadian Minister of Justice and the related documents were all sent by the Colonial Office to the Law Officers of the Crown on 26 February. An enclosed letter,[65] written by Herbert, drew attention to the Canadian authorities' preference for an Imperial act, and their opinion that, once the territories had been properly transferred, the BNA Act of 1871 would be sufficient to permit the Dominion to create provinces therefrom. The law officers were asked to state if they believed further Imperial legislation necessary, and the letter concluded, "It appears to Sir Michael Hicks Beach to be for obvious reasons undesirable to have recourse to legislation by the Imperial Parliament unless such a course is unavoidable." What the "obvious reasons" might be was not further enlarged upon.

The reply of the law officers,[66] dated 3 April, confirmed their former opinion that Her Majesty could by order in council annex the territories in North America belonging to the Crown to Canada. So far as the other matter was concerned, regarding the erection of such territories into provinces, they admitted that their "attention had not been drawn" to the BNA Act of 1871, and they thought that this statute would in fact give Canada full executive and legislative authority over these territories after their annexation.

The substance of the law officers' report was communicated by Hicks-Beach to the Marquis of Lorne,[67] who had succeeded Lord Dufferin as Governor General in November 1878. Sir Michael added:

> I shall be prepared, therefore, should your Government desire it, to take the necessary steps forthwith for effecting the annexation to Canada of the territories in question by Means of an Order of Her Majesty in Council; – but as Imperial Legislation is not necessary for this purpose it will of course not be advisable to have recourse to it.

Evidently fearing that reservations might still be held in Canada about the proposed order in council, Sir Michael wrote a further, confidential note to the Governor General[68] just one day later, which reveals clearly his anxiety that the change be accepted.

> Referring to my Desp. no. 106 of the 18th inst't. intimating the opinion of the Law Officers of the Crown respecting the annexation of certain territory to Canada by means of an Order in Council, I anticipate that your Gov't will share the satisfaction with which I have received this advice. There are obvious reasons which make this course of action preferable to attempting to secure the same object by the introduction of a Bill into the Imperial Parl't. Questions might be raised in the discussion of such a measure which might, in the great press of business, not improbably lead to the abandonment of the project; and I shall be glad to learn that your Gov't concur in my proposal to obtain an Order in Council for the purpose.

The Governor General's reply,[69] written more than six months later on 5 November, enclosed a copy of an order in council[70] approved the day before. The order embodied a memorandum by Prime Minister Macdonald, which stated that the information about the opinion of the law officers respecting the annexation was "in the highest degree satisfactory" and requested an order in council of Her Majesty's government for the purpose of such annexation.

On 6 February 1880, the Colonial Office sent to the law officers a draft copy of the proposed order in council,[71] requesting their opinion as to whether it would be "proper and sufficient" for its purpose. The draft was practically identical to the order as finally approved, except that the effective date of the annexation, which had not yet been decided upon, was left out. It is noticeable that the description of the boundaries of the territories to be annexed abandoned earlier attempts at more precise delimitation and employed the extremely vague terminology that appeared in the final order in council. There appears to be no record of a reply from the law officers; it may be presumed, however, that their endorsement was given, in view of the above-mentioned similarity of the draft to the order as finally passed.

A draft copy of the order was sent on 24 July to Sir John A. Macdonald, who was in England at the time, with the request that he suggest an effective date for the annexation. Macdonald's reply on 28 July[72] indicated that he thought the precise date immaterial, but should Lord Kimberley (the new Colonial Secretary) approve, he would suggest the first of September following. This date was immediately inserted in the draft, and Lord Kimberley sent a copy on the same day to the Lord President of the Council, with the request that it be submitted to Her Majesty at the council's next meeting.[73]

The order in council[74] was approved only three days later, indicating that it was handled without delay. Since it is unquestionably one of the key documents in the entire story of Canada's effort to acquire title to these northern regions, it is worth reproducing in full:

> At the Court at Osborne House, Isle of Wight, the 31st Day of July, 1880.
>
> Present:
>
> The Queen's Most Excellent Majesty,
>
> Lord President,
>
> Lord Steward, Lord Chamberlain.
>
> Whereas it is expedient that all British territories and possessions in North America, and the islands adjacent to such territories and possessions which are not already included in the Dominion of Canada, should (with the exception of the Colony of Newfoundland and its dependencies) be annexed to and form part of the said Dominion.
>
> And whereas, the Senate and Commons of Canada in Parliament assembled, have, in and by an Address, dated May 3, 1878, represented to Her Majesty 'That it is desirable that the Parliament of Canada, on the transfer of the before-mentioned territories being completed, should have authority to legislate for their future welfare and good government, and the power to make all needful rules and regulations respecting them, the same as in the case of the other territories (of the Dominion); and that the Parliament of Canada expressed its willingness to assume the duties and obligations consequent thereon;'
>
> And whereas, Her Majesty is graciously pleased to accede to the desire expressed in and by the said Address: Now, therefore, it is hereby ordered and declared by Her Majesty, by and with the advice of Her Most Honourable Privy Council, as follows:
>
> From and after September 1, 1880, all British territories and possessions in North America, not already included within the Dominion of Canada, and all islands adjacent to any of such territories or possessions, shall (with the exception of the Colony of Newfoundland and its dependencies) become and be annexed to and form part of the said Dominion of Canada; and become and be subject to the laws for the time being in force in the said Dominion, in so far as such laws may be applicable thereto.
>
> (sgd) C. L. Peel.

Lord Kimberley sent the approved order to the Marquis of Lorne in a dispatch dated 16 August,[75] and it was published in the *Canada Gazette* on 9 October. Thus the formalities connected with the transfer were finally brought to a conclusion.

Comments

The correspondence summarized above appears to give a fairly clear picture of the rather involved negotiations leading to the transfer. However, several aspects of it merit further comment.

1. One of these is the extraordinary amount of time required to complete the transfer. The first official suggestion of a transfer

was made by Lord Carnarvon in his dispatch of 30 April 1874, and afterwards a sense of urgency is sometimes discernible in the remarks of officials on both sides of the Atlantic,[76] yet well over six years elapsed before the order in council was finally signed on 31 July 1880. The most obvious explanation, evident from the correspondence, is undoubtedly the correct one; the British and Canadian authorities spent a good deal of time trying to determine what territories would be subject to the transfer, and then encountered more delay trying to decide whether an Imperial act or order in council should be used to effect it. Furthermore, it was a move initiated by British rather than Canadian statesmen, the Dominion government for a considerable time showed little interest or concern, and it fell to the lot of a few Imperial officials, principally colonial ministers Carnarvon and Hicks-Beach, to push matters along and occasionally prod the rather indifferent Canadians into action.

2. The absence of precise territorial delimitation in the order as finally constructed has aroused comment,[77] and is certainly inconsistent with the earlier attempts to avoid leaving anything in doubt. The Colonial Office enlisted the help of the Hudson's Bay Company, the Admiralty, and the Canadian government, as well as its own personnel, in order to determine what Arctic territories were British property, and throughout most of the correspondence the quest continues for an exact definition of the territories being transferred. It is also evident in the Canadian joint address of 3 May 1878, and the remarks of the members who spoke during the debate when the address was accepted indicate their belief that a major benefit of the transfer from Canada's point of view would be the clarification of her northern boundaries. Nevertheless, all such attempts were abandoned at the end, and in the final order the British authorities resorted to the almost meaningless expression "all British territories and possessions in North America, not already included within the Dominion of Canada, and all islands adjacent to any of such territories or possessions ... (with the exception of the Colony of Newfoundland and its dependencies)"[78] in naming the territories subject to the transfer. Why the change?

Here again the answer, or much of it, seems obvious. In his influential 1905 *Report upon the Title of Canada to the Islands North of the Mainland of Canada*, Dr. W. F. King (the Chief Astronomer in the Department of the Interior at the time) suggests that Great Britain doubted the validity of her title to all the lands within the limits that had been proposed and hence declined to make a precise delimitation, although she did want to transfer to Canada whatever possessions she had in this quarter.[79] In a 1921 memorandum, Hensley R. Holmden, Associate Archivist in charge of the Maps Division, who in general agrees with King, observes that the British did not know which of their Arctic territories had not already been annexed to Canada, and that in any case an exact definition could not be given of territories that were then still largely unknown. For these reasons, he is certain that the order in council was intentionally phrased in imprecise terms.[80] All these points are borne out by the correspondence, which indicates that at the start the authorities wanted a precisely worded document, and gave up only when it became obvious that this would be impossible to achieve in satisfactory fashion. It is also clear that the Admiralty hydrographer's report of 23 January 1879, with its suggestion that the British claim stop at 78°30' N in deference to American explorations farther north, caused second thoughts about the wisdom of an exact claim. At any rate, this marks the approximate point where attempts at precise delimitation were abandoned.

Whether there were other, more obscure reasons for the change is difficult to say. The British authorities may have been genuinely reluctant to claim territories where the American title might be stronger than their own, or possibly, in more Machiavellian fashion, they may have hoped that by an indefinite claim rights could be gained, in the passage of time, that Britain did not at the moment possess. There is the further possibility, mentioned by neither King nor Holmden, that they may not have wanted to give up all chance of a claim to part of Greenland, and so avoided precise geographical delimitation in order to keep that prospect open for the future.[81] Whatever the full explanation may be, the vagueness of the order in council as finally adopted gave rise later on to serious doubts as to what had actually been transferred to Canada.

3. Another apparent inconsistency, mentioned by King[82] and discussed at some length by Holmden,[83] is the abandonment by the Imperial authorities of an act of Parliament (which they themselves had suggested in the first place) in favour of an order in council to bring about the transfer. Again there appears to be no real mystery involved, in the light of what is revealed in the correspondence. An act was suggested by Lord Carnarvon on 6 January 1875, and during early negotiations it was assumed on both sides of the Atlantic that this device would be used. On 22 February 1878, shortly after Hicks-Beach had become Colonial Secretary, the alternative suggestion of an order in council was made at his direction, with reference to earlier opinions given by the law officers of the Crown in rather similar cases, on 8 November 1866, and 8 May 1871.[84] On two later occasions (28 May 1878 and 3 April 1879), the law officers reaffirmed that a transfer by order in council would be valid (thus removing the doubt that had bothered the Canadian authorities), whereas the Canadian Minister of Justice cited the BNA Act of 1871 as evidence that Canada could create provinces from the new territories once the transfer had been completed (thus clearing up the point that had escaped the law officers themselves). In the end, both sides were satisfied that the order in council was in all respects adequate, and Sir Michael, who appears to have been the chief sponsor of the change, had won his point. His motives are indicated in several of his letters, notably that of 19 April 1879, where he speaks of "obvious reasons which make this course of action preferable" and worries over the possibility that "questions might be raised in the discussion of such a measure (i.e. an act) which might, in the great press of business, not improbably lead to the abandonment of the project." There is perhaps room for a certain amount of curiosity about his "obvious reasons" and what it was he actually feared most – delay or defeat in Parliament, excessive or unfavourable publicity, a strong public reaction against the project in either Great Britain or the United States – but it at least seems clear that he preferred the order in council because he thought it would be quieter, faster, and more certain of passage.

4. Another feature that seems rather odd is that the law officers could have overlooked the BNA Act of 1871, since it had been passed to meet a situation rather similar to that which they were anticipating when they gave their opinion (28 May 1878) that further Imperial legislation would be necessary after a transfer by order in council if it were desired to create provinces from the new territories. The circumstances surrounding the passing of this act are briefly as follows.

In 1870, while the Manitoba Bill was under discussion, the question was raised as to whether the Parliament of Canada had authority thus to create provinces from unorganized territories and to give them representation in the Dominion Senate and House of Commons.[85] The matter was taken under consideration, and on 3 January 1871 Governor General Lord Lisgar sent Colonial Secretary Lord Kimberley[86] an approved minute of council[87] on the subject, with an attached report, dated 29 December 1870, from the Minister of Justice (Sir John A. Macdonald). In his report, Macdonald noted the difficulty that had arisen and the fact that the BNA Act of 1867 did not specifically provide for the representation of the territories in the federal Parliament, and then recommended that

> the Earl of Kimberley be moved to submit to the Imperial Parliament at its next Session, a Measure
>
> 1. Confirming the Act of the Canadian Parliament 33rd Vict. chap. 3 above referred to as if it had been an imperial Statute and legalizing whatever may have been done under it, according to its true intent.
>
> 2. Empowering the Dominion Parliament from time to time to establish other Provinces in the North Western Territory ... and also empowering it to grant such Provinces representation in the Parliament of the Dominion.

A suggested draft of the requested bill was sent by Lord Kimberley to Lord Lisgar on 26 January,[88] and a Canadian order in council was passed on 27 February,[89] embodying the substance of Kimberley's draft in another that Lisgar returned to him on 2 March.[90] The draft bill, in slightly changed form, was inserted in a joint address to the Queen from the Senate and House of Commons on 13 April,[91] and sent by the Governor General to Kimberley on 18 April.[92] The BNA Act of 29 June 1871 followed.[93] The sections most relevant here read as follows:

> Whereas doubts have been entertained respecting the powers of the Parliament of Canada to establish Provinces in Territories admitted, or which may hereafter be admitted into the Dominion of Canada, and to provide for the representation of such Provinces in the said Parliament, and it is expedient to remove such doubts, and to vest such powers in the said Parliament:
>
> Be it enacted....
>
> 2. The Parliament of Canada may from time to time establish new Provinces in any territories forming for the time being part of the Dominion of Canada, but not included in any Province thereof, and may, at the time of such establishment, make provision for the constitution and administration of any such Province, and for the passing of laws for the peace, order, and good government of such Province, and for its representation in the said Parliament....
>
> 4. The Parliament of Canada may from time to time make provision for the administration, peace, order, and good government of any territory not for the time being included in any Province.

The act also stated (section 5) that both the Rupert's Land Act and the Manitoba Act were to be deemed "valid and effectual for all purposes whatsoever."[94]

Thus, if the BNA Act of 1867 had failed to give Canada the power to create provinces from territories that had been or might be annexed to it, the act of 1871 would seem to have remedied this deficiency.

Conclusion

The documents referred to in the preceding pages appear to throw a good deal of light upon the transfer, its background, and certain other matters related to it. It is clear that Britain decided, after receiving two embarrassing and potentially troublesome applications for land and other privileges, to make Canada the proprietor of all British possessions in this area that had not already been placed under Canadian jurisdiction. There could possibly be something to Holmden's suggestion that Great Britain believed such a transfer would enable her to appeal to the Monroe Doctrine for settlement in case of a dispute with European powers.[95] It was an American, however, who made the original non-British application for a concession, and it is evident that the major concern of the British authorities was with the United States.[96] They may have thought that by quietly transferring Britain's rights in this region to Canada they would be in a better position to forestall or defeat any attempt by the United States, whether based upon the Monroe Doctrine or not, to assert American sovereignty there. Furthermore, the fact of the transfer might in itself imply that the territories in question were subject to measures of sovereignty and control, both before and after the transaction was completed.

Regarding the legal status of the transfer, the total evidence of the preceding pages would certainly indicate that, although it was attended by a good deal of delay and confusion, the transfer itself was valid enough as a voluntary gift to Canada of whatever rights Britain possessed. What was in doubt, then and later, was the completeness of Britain's own title at the time of the transfer, as well as the extent of the territories subject to the transaction. Holmden puts the matter succinctly enough: "The Imperial Government did not know what they were transferring, and on the other hand the Canadian Government had no idea what they were receiving."[97]

2

A Period of Relative Inactivity and Unconcern, 1880–95

In a period of just ten years, the young Dominion of Canada found itself responsible for virtually the northern half of the continent and adjacent islands, except Newfoundland, Alaska, and Greenland. Steps were speedily taken to develop the more fertile, habitable parts of the transferred territories and bring them under control, and progress in these parts, mainly the western Prairies, was rapid. But in the remoter northerly parts, especially the islands, very little was done in consequence of the transfer for fully fifteen years after 1880, and the Canadian government left the islands to keep "the noiseless tenor of their way." This inactivity left the impression afterwards in some quarters that the Canadian authorities doubted the legality of the transfer and felt inhibited in assuming full responsibility until these doubts had been set at rest by the passing of the Colonial Boundaries Act by the Imperial Parliament in 1895.

One leading figure who seems to have held this view was Dr. William Frederick King, Canada's Chief Astronomer at the turn of the century and author of the familiar *Report upon the Title of Canada to the Islands North of the Mainland of Canada*, which became, after its publication in 1905, probably the most highly regarded work on the subject.[1] Some aspects of King's report were questioned by Hensley R. Holmden, Associate Archivist in charge of the Maps Division at the Public Archives, in his *Memo re the Arctic Islands*, written in 1921.[2] But King's *Report* was published, even if only in a limited, confidential edition, while Holmden's *Memo* was put out only in manuscript form for the benefit of a few government officials who were engaged in some troublesome business concerning the islands at the time. Thus King's *Report* became relatively familiar to government and later to academic people, while Holmden's *Memo* was left to gather dust on archives shelves. Little other writing was done on the matters discussed in the two reports, and the net result was that King's document acquired an aura of unassailable authenticity and infallibility which was in some respects exaggerated. For example, it is easy to show, as Holmden did, that King was largely mistaken in his belief about the basic reason for the Canadian government's inactivity respecting the Arctic Islands during the fifteen years after 1880. However, this explains only one aspect of an extremely complicated situation.

Shortly after the 1880 transfer, the Canadian government attempted to find out what might be done in the newly acquired territories. The Minister of Justice, Alexander Campbell, carried on a correspondence with the Hudson's Bay Company in the hope of acquiring information about the inhabitants which might aid in planning any necessary action.[3] Company officials could tell him little, however, and finally he recommended that no steps should be taken to legislate for these regions until circumstances should warrant such activity. His recommendation was embodied in an order in council, promulgated on 23 September 1882, and forwarded to Secretary of State for the Colonies the Earl of Kimberley two days later[4]:

> The Committee of Council have had under consideration a Despatch dated 16th August 1880, No. 131, from the Earl of Kimberley, enclosing an Order of Her Majesty in Council dated the 31st of July 1880, annexing to the Dominion of Canada from the 1st September 1880 such British possessions in North America (with the exception of the Colony of Newfoundland and its dependencies) as are not already included in the Dominion.
>
> The Minister of Justice to whom the said Despatch was referred with a view to endeavour to obtain information regarding the occupants of the country North and North West of Hudson's Bay, and their habits and pursuits, reports that immediately after the reference he entered into a correspondence with the principal officer of the Hudson's Bay Company on the subject, and that gentleman very kindly caused Circulars to be addressed to such of the Agents of the Company as were likely to be able to furnish information on the points under consideration. On the 22nd of July last the Chief Executive Officer of the Company, Mr. James Grahame, addressed a letter to him, the Minister, informing him that the parties to whom he had referred the enquiries were unable to furnish the required information.
>
> *The Minister is not aware of any other source where such information as is desired may be sought, and he advises that no steps be taken with the view of legislating for the good government of the country until some influx of population or other circumstance shall occur to make such provision more imperative than it would at present seem to be.*
>
> The Committee concur in the report of the Minister of Justice and advise that a copy of this Minute when approved be transmitted to her Majesty's Secretary of State for the Colonies.[5] [emphasis added]

Here, it would seem, lies the basic reason for the almost total lack of activity on the part of the Canadian government in the new territories for about fifteen years after 1880: no need for it could be found. It was not, as King apparently thought, doubt that the transfer was valid.[6]

King also misinterpreted and overestimated the relevance of the British Colonial Boundaries Act of 1895.[7] The act itself is very short, its main clause stating:

> 1. – (1.) Where the boundaries of a colony have, either before or after the passing of this Act, been altered by Her Majesty the Queen by Order in Council or letters patent the boundaries as so altered shall be, and be deemed to have been from the date of the alteration, the boundaries of the colony.

FIGURE 2-1: DR. W. F. KING. *NATURAL RESOURCES CANADA*.

> Provided that the consent of a self-governing colony shall be required for the alteration of the boundaries thereof.
>
> In this Act "self-governing colony" means any of the colonies specified in the schedule to this Act.
>
> The self-governing colonies specified in the accompanying schedule were Canada, Newfoundland, New South Wales, Victoria, South Australia, Queensland, Western Australia, Tasmania, New Zealand, Cape of Good Hope and Natal.

About three weeks after the act was passed, Britain sent a copy to Canada, accompanied by a copy of a circular from Colonial Secretary Joseph Chamberlain which read:

> The Law Officers of the Crown having recently reported that where and Imperial Act has expressly defined the boundaries of a Colony, or has bestowed a Constitution on a Colony within certain boundaries, territory cannot be annexed to that Colony so as to be completely fused with it, as, e.g., by being included in a province or electoral division of it without statutory authority, it followed that certain annexations of territory to colonies falling within the above category which had been effected by Order in Council and Letters Patent, accompanied by Acts of the Colonial Legislatures, were of doubtful validity, and this Act has been passed to validate these annexations, and to remove all doubts as to Her Majesty's powers in future cases.[8]

Dr. King seemed to assume in his report that the Imperial Parliament passed the Colonial Boundaries Act specifically or essentially to remove any doubt about the validity of the transfer of 1880.[9] Holmden disagreed with this interpretation, noting that by the time the order in council of 31 July 1880 was passed the authorities in both Great Britain and Canada were satisfied that the transfer could be legally accomplished in this manner, and their remaining doubts related to the uncertain boundaries of the lands transferred in both 1870 and 1880. He believed that although the Colonial Boundaries Act would clear up any doubts about the validity of the transfer in 1880, it was not "intended to apply to Canada."[10]

It seems to me that Holmden is generally correct, except that the act was obviously intended to be applicable to Canada, since Canada was one of the self-governing colonies named in the accompanying schedule. Perhaps he meant that in passing the act the Imperial authorities did not have Canada primarily in mind. Remarks passed in the British parliament when the proposed measure was being discussed provide strong evidence that the territories subject to this transfer were not the primary concern, since the colonies specifically mentioned were New Zealand, some of the Australian colonies, Cape Colony, and Natal.[11]

Nevertheless, and in spite of the foregoing (and contrary to Holmden's view in 1921), additional evidence suggests that doubts about the 1880 transfer did figure into Britain's decision to enact the Colonial Boundaries Act. If Dr. King was partly off the track in his assessment of this connection, he was to a large extent only reflecting the view of it which had been taken by the authorities in London in 1895. On 21 May, Henry Jenkyns at the Office of the Parliamentary Counsel wrote a memo on the proposed act which was sent as a dispatch to Ottawa on 29 May. The most relevant parts of it read as follows.

> It appears from three reports from the Law Officers, dated respectively the 25th August 1894, the 27th February 1895, and the 27th February 1895 [*sic*], that the law as to the alteration of the boundaries of colonies is as follows: –
>
> I. Where an Imperial Act has expressly defined the boundaries of a colony or has bestowed a constitution on a colony within certain boundaries, territory cannot be annexed to that Colony so as to be completely fused with it, as e.g., by being included in a province or electoral division of it, without statutory authority ...
>
> II. But the Queen can, unless restrained by an Imperial Act, give to any such colony as above mentioned and the colony can accept the administration and government of any territory. The most solemn mode of such acceptance is colonial legislation.
>
> In such a cse [*sic*] the territory is not incorporated with and does not become part of the colony, but is only administered by the same government.
>
> III. The same law appears to apply –
>
> (a) Where the boundaries have been fixed by Order in Council or letters patent issued in pursuance of statutory authority....
>
> V. An annexation, even if irregular in the outset, may possibly, if followed by a de facto incorporation for a long period of time, acquire, like any other constitutional changes, validity through usage....
>
> It follows from the above that certain annexations of territory by Order in Council and letters patent accompanied by Acts of the Colonial Legislatures are invalid. For instance –

(a) The annexation to Canada of all British territory in North America and of the adjacent islands by Order in Council of the 31st July 1880 (the limits of the Dominion having been fixed by the British North America Acts, 1867 and 1871).

(b) The annexation to Queensland of all islands within 60 miles of the coast of Queensland …

(c) The annexation to New Zealand of the Kermadec Islands.…

It will be observed that the Bill applies only where the boundary has been fixed by or under an Act of Parliament, and does not touch the case where the boundaries have been already fixed by the prerogative power of the Queen.[12]

Thus, if doubts about the "sufficiency" of the 1880 order in council were in any way justified, the Colonial Boundaries Act of 1895 retroactively removed the need for them. One may assume, however, that the above documents were received in Ottawa with consternation, even if the presumed insufficiency was being corrected. Particularly unsettling must have been the categorical statement in Jenkyns' memo that the transfer of 1880 was one of the annexations by order in council now regarded as "invalid." The obvious issue, which must have troubled Canadian officials greatly, is simply this: Was the confirmation provided by the Colonial Boundaries Act really necessary for the 1880 transfer? A number of questions and comments spring immediately to mind.

1. One of the most fundamental, and most disturbing, questions is the following. How is it that the transfer could be pronounced valid, after full consideration and on repeated occasions, by law officers in the 1870s, and then pronounced invalid by law officers in 1895? A question, which cannot be answered from the documents cited, is whether the revised 1895 opinion about the transfer was actually that of the law officers themselves or a conclusion reached through analogy by Colonial Office officials.

2. Even if the annexation of 1880 was "irregular in the outset," would it not have acquired "validity through usage," in accordance with the fifth point in Jenkyns' memo? After all, it had been treated as valid for fifteen years.

3. Considering that the order in council had been judged adequate in all respects in 1880, could a reversal of opinion by the law officers or someone else in 1895 have the retroactive effect of making it invalid?

4. Were the law officers and others aware in 1895 of the purpose and significance of the BNA Act of 1871 in connection with territories admitted into the Dominion of Canada? This act had been overlooked by the Law Officers of the Crown in the 1870s. It is mentioned once in the correspondence presently under discussion, but in a somewhat different context. It would be remarkable, to say the least, if the relevance of the act was overlooked a second time in 1895.

5. Assuming that the authorities in 1895 were fully aware of the BNA Act of 1871 and its purpose, why did they not accept it as covering the territories subject to the transfer of 1880? The following is surmise, but may suggest an answer. The act of 1871 dealt with territories "admitted, or which may hereafter be admitted" into the Dominion, and authorized the Parliament of Canada to create provinces from them and otherwise administer and govern

them. Presumably, then, all would be in order after they had become part of the Dominion, so long as they had been admitted into it by legal and constitutional means. But if they had not, the BNA Act of 1871 could not in itself legitimize their entry. Perhaps this was what was seen as the fly in the ointment in 1895.

6. Did the fundamental circumstances which the Colonial Boundaries Act was intended to take care of really exist in connection with the transfer of 1880? It would seem that they did not. The documents make clear that the act was designed to correct situations where an Imperial act had "expressly defined the boundaries of a colony," and where subsequently territory had been annexed the colony without statutory authority, for example by order in council, so as to be "completely fused" with it, by being included in a province. Neither of these basic circumstances existed in the case of the 1880 transfer. It is true that the Province of Canada was admitted to Confederation with the boundaries of former Upper and Lower Canada, these becoming Ontario and Quebec respectively; but the northern boundary with the HBC territories was not specified, either before, at the time of, or after Confederation. The BNA Act of 1867 gave statutory authority for the admission by order in council of Rupert's Land and the North-Western Territory to Canada (art. 146), and the BNA Act of 1871 confirmed the power of the Parliament of Canada to create provinces from territories within Canada and govern non-provincial territories. But nowhere in either act was there, as apparently suggested in Jenkyns' memo, any definition of the territorial limits of either Rupert's Land or the North-Western Territory. And these, rather than any province or provinces, were adjacent to the territories involved in the transfer of 1880. As for the second point, the territories subject to the transfer had purportedly been annexed simply as territories, and had not been fused with any province. This would have been difficult, because the vast expanse of the former HBC empire intervened between them and the existing provinces. There was nothing to suggest that they were supposed to have been fused with any of the provinces, or even with these HBC lands.

In sum, it seems clear that if there were any flaws in the constitutional aspects, or the mechanics, of the transfer of 1880, these flaws were overcome by the Colonial Boundaries Act of 1895. But this act, evidently necessary for a number of annexations in other parts of the Empire, does not seem to have been really needed so far as the transfer of 1880 was concerned. It was designed to deal with cases where Imperial legislation had precisely defined colonial boundaries, but there had been no such definition of the northern boundaries in British North America. It was designed also to take care of cases where territories had been "completely fused" with existing colonies as parts of provinces, etc., but there had been no such fusion in 1880. The transfer had been judged entirely satisfactory when it was made and had been so regarded afterwards, and the BNA Act of 1871 covered the situation so far as later developments were concerned. For these reasons it is difficult to see that there was anything particularly wrong with the transfer in an internal, constitutional sense. If there was, surely it amounted to no more than a minor technicality.

What was wrong with the transfer, as already indicated, was that it purported to annex to Canada, in the vaguest and most imprecise way, unnamed territories of unknown and unspecified extent, to which Great Britain's title was uncertain, and for which no boundaries were given. In this sense it was vulnerable to the charge that it was not really a transfer at all. This deficiency had a more international aspect, and if other states had become interested in establishing serious claims within the archipelago during the years immediately following the transfer, Great Britain and Canada might have found that their arrangement was by no means immune to challenge. Ironically enough, this could have happened given foreign explorers' activities during the early 1880s (see chapter 6). On the whole, however, if Canada was doing little to consolidate her claim to the archipelago during these years, other states were doing very little that would give them a basis for making counterclaims.

The Expeditions of Lieutenant A. R. Gordon: 1884, 1885, 1886

A series of three Canadian expeditions to Hudson Bay and Strait during the successive years of 1884, 1885, and 1886, all commanded by Lieutenant Andrew Robertson Gordon of the Royal Navy and supervised by the federal Minister of Marine and Fisheries, stands as a rare example of Canadian activity in the Arctic.[13] A select committee of the Canadian House of Commons had conducted an inquiry in February and March 1884 into the possibilities of commercial navigation in Hudson Bay and Strait, and reported optimism about the prospect of developing this passage as the shortest sea route between the Canadian Northwest and Great Britain. The committee had further recommended that immediate steps be taken to conduct investigations and observations over a three-year period to ascertain the feasibility of the route.[14] Lieutenant Gordon's three voyages were primarily concerned with carrying out the recommendations of the report, and were thus chiefly occupied with observing navigation and weather conditions in these waters.[15]

Using the chartered steamers *Neptune* in 1884 and *Alert* (of the Nares expedition) in 1885 and 1886, Gordon cruised extensively in Hudson Strait and Hudson Bay, and visited numerous points, including Port Burwell, Chesterfield Inlet, Marble Island, Churchill, York Factory, and Digges Island. Groups of observers were left at half a dozen points in the strait in 1884, relieved in 1885, and the relieving parties picked up in 1886. They took note of navigation conditions, including water currents and ice, weather, flora and fauna, natural resources, and the native population; Gordon himself also wrote lengthy memoranda on these matters. Dr. Robert Bell of the Geological Survey, who accompanied the expeditions, furnished detailed geological reports. In 1886, Gordon surveyed the mouths of both the Churchill and the Nelson-Hayes river systems as prospective harbours and sites for the terminus of the projected Hudson Bay railway, and he emphasized that in his view Churchill was by far the more suitable of the two.[16] He also advised that a four-month navigation season, from July through October, was the maximum that could be expected – with delays in July and difficulties in October.[17]

Some authors have supposed that Gordon's three voyages were directly connected with the transfer of 1880 and Canada's assumption of responsibility in the newly acquired territories.[18] I can find little to justify this supposition since, as Gordon's narratives and other evidence make clear, the voyages were designed primarily to gather information about navigation in Hudson Bay and Strait, and they penetrated no farther north. In his 1884 report, Gordon himself noted that "the primary object of the whole expedition is to ascertain for what period of the year the Straits are navigable."[19] Dr. Bell, in his

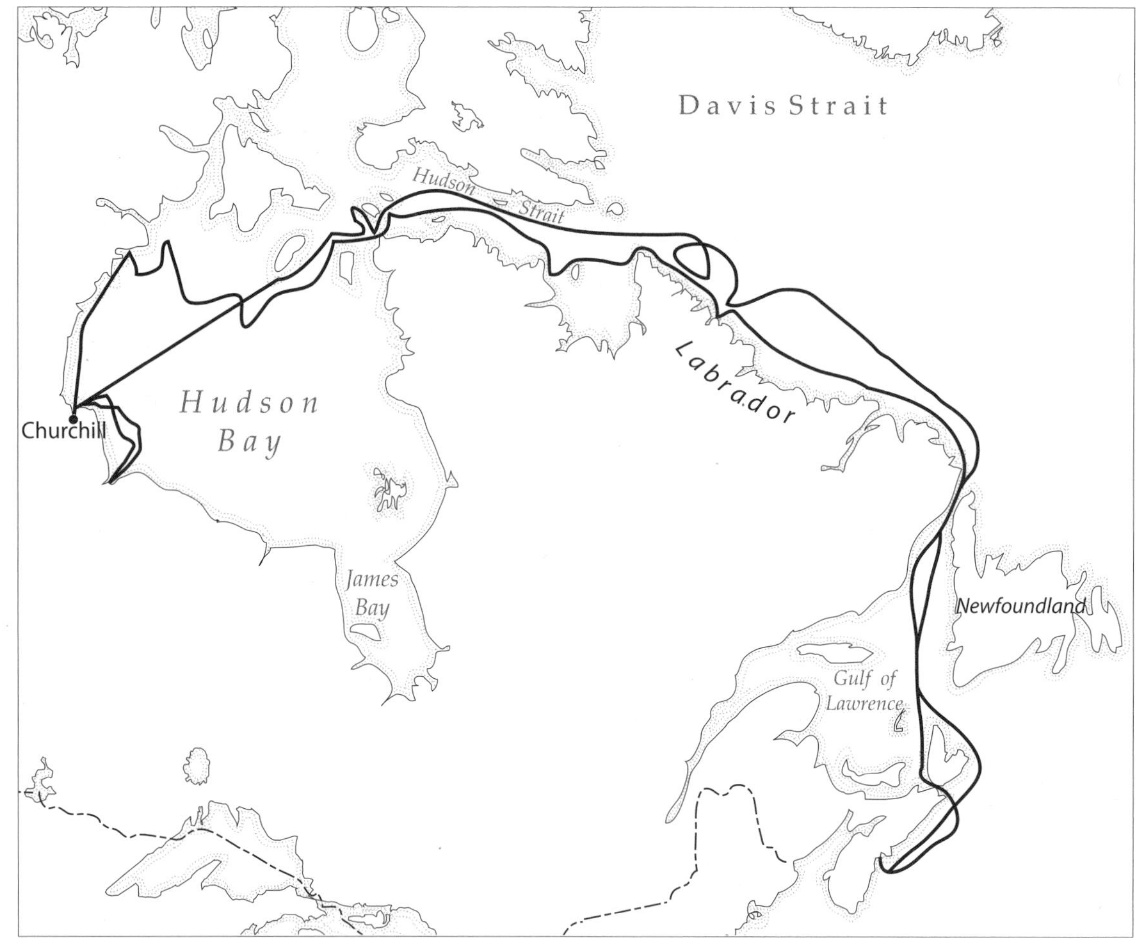

FIGURE 2-2: CHART SHOWING THE TRACK OF THE DSS *ALERT* HUDSON'S BAY EXPEDITION 1886. *JENNIFER ARTHUR-LACKENBAUER* BASED ON A. R. GORDON, *REPORT OF THE HUDSON'S BAY EXPEDITION OF 1886 UNDER THE COMMAND OF LIEUT. A. R. GORDON* (OTTAWA: DEPT. OF MARINE AND FISHERIES, 1887).

report for the same year, stated "that the main object of the expedition, sent out by steamship the present season, was to establish six observatory stations on the shores of Hudson's Strait ... all with a view to throw additional light on questions regarding the navigation of these waters."[20] Minister of Marine and Fisheries George Eulas Foster instructed Gordon prior to the 1886 voyage to "bear in mind that it is the wish of the Department to demonstrate as far as possible the navigability of the Straits, for purposes of commerce."[21] A few weeks earlier, Foster had emphasized the same point in the House of Commons in his reply to a question about the voyages of 1884 and 1885. "In sending the *Alert* to visit the Hudson's Straits last year," he explained, "it was intended by the Government that the navigability of these waters should be tested by that vessel, as that was the primary object of fitting out the expedition to the Hudson's Bay and Straits in 1884–85."[22] Unless there is other evidence as yet unrevealed, there would seem to be no reason why the above statements should not be taken at face value, and therefore it is probably safe to conclude that from the Canadian government's point of view the voyages of Gordon were not directly connected with the 1880 transfer of the Arctic Islands.

Even so, Gordon became concerned about the assertion of Canada's jurisdiction in the regions he visited. In his 1884 report, he took note of the profitable whaling and fishing industries carried on freely by American citizens and by the HBC. With regard to the Americans in particular, he wrote:

> I have the honour to urge that in any negotiations with the Government of the United States, relative to a treaty of reciprocal trade, due allowance should be made for the great value of the fisheries of Hudson's Bay.
>
> If American whalers are to be permitted to continue to fish in those waters, arrangements should be made by which Canada would receive a substantial equivalent for the privilege.
>
> I would further suggest that unless a very large consideration is granted in return for the privilege, the Canadian Government should reserve the right to make and enforce such regulations as will prevent the extermination of these valuable mammals from our northern waters.[23]

He also observed that Newfoundland authorities were collecting customs duties in their Labrador ports on goods destined for consumption at Fort Chimo in Canadian territory, and that although the HBC had to pay duties to the Canadian government on trade goods imported into Hudson Bay, the American whalers were bringing in such goods, evidently including liquor, and paying nothing.[24]

Gordon apparently made no formal proclamations of Canadian sovereignty during his three expeditions, unlike his successors William Wakeham, Albert Peter Low, and Joseph-Elzéar Bernier, but he did protest that the waters of Hudson Bay were wholly within Canadian territory and should be so regarded. A passage in his 1885 report reads as follows:

> The waters of Hudson's Bay are wholly within the Dominion, and the right of Canada to protect these waters and keep them for her own citizens is, I think, unchallenged. In the case of the White Sea in Northern Russia, the Russian Government charge high licenses for the privilege of fishing, and prescribe the methods to be used in capturing the fish. I would strongly urge the advisability of protecting these fisheries; and in any negotiations with the United States Government in reference to right of United States citizens to fish within the territorial waters of Canada, the value of the Hudson's Bay and Straits region as a fishing ground should be strongly insisted on; and under any circumstances, our Government should retain the right to prescribe the methods which may be used.[25]

In his 1886 report, Gordon returned to the same themes and embodied his earlier points in a series of formal recommendations, adding his opinion that a Canadian government vessel should visit the region annually to regulate the fisheries and for any other purposes necessary.[26] Obviously the Canadian government did not carry out promptly all his recommendations (particularly regarding annual voyages), but they remain interesting and significant in the light of later events.

Other Activities, Mainly in Former HBC Lands (1880–95)

34

Other Canadian expeditions during this period were concerned essentially with the northern mainland rather than the Arctic islands. Most of them were carried on by members of the Geological Survey, and thus were primarily scientific in character. Among the more important were those of Joseph Burr Tyrrell in the so-called Barren Grounds west of Hudson Bay in 1892, 1893, and 1894. He was accompanied in 1893 by his younger brother James Williams (J. W.), who had been with Gordon in 1885–86. In 1887–88, Dr. George Mercer Dawson, William Ogilvie, and Richard George McConnell carried out extensive surveys along the Yukon and Mackenzie Rivers and their tributaries. Other members of the Geological Survey were at work elsewhere in the North, notably Dr. Bell and A. P. Low in the Hudson Bay region. For the most part, these expeditions were not directly connected with the Canadian assumption of responsibility in the newly acquired regions, but they did constitute significant initial attempts to reveal the geography and natural resources of remote parts of the lands acquired in 1870. For example, J. W. Tyrrell mentioned building cairns and raising the flag in various places as traditional symbols of sovereignty,[27] and Ogilvie completed the specific task of locating the 141st meridian as the boundary between Alaska and Canadian territory.[28]

Responsibility for the maintenance of law and order in the Canadian North fell to the Royal Canadian Mounted Police when its authority extended to this region. Created as the North West Mounted Police (NWMP) in 1873 by a federal act[29] and a federal order in council,[30] it was conceived as a police force in and for the Northwest Territories. Initially, however, the NWMP's primary responsibility was to establish law and order in the comparatively small portion of the North-West Territories which lay immediately north of the American border and between the newly created provinces of Manitoba and British Columbia. For about twenty years their chief concern was with this rapidly developing region. During these stirring times the NWMP had conspicuous success in maintaining law and order on a frontier previously lacking both, and, incidentally, in building for themselves a solid reputation for justice, fair play, and devotion to duty.

In the summer of 1890, Inspector J. V. Bégin carried the force's flag for the first time to Hudson Bay, making a long patrol overland and by river from Norway House at the outlet of Lake Winnipeg to York Factory and back.[31] In so doing he started the movement northwards of the NWMP, which was eventually to extend their supervision to the farthest extremities of the Canadian Arctic. In 1893, Inspector D. M. Howard and eight constables were sent to establish a post at Athabaska Landing, on the Athabaska River, with subsidiary detachments at Lesser Slave River and Grand Rapids. These were the most northerly posts at that time but were kept open only during the summer.[32]

There does not seem to be a great deal more of relevance to say about the northern territories during the period 1880–95. Canada's main interest was in the more southerly, fertile parts of the HBC lands transferred in 1870, and activity was concentrated therein. Such activity as was carried on in the more remote parts of former Rupert's Land and the old North-Western

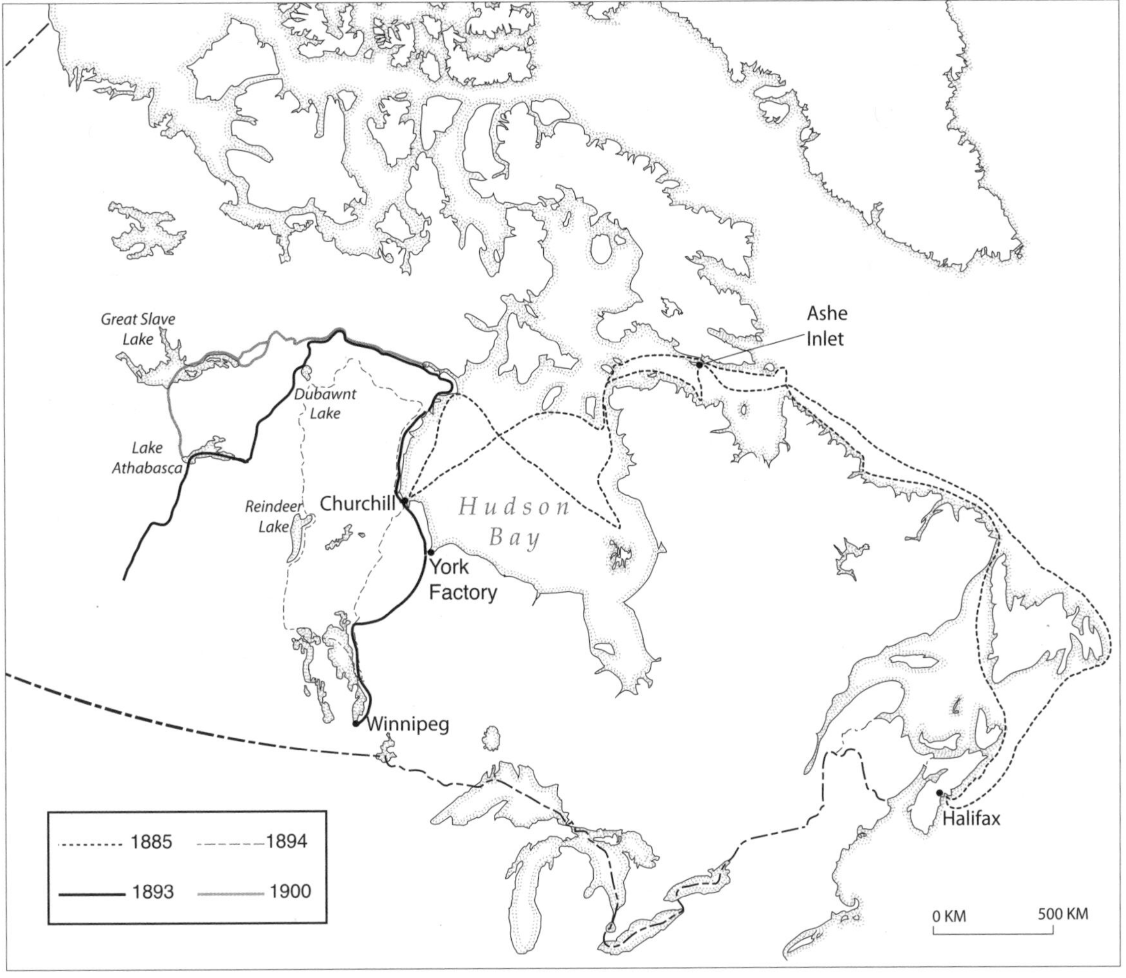

2-3: THE 1893 AND 1894 TYRRELL EXPEDITIONS. *JENNIFER ARTHUR-LACKENBAUER.*

Territory was not primarily intended to assert Canadian ownership and rights of jurisdiction, and the Arctic islands were ignored almost completely. Hensley Holmden, in commenting upon the apparent lack of action by the Canadian Government between 1882 and 1895, "found no despatch or Minute of Council dealing in any way, or even relating to the question of the extension of Canada's boundaries towards the North and northwest" during these years.[33] Similarly, W. F. King observed that although the *Revised Statutes* of 1886 took account of the withdrawal of Manitoba and Keewatin from the Northwest Territories, they made no provision for the inclusion of the territories subject to the transfer of 1880.[34] The organization and administration of the Dominion's northern inheritance remained incomplete.

3

Organization and Administration of the NWT, 1895–1918

Canada's attempts to make definite provision for the organization and administration of the northernmost territories may be dated from the promulgation of a federal order in council on 2 October 1895 which formed the hitherto "unorganized and unnamed districts of the North-west Territories" into the four provisional districts of Ungava, Mackenzie, Yukon, and Franklin.[1] Franklin was stated to be "of indefinite extent," but, apart from some coastal and Hudson Bay islands, it was defined so as to include the entire arctic archipelago, as it was then known.

The circumstances surrounding the promulgation of this order in council, and the reasons for it, have remained rather mysterious. Dr. William Frederick King, in line with his belief that Canada regarded the transfer of 1880 as incomplete until the British Parliament passed the Colonial Boundaries Act, seems to take the view that the Canadian order in council was a direct consequence of this British act.[2] Hensley R. Holmden, on the other hand, believes that the close proximity in time between the act and the order in council was pure coincidence. Although the Colonial Boundaries Act was dated 6 July 1895, a copy of it was not sent to Canada until 26 July, accompanied by the circular from Colonial Secretary Joseph Chamberlain discussed in the previous chapter. Although the Canadian order in council organizing the territories was not issued until 2 October 1895, it was proceeded by (and evidently resulted from) a report submitted earlier by Canadian Minister of the Interior Thomas Daly which advised the government to organize the four provisional districts. The odd feature pointed out by Holmden is that this report is also dated 26 July 1895 – the same date that Chamberlain's circular and the copy of the colonial Boundaries Act were sent to Canada. If the order in council was a consequence of Daly's report, and if Daly's report was a consequence of the Colonial Boundaries Act and Chamberlain's circular, then the latter must have been sent to Canada by transatlantic cable and Daly must have handed in his report and recommendations on the same day. Holmden, after asking if there was any "common inspiration" in these events, implies that there was none, noting "there is nothing in the Order in Council to show that it was prompted by the passage of the Imperial Act."[3] He prefers to believe that it was a motion by the Hon. David Mills, the Liberal member for Bothwell, in the House of Commons on 28 May 1894 requesting "copies of all correspondence since 1867, between the Government of Canada and the Imperial Government in reference to Her Majesty's exclusive sovereignty over Hudson Bay,"[4] and ensuing remarks by Mills and Minister of Marine and Fisheries Sir Charles Tupper which "called attention to Canada's possessions in the far north." In Holmden's view, these remarks and the events that provoked them caused Daly to make his report.[5]

Holmden notes that Parliament agreed to and "brought down" Mills's motion but adds that the requested papers were destroyed in the 1916 fire that burned the Parliament building.[6] The remarks by Mills and Tupper to which he attached such importance went as follows:

> *[Mr. Mills] said*: This, Mr. Speaker, is a matter of very considerable importance. The Government, of course, know right well that Hudson's Bay has always been claimed by Great Britain as part of the sovereignty of the Crown ever since the discovery of the bay. It was a matter of dispute for some time, during a former century, between Great Britain and France as to whom this bay, of right, belonged; but that question was settled in favour of the British contention by the Treaty of Utrecht in 1713, and since then I believe, it has been recognized as between Great Britain and France and acquiesced generally by christendom that this is a portion of the British possessions in North America. I understand, Mr. Speaker, that lately American vessels have been going in there, engaged in whale, porpoise, and other fishing operations, and I do not understand that any steps have been taken by the Government to assert the jurisdiction of Canada over these waters. Now, the whole coast of Hudson's Bay lies within British territory. The bay is a land-locked bay, only connected with the high seas by the narrow passage of water called the Hudson's Straits. But, Sir, if the ships of foreign countries are allowed to go into these waters without question, and without taking out any license, to engage in fishing operations there, it might very well be, at no distant day, according to the rules of acquiescence, that the parties whose ships so engaged might claim to go there, as a matter of right, regarding these waters as part of the high seas. I think it is important to know how far there has been any departure from the long and continuous contention that these are British waters. Under the modern doctrine there has been a disposition to limit the rights of states to waters within their own territory and upon their own coasts, and it is important to know whether any correspondence has taken place between the Government of Canada and the Government of the United Kingdom with reference to our sovereignty over these waters as part of the territory of Canada. I am not going to detain the House with any statement of the elementary principles of international law applicable to the case. These are generally well known. What it is important to know is what steps the Government have taken to assert their authority and to prevent any rights or pretentions of rights being acquired by any other people or community on the ground of acquiescence and because of our indifference with regard to these matters. There is no difference in point of law, between the rule of acquiescence as applicable between

private individuals and between states. It is therefore of consequence that we should not, by our indifference, permit any loss to be sustained by the Canadian people, and for this reason I move for this correspondence. I assume that the Government have not been indifferent to the rights of the people of Canada; I assume that the Government have not, by negligence, or by sleeping upon their rights, permitted rights of other parties to spring up. It is true that it may involve some expense to this country to exercise proper police supervision over the waters of Hudson's Bay. It seems to me, however, that on account of the narrowness of the straits which connected this bay with the Atlantic, that right should be very easily exercised, and at no great expense to the country. But whether that expense be more or less, I think it is important that it should be incurred for the purpose of maintaining our rights; and I am sure that the House and the public would not be indifferent to the maintenance of the sovereignty of Canada over these waters. I am told that they are valuable at the present time, that the whale fisheries and porpoise fisheries are both extensive, and that the hair seal fisheries in the vicinity are also extensive, and have of late years greatly increased. This being so, and it being probably that at no distant date the bay will be connected with the settled portions of Canada by railway communication, it is highly important that our exclusive jurisdiction over those waters should not be lost, and for these reasons I move the motion now in your hands.

Sir Charles Hibbert Tupper: The importance of this question is fully recognized by the Government. The hon. Gentleman has referred to the fisheries of the Hudson's Bay and the Canadian interests in those waters, and it is perhaps only right that I should say in advance of the return being brought down, that the question has received due attention, and its importance is fully recognized. The hon. Gentleman has referred to the invasion of our territorial rights by fishing and hunting that are carried on in Canadian waters in Hudson's Bay by foreign fishing vessels. I may say that from time to time rumours of that character have reached me. The remoteness of the region, however, has made it extremely difficult to ascertain with any degree of accuracy the correctness of these rumours. Some steps have been taken, through the agency of the Department of Marine and Fisheries, to publish notices that the laws of Canada apply in those waters; but it is only fair to say that since we are not as yet familiar with either the time that those vessels are likely to arrive or the portions of the bay where they may be found at any time, these notices have been to a great extent formal. Nevertheless, so far as the records of my department show, there had been no inaction in that connection that would in the slightest degree prejudice the rights of Canada over this region. On one or two occasions we have, through the agency of the Hudson's Bay Company and through the Indian Department, endeavoured to obtain full information in regard to the illicit trading which is said to have been carried on by small foreign vessels going there possibly to hunt, or engage in the whale or porpoise fishery, but the result of those efforts so far has not been such as to give us much definite information. Even the Hudson's Bay Company officials themselves, though they believe and assert that a good deal of smuggling is carried on in violation of our revenue laws, have not been able, up to date, to furnish such information as would enable us to take definite action. However, the whole subject and the important interests that are there involved have been under consideration for some time with the object of ascertaining what definite course should now be taken in regard to the various propositions for protecting such rights as we think should be conserved, for instance, the very question of jurisdiction to which the hon. gentleman has referred, and propositions relating to the establishment of a revenue ship for the purpose of maintaining those rights. There would be ample opportunity to assert exclusive sovereignty over those waters because of the narrow approaches to the great waters of the bay. Most of the channels are under six miles in width, and all, I think, are outside the main entrance of the Hudson's Bay itself. So that when it becomes necessary actively to assert such rights as we possess, there would be, as the hon. gentleman says, no great difficulty; and I am inclined to agree with him in the view that no great expense would be entailed. The papers, so far as they relate to the various departments, will, no doubt, be soon collected and brought down, in answer to the hon. gentleman's motion.[7]

Holmden does not give any further evidence to support his belief that these speeches, along with the related circumstances, led to the promulgation of the order in council of 2 October 1895 and an apparently new interest in the most northerly territories. Other evidence not only strengthens his contention but also helps to make the pattern of developments logical and understandable. The remarks by both Mills and Tupper about the activities of American whaling ships in Hudson Bay, for example, call to mind the complaints and recommendations of Lieutenant A. R. Gordon a few years earlier. The same question was brought up in the House of Commons on 27 June 1892, when reference was made to complaints by Lieutenant-Governor John Christian Schultz of Manitoba and Keewatin to the Minister of the Interior about the same activities. Schultz mentioned the matter frequently in his reports (see chapter 4 on whaling) and seems to have been largely responsible for bringing it to the attention of the authorities in Ottawa in 1890 and 1891.[8] In 1894 he again urged the government to stop the American whaling fleet's wanton destruction of sea life and illegal trade with Inuit.[9] Deputy Minister of the Interior Alexander Mackinnon Burgess underlined both of these points in his own report dated 17 April 1895,[10] which would presumably have been in Daly's hands long before he made his own report to the cabinet on 26 July.

The reports of the Department of the Interior also indicate a rising concern over the Alaska boundary and the Yukon gold mining industry. Deputy Minister Burgess noted that William Ogilvie, in his 1887–88 survey, had found that the 141st meridian crossed the Yukon River about ninety miles farther down the river than it was shown on American maps, and that some of the best gold-bearing districts were really in Canadian territory.[11] Four years later, he commented upon the British-American convention of 22 July 1892, which provided for a joint survey of the Panhandle boundary and the appointment of Dominion Chief Astronomer W. F. King and Dr. Thomas C. Mendenhall as British and American commissioners respectively.[12] In his 1895 report, he gave details about the importation of merchandise into the Yukon by American concerns via the Yukon River and the coastal mountain passes without paying duty, and also about the illicit traffic in intoxicating liquor. Therefore, he said, the facts clearly established that

> the time had arrived when it became the duty of the Government of Canada to make more efficient provision for the maintenance of order, the enforcement of the laws, and the administration of justice in the Yukon country, especially in that section of it in which placer mining gold is being prosecuted upon such an extensive scale, situated near to the boundary separating the North-west Territories from the possessions of the United States in Alaska.[13]

Inspector Charles Constantine of the North West Mounted Police (NWMP) had already been sent to the Yukon in the spring of 1894 to investigate and report, and in June 1895 was sent back at the head of twenty members of the force to represent the Canadian government temporarily in all respects. At the same time William Ogilvie was also sent back to locate the 141st meridian both south and north of the Yukon River, preferably with American co-operation.[14]

Other factors may also have contributed to the Canadian government passing Order in Council No. 2640 of 2 October 1895, but on the basis of the evidence discovered these were the important ones.[15] The order in council recommended the establishment of four new provisional districts in the hitherto "unorganized and unnamed districts of the North West Territories":

Ungava, which was stated to be "of indefinite extent," included the territory enclosed by Hudson Strait on the north, Hudson and James Bays on the west, the uncertain northern boundary of Quebec on the south, and the equally uncertain western boundary of Labrador on the east. The islands in Hudson Strait, Hudson Bay, and James Bay less than three sea miles from the coast were to be included within Ungava; those beyond this limit would fall under the control of the Dominion government.

The *Yukon District* was bounded by the 141st meridian (Alaska) on the west, the 60th parallel on the south, an irregular line along the summits of the mountain ranges west of the Mackenzie River on the east, and the Arctic Ocean on the north, with a small portion on the southwest against the Alaskan Panhandle undetermined because it was in dispute with the United States. The order specified that the district should include Herschel Island and all other islands within three geographical miles of its Arctic coast.

The *Mackenzie District* was to comprise the area enclosed by the Yukon District boundary on the west, approximately the 60th parallel (actually the 32nd correction line of the Dominion lands survey) on the south, the 100th meridian on the east, and the Arctic Ocean on the north. Like the Yukon, Mackenzie was to include all islands within three geographical miles of its Arctic coast.

The *District of Franklin*, which also was stated to be "of indefinite extent," was to be bounded as follows:

> Beginning at Cape Best, at the entrance to Hudson Strait from the Atlantic; thence westerly, through said Strait, Fox Channel, Gulf of Boothia, Franklin Strait, Ross Strait, Simpson Strait, Victoria Strait, Dease Strait, Coronation Gulf, and Dolphin and Union Strait, to a point in the Arctic Sea, longitude about 125° 30' West, and in latitude about 7° north; thence northerly, including Baring Land, Prince Patrick Island, and the Polynea Islands; thence north-easterly to the "farthest of Commander Markham's and Lieutenant Parry's sledge-journey" in 1876, in longitude about 63 1/2° West, and latitude about 83 ¼° north; thence southerly through Robeson Channel, Kennedy Channel, Smith Sound, Baffin Bay, and Davis Strait to the place of beginning.

The order in council also recommended the enlargement of the already existing districts of Athabaska and Keewatin, by adding to them the large remaining areas directly north of Saskatchewan and Ontario respectively. It was evidently intended that the addition to Athabaska would be accomplished by the order in council itself, and the enlarged district would comprise the territory enclosed by British Columbia on the west, Alberta and Saskatchewan on the south, the 100th meridian on the east, and the 32nd correction line (Mackenzie) on the north. The addition to Keewatin would be brought about at the next session of Parliament by a federal act (presumably because this was how Keewatin had been created), and this district would thereafter comprise those territories enclosed by Ontario (as constituted by the Imperial act of 1889), Manitoba, Saskatchewan, the 100th meridian, and the Arctic, Hudson Bay, and James Bay coasts. The order concluded that "should the foregoing recommendations be adopted, the whole of the unorganized and unnamed portions of Canada will have been divided into Provisional Districts."[16]

Boundary Corrections and Adjustments (1895–1918)

As events turned out, however, no steps were taken to carry out the recommendations of the 1895 order in council, and instead another order in council was issued two years later, on 18 December 1897, to rectify mistakes which had been made in the first one.[17] The opening sentences of the new order give some indication as to why it had been found necessary:

> On a Report dated 10th December, 1897, from the Minister of the Interior, stating that by Order in Council of the 2nd October, 1895, the unorganized portions of Canada were divided into Provisional Districts, four new districts being created and changes made in the

boundaries of one of the old districts. It was further provided that at the next session of Parliament, a Bill should be introduced having for its object the addition of territory to the District of Keewatin. Shortly after the date of the above Order deficiencies were found in the descriptions of the district boundaries, and as doubts existed as to the form of the proposed amendments to the Keewatin Act, no steps were taken to carry out the directions of the Order.

The Minister recommends that the Order in Council of the 2nd, of October, 1895, be canceled, and that such legislation as may be necessary be introduced at the next session of Parliament to authorize the division of the portions of Canada not comprised within any Province into nine Provisional Districts in accordance with the annexed description and map.

The deficiencies in the 1895 order in council may be summarized as follows. The order had stated that the new districts of Ungava, Mackenzie, and Yukon should include all islands in Hudson Strait, Hudson Bay, James Bay, and the Arctic Ocean within three miles of their coasts ("sea" miles in the case of Ungava, "geographical" miles in the cases of Mackenzie and Yukon). The islands more than three miles from the Ungava coast, in Hudson Strait and Bay and James Bay, had supposedly been accounted for, as the order stated specifically that they were to be under the control of the Dominion Government. However, the attached map showed islands much more than three miles from the coast in Hudson Strait and Bay as part of Ungava. Also, although the recommended boundary for Keewatin was to follow the western shoreline of Hudson Bay, the same map showed Southampton and other islands in the Bay as territories to be added to this district. So far as the islands more than three miles from the Yukon and Mackenzie coasts were concerned, it appeared that no specific provisions had been made for them. Franklin District was to extend west only as far as 125° 30', but the western boundary of the Yukon was 141°, and thus there obviously more than three miles from the coast, between 125° 30' and 141°, which had not been included in any of the new provisional districts. Also, the southern boundary of Franklin had not been clearly defined, other than that it was to run though the channels north of the mainland, and thus it could be argued that this district would not necessarily include all islands north of Mackenzie beyond the three-mile limit. If the boundary were presumed to run through the middle of the channel separating the archipelago from the mainland, then wherever this channel was wider than six miles all islands north of Mackenzie between the three-mile limit and the mid-channel line would be excluded from both districts. And no mention whatever had been made of the islands north of the Keewatin coast. Finally, the order in recommending

> the division of "the unorganized and unnamed districts of the North-west Territories" into the four provisional districts of Ungava, Franklin, Mackenzie, and Yukon seemed to assume that the archipelago was already a part of the Northwest Territories, even though, as already noted, the statutory definition of the Northwest Territories had actually excluded the archipelago.[18]

By the new plan Keewatin, and also the eastern part of Mackenzie, were to be extended northward to the middle of the channel separating the archipelago from the mainland – to what would be the southern limit of Franklin. Farther west, in the Beaufort Sea area, Mackenzie and Yukon were to include all islands within twenty miles of the coast. The boundary between Mackenzie and Yukon was to be altered so as to follow a watershed line rather than the summit of the highest range of mountains. Keewatin was to receive the territory between northwestern Ontario and Hudson Bay that the order in council of 1895 had recommended should be added to it, and also those parts of James and Hudson Bays west of an irregular line drawn through the middle of James Bay and then through Hudson Bay, Foxe Channel, and Frozen Strait to the head of Repulse Bay. Keewatin would lose Melville and Boothia Peninsulas, however, which were assigned to Franklin. Ungava was to be extended to the middle of Hudson Strait (the southern boundary of Franklin), and to the eastern boundary of Keewatin in Hudson and James Bays. Franklin, besides gaining Melville and Boothia Peninsulas, was to be extended westward to the 141st meridian, and would include "all those lands and islands comprised between the one hundred and forty-first meridian of longitude west of Greenwich on the west and Davis Strait, Baffin Bay, Smith Sound, Kennedy Channel and Robeson Channel on the east which are not included in any other Provisional District." No northern boundary was mentioned. The order also described the boundaries of Assiniboia, Saskatchewan, Alberta, and Athabaska, but said that these districts would "remain as they were established by the Order in Council of the 2nd October, 1895, and previous Orders."

Thus the order in council of 1897 overcame the deficiencies in that of 1895 and, without overlapping, included within one or another of the several provisional districts all previously unorganized lands and islands to which Canada laid claim between Davis Strait and the 141st meridian.[19] The 1897 order also asked for "such legislation as may be necessary" to authorize the new division, and this legislation did not materialize. Thus, as historian Lawrence Johnstone Burpee observed, it might appear that the districts had no legal existence except insofar as they were created in 1882. Nevertheless, the federal government evidently considered the orders in council of 1895 and 1897 to have taken effect when it redefined the districts in 1918.[20]

The enactment of the Yukon Territory Act on 13 June 1898 introduced further complications.[21] This measure, passed while the Klondike Gold Rush was at its height, removed the Yukon from the rest of the Northwest Territories and constituted it a separate territory with a local government of its own, under a commissioner and council. A preliminary step in providing for law and order in the Yukon had already been taken almost one year earlier, when a Dominion order in council (16 August 1897) had created the so-called "Yukon Judicial District," with a resident judge.[22] This order, in describing the limits of the new judicial district, had duplicated exactly the description of the

FIGURE 3-1: MAP SHOWING THE NEW PROVISIONAL DISTRICTS OF UNGAVA, YUKON, MACKENZIE, FRANKLIN IN 1897. *JENNIFER ARTHUR-LACKENBAUER.*

Yukon Provincial District given in the defective order of 2 October 1895. The act of 1898 in defining the Yukon Territory reverted, apparently by oversight, to the definition in these two orders in council instead of following that of the corrected order of 18 December 1897. Thus the act included within the new Yukon Territory only those islands which were located within three geographical miles of its coast. W. F. King pointed out this error[23] and suggested that since the 1898 measure was a parliamentary statute it would have annulled the order in council of 18 December 1897, at least insofar as the Yukon Territory was concerned. It might even have annulled the order altogether with respect to the definition of northern boundaries, not only for the Yukon but also for the other districts. The act did not mention these other districts, but if it did annul completely the boundary provisions in the corrected order in council of 1897, King asked, were the boundaries of 1895 once again in force for them as well as for the Yukon? Or did the act recreate the boundaries of 1895 only for the Yukon, leaving the other districts as redefined by the corrected order in council of 1897? Here King pointed to what he thought was a basic difference in principle between the order in council of 1895 and that of 1897. Where the former claimed the northern mainland, the offshore islands within three miles, and the Arctic Archipelago as a separate territory divided from the mainland by a channel which in some parts became high sea, the latter claimed all land, both continental and insular, within certain prescribed limits. Dr. King seemed to lean to the view that the act of 1898 renounced the principle of the order of 1897 and adopted that of the order of 1895, and thus itself asserted a principle which "would involve the abrogation of the Order in Council of 1897, as regards the whole northern limit of Canada."[24]

Another Yukon Territory Act was passed in 1901,[25] the final two sections of which were obviously intended to correct the flaw in the act of 1898. Again it was open to doubt whether the object had been achieved. The new act extended the northern boundary of the Yukon Territory to include the islands within twenty (rather than within three) miles of the coast, in line with the order in council of 18 December 1897. Dr. King, still doubtful, held that the act of 1901 would have no other re-enacting effect upon the order in council of 1897, and if the latter were completely annulled by the act of 1898, then all the islands east of the Yukon coast and beyond the three-mile limit (except those which might be included in Franklin District) would be left outside Canadian jurisdiction, because the act of 1901 reaffirmed the twenty-mile limit only for the Yukon itself.[26]

Thus, as matters stood after this act had been passed, the Canadian authorities had tried by means of three orders in council and two acts of Parliament to achieve a satisfactory delimitation of Canada's northern territories. If Dr. King's interpretation is well founded, the situation in 1901 remained as confused as it had been in 1895. One may add that the failure to enact the legislation requested in the order in council of 18 December 1897 would certainly appear to have left the authority of that document in doubt, and it is particularly difficult to see how its provisions could have applied to Keewatin, which had been created and defined by act of parliament.[27]

Another chunk was bitten from the Northwest Territories in 1905, when the provinces of Alberta and Saskatchewan were created from the former districts of Alberta, Athabaska, Assiniboia, and Saskatchewan.[28] During the years immediately preceding 1905 there was much dispute over various aspects of this project, for example, the number of new provinces that should be created and the boundaries they should have.[29] Under the terms of the solution finally adopted by the federal government, the two new provinces assumed their present form, extending north to the 60th parallel (which now replaced the 32nd correction line as the northern boundary for these units), and being separated by the 4th meridian in the system of Dominion Lands Surveys (the 110th meridian of longitude).[30] The boundary line between Manitoba and former Assiniboia became the boundary line between the provinces of Manitoba and Saskatchewan. This line (the centre of the road allowance between the twenty-ninth and thirtieth ranges west of the principal meridian) was extended northward until it met the 102nd meridian, and then was prolonged on this meridian due north as far as the 60th parallel, continuing in its extension to form the eastern boundary of Saskatchewan. Small portions of former Saskatchewan and Athabaska were cut off east of this line, and the separated parts were apparently added to Keewatin,[31] which was re-annexed to the Northwest Territories by order in council four days after the Alberta and Saskatchewan Acts were passed.[32]

On the same day that the provinces of Alberta and Saskatchewan were created, a Northwest Territories Amendment Act was passed, which defined the remaining Northwest Territories in the following terms:

> The North-west Territories shall hereafter comprise the territories formerly known as Rupert's Land and the North-western Territory, except such portions thereof as form the provinces of Manitoba, Saskatchewan and Alberta, the district of Keewatin and the Yukon Territory, together with all British territories and possessions in North America and all islands adjacent to any such territories or possessions except the colony of Newfoundland and its dependencies.[33]

This evidently constitutes another attempt to achieve a satisfactory description of Canada's northern possessions. The terminology of the act is such that it might have taken care of the point about the offshore islands which was in doubt in 1895, 1897, 1898, and 1901, but it was imperfect in other respects. It revived (and almost duplicated) the language of the original Imperial order in council transferring Britain's Arctic territories to Canada in 1880, and thus was subject to that document's deficiencies.

The Northwest Territories Act of the *Revised Statutes of Canada* (1906) further defined the Northwest Territories,[34] but it differed little from the one just discussed, except that it included Keewatin as part of the Territories[35] in accordance with the order in council of 24 July 1905. It also excluded from the Territories any islands belonging to the provinces, a point which apparently had been overlooked before. The islands in question were not further identified.

In 1912 the Northwest Territories were again reduced, when the provinces of Manitoba, Ontario, and Quebec were all enlarged at their expenses.[36] The northern boundary of Quebec had already been extended in 1898, when it was fixed at the Eastmain and Hamilton Rivers and the parallel of latitude (approximately 52° 55') joining Lakes Patamisk and Ashuanipi at the sources of these two rivers.[37] By the act of 1912,[38] Quebec was again extended northward to swallow up the entire Ungava peninsula, all the way to Hudson Bay and Strait, leaving out whatever portion of the disputed territory in the northeast might be the property of Newfoundland. Matters were otherwise uncomplicated here because Quebec had no provincial rival. Such was not the case farther west, where Saskatchewan, Manitoba, and Ontario all contended vigorously for the available territory. It was impossible to satisfy completely the conflicting claims of all the provinces; the solution adopted by the federal government was to pay no heed to the demands of Saskatchewan but rather to divide between Manitoba and Ontario all of southern Keewatin up to the 60th parallel of latitude.[39] The 60th parallel thus became the dividing line between the four western provinces and the Northwest Territories, all the way from the northwestern extremity of British Columbia to Hudson Bay. The division of territory between Manitoba and Ontario was accomplished by extending their common boundary line due north along the meridian where it had been fixed by the Ontario Boundary Act in 1889 as far as the twelfth base line of the system of Dominion Land Surveys, from which point it was continued northeasterly in a straight line to the easternmost point of Island Lake, and thence again northeasterly in a

FIGURE 3-2: MAP OF CANADA IN 1912. *JENNIFER ARTHUR-LACKENBAUER.*

straight line to the point where the 89th meridian intersected the southern shore of Hudson Bay. None of the islands off the coast in Hudson and James Bays and Hudson Strait were given to the provinces at this time, although Quebec, in particular, had pushed strongly for this. Prime Minister Borden justified the denial by citing the difficulty of describing the islands with sufficient accuracy and the possibility that they would be needed for Dominion purposes in connection with navigation and defence.[40]

Manitoba and Ontario had thus by 1912 assumed their modern configurations. Quebec, however, by a 1927 opinion of the Judicial Committee of the Privy Council, lost a considerable amount of the territory along her northeastern border which was in dispute with Newfoundland, and which both she and Newfoundland had been claiming since 1763.[41]

The elimination of the District of Ungava in 1912[42] left Mackenzie, Keewatin, and Franklin as the only remaining units of the Northwest Territories and the only parts of Canada (except the Yukon Territory) without provincial status. These three provisional districts were again defined by an order in council of 16 March 1918, which was not effective until 1 January 1920.[43] By its terms they were to comprise the following territories: (1) Mackenzie was to be bounded on the west by the Yukon Territory, on the south by the 60th parallel, on the east by the second meridian in the system of Dominion land surveys (i.e., 102° West longitude), and on the north by the continental shore of the Arctic Ocean. (2) Keewatin was to be bounded on the north by the continental shore of the Arctic Ocean (excluding Boothia and Melville Peninsulas) and a somewhat irregular line from Repulse Bay to Cape Wolstenholme at the northwestern extremity of Quebec, on the east and south by the shoreline boundaries of the provinces of Quebec, Ontario, and Manitoba, and then by the 60th parallel forming the northern boundary of Manitoba, and on the west by Mackenzie District. (3) Franklin was simply stated to consist of "that portion of the Northwest Territories not included in the provisional districts of Mackenzie and Keewatin." Presumably this was intended to mean Boothia and Melville Peninsulas plus the entire Arctic Archipelago, including the islands in Hudson Strait but excluding the islands in Hudson and James Bays which had been assigned to Keewatin. Evidently Franklin was supposed to include the islands in the channel immediately north of Keewatin and Mackenzie. On the other hand, nothing was said specifically about the islands north of the Yukon coast, and one would presume that all those less than twenty miles from the shore would remain within that territory under the terms of the act of 1901.[44]

It seems evident that the principal purpose of the order in council was to assign all islands in Hudson and James Bays to Keewatin, and, by implication and with the possible exception noted above, all other islands north of the continental shoreline to Franklin. A section of the preamble suggests obliquely that this was so: "And Whereas it is considered that a revision of the provisional districts is expedient and that their boundaries should be made coterminous with those of the provinces." It is also evident, as Burpee observed,[45] that the adoption of this order in council indicates that the Dominion authorities still held the opinion that districts could be created and defined by this means. It does not appear, however, that the order in council itself conflicted directly with previous legislation on the same subject, notably the Northwest Territories Amendment Act of 1905 and chapter 62 of the *Revised Statutes* of 1906. These statutes attempted, in rather imprecise fashion, to describe the overall composition of the Northwest Territories as a unit, without saying anything about the boundaries of the individual districts. On the other hand, the order in council of 1918 attempted to define the district boundaries. The definitions of Mackenzie and Keewatin were clear enough, but that of Franklin, as in previous instances, remained extremely vague.

Whaling and the Yukon Gold Rush

Although Canada undertook to organize her northern territories in 1895, this was done in such haphazard and erratic fashion that there were continuing doubts as to the legality and effectiveness of various aspects of the action taken. In addition, there were circumstances relating to the activities of foreign states and nationals which contributed to Canada's growing concern over the status of these northern regions.

Foreign Whalers in the North

It appears that the first whalers in the Arctic waters west of Greenland were Dutchmen who began to move into Davis Strait from the waters east of Greenland in or about 1719, after the Spitsbergen whaling industry had begun to decline.[1] Later in the century they were joined by British whalers who, after a revival of British Arctic whaling about mid-century, began to move into Davis Strait starting in 1773. The British gradually took over Arctic whaling from the Dutch, not only in this strait but in northern waters generally, and by the end of the Napoleonic Wars had practically completed the process. During these years parliamentary legislation regulated and supported the British industry, most notably in a 1786 statute which consolidated and revised former acts and became the fundamental law on the subject.[2] Although William Baffin had observed large numbers of whales in northern Baffin Bay during his Arctic voyage of 1616 and had recommended that a whaling enterprise be undertaken there,[3] for fully two hundred years afterwards the whalers did not go beyond Davis Strait and the coastal waters of southern Greenland. Ross and Parry finally showed them the way into Baffin Bay and Lancaster Sound in 1818 and 1819. An era of great activity followed, and the first half of the nineteenth century saw the high tide of British Arctic whaling. During this entire period the only kind of vessels used were sailing ships. The steamship was tried for whaling in northern waters for the first time in 1857, and steam quickly replaced sails, the transfer being practically completed within two decades. The boom in Arctic whaling was followed by a period of doldrums, so serious that by about 1875 English whalers had virtually abandoned the industry, although the more persistent and enterprising Scotsmen continued and in some cases did well. American whalers began to operate in Davis Strait as early as 1732, but later in the century they deserted this area and did not return until 1846. Thereafter they concentrated their activities on the west side of the strait, especially Cumberland Sound, where Chief Mate Buddington initiated the

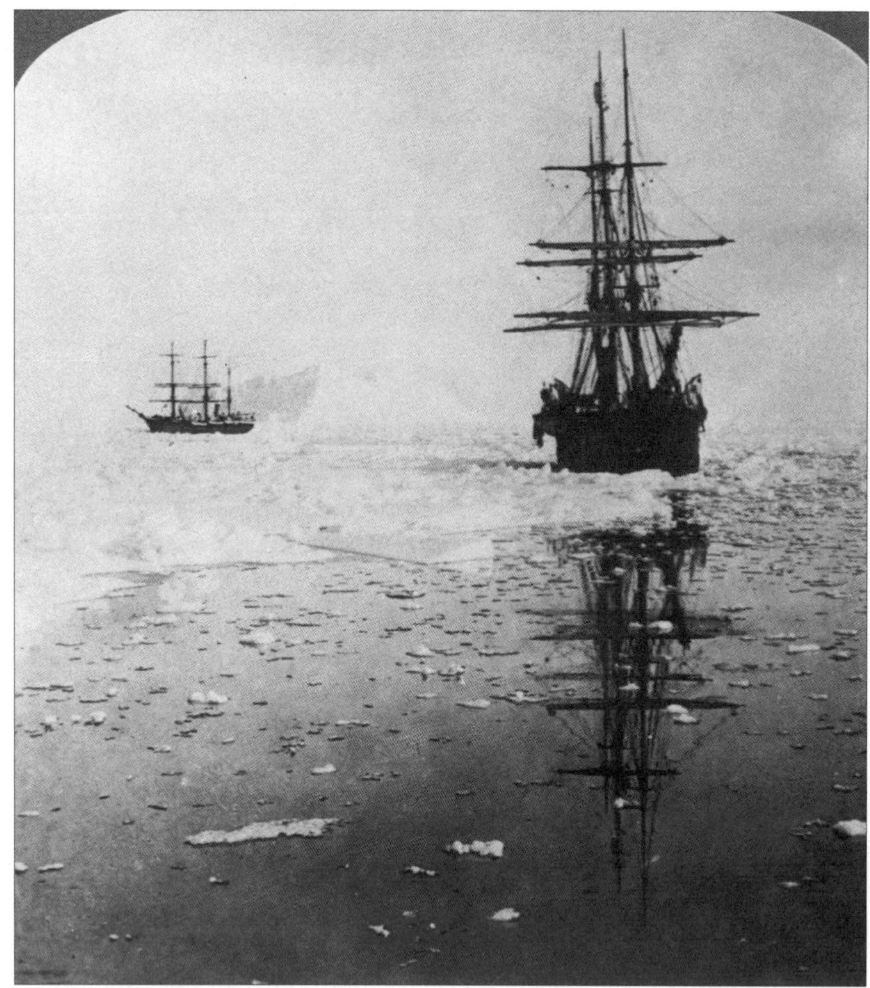

FIGURE 4-1: WHALERS *DIANA* AND *NOVA ZEMBLA*, DEXTERITY HARBOUR, BAFFIN LAND, 1899. *GLENBOW NA-1518-1*

practice of wintering on the whaling "grounds" in 1853.[4] The Americans eventually transferred their own attention to Hudson Bay and left Davis Strait to the Scots, who began to develop "land stations" on Baffin Island, maintaining permanent posts operated inexpensively by a few whites with Inuit help.

The Hudson's Bay Company (HBC) attempted to establish a whaling industry in Hudson Bay at an early stage, but their efforts were spasmodic and generally on a small scale. It concentrated its initial efforts in the Churchill River region, and a small quantity of white whale blubber was shipped to England as early as 1689 – the year of the company's first attempt to establish a post on that river.[5] In later years whaling was carried on periodically from several of the company's posts around the bay, and also in the waters north of Churchill, but it never assumed the important role that early company enthusiasts had envisaged.[6] John Rae told of the large numbers of whales in the northwestern part of the Hudson Bay in his accounts of his expeditions of 1846–47 and 1853–54, and thus helped to publicize the possibilities of whaling in this region.[7]

Two American whalers entered Hudson Bay in 1861 and apparently wintered there, thus initiating American activity which virtually monopolized whaling in the bay. By 1864 there were fifteen American whalers in Hudson Bay. One of them, the *Pioneer*, returned with what was described as the most profitable cargo ever obtained by an American whaler.[8] The American practice was to winter in the bay, and this necessitated provisioning their ships for at least two seasons. After the 1870s, however, whaling in both Davis Strait and Hudson Bay went into decline. By 1906, British whaling in Canadian Arctic waters had practically ended.[9] American whaling in Hudson Bay had also become inconsequential, with William Wakeham reporting only three American ships there in 1897,[10] and Albert Peter Low one in 1903–4.[11]

American whaling north of Bering Strait began in the 1840s, with the successful Arctic cruise of the Sag Harbor bark *Superior*, and developed rapidly thereafter.[12] At first most of the ships were based in New England ports, but San Francisco became a whaling port in 1850 and after the Civil War became the principal base for whaling in the North Pacific and Western Arctic.[13] The first whalers ventured to the east of Point Barrow in 1854, and in 1889–90 the schooner *Nicoline* of San Francisco began the practice of wintering in the region by spending that winter at Elsom Bay, just east of Point Barrow. The same ship moved eastward and wintered the next year at Canada's Herschel Island, in company with two new arrivals from San Francisco, the *Grampus* and the *Mary D. Hume*.[14]

Herschel Island became the winter rendezvous for American whalers in the western Arctic, with as many as fifteen steam and sailing ships spending the season there together. Captains and officers (some with wives along), the crews, and local Inuit combined forces to create a "Gay Nineties" atmosphere vastly different from, but not unworthy of, more populous southern centres. The island also became the local headquarters for whaling, and from it the whalers penetrated eastward along the coast to Amundsen Gulf and across to Banks Island. The general decline in whaling soon began to affect this region as it affected others, once substitutes for both whalebone and whale oil came into common use. Soon after the high tide of the 1890s, American whaling in the Beaufort Sea began to lose its importance, and within a few years it became almost non-existent.[15]

One of the first Canadian officials to become concerned about the unregulated activities of foreign whalers in Canada's northern waters was Lieutenant A. R. Gordon. In his reports on his voyages of 1884, 1885, and 1886 (described in chapter 2), he argued that the waters of Hudson Bay were wholly Canadian. Therefore, he urged that American whaling and fishing in the bay and strait should be strictly supervised, with regulations imposed, a levy of customs duties, and an annual patrol by a Canadian government ship.[16]

On 16 April 1888, the following exchange took place in the House of Commons between Guillaume Amyot, the Conservative member for Bellechasse, and Minister of Marine and Fisheries George Eulas Foster:

> *Mr. Amyot asked*, Whether it is the intention of the Government to prevent the whale fishery from being carried on during a certain period in Hudson Bay and vicinity? In case permission is granted to foreigners to engage in such fishery in Hudson Bay and vicinity, whether it is the intention of the Government to impose a license fee upon each vessel so engaged, and to prescribe the

> method in which such fishery shall be conducted?
>
> *Mr. Foster.* It is not the intention of the Government to take any steps in the direction at present....
>
> *Mr. Amyot asked,* Whether it is the intention of the Government to lease out the salmon rivers emptying into the Hudson Bay or in its vicinity?
>
> *Mr. Foster.* That is under the consideration of the Government.[17]

It would appear that Amyot was well acquainted with Gordon's voyages, since his questions followed very closely a summary of recommendations Gordon submitted in his report on his expedition of 1886.[18] The lack of official concern suggested by Foster's first answer would undergo considerable change before long.

Lieutenant-Governor John Schultz of Manitoba and Keewatin also became worried at a comparatively early stage over the activities of foreign whalers in Canada's northern waters. He mentioned the matter frequently in his reports and seems to have been largely responsible for bringing it to the attention of the authorities in Ottawa. In his concluding report for 1890, for example, he took note of "a decrease of walrus, seal and whale off the east and north-east sea coast of the district, caused it is said, by the increasing and unceasing efforts of whalers in Fox and other northern channels."[19] In his final report for the following year he went into greater detail:

> With reference to what I stated in my final report for 1890, I have since received from Churchill and other quarters fuller information, and hence advised you that, while American whalers have ceased to visit that part of Keewatin sea coast south of the mouth of Chesterfield Inlet, it is simply because they have exhausted that area, and confined their efforts to the still more northern Canadian waters of Fox and other channels, Rowe's Welcome and Lyon Inlet, leaving the more southern water referred to, in which they had carried on their operations without the slightest reference to the distance from shore; while, to enable them to avoid late navigation of Hudson Straits they frequently wintered, as I advised you, in one of the harbours of the Marble Island, where they traded to the Esquimaux with goods upon which no duty was paid, thus violating the revenue laws of Canada, and injuring the trade of a Canadian-English company who traded with goods upon which duties had been paid.[20]

In his own report for the same year, Deputy Minister of the Interior Alexander Mackinnon Burgess simply remarked that Schultz had made reference to "the illegal operations of American whalers along the more northerly sea coast of the district."[21]

News that American whalers had in 1890–91 begun the practice of wintering at Herschel Island arrived quickly, though in roundabout fashion, to the Canadian government. On 5 December 1890, Captain David Gray of Peterhead, Scotland, sent Secretary Dugald Graham of the Edinburgh Fishery Board a clipping copied from the *Times* of 29 November, which announced that three American whaling ships were wintering at the mouth of the Mackenzie River. In his accompanying letter he complained that whales in northern waters would soon be

FIGURE 4-2: WINTER QUARTERS AT HERSCHEL ISLAND, PAINTED BY JOHN BERTONCCINI. *NEW BEDFORD WHALING MUSEUM COLLECTION, 1971-15*

exterminated and, referring to the "highhanded manner" of the Americans in connection with sealing, maintained that "our ships have as much right to anchor at the Pribyloff Islands and kill seals as the Americans have to anchor in our harbours and bays to kill whales." The office of the Secretary for Scotland sent a copy of Gray's letter to the Colonial Office, which in turn sent word to Canadian Governor General Lord Stanley. The matter became a subject for Cabinet discussion in Ottawa, resulting in the following order in council promulgated on 29 April 1891.

> The Committee of the Privy Council have had under consideration a Despatch dated 16th January 1891, from the Right Honourable the Secretary of State for the Colonies respecting the rumours that three United States Whalers had proceeded to the mouth of the Mackenzie River, to winter there....
>
> The Minister under these circumstances submits that proper notice be given through the Canada Gazette of the law and regulations bearing on such matters, and that with the concurrence of the Minister of Customs and the Minister of Inland Revenue, a special Messenger be despatched from Fort Macpherson, or the nearest point from which a messenger can be despatched, for the purpose of warning all parties concerned against the killing of Whales and the illegal traffic in liquor, and fire arms, the result of his journey to

> be reported, and that the expenses of this Mission be charged to "Unforseen Expenses."[22]

This order in council recommended that the government issue official notice of the whaling laws, and Minister of Marine and Fisheries Charles Tupper signed a public note to that effect on 6 July 1891. The notice called attention to several chapters of the *Revised Statutes of Canada*, specifically chapters 94 (*An Act Respecting Fishing by Foreign Vessels*), 32 (*An Act Respecting the Customs*), 43 (*An Act Respecting Indians*), 50 (*An Act Respecting the North-West Territories*), and 53 (*An Act Respecting the District of Keewatin*), and pointed out relevant provisions in each. These included licensing, searching, fining, and seizure of foreign fishing vessels in Canadian waters (chapter 94), the requirement that all goods imported into Canada (whether dutiable or not) must be brought in at a port of entry with a custom house (chapter 32), the regulations forbidding the supply of intoxicants to Indians (chapter 43), and the regulations prohibiting the unauthorized manufacture or trade of intoxicants in the Northwest Territories and Keewatin (chapters 50 and 53).[23]

Another order in council on the subject was issued on 12 September 1892:

> The Committee of the Privy Council have had under consideration a communication from the Lieut. Governor of Manitoba, relative to the trespassing of United States Whalers at Herschell Island, near the mouth of the Mackenzie River, in the Arctic Ocean, and to their trading with the Esquimaux of the North Arctic Coast, and Canadian Indians on the coast of Hudson's Bay, also drawing attention to the injurious effects which a continuance of this contraband traffic must have on these Indians, who are described by the Right Reverend Bishop Bompas, as an excitable, quarrelsome and treacherous people....

After quoting part of the order in council of 29 April 1891, and referring to the notice published in the *Canada Gazette* of 25 July 1891, the order recounted that posters containing this notice had been sent to the Commissioner of the HBC at Winnipeg, with the request that he have them posted at suitable company stations, and that he also send a special messenger from Fort McPherson to the Arctic coast to warn against killing whales.[24]

On 11 April 1894, in the course of a speech advocating the development of the Hudson Bay shipping route, Senator John Ferguson of Niagara read from a petition by the Geographical Society of Quebec which said that "the said fisheries [in Hudson Bay] are reported to have been practically monopolized by foreigners, without any hindrance whatever, for nearly half a century." The petition went on to observe that American whalers had taken cargoes valued at $1,371,000 from Hudson Bay during the eleven years preceding 1874.[25]

The important exchange between David Mills and Sir Charles Tupper in the House of Commons on 28 May 1894, already referred to in chapter 3, was occasioned largely by reports of the activities of American whalers in Hudson Bay:

> *Mr. Mills*: I understand, Mr. Speaker, that lately American vessels have been going in there, engaged in whale, porpoise, and other fishing operations, and I do not understand that any steps have been taken by the

Government to assert the jurisdiction of Canada over these waters....

Sir Charles Tupper: I may say that from time to time rumours of that character have reached me. The remoteness of the region, however, has made it extremely difficult to ascertain with any degree of accuracy the correctness of these rumours. Some steps have been taken, through the agency of the Department of Marine and Fisheries, to publish notices that the laws of Canada apply in those waters; but it is only fair to say that since we are not as yet familiar with either the time that those vessels are likely to arrive or the portions of the bay where they may be found at any time, these notices have been to a great extent formal.[26]

Lieutenant-Governor Schultz returned to this theme in his report of 31 December 1894, for the year just ending, and put his case bluntly and in considerable detail:

> After a cessation of their efforts for a number of years, American whalers have again resumed their former practice of wintering their ships at Marble Island, from which part of Canada, it will be remembered, the almost complete denudation of sea animal life in our great Canadian inland sea was effected, and our Customs regulations and some other laws especially relating to Indians completely ignored. The two whaling ships which wintered in our harbour on that island last winter [1893–94], no doubt pursued the same methods as those of past years, and though their presence there and the employment by the Hudson Bay Company of their whaling ship the "Perseverance," for the past two seasons, is a gratifying evidence that during these years of rest from pursuit and attack, the whale, walrus and seal have increased in the north-western waters of the bay, yet I have again to repeat the warning given so many times since I first brought the matter up seventeen years ago that, without some control is exercised over the present method of killing these animals which will allow them a fair chance of escape and of restocking these once valuable waters, the merciless bomb-lance and gun and other appliances which give these creatures no chance of life at all, will speedily destroy the last hope of restocking these Canadian waters.
>
> As Canada may be said to possess the last remaining fur preserve of the world, so too does it seem that the tidal channels of her Arctic archipelago are destined to be the last home of these leviathians [*sic*], who, within the memory of living men, have been driven from Newfoundland latitudes to the places where their remnants have sought retreat. On the eastern and western verge of our wide group of Arctic islands they are now to be found in larger numbers than in any other seas; and now that after some years of rest they show a disposition to resume these former feeding grounds in the bay, some effort should be made, if the power belongs to Canada, to limit the catch

and define the method of their being taken, in accordance with the principle which dictates the restrictive enactments for the preservation of our freshwater and other food fishes. Our Canadian harbour in Hudson Bay (Marble Island) should at least not be used to further the work of destruction, especially when it is also used in winter as a trading station for the procuring of Canadian furs and other articles which have been bartered for with goods which have contributed nothing to our revenue, and other articles, the sale or giving of which is in contravention of our Indian and other enactments.

While alluding to this violation of our laws by foreign whalers, I have had occasion from time to time to call your attention to the large and lucrative catch of sea animals by the foreign whaling fleet, which, having its headquarters at San Francisco, annually enters the Arctic sea through Behring straits in pursuit of whalebone, oil, ivory, etc. So long as this fleet was limited to the short season when Point Barrow could be safely passed and repassed, and many belated ships were crushed on the shallow and dangerous Arctic Alaskan coast, there was little danger of the denudation of these seas; but the loss of life was so great and the crushed ships so many that the government of the United States decided to build and maintain a permanent relief station of Point Barrow (see my report of the cruise of the United States SS. "Thetis," map of coast, ice movements, plan and soundings of harbour on Herschel Island, etc.), and the United States SS. "Thetis," being detailed to escort the store ships and the artisans to build the relief station, sailed eastward after doing so to be near the fleet should her services be required by disabled ships, and while thus engaged found, sounded and mapped the valuable harbour on the Canadian island lying near our Arctic coast, and about one hundred miles west of one of the mouths of the Mackenzie river, known as Herschel island. No more perfect Arctic harbour could be found, as it was on the southern side, near enough to the Arctic coast to maintain daily communication with the Eskimo, and far enough to allow late fall entry and early spring departure, and excellent entrance and deep water with good holding ground within. Foreign whalers have been quick to see its advantages, as giving them nearly double the length of their fishing season, and they had long known that great advantage afforded in point of extent of fishing waters by the early spring rush of the waters of this mighty river setting back the elsewhere closely impinging permanent icepack; so that last winter four whaling ships wintered in this Canadian haven, seven ships the winter before, four in the previous winter, and two ships in the winter before that again.

From sources of information which I believe to be entirely reliable (see copies of letters sent me by Arctic bishops, explorers, and others, which were transmitted to you) I have reason to believe, in fact, my last communication upon the subject leaving no room for doubt, that from the first these vessels have traded with the Eskimo on our Arctic coast, carrying on a barter with the articles upon which no duties have been paid, and furnishing as matters of trade or reward for inland trading expeditions, magazine rifles, fixed ammunition and intoxicants, thus violating the laws of Canada and defrauding her revenue, as well as very materially interfering with the trading operations carried on by those who have had to transport their goods from Montreal to the Arctic circle, and who have, so far as I am aware, observed all the regulations in force regarding traffic with the Indians, as well as paid duties on their goods.

An idea of the valuable nature of the sea and sea coast products carried to San Francisco by the foreign whalers in question may be had from reports believed to be reliable, as to the large quantity and value of only one of such articles brought to San Francisco by a single whaler which had wintered at Herschel Island.

I am aware, of course, of the great difficulty which will be found in endeavouring to enforce Canadian rights on this distant sea, and that the Government have had this subject under consideration; but if the rich whaling grounds near the estuary and off the mouth of the Mackenzie and as far east as Cape Bathurst are to be preserved for Canadian use, some restrictive measures must be adopted to prevent the wholesale destruction of the valuable species of that region with the deadly bomb-lance and swivel gun of the pursuing whaleboats.[27]

Deputy Minister of the Interior Burgess underlined the principal points made by Schultz in his own report for the same year:

His Honour calls attention to the fact that, after a few years cessation, two American whale ships wintered at Marble Island in Hudson's Bay during 1893–94, and no doubt pursued the same destructive methods as in past years which caused the almost complete extinction of animal life in these waters; and he repeats the warning that unless some control is exercised over the present mode of killing the seals and walruses they will soon become utterly exterminated. These foreign seamen not only capture and kill whales and seals in our waters, but also obtain from the Indians furs and other articles in exchange for goods upon which no duty is paid. A great proportion of these goods are of classes which are prohibited by our laws from being introduced among the Indians.

Attention is also called to the fact of the American whaling fleet annually entering the Arctic Ocean from Behring Sea, and carrying on the same destructive methods of capture and the same illegal traffic with the Eskimos. This has been going on to a much increased extent of late owing to the discovery of the important Arctic harbour on Herschell Island, about one hundred miles west of one of the mouths of the Mackenzie River, where numbers of these whaling vessels pass the winter.[28]

J. C. Patterson, who succeeded Schultz as Lieutenant-Governor of Keewatin, referred briefly to the American whalers in Hudson Bay in his report for 1896:

> I am informed that in past years a considerable traffic in intoxicating liquors was indulged in by American whaling vessels which wintered on the shores of the northern part of Hudson's Bay. These vessels, not being under the British flag, have for some time carried on a considerable trade in these Canadian waters, and their crews, it is stated, have shown but little respect for our Canadian laws or the regulations regarding the aborigines of the country, while they were not contributors in any way to the revenues of the Dominion. Whether there has been any recurrence of this traffic in that remote part of the district during the past season I am, as yet, without information.[29]

Burgess also referred briefly to the matter in his report for the same year:

> His honour's predecessor, the late Sir John Schultz, during his term of office, called the attention of the department to the illegal traffic carried on by American whalers who were in the habit of wintering at Marble island in Hudson's Bay. These people introduced intoxicating liquors among the Indians, and traded with them, giving them in exchange for valuable furs goods which they brought into the country free of customs duty. No recurrence of this offence has been reported during the past year.[30]

Further reference to the Herschel Island situation was made in the House of Commons on 12 April 1897.

> *Mr. [Thomas Osborn] Davis asked*: Is the Department of Customs aware that smuggling is being carried on by the crews of American whalers from Herschel Island into Mackenzie River Basin?
>
> *The Controller of Customs (Mr. Paterson)*: It was reported to the department in December, 1895, that illegal trade was being conducted by United States whalers at the mouth of the Mackenzie River. On 5th March, 1896, the department received a letter alleging that smuggling was going on at Herschel Island.[31]
>
> The Controller of Customs was obliged to answer a similar question about two months later, on June 21, posed by Mr. [Frank] Oliver of Alberta.
>
> *Mr. Oliver asked*: 1. Is the Government aware that a considerable trade is done by United States whalers at the mouth of the Mackenzie River without duty being paid? 2. Is it the intention of the Government to protect Canadian trade revenue by establishing a customs office here?
>
> *The Controller of Customs (Mr. Paterson)*: 1. The Department of

> Customs has been informed that illegal trading is being carried on at the mouth of the Mackenzie River by United States whalers. 2. The question of establishing a customs office there will receive consideration.[32]

Inspector Charles Constantine, commander of the North West Mounted Police (NWMP) force which had been sent to the Yukon in 1895, commented on the matter in his report of 20 November 1896. His report, based only upon hearsay, was written at his base at Fort Constantine on the Yukon River, and he had not been to the Arctic coast. He said, *inter alia*:

> The territory about the mouth of the Mackenzie River and Herschel Island is one that the attention of the government is called to. Twelve whalers, steam and sailing, wintered there last winter. The crews number from 1,000 to 1,200, these vessels do not leave winter quarters till about the middle of end of July. Each year a vessel is loaded at and despatched from San Francisco with supplies for this fleet, of which cargo liquor forms a large share. This liquor is sold or traded to the natives for furs, walrus, ivory bone and their young girls who are purchased by the officers of the ships for their own foul purposes. The natives have also learnt to make liquor from dried fruit, sugar or molasses. They are very violent and dangerous when in liquor. Last winter, it is reported, that one had tied up his daughter by the heels, and whipped her to death. Mr. Whittaker (a missionary) and the ships' captains tied up the man, and whipped him. The result was that the natives threatened to make the missionary leave the island, if not worse.

Constantine also reported that deserters from the whaling ships were coming overland and by river to the Yukon placer mines, and advised that an armed government vessel should be sent to those waters to keep order.[33]

The Yukon Gold Rush

When Great Britain and Russia established the 141st meridian as the dividing line between their territories in northwestern North America in 1825, the region through which the line passed was still virtually unexplored and unknown. The Russians, who were already familiar with much of the Alaskan coast, subsequently explored the interior, and in 1838 an employee of the Russian American Company named Malakoff (or Malakhof) ascended the Yukon River as far as the site of Nulato. Four years later, the company established a trading post at Nulato, several hundred miles up the Yukon and about eighty miles from Norton Sound – the farthest inland and the most northerly of the company's posts.[34] In 1866–68, Smithsonian scientist Dr. William Healey Dall of the American Western Union Telegraph expedition, which was connected with a plan for an overland telegraph line from America to Europe via Bering Strait, led a party up the Yukon as far as the HBC post Fort Yukon, at the junction of the Yukon and the Porcupine Rivers.[35] In the spring of 1867, two Canadian members of the party, Frank Ketchum and Michael Labarge, went farther upstream to another HBC post, Fort Selkirk, at the juncture of the Lewes and the Pelly.[36] Another member of the party, the English artist

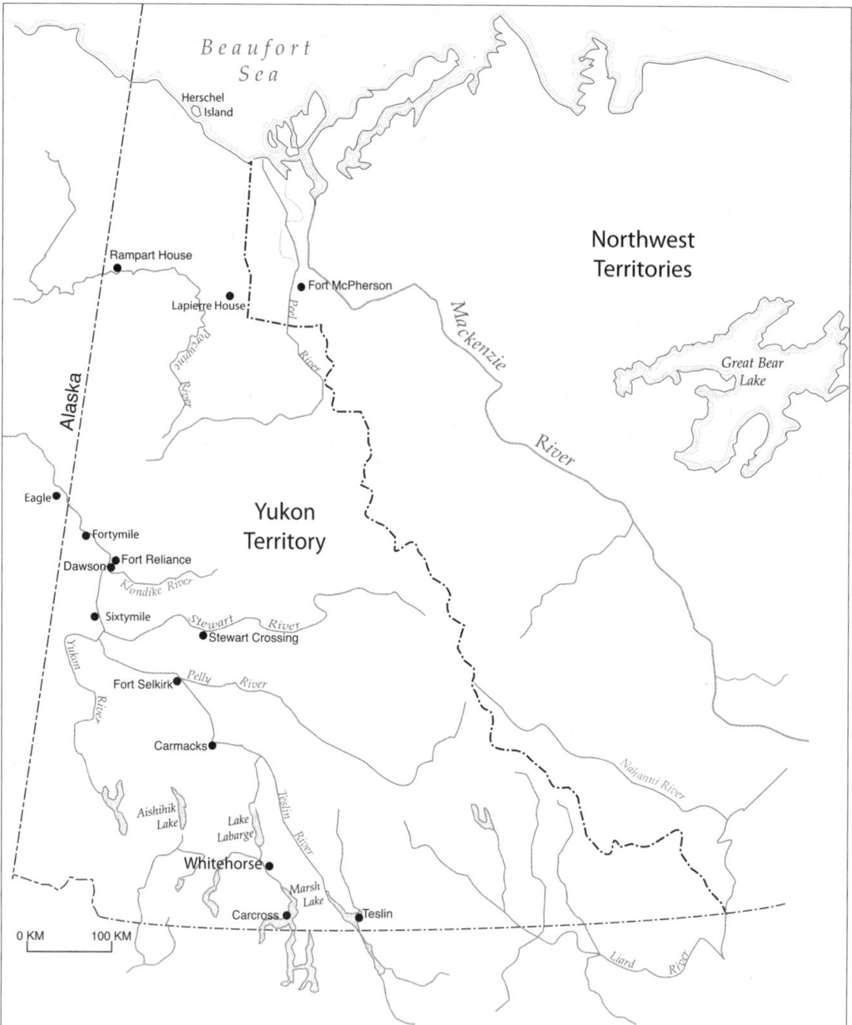

Figure 4-3: Map of the Yukon after 1901. *Jennifer Arthur-Lackenbauer.*

Frederick Whymper, asserted that the mouth of the Tanana (240 miles above Nulato) was the farthest point ever reached by Russian traders, and that occasionally HBC men reached the same point from the east.[37]

In the meantime, the HBC was approaching the Yukon from the opposite direction. In 1840, clerk Robert Campbell made his way from the headwaters of the Liard River to a tributary of the Yukon, which he named the Pelly after the company's governor. In 1843 he reached the junction of the Pelly and the Lewes (i.e., the Yukon), and he established Fort Selkirk at this spot four or five years later.[38] In 1842, John Bell crossed from the Peel River, a tributary of the lower Mackenzie, to the Porcupine, which he descended for some distance. In 1846, he repeated his exploit and descended the Porcupine to the Yukon, where Alexander Hunter Murray founded Fort Yukon the following year. In 1850, Campbell went downstream from Fort Selkirk to Fort Yukon, this proving that the Lewes-Pelly and the Yukon were the same river.[39]

For a few years the HBC had the Yukon region practically to itself and dominated its trade. Besides Fort Selkirk and Fort Yukon, they had Fort McPherson on the Peel River, and Lapierre House across the mountains on the upper Porcupine. Fort Selkirk was pillaged by coastal Tlingit First Nations in 1852,[40] however, and Fort Yukon eventually had to be given up because it was located far to the west of the 141st meridian. This had been known for some time, but little was done about it as long as the Russian occupation lasted. In August 1869, however, two years after the Americans had purchased Alaska, Captain Charles Walker Raymond of the US Corps of Engineers notified the agent of the HBC at Fort Yukon "that the station is in the territory of the United States; that the introduction of trading goods, or any trade by foreigners with the natives, is illegal, and must cease; and that the Hudson Bay Company must vacate the buildings as soon as practicable."[41] The company moved the post successively to two sites farther up the Porcupine in what was thought to be British territory, but an approximate determination of the boundary line in 1889 showed that it was still in Alaska, so it was again moved up the river to a point just east of the 141st meridian. Identified as Rampart House, it was abandoned by the HBC a few years later.[42]

Prospector George Holt first reached the headwaters of the Lewes, or Yukon, from the Lynn Canal around 1878.[43] Over the next several years, miners and prospectors similarly entered the Yukon country, most of them traveling via the Chilkoot Pass. Thus, when Lieutenant Frederick Gustavus Schwatka of the US Army crossed the Chilkoot Pass in 1883 and descended the river, making the first survey of it, he had been preceded by a considerable number of others.[44] This was, in brief, the situation at the time of the great coordinated expedition of George Mercer Dawson, William Ogilvie, and Richard George McConnell in 1887–88.

The background and purpose of this expedition were set forth by Deputy Minister of the Interior Burgess in his department's annual report for 1886:

> For several years past reports have been reaching the Department from various quarters to the effect that explorations conducted by prospectors in that part of the valley of the Yukon River lying within Canadian territory have indicated the district to be of great economic value and capable of development, particularly in regard to its mineral resources; and it had become apparent that it would be of importance to the Dominion that the region should be thoroughly explored and that accurate information should be obtained with respect to it at as early a moment as possible. In May last Messrs. J. C. Phinney & Co., bankers and brokers, of Seattle, Washington Territory, wrote to the Department stating that they were satisfied, from explorations conducted on their behalf, that the district was rich in mineral deposits.... In view of the facts thus elicited and of other information in your possession in regard to the Yukon, region, I received in September last your instructions to proceed with the organization of a joint geological and topographical expedition, which should start out early this spring. This expedition will be conducted by Dr. G. M. Dawson, Assistant Director of the Geological Survey, and Mr. William Ogilvie, of the topographical corps of the Department.[45]

The three sections of the joint expedition all carried out their responsibilities with determination and success. Dawson left Ottawa on 22 April 1887, travelled by rail to Vancouver, by boat to Wrangell, then via the Stikine, Dease, Frances, and Pelly to Fort Selkirk, where he rendezvoused with Ogilvie on 13 August. They headed up the Lewes and over the Chilkoot Pass to Lynn Canal, arriving on 19 September.[46] His assistant McConnell accompanied him to the mouth of the Dease, after which he descended to Liard to where it joins the Mackenzie at Fort Simpson, wintered at Fort Providence on Great Slave Lake, descended the Mackenzie the following spring, crossed the portage between Fort McPherson and Lapierre House, descended the Porcupine to the original Fort Yukon, and then ascended the Yukon and crossed the Chilkoot Pass, reaching salt water on 15 September 1888.[47] Ogilvie's route, approximately the reverse of McConnell's, was from the Lynn Canal across the Chilkoot Pass and down the Yukon to the 141st meridian, which he located during the winter, then via the Tatonduk and upper Porcupine Rivers, Lapierre House, and Fort McPherson to the Mackenzie, and finally up the Mackenzie and overland to Edmonton, which he reached on 23 December 1888.[48]

The principal outcomes of the expedition, apart from its detailed surveys of hitherto largely unknown country, were the varied geographical, geological, meteorological, and other information it brought back, its first-hand observation of trading, prospecting, and mining activities, and Ogilvie's identification of the boundary line where the 141st meridian crossed the Yukon River. Increased prospecting and mining, combined with continued uncertainty about the location of the international boundary, had created a situation of growing concern to the Canadian government. Burgess, in his 1887 report, observed that a considerable population of miners had "for the past three seasons been at work upon the placer diggings in that region, a large number of them within what is well known to be Canadian territory."[49] A year later, with reference to Ogilvie's assignment, he wrote that "an approximate calculation shows that the boundary is nearly ninety below the point where it is marked on the United States maps. This is of great importance, as the line passes through the best gold bearing districts yet discovered in the country."[50]

The date of the first discovery of gold in the Yukon is uncertain. In his account of his 1866–67 travels in Alaska, Frederick Whymper mentioned that "minute specks of gold have been found by some of the Hudson's Bay Company men in the Yukon, but not in quantities to warrant a 'rush' to the locality."[51] Dawson later commented that he had been able to find no earlier reference to the discovery of gold in any part of the Yukon waters than that by Whymper.[52] According to Pierre Berton, Robert Campbell found traces of gold at Fort Selkirk, and sixteen years later the Reverend Robert M. McDonald was reported to have seen it in abundance near Fort Yukon.[53] Dawson, however, dates the real initiation of gold mining in the Yukon to 1880, when a large party of prospectors crossed the Chilkoot Pass. From that time on, he said, miners entered the country in increasing numbers.[54] Within a few years their searches had extended to the Big Salmon, the Pelly, the Lewes, the Stewart, Forty-mile Creek, and other streams in the vicinity. Gold was found literally "anywhere" and "everywhere" along some streams, but only occasionally in paying quantities.[55]

Contrary to popular impression, gold prospecting and mining had reached significant proportions in the Yukon before the sensational Klondike discovery of 1896. In his annual report dated 28 December 1895, Burgess noted the steady yearly increase in the number of gold miners in the Yukon, referring to estimates that at the beginning of the previous season there had been at least 1,000 of them and that $300,000 in gold had been produced in 1894. He also disclosed details about the carrying into the territory by American companies of goods, via both the Yukon River and the mountain passes from Lynn Canal, upon which no duty was being paid, and about the existence of an illicit traffic in intoxicating liquors.[56] These facts clearly established, he said:

> first, that the time had arrived when it became the duty of the Government of Canada to make more efficient provision for the maintenance of order, the enforcement of the laws, and the administration of justice in the Yukon country, especially in that section of it in which placer mining for gold is being prosecuted upon such an extensive scale, situated near to the boundary separating the North-west Territories from the possessions for the United States in Alaska; and second, that while such measures as were necessary to that end were called for in the interests of humanity, and particularly for the security and safety of the lives and property of the Canadian subjects of Her Majesty resident in that country who are engaged in legitimate business pursuits, it was evident that the revenue justly due to the Government of Canada, under its customs, excise and land laws, and which would go a long way to pay the expenses of government, was being lost for the want of adequate machinery for its collection.[57]

Burgess also underlined the need to continue Ogilvie's determination of the 141st meridian south and north of the Yukon River, preferably in co-operation with the United States, especially because an American expedition had already made its own placing of the boundary line across several of the Yukon rivers. (He referred, evidently, to the McGrath-Turner expedition of 1889–91, which had obtained results similar to those of Ogilvie in 1887–88.)[58]

In short, the Klondike discovery was not a totally unheralded event, falling like a bolt from the blue upon the Canadian government and creating a host of problems where none had existed before. Rather it was a spectacular fulfillment, or outcome, or effort which had been in progress for some time. And, of course, it multiplied many times over problems which already existed. Whether the key discovery was that of Robert Henderson on Gold Bottom Creek sometime in the summer of 1896, or that of George "Siwash" Carmack on nearby Rabbit Creek a few weeks afterwards on 16 August, has been debated ever since. Regardless, the consequence was one of the most remarkable gold rushes of all time.[59] During that fall and winter, prospectors flocked to the Klondike from elsewhere in the Yukon and Alaska, to be joined the following year by fortune hunters from literally everywhere as news of the momentous discovery seeped through to the outside world. The town of Dawson, which sprang up immediately at the confluence of the Klondike and the Yukon, grew from nothing to an estimated 17,000 people in July 1898.[60] (Other estimates went much higher, but in the circumstances were unreliable.) Dawson reached its peak in 1899, and for a time was the most populous centre in Canada west and north of

Winnipeg. How many people altogether joined the gold rush remains unknown; one estimate was that at least 100,000 started for the Klondike from different parts of the world.[61] Many failed to arrive, and others did not stay long enough to become part of the community. Few were Canadians, and of the polyglot remainder the overwhelming majority were American.[62] Estimates of gold production varied greatly and were doubtless exaggerated in many cases. Those of the Canadian Department of the Interior, for the period 1 July 1897 to 30 June 1903, gave a value of gold produced totalling $51,305,959.51, from 66,509 recorded claims, with $2,827,070.93 paid in royalties.[63]

The rush began in a situation of almost total absence of facilities to maintain law and order, to provide necessary administrative and governmental machinery, or to supply elementary needs of food, clothing, and shelter to the growing swarms of miners who tumbled pell-mell into Dawson, often with the barest minimum of experience, know-how, and equipment.[64] In the circumstances, things were almost certain to get worse before they got better. Matters were further complicated by the nature of the incoming horde which – typical as it was of the average frontier boom town – contained the usual generous proportion of speculators, adventurers, profiteers, gamblers, thieves, prostitutes, and ne'er-do-wells. The inevitable result was a period of chaos and confusion in Dawson and throughout the Klondike.

The Northwest Mounted Police and the Gold Rush

Yukon gold caused the extension of NWMP activity to the Canadian Arctic. As described above, gold had been known to exist in the Yukon for over a quarter of a century before the Klondike discovery in 1896, and during these years had been mined on a steadily increasing scale, but the miners who drifted into the region had carried on without benefit of any organized government or law except for what they arranged in ad hoc fashion among themselves. The growing number of prospectors and the increase of crime, the latter doubtless exaggerated by lurid reports seeping out of the mining camps, compelled the Canadian government to look into the matter. In May 1894, Inspector Charles Constantine of the Regina Division was sent to the Yukon to make an investigation.[65] Accompanied by Staff Sergeant Charles Brown, he proceeded by way of Victoria, the "Inside Passage," the Chilkoot Pass, and the Yukon River, and by 7 August had reached Fort Cudahy near the mining camp of Fortymile, not far from the Alaska border. Staying only until 3 September, and leaving Brown to look after the collection of customs duties, he returned to "civilization" by descending the Yukon River and then taking ship to Victoria, which he reached on 2 October. His lengthy report, written at Moosomin on 10 October, went into considerable detail about all aspects of the country which he thought required comment, and recommended in particular that a force of about fifty NWMP should be sent there to keep order.[66] The government acted promptly by sending Constantine back next spring as its official representative in charge of a force of nineteen NWMP members. Taking the long sea route from Seattle to St. Michael and then up the Yukon River, they reached Fort Cudahy on 24 July and immediately began construction of Fort Constantine nearby – by far the most northerly NWMP post at the time. Constantine, a rough-hewn, humourless, no-nonsense type, immediately set about establishing his authority. Armed officially with the powers of

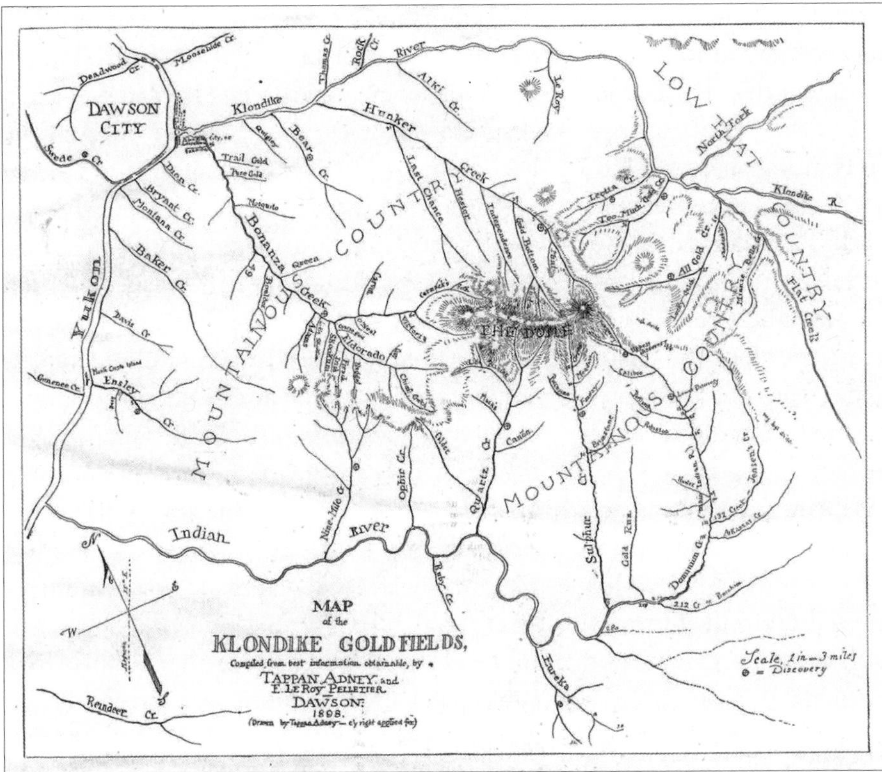

FIGURE 4-4: "MAP OF THE KLONDIKE GOLD FIELDS," *HARPER'S WEEKLY* (MAY 1898).

magistrate and customs officer as well as commander of the police force, he soon succeeded in imposing a large measure of control over the mining camps.[67]

After George Carmack made his fabulously rich gold strike beside Bonanza Creek, the already considerable stream of prospectors, gamblers, traders, adventurers, and others into the Yukon soon assumed the proportions of a flood, and Dawson City at the mouth of the Klondike, which did not exist when the strike was made but sprang up immediately afterwards, mushroomed to a roaring boom town. Reports from Constantine[68] and others, including Canadian government surveyor William Ogilvie,[69] brought home to the authorities in Ottawa that a difficult and potentially very dangerous situation was on their hands, and they decided that increased surveillance was essential. One of the obvious means of doing this was to send in more police.

Inspector W. H. Scarth arrived at Fort Constantine with the first body of reinforcements, twenty strong, in June 1897; Inspector F. Harper arrived with twenty more in October. That month, Minister of the Interior Clifford Sifton also arrived for a hasty inspection with Major James Morrow Walsh, a former inspector in the NWMP who had just been appointed Commissioner of the recently created Yukon Territory.[70] They were accompanied by Inspector Zachary Taylor Wood and another band of Mountie reinforcements. By the end of 1897, eight officers and eighty-eight men of the NWMP were serving in the Yukon (under the Commissioner of the Yukon rather than under the Commissioner of the NWMP), and by the end of the following year the total had increased to ten officers and

254 men. During the summer of 1897, the police built Fort Herchmer at Dawson and transferred their regional headquarters there from Fort Constantine. Other detachments opened while the gold rush was at its height, including Chilcoot Pass, White Pass, Lake Bennett, Tagish, Ogilvie, Fort Selkirk, and Whitehorse. There were about thirty detachments and outposts altogether, almost all of them being located in the mountain passes and along the Yukon River from its source just north of the passes to the Alaska border, as well as on some of its tributaries.[71]

On 4 July 1898, William Ogilvie was appointed Commissioner of the Yukon to replace Major Walsh, who had evidently indicated his wish to resign. The top official in the territory now became a civilian having no previous or current connection with the NWMP.[72] On 7 July, the redoubtable Superintendent Samuel Benfield Steele, who had been sent to the Yukon the preceding February to "hold the pass,"[73] was appointed to command all police in the Yukon under the general authority of the commissioner, thus becoming Constantine's replacement.[74] The authorities on the scene always had their hands more than full, especially during the first two or three years of the rush. Thanks to the presence of the NWMP, however, matters were kept under reasonable control and the Yukon was spared the outright lawlessness that characterized life in American centres such as Skagway, only a few miles across the undetermined border line.[75]

Most of the newcomers to the goldfields, police and civilians alike, went in either through one of the mountain passes from the Pacific seaports or else up the Yukon River. Attempts were made to cross over from the Prairies or from the Mackenzie River, usually with disastrous results, as the intervening country was then practically unknown. Acting upon the government's request that the NWMP examine the practicability of an overland route, Commissioner Lawrence Herchmer picked Inspector John Douglas Moodie to test it by leading a patrol from Edmonton through the wilderness all the way to the Yukon. Moodie's small party, which included Constable Francis Joseph Fitzgerald and Special Constables Frank Lafferty and Henry Tobin, both graduates of Royal Military College, successfully completed the patrol, but only after a difficult, dangerous journey spanning from 4 September 1897 to 24 October 1898. In the meantime, three support patrols under Inspector W. H. Routledge, Inspector A. E. Snyder, and Sergeant Major A.E.C. Macdonell made successful trips to Fort Simpson, Fort St. John, and Dunvegan respectively, although upon their return they could report little about Moodie except that he had disappeared into the little-known country beyond Fort St. John. The obvious conclusion to be drawn from Moodie's successful but perilous journey was that although it was possible to go from Edmonton overland to the Yukon, it would be extremely unwise for the gold seekers to make the attempt. Entry through the coastal mountain passes or up the Yukon River, in spite of the inconveniences associated with each route, proved less difficult and less time consuming in the long run.[76]

Thanks largely to the NWMP and a few capable and conscientious public servants, the difficult period of chaos and confusion was remarkably short, and internally the Yukon was soon quiet and stable. On the other hand, problems with external aspects, or international implications, such as access, river transportation, and customs, tended to become associated with the Alaska boundary dispute, which was now approaching its climax.

One such problem involved the transportation of goods and personnel through the

Panhandle on their way to and from the goldfields. On 23 July 1897, C.F.F. Adam at the British Embassy in Washington sent a letter to Secretary of State John Sherman, on behalf of the Canadian government, requesting permission for the Canadian Pacific Navigation Company to send a steamer from Victoria to Dyea, with passengers and freight destined for the Klondike. The company proposed that the shipment should be bonded through the Panhandle without being subjected to customs duties, and it offered to pay to have an American official accompany the shipment until it was within undisputed Canadian territory.[77] On 28 July, Acting Secretary of State Alvy Adee replied favourably, saying that Dyea had been made "a subport of entry" to facilitate business,[78] and soon Skagway was similarly opened. As one commentator remarked, by making the request "the Canadian Government had implicitly recognized American jurisdiction over the head of Lynn Canal."[79] On 11 August, Adam further requested, on behalf of Canada, American permission for the Canadian government to build a telegraph line from the head of winter navigation on the Lynn Canal across the most suitable pass and into the interior, to establish more efficient communication with the Klondike.[80] This request was also granted on 14 September,[81] but in this instance both request and acceptance reserved the boundary rights or claims of both countries.

Not long afterwards the shoe was on the other foot, when the American government requested Canadian permission to send a relief expedition to the Yukon through Canadian territory. Secretary of State Sherman's letter to British ambassador Sir Julian Pauncefote on 20 December 1897 drew attention to an act of Congress, approved just two days earlier, which appropriated $200,000 to purchase relief supplies for people "in the Yukon River country, or other mining regions of Alaska" and noted that with Canada's permission the goods would not only be sent over Canadian territory but also would be made available there.[82] On 27 December, Pauncefote replied that the Canadian government would permit the entry of the goods, duty free and accompanied by American escorts, but that a Canadian officer should accompany each convoy.[83] Yukon Commissioner James Morrow Walsh was displeased with the idea, doubtless lacking complete information about it. He wrote to Minister of the Interior Clifford Sifton:

> If a foreign expedition is to pass over this district, I consider it my duty to go and see what it is, the number of troops the party consists of, what part of the territory it is to pass over, its authority for doing so, the length of time it is to be in the district, from what point it will depart, and what stores it is carrying. There is not the slightest necessity for an expedition of this kind.

Walsh added that the United States could contract to send supplies over the mountain passes and down the Yukon River, that the danger of shortage was for the following rather than the present year, and that the Americans could best send supplies up the Yukon. In due course, however, he learned to his great relief that this "inexplicable" expedition had been abandoned.[84]

The matter of navigating the northwestern rivers flowing through Canadian and American territory had been settled previously in satisfactory fashion. Article 26 of the Washington Treaty (8 May 1871) had provided that:

> The navigation of the Rivers Yukon, Porcupine, and Stikine, ascending and descending from, to, and into the sea, shall for ever remain free and open for the purposes of commerce to the subjects of Her Britannic Majesty and to the citizens of The United States, subject to any laws and regulations of either country within its own territory, not inconsistent with such priviledge of free navigation.[85]

This stipulation was understood to secure "the right of access and passage" but not "the right to share in the local traffic" between American or Canadian ports. After further discussion, both governments made additional regulations on the subject in 1898.[86]

One dispute which was ultimately settled by arbitration involved a claim by the British government for Crown dues on (or alternatively the value of) 68,500 feet of lumber cut without permit or authority by Howard Mountain in the Yukon Territory, sold by him to contractor O. N. Ramsay, and sold in turn by Ramsay to the US military authorities in Alaska in 1900. Mountain left for San Francisco without paying the Crown dues, and both Ramsay and the American military authorities refused to pay the Canadian authorities. The decision of the arbitration tribunal, given after long delay on 18 June 1913, was that Great Britain could not claim for the value of the timber because for a period of about thirteen years she had claimed only for the dues upon it, and that the American military authorities could not be held responsible for the negligence or dishonesty of either Ramsay or Mountain.[87]

Particular cases of this sort were of small importance compared with the larger dispute over the Alaskan boundary, however, which had been developing while affairs in the Yukon itself had been gradually approaching a state of stability.

5

The Alaska Boundary Dispute

The Alaska boundary controversy had its origins in complications associated with the period of Russian dominion in Alaska. While explorers from western Europe were moving across the vast expanses of North America and up its Pacific coast towards the northwestern extremity of the continent, Russian adventurers were approaching the same region from the opposite direction, and they got there well in advance of their rivals. In 1639, only about sixty years after the Stroganovs and Yermak the Cossack started the great march from Muscovy eastward across Siberia, a small party under Andrei Kopilov is said to have reached the waters of the Pacific and founded the post of Okhotsk.[1] The Cossack Simeon Dezhnev in 1648 sailed a vessel around the northeastern extremity of Siberia from the Kolyma River to south of the Anadyr, according to records discovered nearly one hundred years after the event is supposed to have taken place. He thus proved that Asia did not join North America in that region.[2] There was desultory Russian activity around the Sea of Okhotsk and in Kamchatka Peninsula during the following years, but the next major advance came with the two great voyages of Vitus Bering. Acting on instructions given by Peter the Great just before his death in 1725, this Danish captain, with his lieutenant Alexei Chirkov, sailed from Kamchatka in 1728 and followed the Siberian coast through Bering Strait, reaching 67° 18' N latitude before turning back. In 1741, after years of delay, they set out from Kamchatka again. Although their two ships became separated, they both succeeded in reaching and cruising along the southern coast of Alaska and the Aleutian Islands, thus accomplishing the modern discovery of North America from the Asiatic side.[3]

After Bering's second voyage, Russian explorers and traders sailed from Okhotsk and Kamchatka to Alaskan waters in increasing numbers, and they gradually extended their activities along the Aleutian chain and to the mainland.[4] Among the key events were the establishment of the first permanent Russian post at Three Saints Bay on Kodiak Island by Gregory Shelikhov in 1784, Gerassim Pribilov's discovery of the Pribilov Islands in 1786, and Alexander Baranov's establishment of a new headquarters, Mikhailovsk (later Novo Archangelsk), on the island of Sitka in 1799. The Russians were primarily interested in furs, especially those of the sea otter; in pursuit of this trade, they not only subdued the indigenous residents with much brutality but also fell into serious quarrels among themselves. They had also to withstand an increasing challenge from foreign rivals, notably British, Spanish, French, and American. In the latter part of the eighteenth century, Cook, Clarke, Portlock and Dixon, Meares, Vancouver, Pérez, Heceta, Quadra, Martinez, Haro, Fidalgo, Malaspina, Caamaño, La Pérouse, Marchand, and others were active in Alaskan waters and interested in the region.[5] To eliminate internecine strife among themselves, to combat the intrusions of foreign interlopers, and to maintain better control and management of the fur trade, several leading Russian companies took the initiative and in 1798 consolidated into a single organization. On 8 July 1799, an imperial ukase issued by Emperor Paul I confirmed the consolidation and granted the new organization the title "The Russian American Company."

The ukase bestowed upon the Russian American Company a monopoly charter for a period of twenty years over all enterprises, including hunting, trading, settlement, and industry, on the coast of America north of 55° N latitude and the chain of islands extending across the northern Pacific and southwards to Japan. The company could make new discoveries not only north of 55° but south as well, and it could claim and occupy the lands discovered as Russian possessions if they were not already the property of some other nation. It also had judicial, military, and administrative authority in these regions.[6] As the British pointed out in the Fur Seals Arbitration, however, and as had been recognized in the United States at an earlier time, the ukase was intended primarily to regulate the activities of Russian subjects, rather than to interfere with the rights of foreigners.[7]

The ukase did eliminate most of the quarreling among the Russian traders themselves, but it had little effect upon foreign traders (mainly British and American) who came to Alaskan waters. As a result, officials of the Russian American Company complained to their government, which endeavoured – without success – to support their cause through the medium of diplomatic protests.[8] In the meantime, the Russian company tried to extend its own sphere of activity, and in 1812 it established Fort Ross at Bodega Bay on the California coast, this marking approximately the southern limit of Russian enterprise in the region. Primarily to check the "secret and illicit traffic" of foreigners, Emperor Alexander I issued a sweeping ukase on 16 September 1821, which purported to grant Russian subjects the exclusive right to the "pursuits of commerce, whaling, and fishery, and of all other industry on all islands, ports, and gulfs including the whole of the northwest coast of America, beginning from Behring's Strait to the 51° of northern latitude," and also the Aleutian Islands and Kurile and other islands off the Siberian coast, from Bering Strait to Urup Island in the Kuriles at 45° 50'. The ukase also prohibited all foreign vessels from landing on all these coasts and islands, and also from approaching them within one hundred "Italian miles," on pain of confiscation.[9] Nine days afterwards, the Tsar issued a second charter to the Russian American Company, renewing the monopoly privileges it had been granted in 1799 for a further period of twenty years. The area subject to the monopoly would be governed by the ukase of 1821 rather than by that of 1799, and thus it would extend down the Pacific coast of North America to 51° (i.e., the northern tip of Vancouver Island) rather than just to 55°.[10]

Both the British and American governments protested strongly against these measures as quickly as possible after receiving official notification of them. Although efforts to coordinate their protests fell through because of the evident conflict between their own claims, their separate negotiations soon caused the Russian government to moderate its stand. In a letter to Russian Ambassador Pierre de Poletica on 25 February 1822, American Secretary of State John Quincy Adams expressed his president's concern about the terms of the ukase and inquired whether he was "authorized to give explanations of the grounds of right, upon principles generally recognized by the laws and usages of nations, which can warrant the claims and regulations contained in it."[11] De Poletica's "explanations," given in a letter of 28 February,[12] were firmly rejected by Adams in a further letter of 30 March,[13] and lengthy negotiations followed which involved mainly a Russian retreat from their original position. While this dispute was in progress, and partly because of it, President James Monroe proclaimed his famous "doctrine" to the effect that the American continents were "henceforth not to be considered as subjects for future colonization by any European powers" in his message to Congress on 2 December 1823.[14] When the two powers agreed upon a settlement, as embodied in the treaty of 17 April 1824, Russia abandoned her extreme claims. It specified that the entire Pacific Ocean should be open for navigation and fishing by the citizens of both nations. The treaty also established the parallel of 54° 40' N latitude as the dividing line between Russian and American settlements on the northwestern coast of North America and adjacent islands.[15]

The British government received official word of the ukase on 12 November 1821 in a letter from Russian Ambassador Baron de Nicolay to Foreign Secretary Lord Londonderry (Viscount Castlereagh).[16] Londonderry was advised by King's Advocate C. Robinson to declare Britain's intention of upholding ordinary principles of international law and protesting any infringement of British rights.[17]

Ambassador Sir Charles Bagot in St. Petersburg informed him that the main purpose of the ukase was to prevent the "commerce interlope" of American adventurers and that the justification for the measure was supposed to be Article 12 of the Treaty of Utrecht.[18] He then wrote to the new Russian ambassador Count Christopher Lieven on 18 January 1822 "to make such provisional protest against the enactments of the said Ukase as may fully serve to save the rights of His Majesty's Crown." Specifically, he said that Great Britain reserved all her rights regarding Russian claims to exclusive sovereignty over the land and exclusive right of navigation in the water, as described in the ukase, and could not admit that non-Russian trade therein was illicit or that Russia could legally prevent foreign ships from approaching within one hundred Italian miles of the coast.[19]

The Russian claims, and also those of the Americans in the same region, greatly concerned the Hudson's Bay Company (HBC), which had joined with the Nor'Westers in the territories west of the Rocky Mountains.[20] Later in 1821, the new coalition received Imperial authorization to monopolize trade in these same territories.[21] Deputy Governor J. H. Pelly wrote urgently to Londonderry on 27 March 1822 to put the company's case before him,[22] and in this and later communiqués,[23] he included much supporting evidence which, although it was not always strictly accurate, the British government relied upon extensively in developing its own case.

The Duke of Wellington, who had been appointed to represent Great Britain in conferences at Vienna and Verona following the suicide of Londonderry in August 1822,[24] was given verbal assurances by Count Lieven that the Russian emperor "did not propose to carry into execution the Ukase in its extended sense" and that Russian ships "had been directed to cruise at the shortest possible distance from the shore."[25] The new Foreign Secretary, George Canning, derived similar impressions from a talk with Count Lieven, and he was confident that, so far as their extreme claims at sea were concerned, the Russian government was "prepared entirely to waive their pretensions."[26]

Wellington was far from satisfied, however, with verbal assurances that left the ukase itself in being. In a note to Russian Foreign Secretary Count Karl Nesselrode on 17 October, he expressed strong objections to the claims of exclusive sovereignty, as set forth in the ukase, over both land and sea.[27] When Nesselrode replied in rather conciliatory fashion, offering to negotiate boundaries but in effect reasserting the terms of the ukase,[28] Wellington countered by restating his objections in a stiff note to Count Lieven. He also wrote, in blunt language more characteristic of the general than the diplomat:

> I must inform you that I cannot consent, on the part of my Government, to found on that paper the negotiations for the settlement of the question which has arisen between the two Governments on this subject…. I think, therefore, that the best mode of proceeding would be that you should state your readiness to negotiate upon the whole subject, without restating the objectionable principle of the Ukase, which we cannot admit.[29]

One day later, Wellington sent word to Canning that he had won his point and that the Russian emperor now desired to negotiate "upon the whole question of the Emperor's claims in North America."[30] Russia was willing to abandon completely her "extravagant assumption of maritime jurisdiction,"[31] but Sir Charles Bagot, the British Ambassador to Russia, who had been given the responsibility of conducting negotiations,[32] had much greater difficulty in arranging an agreeable disposition of the claims to land. Canning had directed him to suggest the 57° parallel as the dividing line,[33] whereas the Russian officials had spoken among themselves of the 55th degree, or preferably "the southern point of the archipelago of the Prince of Wales and the Observatory Inlet," as the most northerly limit they could concede.[34] In preliminary conversations with Nesselrode and Poletica, Bagot indicated that although Britain had always claimed up to 59° N latitude, she would accept a line at 57°, or perhaps at Cross Sound at 57-½°, with a meridian line drawn north from Lynn Canal at about 135° W longitude.[35] Poletica, who had been designated to carry on negotiations for Russia, replied with suggestions that his government would like to fix the line of latitude at 55° or 54°.[36]

In the formal talks that followed, Bagot modified the British proposals on three occasions. He found the Russians adamant, at least so far as the southern boundary was concerned. On the other hand, they were less worried about the eastern boundary, and from the start they were willing to accept a line that would leave the entire Mackenzie River in British possession.[37] Bagot's three modifications were:

(1) a line through Chatham Strait and Lynn Canal, northwest to the 140th meridian and along that meridian to the Arctic Ocean;

(2) a line through Sumner Strait north of Prince of Wales Island to the mainland coast, then northwest following the sinuosities of this coast at a distance of ten marine leagues from shore as far as the 140th meridian, and then along this meridian to the Arctic Ocean; and

(3) a line south and east of Prince of Wales Island through Dixon Entrance and Clarence Strait to

> Sumner Strait, and then as in (2) above.[38]

The Russians proposed a line running from the southern extremity of Prince of Wales Island to and up Portland Canal, along the mountains paralleling the coast to the 139th meridian, and thence along this meridian as far as the Arctic Ocean.[39] Feeling that he had already conceded more than he was authorized to do, Bagot suspended negotiations for the time being. On 29 March 1824, he wrote to Canning saying that he had "entirely failed" to get an acceptable agreement from the Russians.[40]

After receiving advice from the HBC,[41] Canning decided that it would be wise to bring matters to a conclusion largely on Russian terms, although with some "qualifications." These qualifications were mainly (1) a more definite description of the Russian strip of territory on the mainland, with its width to be limited to a maximum of ten leagues; (2) a more westerly meridian of longitude for the boundary in the northwest; (3) free use of all rivers flowing through the Russian strip and of all Russian waters; and (4) trade advantages not inferior to those granted to any other nation.[42] With new instructions along these lines to guide him, Bagot tried once more. The negotiations broke down on his insistence that Britain should have a perpetual right of access to the part of the Novo Archangelsk and to navigation and trade along the coast of the strip or *lisière*, as well as a temporary right, which was to be reciprocal, to visit all other parts of the northwestern coast.[43] Shortly afterwards, Bagot was transferred to a different post, and Canning sent his cousin Stratford Canning to St. Petersburg as special emissary to finalize an agreement.[44] With Bagot's last demands put aside, a treaty was framed without great difficulty and signed on 28 February 1825.

Apart from being obliged to bow to Russian wishes regarding the southern boundary and the creation of the *lisière*, the British could point with satisfaction to the acceptance of much of what they wanted in the arrangement that was made. The treaty recognized their freedom to navigate, fish, and trade throughout the Pacific Ocean, thus removing the most objectionable feature of the 1821 ukase. It limited the breadth of the *lisière* to a maximum of ten marine leagues; it conceded their right to navigate "for ever" the rivers flowing through the *lisière*; and it moved the northwestern boundary westward to the 141st meridian. It also omitted, at British insistence, an article in a Russian "counterdraft" of 21 August 1824, which seemed to imply that freedom of navigation in Bering Strait was being conceded "as a boon from Russia."[45]

Article 1, regarding freedom of navigation, fishing, and trading throughout the Pacific, and Article 2, regarding the requirement of permission to land at each other's establishments, were almost identical with the same articles in the Russian-American treaty of the preceding year. The important provisions for the boundary line were in Articles 3 and 4:

> 3. The line of demarcation between the possessions of the High Contracting Parties, upon the coast of the continent, and the islands of America to the north-west, shall be drawn in the manner following:
>
> Commencing from the southernmost point of the island called Prince of Wales Island, which point lies in the parallel of 54 degrees 40 minutes, north latitude,

> and between the 131st and 133rd degree of west longitude (meridian of Greenwich), the said line shall ascend to the north along the channel called Portland Channel, as far as the point of the continent where it strikes the 56th degree of north latitude; from this last-mentioned point the line of demarcation shall follow the summit of the mountains situated parallel to the coast as far as the point of intersection of the 141st degree of west longitude (of the same meridian); and, finally, from the said point of intersection, the said meridian line of the 141st degree, in its prolongations far as the Frozen Ocean, shall form the limit between the Russian and British possessions on the continent of America to the north-west.
>
> 4. With reference to the line of demarcation laid down in the preceding Article it is understood:
>
> 1st. That the island called Prince of Wales Island shall belong wholly to Russia.
>
> 2nd. That whenever the summit of the mountains which extend in a direction parallel to the coast, from the 56th degree of north latitude to the point of intersection of the 141st degree of north latitude to the point of intersection of the 141st degree of west longitude, shall prove to be at the distance of more than 10 marine leagues from the Ocean, the limit between the British possessions and the line of coast which is to belong to Russia, as above mentioned, shall be formed by a line parallel to the windings of the coast and which shall never exceed the distance of 10 marine leagues therefrom.[46]

What the treaties of 1824 and 1825 meant to Great Britain, so far as boundary problems were concerned, was that henceforth any such problems north of 54° 40' would be with Russia, and any south of 54° 40' would be with the United States. In this connection, it is necessary to recall that in earlier times two other nations, France and Spain, had shown developing interest in this region, but by now their pretensions had been eliminated. During the eighteenth century, French explorers and fur traders led by the Vérendryes had moved westward across the continent and had almost reached the Rocky Mountains, but any further action France might have taken on the other side of the Rockies became an impossibility after the Seven Years War and the Peace of Paris in 1763. Henceforth, the possibility of French involvement was limited to whatever fishing and trading interests might develop as a result of sea voyages, such as those of La Pérouse and Marchand. Spain had been the first European state to sail in the waters west of North America, and she had gradually extended her activities and aspirations northward by both land and sea, but the treaty of 22 February 1819 with the United States placed the northern boundary of her Pacific coast territories along the parallel of 42°.[47] Her position respecting more northerly regions thus became comparable to that of France.

For Great Britain and the United States, the question of boundaries west of the Rocky Mountains involved the whole of the so-called "Oregon country," from the northern limit of

Spanish territory to the southern limit of Russian territory, that is, as these limits came to be determined, from 42° to approximately 54° 40'. By the convention on 20 October 1818, the 49th parallel was established as the dividing line between British and American territories from the Lake of the Woods to the Rocky Mountains. Since agreement could not be reached on the territories west of the mountains, it was stipulated that these territories should be open for joint occupation for a period of ten years:

> It is agreed, that any country that may be claimed by either party on the northwest coast of America, westward of the Stony Mountains, shall, together with its harbours, bays, and creeks, and the navigation of all rivers within the same, be free and open, for the term of ten years from the date of the signature of the present convention, to the vessels, citizens, and subjects of the two Powers.[48]

When it became apparent that no definitive settlement could be made before the ten years had expired, another convention was signed on 6 August 1827, extending the provisions of the above-quoted third article indefinitely, but with the prevision that either party could terminate the arrangement after one year's notice.[49] The Oregon Treaty of 15 June 1846 fixed the reminder of the boundary by extending it along the 49th parallel from the Rocky Mountains to the middle of the channel separating the continent from Vancouver Island, and thence through the middle of this channel to the Pacific Ocean, so as to leave all of the island as British territory.[50] Apart from the dispute over San Juan Island, which was settled by arbitration in 1872, British and Canadian boundary disputes in this part of the continent were henceforth to be over the Alaskan Panhandle, first with Russia and then, after 1867, with the United States.

Disagreement with Russia was not long in coming after the treaty of 1825 had been signed – not so much over the boundary, however, as over the interpretation of the treaty and what it implied for navigation and trade. The HBC began to construct a chain of posts along the coast north of the Columbia River, and in 1834 it sent Chief Trader Peter Skene Ogden in the brig *Dryad* to build a fort on the Stikine River. Although the fort was to be constructed on British territory, up the river and beyond the point where it flowed into the Russian *lisière*, Lieutenant D. F. Zarembo of the armed ship *Chichagov* refused, with threat of force, to let Ogden proceed. Ogden was obliged to retreat without carrying out his assignment, and the HBC appealed to the British government for help, claiming damages of more than £22,000. The company charged specifically that the Russians had violated three provisions of the 1825 treaty: Article 6 guaranteeing British subjects freedom of navigation in the rivers crossing the *lisière*, Article 7 guaranteeing for ten years freedom to fish in the coastal waters of the same, and Article 11 renouncing use of force.[51] The British government pressed these charges upon the Russian government, which initially admitted their validity but then tried ingeniously, although with lessening confidence, to avoid admitting the claim for damages.[52] Finally, through direct negotiations between the HBC and the Russian American Company in St. Petersburg and Hamburg, and doubtless to the great relief of the Russian government, the two companies themselves were able to make a settlement. By an agreement signed at Hamburg on 6 February 1839, the Russian American Company leased to the HBC the coastal strip north to Cape Spencer for ten years beginning

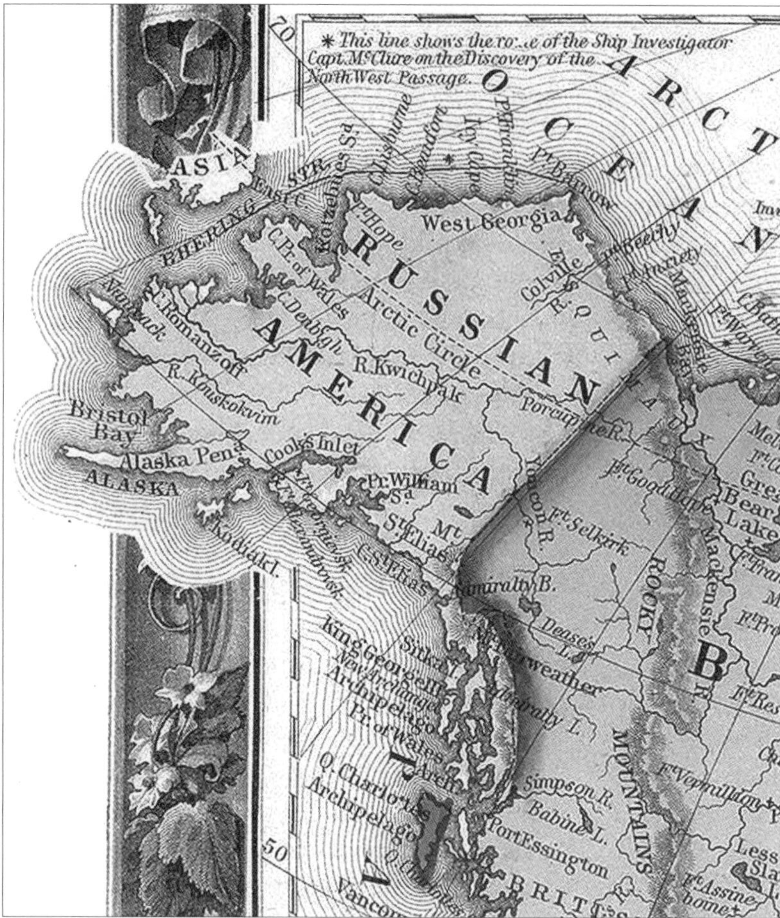

Figure 5-1: Russian American in 1860. Excerpt from the "Map of North America. Showing its Political Divisions, and Recent Discoveries in the Polar Regions," in Mitchell's *New General Atlas, Containing Maps Of The Various Countries Of The World, Plans Of Cities, Etc.* (New York: S. Augustus Mitchell, Jr., 1860).

on 1 June 1840, in return for an annual rent of 2,000 otter skins plus the guaranteed sale of various commodities including food and more otter skins. The HBC also relinquished its claim to damages for the *Dryad* affair.[53] The lease was renewed or extended in 1849, 1858, 1862, 1865, and 1866 for varying lengths of time, the last to terminate on 31 May 1867.[54] It was thus still in existence when the sale of Alaska was made. One of the interesting sidelights of the *Dryad* episode, of considerable consequence for the later events, was that both British and Russian officials in their negotiations not only accepted the existence of the *lisière* but also seemed to agree that its breadth along the Stikine should be ten marine leagues.[55]

Through arrangements initiated before the Crimean War broke out in 1853, the two companies maintained an agreement that their possessions on the northwest coast of America should be neutralized. Both the British and Russian governments approved the agreement, although the British refused to extend it to the adjacent high seas and joined their French allies in attacks upon Russian establishments on the Kuriles and the Siberian coast.[56]

The sale of Alaska to the United States in 1867 brought to an end the proximity of British and Russian territory in North America and meant that henceforth British and Canadian dealings in this part of the continent would be with the United States. In 1862, the HBC had informed the Russian American Company that it did not plan to renew the lease arrangement;[57] although the lease was renewed for a period of two years, every indication suggested that further renewals were doubtful.[58] For this reason and various economic, political, and strategic considerations, the Russian government began to give increasing thought to disposing of its distant colony. The idea of selling it to the United States, far from being new, had been under contemplation for at least several years; nevertheless the actual negotiations for the sale took place rather quickly early in 1867.[59]

At four o'clock in the morning on 30 March 1867 at Washington, DC, Secretary of State Seward and Russian Ambassador Baron de Stoeckel signed the document providing for the cession of Alaska to the United States in return for $7,200,000 in gold.[60] Ratifications were exchanged on 20 June, and the formal ceremony of the transfer took place at Sitka (Novo Archangelsk) on 18 October.[61] Article 1 of the treaty specified that the land being transferred comprised "all the territory and dominion now possessed by his said [Russian] Majesty on the continent of America and in the adjacent islands" and that its eastern limit should be "the line of demarcation between the Russian and the British possessions in North America, as established by the convention between Russia and Great Britain, of February 28–16, 1825, and described in Articles III and IV of said convention." The treaty did not specifically retain any other existing arrangements between Great Britain and Russia, and Article 6 stated that the cession was to be "free and unencumbered by any reservations, privileges, franchises, grants, or possessions, by any associated companies, whether corporate or incorporate, Russian or any other." After the expiration of its third charter on 1 January 1862, the Russian American Company had existed only "on sufferance,"[62] and although steps were taken to renew the charter in 1866, these were nullified by the cession.[63] Also nullified was the still-existing lease of the *lisière* by the HBC, along with new plans by the British company for yet another extension of the lease.[64] Nevertheless, HBC officials assumed that the United States would be bound by the Anglo-Russian treaty of 1825 as Russia's successor, and when their steamship *Otter* was deterred by American regulations and dues from ascending the Stikine River in 1867, they protested to the British government that the Americans were violating the treaty. They were informed that by the terms of the cession the United States was bound only by the boundary provisions of the 1825 treaty and that Russian concessions including the right of navigation were no longer in effect.[65]

Apart from the *Otter* affair and a few other events, such as the expedition of Captain Raymond in 1869 to remove the HBC from its post at Fort Yukon, the change of ownership in Alaska caused little difficulty over the boundary for several years. The transfer of Rupert's Land and the North-Western Territory to Canada, along with the extension of British Columbia's northern boundary to the 60th parallel, eliminated the HBC as a political factor in the area almost as thoroughly as the sale of Alaska had eliminated the Russian American Company. There was little American interest in the newly acquired territory, and less American immigration into it, while the majority of Russians departed. As time went on, however, a succession of events focused attention upon boundary problems once more.

On 11 July 1872, Lieutenant-Governor Joseph W. Trutch of British Columbia forwarded a copy of an address from his legislature to the Dominion government in Ottawa asking that, in view of the recent mineral discoveries in the northern part of the province and the undefined state of the boundary with Alaska, steps be taken to have this boundary properly marked out.[66] Under instructions from the British government, Ambassador Sir Edward Thornton broached the idea of a joint commission in Washington, where it was favourably received, but the proposal fell through because of the unwillingness of Congress to grant the necessary funds for the survey. American officials had suggested that it might be sufficient to locate only particular points, such as those where the boundary line crossed some of the important rivers including the Stikine, but Secretary of State Hamilton Fish feared, rightly, that even this would be considered too expensive by Congress.[67]

In January 1874, the British Columbia legislature presented another address to the Lieutenant-Governor requesting a delimitation of the boundary, and again Trutch sent it to Ottawa, with no more significant result than the first time.[68] Acting on its own, however, the Canadian government in November 1873 appointed Captain Donald Roderick Cameron, who was not only Her Majesty's North American Boundary Commissioner but also the son-in-law of Charles Tupper, to report on the cost and time that a joint commission would require to fix the boundary line.[69] Cameron's report was not submitted until February 1875, and since his estimate of cost ranged from $425,000 to $2,230,000 and of time from two to seven years, it was too vague to be of much help.[70] John Stoughton Dennis, the Surveyor General of Canada, had also submitted a report a year earlier which accepted the American suggestion that only particular points along the boundary needed to be fixed, and he advised that it was unnecessary then "and it may be for all time" to do more.[71]

This point of view was not to prevail. In a conversation with Ambassador Thornton on 23 September 1875, US Secretary of State Hamilton Fish informed him of reports from Sitka to the effect that a party of British subjects had settled on the Stikine below the Canadian custom house and that both the settlement and custom house were within ten marine leagues of the coast and thus on American territory. Thornton replied that the occurrence showed the wisdom of the British recommendation that the boundary should be determined without delay, and he suggested that both countries send officers to settle the problem.[72] Trouble also arose over the trading post of a Canadian named Buck Choquette, which was located on the Stikine about two miles above the custom house, left isolated in 1876 when the Canadian authorities moved it ninety miles upstream. Claiming that his post was clearly within Alaska, American officials ordered Choquette to pay duty on his goods or remove them by spring 1877. Choquette insisted that his post was in British Columbia and held his position when the American customs official at Sitka, hearing that the Canadian government had ordered a survey of the Stikine, temporarily suspended any attempt at enforcement of his decree.[73]

More serious was the case of Peter "Bricktop" Martin, who in 1876 was sentenced to fifteen months' imprisonment on two convictions at Laketon in the Cassiar mining district of British Columbia. Then, after momentarily escaping from and wounding his escort while being taken out via the Stikine River to the Victoria jail, he was convicted of these new offences at Victoria and sentenced to an additional twenty-one months. Secretary of State Fish demanded the release of Martin on grounds that his escape and recapture had taken place on American territory within the Alaskan Panhandle, a point British and Canadian authorities were not willing to concede. A considerable correspondence ensued, with Ambassador Thornton renewing British suggestions for an accurate delimitation of the boundary line.[74] On 3 March 1877, in an attempt to locate the boundary at least at the point in question, the Canadian government appointed a civil engineer named Joseph Hunter to make a survey of the lower Stikine.[75] Hunter's report, composed after a very rapid and efficient survey, was handed in the following June.[76] In a separate note, he advised that the escape and recapture of Martin had almost certainly taken place on Alaskan soil.[77] Influenced also by a dispatch from Colonial Secretary Lord Carnarvon recommending Martin's release,[78] the Canadian government agreed to set him free shortly afterwards.[79] In February 1878, the American government accepted a suggestion, presented by Thornton on behalf of the Canadian government, that Hunter's demarcation of the boundary at the Stikine should be accepted as a provisional line for that area.[80]

There was confusion and uncertainty not only over the boundary at the Stikine but also over navigation rights upon it. When American customs officials in the Panhandle asserted their intention in 1873 of preventing foreign ships from carrying freight through the American part of this river, Thornton protested on grounds that Article 26 of the Treaty of Washington (8 May 1871) guaranteed free navigation of the Stikine (as well as the Yukon and Porcupine) to subjects and citizens of both Great Britain and the United States.[81] In January 1874, Fish informed Thornton that the customs officials had been instructed "to act in accordance with the provisions of the Treaty of Washington."[82] As already noted, HBC officials had assumed at the time of the cession of Alaska that they would retain their rights under the Anglo-Russian treaty of 1825, but they learned from the British government in 1868 that although the United States was bound by the boundary provisions of this treaty (which were reproduced in the treaty of 1867), other Russian obligations, including those connected with navigation, had not been passed on. Nevertheless, the British government later took the view that although by Article 6 of the 1867 treaty Russia ostensibly revoked the navigation rights granted Britain in 1825, it could not do this legally without British consent. In reality, Britain itself had admitted the abrogation of these rights by the negotiation of the Treaty of Washington in 1871 and by the terms of the treaty itself. Therefore, whatever British rights of this kind presently existed were derived only from the Treaty of Washington, specifically Article 26.[83]

British thought and action on this subject were highly unsatisfactory to some Canadian officials, notably Minister of Justice Edward Blake, who maintained that British rights had continued unimpaired and unrestricted after 1867 but had been given away in return for very little in 1871.[84] The differences between the relevant sections of the treaties of 1825 and 1871 were in fact of considerable significance, since the earlier treaty gave British subjects unrestricted rights of navigation upon all rivers flowing through the *lisière*, whereas the later treaty gave them rights of navigation for commercial purposes only, upon only three specified rivers, and also conceded reciprocal rights to American citizens in the Canadian parts of these rivers.[85] The British government cited the restriction of navigation in the Washington treaty to commercial navigation only as an additional reason for setting Martin free,[86] but it does not appear that the broader question of American inheritance of Russian responsibility was ever conclusively settled.

Little of note respecting the boundary occurred for several years, although some interested individuals realized the danger of leaving it unfixed. Among these was William H. Dall, then a member of the US Coast and Geodetic Survey, who in April 1884 wrote to Canada's George Dawson suggesting that "the matter of the boundary should be stirred up. The language of the Treaty of 1825 is so indefinite that were the region included for any cause to become suddenly of evident value, or if any serious international question were to arise regarding jurisdiction, there would be no means of settling it by the Treaty." He remarked that since there was no natural boundary and since the "long caterpillar" of mountains on Vancouver's charts had no existence as such, the United States would undoubtedly wish to fall back on the wording of the 1825 treaty: "line parallel to the winding of the coast and which shall never exceed the distance of ten marine leagues therefrom." Even this would be impracticable to trace; therefore determinable boundaries should be agreed upon, and perhaps Dawson would "be able to set the ball in motion on your side."[87] It does not appear that the suggestion as made had any immediate consequences in Canada, but the importance of a settlement was apparent to Thomas F. Bayard, the new American Secretary of State, who after consulting with Dall wrote a letter to Ambassador Edward John Phelps in London asking him to suggest to the British government the appointment of an international commission to fix the boundary line.[88] President Grover Cleveland also referred to the matter with some urgency in his first annual message to Congress on 8 December 1885.[89] Impressed by the new American attitude, Lord Salisbury readily agreed to consider Bayard's suggestion.[90] Later, after consultations between British and Canadian officials, word was sent to Washington that the Canadian government would prefer a preliminary survey that could lead to more definitive action afterwards.[91] In the course of the correspondence which followed, Lord Salisbury drew attention to certain remarks made by Lieutenant Frederick Schwatka in his report of his journey through the Yukon and Alaska in 1883, which located Fort Selkirk in Alaska and fixed Perrier's Pass (on the Chilkoot Trail) and 140° W longitude as part of the international boundary. Salisbury noted that Fort Selkirk was actually well within British territory and that Great Britain was not prepared to accept Schwatka's two points as fixing the boundary. Carefully denying that any importance was attached to the omission, Salisbury also observed that Schwatka had failed to inform British authorities of his desire to travel in British territory.[92] Much more significant than the Schwatka affair, however, was the conference held in Washington in late 1887 and early 1888 to settle North American fisheries rights and other outstanding questions between Great Britain and the United States. Participants arranged to bring together Dawson and Dall as experts to discuss the Alaska boundary, and it was through their discussions in Washington that irreconcilable differences of opinion respecting the boundary were brought into the open. In this development the so-called "Coast Doctrine"[93] of Donald Cameron, formerly Boundary Commissioner and now a general, looms very large.

Cameron, who had been appointed an adviser to the Canadian government on the Alaskan boundary and had given the matter much thought, explained his rather facile solution to the Panhandle problem in a lengthy report written in 1886.[94] The main question involved the interpretation to be given the expression "*la côte*" ("the coast" as used in the Anglo-Russian convention of 1825). Cameron disposed of the question neatly and in a fashion decidedly favourable to Canada by concluding that "the coast" meant the general coastline of the continent, cutting across both promontories and inlets but going around neither. He put forward his argument plausibly and forcefully:

> It can easily be shown that the general coast line of the continent, exclusive of inlets, creeks, and similar narrow waterways, is the sense in which the words were used.... [T]he line, whether marked by mountains or only by a survey line, has to be drawn without reference to inlets.... None of the inlets between Portland Channel and the Meridian of 141° W long. are six miles in width, excepting, perhaps, a short part of Lynn Canal. Consequently, with that possible exception, the width of territory – on the coast assigned under the Convention to Russia – may not be measured from any point within the mouths of the inlets. All the waters within the mouths of the inlets are as much territorial waters, according to any universally admitted international law, as those of fresh-water lake or stream would be under analogous circumstances.[95]

Thus, according to Cameron's interpretation of the convention, inlets less than six miles in width were to be British territorial water, and accordingly Canada would have access to salt water at various places along a relatively narrow panhandle. This was the Coast Doctrine, "in all its mad beauty," as one commentator has remarked,[96] and Dawson adopted this solution to the boundary problem in seemingly uncritical fashion from his former chief and attempted to sell it to Dall during their Washington discussions in February 1888.

It was not difficult for Dall to point out in reply that the history of British-Russian negotiations leading up to the convention showed that "Russia needed, asked, and obtained the possession of the entire undivided coast margin."[97] If the six-mile principle had been applicable and had been applied consistently, most of the offshore islands as well as the inlets would have become subject to British sovereignty. Furthermore, if the inlets had been intended to be British property, then there would have been no need for any special provisions, such as those in the convention, to enable her to reach them. He went on:

> It is, of course, in view of all the facts, nothing less than preposterous to suppose that Russia would have accepted a treaty which cut her "strip" of main-land into several portions, or that Great Britain, having the right to occupy with trading posts the richest fur region of the archipelago, and represented by the Hudson's Bay Company, the keenest corporation of that period, should nevertheless not only not assert and use these rights, but on the other hand pay money and otter skins for these very privileges to a foreign and competing corporation.[98]

Dall also disagreed with Cameron and Dawson on other points, notably the identification of Portland Channel or Canal, but the most fundamental disagreement respected the *lisière*. He put forward his views in several memoranda to Secretary of State Bayard, which were published in US Senate documents[99] and later in the documents of the Alaska Boundary

Case. Obviously the arguments of Dall on the one side, and Cameron and Dawson on the other, were well known to responsible officials in both Canada and the United States (although probably not to the general public). It seems very unfortunate, in retrospect, that the vacuity and unreality of Cameron's case, and the cogency and logic of Dall's, were not fully appreciated and acknowledged at the time in Canada as well as in the United States. Had this been the case, much of the trouble over the Alaska boundary might have been avoided.

In the meantime, the British Columbia government had adopted and put forward a proposition with even less substance than Cameron's. It was based upon a report written in 1884 by Judge John Gray of the Supreme Court of that province, which argued that the boundary line should not ascend Portland Channel as Article 3 of the Anglo-Russian treaty of 1825 said it should. Instead, Gray suggested that it should go through Clarence Strait just east of Prince of Wales Island and strike the mainland at 56° N latitude, thus making Revillagigedo Island and a large chunk of the mainland part of British Columbia. Gray claimed that the words "Portland Channel" had not really been in Article 3 of the treaty at all but rather were a "subsequent interpolation" because, looking at the rest of the article, a line ascending "to the north" from the "southernmost point" of Prince of Wales Island would not go up Portland Channel, and even if it did, the channel would not take it "as far as" 56°. Gray had an even more vivid imagination than Cameron; nevertheless, in spite of the transparent inaccuracy of his claim, some Canadian government officials took it seriously, and even Dawson recommended that it should be left for the Americans to refute.[100]

Although the Dall-Dawson discussions had shown the wide divergences between American and Canadian views on the Alaska boundary and had, so to speak, established the lines of battle, little of note developed for several years. On 10 September 1888, the Canadian government had received a report that the Alaskan authorities were about to grant a charter for the construction of a trail from Lynn Canal through White Pass to the interior of Alaska. British Ambassador Sir Lionel Sackville-West protested to Secretary of State Bayard that the territory in question was British.[101] Bayard could only reply that the "vague and indefinite" rumour had not come to the notice of his department.[102] On 5 June 1891, Ambassador Julian Pauncefote called the attention of Secretary of State James G. Blaine to a published report of the US Coast and Geodetic Survey referring to a planned survey of the frontier "about 35 miles" from the coast and to the Canadian government's feeling that "the actual boundary line can only be properly determined by an International Commission."[103]

In February 1892, a conference took place in Washington between Secretary of State Blaine, his adviser J. W. Foster, Ambassador Pauncefote, and Canadian ministers John Thompson, George Foster, and Mackenzie Bowell, its outcome being an agreement for a joint survey of the Alaska boundary line.[104] This agreement was formalized by a convention signed at Washington the following 22 July, which provided for a survey of the territory adjacent to the boundary line

> from the latitude of 54° 40' north to the point where the said boundary line encounters the 141st degree of longitude westward from the meridian of Greenwich … with a view to the ascertainment of the facts and data necessary to the permanent delimitation of said boundary line in accordance with the spirit and intent

> of the existing Treaties in regard to it between Great Britain and Russia and between the United States and Russia.[105]

The convention stipulated that the survey was to be completed in two years, but this allotment of time was insufficient so a supplementary convention was signed at Washington on 3 February 1894, extending the time limit to 31 December 1895.[106] As commissioners, the British government appointed Canada's chief astronomer Dr. W. F. King,[107] and the American government appointed Superintendent of the US Coast and Geodetic Survey Thomas Corwin Mendenhall,[108] the latter being replaced by William Ward Duffield in June 1895.[109] Duffield and King duly submitted a joint report, accompanied by maps and photographs, on 31 December 1895.[110] In accordance with the terms of the convention, the survey made no attempt actually to fix the boundary line, and its main value lay in the provision of necessary information about the territory in dispute.

The spectacular gold strike on the Klondike River in 1896, and the inevitable rush that followed, gave a new note of urgency to the need for settlement of the boundary problem. The shortest and fastest route to the region from the west coast of both Canada and the United States passed through the Lynn Canal and over the mountain passes to the headwaters of the Yukon, thus emphasizing in dramatic fashion the importance of the whereabouts of the frontier and also related questions of access, jurisdiction, and customs. Before long, a variety of complaints and rumours of actual or threatened clashes were filtering back to Ottawa and Washington, and it required little imagination to appreciate that the possibility of real trouble had greatly increased.

The portion of the boundary line running north along the 141st meridian from Mount St. Elias posed a much smaller problem than the irregular portion extending southeast from the same mountain, which was supposed to show the limit of the Panhandle to its southern extremity. In the first case, it was only a matter of locating a boundary that was defined in such a way that disagreement about it was, if not impossible, at least most unlikely. In the second case, it was necessary to reach agreement on where the boundary was supposed to run before the practical problem of marking it on the ground could be undertaken. On 1 June 1895, the Canadian government passed an order in council which took note of the need to determine the location of the 141st meridian and observed that William Ogilvie had already been dispatched to continue the survey he had begun in 1887–88, when he had fixed the intersections of the 141st meridian with the Yukon River and Forty-mile Creek. The order also recommended seeking the co-operation of the United States, preferably in joint action on the survey or, failing that, in temporary recognition of Ogilvie's work without prejudice to the rights of either country when a joint survey should be made at a later date.[111] The British government proposed this to the United States on 20 August 1895,[112] and after consideration the American government replied favourably on 11 March 1896, proposing a more limited joint survey that would concentrate initially on fixing principal points along the 141st meridian. An order in council issued by the new Laurier administration on 28 September 1896 recommended acceptance of the American proposal, observing that the preceding Conservative government had taken the same view.[113] On 30 January 1897, a convention was signed in Washington for "the demarcation of so much of the 141st meridian of west longitude as may be necessary for the determination of the boundary,"[114] but the convention was not ratified by the American Senate, and joint action on this part of the boundary did not take place until after the dispute over the Panhandle had been settled.

Dyea and Skagway, the principal ports of entry at the head of the Lynn Canal for miners and goods bound for the Yukon, quickly took on boom town characteristics. The refusal of American officials to allow Canadian vessels to land at these ports caused a chorus of Canadian complaints, and Canadian Commissioner of Customs John McDougald wired the Treasury Department in Washington on 22 July 1897, asking permission for Canadian goods to pass through to the Yukon without payment of customs duties, on condition that the parties concerned pay for American officers to accompany the goods.[115] Assistant Secretary of the Treasury W. B. Howell wired back promptly suggesting that Dyea be made a sub-port of entry under these conditions,[116] and a day later he sent another wire saying that this had been done.[117] About a month later, another Canadian request was made for the same privilege at Skagway,[118] eliciting the response that this had already been done.[119] Needless to say, these requests were afterwards used by the United States to buttress her case for ownership of all the land on the shores of the Lynn Canal.[120]

On 23 February 1898, the British government proposed to the American government that the determination of the boundary south of Mount St. Elias "should at once be referred to three Commissioners (who should be jurists of high standing), one to be appointed by each Government, and a third by an independent Power," the commissioners to begin immediately by fixing the frontier at the heads of inlets used for traffic to the Yukon. The proposal added that, pending this settlement of the boundary, Great Britain would view a *modus vivendi* with satisfaction.[121] On 18 April 1898, Ambassador Pauncefote presented to the American Secretary of State a memorandum noting the Canadian government's fear that divergent views on the boundary would prevent any accomplishment under the 1892 convention, but he also expressed its willingness to accept a provisional line "at the Watershed at the first summit north of Dyea" without prejudice to the claims of either party.[122] The American government consented to this suggestion in a note dated 9 May.[123] Later in May, a series of meetings were held in Washington, at which arrangements were made for the establishment of a joint high commission to settle the principal outstanding problems between Canada and the United States, the Alaska boundary being one of them. A protocol of proceedings and conclusions was signed on 30 May, both parties appointed high commissioners, and each sent the other a memorandum of its views.[124]

Under the terms of the protocol, the joint high commission of six American and six British appointees held meetings in Quebec City between 23 August and 10 October 1898, and in Washington between 9 November 1898 and 20 February 1899. Attempts were made to deal comprehensively with the dozen or so subjects listed for discussion on the lengthy agenda, including Bering Sea fur seals and Atlantic fisheries. It proved impossible to reach agreement on the Alaska boundary question, however, and on this stumbling block the entire conference foundered. Lord Farrer Herschell, head of the British-Canadian delegation, had been persuaded (evidently against his better judgment)[125] to put forward a combination of the British Columbia government's and Major General Cameron's claims in extreme form. These claims had been adopted and given authoritative expression by Canadian Minister of the Interior Clifford Sifton and would have

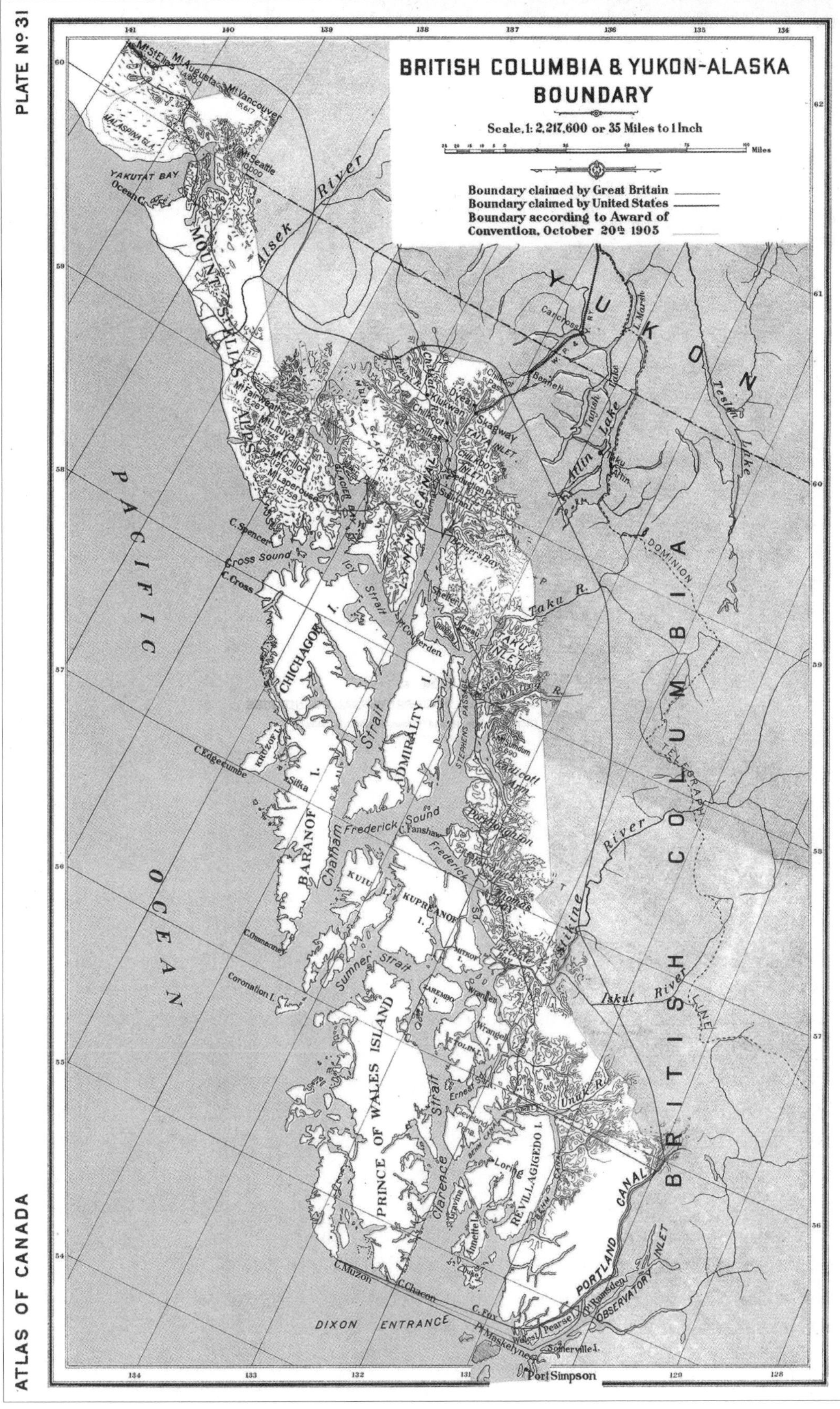

FIGURE 5-2: MAP OF U.S. AND CANADIAN CLAIMS AND THE ACCEPTED BOUNDARY. *NATIONAL ATLAS OF CANADA, 1906.*

made the boundary run through Clarence Strait east of Prince of Wales Island instead of up Portland Channel, and then across the promontories of the coast so as to leave all the major inlets in British (Canadian) possession.[126] Not surprisingly, the Americans firmly rejected this proposition. The Canadians were particularly anxious to have direct access to salt water from the Yukon, and Herschell proposed that the United States should cede to Canada Pyramid Harbour on Chilkat Inlet at the upper end of the Lynn Canal, with a strip of land along the Chilkat River and Pass to connect the port with the Yukon. The Americans countered with offers of free use of all ports on the Lynn Canal and a fifty-year lease of Pyramid Harbor and the desired strip.[127]

As the impossibility of compromise became increasingly evident, the British delegation proposed on 16 December (and repeatedly afterwards) that the entire Panhandle boundary should be submitted to arbitration by legal experts.[128] Much haggling ensued over the terms of the proposed arbitration, with the Americans insisting that the headwaters and shore of Lynn Canal should not be subject to determination. The British wanted to associate an Alaska boundary compromise with the proposed abrogation of the Clayton-Bulwer Treaty of 1850 relating to a Panama Canal, but the Americans wanted to keep the issues separate. The United States had its way, as Great Britain signed a new treaty on 18 November 1901, providing for American construction of the canal, before the Alaska boundary dispute had been settled.[129] The Americans had hoped that Lord Herschell would be more reasonable to deal with than the Canadian delegates, whom they expected to be difficult, but as events turned out they found Herschell "more cantankerous than any of the Canadians."[130] Since there appeared to be good prospects for progress on the other matters before the commission, the Americans wanted to proceed with these even if the Alaska boundary remained unsettled, but the British-Canadians insisted that only a package deal could be accepted. The deadlock on the Alaska boundary being insurmountable, the meetings broke off on 20 February 1899 without achievement.[131]

On 20 March 1899, Secretary of State John Hay wrote a note to Pauncefote suggesting a provisional boundary line around the head of Lynn Canal "at the water shed on the summit of White and Chilkoot Passes, and at a point thirty marine miles from Pyramid Harbour on the Chilkat Pass and otherwise known as the Dalton Trail."[132] Pauncefote referred this suggestion to the Canadian government, which was willing to accept the watershed for White and Chilkoot Passes as a provisional line, but contended that for Chilkat Pass the boundary should be placed provisionally "at the crest of the mountains nearest to the coast." The entire boundary line from Prince of Wales Island to Mount St. Elias, however, should be determined by arbitration.[133] On 13 May, Francis Hyde Villiers, the Assistant Under Secretary at the Foreign Office writing on behalf of Lord Salisbury, sent a note to US Ambassador Joseph Hodges Choate informing him that the Canadian government had agreed that the Alaska boundary dispute could be referred to arbitration at once along the lines of the Venezuela-British Guiana boundary arbitration treaty (thus separating it from the other points at issue) and that the Canadians were willing to proceed with these other matters as soon as an arbitration agreement had been reached.[134]

Lord Salisbury wrote a further note on 1 July, emphasizing that settlement of the Alaska boundary problem seemed impossible except through arbitration and proposing formally that the Venezuela treaty should be applied.[135]

The American government was not inclined to accept the Venezuela treaty as a definitive guide, however, on grounds that – unlike the British-Venezuelan territorial dispute – the dispute over the Panhandle strip was new and no protest over occupied settlements therein had been made until recently.[136] On 17 August, Sir Wilfrid Laurier, in explaining his Cabinet's rejection of a British proposal that Canada should have a perpetual lease of half a square mile on the Lynn Canal and a railway right-of-way to the Yukon, reiterated the Canadian contention that "the only solution is a reference of the whole matter to arbitration."[137]

After much bargaining over Hay's proposal of 20 March 1899, the parties agreed to a *modus vivendi* on 20 October of the same year, setting a provisional boundary line around the head of Lynn Canal. On the Dyea and Skagway Trails, the line was placed at the summits of the Chilkoot and White Passes, respectively, as Hay had suggested, while in the Dalton Pass–Chilkat River region it was to run along the right (south) bank of the little Klehini River to its junction with the Chilkat and from there eastward to the summit of a specified prominent peak. The document stated clearly that the arrangement was without prejudice to the claims of either party in the permanent fixing of the boundary.[138]

For over three years, however, little progress towards a permanent settlement was made. Negotiations continued in desultory fashion, one of the principal points at issue being the composition of the proposed arbitration tribunal. Early British proposals for such a tribunal had taken a variety of forms:

(a) "three Commissioners (who should be jurists of high standing), one to be appointed by each Government, and a third by an independent Power";[139]

(b) "legal experts" or "legal and scientific experts" without specification as to number;[140] and

(c) three "eminent" jurists or jurists "of repute," one to be appointed by the United States, one by Great Britain, and the third by the other two.[141]

Proposals (b) and (c) had been put forward by the British-Canadian representatives on the joint high commission suggesting "four members – two to be named by each Government, one to be a legal expert and one an expert of established reputation in the science of geography and geodesy"[142] and then an arbitral tribunal of "six impartial jurists of repute," three to be nominated by Great Britain and three by the United States.[143]

The basic British-Canadian and American concepts of the tribunal were radically different, and each side held to its own point of view with tenacity. The British, and more particularly the Canadians, wanted an odd-numbered tribunal with a neutral member, believing that there would be a better chance that such a body would reach a decision and also that in case of a division there would be a better chance that an impartial vote would determine the majority. The Americans, feeling at heart that reference of the matter to a tribunal would in reality constitute an unwarranted concession on their part, held out for an even-numbered tribunal without a neutral member so that their appointees could not be outvoted.[144]

The Spanish-American War had tended to draw American attention away from other issues in 1898; the Boer War similarly attracted

British attention between 1899 and 1902. The stubborn but futile British and Canadian attempt to relate the abrogation of the Clayton-Bulwer Treaty to the Alaska boundary dispute was another reason for loss of time. There were distracting elections in all three countries in 1900: in Great Britain in October and in the United States and Canada in November. The assassination of President William McKinley in September 1901 threw American affairs into momentary disarray, but the succession of Vice President Theodore Roosevelt to the presidency brought to office a much more belligerent defender of American interests than McKinley had been. Roosevelt soon made it evident that he felt there was nothing of importance to arbitrate in the Alaska boundary dispute, and if there was to be a settlement, it must be on American terms.

The uncompromising attitude of President Roosevelt caused concern in both Canada and Great Britain. In March 1902, he gave orders for the dispatch of additional troops to Alaska,[145] and from time to time he made aggressive statements, the general tenor of which was to the effect that the Canadians "did not have a leg to stand on" in their contentions.[146] Prime Minister Laurier went to London in 1902 to attend the colonial conference which was meeting that year, and while there, evidently under British pressure, he agreed to accept the American demand that the proposed boundary commission should have an even number of members, all of whom would be appointed by the parties to the dispute.[147] This concession removed one of the major points of disagreement, and henceforth events moved more rapidly.

On 17 October 1902, Secretary of State Hay reiterated an earlier American proposal that, instead of rendering a decision, the members of the tribunal "should merely place their reasoned opinions on record."[148] The Canadian government replied that it "would be disposed to consider it favourably, provided the reference to the Tribunal should include all aspects of the question."[149] On receiving word of this from the British government, Hay indicated his own concurrence, although he would have to consult the president about it. He also gave British Ambassador Sir Michael Herbert the impression that he would now accept a decision of the judicial tribunal as final.[150] Negotiations now focused mainly on a draft treaty, which would specify precisely the terms of reference under which the tribunal would function, and the points of dispute about the boundary, which it would undertake to resolve. On 23 January 1903, Foreign Secretary Lansdowne cabled instructions to Herbert to sign the treaty as it had been framed,[151] and this was done the following day.[152]

The Case

The treaty provided for the immediate appointment of "six impartial jurists of repute," three by His Britannic Majesty and three by the President of the United States, who were to "consider judicially the questions submitted to them," and who would decide all questions by majority vote. Each of the two high contracting parties was to appoint an agent and whatever counsel it wished, and each was to pay for their services as well as for the services of its appointees to the tribunal. The written or printed case of each party, accompanied by all documentary evidence, was to be presented within two months of the date of ratification of the treaty; within two months of this date of presentation, although with provision for a time extension, each party was entitled to present a counter case with additional documentary evidence.

Within two months from the expiration of the time allowed for delivery of the counter cases, each party was obligated to present a written or printed argument which it could support before the tribunal by oral argument of counsel. The tribunal was to assemble in London as soon as possible and, subject to a provision for extension of time by agreement of the two parties, render its decision within three months of the conclusion of the arguments. The decision was to be final and binding, and upon receiving it both parties immediately were to appoint scientific experts to lay down the boundary line in conformity with its terms. Article III of the treaty specified that the tribunal should consider, in settling the questions submitted to it, the treaties of 1825 and 1867, and particularly the third, fourth, and fifth articles of the 1825 treaty, which were reproduced word for word in French from the original text. The specific questions which the tribunal was to decide were set down in precise terms in a key article of the convention:

> Article IV. Referring to Articles III, IV, and V of the said Treaty of 1825, the said Tribunal shall answer and decide the following questions: –
>
> 1. What is intended as the point of commencement of the line?
> 2. What channel is the Portland Channel?
> 3. What course should the line take from the point of commencement to the entrance to Portland Channel?
> 4. To what point on the 56th parallel is the line to be drawn from the head of the Portland Channel, and what course should it follow between these points?
> 5. In extending the line of demarcation northward from said point on the parallel of the 56th degree of north latitude, following the crest of the mountains situated parallel to the coast until its intersection with the 141st degree of longitude west of Greenwich, subject to the condition that if such line should anywhere exceed the distance of 10 marine leagues from the ocean, then the boundary between the British and the Russian territory should be formed by a line parallel to the sinuosities of the coast and distant therefrom not more than 10 marine leagues, was it the intention and meaning of said Convention of 1825 that there should remain in the exclusive possession of Russia a continuous fringe, or strip, of coast on the mainland, not exceeding 10 marine leagues in width, separating the British possessions from the bays, ports, inlets, havens, and waters of the ocean, and extending from the said point on the 56th degree of latitude north to a point where such line of demarcation should intersect the 141st degree of longitude west of the meridian of Greenwich?
> 6. If the foregoing question should be answered in the negative, and in the event of the summit of such mountains proving to be

in places more than 10 marine leagues from the coast, should the width of the *lisière* which was to belong to Russia be measured (1) from the mainland coast of the ocean, strictly so-called, along a line perpendicular thereto, or (2) was it the intention and meaning of the said Convention that where the mainland coast is indented by deep inlets forming part of the territorial waters of Russia, the width of the *lisière* was to be measured (a) from the line of the general direction of the mainland coast or (b) from the line separating the waters of the ocean from the territorial waters of Russia, or (c) from the heads of the aforesaid inlets?

7. What, if any exist, are the mountains referred to as situated parallel to the coast, [and] which mountains, when within 10 marine leagues from the coast, are declared to form the eastern boundary?[153]

The selection of the "six impartial jurists of repute" became a matter of bitter controversy and recrimination. For Canada, it left the most lasting scars of dissatisfaction and ill feeling. On 14 February, Ambassador Herbert sent a cable to the Marquis of Lansdowne saying that he had learned that day from Secretary Hay that President Roosevelt would probably appoint as American members of the tribunal Senator Henry Cabot Lodge of Massachusetts, Senator George Turner of Washington, and Secretary of War Elihu Root.[154] Four days later, the news was relayed to the Canadian government,[155] which protested strongly on the reasonable grounds that it had agreed to the tribunal on the understanding that the appointees would be "impartial jurists."[156] As a matter of fact, all three were eminent lawyers, but they could hardly be considered impartial, since all three were currently political rather than legal in their primary responsibilities. Root, although highly esteemed abroad as well as at home, was circumscribed through being a member of Roosevelt's Cabinet. Both Lodge and Turner had already publicly committed themselves to the American side of the case. Furthermore, Lodge was well known to be an aggressive Anglophobe, and Turner represented the state which had the most direct interest in Alaskan affairs. The British government, although "as much surprised" as the Canadians at the disheartening turn of events, stressed the "difficulty" of the situation and their earnest desire "to have the concurrence" of the Canadian government in dealing with it.[157] They had already foreshadowed their ratification of the treaty in the Speech from the Throne on 17 February, before communicating the news of Roosevelt's selections to Ottawa; the ratifications were duly exchanged in Washington on 3 March, while the situation was still under the consideration of the Canadian government.[158]

Partial explanations for Roosevelt's appointments have been offered by suggestions that he first asked at least two[159] (and perhaps all[160]) of the members of the Supreme Court to serve and met with refusal in each case. Whether he was merely going through the motions is a valid question. At any rate, he was undoubtedly concerned about the problem of securing the Senate's approval of the treaty, and Lodge recounted afterwards that he had impressed upon the president the virtual impossibility of getting this approval unless the appointments were satisfactory from that body's point of view. Lodge recalled that the treaty had been put in his charge, and when several senators, especially from the Northwest, informed him that they would have to have assurance about American representation on the tribunal, he obtained permission from the president to tell them in confidence whom the appointees would be. This information quieted their objections, and the Senate ratified the treaty on 11 February. One American who was not pleased with the appointments was Secretary Hay who, according to Lodge, "was extremely displeased and protested in the strongest way to the President against Mr. Root, and even more strongly against me, taking the ground that our opinions were already well known, which was also true of Senator Turner."[161]

Typical of angry Canadian comment was the following, which John W. Dafoe of the *Winnipeg Free Press* received in a letter written to him "about this time" by Minister of the Interior Clifford Sifton:

> As you have no doubt already sized the matter up, the British Government deliberately decided about a year ago to sacrifice our interests at any cost, for the sake of pleasing the United States. All their proceedings since that time were for the sake of inveigling us into a position from which we could not retire....
>
> It is, however, the most cold-blooded case of absolutely giving away our interest, without even giving us the excuse of saying we have had a fight for it, which I know of, and I do not see any reason why the Canadian press should not make itself extremely plain upon the subject. My view, in watching the diplomacy of Great Britain as affecting Canada for six years, is that it may just as well be decided in advance that practically whatever the United States demands from England will be conceded in the long run, and the Canadian people might as well make up their minds to the now.[162]

The British government was convinced that it would be useless to press the United States to change the American representatives on the tribunal and extremely unwise to break off negotiations altogether, but it dropped a broad hint to the Canadians that retaliation might be made by appointing "representatives appropriate to the altered circumstances of the case."[163] The Canadian government declined to accept the suggestion, however, and held to the view that if the case were to proceed, "only Judges of the higher Courts, who in the best sense of the words would be impartial jurists of repute, should be chosen."[164] In accord with Canadian wishes, the three men appointed were Lord Alverstone, Lord Chief Justice of England; Sir Louis Jetté, former judge of the Superior Court of Quebec and currently Lieutenant-Governor of that province; and John Douglas Armour, justice of the Supreme Court of Canada.[165] On the death of Justice Armour in July 1903, Allen B. Aylesworth, KC, of the Ontario bar, was appointed to replace him.[166] Clifford Sifton was named agent for the British-Canadian side, with Under Secretary of State Joseph Pope and Chief Astronomer W. F. King to assist him. Senior members of counsel were Attorney General of England Sir Robert Finlay, Solicitor General of England Sir Edward Carson (replacing former Canadian Liberal leader Edward Blake, who was forced to retire because of illness), and Christopher Robinson of Toronto. The junior members, several of whom were destined to achieve distinction in their own rights, were Lyman P. Duff, Aimé Geoffrion, and F. C. Wade of the Canadian bar and John A. Simon and S. A. Rowlatt of the English bar. General John W. Foster acted as agent for the United States, with several experts to assist him; the American counsel were Jacob M. Dickinson, David T. Watson, Hannis Taylor, and Chandler P. Anderson.[167]

Preparation of the cases, counter cases, and printed arguments occupied approximately six months after the exchange of ratifications on 3 March. The British-Canadian side tried repeatedly for extensions of time and for postponements of the date when the oral arguments would begin, but the Americans refused to accommodate them. Secretary Hay was personally inclined to grant the requested additional time,[168] but others, including Lodge and the president himself, took the hard line that none should be allowed.[169] Hay's position became so uncomfortable that he offered his resignation, but the president declined to accept it.[170] Evidently the main reason for the American refusal was that the members of its tribunal wanted to leave England in October so as to be back in the United States for the approaching sessions of Congress – a revealing indication, no doubt, of the "judiciality" of Roosevelt's appointments.[171]

While the preparation of the cases was in progress, Roosevelt issued a barrage of letters, statements, and instructions which left no doubt about his own stand. On 25 March 1903, for example, he sent "personal and confidential" instructions to the three American commissioners on the tribunal, in which he described the Canadian claims as untenable and the Canadian position as far from judicial. He also insisted that the question of Canadian ownership of salt water harbours should not be open for discussion. In rather contradictory fashion, however, he said:

> You will of course impartially judge the questions that come before you for decision....There is entire room for discussion and judicial and impartial agreement as to the exact boundary in any given locality.... In the principle involved there will of course be no compromise.[172]

On 25 July, Roosevelt wrote a letter to Justice Oliver Wendell Holmes of the US Supreme Court, who was in England at the time, saying that although he wished to make one last effort to reach a settlement through the tribunal, he wanted it distinctly understood that if there was disagreement, he would get Congress to give him authority "to run the line as we claim it, by our own people, without any further regard to the attitude of England and Canada." Since he also made clear that Holmes was "entirely at liberty" to pass the information on to Colonial Secretary Joseph Chamberlain, the judge took this extraordinary step.[173] On 26 September, he wrote in similar vein to Henry White, Secretary of the American embassy in London, and suggested that White impart its contents to Prime Minister Balfour.[174] The president also asserted his willingness to resort to force of arms, and in a letter to Senator George Turner, he remarked that in case of disagreement he was ready to "send a brigade of American regulars up to Skagway and take possession of the disputed territory and hold it by all the power and force of the United States."[175] There can be little doubt, as Philip Jessup remarks, that the British government was made thoroughly aware of the Rooseveltian viewpoint.[176]

In this general atmosphere of anxiety, suspicion, and antagonism, which fortunately did not seem to affect the proceedings themselves, the tribunal met for the first time at the Foreign

Office in London on 3 September 1903. On the motion of Elihu Root, Lord Alverstone was unanimously elected president of the tribunal, and it was agreed that oral arguments would begin on 15 September and continue thereafter on weekdays, Monday through Friday, until finished. Finlay, Robinson, and Carson spoke for the British-Canadian side and Watson, Taylor, and Dickinson for the American side, in each case in the order just given, with the first group having the first, third, and fifth places and the other the second, fourth, and sixth. The printed cases, counter cases, and arguments had been prepared with great care and in great detail, considering the limited amount of time available, and the oral arguments, although unequal as to length and also as to merit, developed the main issues of the controversy thoroughly. The oral argument ended on 8 October, and the decision of the tribunal was handed down on 20 October.

The printed materials and the oral arguments all devoted considerable attention to the historical background of the case and other relevant or supporting information, but necessarily the major concentration was placed upon the seven specific questions which the tribunal was called upon to answer. It may be convenient here also to concentrate upon these seven questions, which in summary were handled as follows.

On the first question, regarding the beginning point of the line, there was virtual argument and consequently little discussion. Article 3 of the 1825 treaty had identified "the southernmost point of the island called Prince of Wales Island" as the spot where the line should begin. As the British case observed, the United States had once attempted to apply this description to Wales Island at the outlet of Portland Channel but had abandoned the attempt, and both sides now accepted the much larger Prince of Wales Island north of Dixon Entrance. A further point of confusion, regarding the choice of the beginning point from two promontories, was eliminated without much difficulty. The southern extremity of Prince of Wales Island was actually Cape Chacon, while Cape Muzon (although a short distance further south) was the southern tip of nearby Dall Island. The British, however, were willing to admit that neither Captain George Vancouver, who surveyed the island in 1793, nor the negotiations in 1825, realized that Dall Island was separated from Prince of Wales Island, and thus they conceded that the more southerly Cape Muzon was the legitimate beginning point according to the intent of the treaty.[177]

The second question, regarding the identity of Portland Canal, caused more disagreement within the tribunal than any other – to such an extent that in the end the Canadian members refused to sign the award. The British-Canadian side argued that the true Portland Canal was the one that had been surveyed and given this name by Captain Vancouver in 1793 and that his identification of it had been known and used by the negotiators who made the treaty of 1825. They claimed that Vancouver himself had identified it as the long passage that extended all the way from its upper end close to 56° N latitude to open water, passing north of Pearse, Wales, Sitklan, and Kannaghunut Islands. Thus these islands were British territory. In making this claim, they relied heavily upon a statement in Vancouver's own narrative, where he referred to this passage as "that arm of the sea, whose examination had occupied our time from the 27th of the preceding to the 2d. of this month … which, in honor of the noble family of Bentinck, I named Portland's Canal."[178] Their contention was strongly supported by this and other evidence, and the other side did not question that Vancouver's route down the passage had taken him north of all four islands. They also held that Vancouver's Observatory Inlet, just south of Portland Canal, extended all the way from its inner extremity to the main outlet south of Point Wales on Wales Island, and they cited as their main evidence another statement in Vancouver's narrative ("The west point of Observatory inlet I distinguished by calling it Point Wales").[179] They discounted the importance of post-1825 maps and interpretations, saying that these could not have had any bearing upon the negotiations leading up to the treaty in that year. They also maintained that the expressions "Portland Canal" and "Portland Channel," both of which had been used, had the same meaning.[180]

The American counsel agreed with the British so far as the upper part of Portland Canal was concerned, but they maintained that in its lower reaches it turned south between Pearse Island and Point Ramsden, and from there to open water was actually what the British called the lower part of Observatory Inlet. Thus a line drawn through the American "Portland Canal" would give the four islands in question to the United States. To the Americans, Observatory Inlet was only that part of the British Observatory Inlet which extended northeast of Point Ramsden. What was important, they said, was the Portland Canal of the negotiators in 1825, maintaining that these men must have seen Portland Canal either as the entire estuary from the mainland (including the four islands and also the upper part of the British Portland Canal) or simply as the upper part alone, with the large estuary being left unnamed. In either case, the boundary line should follow the main passage south of the four islands.[181] Senator Turner raised the further question as to whether Vancouver, in naming Portland Canal, considered its opening to be the narrow, island-filled passage north of Kannaghunut and Sitklan Islands, through which he sailed, or the shorter, broader, clearer, more navigable Tongass Passage between Sitklan and Wales Island, which he saw but did not sail through on his way out of Portland Canal.[182]

The answer to the third question, regarding the course the line should take from its beginning point to the entrance of Portland Canal, depended largely on the answer to the second. The British-Canadian counsel argued that the words "54 degrees 40 minutes" in Article 3 of the 1825 treaty were only intended to aid in identifying the beginning point at the southern extremity of Prince of Wales Island and were not intended to describe the course to be followed. The line between the two points in question should be the shortest and most direct possible, and since a straight line from Cape Muzon to the entrance of Portland Canal (as interpreted by the British) would cut off Cape Chacon and some small islands nearby, it would be necessary to draw two straight lines, one from Cape Muzon to Cape Chacon and another from Cape Chacon to the channel entrance.[183] The Americans at first simply asked that the line should run "in an easterly direction" to the middle of the entrance of what they conceived to be Portland Channel, but later they advanced the argument that the line was intended to run along the parallel of 54° 40', which would in fact take it very close to the point they wanted it to reach.[184]

The fourth question, regarding the point on the 56th parallel to which the line should be drawn from the head of Portland Channel, and the course this line should follow, resulted from the false assumption in the negotiations leading up to the treaty of 1825 that Portland Channel extended up to 65°. Actually only a few miles intervened, in a direct line, but the opposing views as to how the discrepancy in the treaty should be resolved differed radically.

The British argued "that the point in the 56th parallel to which the line should be drawn is the point from which it is possible to continue the line along the crest of the mountains situated parallel to the coast, and, accordingly, that the point at which the 56th parallel and the crest of the coast mountains coincide is the point in question."[185] Since they were contending for a very narrow, broken coastal strip, governed by a line of mountain crests very close to water's edge, they located the point in question far to the west of the head of Portland Canal, actually on Cleveland Peninsula to the northwest of Revillagigedo Island. The intervening distance was about seventy miles, and they proposed to bridge it by a straight line which would run only slightly north of due west. The Americans maintained that the logical interpretation of the treaty was that the line should be continued in the direction it was following along Portland Channel until it struck the 56th parallel, without immediate regard to mountains, and that it should then be taken directly to the appropriate mountain top in the coastal chain, which they, of course, located much farther inland than the British did. They held that the British line was not only illogical but in violation of the treaty, since it would cross salt water and also a small island north of Revillagigedo Island.[186]

The fifth question was long and involved, but in essence it amounted to whether it was the intention and meaning of the 1825 convention that Russia should have a continuous strip of coast on the mainland, not more than ten marine leagues in width, separating the British possessions from salt water. This was clearly the most important question put to the tribunal, and the outcome of the entire controversy depended to a large extent on its answer. (The sixth and seventh questions were obviously closely related to it and largely dependent upon it; hence most of the arguments treated the three together, with most emphasis falling upon the fifth.)

The British-Canadian side argued that the answer to the fifth question should be in the negative. They held that the words "ocean" and "coast" as used in the treaty of 1825 in reference to the boundary must refer to the same line, since where one ends the other begins. These words could not have been intended to apply to the water and land of the deep inlets, however, so the boundary line must cut across these inlets, making everything on the inner side British. It would be impossible to draw a ten-marine-league line parallel to all the windings and indentions at the edge of tide water or salt water; on the other hand, it would be quite possible to draw it parallel to the "general coast," and since the possible rather than the impossible was contemplated, the line should be drawn in this fashion, cutting across both deep inlets and long promontories. This would admittedly have left Russia with a narrow, broken strip, while Britain would

have access to salt water in a number of places. However, the only difficulty in accepting this lay in reading into the treaty a controlling principle that British territory should at no point touch salt water, and this principle was nowhere stated in the treaty. The establishment of the *lisière* had nothing to do with British access to and use of the sea; what Russia wanted was to stop Britain from having liberty to settle and trade near her own establishments on the islands. Russia herself had no settlements on the mainland in this region and was not in possession of it, and in fact had only Sitka as a genuine possession on the adjacent

> islands. Maps and documents had no value insofar as they misrepresented or contradicted the treaty; neither had later American acts of possession and administration insofar as they were done in the face of Canadian protests or while the countries were at issue on the question. Canada had protested certain American action, but could not be held responsible for not protesting others of which she had known nothing. Canadian admissions of American possession could not be taken also as admissions that mere possession precluded questions of right.[187]

The American side argued that the fifth question should be answered in the affirmative: that the 1825 convention was intended to give, and that it had given, a continuous strip of coast on the mainland to Russia which shut off the British territories from salt water. They maintained that Russia's primary object in the negotiations leading up to the treaty had been to secure such a strip, that Britain in the end had agreed that she should have it, and that the agreement had been written into the treaty and clearly understood on both sides. In purchasing Alaska in 1867 and acquiring all Russian rights therein, the United States had relied upon this interpretation of the treaty; both Russia before 1867, and the United States for fully thirty years afterwards, had acted under the assumption that they had full sovereignty over an unbroken coastal strip, without any formal protest of objection from Great Britain. On the contrary, British and Canadian official acts, declarations, and publications after 1825 consistently demonstrated their acceptance and recognition of first Russian and then American title, and the American case and counsel pointed to the implications in this direction of episodes such as the *Dryad* affair, the lease of the *lisière* by the HBC, the Peter Martin affair, and the Hunter survey. Governments, geographers, cartographers, and historians, including British and Canadian, had all given either implicit or explicit endorsement to the American contention, which was fortified by substantial and continuous measures of occupation and administration. Although American officials had become aware of the Canadian challenge, notably as a result of the Dall-Dawson discussions in 1888, the American government had received no distinct, official announcement of any British claim at variance with the concept of an unbroken *lisière* until 3 August 1898, on the eve of the meeting of the joint high commission. On the subject of the coastline,

> there are but two possible coast lines known to international law. One is the physical coast line traced by the hand of nature, where the salt water touches the land, which exists for the purpose of boundary: the second is the political coast line – that invisible thing superimposed upon the physical coast by the operation of law, which exists for the purpose of jurisdiction.[188]

In this case, there was already a political coastline, which lay outside the archipelago, so there could not possibly be a second political coast lying behind it. In any event, the coastline of relevance here was the physical coastline, where land and salt water met, and there could be no such thing as a general trend of the physical coastline. "Ocean" is to be considered as analogous to "man" in that each word comprehends not only the main body but also the arms or limbs.[189]

The British-Canadian side pointed out that the sixth question had to be answered only if two conditions were fulfilled: (a) that the fifth question had been answered in the negative and (b) that the summit of the mountains in question proved to be in some places more than ten marine leagues from the coast. Since they requested the first and anticipated the second, they took the view that the sixth question required an answer. It had been badly framed, and its wording gave everyone concerned a certain amount of difficulty, but according to their interpretation the alternatives it posed in Parts 1 and 2(a) were essentially the same, and thus there were really three alternatives: 1 and 2(a) together, or 2(b), or 2(c). That is to say, if the above two conditions were fulfilled, the width of the *lisière* could be measure from the line of the general direction of the mainland coast (1 and 2[a]), or from the line separating the waters of the ocean from the territorial waters of Russia (2[b]), or from the heads of the inlets (2[c]). They held, of course, that the measurement should be taken from the line of the general direction of the mainland coast according to the first alternative, and thus the upper part of the deeper inlets would be British. In cases where the line of mountains cut across the inlets, the waters inside this mark would also be British.[190]

Since the Americans argued that the fifth question should be answered in the affirmative, it follows that according to their view the sixth question did not require an answer. But if the tribunal should decide against them on the fifth question, the sixth had to be answered, and they held that the width of the *lisière* should be measured from the heads of the inlets – in which case the result would be approximately the same as if they had won the answer to the fifth. They maintained that a boundary line placed according to the British contention would be in direct conflict with the plain intent and meaning of the treaty of 1825 and that it would be utterly unreasonable to suppose that the Russians had conceded such a line to the British, since it would have deprived them of practically every safe harbour and anchorage on the mainland coast.[191]

On the seventh question, of the existence and identity of mountains forming the eastern boundary, the British-Canadian side contended that there were such mountains which fulfilled the requirements of the treaty and that they lay parallel to the general coast all the way along the *lisière* north of 56°. These mountains were to constitute the boundary within the ten-marine-league distance from the coast, and this distance was to be invoked only as a limit to mark the maximum possible breadth of the strip when the mountain chain went beyond it or ceased altogether. It was not necessary that this mountain chain should be completely continuous and unbroken; on the contrary, the line it made could continue across rivers, valleys, and inlets. The expression "la crête des montagnes" or "the summit of the mountains" in the 1825 treaty meant the tops of the mountains adjacent to the sea; the best evidence of this was that although Britain had suggested a line along "the base of the mountains nearest the sea," at Russian insistence the line was moved to the summit of these same mountains. Thus the strip would be very narrow throughout most of its length. The line would connect the summits of appropriate mountains next to the coast, and although it could not be argued that there was anything definite about the choice of such mountains, nevertheless the treaty clearly meant that this was the way the line should be drawn.[192]

The Americans argued that the contracting parties in 1825 intended that the width of the *lisière* should be consistently ten marine leagues measured from tide water, unless within that distance there was wholly or in part a continuous range of mountains extending the full length of the strip. The negotiators had believed that such a range existed, but in fact it did not, and nothing could be distinguished beyond a veritable sea of mountains. Thus ten marine leagues, rather than an imaginary range of mountains, became the controlling feature and should be applied throughout. They maintained that the British-Canadian side was mistaken in translating "la crête des montagnes" to signify the tips of individual mountains; rather it signified a continuous mountain ridge, which also was non-existent. Therefore the proposal to form the boundary line by connecting arbitrarily selected mountain tops was invalid. The other side was also mistaken in assuming that the mountain range nearest the sea, if one existed, should be taken. What was contemplated in 1825 was a principal range farther from the coast, as depicted on the maps of the time.[193]

Running through the case, and recurring continually, was the question as to whether Britain (and then Canada) had understood and accepted the concept of the unbroken *lisière* during the approximately sixty years before it began to emerge clearly as a major issue – and, more specifically, the precise point in time when they gave definite and formal notice that they disputed it. As noted above in my comments on the fifth question, the British-Canadian side attempted to establish that they had made clear their own point of view about the *lisière* and had protested against what they regarded as unwarranted American occupation of it. They referred particularly to such matters as Joseph Hunter's survey of the boundary at the Stikine River in 1877, working from "the general direction of the coast";[194] the British government's protest in 1887 regarding Schwatka's unauthorized fixing of the boundary during his 1883 reconnaissance;[195] Dawson's firm expression of opinion about the coastal strip during his discussions with Dall in 1888;[196] the British protest over the projected construction by Americans of a trail from Lynn Canal over the White Pass in 1888;[197] the convention of 1892 which dealt with an "existing boundary" that required only "permanent delimitation";[198] and Lord Salisbury's dispatch of 19 July 1898, which stated clearly the British view that the provisional boundary which had been agreed upon at the head of the Lynn Canal was more than one hundred miles from the ocean.[199] As evidence that the Canadian contention had come to the notice of official circles in the United States, they pointed out that the American president had laid the report of the 1887–88 conference (with some of the Dawson-Dall documents) before Congress[200] and that the Canadian claims had been referred to in Congress on at least two occasions. On 3 January 1896, Senator Watson C. Squire read a report to the Senate about the "pretensions of Canada" to canals, bays, and inlets, and the Canadian claim that the boundary line should "follow an alleged range of mountains arbitrarily crossing and cutting off the heads of bays and inlets, the ownership of which by the United States had hitherto been unquestionable."[201] On 12 February of the same year, Mahlon Pitney, a New Jersey representative, spoke in the House of Representatives regarding the Canadian claim that "there is a range of mountains very near to the coast of the mainland, and … a line should be run there near the coast, which would leave in British territory a large part of Taku Inlet, and a large part of Lynn Canal."[202]

The Americans contended that the evidence presented by their adversaries was of little or no validity. The point fixed by Hunter on the Stikine had clearly been accepted by the United

States as a temporary boundary only; the alleged "protest" over Schwatka's reconnaissance evidently had nothing to do with the coast and coastal waters, and if it had such purpose, this was "so artfully veiled as to make it entirely indiscernible"; the Dall-Dawson discussions were entirely unofficial and were clearly understood to be so by both sides; the "protest" over the projected White Pass trail was finally presented only as dealing with a rumour which the American government found so "vague and indefinite" that it did not take the matter seriously; the British had not put forward their new interpretation of the "existing boundary" at the 1892 conference, and there had been no real divergence of opinion on the subject. On the available evidence it was fair to conclude that the British and Canadians, like everyone else, had accepted the concept of the unbroken *lisière* for fully sixty years after the convention of 1825, and even when contrary theories were formulated following Cameron's 1886 report, they were put forward in such vague, variable, and unofficial fashion that the United States paid little heed to them. In fact, the first official notification the American government had that the continuous coastal strip was disputed came via Lord Salisbury's note of 19 July 1898, which was evidently communicated to them on 1 August following.[203]

The Americans were able to cite an impressive array of documents and statements by British and Canadian officials, some of them quite recent, which indicated not only their acceptance of the unbroken *lisière* and their failure to protest it but also their doubts and uncertainties about their own stand. For example, the Americans cited a remark by former Canadian Minister of the Interior David Mills in the House of Commons on 10 March 1879:

> Ultimately the points in dispute between the two Governments were disposed of in the Treaty of 1825, which gave to Russia a narrow strip of territory upon the coast south of Mount St. Elias, extending as far south as Portland Channel, upon the express condition that all the rivers flowing through this Russian territory should be open to navigation by Great Britain, for all purposes whatsoever.[204]

They interpreted this, of course, as an admission that there was a continuous strip of Russian territory through which the rivers flowed and which would make almost impossible the existence of British bays and inlets sandwiched between this strip and the Russian islands.

On 29 February 1892, Liberal Senator Richard William Scott, Leader of the Opposition in the Senate, spoke as follows in reference to the conference which had just been held in Washington:

> There was no dispute as to the boundary of Alaska.... It was settled in the treaty of 1825. The line was defined, but not marked out .... It is purely a question of survey. The terms of the treaty are not disputed.... I have never heard of any dispute as to the interpretation to be given to the treaty, because the treaty is plain and speaks for itself.[205]

On 11 February 1898, the following exchange took place in the House of Commons:

> *The Minister of the Interior (Mr. Sifton)*: I believe our contention is that Skagway and Dyea are really in

> Canadian territory, but as the United States have had undisputed possession of them for some time past, we are precluded from attempting to take possession of that territory.
>
> *Sir Charles Hibbert Tupper*: May I be excused for saying that I do not think the hon. Minister meant to say "undisputed possession."
>
> *The Minister of the Interior*: There have been no protests made. It must be taken as undisputed when there has been no protest made against the occupation of that territory by the United States.
>
> *Sir Charles Hibbert Tupper*: A claim, I suppose, was made and adhered to?
>
> *The Minister of the Interior*: There is nothing in the records to show that any protest has been made – an unfortunate thing for us, but it's a fact....[206]

A few days later, replying to a query about the reported intention of the American government to send two companies of troops to Dyea and Skagway, Prime Minister Laurier remarked:

> My hon. Friend is aware that, although this is disputed territory, it has been in the possession of the United States ever since they acquired this country from the Russian Government in 1867, and, so far as my information goes, I am not aware that any protest has ever been raised by any Government against the occupation of Dyea and Skagway by the United States....[207]

On 7 March of the same year, replying to Tupper's question about the choice of the Stikine River over Lynn Canal for a Yukon railway and anticipated American frustration of the plan, Laurier answered in rather confused, or confusing, fashion:

> But if we had adopted the route by the Lynn Canal, that is to say, had chosen to build a railway from Dyea by the Chilkat Pass up the waters of the Yukon, we would have to place the ocean terminus of the railway upon what is now American territory. I agree with the statement which has been made on the floor of this House, on more than one occasion, that Dyea, if the treaty is correctly interpreted, is in Canadian territory....
>
> Now I will not recriminate here; this is not the time nor the occasion for doing so; but so far as I am aware no protest has ever been entered against the occupation of Dyea by the American authorities; and when the American authorities are in possession of that strip of territory on the sea which has Dyea as its harbour, succeeding the possession of the Russians from time immemorial, it becomes manifest to everybody that at this moment we cannot dispute their possession, and that before their possession can be disputed, the question must be determined by a settlement of the question involved in the treaty. Under such circumstances, Dyea was practically in American territory – at all events, in possession of the Americans.[208]

These and other such statements resurrected by the Americans had a decidedly weakening effect on the Canadian case.

A reasonable summary of the issue would appear to be that the British and Canadians were right, at least for the period after about 1886, in maintaining that they had raised questions about the *lisière* and advanced views regarding it contrary to the American view. They were also right in insisting that they had made known these views to American officialdom. On the other hand, the Americans were right in maintaining that all evidence pointed to general and official British and Canadian acceptance of the unbroken *lisière* for about sixty years after the 1825 treaty and that although they had been made aware of contrary views in recent years, they had not received them in formal and official fashion until 1898. On this particular matter, the Americans had the better argument.

As the oral arguments proceeded, the irreconcilable differences of opinion within the tribunal itself became increasingly apparent. It was widely assumed that in all probability the three American members would vote solidly in favour of the United States' claims. This would mean that the questions would be decided by a four to two majority in favour of the United States, or left unsettled by a three to three tie, depending upon the decisions made by Lord Alverstone. He was not only the president of the tribunal but also the central figure in the manoeuvrings and negotiations behind the scenes which were directed mainly towards winning his vote.

President Roosevelt's crude efforts to dictate the course of action the American members of the tribunal should follow, and to browbeat the British government, have already been noted.[209] He continued in this vein during the oral arguments. On 3 and 5 October, he wrote letters to Root and Lodge, respectively, remarking in the one to Lodge: "The plain fact is that the British have no case whatsoever.... Rather than give up any essential, we should accept a disagreement.... We must not weaken on the points that are of serious importance."[210] Secretary Hay, although trying hard to keep the president within bounds,[211] also sent communiqués to Henry White and Ambassador Choate at the embassy in London to firm up their resolution on the major issue and to instruct them regarding American procedure. On 20 September, Hay wrote a letter to White, hoping that its contents "might indiscreetly percolate through to Balfour."[212] He stated in categorical terms that the disputed territory in the coastal strip was American and that if the tribunal failed to decide the question, the United States would not submit it to adjudication again but would simply continue to hold the land.[213] On 16 October, he sent word to Choate, in response to the ambassador's request for instructions, that if the tribunal granted the unbroken coastal strip to the United States, the president would accept a decision favourable to the other side on the Portland Canal.[214]

The three American commissioners kept in close contact with one another and also maintained a close liaison with Choate and White at the embassy so that they all presented a united American front. Lodge in particular sent frequent communiqués to Roosevelt to keep him informed about how the case was developing.[215] Henry White observed afterwards that on the occasions when it was necessary to convey some delicate intimations to Lord Alverstone about the stand he should take, "it was always Cabot who was deputed to do it. He has shown great tact and considerable diplomacy throughout."[216] Other accounts, including Lodge's own, do little to dispel the impression that he had an active and influential role in behind-the-scenes proceedings.[217] On 2 October, having become very worried about the way the oral arguments were proceeding, he wrote anxiously to White, asking him to let Prime Minister Balfour know how serious the situation had become and suggesting that he try to get Balfour to speak or write to Alverstone in the following vein: "We know you are going to decide this question impartially on the law and facts. We, of course, should not think of seeking to influence your opinions on any point. But it seems right that you should know that a failure to reach a decision would be most unfortunate."[218] On the same day, Root also wrote to White suggesting that he see Balfour. Although he should avoid saying anything to the prime minister that "might be misconstrued as being in the nature of a threat," Root instructed that "the Foreign Office should know how serious the consequences of disagreement must necessarily be."[219] White spent the following weekend at Balfour's country estate, and in a long conversation on 4 October, the prime minister said that he attached far more importance to the agreement of the tribunal than to any other current problem. Two days afterwards, his confidential secretary told White that he had seen Alverstone twice.[220]

On 9 October, the day after the tribunal heard the last of the oral arguments, Lodge and Balfour had a meeting at White's home in which both spoke of their extreme anxiety over the consequences of failure to reach a settlement.[221] Five days later, when it appeared that the six commissioners were deadlocked, Choate had an interview with Lord Lansdowne and strongly pressed Roosevelt's views upon the foreign secretary. He left satisfied that Lansdowne and Balfour would emphasize to Alverstone the need for a settlement. According to Choate's account, he and Lansdowne reached the amazing agreement that if the commissioners failed to settle the question of the boundary line, they would undertake to do it themselves.[222]

The foregoing shows the nature and extent of American pressure with sufficient clarity. What about Canadian? From the start it seemed apparent, at least in the American view, that the Canadians would adhere united and stubbornly to their own contention and would use all possible means to avoid defeat. Lodge wrote to Roosevelt that the Canadians were so "perfectly stupid" that they could not see that "a disagreement deprives them of their only chance to get out of the matter creditably";[223] in his later recollections, he remarked that "the two Canadian representatives would yield absolutely nothing on any point" and "there was no possibility of any agreement whatever between the Canadians, who would assent to nothing, and the American commissioners."[224] The Canadians were "filling the newspapers with articles of the most violent kind, threatening England with all sorts of things if the decision should go against Canada," and England was "so afraid of Canada" that the pressure might be effective.[225] In a letter to White, Secretary Hay remarked, "I see the Canadians are clamoring that he [i.e., Alverstone] shall decide not according to the facts, but 'in view of the imperial interests involved.'"[226] As the case proceeded, the American commissioners reported Alverstone's complaints to them about the Canadian pressure being exerted upon him.[227] According to Lodge, Alverstone admitted "that he was in a very trying and disagreeable position; that the Canadians were putting every sort of pressure and making every kind of appeal to him."[228]

These reports emanated from American sources, of course, and it is conceivable that they could have been distorted, or exaggerated, or inaccurate in some degree. But in the final stages, if not before, Canadian pressure from high political authorities became as blatant and uninhibited as American. On 7 October, Sifton cabled Laurier from London:

> I think that Chief Justice intends to join Americans deciding in such a way as to defeat us on every point. We all think that Chief Justice's intentions are unjustifiable, and due to predetermination to avoid trouble with United States. Jetté and Aylesworth are much exasperated, and considering withdrawing from Commission.[229]

Laurier replied:

> Our Commissioners must not withdraw. If they cannot get our full rights let them put up a bitter fight for our contention on Portland Canal, which is beyond doubt: that point must be decided in Canada's favor. Shame Chief Justice and carry that point. If we are thrown over by Chief Justice, he will give the last blow to British diplomacy in Canada. He should be plainly told this by our Commissioners.[230]

Any assumption or recognition here of impartiality or judiciality on the part of the Canadian commissioners would be difficult to detect. The same tendency to identify them with the Canadian point of view, and to instruct them, is evident in a later exchange between the same two leaders. On 17 October, after the tribunal had made its decisions but before the award had been made public, Sifton sent another cable to Laurier:

> Chief Justice has agreed with American Commissioners. Their decision will be to give us Wales and Pearse Islands, but give Americans two islands alongside, namely, Kanaghannut [*sic*] and Sitklan which command entrance to canal and destroy strategic value Wales and Pearse. Remainder of line substantially as contended for by Americans, except that it follows watershed at White Pass and Chilkoot. Our Commissioners strongly dissent. Decision likely to be Tuesday next. I regard it as wholly indefensible. What is your view? Course of discussion between Commissioners has greatly exasperated our Commissioners who consider matter as pre-arranged.

Laurier replied by cable the following day:

> Concession to Americans of Kanaghannut [*sic*] and Sitklan cannot be justified on any consideration of treaty. It is one of those concessions which have made British diplomacy odious to Canadian people, and it will have most lamentable effect. Our Commissioners ought to protest in most vigorous terms.[231]

The Canadian commissioners did protest, publicly, "in most vigorous terms," but how much Laurier's message might have had to do with their protest is uncertain.

Lord Alverstone, the key figure in the proceedings, was under severe and conflicting pressures from literally all sides – from the American and Canadian members of the tribunal itself, from various external American and Canadian influences including politicians and newspapers, and from his own government. In the circumstances, it would have been almost miraculous if he had not reacted to the stresses and strains in some fashion. Nevertheless, his conduct of the oral arguments appears to have been consistently impartial, open-minded, courteous, and capable; anyone reading the lengthy record of the hearings cannot help but be impressed by the quality of his performance. The charge that has been most frequently levelled against him is that he permitted himself to become wrapped up in the bargaining, manoeuvring, and wheeling and dealing that went on behind the scenes and that he abandoned his assigned role as impartial judge to become a sort of umpire or conciliator between two quarrelling groups, with the purpose of securing a negotiated or compromise agreement rather than rendering his own judicial decision. A leading Canadian commentator has said that he was revealed "not as the inflexible judge but as the adroit and pliable adjuster of difficulties."[232] The evidence certainly gives some support to the accusation, but, giving full consideration to the situation in which he found himself, Lord Alverstone was more sinned against than sinning.

On 13 September, shortly before the oral arguments began, Alverstone asked Joseph Pope confidentially if he "thought Canada would be satisfied if we could get Wales and Pearse Islands and a mountain line. I said that I feared not. He asked which would they prefer that or an absolute draw – 3 and 3 all round. I said I thought the latter. Personally I would greatly prefer the former, which I thought was all we could expect, but I added people were as unreasonable in Canada as elsewhere and that the inlets were the question." This conversation occurred during a weekend visit, and afterwards Pope wrote of it: "The position, at times, was most embarrassing, and Lord Alverstone very improperly took advantage of old personal friendship to put to me questions he should not have asked…. I found when I got back to town that Lord Alverstone had been talking to others besides myself, and that his views as to the ownership of the heads of inlets were more or less known."[233]

Senator Lodge said in his *Memoir* that Alverstone told him on the first day of the oral arguments that "of course the oral arguments may entirely change my views, but on the cases as presented to us by the agents, Canada has no case…. You understand that this is entirely subject to change, which may come from hearing the oral arguments.[234] Henry White wrote to Secretary Hay on September 19 that "Alverstone is getting daily into closer personal touch with Cabot and Root and has already spoken quite freely to them…. There seems to be unanimity in thinking the Canadians have a good case upon the Portland Canal or channel, and Alverstone has intimated that he is with us on the main question."[235] On the same day, he wrote a similar message to President Roosevelt.[236] The frequent communiqués of Lodge suggest Alverstone's willingness to negotiate. On 24 September, Lodge wrote to Roosevelt that Alverstone had told him he felt bound to

> hold that the line goes round the heads of the inlets, which is, if course, the main contention. He takes very decisively the British view on the Portland Canal. He wants to answer question 7, however, by picking out a series of mountains which will reduce the strip running around the heads of all the inlets to as narrow boundaries possible, his idea being, I presume, to try to let the Canadians down as easily as possible in this way, after having decided against them on the main point.[237]

On 2 October, Lodge reported to White that Alverstone had told him he was "nearer than ever to our view of question 7, while he is as firm as ever on his main contention of the line going round the head of the inlets which is involved in the reply to question 5."[238]

It is understandable that the members of the tribunal would exchange opinions among themselves, but one gets the impression of a good deal of loose and uninhibited communication on Alverstone's part. This is difficult to reconcile with his own claim (in a cable to Laurier on October 13) of complete circumspection and silence in the matter. On 12 October, Adam C. Bell of Pictou asked in the House of Commons in Ottawa for information about a report in the press that a majority of the Alaska commission were about to give judgment against the Canadian contention. "It is understood that Great Britain's representative on the commission, Lord Alverstone, has privately intimated to diplomatic and colonial office officials that he is convinced that a stronger case is made out by the United States, and that he intends to give judgment accordingly," Bell noted.[239] A cable was promptly sent to London, and Laurier read Alverstone's reply in the Commons on 13 October: "There is not the slightest foundation for statement attributed to me.... I have made no communication of any kind to any diplomatic or colonial officials, or to any person respecting the case. The report is an absolute fabrication."[240] Robert Laird Borden asked on 12 October about a somewhat similar indiscretion attributed to Aylesworth, but Laurier declined to give any credence to the report and apparently no inquiry was made. Neither, apparently, did Aylesworth issue any denial.[241]

The six members of the tribunal carried on their deliberations after the oral arguments ended on 8 October, in the midst of all this speculation, rumour, pressure, and intrigue, and obviously contributed a good deal themselves to the general atmosphere of anxiety and uncertainty. By 17 October, the main decisions had been made, and as noted Sifton sent word of them to Laurier by cable. On 20 October, the award was formally pronounced, the substantive part of it being as follows:

> In answer to the 1st question –
>
> The Tribunal unanimously agrees that the point of commencement of the line is Cape Muzon.
>
> In answer to the 2nd question –
>
> The Tribunal unanimously agrees that the Portland Channel is the channel which runs from about 55° 56' north latitude, and passes to the north of Pearse and Wales Islands.
>
> A majority of the Tribunal, that is to say, Lord Alverstone, Mr. Root, Mr. Lodge, and Mr. Turner, decides that the Portland Channel, after passing to the north of Wales Island, is the channel between Wales Island and Sitklan Island, called Tongass [Passage]. The Portland Channel above mentioned is marked throughout its length by a dotted red line from the point B to the point marked C on the map signed in duplicate by the Members of the Tribunal at the time of signing their decision.
>
> In answer to the 3rd question –
>
> A majority of the Tribunal, that is to say, Lord Alverstone, Mr. Root, Mr. Lodge, and Mr. Turner, decides that the course of the line from the point of commencement to the entrance to Portland Channel is the

line marked AB in red on the aforesaid map.

In answer to the 4th question –

A majority of the Tribunal, that is to say, Lord Alverstone, Mr. Root, Mr. Lodge, and Mr. Turner, decides that the point on the 56th parallel of latitude marked D on the aforesaid map, and the course which the line should follow is drawn from C to D on the aforesaid map.

In answer to the 5th question –

A majority of the Tribunal, that is to say, Lord Alverstone, Mr. Root, Mr. Lodge, and Mr. Turner, decided that the answer to the above question is in the affirmative.

Question 5 having been answered in the affirmative, question 6 requires no answer.

In answer to the 7th question –

A majority of the Tribunal, that is to say, Lord Alverstone, Mr. Root, Mr. Lodge, and Mr. Turner, decides that the mountains marked S on the aforesaid map are the mountains referred to as situated parallel to the coast on that part of the coast where such mountains marked S are situated, and that between the points marked P (mountain marked S, 8, 000) on the north, and the point marked T (mountain marked S, 7, 7950), in the absence of further survey, the evidence is not sufficient to enable to Tribunal to say which are the mountains parallel to the coast within the meaning of the Treaty.[242]

In essence the award amounted to this. The six commissioners accepted unanimously the point of commencement that both sides had argued for in Question 1, there being no serious controversy here. They also accepted unanimously the British contention for Portland Channel, through most of its length, and of Pearse and Wales Islands, in Question 2, this involving a rejection by the three American commissioners of the American claim. In all other cases, Lord Alverstone joined with the three Americans to outvote the two Canadians. The answers to Questions 3 and 7 did not give decisive victory to either side and might be termed compromises. The answer to what was left of Question 2 (the outlet of Portland Channel and the ownership of Sitklan and Kannaghunut Islands) and to Questions 4, 5, and 6 constituted clear-cut American victories.

Aylesworth and Jetté were so displeased with the outcome of the tribunal, especially with what they regarded as the non-judicial division of the four islands at the entrance of Portland Channel and selection of the mountain line, that they refused to sign the award. They also wrote strongly worded dissenting opinions and issued public statements justifying their stand. Alverstone and the American commissioners also wrote their own opinions: Alverstone individually, the Americans as a group.

Aylesworth was bitterly critical of Lord Alverstone for his abandonment of his earlier view that the British contention regarding Portland Channel was entirely correct and the four disputed islands should thus all be Canadian, and for his acceptance of the American demand that Tongass Passage should be named the entrance of Portland Channel, thus making Sitklan and Kannaghunut Islands American territory. This, Aylesworth said, "is no decision upon judicial principles; it is a mere compromise dividing the field between two contestants.... nothing less than a grotesque travesty of justice."[243] He disputed also the majority decisions on Questions 5, 6, and 7. In his comments, he adhered rigidly to the Canadian claims that (1) the 1825 convention had not been designed to give Russia a continuous strip of coast on the mainland, (2) the strip should be measured from the general direction of the mainland coast and thus would be broken by the inlets, and (3) the mountain line should run along the tops of the mountains nearest the sea.

Jetté's opinion consisted largely of lengthy and rather pointless repetition of the 1825 treaty, the convention of 24 January 1903, the arguments of the two sides, and the award. In essence, he took essentially the same stand on the specific questions as Aylesworth. Regarding the majority decision to divide the four islands, he found that "it was totally unsupported either by argument or authority, and was, moreover, illogical."[244] On Question 7, he observed correctly that the decision of the majority to choose certain mountains was adverse to the American contention that the treaty called for a continuous chain of mountains and that no such chain was identifiable. He could not accept the arbitrary choice of a mountain line which "although it does not concede all the territory they claimed to the United States, nevertheless deprives Canada of the greater part of that to which she was entitled."[245]

The American commissioners wrote joint opinions on the second and fifth questions. On Question 2, they explained their rejection of both the American contention that Portland Channel lay south of all four disputed islands and the British that it lay north of them and their opting for Tongass Passage as the "true entrance" of Portland Channel so that the islands were divided. Their explanation followed essentially the line of reasoning that Senator Turner had indicated in his remarks before the tribunal.[246] In accounting for their acceptance of the American argument on the fifth question, that is, that the 1825 treaty conceded a continuous Russian mainland strip running around the heads of the inlets, they did little more than reiterate the main points made by the American side during the case, with emphasis upon the factors of original understanding and long, unchallenged possession.[247]

The two opinions written by Lord Alverstone were also concerned with the second and fifth questions. He reached the same conclusions as the American commissioners, but his written comments suggest a different line of thought in each case. His approach to the second question is in fact difficult to detect if one has only his written opinion for guidance. For the fifth question, it is clear that while he concurred with the Americans in his emphasis upon the importance of the original intent of the 1825 treaty, he was much less impressed than they were with the significance of such things as subsequent actions and mapmakers' interpretations.[248]

Alverstone's reversal on Portland Channel and the four islands, and his questionable behaviour in connection with this change, provoked Canadian resentment more than anything else and precipitated the bitter aftermath that followed. During the course of the oral arguments, he had made no secret of his conviction that the British contention regarding Portland Channel was the correct one and thus the four islands should be Canadian; his memorandum on the subject, which he apparently read to the other commissioners on 12 October,[249] embodied this view. Yet, when the vote was taken, he joined with the three Americans to identify Tongass Passage as the entrance of Portland Channel, thus conceding the two small, outer islands to the United States. The usual explanation for this odd turnabout is that the American commissioners, finding the American argument on Portland Channel untenable and Alverstone stubbornly determined to deny them as wide a *lisière* as they wanted, demanded the two outer islands as compensation, and Alverstone's surrender on this point gave the resulting compromise arrangement. He wrote a memorandum afterwards in which he said that one of the American commissioners told him that if the islands were not divided, they would not sign the award, and he defended his action on grounds that it was necessary and the two tiny islands were of no value anyway.[250]

Alverstone was subjected to severe public criticism by the two Canadian commissioners and by many senior Canadian officials, including Sifton and Laurier, for his compromises on the four islands and the mountain line. Aylesworth and Jetté took the extraordinary step of issuing a public statement criticizing the award and justifying their refusal to sign it, in which they said:

> We do not consider the finding of the tribunal as to the islands at the entrance of Portland Channel or as to the mountain line a judicial one, and we have therefore declined to be parties to the award.... We have been compelled to witness the sacrifice of the interests of Canada, powerless to prevent it, though satisfied that the course the majority determined to pursue in respect to the matters above specially referred to, ignored the just rights of Canada.[251]

Hurt and angered by the storm of criticism that descended upon him, in which the Canadian press enthusiastically joined, Alverstone wrote letters to Jetté, Aylesworth, Laurier, and Sifton in which he defended the decisions he had made. The replies he received showed their rejection of his attempts at self-justification, and when Laurier expressed frankly his view that the decision on Portland Channel and the two islands could not be supported on judicial grounds, Alverstone wrote back, "I desire to state most emphatically that the decisions, whether they were right or wrong, were judicial and founded on no other considerations. I alone am responsible for them."[252] He also commented publicly on the matter in a speech at a dinner in London. "If when any kind of arbitration is set up, they don't want a decision based on the law and the evidence," he proclaimed, "they must not put a British judge on the commission."[253] In his memoirs, Alverstone commented in a general way upon the case and still defended his impartiality:

> I came to the conclusion that I could not support the main contention of Canada as regarded the boundary, and acting purely in a judicial capacity, I was under the painful necessity of differing from my two Canadian colleagues.... I only came to this decision with the greatest reluctance, and nothing but a sense of my duty to my position influenced me. I mention this because my conduct in giving this decision was the subject of violent and unjust criticism on the part of some Canadians.[254]

In spite of Alverstone's protest, it seems beyond doubt that the decision on Portland Channel and the islands was a last-minute compromise that he made in the face of severe pressure from the American commissioners and perhaps from his own government. A few years afterwards,

Canadian lawyer John Skriving Ewart (a tireless advocate for Canadian independence), in a viciously worded article which according to one leading commentator has been considered "a classic work of legal reconstruction,"[255] put forward a strong argument that Alverstone's opinion espousing a division of the islands was in reality his earlier opinion advocating the award of all four to Canada, but slightly and illogically revised and generally inconsistent with the new conclusion. Ewart's basic argument ran thus: "With the change of one word in one clause; the omission of two words in another clause; and the interjection of one whole clause, *this second judgment of Lord Alverstone is really his first judgment.*"[256] In spite of the vitriolic and polemical style of the article, Ewart's argument, which he set forth in minute detail, certainly had a ring of authenticity. It was shown to be essentially sound in 1914 when Frederick Coate Wade, one of the Canadian counsels in the case, published (for the first time according to his own claim) Alverstone's earlier opinion, which conformed essentially to the reconstruction Ewart had made.[257] Recalling a comment in Aylesworth's opinion,[258] Ewart also charged that in identifying Portland Channel in his second judgment, Alverstone had at first written, "The channel which runs to the north of … the islands of Sitklan and Kannaghunut and issues into the Pacific between Wales and Sitklan Islands." Subsequently, he was permitted to eliminate the words "Sitklan and Kannaghunut" so that his award conformed with his second decision and with geographical possibility.[259] To reiterate, the opinion Alverstone finally gave was a hasty last-minute compromise, made in the face of severe pressure. There remains the possibility, of course, that it also represented a genuine change of view on his part, and thus it could have been based upon judicial considerations.

This brings up again the provocative question posed by Senator Turner during the oral argument as to whether Captain Vancouver, when naming Portland Channel, considered its opening to be the passage north of Kannaghunut and Sitklan Islands, out of which he sailed, or Tongass Passage between Sitklan and Wales Islands, which he saw but did not sail through when leaving Portland Channel.[260] The question appeared to embarrass both Sir Robert Finlay and Sir Edward Carson, who had obvious difficulty finding a satisfactory answer. Turner suggested that although it was quite clear Vancouver had gone out through the northern channel, there was no conclusive evidence as to which route he had taken on his return trip, and it was on the return trip that the name was given. He had not chosen the northern channel on his outward trip because it was the better one but simply because it was the direction he wanted to take, and in fact Tongass Passage was broader, clearer, and more navigable than the other one. The element of time might also have favoured his being opposite Tongass Passage when the channel was identified. Turner was thus able to cast at least a measure of doubt upon the British contention for the entrance of Portland Channel, and in the final decision, of course, the majority opted for Tongass Passage.

The matter is important because the choice of Tongass Passage gave Aylesworth his specific reason, according to his own statement, for refusing to sign the award. In his dissenting opinion he wrote, "It is a line of boundary which was never so much as suggested in the written Case of the United States, or by Counsel, during the oral argument before us. No intelligible reason for selecting it has been given in my hearing. No Memorandum in support of it has been presented by any member of the Tribunal." In a technical way he may have been right, since the suggestion was put forward by a member of the Tribunal rather than of Counsel, and orally rather than on paper. Otherwise, the evidence is against him. Further on, he continued, "The sole question presented to us for decision on this branch of the case was whether the Portland Channel of the Treaty lay north of the four islands or south of the four, and until today it has been uniformly admitted by everybody that all four of these islands belonged, all together, either to Great Britain or to the United States."

Obviously both parts of this statement are incorrect. This was not the question presented to the tribunal, as a glance at the treaty will show. The precise wording of the question was simply, "What channel is the Portland Channel?" Aylesworth's concept of the possible alternative answers had obviously not been "uniformly admitted by everybody." It is difficult to understand how he could have made the above statements, because he was present and made comments on both occasions when Turner raised the issue.[261] Regrettably, Aylesworth's view of this aspect of the case has been widely and uncritically accepted by many Canadian writers. James White, for example, wrote in his *Boundary Disputes and Treaties* that "there was no evidence presented by either nation, nor can any be found, that would indicate that Portland Channel was ever considered as passing between Sitklan and Wales Islands, as decided by the tribunal."[262] Even Sir Joseph Pope, who was at the tribunal, took no note of Turner's suggestion: "At no stage of the proceedings was such a claim ever put forward by the American counsel. Nobody on either side ever suggested such a thing as a division of these four islands."[263] Ewart in his categorical fashion stated that Alverstone agreed to locate the channel entrance "at a place for which there was not a tittle of evidence, which the Americans had never claimed, and in favor of which American counsel had not advanced a single argument.... Division was never thought of or suggested by anybody until the compromise was agreed to."[264] After remarking elsewhere that "until that moment there had not been a suggestion that the line could possibly run anywhere but north or south of all four islands," Ewart adds the footnote that "Mr. Turner's interpolations at pages 77 to 79 do not affect the correctness of this assertion." Thus, having discovered the evidence that destroyed the point he was trying to establish, he blithely chose to ignore it.[265] Why the Canadians at the tribunal, especially Aylesworth, failed to give due consideration to this evidence in their savage criticism of this part of the award is a question. Their failure to do so undoubtedly had an unfortunate effect, because it gave rise to a popular Canadian folk-tradition about the division of the islands which is not entirely warranted by the facts.

In time, it became clear that the importance both sides then ascribed to Sitklan and Kannaghunut Islands was wholly imaginary. The two islands are practically valueless, strategically and otherwise. In his opinion, Aylesworth described them as being "of the utmost consequence, for they lie directly opposite to, and command the entrance to, the very important harbour of Port Simpson, British Columbia,"[266] which was then planned as the western terminus of the Grand Trunk Pacific Railway. Others took a similar view. As events transpired, however, the railway was diverted to Prince Rupert, the United States did not fortify the islands, and practically nothing happened to disturb their customary tranquility, isolation, and insignificance. As a matter of fact, word had been sent from Washington that the British contention as to Portland Channel could be conceded,[267] and it would thus appear that in demanding the two outer islands the

American commissioners were acting on their own. All told, the furor over Sitklan and Kannaghunut constitutes the silliest aspect of the entire case, and it is debatable who behaved the more discreditably in the affair: the American commissioners for insisting upon having them or the Canadian commissioners for raising such an outcry over not getting them.

The objections of the Canadian commissioners to the majority's decision fixing the mountain line were much more solidly grounded, and it is unfortunate that they did not concentrate more exclusively upon this aspect of the award. The selection of particular mountain peaks was necessarily quite arbitrary, and any number of alternatives could easily have been found. If the majority had stated frankly that in the absence of adequate information their aim was simply to make as equitable and just a placing of the line as was possible in the circumstances, their decision might have been less objectionable. Their categorical assertion that the mountains they chose *were* "the mountains referred to as situated parallel to the coast"[268] was sheer effrontery, and the fact that they could not complete their own line suggests strongly that the inadequacy of their knowledge about the part they could not locate extended in reality to the part they did locate. The line they chose made an almost equal division of the disputed territory between the Canadian and the American claims, but there would appear to be strong grounds for holding that a just division would have given Canada considerably more. Granting that the strip was intended to be unbroken, it is also clear that it was intended to be narrow. The best evidence of this is that when the Russians objected to the British proposal for a boundary following the base of the coast mountains because it might go right down to water's edge, they themselves proposed as a corrective a line following the tops of these same mountains.[269] As Sir Robert Finlay said in his argument, "You start from the margin of the sea, you go up to the summit of the mountains, and there you have got your *lisière*."[270]

Considering all the issues disputed during the case, about the most certain thing is that the convention of 1825 was intended to give Russia an unbroken strip of mainland coast and that, consequently, Question 5 as put to the tribunal required a positive answer. It is here, regrettably, that the performance of the two Canadian commissioners became most questionable. Virtually all other matters before the tribunal were genuine issues that required settlement, including the beginning point of the boundary line, the identity of Portland Channel, the course of the line from the beginning point to the entrance of Portland Channel and from the head of Portland Channel to the 56th parallel, the existence and location of the mountain range in the treaty, and the breadth and exact delimitation of the *lisière*. Unfortunately, most of them did not lend themselves to settlement in strictly judicial terms. But the matter of the unbroken coastal strip was not in reality a legitimate issue, and it would probably have been better if it had not been permitted to assume the status of one. The background of the case shows clearly that President Roosevelt was right in his contention that this was a trumped-up claim on Canada's part and if (in line with his view that it was not justiciable) he had refused to let it go before the tribunal, he would have given it no more than the treatment it deserved. This in no way excuses his behaviour after he had agreed to let it become part of the arbitration, but that is another matter.

The genesis of the "Coast Doctrine" upon which Canada relied is in itself surprising. In any such situation, a General Cameron is likely to make his appearance, bring forth an idea that seems to fit the needs of the moment, and give it the aura of substance and legitimacy. What is truly remarkable, however, is the manner in which this peculiar notion permeated and infected thought, judgment, and policy in the higher echelons of Canadian officialdom and government, from George Mercer Dawson through to Clifford Sifton, until it became official in every sense of the word. Equally remarkable is that, although it was trumpeted loudly in public by leading figures, in private many of them were willing to concede that it lacked validity. There seems to be little doubt that Laurier and Joseph Pope, among others, realized that the Canadian claim to the inlets was invalid in a legal sense and that responsible British officials took the same view.[271] The invalidity of the Canadian contention has also been generally recognized by qualified Canadian authorities who have since written on the subject, although some seem to have made this admission more or less as an afterthought, following the familiar complaints about how badly Canada was treated. It is also worth reiterating, while speaking of aspects of the case which seem incomprehensible today, that the American W. H. Dall had pointed unerringly to some of the major flaws in Cameron's theory in his discussions with Dawson in 1888, and the details of these discussions were well known to the Canadian government. If more attention had been paid to his arguments, a good deal of unnecessary trouble might have been avoided.

H. George Classen, in his study of the Alaska boundary dispute, makes the following penetrating comment on the issue of the coastal strip, and in so doing shows effectively the foolishness of the Canadian claim:

> There is no doubt whatever that the United States was right when it claimed that the treaty had conceded to Russia, and thus to the United States, an unbroken strip of mainland coast from the mouth of Portland Channel to the 141st meridian. When the treaty-makers of 1825 spoke of "sinuosities of the coast" they meant just that; and when they spoke of the "coast" they meant the physical coast and not the abstract, artificial construct of the Canadian claim....
>
> To imply, as the Canadian claim did, that the map-makers had for over sixty years misinterpreted the Treaty of 1825 without being corrected by anyone; that Russia had bargained so tenaciously for the longest possible mainland strip only to leave in the hands of Britain every desirable harbour on that coast and to content itself with the useless promontories; that the Hudson's Bay Company expedition of 1834 was prepared laboriously to work its way up the Stikine in open boats lowered from the *Dryad* when the ship could have sailed freely up any inlet into British territory; that the treaty would make a special point of conceding to Britain the right to navigate the rivers without mentioning the "territorial" inlets – all this deserves only one description: it was absurd.[272]

Yet this is the interpretation of the treaty that the two Canadian commissioners, "sitting judicially, and sworn to so determine and answer the questions submitted,"[273] and with all the ascertainable facts before them, decided should be validated when they refused to join the majority in answering "Yes" to Question 5 – the most important issue before the tribunal. Is it not in order to ask, then, how impartial, in actual fact, were our "impartial jurists of repute"? Or, if they meant to be impartial, how reputable was their judgment?

The same question may be pursued regarding their overall performance in the case and the award. The popular Canadian tradition has been that the American commissioners, under instructions from President Roosevelt, upheld the American claims with utmost rigidity from beginning to end, that Lord Alverstone thought only of a settlement and thus had no firm principles or views to uphold, and that the Canadian commissioners were the only ones to look at the case with firmly judicial and impartial eyes. The truth of the matter is considerably different. Alverstone was undoubtedly the most willing to compromise, but he also had the soundest and most impartial judicial appreciation of the case, and the final award was not greatly at variance with his frequently expressed opinion as to what it ought to be. Roosevelt had told the American commissioners that there should be no yielding on the principle of the *lisière*, but this was a view they should have taken on purely judicial grounds anyway. Otherwise, even though stubbornly pro-American in their attitude, they seem to have taken the posture that the remaining issues were open for adjudication.

Of all the questions in dispute, only two – the identity of the upper part of Portland Channel and the existence of the unbroken *lisière* – could be answered judicially and at the same time decisively. As the oral arguments clearly demonstrated, information was so imprecise and incomplete that clear-cut judicial answers were impossible to the other questions. That being the case, the only approach the tribunal could take to reach a decision, if it was to make one, was to search for the best answers that could be found in the existing circumstances, paying due heed to all relevant facts and evidence. This, in turn, might make inevitable certain elements of concession and compromise. The only alternative was to hand the dispute back to the respective governments for settlement at a political or diplomatic level. The tribunal could hardly have been blamed if it had done this, and it may well be censurable in some respects for not having done so. Looking at the award as given, however, the American commissioners in the end did concede a good deal, either by conviction or by compromise, on the issues concerning the identity of Portland Channel (Question 2), the line to Portland Channel (Question 3), the existence of a mountain line (Question 7), and the ten marine leagues and the width of the coastal strip (Questions 5 and 7). On the other hand, the Canadian commissioners yielded not one jot or title of the Canadian claims, but rather clung inflexibly to the Canadian case throughout, as if they were impervious to argument, evidence, or reason. Their refusal to compromise on judicial principle does them credit, insofar as this really accounts for their stand, but otherwise their stiff-necked, narrow-minded identification of a fair judgment with Canadian interests says little for their impartiality, or judicial perception, or both.

There was plenty of irresponsible and threatening talk on both sides of the 49th parallel during the affair, in both official and unofficial circles. Here again the Canadian tradition of self-righteousness is somewhat at variance with the facts. American intransigence, greed, belligerence, and bluff, insofar as they made themselves evident, were on the whole pretty well matched by Canadian, the main difference being that the United States was in a position to carry out its threats and Canada was not. This feature, real and dangerous at the time, was often discounted or ignored by.angry Canadians. For example, Seymour Eugene Gourley of Colchester proclaimed in the House of Commons in February 1902:

> What we want now is a full discussion in this House so that this ministry will know that the time has come when if they sacrifice one foot of Canada soil we will hang them as high as Haman. If it is necessary to fight the Yankees we will fight them within twenty-four hours, and after six months we will capture their capital and annex their country to Canada.[274]

When news of the award came, the same speaker lectured the House again in the same vein and had a little help:

> We are not a weak colony. Six millions of free people would beat the United States single-handed in the contest….
>
> *Mr. [Samuel] Hughes (Victoria)*: We beat them in 1812, when they were relatively forty times as populous as they are now.
>
> *Mr. Gourley*: Of course. And we could do it again.[275]

Perhaps, in retrospect, we should thank beneficent providence for the much-maligned Lord Alverstone.

Prime Minister Laurier, although expressing disappointment in the outcome of the case, was more concerned about the root problem of Canada's relationship with the Mother Country and its need for a greater measure of independence in foreign affairs:

> I have often regretted also that we have not in our own hands the treaty-making power, which would enable us to dispose of our own affairs…. But we have no such power, our hands are tied to a large extent owing to the fact of our connection – which has its benefits, but which has also its disadvantages….
>
> It is important that we should ask the British parliament for more extensive power, so that if ever we have to deal with matters of a similar nature again we shall deal with them in our own way, in our own fashion, according to the best light that we have.[276]

It was Henri Bourassa, however, who had been connected with the joint high commission in 1898 and had obviously made himself familiar with the historical background of the dispute, who in an able summary reduced the case to its most basic features and set them before the House:

> I think no other conclusion can be drawn by any unbiased mind than that it was clearly the intention of the parties that the strip of land should be uninterrupted, and that Great Britain would not have any right whatever to the inlets that penetrated the coast….
>
> Much has been said about the importance of these two little islands, Kannaghunut and Sitklan. As far as their intrinsic value is concerned, I think every body will agree that they are of no value whatever. To speak of their strategic value is to my mind going a little beyond the mark.[277]

Regarding the substance of the entire award, Canada might fairly have received somewhat more – perhaps the two tiny islands, certainly a larger share of the disputed *lisière*, possibly (because of what has been called a slip on Lord Alverstone's part) a little more territory in the Chilkat River region. Allegedly, in drawing the boundary here, Alverstone overlooked the *modus vivendi* line of 1899, and the American commissioners conveniently neglected to draw his attention to it.[278] The *modus vivendi* line was clearly understood to be provisional only, however, and since the commissioners were attempting to place the line along mountain tips, it is unlikely that Alverstone's oversight (if it was that) would have made any difference. In any case, all these additions would not have given Canada what she really wanted: an outlet or outlets to salt water. Canada's counsel at the tribunal, especially Sir Robert Finlay and Sir Edward Carson, did a magnificent job of presenting her case for the inlets, untenable as it was, in the most favourable light. It was a hopeless task. The only way she might have gained the desired access to tidal water would have been through a diplomatic arrangement of the sort that failed to materialize in 1899. It might have been much better if she had sought, through negotiation, a reasonable modification of an existing but disadvantageous situation, instead of pinning her hopes stubbornly on a spurious legal case.

As a final comment, it is obvious now, and should have been obvious then, that Canada's real grievance could not justly be laid at the door of the United States for what had happened since 1867, but rather concerned what had happened long before. In other words, the real fly in the ointment was the treaty of 1825. Britain, interested mainly in securing Russia's withdrawal from her extravagant pretensions in North Pacific waters, made the unnecessary concession on the mainland that led to all the trouble. Although the two were not logically related and should not have been associated, it is clear that Britain, anxious to gain the one, was not greatly disturbed about conceding the other, and thus let Russia make off with a large strip on the mainland to which she had no more claim than Britain had. If justice had been done, Russia would have received no compensation whatever for abandoning her extreme maritime claims, and the Alaskan coast would have been a separate issue. Here the pretensions were about equal: Britain had no establishments within about two hundred miles on the mainland; Russia had only one real post on the adjacent islands; and neither had established any permanent presence whatever in what became the disputed *lisière*. So far as the coast was concerned, both were starting practically from nothing. The British concession was particularly deplorable because, in spite of Russian arguments to the contrary, British ownership of the mainland coast would not in itself become ruinous to Russia's position on the islands, even if Russia had been clearly entitled to them. On the other hand, Russia's deliberate purpose in seeking a coastal strip was to bar forever British access to salt water in the region, frustrating British commerce and enterprise. Britain's abandonment of the issue becomes even more incomprehensible given that it was in a favourable strategic position to make larger demands in the region – and to back them up with naval force if the need arose. Ironically, if the HBC had had the initiative and foresight to establish even a single post on the upper Stikine River between 1821 and 1825, the entire outcome might have been changed. No doubt the dispatch of a British ship or two, from the many left idle after the end of the Napoleonic Wars, would have had an even more marked effect. Even without any such devious or threatening devices (which would not, of course, have been in any way exceptional in the diplomacy of the time), a British diplomatic stance as firm and uncompromising as that of the Russians would in all probability have brought about a result more favourable to Britain – and ultimately to Canada. Here, in truth, was the real nucleus of all the trouble over the Alaska boundary.[279]

6

Foreign Explorers in the Canadian North, 1877–1917

The history of exploration in the Canadian Arctic in the half-century after Confederation is not simply a Canadian story. Various foreign explorers were active in the region, searching for clues to the fate of the Franklin expedition, conducting scientific research, discovering unknown coasts and claiming islands for their home country, and even transiting the Northwest Passage for the first time. Some of these explorers are well known, others less so. Cumulatively, their activities raised significant awareness about the Canadian North and gave Canadian authorities some reason to fret over the situation in the territories for which they had recently assumed responsibility.

The Howgate-Tyson Expedition (1877–78)

An expedition which has remained rather obscure was that organized by Captain Henry W. Howgate of the US Army and led by the whaler George Tyson in 1877–78.[1] Howgate had conceived the idea of establishing a temporary Inuit colony in Lady Franklin Bay to aid a project for science and exploration; the expedition of 1877 was privately planned as a preliminary step he hoped would subsequently receive the official blessing and support of the American government.[2] The choice of Tyson, well known for his role in the recovery of *HMS Resolute* and his drift through Baffin Bay on the return trip from Hall's third expedition, was probably an unfortunate one, for, as his narrative reveals, he had little liking for his Inuit "colonists" and little desire to associate with them.[3] He took the fifty-six-ton schooner *Florence* and a small crew of twelve to Cumberland Sound in the summer of 1877 and wintered there, maintaining contact with the wintering whalers and less enthusiastically with the local Inuit. Unfortunately for the project, Congress did not grant the desired assistance,[4] even though various government departments had helped to outfit the preliminary expedition,[5] and thus the plan could not be carried through. Having transported some Inuit, dogs, and equipment to a Greenland port for the anticipated rendezvous with the main expedition in the summer of 1878, Tyson waited for its arrival in vain. When it became clear that it was not going to show up, he took his "colonists" back to Cumberland Sound, dumped them ashore, and gladly abandoned the project. Interestingly enough, all this happened while British officials were fretting

THE AMERICAN FRANKLIN SEARCH EXPEDITION: CROSSING SIMPSON'S STRAIT IN KAYAKS.
FROM A SKETCH BY MR. H. W. KLUTSCHAK.

FIGURE 6-1: H.W. KLUTSCHAK, "THE AMERICAN FRANKLIN SEARCH EXPEDITION: CROSSING SIMPSON'S STRAIT IN KAYAKS," WOOD ENGRAVING IN *THE ILLUSTRATED LONDON NEWS*, 8 JANUARY 1881. *OSHER MAP LIBRARY AND SMITH CENTER FOR CARTOGRAPHIC EDUCATION AT THE UNIVERSITY OF SOUTHERN MAINE, OML-1881-22. IMAGE: 15.013.*

over how they could best arrange a transfer of their rights in the Arctic islands to Canada. If the American "colony" had materialized, the problem would doubtless have become more complicated.

Frederick Schwatka (1878–80)

Of the numerous expeditions which searched for relics of the Franklin disaster, the last that went out deliberately for this purpose was the one commanded by Lieutenant Frederick Schwatka of the 3rd US Cavalry in 1878–80.[6] The motivation for the expedition was an Inuit report brought back by the whaler Captain T. F. Barry after a trip to Repulse Bay in 1871–73, which said that they had been visited years before by a white man in uniform who had left many papers in a cairn. Schwatka obtained leave of absence to conduct the expedition, which was sponsored mainly by the New York shipping merchants Morrison and Brown, and was taken to Depot Island north of Chesterfield Inlet in the schooner *Eothen* by Captain Barry in the summer of 1878. From this base, he set out on 1 April 1879, with three white men and thirteen Inuit, the party including the expedition's chronicler William Henry Gilder, "Eskimo Joe" (who had been the faithful companion of Charles Francis Hall), and Joe's wife "Neepshark." The entire summer was spent searching King William Island and the nearby mainland coast, and it was not until 4 March 1880 that they arrived again at Depot Island, having sustained themselves almost entirely by "living off the country" during their record-breaking sledge journey of 3,251 statute miles in over eleven months, and having made the return trip in temperatures as low as –71°F (–57°C).[7] Their search was more detailed and thorough than any of the preceding ones. Unfortunately, although they found more relics, they discovered no written records that might have thrown further light upon the fate of the lost expedition. They built some cairns and indulged in a display of the American flag on 4 July when it "waved from the highest point of King William Land,"[8] but it would appear to be an exaggeration to suggest that these gestures were intended to claim territory.[9] In Gilder's view, the most important result of the expedition was that they had ascertained (to their own satisfaction at least) that the Franklin records had been lost in Starvation Cove west of Richardson Point.[10]

Adolphus W. Greely (1881–84)

In 1875, a far-reaching proposal for a change of emphasis in polar exploration was put forward by Austrian Navy Lieutenant Karl Weyprecht, who, with his fellow country man Lieutenant Julius Payer, had been to Novaya Zemlya in 1871 and had recently returned from their joint discovery of Franz Josef Land in 1872–74.[11] Addressing a German scientific conference at Graz, Weyprecht suggested that henceforth the primary objective of polar exploration should be scientific investigation and that geographical discovery, which often amounted only to sighting new coastlines and reaching high latitudes, should be a matter of secondary concern, important mainly in enlarging the scope of scientific inquiry. If maximum results were to be obtained, he argued, the scientific program should be comprehensive, co-operative, and international in scope.[12] The International Meteorological Congress approved this broad concept at its meeting in Rome in 1879, and later conferences at Hamburg in 1879 and Berne in 1880 gave it substance and form. The outcome was the First International Polar Year of 1882–83, in which eleven nations established fifteen observatory stations in the polar regions: two in the Antarctic and the rest in the Arctic. This pioneering project gathered a great deal of valuable information and served as a model for the Second International Polar Year in 1932–33 and the International Geophysical Year in 1957–58.

Five of the stations were in North America, including one in Alaska, one in Greenland, and three in the Canadian Arctic. The United States maintained a small party under Lieutenant Patrick Henry Ray of the Eighth Infantry at Point Barrow from September 1881 to August 1883,[13] and Professor Adam F. W. Paulsen took charge of a Danish Station at Godthaab from August 1882 to August 1883. A small British-Canadian Station at Fort Rae on Great Slave Lake functioned under Captain Henry Philip Dawson from August 1882 to September 1883, while Germany maintained a station under Dr. Wilhelm Giese at Kingua Fiord in

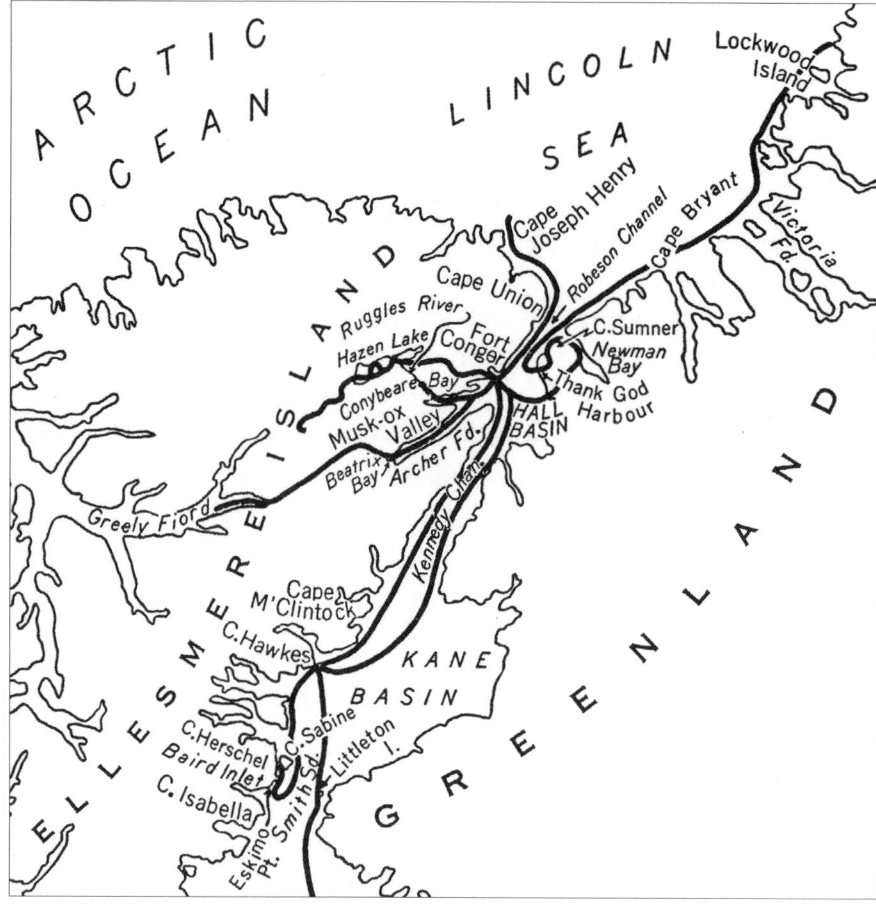

Figure 6-2: The Greely expeditions, 1881–84. Andrew Taylor, *Geographical Discovery and Exploration in the Queen Elizabeth Islands* (Ottawa: Department of Mines and Technical Surveys, 1964), 84. *By permission of Natural Resources Canada.*

Cumberland Sound, Baffin Island, during approximately the same period. In addition to carrying out observations, Giese with Leopold Ambronn explored the interior of Cumberland Sound, and helped by the Moravian missionaries, Dr. Robert Koch made supplementary observations in Labrador.[14] The fifth North American station, which because of its achievements and its ultimate tragedy probably made a deeper and more lasting impression than the other fourteen stations put together, was also an American undertaking. This was the one in Lady Franklin Bay, under the command of US Cavalry Lieutenant Adolphus W. Greely.[15]

The expedition actually originated as the brainchild of the Arctic enthusiast Captain Howgate,[16] who strongly supported some of Weyprecht's views but had failed to secure government support for his colonization and exploration scheme in 1877 and 1878.[17] Howgate persisted but was again unable to persuade Congress to pass the necessary bill in 1879.[18] In May 1880, however, he saw the US government authorize the establishment of a temporary observation station in Lady Franklin Bay as an American contribution to the International Polar Year.[19] To his embarrassment, the navy condemned his chartered ship *Gulnare* as unseaworthy. Although he sent her out under his own authority, she returned after getting no farther than Greenland. In March 1881, Congress voted $25,000 for an expedition which would be official in every respect. Greely, who had already been chosen in 1880 but had declined to go when the *Gulnare* was condemned, now eagerly accepted the command.[20]

The personnel of the expedition were taken to Lady Franklin Bay during the summer of 1881 in the steamer *Proteus*, which departed as soon as their habitation, Fort Conger, was under construction. The party of twenty-five included Greely, two second lieutenants, the surgeon Dr. Octave Pavy (who had been left by the *Gulnare* in Greenland), two Greenland Inuit, and nineteen army non-commissioned officers and privates. The plan anticipated that they should be visited by a relief ship in 1882 and taken out in 1883, but incredible bad luck and bungling on the part of others left them in complete isolation for almost three years. During the first two seasons they accomplished a great deal, not only in carrying out to the letter the comprehensive plan of scientific observations but also in exploration. In the spring of 1882, Dr. Pavy was stopped four miles offshore from Ellesmere Island, at 82° 56' N, and thus failed in his attempt to beat Markham's record north of Cape Joseph Henry. On the other hand, Second Lieutenant James B. Lockwood, Sergeant David L. Brainard, and "Eskimo Fred" (Frederick Thorlip Christiansen) succeeded magnificently in their trip along the north Greenland coast, reaching Lockwood Island at 83° 24' N 40° 46' W, which was approximately 150 miles beyond Beaumont's farthest east and four miles beyond Markham's farthest north. In the spring of 1883, the same trio attempted to beat their own record along the same coast, but they were stopped by open water off the Black Horn Cliffs. In 1882, Greely himself made two trips to Lake Hazen; a year later, Lockwood, again with Brainard and "Eskimo Fred," penetrated still further in the same direction to Greely Fiord, leading to the opposite side of the island.[21] Although the sledging parties raised ceremonial flags to mark their discoveries and assigned generally American names to them,[22] they do not appear to have made any formal claims to land; Greely's orders show clearly that the authorities in Washington were concerned with scientific research and discovery rather than the acquisition of polar territory.[23]

Notwithstanding the expedition's great success in both these fields, it was troubled throughout by dissension and ended in appalling tragedy. A private named Clay was sent back on the *Proteus* in 1881 on grounds of incompatibility, and second-in-command Lieutenant Frederick F. Kislingbury, who "resigned," would have gone too but for the fact that he missed the ship. Dr. Pavy, who was in continual disagreement with Greely, also wanted to quit but was held in the service pending court martial; Sergeant David Linn was reduced to private; and there were other frictions, culminating in the shooting, at Greely's order, of Private Charles B. Henry, who persistently refused to stop stealing food during the last terrible days of starvation. This state of extremity was brought about by their retreat from Fort Conger to Smith Sound in August 1883, in conformity with the expedition's official instructions, and by the failure of relief expeditions to keep the appointed rendezvous. The *Neptune* had turned back in 1882, and the *Proteus* had been caught in the ice and sank in 1883, leaving them without shelter upon their arrival in Smith Sound and with food sufficient for only about forty-five days. During the ensuing dreadful winter of cold and starvation, there was miraculously only one death before April, but afterwards they succumbed one by one. When Commander Winfield S. Schley succeeded in reaching them with two relief ships on 22 June 1884, only Greely and six others remained alive in their last camp west of Cape Sabine.[24]

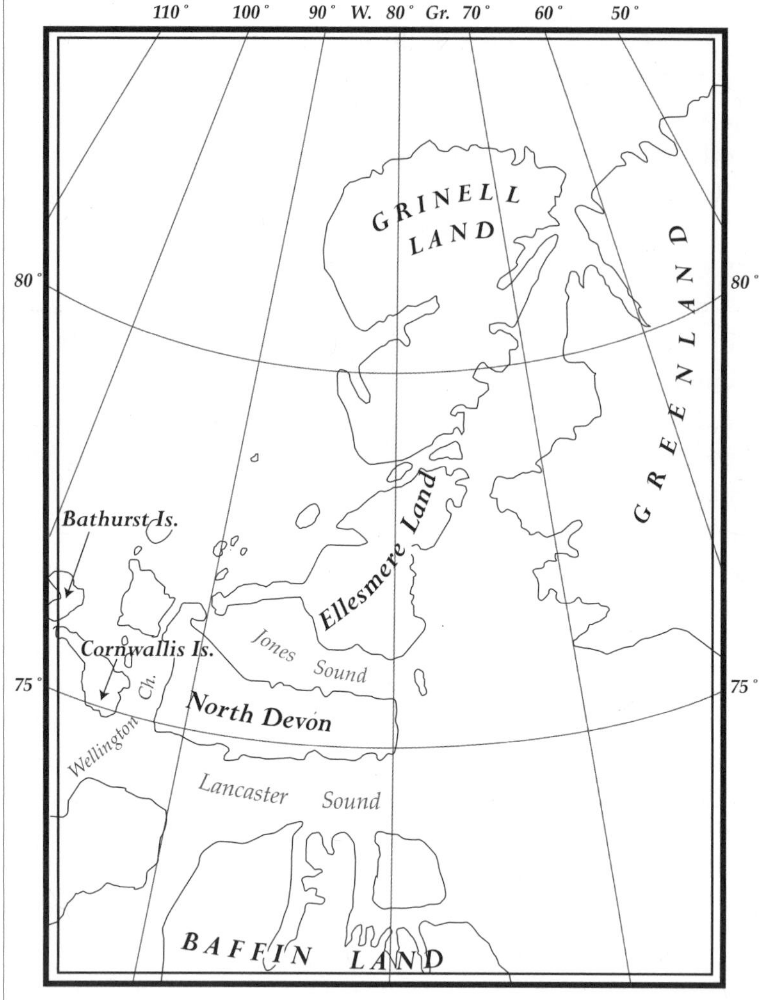

FIGURE 6-3: FRANZ BOAS, SPECULATIVE MAP OF ELLESMERE ISLAND (ENVISIONED AS TWO ISLANDS, ELLESMERE LAND AND GRINNELL LAND). *SCIENCE* 5, NO. 108 (27 FEBRUARY 1885), 171. *JENNIFER ARTHUR-LACKENBAUER.*

Franz Boas (1883–84)

When the *Germania* went to remove the Giese party from Kingua Fiord in 1883, it had aboard the young German Dr. Franz Boas, who, supported by the German Polar Commission, spent the following year in private anthropological and ethnographical research among the Inuit of Cumberland Sound and vicinity.[25]

Otto Sverdrup (1898–1902)

Norwegian Otto Sverdrup was evidently offered the command of an expedition at the suggestion of Fridtjof Nansen, under whom he had served during the first crossing of Greenland in 1888 and later as captain of the *Fram* during her remarkable drift across the Arctic Ocean in 1893–96.[26] As in the drift, the chief sponsors of the 1898 expedition were the consul Axel Heiberg and the Ringnes Brothers brewing firm, while the Norwegian government loaned the *Fram* and donated 20,000 kroner. It was planned that the expedition should proceed to Smith Sound, winter as far north as possible, and then, with no thought of reaching the North Pole, explore along the northern coast of Greenland and if possible down the eastern side. The sponsors wisely left Sverdrup free to change the plan to meet unforeseen circumstances, however, and unable to get through Kane Basin in either 1898 or 1899, he diverted the expedition to Jones Sound, which provided the base for his activities during the final three years.[27] The winter of 1898–99 was spent in Rice Strait, not far from the scene of Greely's disaster on Pim Island. In the spring, two sledging trips were made across King Oscar Land (as he called that part of Ellesmere Island) to Bay Fiord: one under Sverdrup himself and the other under the cartographer Gunnar Isachsen. During the winter, contact was made with Peary's expedition, which was wintering off Cape Hawks some distance north and preparing for an assault upon the North Pole. Peary's evident disapproval of having any possible rival in the area has been given as an additional reason for Sverdrup's move to Jones Sound.[28]

The winter headquarters for 1899–1900 was in Harbour Fiord and for 1900–1901 was in Goose Fiord, both on the south coast of Ellesmere Island. From these bases, spectacularly successful sledging journeys were made during three successive seasons. In 1900, Sverdrup and Ivar Fosheim went up the west coast of Axel Heiberg Island to 80° 55' N, Gunerius (Gunnar) Isachsen and Knut Hassel made a rather hasty trip to the Ringnes Islands, and the geologist Per Schei with Peder Hendriksen undertook a more leisurely scientific examination of North Kent, Buckingham, and Graham Islands. In 1901, Sverdrup and Schei went up Eureka Sound to Butter Porridge Point, locating Greely Fiord and thus linking up with the discoveries of the Greely expedition, while Isachsen and Hassel returned to the Ringnes Islands and went right around them. In 1902, Sverdrup and Schei again sledged up Eureka Sound, this time continuing up the west coast of Ellesmere to Land's End at 81° 40' N, where they were only sixty miles from Pelham Aldrich's farthest in 1876; Isachsen and the zoologist Edvard Bay surveyed part of the north coast of Devon Island; and second-in-command Victor Baumann took Fosheim and the mate Oluf Raanes on a trip to Franklin's old wintering place at Beechey Island. Collectively, Sverdrup's sledging parties had traced almost the entire unknown western coast of Ellesmere Island, discovered and explored Axel Heiberg and the two Ringnes Islands, as well as the hitherto untravelled north coasts of Cornwall, Graham, and Devon Islands, and sighted King Christian Island. The scientific work of the expedition, published between 1904 and 1919, fills four large volumes[29] and seems incredibly comprehensive considering the small size of the crew: sixteen altogether, two of whom died.

Although Sverdrup indulged in the customary building of cairns, depositing of records, displaying of flags, and naming of new lands, it does not appear that he accompanied these actions by any formal ceremonies of taking possession on the ground.[30] Nevertheless, his casual and good-humoured narrative indicates that he felt he was operating in a region unclaimed as well as unknown,[31] and his final statement that "an approximate area of one hundred thousand square miles had been explored, and, in the name of the Norwegian king, taken possession of"[32] shows clearly his intention that the lands he had discovered should be added to the Norwegian kingdom. His claim constituted a principal source of

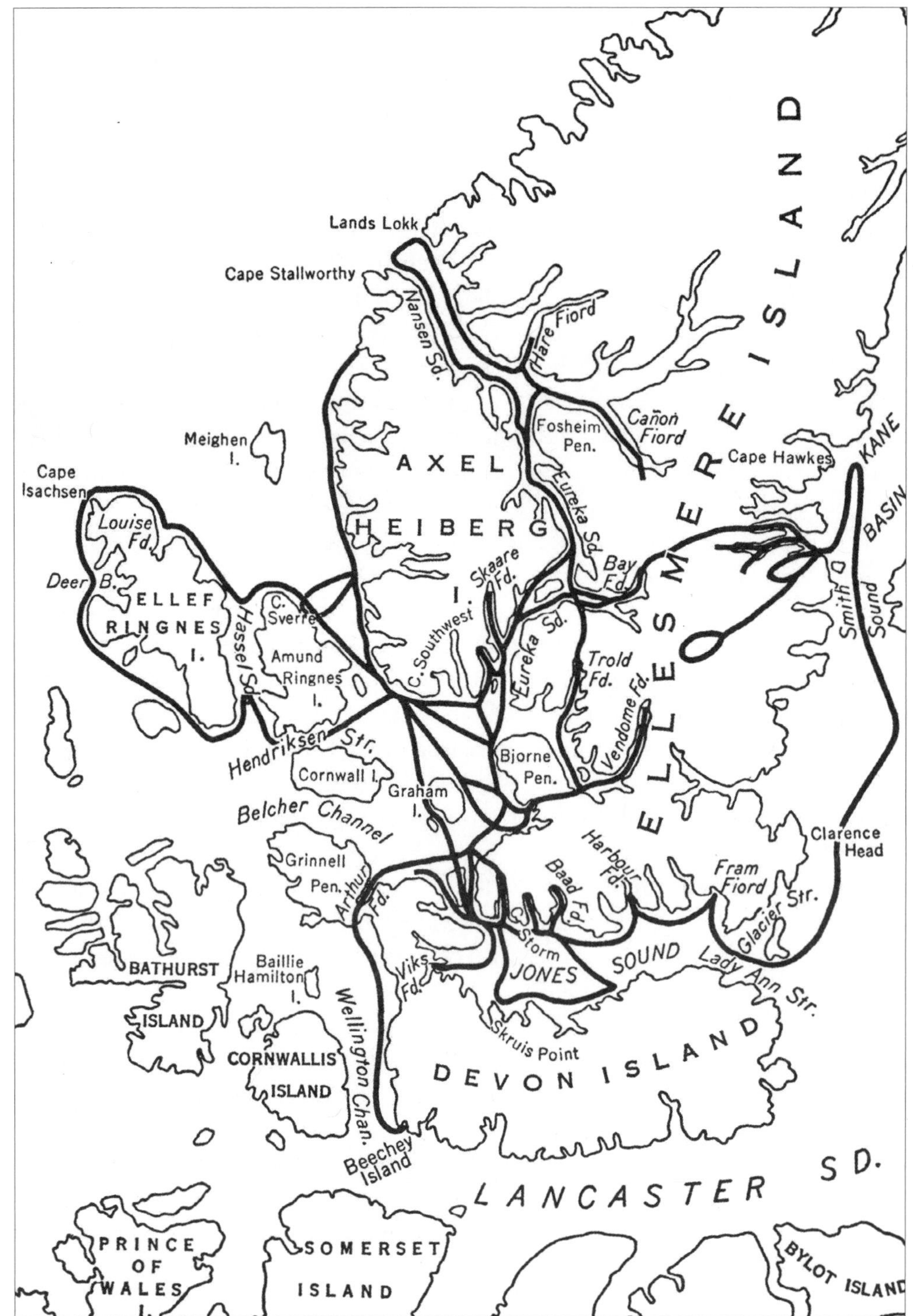

FIGURE 6-4: THE SVERDRUP EXPEDITIONS, 1898–1902. ANDREW TAYLOR, GEOGRAPHICAL DISCOVERY AND EXPLORATION IN THE QUEEN ELIZABETH ISLANDS (OTTAWA: DEPARTMENT OF MINES AND TECHNICAL SURVEYS, 1964), 89. *BY PERMISSION OF NATURAL RESOURCES CANADA.*

worry to Canada in her attempts to gain full sovereignty over the archipelago and remained unresolved until disavowed by the Norwegian government in 1930 (see chapter 12).

Roald Amundsen (1903–6)

Sverdrup's countryman Roald Amundsen is chiefly remembered for his successful dash to the South Pole in 1911, but he had won an earlier distinction in 1903–6 by being the first to take a ship completely through the Northwest Passage. In so doing he accomplished one of the two major aims of the expedition. The other, to pinpoint the North Magnetic Pole, was achieved less authoritatively.[33]

The expedition was financed privately, for the most part, and evidently with considerable difficulty, as is shown by Amundsen's admission that it left Christiania secretly on the night of 16 June 1903 to avoid an impatient creditor who wanted his money without delay.[34] The ship was the tiny 47-ton fishing smack *Gjoa*, with a 13-horsepower motor, and the crew numbered only seven including Amundsen himself. Stopping en route at Godhavn and Beechey Island, Amundsen then followed the route that Franklin had attempted, except that he took the passage east rather than west of King William Island. The winters of 1903–4 and 1904–5 were spent comfortably in the secure little harbour of Gjoa Haven, on the south coast of King William Island, where they found much more game than Franklin's unfortunate crew evidently had done. In the autumn of 1904, Inuit brought them word of "Kabloona" in two ships to the southeast, with whom they attempted to communicate; the following spring an Inuk brought letters from Major J. D. Moodie of the Royal Northwest Mounted Police (as it was renamed in 1904) and Captain J.-E. Bernier, who were wintering in their ship *Arctic* at Cape Fullerton, and also from Captain George Comer of the American whaler *Era*.[35] Since the Canadian expedition was a government patrol, it may be surmised that Moodie and Bernier informed the Norwegians that they were in Canadian waters, but Amundsen's narrative speaks only of his gratitude for the Canadians' offer of assistance and gift of sledge dogs.

Figure 6-5: Roald Amundsen. *Library and Archives Canada / C-000738.*

In the spring of 1904, Amundsen and Per Ristvedt sledged almost to the Tasmania Islands off the Boothia coast in their attempt to locate the North Magnetic Pole. A year later, second-in-command Godfred Hansen and

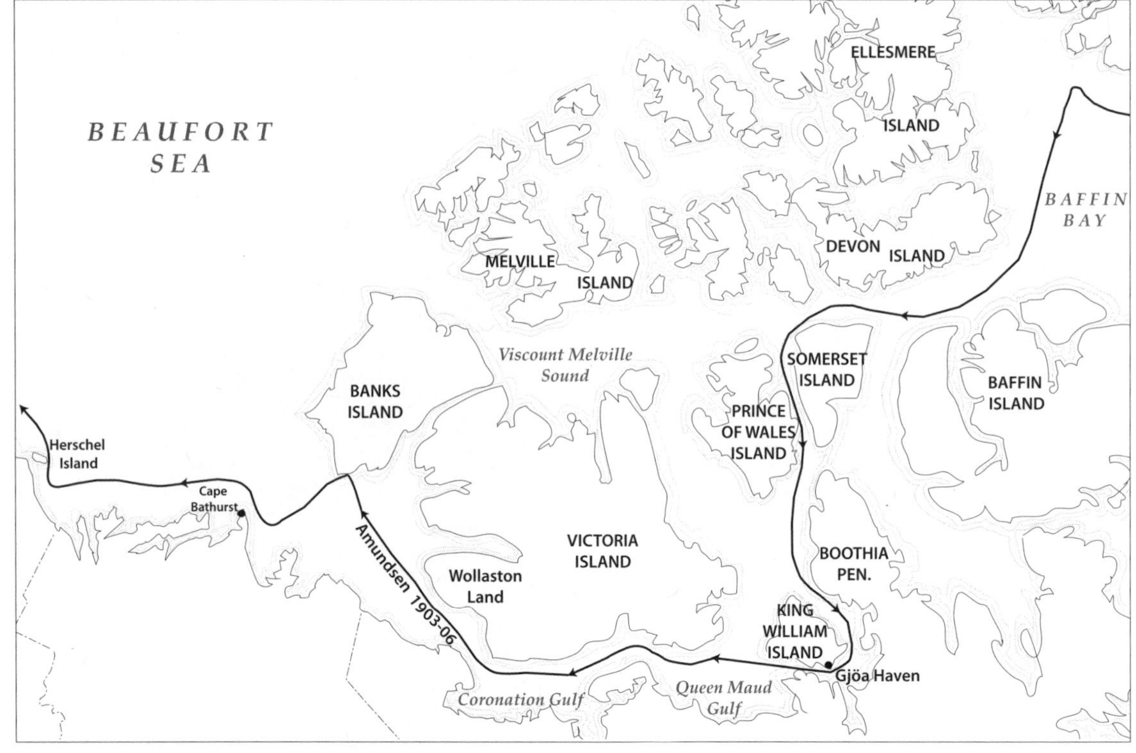

FIGURE 6-6: AMUNDSEN EXPEDITION, 1903–6. *JENNIFER ARTHUR-LACKENBAUER.*

Ristvedt explored part of the hitherto unknown eastern coast of Victoria Island, from Richard Collingson's farthest near Gateshead Island to Cape Nansen at 72° 2' N 104° 45' W.[36] During their third winter, this time near Herschel Island, Amundsen travelled to Fort Yukon and Eagle City to communicate by telegraph with the outside world. Although the expedition lost their magnetic observer Gustav Juel Wiik that March, they completed the passage with their arrival at Nome, Alaska, on 31 August 1903.

Robert E. Peary (1886–1909)

As the name of Amundsen is always associated with the conquest of the Northwest Passage and the South Pole, Robert E. Peary's is inextricably linked to the attainment of the North Pole. He also did noteworthy work in Greenland, to which the first five of his eight Arctic expeditions were directed, and in the Canadian archipelago. His first expedition, in 1886, involved an attempt to penetrate the interior of Greenland as far as possible from Disko Bay, but he was forced to turn back after about 120 miles. In each of his next two expeditions, in

FIGURE 6-7: PHOTOGRAVURE OF ROBERT E. PEARY IN FURS, 1909. *PEARY-MACMILLAN ARCTIC MUSEUM, BOWDOIN COLLEGE.*

1891–92 and 1893–95, he made crossings of north Greenland from Inglefield Bay to Independence Fiord. Two summer cruises, an unsuccessful one in 1896 and a successful one a year later, were devoted to bringing back the largest of the three Cape York meteorites, the two others having been recovered in 1895.[37]

Peary broached a new plan of Arctic exploration that would concentrate upon reaching the North Pole, which he presented at the annual meeting of the American Geographical Society in January 1897. He received vital help from the English newspaperman Alfred Harmsworth, who gave him the stern yacht *Windward*, and from the Peary Arctic Club, organized in the spring of 1898 specifically to promote his project.[38] Setting out in July 1898, Peary spent four years in the north, with winter quarters successively at Cape D'Urville on the east coast of Ellesmere Island, at Etah in Greenland, at Greely's Fort Conger, and in Payer Harbour near Cape Sabine. His attempts to reach his goal fell far short in both 1901 and 1902; nevertheless his achievements were significant.

Most notable were several exploratory trips into the interior of Ellesmere Island: a lengthy journey in 1900 along the north Greenland coast that took him to approximately 83° N 23° W, well beyond Lockwood's farthest in 1882, and (from his own viewpoint most important) an attempt upon the Pole in 1902 that reached almost 84° 18' N above Ellesmere Island, well beyond Markham's farthest in 1876. Peary returned minus his toes, which froze during a winter trip to Fort Conger in 1899, but determined to conquer the remaining 400 miles.

His next attempt was in 1905–6 in the specially constructed *Roosevelt*, which was built largely with funds provided by members of the Peary Arctic Club and was skippered by Newfoundlander Bob Bartlett of the famous Bartlett seafaring family.[39] They succeeded in ramming the *Roosevelt* through the ice as far as Cape Sheridan, where she wintered about two miles beyond the *Alert*'s position, and the great attempt began on 19 February 1906. After leaving the last of his supporting parties behind, Peary with seven Inuit pushed on to a new record of 87° 6' N (32' beyond the Italian Umberto Cagni's farthest in 1900, reached from Franz Josef Land) before shortage of food compelled him to turn back.[40] Drifting east on the return trip, Peary struck Cape Neumeyer at approximately 48° W on the Greenland coast, and then he made his way back to the ship with great difficulty. After only two weeks' rest, he made a trip along the Ellesmere coast which filled in the remaining gap between the farthest points of Aldrich in 1876 and Sverdrup in 1902, but the land he thought he sighted to the northwest – "Crocker Land" – was later found to be non-existent.[41] In one season, however, he had beaten Markham's farthest north, Beaumont's farthest east, and Aldrich's farthest west, thus eclipsing the collective achievements of the three principal sledging parties of the Nares expedition – a striking demonstration of both superior capacity and superior technique, at least in covering distance. Peary's growing obsession with his designs is evident in his hastily written and excited narrative, and his exultant exclamations of "Mine! Mine!" upon reaching new parts of Ellesmere Island seem to indicate a passion for personal glory more than a desire to add new territories to the United States.[42] It is true that he speaks occasionally of planting the Stars and Stripes in new regions,[43] but he apparently made no formal claims in the territories he was first to tread upon.

Peary's final assault upon the Pole was made in 1908–9. Again the expedition was financed largely by members of the Peary Arctic Club, and again he had the *Roosevelt*, the serious damages suffered in 1906 having been repaired.[44] The party included veterans, such as African-American jack-of-all-trades Matt Henson, who accompanied Peary on all his Arctic expeditions except the first, and skipper Bob Bartlett. There were also the two young tenderfeet George Borup and Donald MacMillan, the latter of whom was just beginning his long career of Arctic exploration. Wintering again at Cape Sheridan, Peary made preparations for the earliest possible start from Cape Columbia at the northernmost tip of Ellesmere Island. By now his so-called "Peary system" of rapid and extended Arctic travel had been worked out to a high degree of efficiency. It depended essentially upon the attainment by ship of the farthest possible land base; the maximum use of Inuit, dogs, and sledges; and the help of supporting parties to break trail, build igloos, and deposit supplies.[45] Preceded by six supporting parties, he left Cape Columbia on 1 March 1909 and sent back the six one by one until the last, under Bartlett, left him on 1 April at 87° 46' 49" N. Accompanied only by his chosen group of Henson[46] and four Inuit, Peary pressed on

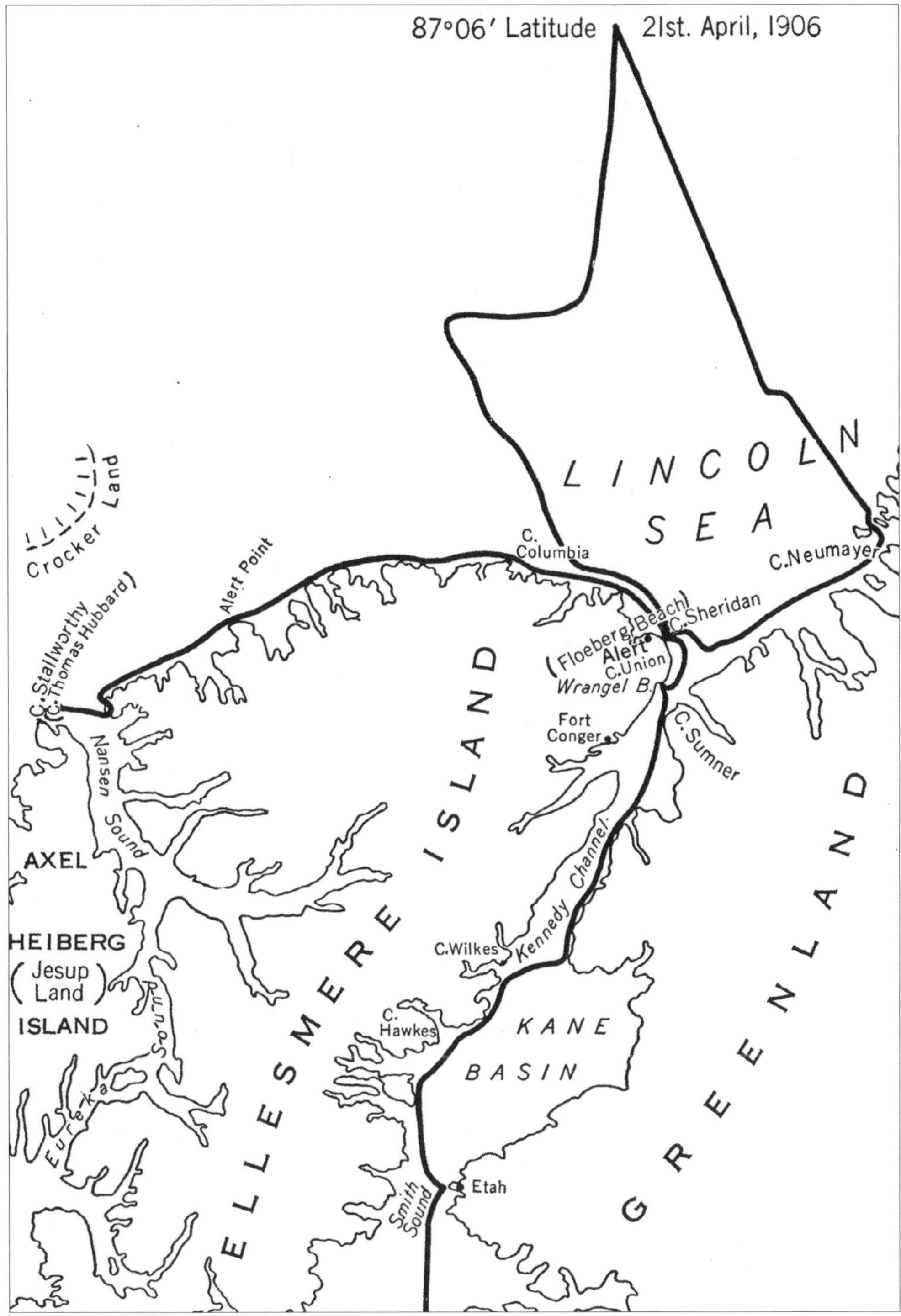

Figure 6-8: Peary expeditions, 1898–1909. Andrew Taylor, Geographical Discovery and Exploration in the Queen Elizabeth Islands (Ottawa: Department of Mines and Technical Surveys, 1964), 68, 73, 78. *By permission of Natural Resources Canada.*

and, according to his calculations, had reached the approximate location of the North Pole by 6 April. The return trip was accomplished without incident and with almost unbelievable speed – Cape Columbia being reached on 23 April and the *Roosevelt* about four days later. The triumph was marred by the death of Professor Ross Marvin while leading his support party back to the ship. (Marvin's two Inuit companions initially stated that he drowned, although in 1926 one of them confessed that he had shot Marvin to prevent him from abandoning the other.)[47]

Peary claimed the entire region, including the North Pole itself, for the United States: a claim that aroused a good deal of legal discussion afterwards. He raised several flags at the Pole, including the American national ensign, and left the following message in a glass bottle:

> 90 N. Lat., North Pole,
> April 6, 1909.
>
> I have to-day hoisted the national ensign of the United States of America at this place, which my observations indicate to be the North Polar Axis of the earth, and have formally taken possession of the entire region, and adjacent, for and in the name of the President of the United States of America.
>
> I leave this record and United States flag in possession.
>
> Robert E. Peary,
> United States Navy.[48]

Dr. Frederick A. Cook (1907–9)

The mysterious and highly controversial figure of Dr. Frederick A. Cook cannot be ignored, even though most authorities have refused to accept his own record of his achievements. Cook had served as surgeon on Peary's Greenland expedition of 1891–92 and on Adrien de Gerlache's Belgian Antarctic expedition of 1897–99, and he had apparently acquitted himself well. In the summer of 1907, he arrived in Greenland on an expedition of his own, and after spending part of the winter near Etah, he disappeared into the interior of Ellesmere Island in February 1908, accompanied by one white man and nine Inuit. All returned or were sent back except two Inuit, and he reappeared with this remnant in the spring of 1909, claiming to have reached the North Pole from the northern extremity of Axel Heiberg on 12 April 1908.[49] There is no doubt that he spent two seasons in the field with limited supplies, a creditable feat in itself, and he may even have gone some distance north of Axel Heiberg, but the contrary testimony of his Inuit and other unsatisfactory evidence overcame the early enthusiastic acceptance of his North Pole claim and most reputable authorities soon discounted it. The principal result was to cast additional doubt upon Peary's achievement, which could not be conclusively verified either, and a bitter dispute between the two explorers and their rival groups of supporters went on for years.

In his narrative, Cook reveals his impression that he was travelling in a No Man's Land, saying that "no nation assumes the responsibility of claiming or protecting" Ellesmere Island,[50] although later he acknowledges his awareness that "Captain Bernier was bound for the American [Ellesmere Island] coast, to

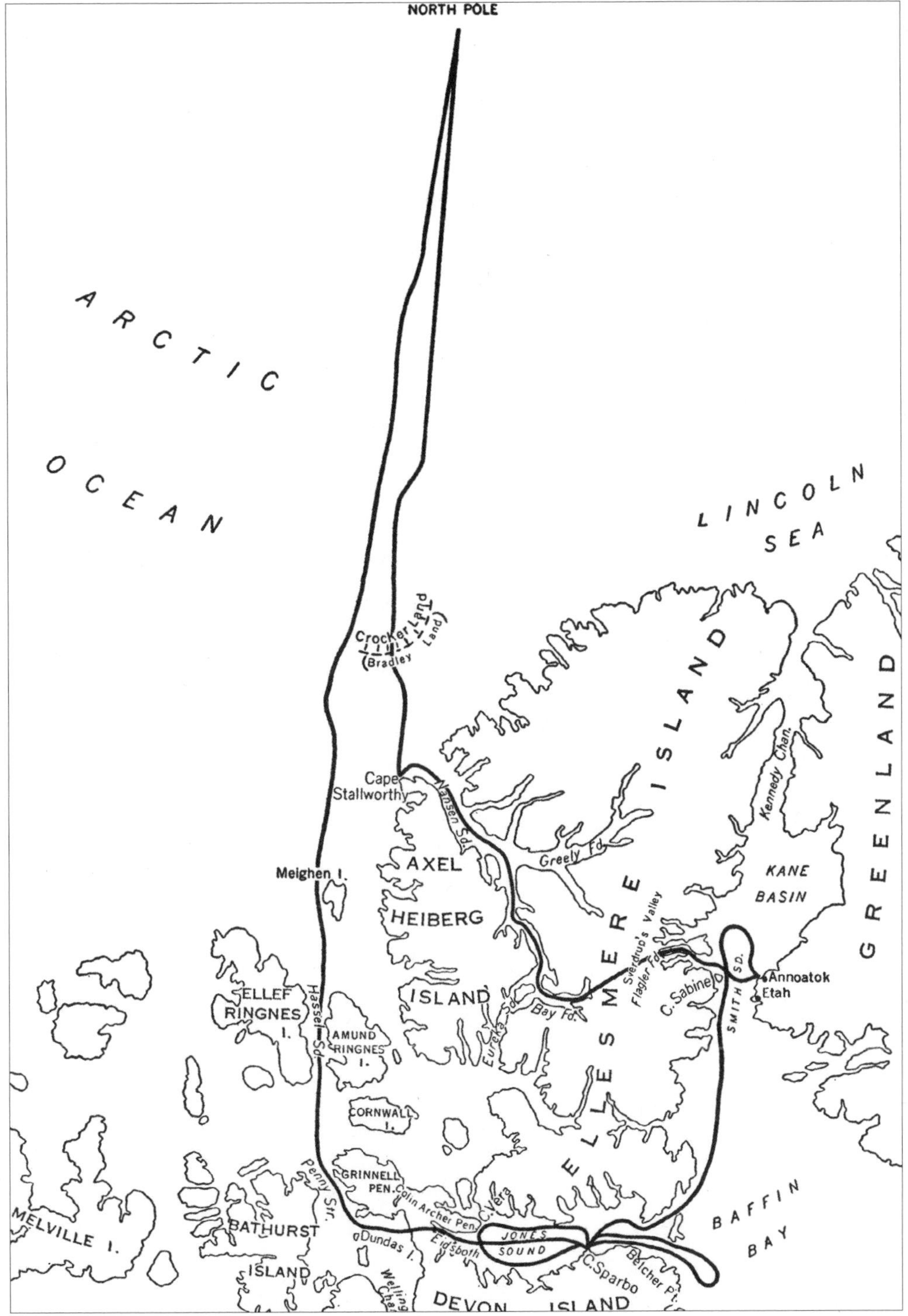

FIGURE 6-9: COOK EXPEDITION, 1907–9. ANDREW TAYLOR, *GEOGRAPHICAL DISCOVERY AND EXPLORATION IN THE QUEEN ELIZABETH ISLANDS* (OTTAWA: DEPARTMENT OF MINES AND TECHNICAL SURVEYS, 1964), 76. *BY PERMISSION OF NATURAL RESOURCES CANADA.*

explore and claim for Canada the land to the west."[51] Cook also disputed Peary's alleged complaint that he should have made an application to seek the Pole, and that he was trespassing upon Peary's prior right, insisting that "the Pole is a place no nation owned, by right of discovery, occupation, or otherwise."[52]

Bernhard A. Hantzsch (1909–11)

A small private expedition that ended disastrously was that of Bernhard A. Hantzsch in 1909–11.[53] A German ornithologist, Hantzsch had been liberally supplied by scientific circles in Germany but unfortunately lost much of his outfit when the ship taking him to Cumberland Sound was wrecked on the outward voyage in the summer of 1909. He spent a difficult winter at Blacklead Island, in continual disharmony with the rest of the white population, and then, accompanied by several Inuit, he explored the Nettilling Lake region and the adjacent shore of Foxe Basin. His crossing of mid-Baffin Island was the first authenticated traverse by a white man. He wintered some distance north of the Koukdjuak River in great hardship and then, having examined the coast to approximately 86° 45' N, died on the return journey in June 1911, apparently of illness and malnutrition.

Donald B. MacMillan (1913–17)

The last major foreign expedition of this period was that led by Donald B. MacMillan in 1913–17. MacMillan had been with Peary in 1908–9 and now undertook an expedition of his own, sponsored privately by the American Museum of Natural History, the American Geographical Society, and the University of Illinois.[54] He planned to remain in the field for two years, or at most three, but through various misfortunes, relief expeditions miscarried in both 1915 and 1916, and his small party was not evacuated until Bob Bartlett arrived with the *Neptune* in the summer of 1917. From their comfortable headquarters, "Borup Lodge" at Etah on the Greenland coast, expedition members completed a considerable number of sledging trips and scientific sorties – the one of most immediate concern to the expedition being MacMillan's long journey in 1914 beyond Axel Heiberg Island. Ethnographer Walter E. Ekblaw examined the Bay Fiord, Greely Fiord, and Lake Hazen region of central Ellesmere Island in 1915. The following year, MacMillan skirted the Sverdrup Islands and made the first landings upon King Christian Island and the north shore of Cornwall Island. In 1917, MacMillan traced the oft-seen but little known eastern coast of Ellesmere Island south of Cape Sabine. The expedition also recorded the discovery of nine new islands.[55] In common with other explorers to this time, MacMillan seems to have proceeded on his expedition under the impression that the part of Greenland in which he would be operating was subject to the laws of no state, but on 11 January 1917, he received the news by sledge that "the United States had acquired, by purchase, the Danish West Indies, conceding to Denmark at this time the right to control all of Greenland."[56] He also mentions his awareness that the Canadian government expedition under A. P. Low "landed and took formal possession of Ellesmere Land in August, 1904."[57] When he searched the site at Cape Herschel, however, he found that the cairn had been demolished and the record had disappeared.

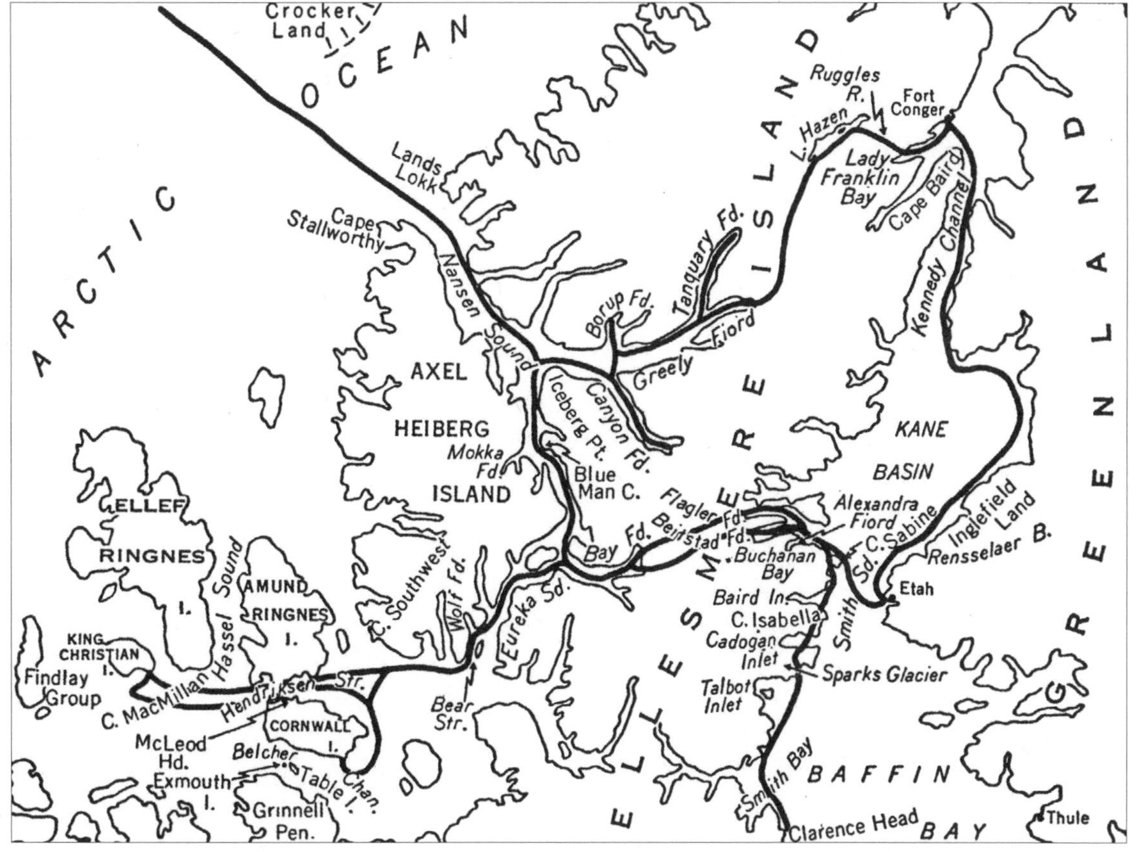

FIGURE 6-10: MACMILLAN EXPEDITION, 1913-17. ANDREW TAYLOR, *GEOGRAPHICAL DISCOVERY AND EXPLORATION IN THE QUEEN ELIZABETH ISLANDS* (OTTAWA: DEPARTMENT OF MINES AND TECHNICAL SURVEYS, 1964), 99. *BY PERMISSION OF NATURAL RESOURCES CANADA.*

7

Canadian Government Expeditions to Northern Waters, 1897–1918

The preceding chapters have attempted to describe events, situations, and disputes that provoked increasing concern on the part of Canadian authorities regarding the security of the more northerly parts of the territories which had been turned over to Canada in 1870 and 1880. The Canadian government's response was the gradual initiation of a program of action, rather limited but nonetheless designed to solidify and consolidate Canadian sovereignty over the territories in question. Some aspects of this program, such as the attempts to organize these territories into districts, define their boundaries, and provide (at least for the Yukon) the basic elements of an administration, have already been described. Other aspects included the dispatch of Mounted Police units to various parts of the North to maintain law and order and the dispatch of government expeditions to northern waters to keep an eye on foreign whalers, traders, and others; to initiate the application of Canadian laws and regulations; and to bring these regions and their inhabitants under Canadian administration more generally. This chapter focuses on these early government expeditions, which eventually developed into the principal device used to assert supervision and control in the Arctic archipelago.

William Wakeham (1897)

The first Canadian government expedition was sent out in 1897 under the authority of the reconstituted Department of Marine and Fisheries[1] and commanded by Dr. William Wakeham (who had been serving as Canada's representative on the International Fisheries Commission). When the project was first discussed in the House of Commons, the stated purpose of the $35,000 requested for it was "to provide for another expedition by water to Hudson Bay, to settle, if possible, the practicability of the route for commercial purposes."[2] Certain questions regarding the navigability of Hudson Bay and Strait had not been conclusively settled by the voyage of Lieutenant A. R. Gordon in the 1880s, particularly because of strong disagreements which had emerged afterwards. Therefore, government officials hoped that the new expedition would provide some definite answers. Speaking in the Commons discussion after the new Liberal Minister of Marine and Fisheries

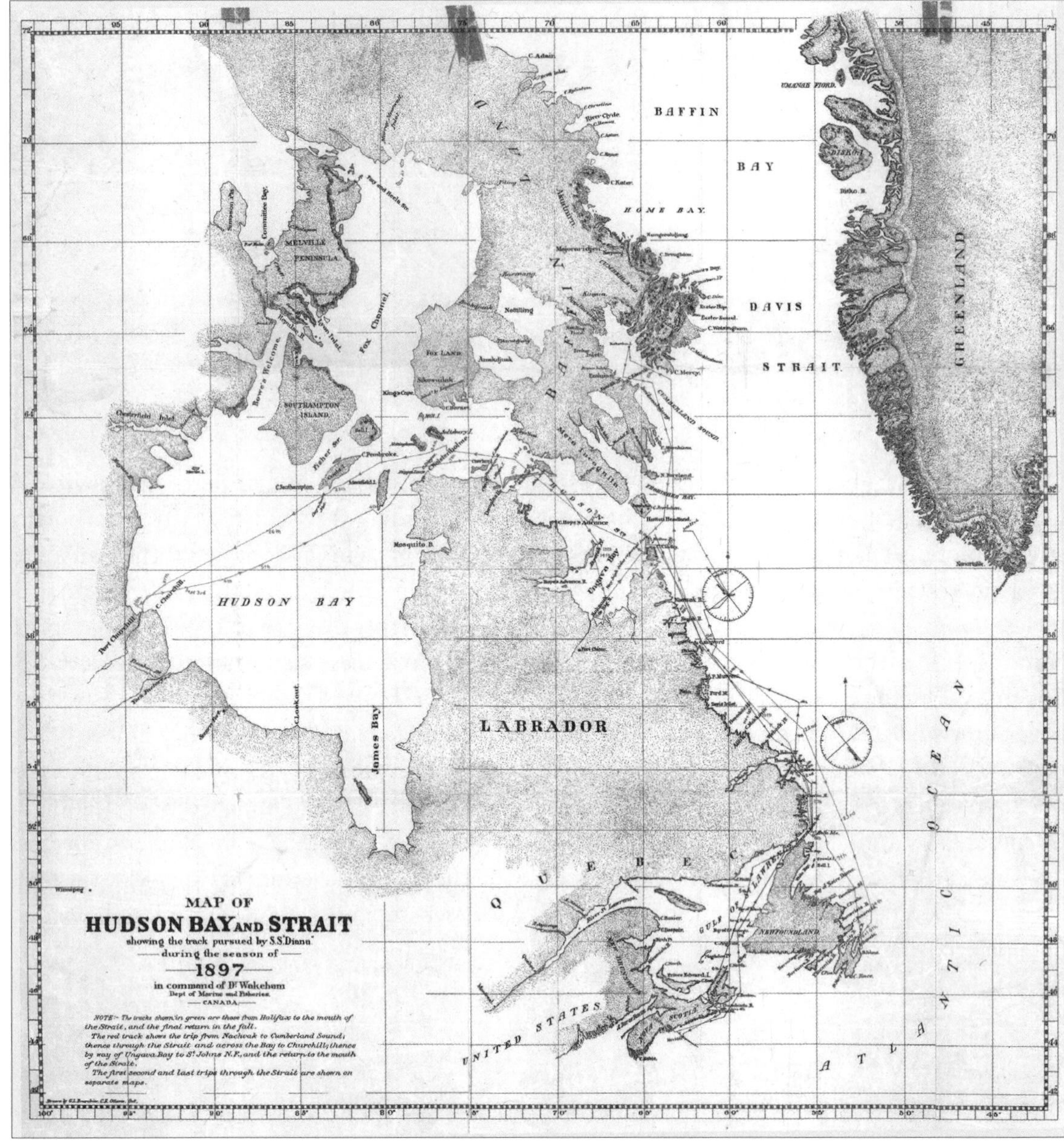

FIGURE 7-1: G.L. BOURCHIER, MAP OF HUDSON BAY AND STRAIT SHOWING THE TRACK PURSUED BY S.S. "DIANA" DURING THE SEASON OF 1897 IN COMMAND OF DR WAKEHAM, DEPT OF MARINE AND FISHERIES, CANADA, IN *REPORT OF THE EXPEDITION TO HUDSON BAY AND CUMBERLAND GULF IN THE STEAMSHIP "DIANA" UNDER THE COMMAND OF WILLIAM WAKEHAM, MARINE AND FISHERIES CANADA, IN THE YEAR 1897*, PUBLISHED IN CANADA *SESSIONAL PAPERS* (NO. 11B), VOL. XXXII, NO. 9, 1898. *COURTESY OF CENTRE FOR NEWFOUNDLAND STUDIES, MEMORIAL UNIVERSITY LIBRARIES. MAP 146.*

Louis Henry Davies, Sir Charles Tupper, who had filled the same post for the Conservative government a few years earlier, remarked: "The hon. Minister will recollect that there was a dispute carried on for years between Admiral Markham and Commander Gordon as regards the result of that investigation, and as to the navigability of these waters for a certain period." George Elliott Casey of West Elgin observed, "There is no doubt that it was the desire on the last occasion to find that the Hudson Straits were not navigable."[3]

Commander William Wakeham was instructed to try to find out if the navigation season recommended by Gordon from approximately 1–10 July to the first week in October could safely be extended.[4] In his post-expedition report Wakeham wrote:

> Now, as I understand the position, there is no question of the navigability of the strait with suitable vessels during a certain season.... I was not sent up to decide whether Hudson Strait could be navigated with suitable vessels within the dates mentioned – that question was settled, but what was required to meet the claims of those not satisfied with the dates above given, was a further test over a longer season, both spring and fall.[5]

Sailing in the chartered steam whaler *Diana*, Wakeham had entered Hudson Strait on 22 June and finally left it on 30 October. Between these dates, he made four round trips through the strait and also visited Cumberland Sound and Churchill. In the meantime, geological parties from the ship under Dr. Robert Bell and A. P. Low conducted investigations in southern Baffin Island and Ungava. Wakeham's firm conclusion, in reference to the navigation season, was that the advice of Lieutenant Gordon had been essentially sound:

> I now conclude this part of the report by saying that I absolutely agree with Captain Gordon in fixing the date for the opening of navigation in Hudson Strait, for commercial purposes, by suitable vessels, at from 1st to the 10th July.... For all the reasons I have enumerated, I consider the 20th of October as the extreme limit of safe navigation in the fall. To such brave and experienced mariners as those who accused Capt. Gordon of timidity because he refused to force the "Alert" through the ice of Hudson Strait in June, after she had lost her stem plate, or who have dubbed the hardy men from Newfoundland who manned and sailed the "Diana," as "feather bed sailors," because we left the strait with the end of October, these conditions are frivolous and will have no influence; but to the ordinary sailor and ship owner, I flatter myself, sir, they will be plain and sufficient.[6]

Although the primary purpose of the expedition was to investigate navigation problems, a further purpose is also evident: to assert and uphold Canadian sovereignty in the region visited. Speaking for the Conservative government in the Senate before the defeat of 1896, well over a year before the expedition set sail, Sir Mackenzie Bowell said:

> It is not the intention of the government at present to dispatch a vessel exclusively for the purpose

> indicated, but the Departments of Customs and Marine and Fisheries have under consideration the propriety of keeping a vessel in Hudson Bay, for some time, for the purpose of protecting the revenue and also for the protection of the fisheries. As most hon. gentlemen who have paid any attention to the matter know, fisherman from the United States have been poaching on our fishing reserves for many years, and taking from those northern waters a good deal of wealth which properly belongs to us.[7]

Obviously the new Liberal administration decided to go ahead with the project, and on 6 May 1897, fisheries minister Davies reported to the House of Commons in the following terms:

> It has been reported to me that some American whalers have for a series of years visited Cumberland Sound, north of Hudson's Bay Straits, and have acted as if they owned the country; and my instructions to Commander Wakeham were to proceed up the Sound, to take as formal possession of the country as possible, to plant the flag there as notice that the country is ours, and take all necessary precautions to inform natives and foreigners that the laws must be observed, and particularly the customs laws of Canada.[8]

In his report, which was addressed to Davies, Wakeham mentions "the instructions contained in your letter of the 23rd of April last," and probably refers to this aspect of them a little further on, where he writes, "when all doubt as to the navigability was passed, I was to leave the strait and proceed on other work; resuming the navigation of the strait in the autumn of the year." But he does not reproduce the instructions, nor do they appear to have been printed in departmental reports or elsewhere.[9] His narrative, however, indicates his activities related to this part of his assignment. He found out as much as he could about whaling, fishing, and trading activities in the parts he visited, called at Hudson's Bay Company and whaling posts, and tried to contact any ships in the region. He learned[10] that only three American whaling ships had been visiting Hudson Bay in recent years and that there were only two whaling posts in Cumberland Sound, both of them Scottish. Consequently, he did not see much reason for alarm over such enterprises, nor did he feel that much revenue was being lost, even though Canadian duties were not being paid on goods brought in. His task of taking formal possession of the territory was performed at Kekerten in Cumberland Sound on 17 August, where, in the presence of the Scottish whaling agent, some Inuit, and his own crew, he raised the Union Jack and declared that "the flag was hoisted as an evidence that Baffin's Land with all the territories, islands and dependencies adjacent to it were now, as they always had been since their first discovery and occupation, under the exclusive sovereignty of Great Britain."[11] It would appear that Wakeham was the first leader of a Canadian expedition to make such a proclamation, under government orders, after the transfers of 1870 and 1880.

Although there had been some anticipation that Wakeham's expedition would initiate a continuing government presence in the Hudson Bay region, this did not turn out to be the case. When Conservative William James Roche asked in the House of Commons on 18 May 1899, "What action does the Government propose to take on the strength of information obtained by the expedition?" Davies replied that "no action is at present contemplated."[12] In fact, no further expedition of this type took place for half a dozen years, the next being that of Albert Peter Low in 1903–4.

Albert Peter Low (1903–4)

In the case of Low's expedition, the priorities were reversed: its primary concern was with the question of sovereignty, and other matters such as navigation were secondary considerations. This was an official Canadian government expedition that had as its deliberate purpose the establishment of Canadian sovereignty over Hudson Bay and at least part of the Arctic archipelago, and as such it constitutes one of the important landmarks in Canada's effort to bring this region under effective control. The government intended it to initiate genuine regulation of the fishing and whaling industry in Hudson Bay and the waters near Baffin Island, establish posts for the collection of customs, and generally impress upon both Inuit and whites in the region that they were subject to Canadian law. In addition, a small staff of scientists would accompany the expedition to bring back as much technical and scientific information as possible in a variety of fields, notably meteorology, navigation, geology, botany, and zoology.[13]

Low was appointed to the command of the expedition early in June 1903, according to his report,[14] but the official order in council confirming the appointment was not issued until 13 August, and he was formally commissioned on the same day. The order in council reads as follows:

> On a Memorandum dated 8th August 1903, from the Minister of Marine and Fisheries, recommending that Mr. Albert P. Lowe [*sic*], of the Geological Survey of Canada, be appointed officer in charge of the Expedition to Hudson Bay and Northward thereof, in the Steamship "Neptune" –
>
> The Minister further recommends that under the provisions of Section 2 of Chapter 95 of the Revised Statutes of Canada, Mr. Lowe be appointed a Fishery Officer for Canada, with authority to exercise therein during his term of office as such Fishery Officer, the powers of a Justice of the Peace for all the purposes of the Fishery Laws and Regulations.
>
> The Minister also recommends that a Commission be issued to Mr. Low conveying the powers above described and such others as may be requisite for him to exercise in his capacity as Officer in Charge of the Expedition in question.[15]

The commission itself was phrased in only the most general terms, however, the operative passage being worded thus:

> We have constituted and appointed, and We do hereby constitute and appoint you the said Albert Peter Low to be officer in charge of the expedition to Hudson Bay and northward thereof in the Steamship *Neptune*,
>
> To have, hold, exercise and enjoy the said office of officer in charge of the expedition to Hudson Bay and

> northward thereof in the Steamship *Neptune* unto you the said Albert Peter Low, with all and every of the powers, rights, authority, privileges, profits, emoluments and advantages unto the said office of right and by law appertaining during pleasure.[16]

Besides Low, who was geologist as well as commander of the expedition, the senior personnel were Major J. D. Moodie of the North West Mounted Police (NWMP), who was appointed a commissioner, customs officer, and stipendiary magistrate, and Samuel W. Bartlett of the famous Newfoundland seafaring family, who was the ship's captain. Officially, the expedition was under the Department of Marine and Fisheries, but several other departments or branches were involved, notably the Department of the Interior and the NWMP. Some of the correspondence, notably that concerning the appointment of Major Moodie, throws a good deal of light upon the background, scope, and purpose of the expedition.

On 30 July 1903, Deputy Minister of the Interior James A. Smart sent the following letter and memorandum to Colonel Fred White, comptroller of the NWMP:

> I beg to enclose you herewith a copy of a memorandum respecting the expedition to Hudson Bay. As you will observe, this memorandum sets out fully the nature of the proposed expedition, as well as the manner in which it is to be conducted. I have written to both Doctor [Robert?] Bell and Colonel [F.] Gourdeau [the Deputy Minister of Marine and Fisheries] asking them to have the necessary instructions to their officers issued at once, and I would be glad if you would adopt the same course with regard to the officers who are to be appointed by your Department.
>
> It is the Minister's wish that the instructions to the Captain who is to be in charge of the vessel should be prepared by yourself, the Deputy Minister of Marine and Fisheries, and myself, and that the same should provide that the Captain in charge of the vessel, the Police Officer, and Mr. Low should constitute a sort of executive committee for consultation in regard to matters of general importance effecting the expedition.
>
> I will be glad to meet you and Colonel Gourdeau at any time which may be found convenient for us to do so, but in the mean time the Minister would be glad if you would take the necessary steps to have your instructions to whoever may be appointed as Police Officer, prepared and issued at once.
>
> As you will observe from the memorandum, the officer of the North West Mounted Police will be commissioned to act as Collector of Customs for the whole Territory, and will also be commissioned as stipendiary Magistrate.
>
> It is the Minister's wish also that copies of all the instructions and commissions should be on file in both the Departments of Marine and Fisheries, and Interior, and I would be glad therefore, if you would kindly furnish me with a duplicate of the same for that purpose.[17]

Memorandum.

During the last year information has been received to the effect that American traders and whalers are in the habit of landing upon Hershell Island, at the mouth of the McKenzie [*sic*] River, and at or near the mouth of the McKenzie River carrying on a whaling, fishing and trading industry, and that the same thing has been going on to some extent on the North West coast of the Hudson Bay and upon the islands North of the Hudson Bay in the Arctic Circle.

There is not believed to be any question as to the absolute title of Canada to these territories and islands but it is feared that if American citizens are permitted to land and pursue the industries of whaling, fishing and trading with the Indians without complying with the revenue laws of Canada and without any assertion of sovereignty on the part of Canada unfounded and troublesome claims may hereafter be set up. The following has therefore been mapped out:

Superintendent Constantine of the North West Mounted Police has been sent overland to the mouth of the McKenzie River and will shortly reach that point. There he will establish authority of the Government and at the earliest possible date will make a report containing the necessary information upon which to base further action. It is believed that next year it will be wise to send an expedition around by way of Behring Straits to establish a permanent post wherever recommended by Superintendent Constantine.

As to the coast and islands Northward from Hudson Bay it is proposed immediately to send an expedition under the Marine and Fisheries Department which shall be for the purpose of patrolling and exploring and establishing the authority of the Government on the points in question.

Scientific observers from the Geological Survey and the Department of Marine and Fisheries will accompany the expedition, also a photographer from the Survey Branch of the Department of the Interior. The object in sending these officers is to collect all possible information in regard to the territory visited and to have the information collected in exact and scientific form so as to be available for future use. It is also proposed to send a commissioned officer of the North West Mounted Police with four or five men who will establish the post at the place found to be most convenient. Materials for permanent buildings will be taken up. The post will be provisional for two years but it is the intention that the patrol will return and visit the post every year. The officer of the North West Mounted Police will be commissioned to act as Collector of Customs for the whole territory and will also be commissioned as stipendiary magistrate. The details as to the working out of the scheme must necessarily be left largely to the experience and judgment of the officers in charge. Mr. Low, of the Geological Survey, who has already explored extensively in the Hudson

Bay district, will be the geologist accompanying the expedition.

The ship commissioned for the expedition is the "Neptune." The officers and crew will consist of- Captain, two mates, chief engineer, two assistant engineers, six stokers, chief steward, two assistant stewards, one cook, assistant cook, boatswain, carpenter, gunner, surgeon and twelve able seamen.

The cost of the expedition, approximately, will be:

Charter of steamer.... $1,800 per month
Wages of crew.... 1,200 per month
Surgeon.... 100 " "
Photographer.... 75 " "
Maintenance of crew and staff.... 700 " "
Coal (200 tons per month).... 1,700 " "
Engine and deck supplies.... 200 " "

Total.... $5,775

It is to be noted that the provisioning and equipment must contemplate absence for two years although in all probability the ship will return next year in the spring and go back in the fall, but there is always a possibility in those waters of a ship being icelocked and ample provision must be made against such a contingency.

It will be understood that our knowledge of the Northern portions of the territories in question being so unexact no very definite instructions can be given as to the location of the post. The Captain in charge of the expedition, the police officer and Mr. Low, the geologist, will be a committee to jointly decide on what shall be done and where the permanent post shall be located. They will further be asked to make a full report as to what should be the policy of the Government in dealing with the administration of these territories, apart from the technical report which each of them will be required to furnish to his own branch of the service.[18]

Colonel White responded with the following instructions to Major Moodie, which were explicit about the role of the NWMP as he understood it:

The Government of Canada having decided that the time has arrived when some system of supervision and control should be established over the coast and island in the northern part of the Dominion, a vessel has been selected and is now being equipped for the purpose of patrolling, exploring, and establishing the authority of the Government of Canada in the waters and islands of Hudson Bay, and the north thereof.

In addition to the crew, the vessel will carry representatives of the Geological Survey, the Survey Branch of the Department of the Interior, the Department of Marine and Fisheries, the Royal Northwest Mounted Police and other departments of the public service.

Any work which has to be done in the way of boarding vessels which may be met, establishing ports on the mainland of these islands and the introduction of the system of

Government control such as prevails in the organized portions of Canada has been assigned to the Mounted Police, and you have been selected as the officer to take charge of that branch of the expedition.

You will have placed at your disposal a sergeant and four constables; you will be given the additional powers of a Commissioner under the Police Act of Canada, and you will also be authorized to act for the Department of Customs.

Mr. Low, the geologist; the captain in command of the vessel; and yourself will be constituted a Board to consult and decide upon any matters which may arise requiring consideration and joint action.

The knowledge of this far northern portion of Canada is not sufficient to enable definite instructions to be given you as to where a landing should be made, or a police post established; decision in that respect to be left to the Board of Three above mentioned, and wherever it is decided to land you will erect huts and communicate as widely as possible the fact that you are there as a representative of the Canadian Government to administer and enforce Canadian laws, and that a patrol vessel will visit the district annually, or more frequently.

It may happen that no suitable location for a post will be found, in which case you will return with the vessel but you will understand that it is the desire of the Government that, if at all possible, some spot shall be chosen where a small force representing the authority of the Canadian Government can be stationed and exercise jurisdiction over the surrounding waters and territory.

It is not the wish of the Government that any harsh or hurried enforcement of the laws of Canada shall be made. Your first duty will be to impress upon the captains of whaling and trading vessels, and the natives, the fact that after considerable notice and warning the laws will be enforced as in other parts of Canada.

You will keep a diary and forward, whenever opportunity offers, full and explicit reports on all matters coming under your observation in any way affecting the establishment of a system of government and the administration of the laws of Canada.[19]

The above documents seem to reveal a certain amount of confusion in the planning and organization of the expedition, particularly with regard to the responsibilities of the departments and individuals involved. For example, although it was clearly specified that the expedition was to be under the Department of Marine and Fisheries, Deputy Minister Smart of the Department of the Interior wrote the letters to the other senior officials asking them to have instructions issued to the officers, and in speaking of the wishes of "the" minister he must surely have been referring to his own minister (Clifford Sifton). Although the order in council noted Minister of Marine and Fisheries Raymond Préfontaine's recommendation that Low be appointed officer in charge of the expedition as well as a fishery officer with the powers of a justice of the peace for all the purposes of the fishery laws and regulations, the memorandum and White's letter to Moodie said that Low be commissioned to act as collector of customs for the whole territory and as stipendiary magistrate. Again, although both the order in council and Low's commission make it clear that he was to be officer in charge of the expedition, both the memorandum and White's letter speak of Low only as geologist, while the memorandum refers to the captain as being in charge of the expedition. Low himself does not seem to have been in any doubt about his position as commander, which was confirmed by the order in council and the commission, and there does not appear to be any evidence that the confusion caused any trouble during the expedition.[20]

Preparations for the voyage were made with as little publicity as possible – and one might almost say in a cloak-and-dagger atmosphere. What was not said publicly at the time, however, was said with emphasis three years later. Replying to repeated charges by the new Minister of Marine and Fisheries Louis-Philippe Brodeur that the Opposition was willing to let the Americans take possession of the northern territories, Conservative Leader Robert Borden spoke as follows:

> Either the hon. minister does not know the history of his own and other departments of the government or else he has taken a course which I would not like to characterize in this House as it deserves. If he knew what he was speaking of, he would know that one of his colleagues came to me some two or three sessions ago and explained that he wanted a certain vote passed for the purpose of patrolling those waters, but that for certain reasons of state he desired that there should be no discussion in the House on the subject. I spoke to my hon. Friends and the vote went through without a word of discussion. That vote was for the very purpose of protecting those northern lands and having the British flag fly over them.... The Minister of the Interior of that day, now the member for Brandon (Mr. Sifton), came to me across the floor, presented to me certain documents of a confidential nature, asked me to consider them and the vote which was to be founded upon them for the purpose of preventing this poaching in northern waters and thus avoid such claims as were made in connection with the Alaskan Boundary. After twenty-four hours consideration, I arranged with gentlemen on this side that, for reasons of state, there would be no discussion when that estimate went through the House.[21]

A little later in the same debate, Borden referred to a confidential memorandum he had been given by a member of the government, and read excerpts from it.[22] These excerpts show that it was the memorandum which Deputy Minister Smart had sent with his letter to Colonel White on 30 July 1903 and which is reproduced above. Borden's statement was supported by other opposition members, among them David Henderson, who remarked:

> I well remember, some two years ago, the circumstances referred to by the leader of the opposition, when we on this side of the House were requested by a minister of the Crown not to discuss the item that was to

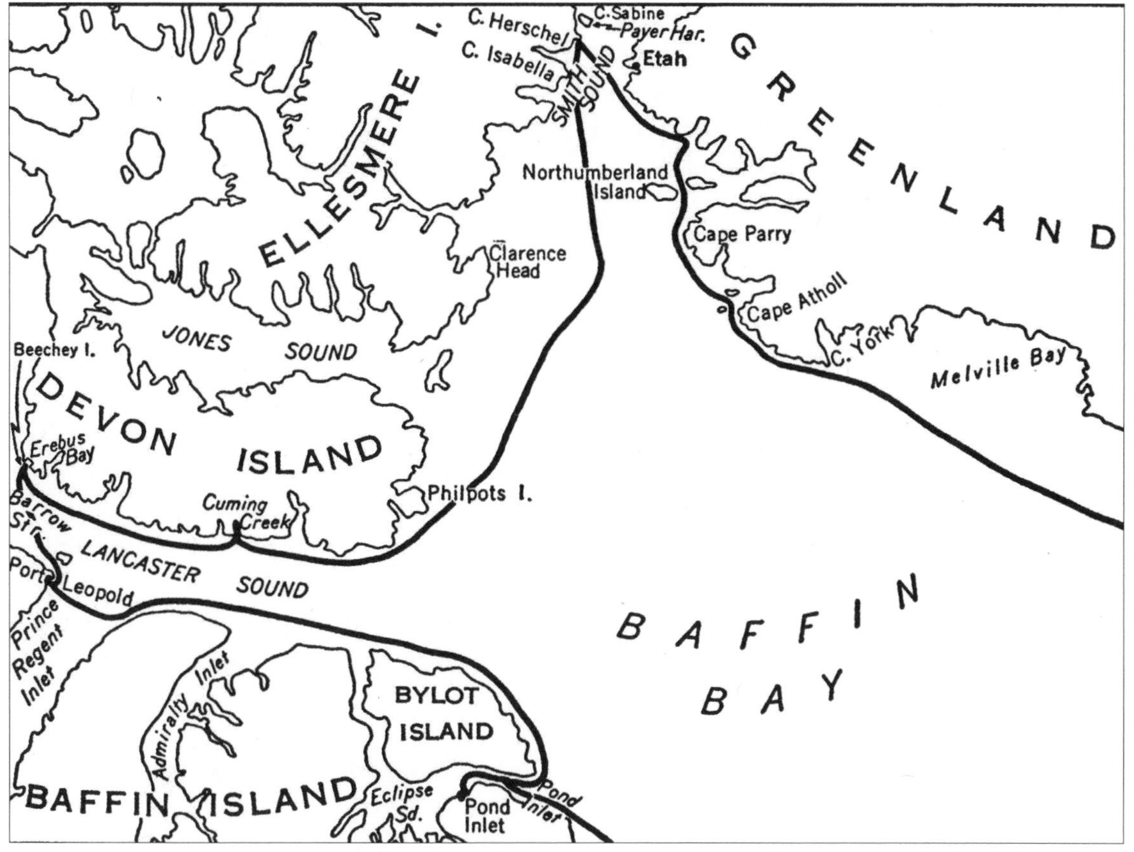

FIGURE 7-2: LOW EXPEDITION, 1904. ANDREW TAYLOR, *GEOGRAPHICAL DISCOVERY AND EXPLORATION IN THE QUEEN ELIZABETH ISLANDS* (OTTAWA: DEPARTMENT OF MINES AND TECHNICAL SURVEYS, 1964), 111. *BY PERMISSION OF NATURAL RESOURCES CANADA.*

> be voted for the purpose of sending out an expedition; we were asked to do so because the government did not wish to show to the people of the United States the weakness of our position; therefore we were asked to remain silent and assent to the item going through.[23]

It seems apparent that whatever the need for secrecy may have been about midsummer 1903, it had disappeared three years later in 1906. Nonetheless, the silence had been broken long before this time. As early as 30 September 1903, during a Commons discussion of Captain J.-E. Bernier's projected expedition to the North Pole, Minister of Marine and Fisheries Raymond Préfontaine had remarked (in reference to Low's assignment) that "at the present time an expedition has left for the northern part of Hudson Bay. And why? Simply to organize that territory, to protect our interests in it and keep it for Canada."[24] Officials felt that once Low was on his way he would be in a position to take the necessary action, and therefore, it was no longer important to keep the project a secret.

The expedition left Halifax on 23 August 1903 and returned on 12 October 1904. Besides Commander Low, Major Moodie, and Captain Bartlett, the ship's company included a crew of twenty-nine, five other members of the NWMP, a scientific staff of five, and an Inuit interpreter picked up at Port Burwell.[25] The *Neptune* proceeded in turn to Port Burwell, Cumberland Sound, Hudson Strait, and Fullerton Harbour at the northwest of Hudson Bay, where the expedition wintered. In the summer of 1904, the ship passed out again through Hudson Strait and northwards to Ellesmere, Devon, Somerset, Bylot, and Baffin Islands, through the Strait again to Fullerton, and then home to Halifax, making frequent stops en route to visit settlements and collect scientific data.

The activities of Low and Moodie during the voyage show how they undertook to carry out their assignment. Low gathered a great deal of information about the regions visited – their geography, geology, and Inuit inhabitants, the work of previous explorers, the Scottish and American whaling industries, the prospects for navigation – and incorporated it in his account of the voyage. On 4 September 1903, the *Neptune* landed near Blacklead Island in Cumberland Sound, and the next day Major Moodie explained the intentions of the Canadian government to the Anglican missionaries and the agent of the Scottish whaling establishment located there.[26] Over the next few days, visits were made to another Scottish whaling station at Kekerten Island, also in Cumberland Sound, and to a station at Cape Haven in Cyrus Field Bay operated by Potter and Wrightington of Boston.[27] In accordance with instructions, Low searched for Captain George Comer of the American whaler *Era* and wintered with him at Fullerton, maintaining good relations throughout their stay together.[28] Major Moodie decided that Fullerton would be a suitable location for a police post and erected a building there, leaving several members of the Mounted Police in charge when the *Neptune* departed in the summer of 1904.[29]

On the east coast of Ellesmere Island, not far from Adolphus Greely's last camp at Cape Sabine, Low took formal possession of the island for Canada. He describes the proceedings in the following words:

> It took little time to attend to the duties of the landing at Cape Herschel, where a document taking formal possession in the name of King Edward VII., for the Dominion, was read, and the Canadian flag was raised and saluted. A copy of the document was placed in a large cairn built of rock on the end of the cape.[30]

Low does not himself give the text of his proclamation, but elsewhere it has been reproduced as follows:

> In the name of His Most Gracious Majesty King Edward VII, and on behalf of the government of the Dominion of Canada, I have this day taken possession of the Island of Ellesmereland, and of all the smaller islands adjoining it, and in token of such formal possession I have caused the flag of the Dominion of Canada to be hoisted upon the Island of Ellesmereland, and have deposited a copy of this document in a sealed metal box placed in a cairn erected on the conspicuous headland of Cape Isabella.
>
> (Sgd) A. P. Low
> Officer Commanding
> The Dominion government's expedition to Hudson Bay and Northern waters.[31]

FIGURE 7-3: HOISTING THE FLAG, ELLESMERE ISLAND, 1904. *LAC PA-038265.*

On 15 August, Low followed a similar procedure at Beechey Island[32] and two days later at Port Leopold, Somerset Island.[33] Low did not land on or claim any of the more westerly islands because his instructions limited the cruise westward in Lancaster Sound to Beechey Island.[34]

The 1903–4 expedition of Low and Moodie may be regarded as a deliberate attempt on the part of the Canadian government to take effective possession of the more easterly islands of the archipelago and to bring their inhabitants and commercial enterprise under Canadian law. The pattern of activity initiated by Low was followed closely by his successor Captain Joseph-Elzéar Bernier, who was in the archipelago as a government agent each year from 1904 to 1911.

Captain Joseph-Elzéar Bernier (1904–11)

Captain Bernier had already had a long and adventurous career at sea before sailing on his first Arctic voyage in 1904.[35] Born in 1852 at L'Islet, on the southern shore of the St. Lawrence about fifty miles below Quebec City, he came from a well-known French-Canadian seafaring family which for several generations had contributed members to the ships that sailed in the St. Lawrence River and Gulf. Bernier himself had become master of a ship at the incredibly early age of seventeen, and he had been all over the globe on scores of voyages. Apparently his interest in Arctic exploration had first been stimulated through witnessing the fitting out of Charles Francis Hall's *Polaris* in the Washington Navy Yard in 1871. Although he had not as yet undertaken any polar expeditions himself, he had steeped himself in Arctic lore and had become a recognized authority on the subject.[36] He became obsessed with the desire to make the first conquest of the North Pole and to plant the British flag there, but he also became convinced, through long study of the problem, that the traditional direct assault upon the Pole by ship and then sledge was not the best method of attack. Taking note of the transpolar drifts of the wreckage of Lieutenant-Commander George W. De Long's *Jeannette* in 1881–83 and of Fridtjof Nansen's *Fram* in 1893–96, Bernier reasoned that if a ship were deliberately put into the right place in the ice north of Alaska it would drift gradually to the northwest and across the Arctic Ocean, passing so close to the North Pole on the way to Greenland or the Greenland Sea that it could be used as a base from which the North Pole could be attained on foot.[37]

Once Bernier had set his mind on this project, he pursued it with the enthusiasm, tenacity, and determination that typified his efforts regardless of the task in hand. In his autobiography, he tells how, after 1872, his cabin aboard ship became an Arctic library. His collection continued during periods ashore, as dockmaster at Lauzon from 1887 to 1890 and as governor of the Quebec gaol from 1895–98. In 1899–1900, he succeeded in salvaging the steamer *Scottish King*, which had been wrecked about forty miles south of St. John's on the Newfoundland coast; his earnings of over $35,000 for this exploit gave him a measure of the financial independence he needed for the promotion of his enterprise. While occupied with these and other activities, he carried on a persistent campaign of tours, lectures, interviews, solicitations, and appeals, not only throughout Canada but in Great Britain and the United States as well, with the object of stirring up public enthusiasm and financial support for his project.[38]

There is much information scattered throughout a variety of sources, but especially in the Laurier Papers, Bernier's own papers, and Hansard, which, when pieced together, tells a great deal about his efforts to bring his expedition to reality and his conviction that it would be important in connection with Canada's sovereignty in these northern regions and the security of her northern frontier. On 5 March 1898, Bernier took his appeal directly to Prime Minister Laurier, apparently for the first time, in a letter accompanied by a detailed plan.[39] The plan itself had changed from the original, since it now involved taking a ship to a point as far to the north as possible beyond the mouth of the Lena, or alternatively to the vicinity of Franz Josef Land, and then leaving the ship and trying to reach the Pole by using houseboat, sledges, kayaks, dogs, and reindeer. Laurier was evidently dubious about the plan, although the reason is not entirely clear, but Bernier kept up the pressure. Among his many public appearances to promote his project were speeches or lectures to la Société de géographie de Québec,[40] la Société littéraire et historique de Québec, the Quebec legislature, the Canadian Institute in Toronto,[41] the Royal Society of Canada,[42] the Royal Colonial Institute in

FIGURE 7-4: CAPTAIN J. E. BERNIER. *LIBRARY AND ARCHIVES CANADA / C-085035.*

London,[43] and, on several occasions, the members of Parliament in Ottawa.[44] Almost without exception, his plans were well received, and the fund of voluntary contributions grew slowly. Bernier lost no opportunity of letting Laurier know about any additional support, either moral or financial, that he received, and there were other testimonials which were apparently unsolicited and unknown to him.

A "Rapport de la Société de Géographic de Québec," dated 23 May 1899, was sent to Laurier as an endorsement of the polar expedition, and it suggests the extent to which Bernier was preoccupied with the political aspects of what he was trying to do. It is also an early formulation of the sector concept which was given such publicity a few years afterwards by Senator Poirier:

> Il est au moins rationnel … que nous prenions possession du pays, îles et mers, etc., du bassin polaire et que nous l'occupions où y ayions au moins droit de cité; avant que nos entreprenants voisins des Etats-Unis, qui s'y préparent, viennent ainsi nous déposséder de notre avoir territorial; car le Canada doit nécessairement, tout en se terminant à l'Ouest au méridien d'Alaska, voir prolonger ce méridien le 140ème [*sic*] jusqu'au Pôle. Vers l'Est ce serait le 60ème méridien séparant le Canada du Groënland.[45]

In an interview published in the *Montreal Witness* on 9 February 1901, Bernier put forward his case in similar terms:

> If the boundary between Canada and Alaska were continued northward it would strike the North Pole. A similar line through Baffin Bay prolonged to the pole should be Canada's northeasterly frontier, and if our expedition reached the pole and we planted the flag there we could claim the whole country to the north of us by right of discovery.[46]

A letter from Bernier to Laurier on 18 February 1903, requesting $100,000 from the government, shows his concern about the recently completed Sverdrup expedition and its implications:

> Je vous envoie une carte géographique faisant voir les bornes du Canada septentrional, telles que je les comprends, et désignant plusieurs

> îles très riches en charbon sur une étendue de douze cent milles, qui ont été découvertes de 1898 à 1902 par M. le capitaine Otto Sverdrup et plusieurs autres explorateurs, et dont je voudrais prendre possession au nom du Canada, auquel elles doivent appartenir.[47]

Among the enticements Bernier extended to Laurier was an offer on 15 April 1901 of the presidency of "The General Committee in Charge of the Canadian North Pole Expedition";[48] an invitation on 28 October 1901 to a lecture he was giving to Governor General and Lady Minto; or, failing that, an invitation to a private lecture for his own benefit later on.[49] Laurier remained elusive and hard to convince. When he received a letter of solicitation from "Executive Commissioner" Joseph Xavier Perrault of "The Canadian North Pole Expedition," the stationery letterhead revealing that the organization was under "the High Patronage of His Excellency the Governor General" and the honorary presidency of Lord Strathcona, Laurier replied on 9 July 1901 in the following vein: "N'oubliez pas cependant qu'il y a une expédition, celle de Peary, partie depuis trois ans. S'il réussi, notre projet n'aura plus de valeur; s'il ne réussit pas, il y aura peu d'espoir pour le succès du capitaine Bernier."[50] Answering a letter from François-Xavier Berlinguet of la Société de géographie de Québec on 12 October 1901, Laurier said bluntly: "je désire immédiatement corriger une erreur.... Le Gouvernement n'a fait aucune promesse au Capitaine Bernier."[51]

From time to time, Bernier's projected voyage was brought up in Parliament, the remarks of the members indicating widespread sympathy with its objectives and its prospects. On 21 March 1901, opposition member Frederick Debartzch Monk asked the government to come to a decision about its course of action respecting the expedition, drawing from Laurier only the non-committal reply that this would be done as soon as possible.[52] Occasional comments thereafter showed that the possible political implications of the project were not being overlooked:

> May 14, 1901
>
> *F. D. Monk (Jacques Cartier)*: Captain Bernier is, I think, pre-eminently qualified to go in search of the North Pole; and if he does not get the necessary encouragement from us, I believe he will get it from the American people. I believe he has already been approached by enterprising American newspapers, with the object of securing his services for that purpose....
>
> *T. S. Sproule (East Grey)*: In the impression of many, the discovery of the north pole would enable us much more easily to determine what is our own in making a dividing line between our territory and that of Russia and the United States....[53]
>
> May 1, 1902
>
> *John Charlton (North Norfolk)*: Aside entirely from the reputation that would accrue to this country from the settlement of a geographical problem which has engaged the attention of maritime nations for generations, we would establish our right to all the territories and islands and seas that might lie between our present northern boundary and the north pole itself – all that vast region between the 141st parallel [*sic*] of

longitude on the west, and Baffin's Bay and Grant land on the east....

T. B. Flint (Yarmouth): There can be no doubt, from a fair understanding of our position as the controller of the northern half of this North American continent, that the jurisdiction of Canada extends to the pole.[54]

On the same occasion, David Henderson, the member for Halton, speculated darkly on the outcome if Bernier should resort to Washington for funds: "If he goes to Washington, there is not the slightest doubt that, within twenty four hours he will have all the money he wants. And the next thing we know we shall have another Alaska boundary question away near the north pole, with commissions sitting at Washington to settle question of our northern boundary."[55] Henderson thought it unlikely, however, that Bernier would seek American help, and his remarks (as well as those of the majority of the members who spoke) were decidedly in favour of the project.

Bernier's expedition was again discussed in the House of Commons towards the end of the session on 30 September 1903, with remarks of similar import being made:

John Charlton (North Norfolk): A successful expedition to the Pole would give Canada a very prominent place among the maritime states, and the discovery of the Pole would give us a standing with regard to territorial acquisition in the north between the northern coast of the continent, which we would not otherwise have....

A. C. Bell (Pictou): If any people in the world should look upon it as their peculiar business, and finally succeed in making that discovery, it is the people of Canada, because of the North Pole when discovered will unquestionably form part of this country.... It may be of great material advantage to Canada to establish finally and indisputably her claim and title to all the lands lying on the north part of this continent....

D. Henderson (Halton): Not long ago I saw in the newspapers that the Americans are talking very loudly of some possessions to which they propose to lay claim, away to the north of this Dominion which properly belong to the Dominion of Canada. Now, if Captain Bernier succeeds in locating the Pole and planting thereon the British flag, taking possession of whatever there is in land or sea, we will certainly have a right to claim possession in the name of the King of England of everything that lies between the North Pole and the now known Dominion of Canada. We will then not be troubled in the future with any Alaska boundary disputes in that direction.[56]

Sir Wilfrid Laurier evidently said as little as possible on the subject, either inside or outside the House, and continued to handle it circumspectly and with great caution. He unburdened himself more openly in a private letter to Senator William Edwards on 29 October 1903, in response to a worried one written by the senator the day before. Probably both men were influenced by the Alaska Boundary Award, which had been handed down about one week earlier.

Rockland, October 28th, 1903

Dear Sir Wilfrid:

At the risk of being regarded as troubling you with what may be thought a very trivial matter, I write a few lines with regard to Capt. Bernier. In view of recent events, would it not be well for an exploring expedition to go to the North with the object of a far more important mission than that of the discovery of the North Pole, and if incidentally the North Pole is discovered, no harm will be done.

In looking up the matter a short time ago, I was surprised to find the extent to which the Americans have been whaling in Hudson Bay and the many years they have been at it. Their aggressive and grasping nature is such that we need not be surprised if shortly they take the position that Hudson Bay is an open sea, and further, that they may lay claim to islands and territory in that North land, said to be rich in coal and a variety of minerals. It seems to me that we should lose no time in asserting our rights, and decidedly so. I would neither wait for nor depend on Great Britain looking after our rights or protecting them. I would do it on our own account.

Bernier has not spoken to me of this matter. I am acting entirely on my own account. I have had a life long experience in handling and managing men and I must say that I have never met the man in whom I would have the same confidence as I would have in Bernier in undertaking an expedition where great hardship is to be encountered and great endurance is requisite. His stability and powers of endurance as well as his ability as a navigator I cannot think can be questioned. There may be features of such an expedition that would require other knowledge than that possessed by Bernier, but in any such lines the necessary assistance could be supplied him. If the Americans are permitted to skirt our Western possessions, for Heaven's sake do not allow them to skirt us all around. They are south of us for the entire width of our country; they block our natural and best possible outlet to the Atlantic; they skirt us for hundreds of miles on the Pacific and control the entrance to a vast portion of our territory, and the next move if we do not look sharply after our interests, will be to surround us on the North. You will have noticed no doubt that they have a Northern expedition fitting out now. Britain's interests are first, ours are secondary. Let us look after our own as best we can.

Most sincerely yours,
Wm. C. Edwards

Ottawa, 29th. October, 1903.

My dear Edwards,

The subject as to which you write me has been engaging our attention. Dr. Ami [Bernier] has talked the matter over with me and proposed a

> plan which does not command [*sic*] itself to my judgment at this moment. The plan which he proposes and which he may also have outlined to you is to get the British Government to issue a proclamation claiming jurisdiction over all the northern Territory. This would simply arouse a storm at this juncture. It is by far preferable to continue the work which we have already commence [*sic*] in that direction. This year we have sent from Newfoundland an expedition to establish a post of the Mounted Police on the Interior shore of the Hudson Bay, and quietly assume jurisdiction in all directions. We have likewise sent over land by the McKenzie [*sic*] river an expedition down to the mouth of the river where we are establishing a post of the Mounted Police. Next year, I propose that we should send a cruiser to patrol the waters and plant our flag at every point. When we have covered the whole ground and have men stationed everywhere, then I think we can have such a proclamation as is suggested by Dr. Ami.
>
> Believe me, as ever,
> My dear Edwards,
> Yours very sincerely,
> Wilfrid Laurier[57]

Laurier's letter evidently provides the key to what actually happened and why, but it provokes other questions. One of these relates to the financing of the expedition, where there are noticeable discrepancies in facts, figures, and dates which do not lend themselves to easy explanation. It is clear that the government eventually decided to provide a large amount of money for an expedition, part of it for the purchase of a ship and part for other expenses. The expedition that materialized was, of course, that of 1904–5 in the German ship *Gauss*, which was purchased and renamed the *Arctic*. Bernier says in his autobiography that Laurier, Borden, and Meighen (who, as a matter of fact, was not yet in the House of Commons) "co-operated in securing a vote of $200,000 to outfit a Canadian Polar Expedition under my command."[58] In the House of Commons on 30 September 1903, Minister of Marine and Fisheries Raymond Préfontaine spoke favourably in a personal way of Bernier's plan and suggested $80,000 as the amount which might be provided.[59] On 12 October 1903, the sum of $100,000 was voted to "cover cost of the extension of the coast service and surveys on the northern coast of Canada," on which occasion Préfontaine replied affirmatively to Conservative member Thomas Simpson Sproule's question as to whether "the government are still carrying on their expedition to ascertain the navigability of Hudson bay and straits."[60] There were no other comments, however, and this would appear to have been the vote for Low's expedition.[61]

On 29 July 1904, the House of Commons voted the sum of $200,000 for "the purchase, equipment, and maintenance of vessels to be employed in patrolling the waters in the northern portion of Canada; also for establishing and maintaining police and customs posts at such points on the mainland or islands as may be deemed necessary from time to time." The only comment was by the Prime Minister himself, who gave a brief explanation of the item, referring to the dispatch of the *Neptune* in 1903 to assert "the undoubted authority of the Dominion of Canada in the waters of Hudson's Bay and beyond" and saying that the *Arctic*, "under the command of Captain Bernier," was now being sent to relieve and replace the *Neptune*. He added that the new expedition was "to patrol the waters, to find suitable locations for posts, to establish those posts and to assert the jurisdiction of Canada," and thus he made it clear that the money was not to be used for a drift across the Arctic Ocean or an attempt upon the North Pole.[62] Strangely enough, about one month earlier, Préfontaine had spoken of a special vote which had been granted in 1903 to purchase a ship (the *Arctic*) and send it to Hudson Bay as a special expedition. He also informed the House that this was "a special expenditure for the general account of three departments" – the Department of the Interior, the Mounted Police, and the Marine Department.[63]

Bernier, assuming that he had at last won government sponsorship and would be able to make his polar drift, went to Bremerhaven in the spring of 1904 and for $70,000 or $75,000 purchased the German ship *Gauss*.[64] This was a recently built steamship with auxiliary sail, which had just returned from a German voyage to the Antarctic and which Bernier thought would be ideally suited to his purpose. Back at Quebec, he supervised preparations for his own expedition, and the ship, renamed the *Arctic*, had been made all ready when special instructions from Ottawa in July abruptly changed all his plans. Bernier was directed, he says in his autobiography, to "proceed to Hudson Bay, practically under the orders of the Mounted Police to ascertain whether a certain well-known and highly respected ship captain was engaged in selling liquor to the natives."[65] Bernier's autobiography tells of his bitter disappointment at this turn of events, which effectively cancelled the polar drift and which came to him, according to his own account, as a complete surprise and a great shock.[66]

Bernier seems to have proceeded until the very last moment under the impression that a polar expedition was really going to be dispatched and that he would be in command of it. On the other hand, judging by Laurier's letter to Senator Edwards quoted above, the Prime Minister, as late as 29 October 1903, was still inclined to reject Bernier's plan and was thinking rather of sending a ship to patrol more southerly waters and plant the flag on the lands encountered. This is, of course, what eventually happened. In his remarks on the subject in the Commons on 30 September 1903, however, Minister of Marine and Fisheries Préfontaine clearly identified the project under discussion with Bernier's polar drift, as did others, and Préfontaine voiced his support of it in this context.[67] Yet on 21 June 1904, he said with equal clarity that the purchase of the *Gauss* was for "a special expedition to Hudson Bay" and that the special vote granted the year before had been for "this expedition."[68] The question arises as to whether the government at one stage had made up its mind to support Bernier's polar expedition and later decided to divert the ship to Hudson Bay (as Bernier obviously believed) or whether in fact there had never been any serious intention of letting Bernier go ahead with his project, and the authorities kept him in the dark about their real intentions until they considered that the appropriate moment had arrived to tell him. Also, if the government did change its mind, when did the change come and in what circumstances? Not very much light was shed upon these matters by L. P. Brodeur, the new Minister of Marine and Fisheries, in his attempt to answer questions put by Leader of the Opposition Robert Borden, during a lengthy wrangle over the expedition on 11 May 1906:

> *R. L. Borden*: On what date was this expedition decided upon?

> *Brodeur*: It was decided upon in the month of June.
>
> *Borden*: What time in June?
>
> *Brodeur*: In the beginning of June....
>
> *Borden*: Was she purchased for this expedition?
>
> *Brodeur*: Yes.
>
> *Borden*: When was she purchased?
>
> *Brodeur*: In April, 1904.[69]

Borden was not slow to point out the obvious discrepancy in Brodeur's answers, and it seems apparent that if the expedition was decided upon in June and the ship was purchased in April, then she could hardly have been purchased with this particular expedition in mind.

Bernier's biographers T. C. Fairly and Charles E. Israel report Bernier as having told a newspaperman years afterwards that he thought his polar expedition was cancelled because of Peary's forthcoming new attempt upon the North Pole and Laurier's fear that a Canadian expedition might run afoul of the Americans.[70] There is certainly truth in this, but it is not the whole story. Other considerations were worrying Laurier and his advisers: the outcome of the Alaska Boundary Case and the anxiety it provoked; concern over American activities in Hudson Bay and Strait and the desire to establish these waters as Canadian; the idea that priority should be given to solidifying Canada's claim to the archipelago and making secure the northern frontier; the lingering feeling that a North Pole expedition was a luxury Canada could do without, at least until matters further south were looked after; and certain reservations about Bernier himself. The last-mentioned consideration suggests the unlikelihood, or impossibility, that Bernier would be taken into the full confidence of the government.

In the circumstances, there was little for Bernier to do but swallow his discomfiture and disappointment. He soon found himself able to adjust to the new circumstances, however, and sought consolation in the decision to devote his efforts in the Arctic "to what after may be regarded as a more important object, that is to say to securing all the islands in the Arctic archipelago for Canada."[71] He was eager to take both the responsibility and the credit for this work, which, he later averred, he "had consistently urged upon the Canadian government for many years before it was finally undertaken."[72]

The expedition sailed from Quebec on 17 September 1904, with Bernier as captain of the *Arctic* and Major Moodie of the Royal Northwest Mounted Police (the prefix "Royal" having been added earlier that year), to Bernier's intense displeasure, in command of the expedition as a whole as well as of the ten members of the Mounted Police who accompanied it.[73] The responsibilities of the expedition were limited to Hudson Bay and Strait, and no attempt was made to sail farther north. The *Arctic* proceeded to Port Burwell and then to Fullerton, where she wintered with the *Era* as the *Neptune* had done the previous year. Leaving Fullerton on 5 July 1905, the *Arctic* failed in an attempt to reach Churchill and then, calling at points on the way, returned through Hudson Strait to Chateau Bay on the Labrador coast where it rendezvoused with the *Neptune* and Captain Bartlett. Major Moodie, who had left the *Neptune* at Port Burwell in August 1904 to return south and join the *Arctic*, now received instructions to rejoin the *Neptune* and go back to Fullerton. Bernier, also under orders from Ottawa, took the *Arctic* back to Quebec for repairs, arriving early in the fall.

During the expedition, relations between Major Moodie and Captain Bernier were perhaps formally correct but at the same time rather strained. This occasioned comment afterwards in the House of Commons. For example, Conservative member Joseph Gédéon Horace Bergeron noted on 28 June 1906: "There was some bad blood on the steamer, there is no doubt about that, though we were not allowed to prove it, between Major Moodie and Captain Bernier. Each of them thought he should command the expedition."[74] In their accounts, neither indulges in open criticism of the other, but the underlying tension is evident. For example, Moodie notes that "on September 17, 1904, I sailed from Quebec in command of the D.G.S. *Arctic*."[75] For his part, Bernier suggests that "Major Moodie, of the Royal Northwest Mounted Police, was sent in command of the government force with myself in command of the *Arctic*.... In connection with the voyage, it is worthy of note that Major Moodie was commissioned by the government to establish Mounted Police stations, and for the *Arctic* under my command to attend to annexing to Canada Arctic territory granted by the Imperial Government."[76] Reading between the lines, one can detect other, though less obvious, disagreements.

In his report, Moodie mentioned the construction of a post at Fullerton the preceding winter and spoke of plans to build "the headquarters of 'M' Division, newly created for service in the Hudson's Bay district" at or near Cape Wolstenholme, as well as another post in Cumberland Sound. He also expressed his view that if the government should intend on having the coasts of Keewatin and Ungava patrolled, it would be necessary to establish small detachments no more than 150 miles apart. The notice forbidding the export of muskox hides "had had good results," but if the animals were to be preserved, it would be necessary to prohibit killing at any time, except by the natives for food. Moodie also noted that the regulations of 1904 regarding the methods of killing whales should be extended to walrus and that he had collected customs duties wherever possible (though very small). He also reported sending some dogs to Roald Amundsen, who was wintering at King William Island, in response to a letter received from him on 16 March 1905.[77]

The atmosphere of secrecy which had surrounded the expedition led to rumours and accusations of extravagance, incompetence, and corruption; afterwards those broke out into the open in a barrage of charges and counter charges which resulted in a parliamentary investigation. Conservative member William Humphrey Bennett fired the opening gun in the House of Commons on 11 May 1906, when he charged that the person responsible for fitting out the expedition had "decided, when he had the public crib to go for, to plunge his hands into it, and to fit out an expedition that the gods themselves might envy."[78] In the discussions that followed over the next two months,[79] opposition members repeatedly hurled accusations that the expedition had been provided for on a ridiculously lavish scale and had cost far too much (one estimate was that it had cost a total of about $285,000); that the purchase of supplies had not been by public tender and thus had gone completely out of control; that the *Arctic* had originally been purchased for a expedition to the North Pole and had then been diverted to Hudson Bay without adequate explanation; that although the *Arctic* had been completely equipped for three years she had returned after only one year; and that there had been dissension aboard the ship and also gross misconduct with Inuit women. With regard to the supplies, opposition critics suggested that both quantities and prices paid had been scandalously high, that not all of them had been put on board, and that there had been profiteering, waste, and theft before, during, and after the voyage so that, according to one estimate, only $36,000 worth were left over at the end.

The evident vulnerability of the government to some of these charges, along with rather suggestive information in the Auditor General's report, gave opposition members plenty of scope to vent their wit and sarcasm on those deemed responsible, and they seized their opportunity with gusto. For example:

> *Samuel Barker (East Hamilton)*: I find there were 40 trousseaus bought at $4 each. Were these for ladies or for the crew?
>
> *L. P. Brodeur*: The wife of Major Moody [*sic*] was on board.
>
> *R. L. Borden*: I don't see why one lady would want 40 trousseaus.[80]
>
> *George William Fowler (King's and Albert)*: Was this steamer ballasted with sugar? I see that they carried seven and a half tons of sugar.[81]
>
> *George Oscar Alcorn (Prince Edward)*: What brought this expedition to so untimely an end? Why did this vessel not complete her three years cruise?
>
> *Borden*: The provisions gave out.[82]
>
> *Brodeur*: Of rum, the English expedition had 800 gallons, while the Canadian expedition had only 100 gallons.
>
> *Borden*: Is that the reason the expedition came back?[83]

The opposition members were particularly incensed over the excess of certain commodities which had been provided, even if the expedition had been equipped for three years rather than one. Conservative member George Taylor quoted figures from the Auditor General's report which gave totals of approximately 8,500 cigars, 400 pipes, 5,000 cigarettes, over 4,000 pounds of tobacco of various kinds, 30 cases and 15 gallons of wines, liqueurs, and champagnes, and 285 gallons and 1 barrel of rums and spirits.[84] In some instances, a rough calculation was sufficient to show that the amounts were not really as excessive as they appeared to be, at least on the basis of a plan for a three-year expedition. In other instances, however, the actual rate of usage made the extravagance appear worse than the figures themselves suggested. Conservative member William Barton Northrup, who had obviously put pencil and paper to work, drove this point home by putting before the House a formidable array of statistics, in the following vein: "Then they took 5,908 pounds of bovril at $1.65 a pound and only used 447 pounds. So at the same rate of usage they had enough bovril to last them for thirteen years." In the same way, he calculated that they had taken enough honey to last for 21 years, enough buckwheat to last for 31, enough chocolate sweets to last for 264 years, and enough beeswax and celery cream to last forever, presumably, since they had used none at all.[85]

It was easy for government spokesmen to show errors or exaggeration in some of the charges. For example, the expedition had forty-eight personnel rather than fifteen as the opposition had originally asserted, the cost of supplies and equipment was not nearly so great as had been claimed, the quantities of many articles were modest in comparison with what other expeditions had taken, and it was absolutely necessary to take a considerable surplus in case of emergency or accident. Other explanations were less convincing: that tenders had not been called because the time was insufficient; that a broken windlass had forced the *Arctic* to return; that all the supplies had been put on board and there had not been profiteering, waste, or theft; and that there had never been a vote or appreciation for an expedition to the North Pole.

In view of the seriousness of the charges, Laurier himself moved for a special committee "to inquire fully into all the circumstances connected with the purchase of said supplies, the disposal of the same, and the different matters above mentioned."[86] The Opposition immediately complained that the scope of the proposed inquiry was too limited, but in the end, after losing an amendment taking for a broader investigation, they accepted Laurier's motion without dissent.[87] As might have been expected, the members of the committee divided along essentially party lines, with Conservatives finding plenty of substantiation for the charges and Liberals finding that they were without foundation. The Conservatives presented a minority report which strongly condemned the organization and conduct of the expedition,[88] but it was easily defeated by an overwhelming preponderance of Liberals, and the favourable majority report was then approved.[89]

One of the most notable features of the investigation was that Bernier emerged from it with his reputation unscathed and even, perhaps, a little enhanced. With one or two exceptions, members on both sides of the House spoke of him in consistently laudatory terms and paid tribute to his competence, reliability, experience, and integrity. This was all the more remarkable because Bernier had more to do with choosing, purchasing, and supplying the *Arctic* than anyone else, and thus he was in an extremely vulnerable position. The general consensus of opinion, however, obviously held that whatever had gone wrong with the expedition was not his fault.[90]

The public criticism and the parliamentary investigation were temporary setbacks for Bernier, and they gave him new hurdles to overcome, but they did not stop him. He had returned from the 1904–5 voyage more determined than ever to load his own expedition to the North, and at last he won his point. The *Arctic* was repaired and fitted out at Sorel, the sum of $30,000 was allotted to cover expenses,[91] and the expedition set off from Quebec on 28 July 1906, with Bernier in command. Under the authority of an order in council on 23 July,[92] he had been given separate commissions as officer in charge of the *Arctic* and as a fishery officer for Canada.[93] None of these documents said anything about taking possession of territory, yet Bernier looked upon this as his major responsibility. "The main purpose of the expedition," he remarked, "was to assert Canadian sovereignty in the insular part of the Arctic north of Canada, by formally taking over the territory ceded to Canada by the Imperial government in 1880."[94] It was, he also declared, "the first arctic voyage of real importance to me"[95] – a fairly clear indication of his feelings about the voyage of 1904–5.

The *Arctic* visited in turn Chateau Bay, the Greenland coast, and Lancaster Sound, and then visited Baffin, Bylot, Somerset, Cornwallis, Bathurst, and Melville Islands, as well as some smaller ones. Winter quarters were established at Albert Harbour in Pond Inlet, near the northern extremity of Baffin Island, in early September, and here the expedition remained until 27 July 1907. After the *Arctic* escaped from the winter ice, it made calls successively at Coburg, Somerset, and Ellesmere Islands; then the expedition turned south, calling at Cumberland Sound and Port Burwell before arriving at Quebec on 19 October. In

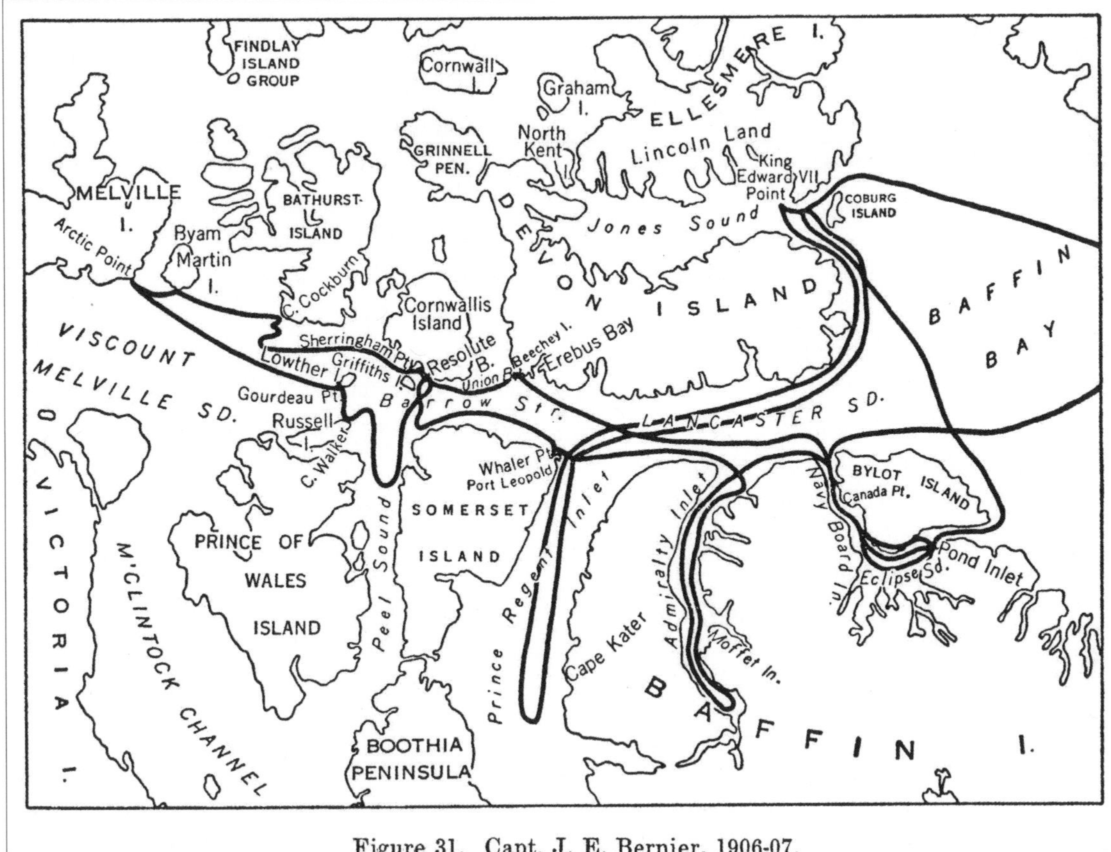

Figure 31. Capt. J. E. Bernier, 1906-07.

FIGURE 7-5: BERNIER EXPEDITION, 1906–7. ANDREW TAYLOR, *GEOGRAPHICAL DISCOVERY AND EXPLORATION IN THE QUEEN ELIZABETH ISLANDS* (OTTAWA: DEPARTMENT OF MINES AND TECHNICAL SURVEYS, 1964), 113. *BY PERMISSION OF NATURAL RESOURCES CANADA.*

the course of the voyage, Bernier landed upon and claimed the following islands: Bylot, Griffith, Cornwallis, Bathurst, Byam Martin, Melville, Lowther, Russell, Baffin, Beloeil, Coburg, Cone, and Ellesmere.[96] In some cases, such as at Griffith, Byam Martin, Lowther, Beloeil, and Cone Islands, he took possession only of the particular island landed upon. In others, such as at Bylot, Cornwallis, Bathurst, Melville, Russell, Baffin, Coburg, and Ellesmere Islands, he went further and purported to take possession not only of the island landed upon but also "the adjacent islands" or "all adjacent islands." In some cases, some of those adjacent islands were named. For example, at Melville Island he took possession of "Melville Island, Prince Patrick Island, Eglinton Island and all adjacent islands," while at Ellesmere Island he named the principal parts of this large island and also nearby islands, including those discovered and claimed by Sverdrup in 1898–1902.[97] Typically Bernier went through a formal ceremony of taking possession, having a cairn erected in a conspicuous place, raising the Canadian flag, making a proclamation, and having the ceremony photographed. In each case, a document of formal possession was drawn up in two or more copies, one of which was deposited inside the cairn. The first such document to be deposited – the one left at Canada Point on the west coast of Bylot Island – is a representative example.

> August 21st, 1906.
>
> This island Bylot Island, was graciously given to the Dominion of Canada, by the Imperial Government in the year 1880, and being ordered to take possession of it in the name of Canada, know all men that on this day the Canadian Government Steamer *Arctic*, anchored here, and I planted the Canadian flag and took possession of Bylot Island in the name of Canada. We built a cairn to commemorate and locate this point, which we named Canada Point, after, and in honour of the first steamer belonging to the Canadian Navy.
>
> Being foggy no latitude was obtained. On the chart this point is located in Long. 80.50 west and 73.22 north Latitude.
>
> From here the *Arctic* will proceed onward through the Navy Board inlet, to the westward into Admiralty inlet, and from these westward to Port Leopold, where we will leave a record of our future work.
>
> Witnessed thereof under my hand this 21st day of August, 1906 A. D., in the fifth year of the reign of His Most Gracious Majesty King Edward VII.
>
> J. E. Bernier
> Commanding Officer, by Royal Commission.
> Fabien Vanasdse, Historiographer.
> Joseph Raoul Pepin, M. D.
> Jas. Duncan, Customs Officer.
> Wingate H. Weeks, Purser.
> Geo. R. Lancefield, Photographer.[98]

The sweeping claim to Ellesmere and nearby islands, which was left at King Edward VII Point on the southern extremity of Ellesmere Island, was worded as follows:

> Proclamation,
> C.G.S. 'Arctic'
> James [*sic*] Sound
> August 12th, 1907.
>
> On this day we landed on this point, on North Lincoln, and annexed the following lands and islands: North Lincoln, Grinnell Land, Ellesmere Land, Arthur Laud, Grant Land, King Oscar's Land, North Kent and several islands, namely, Axel Heiberg Land, Ammund [*sic*] Ringnes Land, Ellee [*sic*] Ringnes Land, King Christian Land, formerly named Finlay Land; North Cornwall, Graham Land, Buckingham Island, Table Island, and all adjacent islands as forming part of the Dominion of Canada. And I hereby annex the above named lands as part of the Dominion of Canada.
>
> J. E. Bernier, Commanding Officer.
> George Hayes, Chief Officer.
> O. J. Morin, Second Officer,
> Wingate H. Weeks, Purser.[99]

Figure 7-6: Large group of Inuit with crewmen of CGS *Arctic* at the ceremonial taking of possession by Capt Joseph-Elzéar Bernier on Baffin Island, 9 November 1906. *Library and Archives Canada / PA-165672.*

Bernier's account does not mention any attempts to take possession of Devon and Somerset Islands, and presumably the reason why he did not trouble to lay claim to them was that Low had already done so. On the other hand, he did take possession of Baffin and Ellesmere Islands even though they had previously been claimed by Wakeham and Low, respectively. In all probability, the explanation for the repetition is that both Baffin and Ellesmere are enormous islands, and the places where Wakeham and Low performed their ceremonies of taking possession are separated by several hundred miles from those where Bernier performed his. Apart from this aspect of repetition or duplication, Bernier seems to have been impressed throughout with the idea that the claims he and Low were making were valid for any purposes and final.

Several whalers met with on the voyage were notified that licences of $50 must henceforth be paid, in compliance with the 1906 amendment to the Fisheries Act,[100] and two licences were sold to each of five Scottish whalers for the years 1906 and 1907.[101] No American whalers were found.[102] Customs duties were collected from the Scottish whalers for goods brought into the area,[103] and an inventory of the goods belonging to the Moravian missionaries at Port Burwell was taken.[104] The Inuit of Baffin Island were told that they must obey the laws of Canada.[105] From the winter base at Albert Harbour, several fairly long exploratory sledge trips were made. Documents left by Low and Moodie on Somerset Island and by Low on Beechey Island were found and reproduced in Bernier's narrative,[106] as were various other records (principally of British expeditions).[107] Altogether, in spite of the dubious value of his proclamations, Bernier made a comprehensive effort to examine and take note of everything he could find in the parts of the archipelago he visited during his voyage of 1906–7 and to establish Canadian law there – insofar as anything could be found to regulate or administer.

The return of the *Arctic* in 1907 was followed by another bitter wrangle in the House of Commons over the submission of an item for $50,000 in the estimates anticipating the next voyage of the *Arctic*. It was intended to "provide for the maintenance of vessels employed in patrolling the waters in the northern portion of Canada, also for establishing and maintaining police and customs ports on the mainland or islands as may be deemed necessary from time to time."[108] The matter at issue, however, was not so much the *Arctic* as the larger question of Brodeur's entire performance in directing the work of his department, and the key point of dispute was whether the estimates should be voted first and departmental information and reports be furnished in full detail afterwards or the information and reports should come first and the voting of the estimates thereafter. In the particular circumstances, Brodeur and his supporters argued for the first alternative, and the Opposition, led by George Eulas Foster, for the second. Opposition members took advantage of the opportunity to deliver extremely caustic remarks about the *Arctic*. George Taylor read with obvious relish a satirical article in the *Toronto Star*:

> The voyage was a great success. There were four meals a day, and the main brace was spliced every hour. It was felt that the captain had established his right to take his ship anywhere that a man may go on pemmican, pâte-de-foie-gras, truffles, and certain other bare necessities of life….
>
> …. Captain Bernier is the greatest island namer and claimer in the business. With its terrific speed – four knots an hour under forced draught – the 'Arctic' can overhaul any island that was ever made. When the 'Arctic' is seen in the offing, bearing down on an island, the island feels at once that it cannot get away from such a relentless pursuer as Captain Bernier.[109]

Foster made his own contribution, in similar vein:

> Captain Bernier took possession of the islands. What he did with them, goodness only knows; but he took possession of them, and the hon. member for Halifax says that they will not be there next year, and next year he will have to go back in search of them and take possession again. If, as he says, they change their

> place of abode every year, there is an absolute reason for a further expedition to capture and take possession of these elusive, floating and shifting islands. Then we will have Captain Bernier with us for ever, or as long as he lives.[110]

After a fruitless discussion that went on continuously from the evening of Thursday, 27 February, until midnight the following Saturday, the House adjourned without deciding the matter.[111] The $50,000 was voted when discussion on the subject resumed a few days later, however, and Brodeur gave a brief summary of plans for the coming expedition of the *Arctic* in the summer of 1908. She was to go to northern waters early in July, patrol the islands in the vicinity of Lancaster Sound which were frequented by whalers, collect licences and customs duties, and if possible go further west and north and claim more islands.[112]

On 20 May, when the estimates for the RNWMP were being discussed, Laurier commented on the situation in the North, his remarks showing clearly that he was firmly convinced that Bernier's expeditions were necessary:

> Since the police have taken possession and asserted our authority, the American whalers have taken licenses from us and have paid customs duties, and our authority is no longer disputed. At first these American whalers were inclined to demur, and I think they made some complaints at Washington; but of late years we have had no trouble…. There was a disputed territory between the United States and Canada, and if we had taken earlier the precaution which to have now taken, of sending men into the country to take possession of it, we would have had Skagway to-day. In the last map issued at Washington, I think by the War Department, there are various islands in the north with American names attached to them, conveying the impression that these lands belong to the United States. Captain Bernier goes north in order to put the British flag and assert our authority on this territory, which we claim as ours…. If we want to assert our jurisdiction in our country, we must be all the time vigilant. Vigilance is the price, not only of liberty but of security as well. I am making no complaint of our American friends, but they are very enterprising, and if they find anything in any place where there is nobody, they are apt to take possession. For that reason the expenditure connected with the expedition of Captain Bernier is well warranted.[113]

Precisely what authority was given to Bernier for the voyage of 1908 is unclear. In a letter of 5 April 1910, to Deputy Minister of Marine and Fisheries Georges-Joseph Desbarats, which accompanied Bernier's report of the expedition, the captain said that the voyage was "for the purpose of patrolling the waters contiguous to that part of the Dominion of Canada already annexed, and for the further purpose of annexing territory of British possessions as far west as longitude 141 degrees."[114] His opening statement in the report read as follows:

> Under a Royal Commission, issued to me to annex lands and territories granted by the British Crown to Canada, and as fishery officer of

> the northern waters of Canada, I commanded the steamer *Arctic*, fitted out and made ready for sea for a two years' voyage under instructions of the Marine and Fisheries Department. Specific instructions were given as to the waters to be patrolled, explored, and lands to be annexed in continuation of the two voyages, already made to the northern waters by the same ship, commanded by myself.[115]

He gave no further identification of the royal commission, and the two commissions included in the report (appointing him officer in charge of the *Arctic* and fishery officer) were actually those for the voyage of 1906–7. These appointments were to be held "during our pleasure," however, and it may not have been considered necessary to reissue or renew them. As already noted, neither of these documents nor the order in council for the voyage of 1906–7 said anything specifically about annexing territory, and Bernier's statement that his authority to carry out this responsibility came from his commission is evidently inaccurate. The "specific instructions" that he mentions must either have been put in another document or given orally. It is also possible, of course, that he put his own interpretation on the instructions he received and saw in them directions which were really not there.

Just before leaving Quebec, he was called into the presence of the Prince of Wales (later King George V), who was visiting the city. Bernier said that he "took advantage of the occasion to indicate to His Royal Highness my plan to take possession for Canada of all the islands discovered and annexed by British explorers, and was warmly commended for my persistence in urging this matter upon the Canadian government."[116]

The expedition departed from Quebec on 28 July 1908, and after cruising along the coast of Greenland and calling at Etah, it entered Lancaster Sound and proceeded westward to a point in McClure Strait south or southwest of Cape Hay. The route through McClure Strait looked inviting and ice-free, but Bernier's orders did not allow for an attempt upon the Northwest Passage, so he turned the *Arctic* about and established winter headquarters at Parry's old base at Winter Harbour on the southern coast of Melville Island. The voyage home began on 12 August 1909, and, after stops including Albert Harbour, Kekerten, Blacklead, and Port Burwell, the *Arctic* arrived at Quebec on 5 October.

During the long stay at Winter Harbour, Bernier sent out sledge parties to take possession of Banks and Victoria Islands. Between 6 April and 9 May 1909, Second Officer O. J. Morin led a small party which under incredibly difficult conditions succeeded in landing upon both and leaving a record of taking possession near Point Russell on Banks Island.[117] Between 1 May and 10 June, Third Officer C. W. Green led another party to McClure's old refuge in Mercy Bay on Banks Island, in the hope of finding relics or remains, but they saw no trace of his ship *Investigator* or of any cache or cairn. A record was left in a cairn at Cape Hamilton.[118] Morin made a second trip to Banks Island between 17 May and 24 June and carried out another search in Mercy Bay. Although he saw debris from the *Investigator*, he found no trace of the ship itself or of any records. A cairn which had been erected by the crew of the *Investigator* was rebuilt, and Morin "officially took possession of Banks island" a second time, leaving a record of the expedition in the cairn.[119] This expedition seems to have been an extraordinary affair,

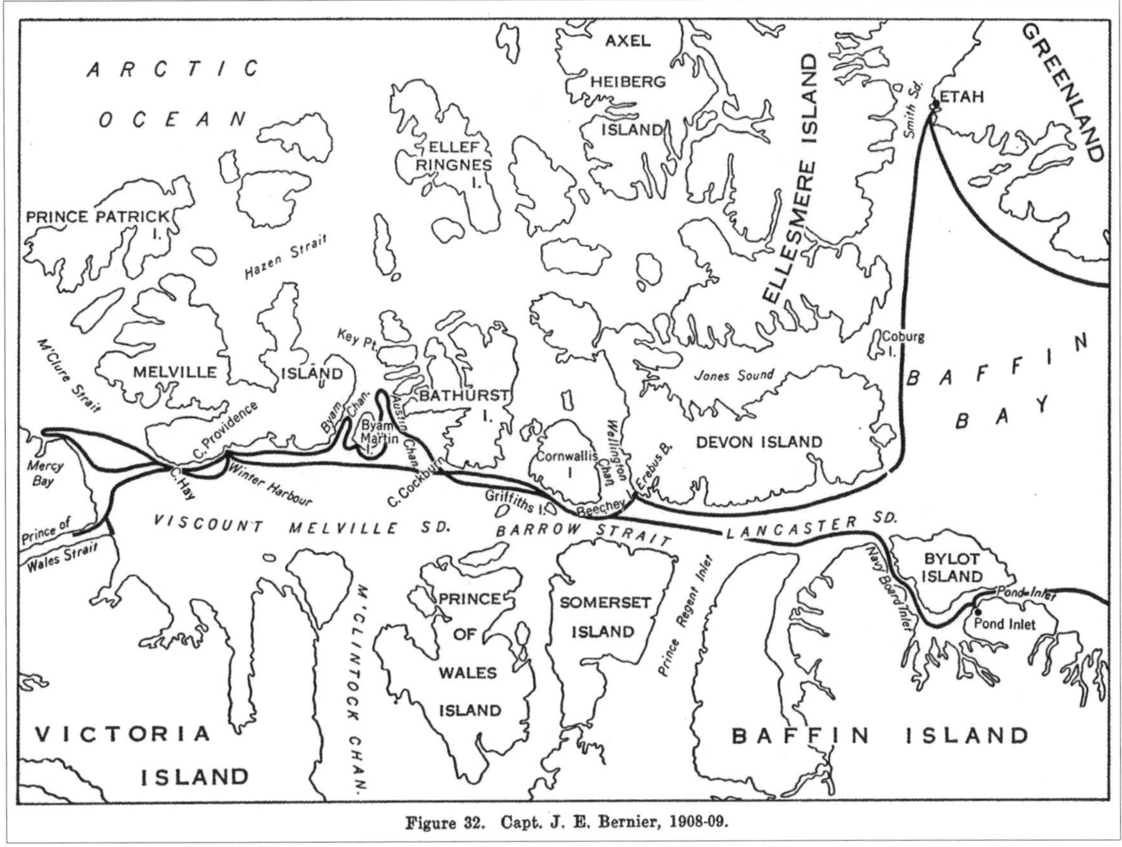

Figure 32. Capt. J. E. Bernier, 1908-09.

FIGURE 7-7: BERNIER EXPEDITION, 1908–9. ANDREW TAYLOR, *GEOGRAPHICAL DISCOVERY AND EXPLORATION IN THE QUEEN ELIZABETH ISLANDS* (OTTAWA: DEPARTMENT OF MINES AND TECHNICAL SURVEYS, 1964), 115. *BY PERMISSION OF NATURAL RESOURCES CANADA.*

having evidently been occasioned by Bernier's dissatisfaction with Morin's first performance, in that his party had left no record of possession on Victoria Island and had simply put the one for Banks Island in a bottle, placed it near a high rock rather than in a cairn, and covered it with stones. On his second expedition, Morin left the document in a cairn, but apparently it claimed only Banks Island, and he did not get to Victoria Island. Nevertheless, Bernier felt able to say that this expedition "was more satisfactory than the first."[120] The attention to detail in the case of Banks and Victoria Islands, and the disregard of such matters in the first sledge party's claim to distant King William Island, is evident. This feature was observable in other claims that Bernier made during his northern voyages.

On 4 March 1909, Bernier's team erected a cross on Northeast Hill at Winter Harbour "to commemorate the annexing of the Arctic archipelago to Canada."[121] Then, on Dominion Day, 1 July, a memorial tablet on Parry's Rock at Winter Harbour was unveiled, revealing an inscription which claimed the entire archipelago for Canada. Bernier wrote:

> At dinner we drank a toast to the Dominion and the Premier of Canada; then all assembled around Parry's rock to witness the unveiling of a tablet placed on the rock, commemorating the annexing of the whole of the Arctic archipelago. I briefly referred to the important event in connection with the granting to Canada, by the Imperial Government, on September 1, 1880, all the British territory in the northern waters of the continent of America and Arctic ocean, from 60 degrees west longitude to 141 degrees west longitude, and as far north as 90 degrees north latitude.[122] That we had annexed a number of islands one by one and a large area of territory by landing, that we now claimed all islands and territory within the degrees 141 and 60 west longitude as Canadian territory, and now under Canadian jurisdiction.[123]

The inscription on the tablet took this form:

> This Memorial is
> Erected today to Commemorate,
> The taking possession for the
> "DOMINION OF CANADA,"
> of the whole
> "ARCTIC ARCHIPELAGO."
> Lying to the north of America
> from long, 60° W. to 141° W.
> up to latitude 90° n.
> Winter Hbr. Melville Island.
> C.G.S. Arctic, July. 1st, 1909.
> J. E. Bernier Commander.
> J. V. Koenig Sculptor.[124]

Clearly Captain Bernier was convinced that this final step, following his earlier claims during the years 1906–9, had secured for Canada all the islands within the stated limits, small as well as large.[125] The question arises as to why he bothered with the preliminary bites at all if he intended throughout to make the final complete swallow. It might reasonably be assumed that Bernier, as a strong exponent of the sector principle which had been pronounced publicly and in categorical terms by Senator Pascal Poirier in February 1907 (see chapter 8), would have found such piecemeal annexations inappropriate and needless. Yet his own accounts certainly leave the impression that he was firmly convinced of the need for and the utility of all that he was doing. In any case, Bernier was in reality an agent for the Canadian government, and to some extent, at least, his actions were directed by government policy. It seems likely that the guiding hand behind the scenes was ultimately that of Laurier himself, and the explanation for what was being done may lie in Laurier's above-quoted letter of 29 October 1903 to Senator William Edwards: "I propose that we should send a cruiser to patrol the waters and plant our flag at every point. When we have covered the whole ground and have men stationed everywhere, then I think we can have such a proclamation as is suggested by Dr. Ami."[126]

Other features of the voyage are worthy of mention. W. E. Jackson, the meteorologist, had a commission as customs officer and took charge of this responsibility.[127] Again licences were sold to whalers, including some Scotsmen and a Harry Whitney of New York. Bernier described the encounter with the latter, who was at Clyde River, Baffin Island, on 5 September 1909, as follows:

FIGURE 7-8: CAPTAIN JOSEPH-ELZÉAR BERNIER AND HIS CREW AT WINTER HARBOUR, MELVILLE ISLAND, 1 JULY 1909. *LIBRARY AND ARCHIVES CANADA / C-001198.*

> I informed Mr. Whitney that I was patrolling Canadian waters, and, as he had on board his vessel a motor whaleboat, it would be necessary for him to take out a fishery license, and that I would issue it. He stated that if it was a regulation, he would pay the legal fee of $50, and take the license. I accordingly issued the license and received the fee.[128]

During his visit at Etah and elsewhere, Bernier informed himself about hunting and whaling in the region, and in his narrative he commented particularly upon the killing of Ellesmere Island muskoxen and other game by the Greenland Inuit and the Peary, Sverdrup, and Cook expeditions. He expressed a strong view that moderate hunting by explorers would be unobjectionable, but it should be kept under Canadian government control:

> I am of the opinion that Canada will not object to hunting, for food purposes, by explorers who prosecute their explorations in the interest of science, but regulations enforcing a judicious course should be adopted, to prevent numbers of Eskimo natives of foreign countries exploiting Canadian territory, and destroying valuable hunting and fishing grounds.[129]

Later he suggested that such regulations would be even more advisable for game-rich Melville Island.[130]

Captain Bernier made his last expedition to the Arctic for the Canadian government in 1910–11. Since the task of formally claiming all the islands of the archipelago was now considered complete, this voyage was mainly a patrol to see that Canadian laws were being observed. It was not the government's intention to adopt a "get tough" policy, however, as shown by the following passage from Deputy Minister of Marine and Fisheries Alexander Johnston's instructions to Bernier:

> You will acquaint any persons whom you may find engaged in the whale fishery in these northern waters that you are patrolling these waters as the duly accredited officer of the Canadian Government, and you will, where necessary, demand payment of license fees for such fishing. If payment be refused you will make a request that such refusal be put in writing. It is not desirable that you should take any action in this regard which would be likely to embarrass the Government.[131]

Bernier was also instructed to attempt the Northwest Passage if possible,[132] but this turned out to be inadvisable because of the extremely large masses of ice blocking McClure Strait. Otherwise the voyage was rather routine. The *Arctic* left Quebec on 7 July 1910, and after reaching a point about thirty miles southwest of Cape James Ross in the unsuccessful attempt to get through McClure Strait, it turned back and wintered at Arctic Bay in Admiralty Inlet, Baffin Island. Again sledge parties were sent out, particularly noteworthy being two expeditions to Fury and Hecla Strait under the leadership of surveyor J.T.E. Lavoie, which discovered that Admiralty Inlet and Prince Regent Inlet were apparently unconnected.[133] When the sailing season opened in 1911, an attempt was made to reach Fury and Hecla Strait through Prince Regent Inlet, but this also was defeated by ice. In the course of the voyage, calls were made at many of the places visited on previous trips, and the *Arctic* was safely back at Quebec on 25 September 1911.

At Albert Harbour in August 1910, Bernier as fishery officer and Lavoie as customs officer boarded the Newfoundland ship *Diana* to look after these responsibilities, and similar duties were performed during the voyage home in 1911 at Kekerten, Blacklead, and Port Burwell.[134] Another Newfoundland ship encountered near Cape Kater off the eastern coast of Baffin Island fled and managed to escape, provoking Bernier to send photographs and a description of her to the department in the hope that she could be identified and action taken.[135] Second Officer Robert S. Janes also met with refusals or excuses when he tried to issue whaling licences to ships at Button Point on Bylot Island, and in one case, he apparently desisted in his attempt because the ship in question was "outside of the three mile limit."[136]

Bernier was not sent back to the Arctic after returning from this voyage, and patrols of the type that Wakeham, Low, and he had initiated were abandoned – at least for the time being. The change of government in 1911 was largely responsible, with the new Conservative administration unimpressed with the need for maintaining such activity. The Conservatives when in opposition had been critical of certain aspects of Bernier's work, which had actually been made possible largely through the personal interest of influential Liberals, such as Préfontaine, Brodeur, and (at least in the later stages) Laurier himself. Not surprisingly, the period of inactivity lasted through the First World War. "The war temporarily put an end to Arctic voyages," Bernier noted, and undoubtedly the shortage of shipping and the pressing need to throw all available men, money, and materials into the war effort would have made such voyages difficult to maintain even had this been desired.

Bernier made several more trips to the Arctic in an unofficial and private capacity before

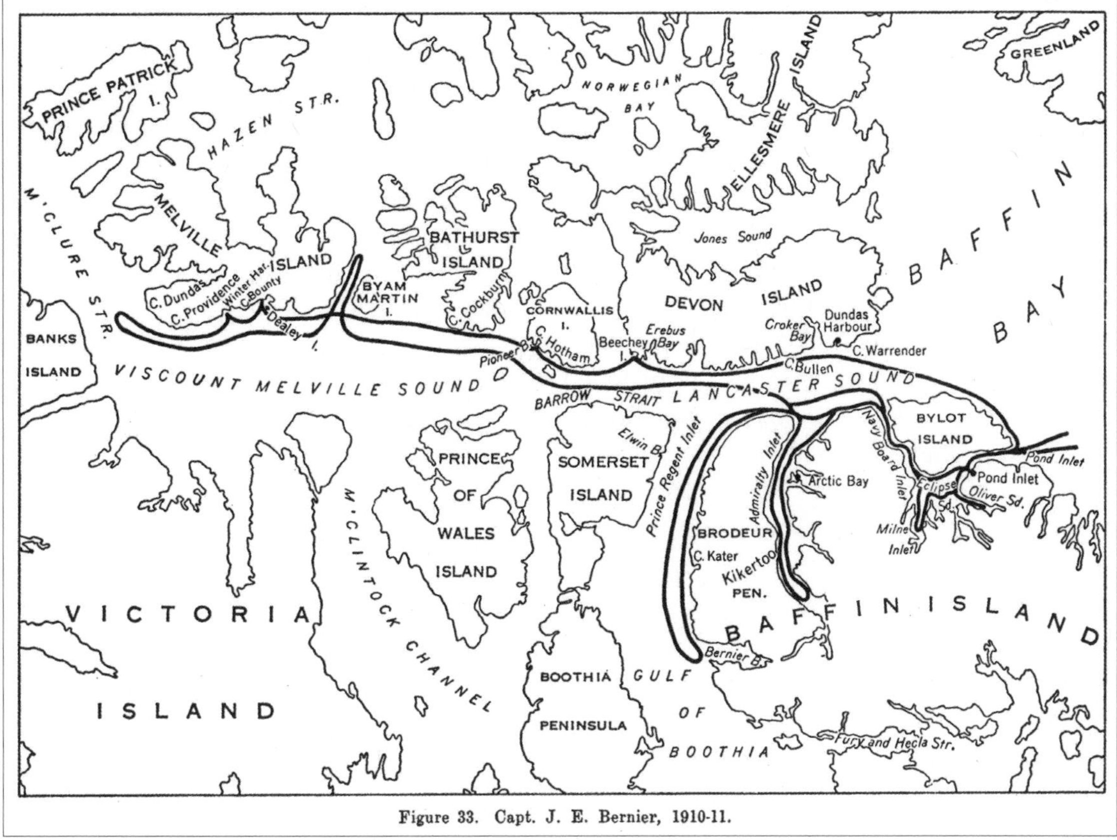

Figure 33. Capt. J. E. Bernier, 1910-11.

Figure 7-9: Bernier expedition, 1910–11. Andrew Taylor, *Geographical Discovery and Exploration in the Queen Elizabeth Islands* (Ottawa: Department of Mines and Technical Surveys, 1964), 118. *By permission of Natural Resources Canada.*

and during the war. The most notable was as commander of the *Minnie Maud* in 1912–13, on an expedition he himself organized to trade and search for gold on northern Baffin Island.[137] Reports by Robert Janes, his second officer on the 1910–11 expedition, that there was gold in the Salmon River valley proved to be inaccurate, but the small party was able to carry on a fairly profitable trade from their winter base at Albert Harbour. The most noteworthy feature of the expedition, however, was a series of remarkable journeys by crew member Alfred Tremblay, who, in almost unbelievably difficult circumstances, covered over 4,000 miles on foot while exploring in northern Baffin Island and Melville Peninsula.[138] He also mapped 3,000 miles of coastline and, after examining Fury and Hecla Strait, reported that although it has a water passage about thirty fathoms deep and is open during some seasons, it could never be relied upon as a shipping route because of permanent ice inside it and also at both eastern and western entrances.[139]

Canadian Arctic Expedition (1913–18)

Although government patrol voyages in eastern Arctic waters were temporarily discontinued in 1911, the official "Canadian Arctic Expedition" under Vilhjalmur Stefansson, which had been planned, organized, and dispatched to the western Arctic before hostilities broke out, continued its activities throughout the war years. Stefansson, born in Manitoba of Icelandic parents and raised in the Dakota Territory, already had a great deal of experience in the North, having made two summer trips to Iceland in 1904 and 1905,[140] an expedition down the Mackenzie River to the Canadian and Alaskan Arctic coast in connection with the luckless Mikkelsen-Leffingwell expedition in 1906–7,[141] and a longer expedition to the same region with Dr. Rudolph Martin Anderson in 1908–12.[142] These expeditions were all privately sponsored and financed: the two to Iceland with Harvard University funds, the one in 1906–7 by Harvard University and the University of Toronto, and that of 1908–12 by the American Museum of Natural History and the Geological Survey of Canada.[143]

For the expedition that he planned to begin in 1913, Stefansson had practically completed arrangements for financial support with the National Geographic Society, the American Museum of Natural History, the Harvard Travelers' Club, and the Geographical Society of Philadelphia. Thus, the expedition was originally conceived as one which would be supported by American institutions. Before these arrangements were finalized, however, Stefansson also approached Prime Minister Robert Borden for additional financial support. Borden responded that he would prefer the Canadian government take over all financial and other responsibility for the expedition because it was going to be conducted mainly in Canadian territory.[144] In Borden's own words, "I told Mr. Stefansson that while the public spirit, sympathy and co-operation of those important institutions were highly appreciated, the Government preferred that Canada should assume entire responsibility for the Expedition, as any lands yet undiscovered in these northern regions should be added to Canadian territory."[145] The upshot was that Stefansson, although remaining completely in charge, found himself commanding an official Canadian government expedition and, at least for certain purposes, acting as a representative of the Canadian government. Among other things, the expedition was authorized to take possession of any newly discovered lands for Canada and to investigate the activities of American whalers in the northern waters of Canada. The order in council of 22 February 1913, confirming the arrangements, made these points sufficiently clear:

> The expedition will conduct its explorations in waters and on lands under Canadian jurisdiction or included in the northern zone contiguous to the Canadian territory. It is, therefore, considered advisable that the expedition should be under the general direction of the Canadian Government and should sail under the Canadian flag....
>
> The expedition would also have occasion to examine into the operations of the American whalers which frequent the northern waters of Canada, and of putting into force the Customs and Fisheries Regulations which these whalers should observe....

> Mr. Stefansson proposes that his personal services should be free to the Canadian Government, but that the Government should provide the necessary funds to pay the expenses of the expedition; Mr. Stefansson to have full responsibility, and to have the choice of the men going on the expedition; and of the ships, provisions, and outfit needed for the trip....
>
> Any new or partly unknown lands which the expedition would touch would be observed, positions fixed, and the British flag would be planted on these lands.
>
> An Officer of the expedition would receive authority as Customs and Fishery Officer, and would be empowered to collect customs dues and fishery dues from the whaling vessels frequenting Canadian northern waters ....
>
> The Committee concur in the foregoing and submit the same for approval.[146]

Mild complications respecting this order in council arose when Canada's Governor General, the Duke of Connaught, sent copies of it to Colonial Secretary Lewis Vernon Harcourt in London on 1 March 1913.[147] Harcourt feared that the Canadian Cabinet might not have adequate formal authority to make the proposed annexations of territory, and on 10 May he replied as follows:

> I have the honour to acknowledge the receipt of His Royal Highness the Duke of Connaught's despatch No. 129 of the 1st of March on the subject of the expedition which the Canadian Government propose to send during the summer to explore the northern seas and the lands which lie to the north of the Continent.
>
> 1. I have read His Royal Highness's despatch with much interest and have communicated copies of it to the Foreign Office and to the Admiralty.
> 2. I take this opportunity of stating that His Majesty's Government have had under their consideration from time to time the question of the position of the territories to the north of Canada. As your Ministers are aware the Order in Council of the 31st July 1880 annexed to the Dominion of Canada all British territories and possessions in North America not already included with the Dominion and all islands adjacent to any such territories or possessions.
> 3. The full extent of the lands thus annexed has nowhere been formally defined and I observe in the fourth paragraph of the approved minute of the Privy Council which accompanied His Royal Highness's despatch, that reference is made to the expedition conducting explorations in waters and on lands under Canadian jurisdiction or included in the northern zone contiguous to the Canadian territory, while it is stated in the eleventh paragraph of the same minute that the

British Flag will be planted on any new or partly unknown lands.

4. So far as the lands on which the Flag is so planted are already, in virtue of the Order in Council, part of Canadian territory no question can arise as to the authority of your Government to deal with the matter, but as it is an established part of the law of the Empire that no Governor has a general delegation of authority to effect annexation of territory, His Majesty's Government are advised that in order to remove any doubt as to the validity of the proceedings of the Canadian Government – with the aim of which they are in full sympathy – it is desirable that formal authority should be given for the annexation of any lands to the north of Canada not already belonging to any foreign power which may not yet be British territory.

5. I have accordingly received His Majesty's commands to convey to the Governor-General authority, with the advice of the Privy Council of the Dominion, to take possession of and annex to, His Majesty's Dominions any lands lying to the north of Canadian territory as defined in the Order in Council of 1880 which are not within the jurisdiction of any civilized power.

6. As it is not desirable that any stress should be laid on the fact that a portion of the territory may not already be British, I do not consider it advisable that this despatch should be published, but it should be permanently recorded as giving authority for annexation to the Governor-General in Council.

7. I have to add that if your Ministers consider it desirable His Majesty's Government will be prepared, when the result of the expedition and the extent of the lands in question are known, to issue a fresh Order in Council supplementing that of July 31st, 1880.[148]

Copies of Harcourt's letter were sent to the several departments most immediately interested, and on 2 June an order in council was promulgated which authorized Stefansson to take possession of new lands for Canada. The key passages of the order, which was based upon a memorandum dated 27 May from Minister of the Naval Service John Douglas Hazen, were as follows:

> The Minister observes that in the course of these explorations it is possible that unknown lands may be discovered and it is advisable that Mr. Stefansson should be given proper authority to take possession of these lands for the Government of Canada, and to annex these lands to His Majesty's Dominions.
>
> The Minister, therefore, recommends that Mr. Vilhjalmur Stefansson be given authority to take possession of and annex to His Majesty's Dominions any lands lying to the

> north of Canadian territory which are not within the jurisdiction of any civilized Power.[149]

Although several departments were involved, the expedition was placed specifically under the direction of the Department of the Naval Service. On 29 May, Deputy Minister G. J. Desbarats wrote a long letter to Stefansson setting down in considerable detail the government's instructions concerning the expedition. These instructions recorded the understanding that there was to be a northern party which would devote itself primarily to exploration of the waters and lands of the Beaufort Sea region and a southern party which would carry on a variety of scientific work along the northern mainland coast. The following brief passage summarizes the basic organization of the expedition:

> The expedition will be under your personal direction and control, and you will give general directions to the various leaders of parties, as may be required.
>
> The Northern party will be under your own immediate charge and control.
>
> The Southern party will be under the direction of Dr. Anderson; the next senior officer of that party being Mr. Chipman, unless some other member is designated by Dr. Anderson.

It was thus made quite clear that Stefansson, besides being directly in charge of the northern party, was in overall command of the entire expedition.[150] Desbarats' letter also noted that the expedition's chief topographer, Kenneth Chipman, had been appointed customs officer based on a recommendation in the February order in council.[151]

The whaling ship *Karluk* was purchased and outfitted at Esquimalt in the spring of 1913. Sailing on 17 June, she joined the *Alaska* and *Mary Sachs*, two smaller vessels which the expedition acquired, at Nome. When the squadron departed from Nome in mid-July, Stefansson had the *Karluk* for the use of the northern party, Anderson had the *Alaska* for the use of the southern party, and the *Mary Sachs*, under Captain Peter Bernard, was to function first as a supply ship and then as a floating base for oceanographic research. It was thus planned that the three ships would operate singly and to some extent independently; however, they and the personnel aboard them became separated in a way that had not been anticipated, with disastrous results.

The *Alaska* stopped at Teller in Bering Strait for needed repairs, but afterwards it succeeded in getting as far as Collinson Point on the northern Alaska coast, about 100 miles west of the Yukon boundary. This became the southern party's winter headquarters in 1913–14. For the remaining two years of this party's work, Anderson made his headquarters at Bernard Harbour in Dolphin and Union Strait, and the *Alaska* took the entire party out through Bering Strait in the summer of 1916. The impressive scientific work of this group was published in a series of voluminous reports by several government departments and agencies over the next three decades.[152]

The *Karluk* was caught in the ice near Camden Bay, about 200 miles beyond Point Barrow, on 13 August. Stefansson and several others became separated from the ship when they went ashore on a hunting trip, and they never saw her again. With Captain Bob Bartlett in command, she drifted to a point about sixty miles northeast of Wrangel Island, where she

FIGURE 7-10: CANADIAN ARCTIC EXPEDITION PARTY, NOME, ALASKA, CA. 1913. *RUDOLPH MARTIN ANDERSON / LIBRARY AND ARCHIVES CANADA / E002712837.*

sank on 11 January 1914. Bartlett took the party to Wrangel Island and then, with only one Inuk as companion, made a difficult winter trip to the Siberian coast and thence to St. Michael in Alaska. From there, news of the disaster was sent by telegraph to Ottawa, and arrangements were made to send several ships to Wrangel Island from Alaska and Siberia. The *King and Winge* succeeded in pushing through the ice and rescuing the survivors early in September, but of the twenty-five who had been on the *Karluk* drift, eleven lost their lives, either trying to reach Wrangel Island or after getting there.[153]

After being separated from his ship, Stefansson spent the following winter on the coast, endeavouring to find men, supplies, and equipment to replace those that had been lost. His task was complicated by the fact that a considerable number of the southern party, led by Dr. Anderson, were now inclined to deny his position as commander and to refuse any materials or co-operation that would help him to carry out the work of the northern party. Nevertheless, by improvisation and by taking advantage of the greater scope for decision and action that fell to him as commander, he was able to accomplish a good deal of what he wanted to do. With the two volunteers Storker Storkerson and Ole Andreasen accompanying him, he made a three-month sledge journey in the spring of 1914 across the ice from the Alaska coast to Banks Island, intending primarily to demonstrate that sea creatures could be secured in sufficient quantities on such a trip to sustain an exploring party. During the next three years, keeping only minimum contact with the mainland, he and small supporting parties maintained themselves in the islands,

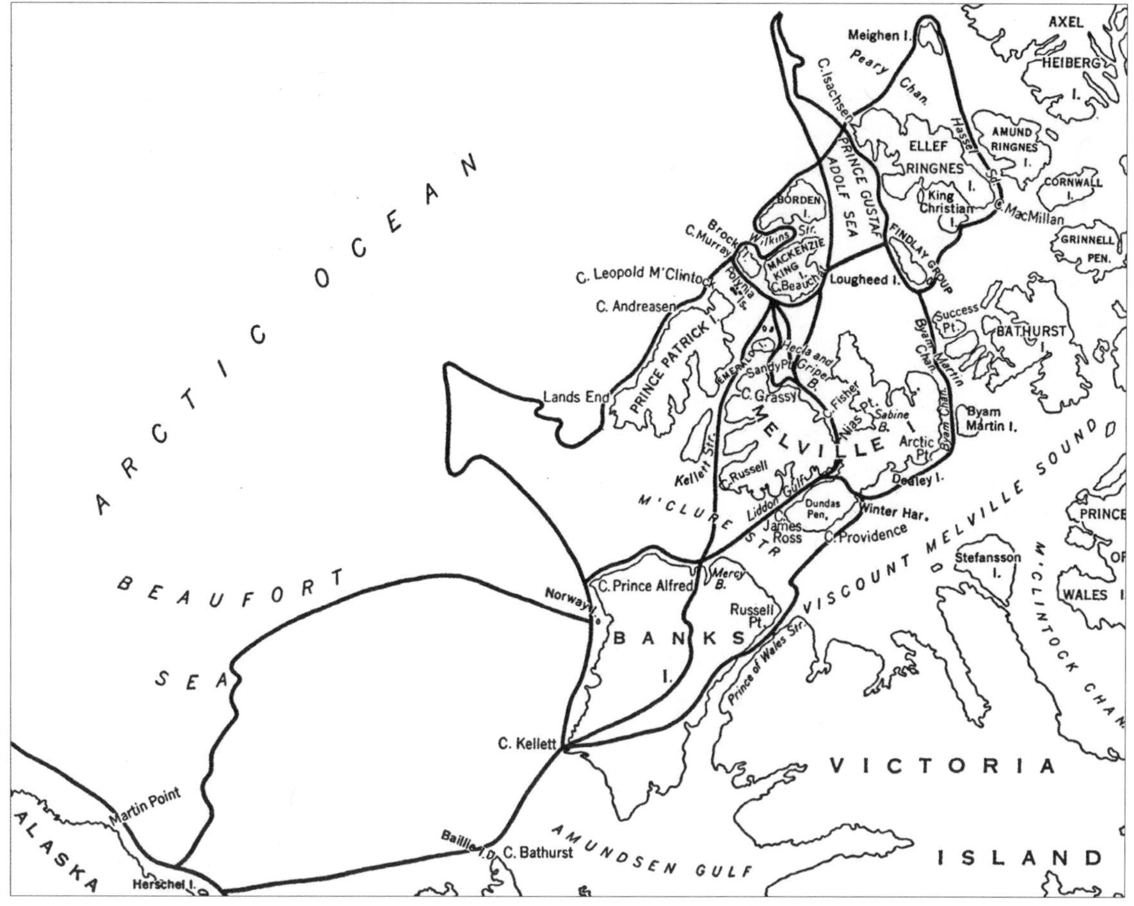

Figure 7-11: Stefansson's expedition, 1913–18. Andrew Taylor, *Geographical Discovery and Exploration in the Queen Elizabeth Islands* (Ottawa: Department of Mines and Technical Surveys, 1964), 121. *By permission of Natural Resources Canada.*

establishing winter bases successively at Cape Kellett on the west coast of Banks Island (1914–15), again at Cape Kellett and also at two other places on or near Banks Island (1915–16), and at Liddon Gulf on the south coast of Melville Island (1916–17). From these bases, Stefansson, with various companions, carried out a succession of exploratory expeditions over the ice of Beaufort Sea and then north of Prince Patrick Island in 1915, across Melville Island and north of the Ringnes Islands in 1916, and again north of the Ringnes Islands to a high of nearly 81° in 1917. The northern party left the islands in the summer of 1917, but an accident to their ship compelled them to spend another winter in the north. Storkerson, who in 1917 had explored most of the unknown part of the northeast coastline of Victoria Island that Godfred Hansen of Amundsen's expedition had been unable to reach in 1905, now used the additional time and opportunity in 1918 to carry out a six-months drift on an ice floe. Stefansson was taken seriously ill and spent long periods of recovery at Herschel Island and Fort Yukon, in consequence not getting back to southern regions until September 1918.[154]

In the present context, two matters connected with this expedition are of particular importance: the sojourn of the party from the *Karluk* on Wrangel Island in 1914 and Stefansson's own discovery of new islands during his sledging trips to the north. The first is important because, perhaps more than any other single factor, it gave Stefansson the impulse and resolve several years later to establish a claim to Wrangel Island, thus setting off a complicated tangle that narrowly missed becoming a major international dispute. The *Karluk* survivors were in actual occupation of the island, which they found completely uninhabited, for a period of almost six months, and during this time they flew the British flag and generally carried on as if they were monarchs of the inhospitable country they surveyed. The second is important because one of Stefansson's main responsibilities, from the Canadian government's point of view, was to discover new islands and claim them for Canada.

On 18 June 1915, while on his spring sledging trip, Stefansson and his three companions sighted new land from the northernmost tip of Prince Patrick Island. The island, which was later christened Brock Island after the director of the Canadian Geological Survey,[155] was claimed by building a gravel mound and depositing in it this record:

> June 20, 2 A. M.
>
> This land was first seen, so far as I know, by Storker Storkerson of the Canadian Arctic Expedition, June 18, 1915, at 2 A. M. from a point on the ice distant from the cairn where this record is left about fourteen miles due west (true). From an ice cake about 40 ft. high, land was seen extending from ExN to NExE. The first man to land here was Ole Andreasen of the same Expedition at 1:50 A. M. June 19th.
>
> "By authority especially vested in me for that purpose, I have to-day hoisted the flag of the Empire and have taken possession of the land in the name of His Majesty King George V on behalf of the Dominion of Canada."
>
> "Vilhjalmur Stefansson,"
> Commander,
> Canadian Arctic Expedition,
> Witnesses: "Storker Storkerson, Ole Andreasen, Karl Thomsen."
>
> Party, dogs (13) and equipment, all well. Shall proceed eastward along this coast some distance, should it prove extensive, and then south across or around Melville Island to the Expedition head-quarters near Cape Kellett, Banks Island.[156]

The next year, Stefansson discovered that there was another, larger island beyond Brock,[157] which was named Borden Island in honour of the Prime Minister.[158] On the 1916 sledging trip, Stefansson discovered more new islands: Meighen and Perley to the north of Ellef Ringnes Island and Lougheed (as distinct from Sverdrup's King Christian Land) to the south of it. He claimed these islands for Canada and left records in cairns, as in the case of the first discovery.[159]

The day after claiming Brock Island, Stefansson expressed his thoughts in a lengthy letter to Prime Minister Borden, which eventually reached its destination. It is worth reproducing in full:

N. Lat. 77° 30', W. Long. 113° Approx.
June 21st., 1915.

Dear Mr. Borden:

I do not know if for the past two years you have taken especial interest in our Arctic Expedition, but I have always felt that the matter of having new land north of Canada discovered and explored by Canadians in the service of the Government, appeared to you an important one. I write this on a land that it has been our fortune to discover and take possession of for Canada. More than anyone else in the Government I have you to thank for the support which has enabled us to accomplish at least part of the purpose of this Expedition, the writing of this letter may therefore seem superfluous, for it is written to urge the fitness and importance of the continuance by Canadians in the service of the Government of the work of exploring the region between the mainland and the pole until the last mystery is unveiled. We shall do what we can next year, but when the three years assigned us are up there will yet remain much to do. We have had misfortunes, but have accomplished a part of our work nevertheless. What you think of how we have met adverse conditions I do not know, and I do not write to plead any personal cause. But I feel strongly not only that Canada should explore the regions to which she lays claim as far as the pole; it is true also that by doing so she makes good her claims. I shall remain ready to volunteer my services for this work, but if it shall seem that my record does not earn further support, then let another carry on the work, so he is a Canadian in Canadian service.

Vilhjalmur Stefansson[160]

Stefansson returned to Ottawa in the autumn of 1918 eager for more Arctic service, but the government was completely occupied with the war and the armistice. In fact, apart from the necessary attention to his own expedition, there had been little visible evidence of official interest or activity in the far north for several years. When activity resumed, it was in circumstances that neither Stefansson nor the government could have foreseen.

8

The Sector Principle and the Background of Canada's Sector Claim

The sector principle or theory has been advocated as a simple, convenient, and logical method of apportioning territory in the polar regions. As such, it ranks as one of the most interesting geographical or geopolitical concepts of the twentieth century, and it has been applied in striking fashion in various instances. It has special significance for Canada because there is a greater area of island territory north of the Canadian mainland than there is north of the mainland of any other state bordering on the Arctic Ocean. If the sector principle came to be generally recognized among the nations and won formal acceptance in international law, Canada's sovereignty over almost all the Arctic territories she has claimed would automatically be validated,[1] and all the effort she has lavished upon cementing her title to them by other means would turn out to have been unnecessary.

In plane geometry, a sector of a circle is a portion of the circle plane bounded by two radii and the included arc, the resulting figure having a shape, to use the common illustration, exactly like that of a two-dimensional representation of an ordinary piece of pie. In spherical geometry, with the third dimension added, a sector becomes a corresponding part of the surface of a sphere. Geographically, a polar sector is a region of similar shape, with either the North Pole or the South Pole at the centre of the circle, usually with two meridians of longitude as the two radii, and usually with either an irregular territorial coastline or a parallel of latitude as the arc of the circle.[2]

The sector principle itself, as put forward by Canadian Senator Pascal Poirier in a Senate speech in 1907,[3] is simple and straightforward. It asserts that each state with a continental Arctic coastline automatically inherits all the islands in the sector between this coastline and the North Pole, which are enclosed by lines of longitude drawn from the eastern and western extremities of the same coastline to the pole. It is apparent, however, that if this concept is followed, Arctic sectors will not be drawn with geometrical precision, owing to the above-mentioned irregularity of the southern boundaries and also the need to take account of other irregularities (for example, the curving water passage between Canadian and Danish Arctic territories). In the Antarctic, the theoretical justification for sectors is missing, since there are no adjacent continental coastlines from which sectors might be drawn, and the only coastline is that of the Antarctic continent itself. Sectors in Antarctica, which are usually based upon lines of latitude in the open sea, have in reality been drawn to mark out coveted parts of the southern continent, where presumably limited amounts of national activity have taken place, rather than in consequence of the principle as conceived for the polar

Figure 8-1: Hon. Pascal Poirier, Senator, May 1892. *Topley Studio Fonds / Library and Archives Canada / PA-033713.*

islands in the northern hemisphere. It should be added, of course, that some of the Antarctic sectors (notably the Australian, New Zealand, Chilean, and Argentinean) are located roughly south of the claimant states, but since the distances in between are approximately 500 or 600 miles at the minimum and several times as much at the maximum, it would appear to be stretching any "principle" based upon the sector concept rather far to assert a claim on that basis.

The sector principle, although generally attributed to Senator Poirier, clearly did not originate with his speech. Poirier himself remarked that it was "not a novel affair" and mentioned a meeting of the Arctic Club in New York the year before, attended by Captain Bernier, where a sector division had been proposed as a means of settling territorial questions in Arctic regions. There are much older precedents, at least for the notion of marking out territories by drawing meridian lines to one of the poles, and in some cases even from pole to pole. In addition, there is a fairly specific background, of uncertain but obvious relevance, to Poirier's proposal as put forward in 1907.

An outstanding early example of a territorial demarcation by means of a meridian line is Pope Alexander VI's famous bull *Inter Caetera* of 4 May 1493, which made a sweeping grant of New World territories to the monarchs of Spain in the following terms:

> We … give, grant, and assign to you and your heirs and successors, kings of Castile and Leon, forever, together with all their dominions, cities, camps, places, and villages, and all rights, jurisdictional and appurtenances, all islands and mainlands found and to be found, discovered and to be discovered towards the west and south, by drawing and establishing a line from the Arctic pole, namely the north, to the Antarctic pole, namely the south, no matter whether the said mainlands and islands are found and to be found in the direction of India or towards any other quarter, the said line to be distant one hundred leagues towards the west and south from any or the islands commonly known as the Azores and Cape Verde.[4]

A little further on, the bull in equally categorical language forbade all persons to go without the permission of the Spanish monarchs "for the purpose of trade or any other reason to the islands or mainlands" beyond the same line.

Portuguese dissatisfaction with this arrangement led to the Treaty of Tordesillas on 7 June 1494, in which Spain and Portugal took the liberty of moving the pope's line to the west, so as to establish a dividing line between Spanish and Portuguese colonial territories that was more agreeable to Portugal. Their representatives "covenanted and agreed that a boundary or straight line be determined and drawn north and south, from pole to pole, on the said ocean sea, from the Arctic to the Antarctic pole."[5] Thirty-five years afterwards, Spain and Portugal established a similar dividing line on the other side of the globe. On 22 April 1529, by the Treaty of Saragossa, Spanish and Portuguese plenipotentiaries covenanted and agreed that

> a line must be determined from pole to pole, that is to say, from north to south, by a semicircle extending northeast by east nineteen degrees from Molucca, to which number of degrees correspond almost seventeen degrees on the equinoctial, amounting to two hundred and ninety-seven and one-half leagues east of the islands of Molucca, allowing seventeen and one-half leagues to an equinoctial degree.[6]

Further examples of the use of meridian lines to demarcate boundaries are to be seen in the British and American treaties with Russia, on the subject of Alaska, during the nineteenth century.[7] The Anglo-Russian treaty of 28 February 1825 fixed the meridian of 141° as the dividing line between British and Russian possessions in the northwestern part of the continent. In the words of the treaty:

> The line of demarcation shall follow the summit of the mountains situated parallel to the Coast, as far as the point of intersection of the 141st degree of West longitude (of the same Meridian); and, finally, from the said point of intersection, the said Meridian Line of the 141st degree, in its prolongation as far as the Frozen Ocean, shall form the

> limit between the Russian and British Possessions on the Continent a America to the North-West.[8]

In the French version of the treaty, the expression "in its prolongation as far as the Frozen Ocean" reads "dans son prolongement, jusqu'à la Mer Glaciale," and much ink has been spilled in the endeavour to find an exact meaning for the two versions. That they were intended to mean the same thing can hardly be doubted but, granting this, several interpretations are at least conceivable:

> (1) "to where land ends and salt water begins,"
>
> (2) "to where the permanent arctic pack, as distinct from seasonally open coastal water, begins,"
>
> (3) "to the main body of the Arctic Ocean, as distinct from Beaufort Sea,"
>
> (4) "as far as the beginning of the Frozen Ocean," and
>
> (5) "as far as and including the Frozen Ocean."[9]

The Russian-American treaty of 30 March 1867, by which the United States purchased Alaska, said that the eastern boundary of the territory was to be the line "established by the convention between Russia and Great Britain, of February 28–16, 1825" and repeated its provisions. The western boundary was also placed on a meridian line, as follows:

> The western limit within which the territories and dominion conveyed, are contained, passes through a point in Behring's straits on the parallel of sixty-five degrees thirty minutes north latitude, at its intersection by the meridian which passes midway between the islands of Krusenstern, or Ignalook, and the island of Ratmanoff, or Noonarbook, and proceeds due north, without limitation, into the same Frozen Ocean.[10]

How far "without limitation" meant is a question that has also been discussed a good deal. It could hardly have been intended to mean "beyond the North Pole," if indeed any particular construction was put upon it. On the other hand, it could reasonably be interpreted to have meant "as far as the North Pole." This is the view taken by US lawyer and treaty expert David Hunter Miller, who wrote, "These words 'without limitation' are pretty strong words. They come very near to fixing the territorial rights of Russia and the United States, so far as those two countries could then fix them, up to the pole."[11]

The foregoing examples show that the practice of marking out territories by drawing boundary lines along meridians of longitude into the polar regions, and in some cases as far as one or both poles, was by no means unknown. Regarding the application of the sector principle to claim all lands between such lines, a number of theoretical explanations, or justifications, or analogies have been offered.

Miller said that Canada's sector claim was not wholly without foundation or precedent and that it bore some analogy to the "back country" or "hinterland" theory regarding territory stretching away from the coast. More accurately, he said, it rested partly on the notion of "territorial propinquity." He added that claims based upon contiguity are not unknown, although there is no well-defined principle to support them, and that Canada's claim in this sense was natural if not logical. He suggested also that the Canadian sector theory was based partly upon the Alaska treaties.[12]

The Soviet jurist W. L. Lakhtine related the sector idea to "regions of attraction," of which he spoke approvingly, saying that "we must disavow the whole triple formula of occupation, i.e., discovery, occupation and notification" and that "the doctrine of occupation of Polar territories must be replaced by the doctrine of region of attraction."[13]

To T.E.M. McKitterick, the sector principle was to be associated with the concept of sovereignty over a hinterland:

> The nearest analogy that can be found in temperate or tropical climates is the old "hinterland" theory. Under this doctrine a state possessing settlements on the coast of a continent could claim sovereignty in some cases limited) over the hinterland, until either the middle line of the continent, the watershed or some other suitable and obvious boundary was reached.... The sector theory is the last survivor of the old "hinterland" principle as applied to continents, and it appears to have no stronger basis in international law than that now discredited theory.[14]

Gustav Smedal summarized the theoretical justifications which have been put forward for the sector principle, mentioning the concepts of the hinterland and of contiguity or propinquity, the difficulties of genuinely effective appropriation in the polar regions, the practicality of the sector principle, and the propriety of leaving the polar regions to nearby states with "sufficient experience" to look after them. In his own view all of them lacked validity.[15]

Friedrich von der Heydte saw the sector principle as relying upon the doctrine of contiguity, which to him was valid if applied with reason. He admitted, however, that it was not applied with reason in the polar regions but rather was exaggerated and abused.[16] Oscar Svarlien also took the view that the sector principle was based essentially upon the doctrine of contiguity,[17] as did L. M. Gould, who wrote:

> The sector principle is apparently derived from the "doctrine of continuity" used in past centuries to justify the extension of colonies into the hinterlands where actual physical control was not possible.... "Contiguity" is a further, more tenuous, extension of the principle of continuity and justifies claim to lands separated even by large areas of oceanic waters, from the claimant state.[18]

H. J. Taubenfeld expressed a similar view in rather similar terms:[19]

> Examples of such bases and precedents for the sector principle are not hard to find. Some of the early colonial grants and charters in North America purported to assign territories stretching far into the interior, and in some cases even from sea to sea. The Second Chapter of Virginia, dated May 23, 1609, granted....
>
> ....all those Lands, Countries, and Territories, situate, lying, and being, in that Part of America called Virginia ... and all that Space and Circuit of Land, lying from the Sea

> Coast of the Precinct aforesaid, up into the Land, throughout from Sea to Sea, west, and Northwest....[20]

Similarly, the First Charter of Massachusetts of 4 March 1629 granted

> all Landes and Hereditaments whatsoever, lyeing within the Lymitts aforesaide, North and South, in latitude and Bredth, and in Length, and Longitude, of and within all the Bredth aforesaide, throughout the mayne Landes there, from the Atlantick and Westerne Sea and Ocean on the Easte Parte, to the South Sea on the West Parte.[21]

Such grants may perhaps be regarded as exaggerated applications of the hinterland concept spoken of by Miller, M. F. Lindley, and McKitterick. In referring to the watershed as a variant of the hinterland, McKitterick cites the Andes as an apparent illustration of its use, saying that "in South America the watershed of the Andes, being in itself a formidable barrier to progress inland, seem to have been the generally accepted division (a fact which would account for the vast size of Portuguese Brazil as compared with the Spanish colonies of Peru and Ecuador)."[22]

On 27 April 1670, Louis XIV granted to the Dutchman Laurens Van Heemskerk a concession of "all the lands which have been and shall be discovered by him in all North America entered from above Canada towards the North Pole, and extending to the South Sea as much and as far as he can reach." Van Heemskerk's ship was caught in a storm, however, and he did not succeed in his plan to sail into Hudson Bay.[23] King Charles II's charter of 2 May 1670 to the Hudson's Bay Company was more modest with regard to the territories bestowed, but less modest in that its validity was not considered to depend upon the factor of discovery. It granted

> the sole Trade and Commerce of all those Seas Streightes Bayes Rivers Lakes Creekes and Soundes in whatsoever Latitude they shall bee that lye within the entrance of the Straightes commonly called Hudsons Streightes together with all the Landes and Territoryes upon the Countryes Coastes and confynes of the Seas Bayes Lakes Rivers Creekes and Soundes aforesaid that are not already actually possessed by or granted to any of our Subjectes or possessed by the Subjectes of any other Christian Prince or State.[24]

The company put its own interpretation on the extent of this grant and, when asked to inform the Lords Commissioners of Trade and Plantations of the limits of its territory in 1750, it stated that it possessed "all the Lands that lye at the North end or on the North side or Coast of the said [Hudson] Bay and extending from the Bay Northwards to the utmost Limits of the Lands there towards the North Pole."[25] As time went on, the company's view of its holdings seemed to crystallize around the concept that, under the charter, Rupert's Land legitimately included all territories draining into Hudson Bay and Strait, and Governor George Simpson firmly stated this claim before the Select Committee of the British House of Commons in 1857.[26]

It was also not unusual for explorers to claim vast expanses of territory stretching far into a continental interior, and in some cases right across it or across adjacent bodies of water. In 1631–32, Captain Thomas James, in the service of some Bristol merchants, wintered on Charlton Island in James Bay and claimed all surrounding territory "westward, as farre as Nova Albion, and to the Northward to the Latitude of 80 Degrees" for King Charles I.[27] On 14 June 1671, Sieur Simon-François Daumont de Saint-Lusson, dispatched by Intendant Jean Talon, made a formal proclamation at Sault Ste. Marie claiming as French all territories bounded by the seas of the North (Hudson Bay and Strait) and the South (the Pacific Ocean).[28] There are many similar cases of sweeping claim by explorers, far too numerous to be recited here.[29] Such claims ranged from completely official all the way to completely unofficial, depending upon individual circumstances.

In the dispute between the United States and Spain in 1805 over the western boundary of Louisiana, American commissioners William Pinckney and James Monroe argued that the principles of the watershed and the middle distance were applicable to the case. They enunciated the two principles in the following terms:

> The first of these is, that when any European Nation takes possession of any extent of Sea Coast, that possession is understood as extending into the interior Country, to the sources of the Rivers emptying within that Coast, to all their branches, and the Country they cover, and to give it a right in exclusion of all other Nations to the same ….
>
> The second is, that whenever one European Nation makes a discovery and takes possession of any portion of that Continent, and another afterwards does the same at some distance from it, where the Boundary between them is not determined by the principle above-mentioned, the middle distance becomes such of course.[30]

In the 1880s, Portugal claimed territories in Central Africa between its coastal colonies of Mozambique and Angola, which would have given her a solid block of land stretching from the Indian Ocean to the Atlantic Ocean. It was able to get recognition of her claim from France[31] and Germany[32] by means of separate treaties in 1886, but Great Britain, who had designs on those territories herself, registered strong objections.[33] The outcome was the Anglo-Portuguese treaty of 11 June 1891, which left Great Britain with a large portion of the disputed territory, and thus kept the two Portuguese colonies separated.[34]

Some of the foregoing illustrations have little or nothing to do with polar territories, but collectively they all indicate that it was by no means unusual to make extensive claims, either to continental territories stretching inland or to island territories extending outward from a coastline. A glance at a few Canadian orders in council and maps will show that there was a developing inclination to apply this approach to the demarcation of Canada's Arctic territories, within sector or other lines, some years before Senator Poirier's speech in 1907.

The joint address of the Canadian Senate and House of Commons on 3 May 1878, asking for the transfer of the Arctic territories, suggested that they should be bounded as follows:

> On the East by the Atlantic Ocean, which boundary shall extend towards the North by Davis Straits, Baffin's Bay, Smith's Straits and Kennedy Channel, including all the islands in, and, adjacent thereto, which belong to Great Britain by right of discovery or otherwise;

> on the North the Boundary shall be so extended as to include the entire continent to the Arctic Ocean, and all the islands in the same westward to the one hundred and forty-first meridian west of Greenwich; and on the North-West by the United States Territory of Alaska.[35]

The order in council of 18 December 1897, redefining the provisional districts, made some use of sector lines, although the earlier order in council of 2 October 1895 had not done so. It stated that the District of Franklin would include "all those lands and islands comprised between the one hundred and forty-first meridian of longitude west of Greenwich on the west and Davis Strait, Baffin Bay, Smith Sound, Kennedy Channel and Robeson Channel on the east which are not included in any other Provisional District." The map accompanying the order showed clearly the sector lines running down the 141st meridian to the mainland coast and down the 60th meridian to the channel separating Greenland from the archipelago, then through the middle of this channel to a point in Davis Strait, and then rather vaguely to the northernmost extremity of Labrador at the eastern entrance of Hudson Strait.[36]

An official Department of the Interior map made by departmental geographer James White in 1904 to accompany Dr. W. F. King's memorandum dated 7 May of the same year and titled "Explorations in Northern Canada and Adjacent Portions of Greenland and Alaska" similarly shows both western and eastern sector lines. However, the eastern line extends south only to the approximate point where it reaches the channel between Greenland and Ellesmere Island.[37] Another version of the same map, but with different detail, shows the sector lines in exactly the same way.

Captain Bernier had been expounding the sector concept for several years before 1907, and he may have planted the germ of the idea in Poirier's mind. La Société de géographie du Québec, which had heard Bernier speak and had evidently fallen under his influence, sent Prime Minister Laurier a report dated 23 May 1899, which strongly endorsed Bernier's plan for a polar drift and also observed, "le Canada doit nécessairement, tout en se terminant à l'Ouest au méridien d'Alaska, voir prolonger ce méridian le 140ème [*sic*], jusque' au Pôle. Vers l'Est ce serait le 60 ème méridien séparant le Canada du Greenland."[38]

On 9 February 1901, the *Montreal Witness*, after an interview with Bernier, quoted him as saying:

> If the boundary between Canada and Alaska were continued northward it would strike the North Pole. A similar line through Baffin Bay prolonged to the pole should be Canada's northeasterly frontier, and if our expedition reached the pole and we planted the flag there we could claim the whole country to the north of us by right of discovery.[39]

Similar statements were made from time to time in Parliament, usually in connection with Bernier and his projects. For example, on 1 May 1902, when Liberal John Charlton was trying to enlist support for Bernier's proposed drift across the Arctic Ocean, he remarked that one of the benefits of the voyage would be that "we would establish our right to all the territories and islands and seas that might lie between our present northern boundary and the north pole itself – all that vast region between the 141st parallel of longitude on the west, and Baffin's Bay and Grant land on the east."[40] In the course of the same debate, Liberal Thomas Barnard Flint of Yarmouth, who also supported Bernier's plan, made a similar comment:

> There can be no doubt, from a fair understanding of our position as the controller of the northern half of this North American continent, that the jurisdiction of Canada extends to the pole. At any rate, if we are the first to circumnavigate the sea and establish the British flag on any point of land discovered there prior discovery and prior occupation will give Great Britain through Canada absolute jurisdiction for all time forward over those regions.[41]

Charlton returned to the subject on 30 September 1903 and spoke in similar vein, saying that "the discovery of the Pole would give us a standing with regard to territorial acquisition in the north between the Pole and the northern coast of the continent, which we would not otherwise have."[42] Conservative Adam Carr Bell remarked:

> Our cousins in the United States have made repeated efforts to discover the Pole, and I think if any people in the world should look upon it as their peculiar business, and finally succeed in making that discovery, it is the people of Canada, because the North Pole when discovered will unquestionably form part of this country....
>
> There can be equally no doubt that it may be of great material advantage to Canada to establish finally and indisputably her claim and title to all the lands lying on the north part of this continent.[43]

He was followed by Conservative David Henderson, who said:

> Now, if Captain Bernier succeeds in locating the pole and planting thereon the British flag, taking possession of whatever there is in land or sea, we will certainly have a right to claim possession in the name of the King of England of everything that lies between the north pole and the now known Dominion of Canada. We will then not be troubled in the future with any Alaska boundary disputes in that direction, but will have the first claim to everything lying between what we now know as the Dominion of Canada and the North Pole.[44]

Conservative Seymour Gourley, in the course of a characteristically dogmatic and chauvinistic speech, contributed that "so far as I am concerned, I will support this proposal because I do not think there is the slightest doubt about Canada owning every foot of territory from here to the North Pole. It is contiguous to Canada, and we own every foot of it by right of discovery and exploration."[45]

Less was said on the subject in the Senate prior to Poirier's famous speech, although on 18 July 1905 the following exchange occurred in that body:

> *Hon. Auguste-Charles-Philippe-Robert Landry*: How far north does Rupert's Land go?

> *Hon. William Templeman*: To the North Pole.
>
> *Hon. Richard William Scott*: This would include through the Arctic oceans.[46]

Senator Poirier himself was one of those who had already spoken of the need to find ways and means of securing Canada's northern territories and her northern frontier. Speaking of the Alaska Boundary Award on 20 October 1903, he made these remarks:

> I think it is time we called a halt and looked forward to see how many other slices we may be called upon to part with.... The next possible arbitration may be concerning Hudson Bay.... Just consider what our position will be if the Americans discover the North Pole and take possession of it.[47]

From all this evidence, and contrary to both the general impression and various particular statements which have been made on the subject, it is clear that the sector principle did not really originate with Senator Poirier's speech on 20 February 1907, or even with Poirier himself.[48] There was actually a long historical background of thought and action, including specific conventions, decrees, and claims, which were probably of genuine though indeterminable significance in providing precedents. In addition there was, as indicated, a specifically Canadian background, which shows that the sector concept had been developing for several years. Nonetheless, Poirier made a more deliberate, precise, and comprehensive exposition of the sector principle than any of his predecessors had done, and as time has passed, it has certainly attracted more attention. It is therefore appropriate, no doubt, that the principle should be generally associated with his name.

Poirier began his speech with the motion that "it be resolved that the Senate is of opinion that the time has come for Canada to make a formal declaration of possession of the lands and islands situated in the north of the Dominion, and extending to the north pole."[49] He referred to various alleged American acts of possession, and he expressed the belief that Canada should take action and assert as publicly as possible her dominion over these lands. Then, recounting at some length the background of exploration and other activity in the region, he proceeded to enumerate the various grounds upon which Canada could claim ownership. The first three of these were discovery, which was almost exclusively British; occupancy, "as much as occupancy can take place"; and Canada's inheritance of all the rights of the Hudson's Bay Company. He then went on:

> We have a fourth claim, we can establish a fourth ground for ownership for all the lands and islands that extend from the arctic circle up to the north pole. Last year, I think it was, when our Capt. Bernier was in New York, a guest of the Arctic club, the question being mooted as to the ownership of Arctic lands, it was proposed and agreed – and this is not a novel affair – that in future partition, of northern lands, a country whose possession to-day goes up to the Arctic regions, will have a right, or should have a right, or has a right to all the lands that are to be found in the waters between a line extending from its eastern extremity north, and another line extending from the western extremity north.

All the lands between the two lines up to the north pole should belong and do belong to the country whose territory abuts up there. Now if we take our geography, it is a simple matter. We find that going around the earth, at the latitude of say between 70 and 80 degrees parallel, all the lands and islands up towards the pole from the 5th to the 32nd degree of longitude east, belong to Norway and Sweden. From the western extremity of the Muskovite empire to its eastern extremity, across Lapland, Archangel and Siberia, that is from about the 32nd to the 190th east, and then overlapping the western hemisphere by ten degrees or 170 degrees west, coinciding with the Behring strait, all north of that tract which is equal to two-fifths of the whole world, is claimed by Russia, Franz Joseph Land excepted. The distance east and west of Franz Joseph Land is about ten degrees. Now, continuing easterly from the Behring strait 170 degrees west to 141 degrees west, we cross the territory of Alaska. That is claimed by the United States, and no one will venture to go up north between those two lines and take possession of any land, or any island that may be discovered between its borders and the north pole. From 141 to 60 degrees west we are on Canadian territory. That is the territory that has been discovered by the seamen of England, that has been traversed by McClure and by Franklin. It is the territory that has been taken possession of by the Hudson Bay Company, and it is the territory that we claim, and I hold that no foreigner has a right to go and hoist a flag on it up to the north pole, because it is not only within the sphere of possession of England, but it is in the actual possession of England. This partition of the polar regions seems to be the most natural, because it is simply a geographical one. By that means difficulties would be avoided, and there would be no cause for trouble between interested countries. Every country bordering on the Arctic regions would simply extend its possessions up to the north pole.[50]

Poirier did not grant a sector to Denmark, and in fact he left the portion from 60° W to 5° E unassigned, even though it contains Danish Greenland. Smedal has suggested that the reason for the omission may have been that Denmark, although possessing Arctic territory, does not itself extend to Arctic regions.[51] It is also noticeable that, except in Canada's case, Poirier was content with approximations – for example, 17° W for the dividing line between the Russian and American sectors. He also overlooked or ignored the fact that once Norway and Sweden separated in 1905, Sweden was shut off from the Arctic Ocean and thus, presumably, would not be entitled to share a sector.

On one important point the Senator's speech was not entirely clear. At the beginning he referred to "the Canadian Arctic waters," and the passage quoted above contains the words: "From 141 to 60 degrees west we are on Canadian territory ... and I hold that no foreigner has a right to go and hoist a flag on it up to the north pole." This could conceivably have been intended to mean that Canada was entitled to everything within the specified boundaries

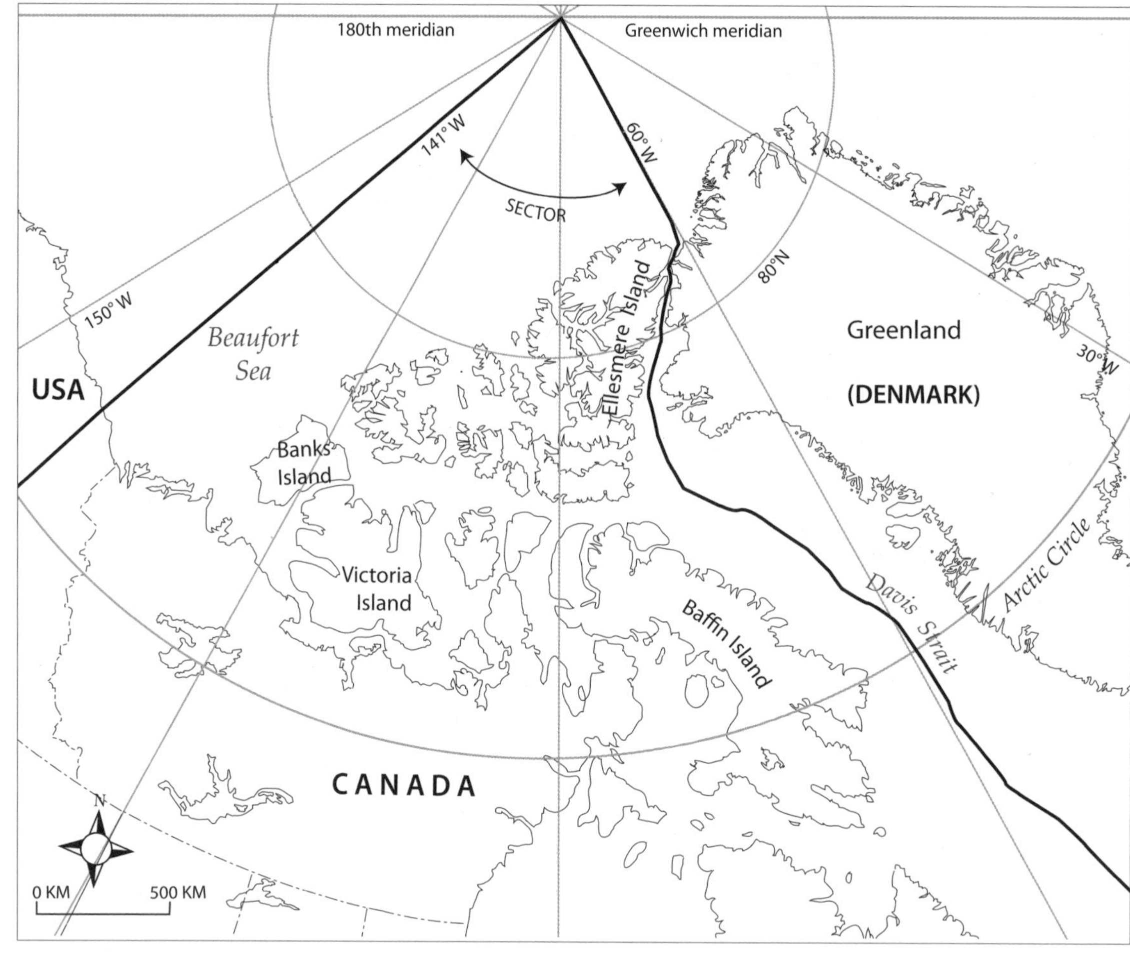

FIGURE 8-2: MAP OF CANADIAN SECTOR. *JENNIFER ARTHUR-LACKENBAUER.*

– in other words, not only land but water and ice as well. In his motion, however, he spoke of "a formal declaration of possession of the lands and islands," and he referred repeatedly to "all the lands" and "all the lands and islands," thus apparently excluding water and ice from what should be subject to Canadian sovereignty. Consequently, it is debatable whether he looked upon the entire sector as Canadian territory or whether he intended to include only the land areas within that sector. It is possible that he had not given much consideration to this distinction, but one might conclude from the general import of his speech that he was primarily concerned with the "lands and islands" that he mentioned so frequently.

This may be a doubtful point, but with regard to another feature of his plan, there would seem to have been no ambiguity. He held that no foreigner had a right to hoist a flag in the Canadian sector between 60° W and 141° W, and, speaking generally of sector states, he asserted, "All the lands between the two lines up to the north pole should belong and do belong to the country whose territory abuts up there." From these and other remarks, it is apparent that he saw Canada, in common with other sector states under the sector principle, as possessor not only of all known islands within the prescribed limits but also of any others, unknown at the time, which it discovered in the future. This aspect of his speech is of particular interest in view of such events as Sverdrup's claim to several islands in the Canadian sector on behalf of Norway several years earlier and Peary's claim to the regions around the North Pole for the United States two years later.

Poirier's motion was not adopted by the Senate on this occasion.[52] He was answered by Senator Sir Richard Cartwright,[53] who, as a senior Liberal and Minister of Trade and Commerce in the Laurier Cabinet, could presumably be regarded as an official spokesman for the administration. Cartwright said in part:

> There is no doubt, I think, that Canada has a very reasonably good ground to regard Hudson Bay as a *mare clausum* and as belonging to it, that everything there my be considered its pertaining thereto. Touching the other point my hon. friend has raised, whether we, or whether any other nation is entitled to extend its territory to the north pole, I would like to reserve my opinion. I am not aware that there have been any original discoverers as yet who can assert a claim to the north pole, and I do not know that it would be of any great practical advantage to us, or to any other country, to assert jurisdiction quite as far north as that. However, I may state to my hon. friend that the importance of having the boundary of Canada defined to the northward has not at all escaped the attention of the government. They have, as the hon. gentleman knows, sent out an expedition very recently to that region, and have established certain posts, and they have likewise exercised various acts of dominion. They have, besides establishing the posts I have referred to, levied customs duties and have exercised our authority over the various whaling vessels they have come across, which, I think, will be found sufficient to maintain our just rights in that quarter. I would think, however, that it was scarcely expedient, for us, bearing in mind that a conference is now going on, to enter into any formal declaration, either on the part of this body or the House of Commons as to the exact limits that we possess thereabouts. I think my hon. friend may rely upon it that the government will take all reasonable precaution to guard against any territory being wrested from us, even if it does appear at present to be of a rather unproductive character.... It is quite within the limits of possibility that further exploration in the Hudson bay, and northward of that, may reveal mineral deposits of very considerable value and importance. The only point to which I would direct his attention is this: That, while negotiations are going on, and while the government are exerting themselves, it may not be the part of policy to formally proclaim any special limitation, or attempt to make any delimitation of our rights there; and therefore, although I can assure the hon. gentleman that due attention will be paid to the matters he has brought before the Senate, and that due precautions will be taken

> to protect and enforce our rights, I think he will do well not to press this motion.[54]

Cartwright got his wish: the motion did not come to a vote. He gave no further details about the "conference" and the "negotiations" which he said were in progress, and it would be interesting to know to what he was referring.[55]

Although Poirier's proposal was thus rejected when it was made, it obviously was not forgotten. Less than two and a half years later, Captain Bernier placed his tablet on Parry's Rock at Winter Harbour, Melville Island, claiming all islands and territory within the Canadian sector for Canada. One cannot help but wonder to what extent there was a direct connection between the two.[56] Bernier commanded an official Canadian government expedition and, at least according to his own statement,[57] had been given a royal commission to annex lands and precise instructions as to what lands to annex. Even though this authority is apparently not to be seen in the documents themselves, it seems unlikely that he would have taken so important a step without some authorization, verbal or other, from the Canadian government, or at least from Canadian government officials.[58]

Another question that provokes curiosity is whether there was any close personal association between Bernier and Poirier, and what the influence of one upon the other may have been. Such an association would be likely, since both were French Canadians (although Bernier was from Quebec and Poirier from New Brunswick), both were keenly interested in Canada's northern regions, and both had had connections with Ottawa for many years. It is tempting to conclude, in spite of the apparent lack of evidence that this was the case,[59] that Poirier (like many others) had become fascinated with Bernier's plans and that Bernier's remarkable energy, enthusiasm, and determination to carry out his northern projects had made Poirier an eager spokesman for his views.

Bernier's enthusiasm, or rather his excess of it, got him into trouble not long afterwards, when he chose the annual dinner of the Arctic Club in New York as the time and place to advance his own idea as to how the sector principle should be put into operation. On 31 January 1910, Conservative member Sam Hughes raised the published reports of this affair in the House of Commons:

> *Sam Hughes*: I desire to call the attention of the right hon. the Prime Minister to the following despatch which appeared in the 'Citizen' and other newspapers on Saturday morning last:
>
> (*Citizen*, Saturday, 29th January, 1910).
>
> New York, Jan. 28 – The question of who has territorial possession of the North Pole has been revived again by Capt. J. Bernier of Canada, who is here to attend the annual dinner of the Arctic club of America to-morrow night. Captain Bernier, will ask Sir Wilfrid Laurier, the Prime Minister of Canada, to request Britain, the United States, Russia, Sweden and Norway and Denmark, all maritime nations bordering on the Arctic sea – to designate official representatives to accompany him on his forthcoming Polar expedition which is to leave Quebec on July 15th next. The principal object of the expedition, he said, will be for a division of the Polar sea in order that Canada and

the other six nations may have their fishery rights properly defined. Captain Bernier will visit both Croker Land, discovered by Peary in 1905, and Bradley Land, which Dr. Cook reported that he sighted, and, after raising the British flag, will proclaim them formally annexed to the Dominion of Canada. Great Britain, he said, formerly ceded to the Dominion all islands in the Arctic sea lying within its lateral boundaries.

I desire to ask the government, whether they have received any such request from Captain Bernier; and if so, is it the intention of the government to remind Captain Bernier that Canada is not yet a nation but part of the British Dominions and intends remaining so, and the expression that Canada is another nation or that Britain is another nation separate from Canada is not applicable to actual conditions.

Sir Wilfrid Laurier: I have seen the despatch mentioned by my hon. friend. I do not know of any such intention on the part of Capt. Bernier as that attributed to him. I do not think that he has any intention of going into international complications. But, if Capt. Bernier spoke as he is reported to have spoken, all I can say is that I think he had better keep to his own deck.

Sir George Eulas Foster: That seems to imply that there is a project on to send Capt. Bernier to the North Pole under sanction of the Dominion government. Is that so?

Laurier: No. Capt. Bernier will go north again this summer to patrol the waters of the north and assert Canadian jurisdiction.

Foster: I think somebody ought to take charge of this gentleman. He seems to be running loose.[60]

Back in Ottawa a few days later, an apparently worried Captain Bernier wrote an explanatory "Memo for the Deputy Minister." The document, dated 8 February 1910, makes rather amusing reading because it indicates that, in spite of his protests and explanations, Bernier had said substantially what he was reported to have said. In part it went as follows:

> I beg to enclose you herewith some cutting, which I took from the New York Newspapers, after the annual dinner of the "Arctic Club", and each paper published its views and comments, on what I have said before the members of the "Arctic Club". This will give you a substantial statement of what I have said which did not compromise neither Sir Wilfrid Laurier, nor the Government.
>
> I mentioned that if an expedition composed of an American, a Canadian, a Dane, a Norwegian, a Swede, & a Russian went to the Pole and filed their separate claim there would be no more fishing dispute in future….
>
> I mentioned also that probably the "Arctic" would sail again for the North and that if I passed close to Bradley land and Crocker land, I would hoist the Canadian Flag on them….
>
> I have never said that I would ask Sir Wilfrid Laurier to ask England, the United States, Russia, Sweden,

> Denmark and Norway to send a representative to come with me, for I do not know the intentions of the Government, only that I am to patrol the Northern Waters....[61]

On 11 February, Bernier wrote an almost identical letter to Laurier himself.[62] He followed this up with another letter on 13 April, enclosing an article from the *New York Times-Democrat* of 28 March on "Ownership of the Poles," which *inter alia* made the significant observation that the United States "cannot afford to have any foreign power taking possession of islands of the Arctic coast of Alaska, even if beyond the three-mile limit."[63]

In spite of the Canadian government's rather negative reaction to Poirier's proposals, and their understandable reluctance to give Bernier complete freedom of voice and action, it is apparent that they had already committed themselves, if not precisely to the sector principle, at least to virtually the same thing. Evidence that this was so is almost conclusive.

On 8 September 1909, the following exchange took place in the British House of Commons:

> *Sir Gilbert Parker* asked the Prime Minister whether the land at the North Pole is considered to belong to the Dominion of Canada; and, if so, providing it is established that Dr. Cook has reached the North Pole and has planted there the American flag, whether that act would, in any way, give the United States any right of possession over that region. [The Hon. Member added, I assume the Prime Minister will understand "land at or adjacent to."]
>
> *The Prime Minister*: I did not understand that. In answer to the first part of the hon. Member's question I do not understand that there is any land at the North Pole.
>
> *Parker*: Adjacent to the Pole.
>
> *The Prime Minister*: Perhaps the hon. Member will put down another question. The second part of the question involves too much hypothetical matter for me to give any definite answer.[64]

Two days afterwards, the following cable was sent in code by Colonial Secretary Lord Eyre Crow to Governor General Earl Grey:

> Following question is to be asked in the House of Commons on Monday next. Begins: Whether Canada makes claim upon all land intervening between the American border and the North Pole and if that claim is made in any treaty or constitutional article or documents, ends. If your Government agrees it is proposed to reply that the Secretary of State for the Colonies understands that the Government of Canada has not made a formal declaration of the exact limits of its possessions northward. See your despatch of 22nd April 1907, No. 188.[65]

There was some discussion in Ottawa, and the next day, 11 September, the Department of External Affairs sent a message to the Governor General advising that "a telegram be sent to the Secretary of State for the Colonies in the following words: – It is understood that Canada claims all lands intervening between the American border and the North Pole."[66] On the same day, Under Secretary of State for External Affairs Joseph Pope wrote a brief memo saying that this answer had been sent.[67] When the question was raised again in the British House of Commons on Monday, 15 September, the answer showed that the wishes of the Canadian government had been taken into consideration:

> *Lord Balcarres (for Sir Gilbert Parker)* asked whether Canada makes a claim upon all land intervening between the American border and the North Pole; and if that claim is made in any treaty or constitutional article or document?
>
> *Colonel Charles Seely*: The Secretary of State understands that the Canada Government have not made a formal declaration of the exact limits of their possessions northwards, but it is believed that they consider themselves entitled to claim all the land referred to by the hon. Gentleman.[68]

Thus, if the activities of Captain Bernier, and especially his claim to all lands and islands in the Canadian sector on 1 July 1909, left any doubt as to the official view of the Canadian government in the matter, the events recounted above would appear to have removed any reasons for such doubt. This authoritative indication of the attitude of the Canadian government is important because it came sixteen years before Minister of the Interior Stewart's remarks in the House of Commons in 1925,[69] which have sometimes been taken as the first official Canadian statements on the subject.

9

Vilhjalmur Stefansson and His Plans for Northern Enterprise after the First World War

Vilhjalmur Stefansson returned from the Arctic in the autumn of 1918 a famous and even influential figure. In spite of the misfortunes and tragedies that had attended his expedition, and in spite of the antipathy and enmity of disaffected members of it, particularly in the southern party, his reputation as a brilliantly successful explorer was still essentially unimpaired. As seen earlier, the Canadian government had accepted his basic concept of the expedition without serious question, and he had been given virtually *carte blanche* in planning, organizing, and equipping it. When difficulties and disasters almost overwhelmed him, moreover, the government stuck with him, and he was thus able to carry out a good part of his own program. In spite of his isolation he was able to maintain periodic contact with Ottawa, and not the least remarkable feature of his performance was the series of detailed reports and communiqués on the expedition and his own experiences which he sent back to Prime Minister Borden and other officials, with incisive, perceptive comments and recommendations regarding government policy in the North. A letter to Borden from the Mackenzie River delta on 8 January 1914 advised protecting Inuit from white man's diseases by placing quarantine officers at Herschel Island and Fort Norman. It also advised conserving their food supply by establishing a partial closed season for caribou, with export of their hides forbidden, and a complete closed season for muskox.[1] In a similar letter to Clifford Sifton, at the time Chairman of the Commission of Conservation, which he wrote on 8 February 1914, at the RNWMP barracks at Fort McPherson, he made essentially the same recommendations.[2] The letter to Borden, which he wrote on newly discovered Brock Island on 21 June 1915, and in which he urged continued northern exploration by Canadians and offered himself for further service, has already been cited.[3] Stefansson himself tells of a letter he wrote to Borden from Melville Island in 1916, in which he claims to have presented to the Prime Minister for the first time a comprehensive exposé of his plans for the North.[4] He was also able, from time to time, to send to Ottawa details of the expedition, which were incorporated in the accounts about it published in the annual reports of the Department of the Naval Service.[5] Thus, although Stefansson himself spent several years in the Arctic islands almost completely separated from all human beings except those in his own party,

FIGURE 9-1: VILHJALMUR STEFANSSON. *RUDOLPH MARTIN ANDERSON / LIBRARY AND ARCHIVES CANADA / E002712840.*

a good deal of information about his experiences reached the "civilized" world and attracted considerable interest and publicity.

Stefansson came back full of plans and projects for the North – and eager to take advantage of every opportunity to put these plans and projects into operation. At first he was interested primarily in bringing them to the attention of the Canadian government, but later he took his case to the public in a great publicity campaign of writing and lecturing.[6] It is no exaggeration to say that many of the ideas he expounded have become familiarly and universally associated with his name. In summary form, his thinking about the future role of the Arctic, and about northern development, was as follows.

He started from the premise that Arctic lands, and the Arctic region in general, were soon going to become much more important than hitherto and would play an expanding role in world affairs. In the air age, which was obviously approaching, the Arctic would no longer be looked upon as nothing more than a forbidding barrier and wasteland, but rather would become a principal (and perhaps the most important) thoroughfare for the world's air commerce. In his own words, he "had come to the view that the earth was now at last a globe for practical purposes."[7] He pointed to the fact, well known but with implications not as yet fully appreciated, that the shortest air routes between the world's largest cities and greatest concentrations of population and industry lay over the Arctic Ocean. In these circumstances it was inevitable that with technological development the Arctic would become a great, centrally located crossroads rather than remaining a sort of backwater or barrier on the periphery of civilization. Stefansson also asserted that in the natural evolution of history the main centres of civilization had been moving steadily northward, from the ancient empires of southern and southwestern Asia to those of Greece and Rome, and then to the modem states of northern Europe such as France, Great Britain, and Germany. He believed that this trend would continue, and, anticipating an increasing realization of the value of such northern lands as Alaska, Canada, Spitsbergen, and Siberia, insisted that there was no real latitudinal limit to northern development. Thus the leading states of the future, or at least a considerable number of them, such as the United States, Canada, Great Britain, Russia, and Japan, would be those located at or near the edge of the Arctic sea, and the transpolar traffic and commerce between and among them would cause this sea to occupy a position comparable to that of the Mediterranean in ancient and medieval times. Planes flying the transpolar routes would require landing fields and refuelling bases, and for these purposes it would be logical to make use of the Arctic islands. The islands would also be valuable as sites for weather stations, and for radio and communications centres. Eventually, when technological development had advanced far enough, submarines would sail under the Arctic ice, not only for military but also for commercial purposes. Stefansson also envisaged the day when giant undersurface tankers and freighters would carry the world's commerce across the Arctic sea.

Stefansson believed that the Arctic region had intrinsic values and potentialities of its own which had not been fully appreciated but would become more evident as time went on. He held that the climate of the Far North, although admittedly rigorous, was not nearly so forbidding as was popularly supposed. Indeed, he insisted that it was no more severe than the climate of much more southerly, subarctic regions that supported large populations. This suggested that the climate of the North would not in itself be a barrier to settlement, and that if and when settlement on a large scale became economically or otherwise desirable, it would take place as naturally as the settlement of the North American prairies. Known resources of value in the Arctic included furs, food from land and sea creatures, and, in some parts, metals and minerals (such as the coal of Spitsbergen). There were also attractive prospects for discovery and development of additional resources, and Stefansson was particularly interested in such projects as the introduction of tame reindeer herds into the North American Arctic, the domestication of the muskox or *ovibos moschatus*, the exploitation of Arctic fisheries, and investigation of the numerous indications of mineral wealth in various parts of the North.

The political and international aspects of the north polar area especially intrigued him. He believed that although Arctic territory had not previously been highly valued, it soon would be; and this would become a region of intense international competition unless steps were taken to remove uncertainties about ownership of land. Although some state or other had claimed practically all known lands and islands, some of these claims were not well established and could easily be challenged. In addition, there were good prospects of discovering other islands as yet unknown, since there was still a large portion of the ice-covered Arctic sea that, so far as records showed, no human being had ever seen. Hence the likelihood that international competition would increase to secure possession of known lands or islands (wherever doubts might exist) and to discover and appropriate new ones. This was a matter of special importance for Canada for several reasons: its central and vulnerable position in the Arctic, her as yet rather dubious claim to a large portion of the known Arctic islands, and also the strong possibility that future discoveries might easily be of islands within or adjacent to the so-called Canadian sector.

Stefansson had given a great deal of thought to these matters, and in his own mind had worked out a program or at least various projects which he thought the Canadian government should undertake. Some of his ideas were already developed in considerable detail; others had as yet taken only vague form; but collectively they amounted to an ambitious and far-reaching plan for Canadian enterprise and development in the North. He wanted to see a continuation of northern exploration, and particularly an expedition that (if possible) he himself would lead. This expedition would have several purposes, including continuing exploration of the little known islands, discovering and taking possession of new ones if any were left to be found, and cementing Canada's claim to the archipelago as a whole. He wanted to establish air bases, meteorological and radio stations, and police posts on the northern islands, to confirm Canadian sovereignty by occupation, and also to facilitate bringing the air age to the Arctic. He was anxious to see the introduction of reindeer herding on a large scale in suitable areas of the Canadian North, and also experimentation with the domestication of the muskox. He urged prospecting for minerals and more thorough investigation of the known indications of them, including the tar sands and oil outcroppings along the Mackenzie River, the copper deposits in the Coppermine region and Victoria Island, and the coal deposits in some of the islands such as Ellesmere and Melville. Already he was forming plans to establish Canadian possession of Wrangel Island, which he did not regard as Russian and thought that Canada could claim on the basis of the temporary occupation of the island by the *Karluk* party in 1914.[8]

These were the most important plans that Stefansson put before the Canadian government upon his return from the North and that he continued to promote, with great determination and persistence, over the following years. Practically all of them quickly became major issues and, regardless of what fate befell them, Canadian government activity in the North for at least the next decade was to a large extent a response – either positive or negative – to them.

Unfortunately for Stefansson, he and his projects had already acquired many enemies and much opposition. Among the leaders were members of the southern party of the returned expedition, especially his former associate and friend Dr. Rudolph Martin Anderson, who found growing support among doubtful and disenchanted senior officials in government. The quarrels that destroyed the harmony of the expedition, especially those between the leaders, were continued after the return to Ottawa, and inevitably came to involve many others. A major dispute broke out over the task of preparing and getting ready for publication the voluminous reports that were to be made about the expedition, especially the scientific aspects of it. There was a move to keep Stefansson out of proceedings, but some of the officials who had been prominently associated with the expedition, notably Deputy Minister G. J. Desbarats of the Department of the Naval Service, insisted that since Stefansson had been placed in full command he could not be denied his rightful place on the publishing committee.[9] It was in these confused and unpleasant circumstances that Stefansson undertook to sell his views on northern enterprise and development to the Canadian government.

Reindeer and Muskox Projects in the North

The importance of the postwar reindeer and muskox projects in northern Canada in relation to problems of Arctic sovereignty should not be overestimated, since there was at most only an uncertain connection between them. Nevertheless, these projects came to the fore at a time when there was renewed concern among Canadian authorities about the security of their northern territories, and to some extent were a manifestation of their desire to occupy these regions and put them to use. Hence a brief summary of the subject is in order. As was so often the case with major plans and problems in the North during and after the First World War, the central figure in these projects was Vilhjalmur Stefansson. There was a background of some importance, however, before he entered upon the scene.

The peoples of northern Europe and Asia, especially the Saami (Laplanders) of northern Scandinavia and the Chukchi of northeastern Siberia, have kept the reindeer in a domestic state for centuries. On the other hand the North American caribou, which is of the same family and is practically identical except that it is a little larger, has never been domesticated (except perhaps in isolated instances). Domestication of reindeer in North America began when Alaska General Agent of Education Dr. Sheldon Jackson, observing first hand the large herds in northeastern Siberia and becoming impressed with the possibilities that the industry might offer for poverty-stricken natives of Alaska, took the initiative in 1891 by having sixteen Siberian reindeer purchased and brought over to the American side. Since Congress had not yet voted an appropriation for this purpose, the initial purchase had to be made with funds contributed privately. This was also the case with the second, larger purchase of 171 reindeer in 1892. The reindeer obtained at this point were taken to Port Clarence Bay, just across the Bering Strait from Siberia, and here the Teller Reindeer Station, the first in Alaska, was established. Congress voted a series of grants starting in 1893, further purchases of Siberian reindeer were made almost annually for about a decade, and trained herders and dogs were imported from Lapland. In due course, herds were established in other parts of Alaska, for the most part in regions adjacent to the Teller Range but also, in an experimental way, in the Aleutians and the Panhandle. Between 1891 and 1915, about 1300 animals were imported. Even though large members were killed for food and skins, natural increase meant that the herds had grown to more than 70,000 animals in 1915, generating great optimism over the future of the reindeer industry in Alaska.[10]

In the meantime another reindeer experiment was being attempted, under considerably less auspicious circumstances, on the other side of the continent. Here the promoter was Wilfred Grenfell, the famous pioneer doctor of Labrador and Newfoundland. Convinced that the vast moss-covered barren lands of these territories would be as suitable for domestic reindeer as for the wild caribou that had inhabited them for centuries, Grenfell consulted with Sheldon Jackson in Washington and then raised sufficient funds to purchase 300 reindeer in Lapland. The animals, accompanied by Saami herders, were transported in 1908 to St. Anthony, near the northernmost tip of Newfoundland, where in five years they increased to approximately 1,500. This fortuitous beginning did not last for various reasons: the absence of Dr. Grenfell during the war, the departure of the Saami herders, a disease which attacked the reindeer, and (perhaps most serious) the indifference and even enmity of the local Newfoundlanders who depleted the numbers through illegal poaching and shooting. By 1917 only about 250 were left. With the consent and co-operation of the Canadian government, as many as could be caught were transferred to Rocky Bay on the north shore of the Gulf of St. Lawrence, later to be transferred again to Anticosti Island. Although his own experiment had ended in failure, Grenfell himself was fully convinced that the feasibility of the idea had been completely vindicated, if the necessary elements of interest and support by the local population were present.[11]

Even less successful was an attempt to start a herd in the vicinity of Fort Smith in the Northwest Territories. In the summer of 1911, fifty reindeer were obtained from Grenfell's herd and transported successively by ship, train, and wagon to Fort Smith. By the time the herd arrived about one-third of them had died and, because of various mischances, only three were left by the autumn of 1913.[12]

No comparable attempts had been made at this time to domesticate the muskox and raise it in captivity. On a much smaller scale, muskox had been kept in at least one zoo (in New York City) with some success, except that they had not reproduced under these conditions.[13] Various explorers had testified as to the docility of the muskox, and Captain Bernier had kept a young calf as a pet during his sojourn on Melville Island in 1908–9.[14]

This was approximately the situation that had been reached when Stefansson returned from the Arctic late in 1918 and embarked on his campaign to interest the Canadian government in his projects to domesticate and raise large herds of reindeer and muskox in the North. Stefansson's own interest in such enterprises had developed during this expedition, as the following entry in his diary indicates. It was written on 29 May 1916, at the northwestern tip of Ellef Ringnes Island, while he was in a mood of deep depression because of a badly injured foot and other frustrations. More optimistically, he wrote:

> A New Domestic Animal seems to me to be placed here ready to our hand in the muskox. I have thought much of this lately, and hope to try to get either the Government or a semi-patriotic commercial company under Government charter to experiment in the matter. It seems to me that the muskox is easier to handle than reindeer, besides producing more meat and the wool in addition. They could undoubtedly flourish wherever they formerly did, if only they will "breed in captivity", of which I have no doubt. The wild oxen of Melville Island act more "tame" than any domestic reindeer in Alaska … and are easily broken to sleds, as shown by experience with them of Illun, who now works for us and once handled two calves on the mainland and used them there for sled work occasionally.[15]

Elsewhere Stefansson recorded that it was in January 1916, while wintering in Banks Island, that his ideas on domestication of the muskox had taken clear enough form to be presented to influential people, including former President Roosevelt, Prime Minister Borden, Canadian High Commissioner in London Sir Richard McBride, and Canadian Bank of Commerce President Sir Edmund Walker.[16] He reproduced a letter of 23 March 1918 from Roosevelt giving at least moral support, and another letter dated 28 October 1918, in which the former president said he would do what he could to influence favourably both Prince Axel of Denmark and the Canadian government with respect to the muskox project.[17]

On 11 November 1918, shortly after his return from the North, Stefansson spoke to the Empire Club in Toronto, and the distinguished audience, overwhelmed with joy at the armistice which had been signed that morning, gave him an enthusiastic reception. He summarized the story of his expedition in a general way,

FIGURE 9-2: MUSKOX ON DEVON ISLAND IN A DEFENSIVE CIRCLE. *PERCY TAVERNER / LIBRARY AND ARCHIVES CANADA / PA-048029.*

but placed particular emphasis on the projects he wanted to initiate. After describing the development of the reindeer industry in Alaska, he went on:

> I now want to mention an even more valuable animal – the muskox. Imagine that you had a cow with a coat of wool that could be shorn once a year and sold. Would that not be a more valuable cow than any you ever saw? Or imagine that your sheep were three or four times as large as they are, and gave milk like the cows, then they would be much more valuable than any sheep you ever saw. And you have a wild animal that meets identically those conditions – with beef identical in taste with your beef and milk with difficulty distinguishable from Jersey milk and wool like the domestic sheep. That animal needs no barn to shelter it, no hay to food it for the winter, for in the farthest islands of the north they now live untended, and fat in any season of the year....
>
> I now propose to go to the Government, and I want the backing of your good-will, as I had it five years ago, to get the Government to undertake this broad-minded thing for the benefit of Canada.... I shall emphasize, by repetition, the fact that ... this

> is about the most important project, in my opinion, that is now before Canada in our period of reconstruction after the war.[18]

In his attempt to win the support of the Canadian government, Stefansson dealt chiefly with Arthur Meighen, at the time Minister of the Interior and thus directly responsible for most aspects of northern administration and development. Meighen was interested and arranged an opportunity for Stefansson to address a joint meeting of the Senate and the House of Commons. This took place on 6 May 1919, in the railway committee room, and Stefansson, as usual on such occasions, made a strong impression.[19] Three days afterwards Meighen wrote a letter to James Stanley McLean, a manager with the Harris Abattoir Company in Toronto, whose services he wanted to secure for the project that was forming in his mind. The letter began as follows:

> I am thinking of recommending to Council, the appointment of a commission to study and report upon the possibilities of developing the muskox and reindeer industry in Northern Canada. Attached hereto, you will find copy of a memorandum furnished me by the Explorer, Stefansson. Recently I had him address the Members of the Commons and Senate, and his speech made a pronounced impression.[20]

On a recommendation from Mr. Meighen, also dated 9 May, an order in council was issued on 20 May appointing a royal commission to investigate the possibilities of raising large reindeer and muskox herds in the Canadian north.[21] The members of the commission, were McLean, John Gunion Rutherford (Ottawa, Railway Commissioner), James B. Harkin (Ottawa, Commissioner of Dominion Parks), and Stefansson. Rutherford, a veterinarian by profession, was appointed chairman. This commission, and the investigation it carried on afterwards, helped to focus public attention upon the North and the problems of conserving and augmenting the resources in animal life there, precisely at the time when the government was becoming increasingly preoccupied with questions of northern administration and jurisdiction.

Although the commission was appointed immediately, it did not meet until the following year. Once it was convened, however, it went about its task with great thoroughness, and lengthy sessions were held in January, February, April, and May of 1920. Testimony was taken from thirty-five witnesses, practically all of them well-known personalities with lengthy experience of one kind or another in the North.[22] Among them were the Anglican missionary W.H.B. Hoare, Bishop Isaac O. Stringer, Captain J.-E. Bernier, Joseph Burr Tyrrell, the American explorer Donald B. MacMillan, and Stefansson's former associate Dr. R. M. Anderson. Almost without exception the witnesses expressed great interest in the project under investigation, and varying degrees of optimism about it. One influential figure who took a rather restrained view was the chairman, Dr. Rutherford, who believed that the reports of enormous herds of caribou in the North were "palpable exaggerations," feared that large numbers of reindeer kept by herders would become wild, and advanced his own more modest idea that "a small herd of reindeer ... could be kept within a given area provided there is sufficient feed" and raised domestically.[23]

In the course of the hearings, some interesting statements were made of relevance to past or future events relating to sovereignty problems. For example, Captain George Comer, whose activities in Hudson Bay had caused so much concern at the time when A. P. Low and Bernier were initiating patrol voyages and who had been regarded as an American interloper, now identified himself as being Canadian-born (although brought up in the United States).[24] Whatever his earlier attitude may have been regarding Canadian claims and interference with his whaling enterprise, Comer now declared himself completely sympathetic with Canadian interests and anxious to eliminate whaling altogether:

> To go back a little farther, there is a little argument between [the] United States and Canada about the right of the Americans to go through and whale in Hudson Bay, keeping outside the three mile limit. We should go ahead and make our docks, occupy the place and clinch the whole thing, and the Americans would not make any claim at all....
>
> ....If I had the making of the laws I would not allow a whale to be killed. I have made my money out of the whaling business, and have seen them killed. Last year two were killed, one got away. Stop that entirely, do not let even our own people kill them. Do not bring up the question at all, as to whether that is a closed sea or not. You will very soon close it, once you put the Wireless on. Do not have any arguments, just go on and take possession.[25]

McMillan, who was to become a problem for the Canadian government later on, also declared his support for Canadian administrative authority and efforts towards conservation in the North, especially in Ellesmere Island:

> I think all expeditions should be prohibited from going into that country, unless on permission obtained from the Dominion of Canada ....
>
> ....If I were coming into Canada, as I had hoped to, I would expect to get permission from the Canadian Government and if they said No, I could not expect to come ....
>
> ....It is the explorer that kills, and he should, as I said before, get into touch with the Canadian Government and get permission to go and get food for himself.[26]

Although the commission's hearings concluded in May 1920, its report was not published until 1922. The hearings themselves apparently attracted little attention, at least in the House of Commons,[27] and the report was available to Parliament long before it was published. On 14 June 1921, Unionist member John Archibald observed that it had been "laid on the Table" some time earlier, and asked if the government proposed to carry out its recommendations. Meighen, now Prime Minister, replied:

> The report, with the evidence supporting it, forms a very voluminous and very valuable document, highly creditable to the chairman and members of the commission and indicating that the utmost possible care and the highest possible thought have been exercised by them in the investigation. On account of its size, however, and the fact that it has only been in our hands for a few days, the

> Government has not come to any conclusion as to whether those recommendations will be followed, and if so, when.[28]

In the meantime, during the period when the commission was still conducting its hearings, Stefansson had severed his formal connection with it and embarked on a project of his own. Having come to the conclusion that the government-sponsored reindeer industry he had originally envisaged would proceed too slowly and on too modest a scale, he decided that he would try to initiate the enterprise himself with private financial backing. He applied to the government for an exclusive lease of a large area in southern Baffin island for grazing purposes and, since his position as promoter of this project was evidently incompatible with his membership in the Reindeer-Musk-Ox Commission, he resigned from the commission on 12 March 1920.[29] Having already approached the Hudson's Bay Company through the company's New York representative, he went to England later in March and succeeded in attracting the interest and support of its directors. After the lease had been granted, the Hudson's Bay Reindeer Company was organized as a subsidiary of the HBC, with headquarters in Winnipeg, and the lease assigned to it. Stefansson himself was to be a director of the new company and its technical adviser.[30]

The lease was granted to Stefansson by order in council on 29 May 1920.[31] It gave him exclusive grazing rights for thirty years on all of Baffin Island south of the 68th parallel: an area of approximately 113,900 square miles. The grazing right was free for the first fifteen years, with an annual rental fee thereafter; and the lease was to be renewable for a further twenty years after the first thirty had expired. In return Stefansson was to see that 1,000 imported reindeer were on the leasehold by 1924 and 6,000 by 1932, at which time the herd was to total at least 10,000. The indenture or contract which formalized the agreement between Stefansson and the Government, and which incorporated the above terms, contained a good deal of additional detail, including provisions for safeguarding the interests of Aboriginal people, incorporating wild caribou into the herds, permitting purchase of reindeer by the government as the herd increased, and restricting the freedom of the lessee to sell or transfer his rights.

The project was undertaken with optimism but soon ended in disaster. Storker Storkeson of Stefansson's 1913–18 expedition was hired as manager and field director at an early stage, and a number of Saami (Lapps) were engaged to serve as herders. Approximately 700 reindeer were purchased in Norway in 1921 and the HBC ship *Nascopie* was used to transport them to Baffin Island in the autumn of that year. Almost everything went wrong from the start. Storkerson resigned before the reindeer had even been purchased, when other people were given the responsibility in his stead of obtaining them and getting them to Baffin Island. Some of the animals did not reach the ship and others died during the sea voyage, so that only about 500 actually reached their destination. The Saami herders, completely unfamiliar with the severe climate of treeless Baffin Island, soon showed themselves to be unadaptable, uninterested, and dissatisfied. The herd scattered far and wide after its arrival, while the Saami built homes and shelters which should have been provided in advance. Only a limited number of reindeer were recovered, and losses continued through absorption by caribou herds and for other reasons. Stefansson himself was occupied with a variety of other projects, and either neglected this one or encountered so many frustrations that he was able to do little to save it. The Saami herders returned to Norway in the fall of 1923, Inuit who replaced them were unable to arrest the decline of the herd, and the company soon became disillusioned and refused to provide either more money or more reindeer. In about two more seasons the herd had disappeared completely, and eventually the lease was cancelled. In this unhappy manner ended the first Canadian attempt at reindeer herding in the Arctic, although Stefansson himself maintained afterwards that the project was sound in principle but had been ruined in execution. This may well have been so, but it does not dispose entirely of the question as to how much responsibility for the failure was Stefansson's own.[32]

In due course the Canadian government undertook officially to establish a reindeer herd in another part of the North, with better success. The *Reindeer-Musk-Ox Commission Report* in 1922 had recommended the establishment of small experimental reindeer herds, in line with Chairman Rutherford's own views, using localities deemed most suitable by government experts. A system should be worked out similar to that so successfully developed in Alaska, including reliance upon missionary bodies for co-operation and help, use of experienced Saami herders, and encouragement of Inuit to participate and also become herders themselves. The commissioners added that, although they had approved the grazing lease granted to Stefansson in 1920, they felt unable to recommend any definite policy regarding such leases, except that henceforth great caution should be exercised in granting them.[33]

After the Baffin Island project had been pronounced a failure, officials with the Department of the Interior contacted Carl Lomen, one of the famous brothers who were known as "The Reindeer Kings of Alaska" who presided over the Lomen Reindeer Corporation. Lomen suggested that reindeer should be obtained from Alaska rather than Norway and driven overland to the area to be stocked. He then followed up this suggestion with the offer that his own company would look after the drive.[34] The Canadian officials were interested but were inclined to proceed very slowly and cautiously. In April 1926, they appointed the Danish-born botanist Alf Erling Porsild and his brother Robert, who had lived in the Arctic for many years and had a sophisticated and scientific knowledge of it, to make a detailed investigation of all aspects of the plan. They first visited Alaska and studied conditions where all the major herds were kept, then travelled over the planned route for the drive from Nome to the Mackenzie delta, and then spent two years examining the large area between the Alaska-Yukon boundary and Coronation Gulf. Altogether they spent May 1926 to November 1928 in the field and travelled a total of 15,000 miles by dog team, canoe, motor boat, pack dogs, and snowshoes. They concluded that the area was well suited to reindeer herding, and they particularly recommended two sections of it: one to the east of the Mackenzie delta and the other north and east of Great Bear Lake.[35] In the summer of 1930, A. E. Porsild surveyed another large area west of the Hudson Bay coast in central Keewatin and also found it suitable for reindeer grazing, although the establishment of reindeer herds would be difficult because of the distance between summer and winter pasture.[36]

After the Porsild brothers had completed their investigation, and acting upon a favourable report of 18 April 1929 by Minister of the Interior Charles Stewart, the Canadian government issued an order in council in May authorizing the minister to contract with the Lomen brothers for the purchase and delivery of 3,000 reindeer at a total price of $195,000.00.[37]

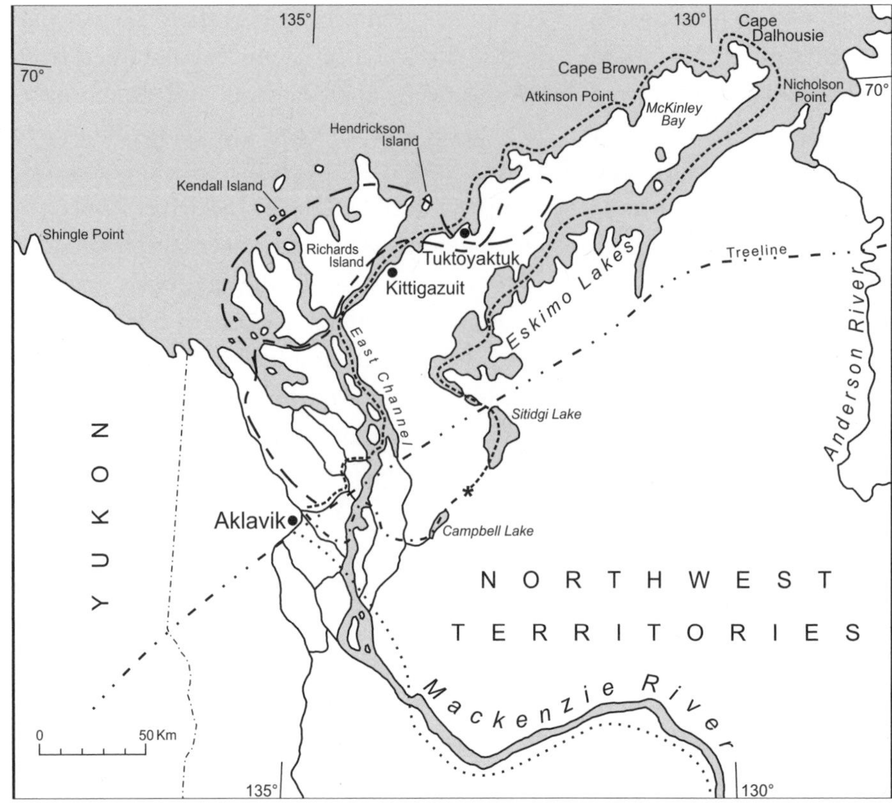

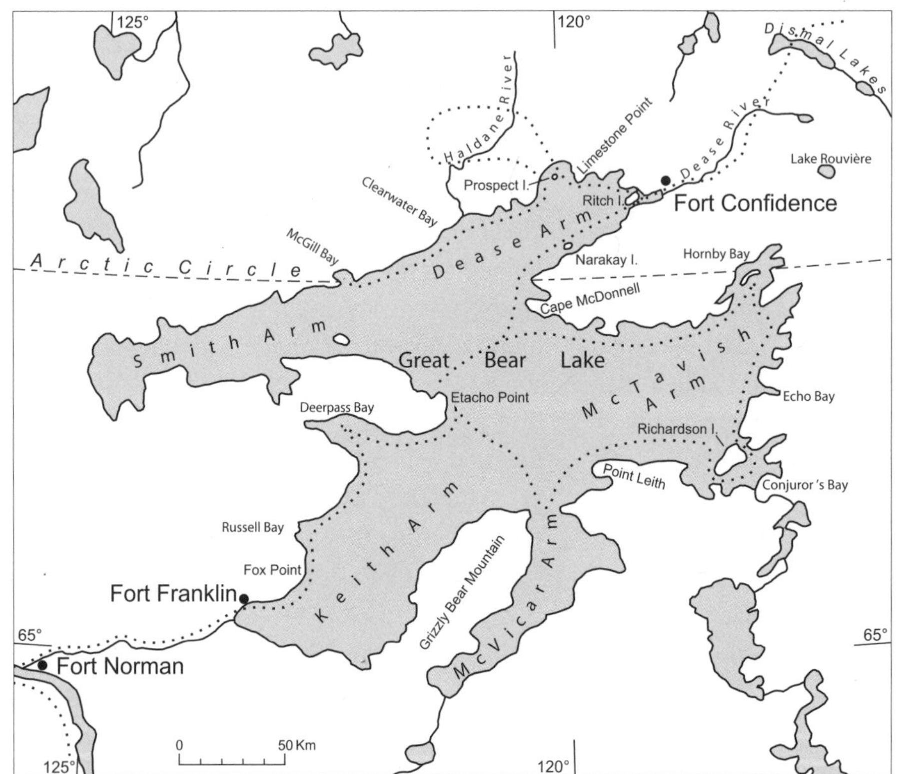

Figure 9-3a, 9-3b: Canadian Reindeer Project investigation routes in the Mackenzie delta, NWT, 1927 (above) and around Great Bear Lake, NWT, 1928 (below). Maps by Ragnar Müller-Wille in Wendy Dathan, *The Reindeer Botanist*, 96, 152. With permission of University of Calgary Press

According to the agreement, the Lomens would take complete responsibility for the drive, and deliver the reindeer on the east side of the Mackenzie delta in 1931. The drive turned out to be a much more difficult and time-consuming task than had been anticipated. The veteran Saami herder Andrew Bahr, who had worked for the Lomens for many years, was placed in charge of the operation; about a dozen Saami and Inuit were hired as his crew; and in the late stages of the drive, when reports were received that Bahr's health was failing, the Lomens' former field superintendent Dan Crowley rushed to the scene to help him. The unbelievably difficult route traced a path from Nabachtoolik near Kotzebue Sound across the interior coast of Alaska to the vicinity of the Arctic coast, and thence eastward to the mouth of the Mackenzie. Owing to the problems encountered, the herd was not driven into the newly constructed corral at Kittigazuit until March 1935. The number of reindeer actually delivered was 2,382, but most of these were young animals born en route, and only about 10 or 20 per cent had begun the drive at Nabachtoolik. Within a few weeks of arrival the herd was increased by over 800 newly-born fawns.[38]

In 1931, A. E. Porsild, who had been sent to Norway to hire experienced Saami herders, returned with three, who helped in the late stages of the drive and then remained with the herd (two for a limited number of years and the third permanently). In line with the original concept that one of the principal purposes of the project would be to provide local Inuit with a self-sustaining industry in which they could participate significantly themselves, young Inuit were from the beginning trained in reindeer handling under the supervision of the Saami; in due course some of them became capable herders. Anticipation that many of them would acquire herds of their own and adopt reindeer "ranching" as a permanent way of life were not realized, however, partly because of Inuit fears respecting economic and other uncertainties which seemed to be inherent in trying to make a living with small reindeer herds, and partly because of their reluctance to abandon their traditional way of life. A few independent Inuit-controlled herds were set up, starting with one on the Anderson River in 1938, but it cannot be said that they were a great success.

For a few years the number of reindeer increased in encouraging fashion, but then the increase ground to a halt. Starting with the 2,382 delivered at Kittigazuit in 1935, the number increased steadily to a total of 6,635 in 1940, including 1,559 in the native herd at Anderson River. However, for various reasons, including inadequate attention, enterprise, and leadership; disregard of scientific selection, culling, and breeding; and the ravages of pests and predators, the three herds that remained in 1963 totalled only 7,000 animals.[39]

The tract of land east of the Mackenzie delta was set up as the Reindeer Grazing Reserve by a federal order in council of 14 December 1933.[40] It comprised about 6,600 square miles, including the Eskimo Lakes region and Richards Island.[41] The pasture resources of the reserve turned out to be both suitable and abundant, and Richards Island proved to be particularly well adapted for summer grazing purposes, both as the locale for the annual roundup and a place where, because of its high winds and proximity to the seacoast, the depredations of insect pests could be reduced. The reindeer were given protection by the Northwest Territories Reindeer Protection Ordinance, promulgated on 18 October 1933, which regulated activities within the reserve and limited the killing of both reindeer and caribou.[42]

As time went on, a mood of pessimism and disillusionment set in, particularly among

FIGURE 9-4: PART OF A FEMALE REINDEER HERD, KITTIGAZUIT, NWT, MAY 1935. *AEP / LIBRARY AND ARCHIVES CANADA / PA-130436.*

some of the government personnel involved with the project, and there were suggestions that the entire operation should be terminated. Eventually it was decided to bring about a fundamental change in policy, with a view to maintaining the industry and improving it. The idea of a government-sponsored and government-supported industry, primarily concerned with training native herders and supplying reindeer meat and by-products, was eventually abandoned in the 1960s.[43]

Reflecting back from the perspective of the early 1970s, it is apparent that even after almost forty years of effort and experiment, the future of the reindeer industry in northern Canada remained uncertain. It survived but did not fulfill the expectations of its founders. In sum, its lack of success can be attributed to:

(1) the absence or constructive policy and firm leadership throughout most of the period;

(2) the disinclination of the local people to abandon their traditional to way of life and adopt this one;

(3) failure to maintain and improve the quality of the animals; and

(4) natural limiting factors such as pests and predators.

There is also a great deal that can be said on the plus side. It has been proved conclusively that the industry is viable in a technical way, so far as the relevant natural conditions or terrain, climate, and pasturage are concerned, and that reindeer can maintain themselves in the region and reproduce in numbers. It is also clear that there is local need and demand for reindeer products, principally meat and hides, but also, in a lesser way, certain subsidiary products such as antlers. The industry has already demonstrated its importance as one of the few renewable resource industries which are possible in the North. It employs people and yields produce, and puts terrain to use which otherwise would remain unproductive. This is particularly important in an area where caribou and other edible creatures of both land and sea are declining in numbers, leaving the local peoples without their traditional means of sustenance. What is needed to make the industry thrive is apparently not yet clear, but the answer may lie largely in the fundamental philosophy or approach that is taken towards it, and the means or methods adopted to carry it forward.[44]

So far as issues of sovereignty are concerned, it is rather difficult to establish any important direct connection between them and the reindeer-muskox projects in the Canadian North. On the other hand it is unlikely that they were completely unrelated. As pointed out, these projects came to the fore largely because of the publicity given to them by Stefansson, at a time when Canadian authorities were extremely worried about the status and security of the northern territories and looked for means to establish undeniable rights of sovereignty over them through genuine occupation and use. Coincidentally, some of the principal figures connected with sovereignty problems, including Borden, Meighen, Harkin, and Stefansson, were also among those most concerned with the postwar reindeer-muskox projects. It is likely that they hoped to find in the establishment of reindeer and muskox herds (especially in any suitable island territories in the North) a further demonstration and manifestation of Canadian sovereignty. As events unfolded, these hopes were not realized. Stefansson's dreams of enormous domesticated herds of these animals came crashing to earth with the failure of his Baffin Island experiment, and the modest and confined project at the Mackenzie delta had very little significance to sovereignty considerations. In the 1920s, however, the idea surely had appeal.

10

Danish Sovereignty, Greenland, and the Ellesmere Island Affair of 1919–21

After the hiatus of inactivity during and just after the First World War, Canadian activity in the North was resumed in circumstances of stress and concern somewhat comparable to those that had existed when the Canadian government first took genuine steps to bring these regions under control about the turn of the century. Now, the causes of worry were such problems as the ultimate fate of Danish Greenland; the apparent disinclination of Denmark to recognize Canadian sovereignty over Ellesmere Island; the international status of the so-called Sverdrup Islands, which had been discovered by this Norwegian explorer during his expedition of 1898–1902; the evident need for Canada to take at least some steps towards occupation and use of her claimed territories in the North generally; the exciting prospect of air travel and transport in and across the Arctic and all that this implied for Canada; and perhaps most important of all, the brooding, restless figure of the explorer Vilhjalmur Stefansson, now an ambitious celebrity, and his determined agitation and planning for northern development (discussed in the previous chapter). The story of how Canadian authorities responded to and tried to solve these problems occupied centre stage through most of the following twenty years.

Danish Sovereignty over Greenland and Canadian Interests

The first major problem in the North to engage the attention of the Canadian government at this time was the question of what should happen to Greenland if Denmark should ever decide to dispose of it. The old Norse settlements in Greenland, which were established by Norwegian-Icelandic sea voyagers some years after their discovery of the island around 900 AD, were first independent, then fell under the sovereignty of the Norwegian Crown about 1260 AD, and then became subject to the union of Scandinavian states formalized by the Treaty of Kalmar in 1397. Contact with the Old World was gradually lost, and the settlements mysteriously disappeared in the early fifteenth century. Communications were re-established some years after the Columbian discovery of America; in 1721, the Norwegian pastor Hans Egede started a new colony, which soon was taken over by what was left of the Scandinavian union. By the Treaty of Kiel in 1814, the monarch of

Denmark-Norway was obliged to cede Norway to Sweden, but he managed to retain Greenland, along with Iceland and the Faeroe Islands.[1] During the later nineteenth and early twentieth centuries, Denmark gradually extended its activity and control in Greenland and then, starting with a request to the United States in 1915, set about securing formal recognition of its title in the island from the interested states. There was some uncertainty, however, whether Denmark was asking for general acknowledgment of her sovereignty over all of Greenland or of her right to extend her sovereignty over all of it. This later became a major issue, especially in the dispute with Norway over Eastern Greenland (see chapter 13).[2]

When Denmark ceded the Danish West Indies in the Caribbean to the United States by a treaty on 4 August 1916, the treaty had appended to it an official declaration by American Secretary of State Robert Lansing to the effect that "the Government of the United States of America will not object to the Danish government extending their political and economic interests to the whole of Greenland."[3] In 1920, similar declarations, essentially unqualified, were made by the French and Japanese governments.[4] In 1920, Great Britain also recognized Danish sovereignty over Greenland, but Britain's recognition was qualified and was preceded by considerable negotiation.

On 3 December 1903, Governor General the Earl of Minto wrote to Colonial Secretary Alfred Lyttelton, enclosing a memorandum which Prime Minister Laurier had handed him that morning concerning "the proposal of the Dominion Government to purchase Greenland." The memo stated that "it has long been apparent to those who have noted the trend of events in the United States that the most popular policy in the Republic is the extension of its territory" and, after citing certain evidence to bear out the contention, went on: "It is obviously in the interest of the Empire that no additional territory should be acquired by the United States in or adjacent to the north half of the continent of North America." Noting that an American attempt some years earlier to purchase the Danish West Indies had been frustrated when the Danish *Landstinget* (the upper house of its legislature) refused to confirm the agreement that had been made, and that American whalers and fishermen were active in the waters west of Greenland, the memo speculated that the United States might try to acquire Greenland. Canada was willing to purchase the island, however, and Laurier suggested that the British authorities ascertain confidentially whether the Danish government would agree to a British acquisition of Greenland for and at the expense of Canada.

At the instance of the Foreign Office, the matter was brought up in Copenhagen by Sir Edward Goschen, His Majesty's Minister in Denmark, with negative results. Johan Henrik Deuntzer, the Danish Foreign Minister, who had told Goschen that "Denmark would never dream of selling that territory" in the autumn of 1903, now reiterated his former statement, adding that "even if the Government wanted to do so, it was certain that the country would not sanction such a sale."[5]

In 1917, the question of Greenland was discussed by a subcommittee of the Imperial War Cabinet. John Douglas Hazen, Canada's Minister of Marine and Fisheries, had presented a paper outlining and assessing the strategic importance of the island. The report of the subcommittee in April of that year stated:

1. That the position of Greenland makes the question of its territorial ownership a matter of great

importance to the British Empire as a whole and to Canada in particular.

2. It is extremely undesirable that Greenland should pass out of the hands of present owner into those of any other Power, even a friendly Power.

3. In the event of any possible sale or disposal of Danish territory in Greenland, we should have a prior claim to its acquisition, and at the first favourable opportunity an undertaking should be secured from Denmark to this effect.[6]

On 10 September 1919, Colonial Secretary Lord Milner sent a confidential telegram to Canadian Governor General the Duke of Devonshire, saying that the Danish government proposed to try to get general recognition of Danish sovereignty over all Greenland at the Paris peace conference. He asked for the Canadian ministers' view in the matter, adding that he inferred from the evidence that they recognized in practice Danish sovereignty over all Greenland.[7] On 27 September, following consultations among Canadian government officials, Devonshire confirmed that Canada had no claim to any portion of Greenland. The Canadian government adhered to the April 1917 report of the subcommittee of the Imperial War Cabinet, however, and considered that recognition of Danish sovereignty throughout Greenland should be conditional on Denmark accepting the recommendations in the subcommittee report.[8]

On 28 January 1920, the Colonial Office sent word to the Duke of Devonshire that the British government was "in full agreement" with the Canadian view but feared that there would be considerable difficulty in getting Denmark to make the desired commitment. Apart from that, Denmark would probably inform the United States and France, which had already committed to recognize Danish rights in Greenland, and this would put the British government in "a somewhat invidious position." The two states mentioned could be sounded out in advance, but this might have the unfortunate result of defeating Canadian wishes.[9]

Great Britain took the lead in opposing Denmark's wish to place the question of Greenland before the powers at the peace conference, on grounds that the delegates wanted to concentrate on matters arising directly out of the war and settle them as quickly as possible.[10] On 16 March 1920, the Danish government sent a note to British Foreign Secretary Lord Curzon, saying that it had decided to submit the question to each of the principal powers separately. Accordingly, the Danes asked the British government for official recognition of Danish sovereignty over the whole of Greenland, which they said (apparently not recognizing the inconsistency) might be given in the same form that the American government used in Lansing's declaration of 4 August 1916.[11] Enclosed with the Danish note was a statement "showing the principles according to which the colony of Greenland is governed, which may prove of interest in dealing with the matter in question" – but which, whether intentionally or not, contained strong evidence that Denmark did not at the time consider that it had full sovereignty over all Greenland:

> As already stated, since the beginning of the eighteenth century Denmark has founded colonies in Greenland. When it became known

FIGURE 10-1: MAP OF GREENLAND SHOWING ROUTES OF THE VARIOUS EXPEDITIONS THAT HAD CROSSED THE GREENLAND ICE TO 1915. KNUD RASMUSSEN, "REPORT OF THE FIRST THULE EXPEDITION," *MEDDELELSER OM GRØNLAND* 51:8 (1915): 285–340.

that there were Esquimaux beyond the territories hitherto under administration, such as Cape York, Danish missionary and commercial enterprise was extended to those localities, which were also formally taken possession of on behalf of the Danish crown.

Danish explorers have visited practically the whole of uninhabited Greenland and made maps of the country, but no formal occupation of the whole of Greenland has actually taken place. In view of Danish sentiments in this matter, as well as the interests of the Esquimaux

> population, it would be desirable if the Danish Government could extend its activity by proclaiming its sovereignty over the entire territory of Greenland.

On 19 May 1920, the Foreign Office sent a reply to Danish minister Erik Wilhelm Grevenkop-Castenskiold, saying that if the Danish government would grant the right of pre-emption to the British Empire in case Denmark should ever wish to dispose of Greenland, the British government would be willing at once to recognize officially Danish sovereignty over the island. The note added that the governments of France, Italy, Japan, and the United States were being informed of the British attitude.[12]

As might have been expected, American officials opposed this British proposition. On 8 June 1920, Ambassador John W. Davis wrote a note to Lord Curzon, informing him that the American government "is not disposed to recognize the existence in a third Government of a right of pre-emption to acquire this territory if the Danish government should desire to dispose of it and accordingly reserves for future consideration what position it may take in the event of a specific proposal for such a transfer."[13] Lord Milner sent a copy of this note to the Duke of Devonshire on 7 July, accompanied by a suggestion from Lord Curzon to adopt "a less formal procedure" by merely notifying the Danish government that "in the event of Denmark parting with the sovereignty over the territory, its acquisition by any third Power could not be recognized in view of its geographical proximity to the Dominion of Canada."[14]

It soon became apparent that Denmark herself was no more inclined to recognize a British right of pre-emption than was the United States. On 20 July, Grevenkop-Castenskiold sent a forthrightly worded note to Lord Curzon, insisting that Danish sovereignty over Greenland had never been questioned by any foreign power; that what Denmark really asked for was "formal recognition of an existing status sanctioned by prescriptive right"; that Denmark's conviction about the matter had already been confirmed by recognition from France, Italy, and Japan; and that Great Britain's wish for a right of pre-emption (the way such qualification made) could therefore not be granted.[15] In these circumstances, Lord Milner wrote to the Duke of Devonshire on 5 August advising that Canada accept Lord Curzon's suggestion,[16] and Devonshire cabled Canada's acceptance on 20 August.[17]

With the consent of Canada thus secured, the Foreign Office sent the following notice of official recognition to Grevenkop-Castenskiold on 6 September 1920:

> With reference to your note No. 202/30/B. 2, concerning the official recognition by His Majesty's Government of His Danish Majesty's sovereignty over Greenland, which you were good enough to address to me on 20th July, I have the honour to inform you that His Majesty's Government recognize His Danish Majesty's sovereignty over Greenland, but in view of its geographical proximity to the Dominion of Canada, His Majesty's Government must reserve their right to be consulted should the Danish Government at any time contemplate the alienation of this territory.[18]

Lord Curzon's suggested reservation was not followed in precise terms. Where he had recommended notifying the Danish government that in the event of the alienation of Greenland "its acquisition by any third Power could not be recognized" by Great Britain, the note of recognition adopted the stronger line that the British government "must reserve their right to be consulted" if Denmark contemplated such alienation.

The events summarized above brought to an end any lingering questions and doubts about Canadian recognition of Danish sovereignty in and throughout Greenland. Henceforth, Canada's concern with Denmark in this region was to be directed primarily to securing similar recognition from Denmark of Canada's rights in Ellesmere Island and also to watching, as an interested observer, the developing dispute between Denmark and Norway over Eastern Greenland.

Vilhjalmur Stefansson and the Ellesmere Island Affair of 1919–21

One of the most important factors, and perhaps the most important, in the revival of Canadian concern about the North after the First World War was the fear of Danish designs upon Ellesmere Island and perhaps other Arctic islands claimed by Canada. It is not easy to date the precise beginning of this alarm, but it is apparent that the figure of Vilhjalmur Stefansson, as well as his campaign for the protection of northern game animals and generally of Canada's interests in the Arctic, looms large in the background. The commission to investigate the possibilities of raising large reindeer and musk-ox herds in the Canadian North, detailed in the previous chapter, is a case in point. Two members of the commission, James Harkin and Stefansson, became much involved in a rather strange and consequence-laden affair, which started out as an attempt to stop the Greenland Inuit from killing excessive numbers of musk-ox on Ellesmere Island. On 11 July 1919, Harkin wrote the following letter to Deputy Minister of the Interior William W. Cory:

> I would recommend that a letter along the lines indicated below be sent to the Danish Government from the Secretary of State for External Affairs. It is understood that Mr. Dagaard Fensen, Direktoren for Styrelson of Koloniere, 1 Gronland, Copenhagen Denmark, is the official of the Danish Government who deals with these matters.
>
> From reports that have been received here from Northern Canada, it is understood that as a result of the visits of Arctic explorers to Greenland and Ellesmere Land the Greenland Eskimos are now crossing to Ellesmere Land more frequently than in the past for the purpose of killing Musk ox. The Government of Canada has created a closed season for Musk ox throughout the Northwest Territories of Canada and the Arctic Archipelago. This was found necessary because of the great decrease in the number of these animals, even in remote districts. Three marked copies of the Northwest Game Act, which applies to Ellesmere land are enclosed.
>
> This question was considered fully at a recent meeting of the Advisory Board on Wild Life Protection and it was decided at this meeting to approach the Danish Government and request their co-operation in

> the protection of the Musk ox on Ellesmere Land. In all probability a great deal of good could be done by having the authorities in Greenland acquaint the Greenland Eskimos with the provisions of the Canadian Northwest Game Act.[19]

Cory responded by writing a letter on 23 July to Under Secretary of State for External Affairs Sir Joseph Pope, incorporating the substance of the above letter and making the same request. He also made the extraordinary suggestion that the Danish government should allow the Canadian government "to station such officers as may be necessary in Greenland for the purpose of protecting the Musk Ox of Ellesmere Land."[20] Governor General the Duke of Devonshire sent the request to London in a dispatch on 31 July, which also formed the subject of notes that Foreign Secretary Lord Curzon sent to the Danish government on 27 August and 5 November. The Danish government conferred with the Administration of the Colonies in Greenland and then sent a reply to Curzon on 12 April 1920, which was transmitted to Ottawa on 26 April. Enclosed with the reply to Curzon was a statement by Knud Rasmussen, explorer and director of the Danish missionary and trade station at Thule, who had also been consulted by the Danish authorities.

Rasmussen's statement, written at Copenhagen on 8 March, described Inuit traditional hunting of the muskox and reindeer (i.e., caribou) in both Ellesmere Island and northwestern Greenland, and the more destructive hunting with firearms by modern expeditions (mainly American) to the extent that the caribou in the region had been exterminated and the existence of the muskox was threatened. The muskox herds were so large that there was no immediate danger of extermination, however, and since Inuit killed muskox mainly to obtain their hides as substitutes for the more desirable caribou hides, Rasmussen was already trying to remedy the situation by importing reindeer hides from northern Europe. His statement ended as follows:

Figure 10-2: W. W. Cory, Deputy Minister of the Interior and Commissioner of the Northwest Territories, 1919-1931. William *J. Topley / Library and Archives Canada / PA-167436.*

> As head of the Thule Station at Cape York I am convinced that it would be impossible without disastrous consequences to prohibit the hunting of the musk ox within the immemorial hunting areas of the esquimaux unless effective

counter-balancing measures as above indicated are previously introduced.

The havoc wrought by white men should also be made good by them. And it would be morally indefensible first to exterminate the reindeer and then to prohibit the hunting of the musk ox.

It is well known that the territory of the polar esquimaux falls within the region designated as "no Man's land" and there is therefore no authority in the district except that which I exercise through my station – an authority which I have hitherto had no difficulty in maintaining chiefly because the polar esquimaux, when reasonably treated, adopt a very rational attitude toward all decisions which the station considers it advisable to take.

The musk ox hunts have hitherto only taken place in the months of March, April and May, during the remainder of the year these animals are practically speaking protected, and it is to be hoped that it will not be long before the station will be able to agree to their complete protection, but this will not be feasible for the reasons already given, before the quantity of hides needed by the population can be provided from elsewhere.

This plan should, it must be hoped, in consequence of the arrangements already made, be realized within a few years.

Fully conscious of the work which is ahead and of the responsibility I assume, I venture to close with the observation that, in order to carry out the protective measures indicated in this statement, I shall need no assistance whatever from the Canadian government.[21]

The reply of the Danish government contained the following statement:

> The Government therefore submitted the matter to the director of the above mentioned Thule station, Mr. Knud Rasmussen, who thereupon has handed to the Administration of the Colonies of Greenland a statement on the subject in which he comes to the conclusion that he will not need the assistance of the Canadian Government in order to carry out the protective measure indicated in his statement.
>
> Having acquainted themselves with the statement in question my Government think that they can subscribe to what Mr. Rasmussen says therein and have instructed me to submit a copy of it to His Britannic Majesty's Government.[22]

Receipt of the Danish notes in Ottawa on 11 May 1920[23] caused a worried reaction on the part of Canadian authorities. By a rather strange coincidence, Harkin had written a memo to Cory one week earlier, noting that no reply from the Danish government had as yet been received and suggesting that a further letter be sent asking for one. His memo also alleged that Rasmussen had sent an expedition of Greenland Inuit to Axel Heiberg Island to kill muskox and to take furs.[24] Harkin immediately showed Rasmussen's statement to Stefansson, who wrote a lengthy memorandum about it on 15 May, contradicting Rasmussen's statement that the danger of exterminating the muskox was not yet imminent and strongly suggesting that the Canadian government should assert "very definite authority" over all the lands to the west of Baffin Bay, Smith Sound, and Robeson Channel.[25] On 16 June, Harkin wrote a memorandum to Cory, which repeated and enlarged upon the substance of Stefansson's memorandum, ending with the following recommendations:

> It seems to me that Canada should in the first place take a very strong stand in regard to its exclusive ownership of and authority over Ellesmere land;
>
> That the Danish Government should be advised that a continuance of the slaughter of musk ox in Ellesmere land by Greenland Eskimos cannot be tolerated because it inevitably will mean the early extermination of the musk ox;
>
> That if Denmark will not immediately agree to entirely stop this slaughter Canada should establish a Mounted Police post in Ellesmere land for the purpose of stopping the slaughter and asserting Canadian authority.[26]

Cory incorporated Harkin's recommendations in a note to Sir Joseph Pope on 23 June and asked on behalf of his minister (Arthur Meighen) "to have an appropriate communication sent through the proper channels at once."[27] This was done by means of a dispatch from Governor General the Duke of Devonshire to Colonial Secretary Lord Milner on 13 July, which repeated the recommendations and asked that the matter be brought to the attention of the Danish government.[28]

A short time after this, on 6 September, Great Britain (with Canada's approval) recognized Denmark's sovereignty over Greenland. As noted above, Britain dropped her earlier demand for a right of pre-emption if Denmark should ever decide to dispose of Greenland, and claimed only the right to be consulted in this eventuality. Obviously, British recognition had been granted without getting any corresponding Danish recognition of Canada's rights either over Ellesmere Island in particular or over the Arctic Archipelago in general, thus failing to ease Canadian worries.

In the meantime, Vilhjalmur Stefansson's potent influence was felt behind the scenes. Stefansson did not believe in wasting time with little fish if he could get the big ones to bite, and at this time he was trying to hook Sir Robert Borden (who had just vacated the prime ministership). On 29 September 1920, Borden wrote a confidential letter to his successor Meighen, as follows:

> Recently I have had some correspondence with Mr. V. Stefansson respecting the introduction to his account of the Arctic Expedition which he has requested me to write. From one of his letters dated 6th September I extract the following: –
>
> "The recognition of the value of the islands north of Canada will come during the next fifty years as the recognition of the value of Alaska has come during the last fifty. It has therefore been for me excellent fortune that the chance fell to me to increase the land area of Canada by the addition of these islands.
>
> "Should the country, upon a fair scrutiny of my work and an estimate

> of the difficulties under which had [*sic*] to be done, consider me worthy of confidence, I should like to devote the next ten years, as I have the last fourteen, to increasing our knowledge of the northern half of our country and to the possible increase of its are [*sic*] by the discovery and exploration of further new lands."[29]

About a month later, on 3 November, Borden wrote another confidential letter to Meighen, again quoting extensively from another letter from Stefansson, who on this occasion was more specific about what he thought should be done:

> In a recent letter from Mr. Stefansson reference is made to the importance of maintaining and strengthening the claims of Canada to which lands in the far North which in future years may have a much greater value than is apparent at present.
>
> I extract from Mr. Stefansson's letter the following: –
>
> "The signs are continually multiplying that other countries are beginning to suspect there may be considerable economic value in even the remotest lands. Any that are hereafter discovered are sure to go to those who discover them, for with a clear realization of their value a discovery is likely to be followed by occupation.
>
> It seems that there are many now in Ottawa who see clearly the importance of making good our claim to Ellesmere Island and the other islands in the vicinity of Greenland. I want to urge the equal importance of an occupation of Wrangel Island and an exploration of the ocean to the north. Ellesmere Island is already valued enough by Denmark for her to question our title, but nobody has as yet taken any steps with regard to Wrangel Island. A quiet occupation by us now will probably not bring forth any protest for several years and by then our title will be clear, especially in view of the fact that it is originally a British discovery and that the only people who have occupied it for any length of time were the members of our expedition in 1914 (they were there six months).
>
> There are two regions in which there seems reasonable prospect of the discovery of new land. One is to the north of Wrangel Island and for this work Wrangel Island should be used as a base. The other is to the northwest of Borden Island (First Land, discovered by us in 1915). For exploration in this quarter a base should be maintained in Melville Island. The domestication of the musk ox in Melville Island could well be undertaken in connection which [*sic*] such a scientific expedition and without greatly increasing the expense or complicating the program."
>
> I feel that a good deal of importance should be attached to these observations and that such steps as are reasonably necessary to attain the object suggested ought to be taken.[30]

Stefansson wrote and spoke persistently in this vein during these months, for the most part to senior government officials or to influential private figures whose co-operation and support he wished to secure. Perhaps his most significant performance came before the Advisory Technical Board, created by the Department of the Interior in June to deal with technical issues (including Arctic sovereignty and related problems), in a special meeting on 1 October 1920.[31] Evidently the meeting was called suddenly and as a matter of great urgency; the chairman of the board, Surveyor General Édouard-Gaston Deville, had received only verbal notification of it, and one of the principal members, Parks Commissioner James Harkin, knew nothing about it until three hours before it began.[32] Stefansson had an opportunity to present his case to this influential group, and he made the most of the occasion. The minutes begin as follows:

> *Chairman* – We have been told that you (Mr. Stefansson) were to speak to this Board so that the Board might report to the Minister.
>
> *Mr. Stefansson* – Yes.
>
> *Chairman* – Perhaps you might explain to the Board what you wish to say.
>
> *Mr. Stefansson* – It starts with Mr. Harkin and myself, we are both members of the Reindeer and Muskox Commission.
>
> I am not sure exactly how it started but I found that the Danes are planning a scientific expedition which is semi-commercial, to cover five years. Now that expedition was thought of years ago. It has been in the air that long. Mr. Rasmussen is to be at the head of it and he was planning originally to come up through, I do not know exactly where – I heard about it eight or ten years ago. The plan then was to explore the mainland of north Greenland and the north coast of the mainland of Canada for purely scientific purposes, but they never got the funds for it and nothing seemed to happen but the country has been branching out in commercial development and they have a trading station on North Star Bay around 77° north latitude on the north coast of Greenland. They are being well supported. The Company is semi-commercial, semi-patriotic and philanthropic. Their aim is scientific as well as a commercial profit. Now they have announced the final expedition is going to cover a term of 5 years. They seem now to be going north to Lancaster Sound. I will name all these islands for you…. These are the islands north of Lancaster Sound. This is what Mr. Harkin and I took up with the Commission, that these people were going to kill a lot of our muskox. They are trying, I believe, to establish trading stations over there and colonize the country with Danish Eskimos from Greenland and that meant the killing of muskox both for food and sale purposes. So, Mr. Harkin here, really knows better than I – I think we sent a note over to them, the note was sent to the Secretary of External Affairs of Denmark, saying, that the muskox is an animal protected under the Game Laws and they must not kill them. Then, I believe a reply came back, which I heard

directly from Mr. Rasmussen, he wrote me in Danish, he said among other things, "There is no question of our breaking Canadian Game Laws because we are not coming into Canada but a part farther north. It is not under Canadian jurisdiction". I have heard since in his communication to you (Mr. Harkin) he referred to it as "No Man's Land."

Mr. Harkin – Yes, he did.

Mr. Stefansson – It amounts to the same thing. It struck me right away that anyone making claim to that country will get ahead of us. We have got a great deal of claim on it, but whether it will be recognized or not is another thing.[33]

In his lengthy address, Stefansson summarized both British and foreign exploration in the Arctic islands, pointed out the vulnerability of the Sverdrup Islands (which had been discovered by Norwegians and were unoccupied by anyone), and, disagreeing with the concept of the sector principle, suggested that Canada might well claim the unoccupied Wrangel Island (see chapter 11) and any new islands which could be discovered. He also implied, erroneously, that there were no treaty provisions between the United States and Russia delimiting their territories or rights in that region.

In the discussion that followed, Harkin remarked that the main question was whether it was worthwhile for Canada to establish her sovereignty over these northern islands, and he expressed his own strong view that it was.[34] Finally Deville, as chairman, put into summary form the three main points upon which the board had to report. They were as follows:

1. Whether steps should be taken by the Government to secure Canadian title to those islands.

2. If the Board is of opinion that such steps should be taken, then what should these steps be.

3. Report as to the advisability of further exploration in those Northern Seas.[35]

It was decided to refer these questions to a subcommittee of the board, which would investigate the whole matter and prepare a report upon it. Those selected for the subcommittee were Deville, Harkin, and four others from the Department of the Interior: Dr. Otto Klotz, Director of the Dominion Observatory and Chief Astronomer; Noel Ogilvie, Superintendent of the Geodetic Survey of Canada; F.C.C. Lynch, Superintendent of the Natural Resources Intelligence Branch; and J. J. McArthur, Commissioner of the International Boundary Survey.[36]

It would appear on the evidence that this performance by Stefansson before the Advisory Technical Board, as well as the resultant appointment of a subcommittee to consider the issued he had raised, initiated the tangled skein of events that followed. In any case, a great flurry of activity behind the scenes went on without let-up for months.

The subcommittee submitted a brief preliminary report, with very little delay, on 13 October 1920, recommending "that the Government should take effectual steps immediately to firmly establish the Sovereignty of Canada with respect to the Northern Islands." It added that it was preparing to submit a specific recommendation as soon as possible "respecting the method of establishing such sovereignty."[37]

Figure 10-3: J. B. Harkin, 1937. *Yousuf Karsh / Library and Archives Canada / accession 1987-054 no. 12326.*

Evidently acting on this recommendation, the Advisory Technical Board sent Deputy Minister Cory a draft memorandum to council on 15 October, authorizing the Minister of the Interior to send an expedition to northern Canada and providing $100,000 to meet preliminary expenses. It considered that the total cost might run to $200,000 or $250,000, but the $100,000 would be sufficient to purchase or charter a ship and provide crew and supplies. On the same day, Cory composed a memorandum to Cabinet incorporating the board's recommendations, at the same time adding his strong advice that "further explorations be carried on." These recommendations must have been considered premature: copies in the Canadian public archives contain notes on them, saying that the board's memo was sent back to it on 16 October "for further attention" and that Cory's memo was "not used."[38] Perhaps nonplussed for the moment, the Advisory Technical Board passed a resolution at its meeting on 20 October, authorizing its chairman to interview the Deputy Minister of the Interior regarding the proposed Arctic expedition.[39]

In the meantime, a continuing effort was being made to obtain as much information as possible about the Arctic islands and to consider all available evidence to meet what some of the board members considered an emergency situation. A technical, non-political report on Ellesmere Island completed on 13 October by Compiler of Geological Information Wyatt Malcolm was circulated,[40] as was a larger, more detailed report on the Arctic islands generally that Malcolm completed on 6 November.[41] W. F. King's 1905 *Report* on Canada's title to the archipelago became urgent reading, and a supplement was prepared summarizing the work of both Canadian and foreign expeditions in the Arctic during the years since King's document had appeared.[42] A letter written by Knud Rasmussen to the Governor of Canada on 10 August 1920, and signed for in his absence by an otherwise unidentified man named Carlaillollr (who also wrote an accompanying letter on 15 September 1920), seemed to cause great apprehension when it arrived in Canada. Rasmussen wrote the letter to say that he might not be able to accept an invitation to appear before the Reindeer-Muskox Commission, which had been holding hearings in Ottawa, but if unable to attend, he would share his views in writing. On the face of it, this was innocent enough, but he gave, without explanation, a sudden and unanticipated journey to northern Greenland as his reason for not getting to Ottawa. Some

Canadian officials saw this emergency voyage as cause for serious alarm.[43]

On 21 October, Harkin wrote a confidential memorandum to Deputy Minister Cory on the subject of an urgent Canadian expedition to Ellesmere Island. He suggested three possible methods of getting there without waiting until next summer: (1) overland from Fullerton near the northwestern extremity of Hudson Bay ("difficult and hazardous.... In an emergency I think Stefansson could make it but I doubt if there is anyone else who could"); (2) by a staunch ship to Bylot Island and the rest of the way either over land and ice, or by plane, or in the ship as soon as navigation opened next summer (the plane trip could be undertaken if it "will not exceed 500 miles"); and (3) by zeppelin from Britain, dropping men and supplies by parachute ("the Imperial Government would expect a guarantee. For advice about the sea voyage into and through Baffin Bay reference should be made to Captain Bob Bartlett, who, although at present in New York.... Of course is a Newfoundlander, not an American").[44]

The following day, Harkin wrote a memo to Cory, evidently by prearrangement, suggesting three reliable sea captains as top possibilities for the position of ship commander if a northern expedition were dispatched. The three were Captain H. C. Pickels of Mahone Bay, Nova Scotia, who was considered the best choice, and the brothers Will and John Bartlett of Newfoundland, who were father and uncle, respectively, of the famous Captain Bob.[45] One day later, Cory wired Canadian government immigration agent W. H. Sullivan in New York, requesting that he contact Pickels immediately after his expected arrival there to ask him to come to Ottawa for consultation.[46] (To look ahead for a moment, Pickels arrived in Ottawa after a few days' delay, and after senior officials had interviewed him and secured testimonials about him, he was given a one-year contract on 16 December 1920 to command the *Arctic* on a northern expedition.[47])

The whole problem was discussed in detail at the seventeenth regular meeting of the Advisory Technical Board on 27 October. Deville brought instructions from the minister and the deputy minister that "immediate action if possible should be taken by the Board." Klotz reported the substance of two letters, which he had recently received from Stefansson. After due deliberation, the board passed the following resolution proposed by Harkin and seconded by McArthur:

> That in the opinion of the Technical Board immediate action should be taken in the matter of occupation and administration of Ellesmere Land for the purpose of definitely establishing Canadian sovereignty therein.
>
> That in that connection the Government should immediately ascertain whether it is practicable to send a boat into Baffin Bay this autumn.
>
> That if reports in that connection are favourable a ship should be forthwith despatched to Baffin Bay with instructions to proceed to Bylot Island.
>
> That as soon as Bylot Island is reached an aeroplane party should be sent to Ellesmere Land to start occupancy and administration.
>
> That an overland party with the same object in view should also be sent from the ship at Bylot Island.
>
> That the ship should proceed from Bylot Island as soon as ice conditions permit, to Ellesmere Land to extend and amplify the work

> of occupation and administration started by the two preceding parties.
>
> That if expert advice indicates that it is not possible for a boat to navigate Baffin Bay this autumn, the British Government should be asked to immediately transport a Canadian party to Ellesmere Land by airship.[48]

Although the records of the meeting do not indicate any disagreement within the board, one important member of it obviously dissented strongly from the proposed course of action. On 29 October, Deville wrote a memo to Cory about the board's resolutions, containing the following:

> I wish to dissociate myself from these resolutions. From the information to which I have had access, I am satisfied that the alleged intention of Knud Rasmussen or of the Danish Government to occupy Ellesmere island or to establish a trading post on it has never existed otherwise than in Mr. Sefanson's [*sic*] imagination. The wild schemes suggested for the immediate occupation of the island can only result, if they become known, in bringing ridicule over the Department.[49]

On 28 October, Loring Christie, Legal Adviser to the Department of External Affairs, wrote a secret memorandum for the Prime Minister entitled "Exploration and Occupation of the Northern Arctic Islands." In the memo, Christie expressed fears akin to those of Harkin. He insisted that it had become "more urgent" for Canada to confirm her sovereignty over the Arctic islands because, according to information possessed by the Department of the Interior, Denmark had gone beyond merely contemplating an expedition to occupy Ellesmere Island and had actually sent it. (In fact, it was reported to have already arrived there.) The only islands that might be in danger were those north of Lancaster Sound. The only threat appeared to be that from Denmark, since neither the United States nor Norway, which had both been more active in the region than Denmark, showed any intention of taking action. Christie recommended that a Canadian government expedition, which would be announced as a continuation of the Stefansson and Bernier expeditions, should be sent north as soon as possible to map known islands and discover new ones, establish customs and game regulations, and construct police posts. He also suggested that Stefansson should be engaged for the exploration work.[50]

In spite of the Advisory Technical Board's recommendation for immediate action, no decision was taken to do anything in precipitous fashion. On 30 October, Cory sent a memo to Deville and Harkin informing them that he had discussed the question of Arctic sovereignty with the minister, and it had been decided that it would be inadvisable to attempt an expedition until navigation opened up in the spring. In the meantime, however, planning and preparation should continue.[51]

This decision was not acceptable to Harkin, who wrote back to Cory on 1 November saying that it was not certain that the Danes had started to occupy Ellesmere Island and that a British or Canadian expedition might still get there first. He therefore advised two things: to get the advice of a reliable ice captain about whether a ship could still be sent into Baffin Bay "this fall" and to ask the British government whether it would transport an expedition to Ellesmere Island by airship.[52]

In the meantime, Stefansson continued to promote his projects by mail and through personal interviews. On 30 October, he sent a letter to Cory, saying that he was writing it at the request of Sir James Lougheed, whom he had interviewed two days earlier.[53] On 3 November, he wrote to Deville suggesting that he should find out from the Department of Marine how long it would take and how much it would cost to put the *Arctic* in seaworthy condition, since she was really "the logical vessel" for the projected northern expedition.[54] On the same day, he wrote a note to Harkin, asking him to send the names and addresses of all the members of the Advisory Technical Board to his secretary, Olive Rathburn, in New York;[55] and at about this time, he sent Deville a complimentary copy of an article he had recently published titled "The Region of Maximum Inaccessibility in the Arctic," which located this region between Alaska and the North Pole.[56] Here, presumably, was where remaining unknown islands were most likely to be discovered. Deville answered Stefansson's letter two days later, saying that the board had already come to the same conclusion about the *Arctic* and, if approval could be obtained, would refit and use her.[57] On the same day, Minister of Marine and Fisheries Charles Colquhoun Ballantyne wrote to Lougheed (the acting Prime Minister at the time) informing him that the *Arctic* could be made available next spring but that it would cost about $35,000 to make her ready for sea service.

In the meantime, Captain Pickels had attended part of the 3 November meeting of the Advisory Technical Board by invitation. The discussion revealed the impracticability of starting a northern expedition at that time, and the members agreed that Harkin should draft a report on the subject of Arctic sovereignty.[58] Preparing this report must have caused Harkin a good deal of mental anguish, judging by the number of preliminary drafts and versions, generally undated and unsigned, which have survived in various collections of documents in the archives.[59] One of these, prepared for the meeting of the Advisory Technical Board on 10 November, seems to represent the outcome of his effort.[60]

In his report, Harkin summarized the background of events that had revived Canadian fears for the security of the northern islands and then proposed a course of action. He started from the premise that although Canadians had generally taken complete British sovereignty over the archipelago for granted, it might well be that under standard rules of international law there was room for grave doubts about it – and Denmark might already have undertaken to appropriate Ellesmere Island. Referring to Dr. King's memo of 1905 as evidence that the problem was not new, he noted that the issue had arisen again when Canada protested to Denmark over the killing of muskox by Greenland Inuit on Ellesmere Island, and he summarized the correspondence and unsatisfactory response of the Danes. Citing Oppenheim's *International Law* as authoritative on the acquisition of territory and the need for genuine occupation and administration, he observed that there was neither occupation nor administration of Ellesmere Island or the other islands of the archipelago. Concentrating specifically on Ellesmere, since this was the one where doubt as to British sovereignty had been raised, Harkin provided an overview of the history of the activity of white men there, which indicated that the British title to the island would be at best inchoate, resulting mainly from rights of discovery and acts of possession. Denmark apparently regarded Ellesmere Island as "No Man's Land," an aspect of the situation "first raised" by Stefansson, whose talk to the

Advisory Technical Board on 1 October 1920 Harkin quoted at length. There were peculiar features about Denmark's behaviour in the matter, such as Rasmussen's letter of 10 August 1920, saying that he was making a hasty trip to Greenland after he had accepted an invitation to testify before the Reindeer-Muskox Commission in Ottawa; the fact that his secretary had held the second letter until September 15 before mailing it; his secretary's statement that Rasmussen had taken all correspondence concerning the matter with him; and Denmark's evident recent attention to questions of international law, as shown by her performance in seeking general recognition of the sovereignty in Greenland.[61] Digressing to discuss in detail matters such as the Monroe Doctrine and the wildlife and mineral resources of Ellesmere Island, Harkin returned to his main theme with a strong plea for action by Canada to establish its sovereignty beyond possibility of doubt. His recommendations were mainly reiterations of what had already been put forward by himself and others: establishment of Mounted Police posts in selected northern locations and extension of their patrols; a special expedition to the most northerly islands; permanent occupation, scientific investigation, and commercial exploitation where possible; establishment of post offices as symbols of sovereignty; and use of aircraft. The project of most immediate importance was to send a government expedition to northern waters as soon as possible the following year. For that purpose, he suggested the *Arctic* with Captain Pickels as skipper.[62]

Harkin's papers include a copy of a letter of 17 November 1920 from Knud Rasmussen to H. G. Henderson of the Governor General's Office (erroneously described as the Secretary of State for External Affairs). In it, Rasmussen said that he had now returned from his journey to North Greenland and was ready to help by giving information to the Reindeer-Muskox Commission. He would not be able to come to Ottawa in person, however, because he had responsibilities with a Danish commission discussing Greenland and, in June 1921, he would be starting a four-year expedition to the Central Inuit and the Arctic Archipelago. Nevertheless, he would send by mail detailed replies to any questions asked of him.[63]

In the meantime, Stefansson's proposal regarding Wrangel Island had been under discussion (see chapter 11). Sir Joseph Pope, who at the suggestion of Lougheed had been attending some of the meetings of the Advisory Technical Board, indicated his disapproval with the idea in a memo to Prime Minister Meighen on 25 November. On the other hand, Pope strongly favoured action in the archipelago north of the Canadian mainland:

> It [Wrangel Island] is far removed from the Dominion – in fact is not even in the western hemisphere, as the 180th meridian of longitude falls upon it. Essentially, it is an Asiatic island.... It was generally considered that any pretensions we might have to this island must be of a very unsubstantial character, and could only result in weakening our legitimate claims to the Arctic islands contiguous to our own territory, for if we can go so far afield as Wrangel to take possession of islands, unconnected with Canada, what is there to prevent the United States or any other power, laying claim to islands far from their shores but adjacent to our own.
>
> Our claim to the islands north of the mainland of Canada rests upon quite a different footing, by reason of their geographical position and

> contiguity.... I think the suggestion to send a Mounted Police force to occupy certain stations on Ellsmere [*sic*] Land and adjacent regions an excellent one, and one which should be no longer postponed. In the past our territorial claims have suffered not a little by inaction and delay, e.g., Alaska and Labrador.[64]

Evidently feeling that there was need for a capable person who could give his undivided attention to the increasing complexities of the projected Arctic voyage, Cory wrote a memo to Commissioner of the International Boundary Survey James J. McArthur on 1 December, asking him to "have the services of Mr. J. D. Craig made available for special work in connection with the northern expedition."[65] The response must have come immediately, because on the same day Cory wrote to Craig asking that he proceed immediately upon the anticipated arrival of Captain Pickels to make the necessary arrangements with him, after consulting with Deville and Harkin.[66] On 4 December, Harkin wrote to Cory referring to the minister's instructions for the preparation of a memo to council about the northern islands and reiterating the legal and other questions that worried him. He suggested that these questions should be brought to the attention of Craig, since responsibility for the preparation of the memo "will now naturally devolve upon" him.[67]

Concern about the secrecy aspect of the proposed expedition was aroused by a letter written to Harkin on 30 November by Dr. Rowland B. Orr, Director of the Ontario Provincial Museum, in which Orr said that he understood a scientific expedition was being sent to Baffin Bay next spring and asked for information about it.[68] Harkin replied promptly, saying in curt fashion that he knew of no information he could give him.[69] He then sent a copy of Orr's letter to Cory, remarking: "I have repeatedly pointed out that in my opinion it is imperative that the utmost secrecy should be maintained with regard to this matter, and that at least from this moment on steps should be taken which will absolutely insure secrecy."[70] Cory advised (too late) that it would be well to delay replying to Orr, but Harkin might inquire where he got his information.[71] When Cory sent Craig to see Harkin on the morning of 6 December about a safe name for the expedition, Harkin suggested that it should be called "The Reindeer Expedition" because many people in Canada and elsewhere knew about the plans for reindeer herds and "this name could be used effectively to camouflage the real purpose of the expedition." Any announcement should be delayed as long as possible, he urged, because if the Danes

> are really now in occupation in Ellesmere Land, or intend to take action in that regard next Spring, even a Canadian announcement of the Reindeer Expedition would arouse suspicion on their part and would probably result in special efforts on their part. If they believe that Canada is still asleep they probably will not hurry.
>
> The United States is undoubtedly in a position to put in claims with respect to Ellesmere Land and I imagine that a reindeer expedition would be a good camouflage insofar as they are concerned.[72]

So far as can be divined from the documents, a lull ensued, and little of significance is recorded during the next four or five weeks. Stefansson was as anxious as ever to get involved in a northern expedition, however, and on 8 January 1921, he wrote to Prime Minister Meighen in the following vein:

> You know my anxiety that Canada shall continue the work of exploration in the North and my eagerness to help in that work. This exploration would be not only for the increase of knowledge but to make good Canadian claims to territories already discovered and to make Canadian any islands that may yet be found.
>
> I have now been ten years in the service of the Government of Canada in exploratory work in the North. This has been without salary. As a result, I am not well off financially. I have now received an offer of wages for lecturing thirty-five weeks next summer and winter that are high from my point of view. I have signed a contract for this work which has a clause providing that it may be cancelled should I go North on a polar expedition the summer of 1921. For that reason it is important for me to know before the end of January whether the Government needs my services. If you think you do, I should consider it both an honor and a public duty to serve either in planning the expeditions or in actual command of them.
>
> I shall hold myself in readiness until February 1st for this Government service and hope the Government can let me know before that time whether those services are wanted.[73]

Meighen had a copy of this letter sent to Minister of the Interior Lougheed on 11 January for his consideration.[74] This was unnecessary: Stefansson had already written a similar letter to Sir James three days earlier.[75] Stefansson also wrote essentially the same letter to Sir Robert Borden,[76] at Borden's own request. Stefansson had evidently been in Ottawa a few days before, and Borden remarked, when sending a copy of the letter to Meighen, that "Stefansson's views as expressed to me seem to have a good deal of cogency, and at any convenient time, I shall be glad to discuss them with you."[77]

As plans for the expedition proceeded, various officials offered advice to achieve different objectives. Dr. Klotz was interested in the possibilities for scientific research and wrote a memo to Craig on 10 January, noting the heavy representation of scientific personnel on earlier expeditions. Although exploration and scientific observation were "a side issue" in the present instance, Klotz noted, the opportunities offered "should be exploited to the fullest extent of the time available."[78] His memo provoked several others on the same subject. The same day, W. Stuart Edwards, Assistant Deputy Minister of the Department of Justice, made the following suggestions:

> (1) In any actual taking possession of the northern islands the settlements established should be at the mouths of the largest river systems, to establish claims to the drainage basins;
>
> (2) A large-scale map should be prepared showing all available data, and as much historical and other information as possible should be acquired;

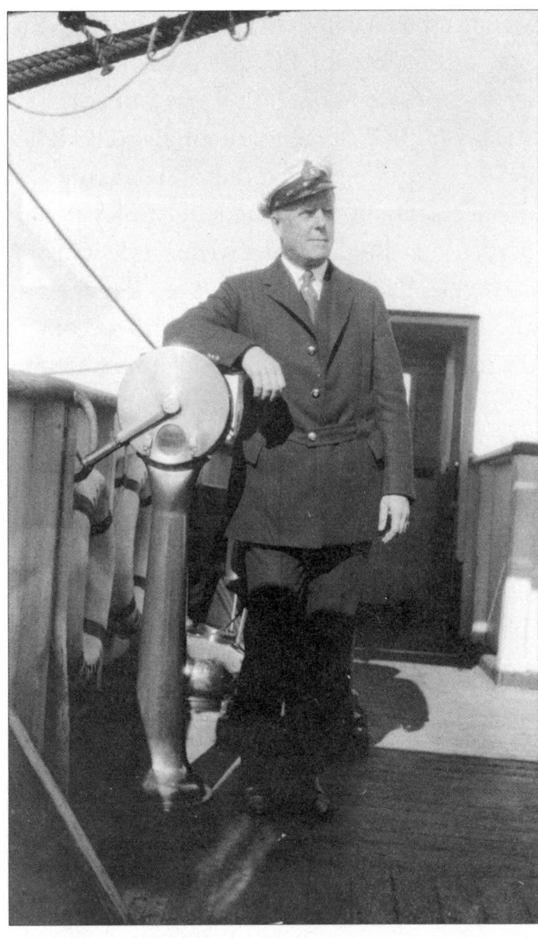

FIGURE 10-5: JOHN DAVIDSON CRAIG ON BOARD THE CGS *ARCTIC*, 1922. *J.D. CRAIG / LIBRARY AND ARCHIVES CANADA / PA-210045.*

(3) The shortest distance from Ellesmere Island to Devon Island and to Greenland should be ascertained;

(4) A comprehensive knowledge of past and present Danish and American activity in the Canadian islands and Greenland should be obtained quickly, that of the United States being particularly important because the *Century Atlas* showed Ellesmere Island in the same colour as the United States and Alaska;

(5) The cooperation of the Department of the Naval Service should be secured; and

(6) The Secretary of State for the Colonies, the British Embassy in Washington, and the Department of Trade and Commerce should all be asked to provide all possible useful information.[79]

On 14 January, Cory wrote a confidential note to Sir Joseph Pope, enclosing part of a New York dispatch of 3 January which had appeared in the *Montreal Gazette* that told of sixteen exploratory expeditions presently being planned or carried out around the world. He drew particular attention to three being prepared by Rasmussen, the Dane Lauge Koch, and American Donald B. MacMillan for different parts of the North American Arctic. Noting that Canada was "vitally interested," Cory suggested that Pope communicate by cipher cablegram with the Home Office in London to find out what he could.[80] Pope threw cold water on the idea, however, expressing that "I really do not see what the Home Office has got to do with the subject" and suggesting instead a letter to the High Commissioner.[81]

On 11 January, Craig wrote a memo to Harkin, referring to "our conversation yesterday with Mr. Cory regarding Mr. Stefansson and the northern expedition" and asking him to draft a letter to Stefansson inquiring whether he would be willing to undertake an exploratory trip to Ellesmere Land. "You have met Mr. Stefansson and have discussed it with him," he added, "and it would seem that you could put the matter up to him in better shape than anyone else."[82] On 12 January, Roy Gibson as acting deputy minister wrote to Harkin making the same request and enclosing a copy of Stefansson's letter of 8 January to Meighen.[83]

The communiqués mentioned in the preceding paragraph seem to have been largely responsible for setting afoot the tangled skein of events that followed regarding this mysterious Stefansson expedition which did not materialize. The truth about this strange affair, in which he figured so largely, was denied to Stefansson; although he remained curious about it and sought the explanation in puzzlement and frustration until the end of his life, he evidently never learned the full story.

Harkin's draft letter to Stefansson was evidently a struggle for him, judging by the pencilled notes in his papers. He also wired Stefansson at the Harvard Club in New York on 15 January, asking him when he could come to Ottawa to discuss matters.[84] Stefansson wired back promptly on 18 January from Petersburg, Virginia.

> Your telegram January sixteenth forwarded stop am lecturing in South till early Feby cant get back New York before fifth or Ottawa before eighth Feby you know my ideas and plans please write me fully on that basis stop use my New York address.[85]

On 21 January, Harkin sent Gibson his completed draft letter to Stefansson with the comment: "I think it is in a safe form." The vital part of it went as follows:

> I infer from your letters upon the subject that you have in mind that exploration work and other work could be carried on under the one commander. It is not considered here that such would be practicable or desirable. The two purposes are entirely different in character and from their nature could not be satisfactorily carried out under the same leadership. The occasion however offers an excellent opportunity for providing for additional exploration in the region immediately to the north and the west of the better known islands. My wire was sent to ascertain whether you would undertake command of an exploration expedition into the area in question. My idea is that the ship provided for the other work could be used to transport your party to a suitable point from which the expedition could take its departure overland under your command. I wired you because I was anxious to go into the details with you personally in connection with this matter.
>
> I notice that your Lecture Bureau contract provides that notice given prior to February 1st would relieve you for northern work. I know that so far as you are personally concerned you recognize that everything in connection with the expeditions is strictly confidential but it is imperative that you should also see that nothing is said to the lecture bureau which will enable it to indulge in publicity which might call attention to these expeditions. There is always a temptation for a lecture bureau to endeavour to get free publicity when opportunity offers and in writing to you upon this subject I take it for granted that you

will take all the necessary safeguards in that connection.

Having reproduced Stefansson's wire of 18 January in his letter, Harkin concluded by observing that, so far as the department was concerned, there was no reason why discussion of the matter should not be delayed until 8 February.[86] The main point that emerges from the letter is that Harkin and his colleagues had already decided that although Stefansson might be considered for an exploratory expedition, the "other work" – that relating to sovereignty – would not be entrusted to him if they could prevent it.

Stefansson replied by telegram on 2 February, from Atlanta, Georgia, saying in part: "Consider it both privilege and duty to accept command expedition to carry out purposes we have discussed and have at heart shall be glad to accept stop lecture managers know nothing our plans there will be no publicity."[87] He followed up this wire with a lengthy letter, written in New York on 7 February, in which he said that he expected to be in Ottawa no later than 14 February and in the meantime was setting down "a basis for discussion." Briefly paraphrased, the points he made were as follows:

(1) it would be fortunate if the expedition were under the Department of the Interior, but it should be outfitted by Desbarats and his subordinates in the Naval Service;

(2) the difficulties of the expedition should not be overestimated, and with proper methods its ends might be achieved with little effort;

(3) it might be necessary to have different commanders in the field, but from Ottawa the work should be planned by someone who thoroughly understood polar conditions;

(4) his acceptance of the command of the exploratory expedition was contingent upon satisfactory backing and support from the government;

(5) there should be during the coming summer "a quiet, entirely unostentatious taking possession of Wrangel Island," which might be carried out by a Canadian fur trader (see chapter 11); and

(6) there should be a public announcement that the Canadian government was continuing scientific exploration in the North, without mention of any political aims, so as to deter competing nations from entering the field.

He concluded with the caution to Harkin, rather ironic in the circumstances, to "remember that this letter is very confidential."[88]

A further exchange of telegrams followed, with Stefansson saying that 14 February would suit him best to meet Harkin in Ottawa, Harkin saying that he was not sure he would be in Ottawa on that date, and Stefansson asking rather curtly, "If you are absent fourteenth when will you be back?"[89] By 17 February, however, Harkin reported to Cory that he had had several conferences with Stefansson; that they had framed a plan for an exploratory expedition to start the coming summer, which might cost a total of $75,000 to $100,000; and that he recommended approval of the plan. He attached to his note a memo by Stefansson which set forth the plan in some detail. Briefly, five men were to go north on the *Arctic* in the summer of 1921, under the command of Fred Lambert of the Geodetic Survey, and establish a main base on Axel Heiberg Island. When the *Arctic* sailed north again in 1922 to take supplies to the police stations which by then would have been established, Stefansson would lead another party of five which would cross Ellesmere Island and join the first party, after which some members of the combined party would carry on extensive exploratory and scientific work north, west, and southwest of the Sverdrup Islands. Lambert would probably return south in 1924 and Stefansson himself probably the following year, perhaps by way of Alaska or Siberia. Harkin remarked in his note, "Of course it is to be distinctly understood that Mr. Stefansson will be in supreme command of the exploratory work of this expedition."[90]

Evidently unaware of the true situation, or only faintly suspicious, Stefansson went ahead with plans for the expedition. On 25 February, he wrote two letters to Cory, one asking for permission to employ E. Lorne Knight (a member of his last expedition) and the other asking for a written commission stating his exact relationship with the Canadian government. On 28 February, he wrote to Harkin suggesting the employment of a young Cornell student named E. P. Wheeler, who like Knight was an American, and saying that although he agreed that the personnel of the expedition should be mainly Canadian, he "would certainly rather take a good man of any nationality whatever than an indifferent Canadian."[91] Cory sent his two letters to Harkin on 1 March, saying, "By a copy of this memorandum I am asking Mr. Craig to call on you in order that something may be drafted."[92]

About this time, the English explorer Sir Ernest Shackleton entered the scene, a development which Stefansson always blamed for the fact that his own expedition did not take place. The true circumstances, however, were somewhat different than Stefansson thought.

Shackleton had had an interview with Prime Minister Meighen in Montreal on 5 February and had asked for financial help from the Canadian government for an expedition he was planning for the Beaufort Sea region. At the same time, he intimated that he understood Stefansson was not interested in taking an active role in such work. The following day, Meighen wrote Sir James Lougheed, then Minister of the Interior, enclosing a memorandum by Shackleton and saying that he (Shackleton) sought an appointment with the minister on Tuesday next. Meighen added, "I told Sir Ernest that I did not understand Mr. Stefansson's attitude in the same way as he did and I was of the opinion Mr. Stefansson was anxious himself to take charge of such work in the North as the Government desired to have done."[93] The Department of the Interior looked into the matter promptly. By 7 February, J. D. Craig was writing at the beginning of a memo to Cory that, "in accordance with your memorandum of this date, I have had a conference with Dr. Deville and Mr. Harkin concerning the proposition of Sir Ernest Shackleton that the Dominion of Canada should contribute towards his proposed Beaufort Sea Expedition." Craig observed that it was impossible to tell from the information provided whether Shackleton would go to the intended region of activity by the west coast or the east coast, but if it were the first, he could not get there in 1921, and if it were the second, he would come into conflict with the department's plans for Stefansson. He thought that Shackleton's expedition might accomplish more from a scientific point of view than Stefansson's, but Stefansson's would be used in connection with the sovereignty question and in any case was already arranged. Therefore, Craig advised that the department should not support Shackleton's expedition unless, perhaps, Shackleton succeeded in getting a large subscription in England and elsewhere.[94]

On 14 February, Lougheed answered Meighen's note, saying that he had had an interview with Shackleton and told him that the government could not at the present time take the action he desired. He added that Shackleton had appeared to understand his explanation and had hinted that he might submit a more limited proposition later on.[95]

The true situation respecting Stefansson is revealed quite clearly in a confidential memo Harkin wrote to Cory on 2 March, after they had met with Lougheed. After some preliminary remarks about the two proposed expeditions and about his fears of Danish and American designs, Harkin continued:

> There is a grave probability that if any aid or recognition is given the Shackleton expedition either (or both) the United States and Denmark may receive advance information from Stefansson, the Canadian Arctic explorer, because Shackleton proposes to explore the identical region that Stefansson also proposes to explore. Stefansson was the first person to specifically call attention to the weakness of Canada's claim to the Northern Islands. No one is more familiar than he with the weakness of our case. He is aware of Canada's plans for remedying that weakness. He therefore is in a position to ruin the Canadian scheme by tipping off the facts to the United States, or Denmark, or in fact any other country that might have ambitions to acquire new territory. Stefansson is a Canadian in the sense that he was born in Canada but that is all. It would therefore be unwise to bank on his Canadian loyalty too much. The Canadian expedition has been developed on the line of keeping him with us through self interest.
>
> Stefansson wrote to both the Premier and Sir James Lougheed asking that he should be made commander of the Canadian expedition. For obvious reasons this was impossible. At the same time it was felt here that Stefansson's friendship must be retained and on the Minister's suggestion he was wired in January to come to Ottawa. It was felt that in the interests of Canada he must be kept enthusiastically with us at least until the *Arctic* got away next June and that to avoid further danger from him it was in Canada's best interests to get him away to the north as soon as possible where he would not be able to damage the Canadian cause. It being impossible to let him take command of the expedition our proposition to him was that he should go up on the *Arctic* as a passenger and then with a small party proceed over the land and the ice to the Beaufort Sea on a new exploration trip. It was felt this would effectually keep him out of the way during the danger period. He suggested a compromise, viz. – that a small advance party should go up on the *Arctic* this year to locate a base for him and that in 1922 he himself should proceed to the base and begin

his exploration. This naturally did not suit us as well as the original idea of his going up in 1921 but it was felt that it would meet our main purposes, viz. – to keep Stefansson silent. Accordingly I recommended it and the Minister approved. At this juncture Shackleton arrived. He of course knew nothing about the title difficulty as regards the north. Presumably he came to Canada for financial aid because he would not raise enough funds in England. His expectation probably is that if he could get recognition from Canada this would stimulate contributions in the Old Country. The purpose of his expedition is solely the securing of scientific information in the Beaufort Sea. So far as this information is concerned there is no pressing need of it. Delay of a few more years in that connection is of no significance to Canada. Therefore in view of Canada's financial position there are no substantial grounds for giving him aid. Equally from the scientific standpoint there is no pressing need of the proposed Stefansson exploration expedition. It has been recommended solely to conserve Canada's interests in the matter of the northern titles.

Both Stefansson and Shackleton propose going to the same area. It is so far unexplored. It cannot be ignored that if the Shackleton expedition is endorsed in any way Stefansson is practically certain to get up in arms. What the result will be is a matter of grave concern to the main issue, viz. – the definite completion of Canadian sovereignty in the north. Even if that point can be safeguarded the situation would still be that Canada in a period of financial stress was financing two expeditions to the same region.

With the authority of the Minister I explained the whole situation to Shackleton. He expressed anxiety to safeguard Canada's interests but advanced the idea that he should be used in connection with the expedition. Finding that his first suggestion that the *Arctic* should be abandoned and his boat used instead was impracticable because his boat was too small for the purpose he suggested that the *Arctic* should establish the two northern police posts proposed and that his boat should establish the two more southerly posts and then proceed on its way towards Beaufort Sea. Apparently this was advanced to give the Government an excuse on which to justify assistance for his expedition. He expressed the opinion that in the short northern season the *Arctic* alone might not be able to establish all four posts this year. Captain Pickels who has been engaged as Master of the *Arctic* has been consulted on this point and contends that there is an ample season of open water to permit of the *Arctic* doing all the work this year.

It is inconceivable that any aid given to Shackleton can be kept so secret that it will not reach Stefansson's ears. What may then happen is left to your own judgment.

Insofar as I may have any responsibility in this matter I consider the

> chance of putting Stefansson in the camp of our enemies is too great a one to be taken. If it is felt some aid must be given Shackleton then at least he should be told that there will be none until 1922. With all talk of the Shackleton expedition dropped we doubtless can keep Stefansson in line until the police posts are established. If it is then considered desirable to assist Shackleton in 1922 and at the same time carry out the arrangements with Stefansson that he too explore Beaufort Sea at least there will be no danger of imperilling the main question, that of the definite establishment of Canadian sovereignty in the north.[96]

On the same day, Harkin wrote another confidential memo to Cory about a news item from Christiania (Oslo), published in the *Ottawa Evening Journal* of 1 March. The news item said that Shackleton was leaving on a new Arctic expedition in May or June, having purchased the Norwegian whaling boat *Foca I.* He would proceed via Hudson Bay, Baffin Bay, and Lancaster Sound to Axel Heiberg Island, and from there he would explore the islands "eastward to Parry Island [*sic*]". The Canadian government had officially informed the *Journal* that it had no connection with the expedition, although Shackleton had approached the Prime Minister and other government officials for help, and thus the announcement from Christiania was "premature." After repeating briefly his fears about Stefansson and generally the substance of the other memo, Harkin continued:

> You are well aware that Stefansson is an exceedingly difficult man to handle. It seems to me that the statement that "the announcement from Christiania is, to say the least, premature" is bound to arouse Stefansson. When he was here a week or two ago he manifested a good deal of nervousness about Shackleton and, therefore, I fear that the newspaper item referred to will aggravate him very much. It seems to me that at all costs we must guard against Stefansson being alienated. I feel quite sure that entirely apart from the Denmark danger Stefansson could very readily convince the United States to send an expedition to Ellesmere Land. That country has probably a better title at present to Ellesmere Land than Canada has. Moreover, the United States have been very anxious to carry on musk ox breeding in Alaska and their Biological Service have asked us to let them have musk ox from Ellesmere Land for that purpose. I feel that if the United States recognized the weakness of Canada's title, as Stefansson knows it, they would not hesitate to try to establish occupation of Ellesmere Land in advance of Canada. Such a possibility suggests very serious and very dangerous complications.[97]

Perhaps the most surprising thing about these remarkable communiqués is their revelation that, although Harkin and others clearly distrusted Stefansson, they were nevertheless willing to take Shackleton, virtually a stranger, into their confidence. A pencilled note on a letter written by Stefansson to Lougheed on 26 February, and sent on to Craig and Harkin, says, "Get him on phone and tell him to pay no attention to reports re Shackleton."[98] The note was unsigned, but it was evidently for Harkin, who must have complied. In a postscript to a letter to Harkin dated 5 March, Stefansson wrote, "Thanks awfully for phoning me last night – I appreciate the thoughtfulness very much."[99] The "thoughtfulness" was obviously not quite what Stefansson imagined it to be.

In the Harkin Papers there is a pencilled memorandum, obviously in Stefansson's handwriting, recording details of a conversation between Stefansson and Harkin in the Chateau Laurier on 11 March. Among the miscellany of details are a list of supplies and equipment needed for the planned expedition, Stefansson's lecture itinerary for the rest of March and part of April (which would take him from Michigan to Florida), and notes about a letter that Stefansson was going to write to colleges and universities about personnel for the expedition.[100] On the same day Stefansson drafted this memorandum, which he sent to Dean Reginald Brock of the University of British Columbia; the presidents of the Universities of Toronto, Manitoba, Saskatchewan, and Alberta; and the principal of McGill University. In the letter, he expressed his preference for young Canadian college graduates, since the expedition was to be "a Canadian enterprise," and he cautioned that the matter was confidential "in so far that I should not like to get any mention of the undertaking into the public press."[101]

On 14 March, Stefansson wrote the following note to Sir James Lougheed. He used his New York stationery, but, according to his lecture itinerary, he would have been at Saginaw, Michigan:

> I have refused a $60,000.[00] a year lecture contract for 1922–23 to take charge of the work of northern exploration which Mr. Cory tells me is definitely decided on.
>
> To Mr. Cory's inquiry (through Mr. Harkin) I have said I prefer to do this work for the Government without salary.
>
> Rather than receive any pay, no matter how great, for mere ordinary work, I prefer to carry on the work of exploration, because I feel I am helping to build the foundation for Canada's greatness. I am proud to have a part in that work, and thank you for the part you have had in its inception.[102]

In the meantime, while Stefansson proceeded with his lecture tour, memos continued to fly back and forth in Ottawa. Harkin wrote one to Cory on 15 March which, after referring to his earlier one of 17 February about Stefansson's proposed expedition, continued as follows:

> You returned this memorandum to me marked A.O.K., B.O.M." I accordingly have proceeded with arrangements in that connection with Mr. Stefansson. The first definite commitment in this matter was made on Saturday. Mr. Stefansson, as you know, wants a man named Knight, who formerly worked with him in the far North, engaged as the practical man though not the Commander of this advance party. On Saturday I found that it was unavoidable to tell Mr. Stefansson to close arrangements with Mr. Knight in that connection. Particularly since the advent of Shackleton I fear there has been more or less of a feeling that once Canada's Police posts have been

definitely established by the Arctic expedition there might be a movement to drop the Stefansson expedition of 1922. As you know I am convinced that so far as any results to be expected from either the Stefansson or the Shackleton expeditions are concerned there is no need whatever to-day of these expeditions, having in mind Canada's financial position. The Stefansson expedition as proposed really has nothing whatever to do with scientific or other results that may be obtained. The position has simply been that Stefansson being thoroughly familiar with the weakness of Canada's case with respect to the North and it not being possible to really look upon him as a real Canadian this expedition idea was developed with a view to providing a positive assurance by this sop to Stefansson's pride and selfishness that there would be no chance of his tipping off the actual situation concerning the north to either Denmark or the United States.

I do not think the proposed Stefansson expedition could be carried out for less than one hundred thousand dollars ($100,000). It is quite a price but I do not think it is too high a one to pay for the assurance that it gives us. Of course I do not know whether this Stefansson expedition has been considered in Council but from the activities with respect to Shackleton I fear there might later on be opposition in Council to seeing the Stefansson expedition through.

It is quite true that insofar as the north is concerned once our police posts are established we will have nothing to fear from Stefansson insofar as the eastern frontier of the Arctic Archipelago is concerned.

I may say that up to date I am convinced that Stefansson is playing the game absolutely loyally to Canada. In this connection it must always be kept in mind that we owe him a debt of gratitude as the man who actually brought the weakness of Canada's case to the Government's attention.

I have before me a memorandum with respect to the organization and equipment of Stefansson's advance party and estimates concerning cost with respect to his main party of 1922 and feel that we must proceed immediately with the arrangements concerning the advance party. As it appears to me that Stefansson is acting in good faith in this matter I feel that I am in a very delicate position when I realize the possibilities of there being attempts to make Canada withdraw from final steps in connection with the expedition. Throughout, practically all the negotiations with Stefansson have been left to me. I therefore feel a keen personal responsibility in connection with the matter of the complete arrangements being fully carried out. Despite the fact that I see no need of this expedition from a scientific standpoint I nevertheless consider that Canada's good faith must be maintained with regard to it.

> Under the circumstances recited I feel that as a go between with respect to Stefansson it is my duty to bring this situation clearly to your attention.[103]

Harkin followed up this memo to Cory with two others of rather similar import, dated 21 March and 22 March. In his memo of 21 March, which was written after he and Cory had seen the minister, he referred to Stefansson's letter of 14 March to Lougheed and said that it would be very difficult to answer. He had gathered from Lougheed that he was not in favour of asking council to finance Stefansson's expedition. Harkin said this was "a complete change of policy." If this meant that the 1922 expedition to Beaufort Sea (to be led by Stefansson) was to be cancelled, then there would be no point in sending an advance party to Axel Heiberg in 1921. Harkin repeated his opinion that the price of the expedition was not too much to pay in order to assure Stefansson's loyalty, although on the other side there was the feeling against paying "hush money." He concluded, "Personally I think it will be far better in the end to definitely decide one way or the other and advise Stefansson rather than go on as at present."[104]

Much of the memo of 22 March went over ground previously covered. He felt strongly that Stefansson's course would be decided "entirely on personal and selfish grounds." Factors that would help to hold him were his ambition to become the "Reindeer King" of Canada, his expectation of additional reindeer leases in the North, and his personal interest in the official reports of his last expedition. If the entry of Shackleton caused Stefansson to think he was being put aside, however, he might go to Denmark or the United States. There was not much real danger in the first possibility, but there might be in the second:

> So far as the United States is concerned official Washington might be considered as unlikely to do anything hostile towards Canada but there would be the greatest danger if Stefansson went to the Hearst outfit. His claims as to the importance of the North Islands both as regards submarines and aircraft would give the Hearst people great material to work with. And it is quite possible they might force official Washington to take action....
>
> There is no doubt that purely as a matter of newspaper enterprise the Hearst people would finance an expedition themselves. It would be great newspaper work for them to have Stefansson in a race with Shackleton.

Harkin repeated his view that if Canada turned Stefansson down it was "obviously taking chances" and that the issue called for "the most careful consideration." Perhaps some alternative could be found:

> If it is definitely decided to turn down the Stefansson expedition the question arises as to whether it is desirable to take any other steps to prevent the possibility of his going over to our enemies. There are a number of items that might be considered: he might be asked to visit Scandinavia and Finland for the purpose of making investigations re. reindeer industry; It might be arranged that the Hudson Bay Company send a boat

to Wrangel Island and Stefansson go along to investigate and report; he might be asked to make a trip across the Barren Lands to study caribou conditions in relation to the reindeer industry; or he might be asked to be a Government candidate at the next election in an Icelandic constituency.

Stefansson's letter to the Minister, it seems to me, was written for the purpose of putting something definite on record, in other words, to overcome the difficulty arising from our negotiating with him re. the expedition but refusing to put anything in writing. Unanswered or evaded it is virtually an admission that we have contracted with him to lead an expedition; and his case is strengthened by the statement that he is sacrificing a $60,000 lecture contract to undertake the expedition.[105]

The deep distrust of Stefansson revealed in these memos fits rather oddly with the admitted conviction that up to date he "is playing the game absolutely loyally to Canada." The memos also suggest that Harkin was undergoing mental conflict regarding the ethics of his own role. The alternative proposals he had in mind for Stefansson are interesting, and it is quite likely that in favourable circumstances some of them might have attracted him.

On 23 March, a memo to Lougheed was drafted under Cory's signature, which was obviously prompted by the memos from Harkin and was intended primarily to clarify whether the minister was opposed to only the Stefansson phase of the proposed exploratory expedition or to both phases of it. The memo said in part:

You made a remark that you would not take this matter to Council. My impression from your remark was that you had in mind only the second part of the expedition, viz. – the trip in 1922 by Stefansson himself. Mr. Harkin got the impression that your remark included the advance party as well.

You will remember that early in February you agreed to this advance party being sent up with a view to guaranteeing Stefansson remaining loyal to us until we had succeeded in establishing our police posts in the North.

The memo noted that if the advance party were still to be sent out in 1921 there would be a great deal of preparatory work to do in a very short time, and asked that "on receipt of this letter" the minister should advise "definitely" as to his views in the matter. However, most of the memo is crossed out and the words "not sent" are pencilled on it, so evidently the matter was dropped for the time being or taken up with Lougheed in some other way.[106]

In spite of these efforts to bring about a decision in the matter, no quick decision was made, and Stefansson's frequent communiqués to Ottawa continued to receive evasive and negative answers. He wired Harkin from Cleveland on 23 March, asking for news.[107] Harkin replied the same day, saying that there was "nothing doing" regarding either Lambert or Alcock, whom Stefansson had suggested for the 1921 Axel Heiberg party, and that he was trying to find a suitable man.[108] Stefansson wired back promptly on 24 March, from Bloomington, Indiana, suggesting Elmer Ekblaw who had been botanist with MacMillan's 1913–17 expedition.[109] Harkin, again replying the same day, said that only a Canadian could be considered.[110] Stefansson sent another wire, also on 24 March, dealing with several matters but emphasizing that the man chosen should be accustomed to outdoor winter life.[111] Harkin wrote a brief letter on 26 March, saying that Stefansson's letter of 14 March to Lougheed had been referred to him because the minister was out of the city. Although the minister would appreciate the "high ground" Stefansson was taking, Harkin advised Stefansson not to turn down the lecture tour because the "unsettled conditions" in Canada might change plans for the expedition.[112] Already, however, Stefansson had hired E. Lorne Knight, a member of his last expedition whom he had been authorized to employ; Knight wrote to Harkin on 27 March saying that Stefansson had accepted him and that he desired instructions.[113]

Harkin wrote a lengthy memo to Cory on 7 April, summarizing the situation as it then existed. He said little about the complications involving Stefansson, however, and the memo was mainly a review of the legal situation as he saw it. To a large extent it simply repeated arguments that had already been made many times by both Harkin and Stefansson, and it suggests that there actually was a good deal of affinity in the thinking of the two.[114]

Stefansson sent another urgent wire on 11 April, this time from Galveston, Texas, saying in part, "Referring your letter it is now too late to retain lecture contracts they were cancelled months ago I assume absolute good faith on part officials now in power and am willing to take chances on change of administration." He asked Harkin to wire a summary of the situation to Beeville, Texas.[115] Harkin sent the wire on to Cory as usual, with the usual request for advice about a reply.[116] There is little documentary evidence that his repeated requests of this kind attracted any helpful response, and it may well be that Cory, lacking a definite Cabinet decision to guide him, was feeling as frustrated over the whole affair as Harkin obviously was.

This pattern of events continued for several more weeks, with Stefansson becoming increasingly anxious and Harkin increasingly embarrassed over his inability to send a definite reply. On 12 April, Knight wrote another letter to Harkin, this time from his home in Oregon, saying that he had had no reply to his letter of 27 March and again asking for instructions.[117] Harkin sent this letter to Cory, again asking for advice about an answer and noting that it had been found necessary to approve the hiring of Knight.[118] Stefansson wired from New Braunfels, Texas, on 18 April to say that he had had no replies from the Canadian university presidents to whom he had written and no reply from Harkin to his telegram of 11 April.[119] Harkin sent the wire on to Cory, saying that he was still without instructions but thought it "important that a message of some kind should go to Mr. Stefansson."[120] On 20 April, Cory returned the communiqués he had received from Harkin, with a memo saying only, "So far we have not received the decision of Council."[121] Stefansson sent two wires from Phoenix, Arizona, on 24 April, one to Cory saying that he had received no replies from Harkin[122] and the other to Harkin saying that he now had answers from the university presidents and that from Toronto strongly recommended Allan, the son of Professor Crawford of that university.[123] Harkin again sent the wire he had received to Cory.[124] Another wire from Stefansson on 3 May announced that he had now heard from all the university presidents and recommended several of the candidates they had named, Crawford being mentioned as one of the two best.[125] Harkin sent it on to Cory with the usual request for instructions, suggesting strongly that "the cards should be laid on the table."[126]

Stefansson's next wire, from Los Angeles on 11 May, said that the time had now arrived for Knight to report to Ottawa according to the arrangement made and that he had resigned the position he had held more than a month ago.[127] Harkin's note to Cory accompanying the wire observed rather bluntly that it was now almost the middle of May and the situation was still "all up in the air."[128] Knight wrote a letter to Harkin from McMinnville, Oregon, on 12 May, saying that he was without funds and had not felt free to take another job; he had written twice already and did not wish to become "a nuisance," but nevertheless he would appreciate some information.[129]

A memo dated 13 May, unsigned but obviously written by Harkin, explained the situation up to that date and strongly recommended that an immediate decision be reached regarding both the northern expedition and the role of Stefansson in it. For the most part, the memo went over ground covered many times before, but it emphasized that the program approved by council "was being carried out without a hitch" until Shackleton appeared on the scene and that although Stefansson was considered "unsuitable" for the command, there was "every evidence" that he had "preserved absolute confidence in connection with this subject." The memo took the view that the *Arctic* should be sent north on a more limited and less expensive trip than that originally planned; but regarding Stefansson, even though to eliminate him at such a late date would seem to him to be "an act of bad faith on the part of the Government," the only advice was to decide promptly one way or the other.[130]

Stefansson sent a wire to Harkin from Lindsey, California, on 17 May, asking him to read the editorial page of the American magazine *World's Work* for May.[131] The editorial, dealing with a proposal that the US Navy send a scientific expedition to the Arctic with a view to claiming lands where oil was discovered, formed a subject for discussion in a typical Harkin-to-Cory memo about a week later. Stefansson had written regarding the proposal: "I can beat them [the Americans] to it if Canada wants me to."[132]

By this time the decision respecting the northern expedition had been taken, and Stefansson's fate was sealed. Stefansson remained unaware of what had happened, and he wired Harkin anxiously on 29 May from Eureka, California:

> Am in very embarrassing situation Knight and various men in Canadian universities whom I approached according our agreement are writing and wiring me stop you should know it is safe to let me know facts even if Shackleton or others have been selected but I must have some word from you stop I have sent in no expense account and shall not but I expect some courtesy you have always shown in our dealings reply Fort-Bragg till Tuesday morning Lakeport Thursday Sebastopol Saturday.[133]

A short note from Cory on 18 May informed Harkin that the expedition was cancelled. The note began as follows: "I herewith return the memoranda relating to the Arctic Expedition. This whole matter has been called off." Little else was said, except that Cory was asking Craig to prepare a memorandum to show the minister's position clearly and that Craig would consult Harkin.[134]

Harkin sent Stefansson the basic news of the cancellation on 30 May in a wire which said only, "Re. your wire twenty-ninth entire expedition abandoned. Am writing."[135] His following letter gave little additional detail, however, and the curt, uninformative tone must have carried quite a sting:

> Doubtless you have received my wire of even date advising you that the entire expedition has been abandoned.
>
> I may say that for some time there had been a great deal of uncertainty. Things were in such condition that it was quite impossible for me to send any satisfactory reply to your several previous messages. Through all the period of uncertainty I personally thought that in the end the decision would be favourable. However as already advised such is not the case.[136]

Stefansson thus received word of the elimination of the expedition upon which he had built such high hopes. It does not appear that Harkin sent him any further information or explanation, or that he asked for any.

In the meantime, while the negotiations with Stefansson were running their course, other important events relating to the expedition were taking place – particularly negotiations with Shackleton.[137] On 15 April 1921, Shackleton (while in Ottawa) put his case directly to Meighen in a lengthy letter, accompanied by a curriculum vitae, a list of the scientific staff who would accompany him, and a copy of Stefansson's letter. He emphasized that he had already secured $125,000 of the $250,000 he needed and would ask the Canadian government for only $100,000. The expedition would be Canadian and for the benefit of Canada, and he pledged to co-operate fully to establish the proposed posts in the North. Even if Stefansson did want to go north, he said, "the shores and the seas are wide, and there is room for all."[138]

On 6 April, Lougheed directed Harkin to prepare a financial statement of the *Arctic* expedition. He submitted an approximate estimate the following day, and he also made a comparative financial statement of the *Arctic* and the Shackleton expeditions, which he presented to the minister on or before 23 April. His figures are difficult to follow, but he apparently concluded that if only one police post was established, the *Arctic* expedition would cost $50,000, while the Shackleton expedition would cost $20,000 plus whatever grant it received. Additional money had already been committed to the *Arctic*, however, and since this money could not be recovered, he seemed to favour the *Arctic* expedition.[139]

Shackleton, like Stefansson, had been doing his best to win the support of influential people who could help him. Three men who seem to have been inclined to support his project were Loring Christie, legal adviser to the Department of External Affairs; John Bassett of the Ottawa office of the *Montreal Gazette*; and Sir John Eaton of the T. Eaton Company. On 9 April, while still in Ottawa, Shackleton sent a handwritten note to Christie saying that he could "carry and place" the one (police) station proposed and that his expedition would be "entirely featured as Canadian."[140] On 11 April, he wired Bassett from New York, asking him to tell Christie that he could relieve the northern party next year "without equipping the ship they proposed to use."[141] He referred, of course, to the *Arctic*.[142] When he had arrived back in England and inspected his ship, however, Shackleton was obliged to cable Bassett saying that he found it impossible to accommodate the proposed party because of their large requirements in coal, stores, and "huts." He presented three alternative requests to Bassett: (1)

to try to obtain $50,000 from the government without any stipulation to carry their party, (2) to obtain $100,000 from the government, in which case he would carry the party on a vessel he would charter himself, or the "most attractive," or (3) to get the government to give him $100,000 or less, provisions already purchased, and magistrate powers, in which case he would make his base and winter on the Ellesmere Island coast and renew the party yearly at cost.[143]

On 3 May, Shackleton sent a further cable to Bassett, evidently in response to a communiqué he had received, saying, "Yes I will undertake this year government Ellesmere proposition and leave main expedition until next year." He went on to detail the difficulties the delay put him in, including his debt to supporters who had provided him with a ship and wanted some action, and his withdrawal "long since" of members of his staff from other occupations.[144] Bassett sent a copy of this cable to Meighen, saying that he would "respectfully suggest that the Government give Shackleton some definite reply as he is anxiously waiting." He added that Sir John Eaton was willing to contribute $100,000 to the expedition.[145] Thus, at this stage, the Stefansson and Shackleton expeditions were in comparable positions.

This correspondence came to Cory's attention, and on 4 May he sent copies of it to Harkin, asking if he knew what proposition had been made to Shackleton. He asked also if Harkin knew about a communication supposed to have been sent to the department about work by the Hudson's Bay Company (HBC) in this connection.[146] Harkin replied in detail on 6 May, saying that he knew nothing about any proposition to Shackleton and, surprisingly, that he had consulted with Christie about it, and Christie said he knew nothing about it either. Christie had expressed the opinion that Bassett had cabled a proposition to Shackleton "on his own responsibility." Harkin knew nothing, either, about any proposition to the HBC involving the question of sovereignty, although he knew from contacts with company officers that they planned to extend their posts northwards. This would constitute occupation, but for sovereignty purposes official government action would have to follow.[147]

In his eagerness and anxiety for a favourable decision, Shackleton attempted to put pressure upon Meighen, and in so doing he probably helped to cook his own goose. On 6 May, he sent Meighen the following cable from London:

> Respectfully urge action and confirmation government support stop it is vital for me to know immediately stop I have fallen in with every line indicated at various interviews with members of council stop during first visit I was told government would support me if I would get adequate outside help stop on receiving this help I returned to Canada the government then suggested that as a reason for their assistance I should carry and place their station thus saving the larger cost of equipping and running the *Arctic* stop I agreed to this and have been holding my ship for final ratification for I realized I could not equip for my long expedition and at the same time carry the large amount of stores and coal which commissioner north west police considered necessary stop therefore I concentrated on helping government plan stop I was given to understand whole matter would come up before council on April eleventh stop time passed stop hearing

> nothing I took the step of holding myself ready to carry out promise to government and to postpone my main expedition until next year having obtained the approval of donors of ship on this side and my Canadian supporters stop in justifyable [*sic*] hope of government support I have taken my principal experienced staff from other occupations and with my ship have been awaiting your decision stop I propose immediately you cable to make necessary accommodation alterations commission ship proceed Canada stop my position is growing equivocal in this country due to delay stop please cable government's definite support and amount bearing in mind the government Arctic expedition would have cost approximately quarter of a million dollars stop urgently awaiting your action.[148]

Meighen's chilly answering cable on 9 May shows clearly that he was in no mood to be badgered into any decision other than one of the government's own choosing. A copy of it in his papers reads as follows:

> Referring your cablegram sixth. Government has made no definite commitment whatever as regards your proposed Expedition and promise of consideration was upon conditions that at no time to date have been complied with Stop Furthermore Government was advised recently on your behalf that you could not go on with your expedition this year Stop Our arrangements now do not admit of assistance your expedition this year.[149]

Not willing to accept rejection, Shackleton protested strongly in another cable on 12 May.

> Keen disappointment adverse decision stop cannot see where I failed to comply with conditions which were firstly reasonable outside help stop secondly scientific personnel to be largely Canadian stop thirdly to carry and lay government station stop the first two conditions were settled before I sailed for England in April stop regarding the third I have held my ship awaiting confirmation of government and that is why the main expedition was postponed stop my message being I would hold main expedition over so as to comply with government plan stop earnestly beg your reconsideration and allow me lay your station stop failing this please cable me definite promise of support next year and meanwhile I will carry on general scientific work as main part of staff is engaged and ship is ready.[150]

Meighen's curt response on 16 May must have ended Shackleton's hopes: "My cable May ninth states our position. Stop. Cannot give any definite promise for next year."[151]

In the concluding scene of this strange drama, there is one feature which seems to stand out clearly. Meighen's cable telling Shackleton the government would give no assistance to his expedition in 1921 was dated 9 May. On the other hand, Cory's note to Harkin saying that the whole matter, including Stefansson's part in it, had been called off was dated

18 May, and it may be assumed that this message was sent without delay. There seems to be no document recording the Cabinet's decision or decisions, but the evidence indicates that Shackleton's expedition had been rejected eight or nine days before the final adverse verdict was pronounced upon Stefansson's.

Neither of the two explorers permitted himself to accept his failure with the Canadian government as a final defeat. Almost immediately, each was planning his next large project, Stefansson the occupation of Wrangel Island and Shackleton the expedition to the Antarctic which resulted in his death early in 1922. In both cases, the change of plans was made with hardly a moment's delay. Shackleton, having received Meighen's final rejection on 16 May, sent a cable the same day to Dr. Alexander Hepburne Macklin, a colleague who was then in Canada, telling him to return immediately to England and prepare for an Antarctic voyage.[152]

While the involved question of the Arctic expeditions was under consideration, officials also looked into Canada's legal position respecting its sovereignty over the northern islands. Not long after being appointed to take charge of planning the proposed expedition, J. D. Craig was asked to make a weekly progress report to the Minister of the Interior. In the first of these reports, dated 4 January 1921, he said, *inter alia*:

> The question of Canada's title to the northern islands is also being looked into from the viewpoint of International law, and an effort is being made to get a memorandum on this point from someone, possibly in the Department of Justice or the Department of External Affairs, whose opinion will carry some weight and so be of practical use as a guide in issuing our instructions.[153]

In his second report, dated 13 January, Craig was able to say that the Deputy Minister of Justice had already forwarded a preliminary memorandum on the Canadian title.[154] The Hon. J. C. Patterson, appointed under Order in Council PC No. 1170 in 1910 to investigate the same subjects, had not made a report, but arrangements were under way to have Loring Christie (then in London) to investigate there.[155]

On 17 January, Craig sent Harkin a detailed list of questions that Christie might be asked to investigate in London.[156] A few changes were made, and the revised list, together with some key documents and papers, was sent to Gibson[157] and then to Deputy Minister Cory[158] on 19 January for transmittal to Christie. In the meantime, a cable was sent to Christie, who had gone to Geneva, to inform him of the work that awaited him in London. Among the key documents and papers were copies of Dr. King's memorandum of 1905, Christie's own memorandum of 28 October 1920, and Harkin's memorandum of 25 November 1920. The questions on the revised list were as follows:

> *Re Dr. King's memorandum.*
>
> 1. Precisely what did Great Britain in 1880 consider as "British territory in North American not already included in the Dominion of Canada"?
>
> 2. Was the Imperial Order in Council of 1880 intentionally indefinite and, if so, why?
>
> 3. What does "adjacent" mean?

4. Is there any reason to differ from Dr. King's interpretation of the intention of the parties to the transfer of 1880?

Re. Mr. Harkin's memorandum.

5. Can Canada of itself, that is without specific instructions from the Imperial Government, take any effective action regarding the sovereignty of lands which may be regarded by other nations as outside of Canada?

6. Were the Low and Bernier expeditions, in this respect, authorized in a form in compliance with the principles of International Law?

7. Is it possible that it might be necessary to repeat all the formal acts carried out by them?

8. What is the situation in regard to Axel Heiberg and the Rignes [*sic*] Islands? Does Norway hold an inchoate title for them?

9. Can Canada take any action looking towards the establishment of a full sovereignty here without specific official endorsation of such action by the Imperial Government?

10. Has Denmark taken any steps to establish sovereignty on Ellesmere Land, or elsewhere? This may be covered by the inquiry being made through Sir Joseph Pope or through Colonel Perry who is referring the matter to Scotland Yard. In this connection see Mr. Harkin's memorandum, page "A" and copy of Rasmussen's letter, paragraph #3. It is very important that information on this subject should be secured and it would seem desirable to make an attempt to ascertain through the British diplomatic representative at Copenhagen, the real object of the Rasmussen expedition.

11. If Denmark has taken any such steps, what are the views of the Imperial authorities in regard to these acts?

12. What steps should be taken by Canada in such an event and how will the Imperial authorities regard the steps that will undoubtedly be taken by Canada to counteract any official action of Denmark along the lines of occupation and administration?

Re. Mr. Christie's memorandum.

13. Are permanent posts necessary for the establishment of effective occupation in the Arctic Zone?

Re. The despatch in the Montreal Gazette.

14. Is there any official knowledge of the United States Expedition and its object?[159]

The plans for Christie's investigation in London were nullified by his return to Canada at the end of January, without having received information prior to his departure from Europe about what was expected of him.[160] In a conversation with Craig, Dominion Archivist Arthur Doughty had already suggested that Christie should get in touch with Henry Percival Biggar, the London representative of the Dominion Archives, to obtain help. On the same occasion, Craig took up with Doughty the question of getting a member of the archives' staff in Ottawa to look into the problem of Canada's title to the Arctic islands, and Doughty replied that although all personnel trained for this sort of research were at the time fully occupied with the Labrador boundary controversy, he nevertheless expected someone to undertake the work shortly.[161] The outcome of negotiations was that Christie undertook to prepare another memo on the subject; Hensley R. Holmden, who was associate archivist in charge of the Maps Division, was engaged to examine historical aspects of the problem from archival and other materials, and arrangements were made to get certain information from London.[162]

Christie prepared his report without delay and had it ready by 17 February.[163] He promptly withdrew it the same day and then submitted a revised version in two separate parts, the first on 17 February and the second on 28 February.[164] The essential change was that a section at the end of the first version strongly condemning the proposal to occupy Wrangel Island was separated and became the substance of the second part of the revised version. Christie had obviously changed his mind. The part of the revised version dated 17 February gives evidence of hasty and rather superficial preparation, and has little of concrete importance in it other than the following advice: first, Canada should take a very firm stand in asserting sovereignty over the northern islands; second, of the three foreign states to be considered, namely the United States, Norway, and Denmark, neither the United States nor Norway had ever shown any serious intention of occupying any of the islands; and third, so far as Denmark was concerned, on every ground Canada should "proceed without hesitation." "If he [Rasmussen] or any of his party is encountered he should be clearly told what our position is, informed of our laws, and requested to conform to them."

The background of the writing of Holmden's memo is also rather confused. In acknowledging receipt of Christie's memo of 17 February, Craig asked him for his opinion about the best way to get the information from London that it had been hoped he would obtain himself before returning to Canada.[165] In his reply on 25 February, Christie referred to the fourteen questions in Craig's memo of 19 January, which had been sent to him in London, and expressed the opinion that the first four should be investigated by the Dominion Archives' representative in London, while the remainder could be handled elsewhere.[166] Craig passed this advice on to Cory on 26 February, suggesting that the first four questions be submitted to Doughty;[167] and Cory complied on 3 March, asking that Doughty have the four questions investigated by his London representative.[168] Holmden, who did the work, carried on his investigation in the Dominion Archives and in the Governor General's secretary's office, and in doing so, he endeavoured mainly to answer five questions which Craig had submitted to Doughty on 21 January.[169] These five questions were, however, identical to the first five on the list in Craig's memo of 19 January. Holmden had a preliminary draft of his "Memo re The Arctic Islands" ready on 14 April 1921[170] and followed it with a larger, more complete version on 26 April.[171] He subsequently added some missing documents after they arrived from England.[172]

Holmden based his answers to Craig's five questions mostly upon Colonial Office documents dealing with the transfer of 1880, which he apparently found either in the archives or in the office of the Governor General's secretary. Briefly summarized, his answers were:

1. In 1880 Britain considered as "British territory in North America not already included in the Dominion of Canada" all unannexed territories and islands, but found it impossible to state precisely what these possessions were.

2. The Imperial order in council of 1880 was beyond doubt intentionally indefinite, because those handling the transfer "could not define, that which in their own minds was indefinite."

3. The word "adjacent" was evidently used regularly to mean "appertaining to" or "of right belonging to" and was applied to islands "lying within, or washed by territorial waters."

4. There would not appear to be any major reason to dissent from Dr. King's interpretation of the intention of the parties in 1880, although Dr. King did not have access to all the correspondence and thus was not completely informed.

5. Canada could evidently do a great deal independently to assert her sovereignty over these northern lands, by establishing patrols, making settlements of Eskimos, exploiting mines, and maintaining law and order.[173]

Holmden went on to discuss other questions relating to the transfer of 1880 and subsequent matters, including the speeches in the House of Commons on Hudson Bay by David Mills and Charles Hibbert Tupper on 28 May 1894, the sector speech of Senator Poirier on 20 February 1907, and the patrol voyages of Wakeham, Low, and Bernier. He ended with several long lists of relevant maps.

His long memo, running to a total of sixty-four pages, is one of the most important works on the subject which has ever been written, especially in its treatment of the official correspondence leading to the transfer of 1880.[174] Unfortunately the memo was never published, and for years about the only work in print on the above-mentioned official correspondence was the partial treatment of it by Albert E. Millward, which was on a much smaller scale.[175] The anxieties of the post–First World War years respecting the security of the northern territories led to the writing of several such memos which never found their way into print, including Wyatt Malcolm's memo of 6 November 1920, Harkin's memo of November 1920, and Christie's memos of 28 October 1920 and 17 February 1921. Holmden's memo was the ablest and had the most fundamental significance.[176]

Besides the political and legal questions bearing upon Canada's position in the northern islands, there was also the practical problem of getting a ship ready to carry out the expedition that had been proposed. This task fell under the direct supervision of J. D. Craig, who was given this responsibility by appointment on 1 December 1920.[177] Almost immediately after the appointment of Pickels as captain of the *Arctic* on 16 December, he and Craig made a trip to Quebec to inspect the ship on 21 December.[178]

Pickels remained to make a more detailed examination, and on 5 January, he reported to Craig that it would cost almost $60,000 to repair, outfit, and supply the *Arctic* for a six months' northern cruise. With the addition of wages and incidentals, he estimated the total cost at $82,615.[179] Craig, in turn, urged the government to allot $85,000 to cover costs.[180] Since the expedition was to be the responsibility of the Department of the Interior, it was necessary to transfer the *Arctic* to this department from the Department of Marine and Fisheries.[181] Later, an additional $70,000 was placed in the main estimates, and this sum was retained (in case of emergency), even after the expedition had been cancelled. The designation "Reindeer Expedition," which had been adopted for the expedition for camouflage purposes, was dropped, and in the estimates the $70,000 appeared under the heading "Northwest Territories Explorations."[182]

With the financial arrangements in place, preparations for the expedition proceeded steadily – although the entry of Shackleton upon the scene soon cast a shadow of uncertainty over its future. There were various suggestions about what might be accomplished by the expedition, especially in scientific work, but Craig took the view that such activities were not the primary purpose of the expedition and that there would be little time for them anyhow.[183] Lougheed concurred with this view and was reported by Cory to agree thoroughly "that this is not a scientific expedition, but one undertaken primarily for the establishment of police posts and the maintenance of British Sovereignty in the Northern Islands."[184] It was then decided to take only a photographer and a cartographer, and other technical and scientific personnel were ruled out.[185] The Royal Canadian Mounted Police (RCMP, the new name given to the RNWMP in 1920) enjoyed a favoured position, and arrangements were made to provide extra space and supplies for them.[186] In spite of the efforts of Craig, Pickels, and others to speed preparation, there remained considerable doubt whether the old *Arctic* could be made ready in time for the voyage, and on 4 May, Pickels wrote an angry note to Craig, complaining of lack of co-operation and effort on the part of the Department of Marine and Fisheries personnel who were supposed to be working on the ship.[187] These difficulties were smoothed over, and Pickels wrote notes to Craig on 18 May and 20 May, reporting that the work was "progressing nicely," *Arctic* had been taken out of dock, and the final phases of outfitting were under way.[188]

On 20 May, Craig wrote Pickels a brief note informing him that the expedition had been cancelled and added his own resigned comment: "There is no use trying to write what I think about it."[189] He enclosed a copy of a memorandum from Cory, advising that the *Arctic* should be kept in good condition in case a northern expedition should become necessary at a later date.[190] For a time the fate of the *Arctic* was in doubt, especially since the Department of Marine and Fisheries was asking that she be returned to them so that she could be used again as a lightship.[191] Cory's wish prevailed, however, and the Department of the Interior decided to retain the ship temporarily and kept it in a state of near readiness in case an emergency demanded a northern expedition at short notice.[192] Captain Pickels, bitterly disappointed as might be expected, reported that the *Arctic* was "in splendid order" and if wanted could be made completely ready for sailing in two weeks.[193] One cause of concern was a rumoured American expedition to the Arctic later that summer under Donald B. MacMillan, although it was also reported that

FIGURE 10-4: KNUD RASMUSSEN. *LIBRARY OF CONGRESS, GEORGE GRANTHAM BAIN COLLECTION.*

the expedition had only scientific objectives (see chapter 14).[194]

While all these preparations had been going on, the responsible Canadian authorities kept their eyes on the Danes and tried to discover what they (and particularly Knud Rasmussen) were doing. On 1 April 1921, Harkin wrote a memo to Cory, suggesting that a code cable should be sent to Sir George Perley in London to ask him to try to get a written application from Rasmussen that would constitute recognition of Canadian sovereignty in any of the northern islands he might visit.[195] About a week later, newspapers carried announcements of Rasmussen's projected expedition to the North American Arctic. Although details were scanty, one report said that the Danish government would contribute 100,000 kroner to support it.[196] On 4 April, Cory cabled the High Commissioner's office in London, and on 25 April, the Governor General cabled Colonial Secretary Winston Churchill about Rasmussen and his expedition. The High Commissioner's office replied to Cory on 28 April, and Churchill replied to the Duke of Devonshire on 29 April, both referring to an interview Rasmussen had had with Sir Henry Lambert at the Colonial Office on 15 or 16 March, in which Rasmussen had indicated no propensity to challenge Canadian authority. Although the British had yet to receive a memorandum of application requested of Rasmussen, both Churchill and Lambert reported that the Dane had "used no language contesting Canada's unrestricted dominion over Ellesmere Land."[197] On 30 April, Ambassador C. M. Marling at Copenhagen reported to Lord Curzon that although the Danish government was contributing 100,000 kroner to the expedition, it was nevertheless purely scientific, and Rasmussen had no official status.[198] Canadian suspicions were not completely put at rest, however, and on 12 May, Craig wrote a memo to Cory, saying that since the Danish government was supporting Rasmussen's expedition and since the requested memorandum had not been received, both he and Harkin felt that the matter could not be overlooked.[199]

On 26 May, after the northern expedition had been cancelled, Harkin wrote a long memo to Cory, reviewing the entire situation and urging that the *Arctic* be used for some kind of a northern patrol expedition, even if no police posts were established. In the memo, he went into detail about the Danish aspect and, in so doing, revealed his extraordinary and almost morbid suspicion and fear of the supposed Danish threat:

When Rasmussen was in London, Sir Ernest Shackleton had an interview with him. One of the early suspicious circumstances in connection with Rasmussen was his sudden decision not to come to America last Summer and his departure for Greenland and the delay of a month by his Secretary in the mailing of his letter to the Musk Ox Commission announcing this change of plans. Shackleton asked Rasmussen why he had so suddenly gone north last Summer and Rasmussen replied that he had gone to investigate the murder of a Greenland Eskimo by one of the McMillan [*sic*] expedition. This was obviously an untruth and an evasion because the murder took place in 1914 and Rasmussen has been up in Greenland practically every year since and so had had ample opportunity to investigate the murder. Moreover the murder took place in Axel Heiberg Land which lies in the Arctic to the westward of Ellesmere Land where Denmark has no jurisdiction.

It seems pretty clearly established that Rasmussen's proposed expedition to the Canadian islands is a scientific one. However it was he who contended that these islands were "No Man's Land" and if he arrived at Bylot Island about August 15th as expected he will have personal evidence that Canada is not administering the north islands. Should Denmark wish to raise the question later on his evidence will be available. It seems unfortunate that this should be the case.

The *Kock* [*sic*] (Danish) expedition left Denmark last year and its departure synchronized with Rasmussen's sudden departure for Greenland last Summer. The announced purpose of this expedition is to make a circular trip in north Greenland. The Colonial Office reports the following from the Royal Geographical Society:

"The Danish State has lent them a ship and the Chairman of his committee is a former rear-admiral of the Danish Navy – the State bears part of the expenses."

This is an expedition that could easily be used for invading the northern islands if the Danish Government has such in mind. If Denmark has any ulterior motives the Rasmussen expedition and Rasmussen proposals re. Conservation of musk ox may only be a blind to distract attention from the *Koch* expedition and give Denmark time to establish occupation in the north. It must be kept in mind that according to the Colonial Office Rasmussen has no official status in Denmark. All in all the attitude of Denmark seems to continue to be suspicious.[200]

Suspicion of Rasmussen was such that on 20 May the Winnipeg office of the HBC cabled the London office, to which he had applied for supplies and transportation during his stay in the North, advising that he should be given no help whatsoever. Harkin advised Cory on 30 May, and Cory agreed that Rasmussen should not be prevented from making his trip so long as Canadian officials were on hand to make him observe Canadian laws.[201] When Edward

Fitzgerald of the Winnipeg office of the HBC learned that Rasmussen had satisfied the British Foreign Office that the expedition was purely scientific, evidently by presenting them with a plan of it, he wired Sir James Lougheed on 4 June asking permission to give Rasmussen any needed assistance.[202] Lougheed replied by wire on 8 June granting the requested permission, provided that Rasmussen accepted Canadian sovereignty.[203]

Rasmussen and the Danish government had become aware, if they were not already, of the extent of the distrust with which Canadian officials regarded their activities in the High Arctic of North America, and they were anxious to demonstrate that this distrust was needless. It is also evident that there was much less worry over the matter in London than in Ottawa. A series of communiqués in early June, starting with the above-mentioned Rasmussen plan presented on 4 June, would appear to have removed all cause for Canadian suspicion, at least insofar as official statements could serve this end. At the same time, unless there is much more to this strange affair than has been revealed, they provide a sort of dénouement to the involved and mysterious business which has formed the subject of the preceding pages.

On 8 June, Colonial Secretary Winston Churchill sent Governor General the Duke of Devonshire a cypher cable, a paraphrase of which read in part:

> Regarding Rasmussen and apprehension that Danish Government may be disposed to question Canadian Sovereignty over Ellesmere Land, a report has been received from His Majesty's Minister at Copenhagen that such a step would be directly against policy of friendship which Danish Cabinet has declared towards the British Empire, and your Ministers may, in his opinion, rest assured that any such action is not the intention of the Danish Cabinet.[204]

This was followed a day later by a "Clear the Line–Urgent" cable, in which Churchill informed the Governor General that the Danish minister had submitted a memorandum "containing definite guarantee by Government of Denmark that expedition has no political or mercantile aims but is of entirely scientific character and that no acquisition of territory whatsoever is contemplated in regions in question."[205] On 10 June, Churchill wrote a short note[206] to accompany a copy of the Danish memorandum, which he sent to inform the Canadian government. The Danish memorandum, dated 8 June, is certainly the key document of the closing stages of the drama and is worth reproducing in full:

> The Government of the Dominion of Canada having apparently entertained some misconception with regard to a Danish scientific expedition which under the leadership of Mr. Knud Rasmussen is about to leave Denmark for the Arctic regions of Canada, the Danish Minister has the honour by order of the King's Government to transmit the following statement to His Britannic Majesty's Government with the request that it may be telegraphed immediately to the Canadian Government.
>
> The entire committee of the Knud Rasmussen polar expedition, with the exception of professor Bøggild and professor Jensen, now absent on leave, has submitted the following

signed statement to the Ministry of Foreign Affairs.

1. The expedition was planned in 1909 by Knud Rasmussen and the late Dr. Stensby [*sic*], professor of geography at the University of Copenhagen;

2. The plan was set forth in 1910 in the Danish scientific journal "Geografisk Tidaskrift";

3. The expedition has a purely scientific character and is unconnected with any political or commercial objects whatever; its chief aim is ethnographical exploration and, in addition, general researches in the interest of natural history.

His Majesty the King has accorded his patronage to the expedition after having received from the committee a detailed explanation of the project in conformity with the foregoing statement.

His Danish Majesty's Government therefore guarantees that the expedition has no political or mercantile aims but is of entirely scientific character and that no acquisition of territory whatsoever is contemplated in the regions in question.

The Danish Minister begs to add that Mr. Knud Rasmussen's expedition is to leave Copenhagen for Greenland, their starting point, on the 16th instant wherefore it would be much appreciated if the consent of the Government of Canada to the landing and further progress of the expedition might be obtained as soon as possible and communicated to this Legation.[207]

Word of the Danish assurance was telegraphed by Lougheed to Fitzgerald on 10 June, and Fitzgerald cabled the London office of the HBC the next day, advising them that the Canadian government agreed that the company might furnish assistance to Rasmussen's expedition, so long as he did not dispute Canadian sovereignty in the northern islands.[208] On 13 June, Fitzgerald informed Lougheed by telegraph that London had cabled back, saying "everything satisfactorily settled Rasmussen expresses many thanks."[209] On 21 June, W. L. Griffith at the Office of the High Commissioner in London wrote a letter to Sir Joseph Pope, saying that although he had at first thought that Rasmussen's neglect to furnish a memorandum might have been calculated, in the light of later events he had concluded that he "was bona fide throughout, and … a man of great intelligence, capacity, and good character."[210]

Nevertheless, suspicion of Rasmussen died hard, at least in some quarters. On 4 January 1922, after the expedition had begun, Harkin wrote a memo to Cory, saying he thought it "at least a matter of bad taste" that Rasmussen should give the name "Danish Island" to an island at the mouth of Lyon Inlet, Melville Peninsula, and advising that the government should "keep a close eye on this expedition."[211] Oswald Sterling Finnie sent a copy of this memo to Commissioner Aylesworth Bowen Perry of the RCMP on 23 January, asking that if possible he should arrange for observation of the expedition.[212] As it proceeded other complaints were raised: that it had flown the Danish flag,[213] that it had interfered with the trade of others,[214] that it had carried on trading itself,[215] and that no licences had been issued to it in 1922.[216] Most of these complaints were cleared up in one way or another: when asked, Rasmussen readily agreed to fly a Union Jack over his Danish flag,[217] the charge that the expedition had engaged in trading activities was repeatedly denied,[218] Rasmussen had asked permission in August 1922 to kill one male muskox for scientific purpose,[219] and he had been granted a hunting and trapping licence for that year.[220]

By April 1925, matters had changed to such an extent that it was Rasmussen who was doing the complaining. Reports about the coming MacMillan expedition indicated that it would receive more favourable treatment than had been extended to him. In a letter to Finnie he wrote:

> All this makes me assume that any new land discovered by him or his expedition will be taken in possession for the U.S.A. If that is so I feel justified in asking how Canada can grant any such right while it was made an absolute condition to me, that I should sign a statement in which I declared that under no circumstances would take possession of any area in behalf of my country Denmark or any other country.
>
> I did sign this statement in London by the High Commission before I left.... I will, as a son of a small nation feel extremely sorry if any explorer from any other country would be given any right which was not given me.[221]

A handwritten note by Finnie on the original of Rasmussen's letter says that he discussed the matter with him while he was in Ottawa between 27 April and 6 May,[222] and it may safely be assumed that the Canadian officials emphasized that they were a good deal more worried about MacMillan than Rasmussen was. The Danish explorer made a favourable impression during his visit to Ottawa, in the course of which, thanks to his intimate knowledge of Inuit and the circumstances in which they lived, he was able to answer the many questions put to him by the Canadian officials. He also reiterated his and Denmark's acknowledgment of Canadian sovereignty over Ellesmere Island in a letter written to O. D. Skelton while still in Ottawa.[223] Over the following years, Rasmussen maintained contacts with people in Ottawa who were concerned with the Arctic, notably O. S. Finnie, and made himself a much respected figure there, enjoying this new status without serious interruption until his premature death in 1933.

The foregoing pages have attempted to document the story of this extraordinary affair, insofar as it can be gleaned from surviving government files and other materials. On at least two key matters probably more could be said: the supposed Danish challenge that touched off the whole business and the cancellation of the *Arctic* expedition in 1921.

To look at the second matter first, the most striking feature about the cancellation of the expedition is that no authoritative or detailed explanation for it has ever been made public. Stefansson was anxious to discover the truth about it, and he remained uneasy and dissatisfied with the partial explanation given him for the rest of his life. He made public his own interpretation of this partial explanation, and although there is obviously much truth in what he says, it is equally obvious that it does not tell the whole story. In his narration, the basic issue was the question of who should command the expedition, with Shackleton becoming his principal rival. The dispute eventually involved (and had to be settled by) the entire Cabinet, with half supporting him and the other half supporting Shackleton. Although not fully informed about the details of the dispute, he had "no reason to doubt what a Cabinet member told me: that, in effect, the two factions said to each other that if they could not agree they might as well do nothing."[224]

This is correct up to a point, but the impression given is inaccurate in some respects, and the affair was much more involved than this would imply. First, Shackleton's expedition was eliminated by Prime Minister Meighen's cable on 9 May 1921, and so Shackleton had ceased to be an active rival when the decision was taken on or about 18 May to cancel the expedition of the *Arctic* to Ellesmere Island.[225] Second, Stefansson was not going to be the overall commander of the *Arctic* expedition anyway, and he knew it, as he had been so informed by Harkin in late January 1921.[226] Craig had been placed in charge of preparing the expedition on 1 December 1920,[227] and he was expedition commander when the *Arctic* finally sailed in 1922. Third, according to Stefansson's own plan agreed upon with Harkin in February 1921, Stefansson himself would not go north in 1921 but would go with a small exploratory party in 1922 and join an advance party which would have established a base on Axel Heiberg Island.[228] Fourth, and rather sad to relate because it went far beyond any suspicions that Stefansson may have had at the time, influential figures who Stefansson thought were for him really had been against him all along (or had turned against him). Harkin, for example, whose thinking on many subjects was akin to Stefansson's, was anxious to send a sovereignty expedition north, but he was determined that Stefansson should not command it. Harkin wanted Stefansson to go north with the expedition, but only to get him away so that, as Harkin saw it, he would be unable to harm Canadian interests. This deep suspicion of Stefansson, so evident in Harkin, was also apparent among many senior officials with responsibilities connected to the expedition, and undoubtedly was relevant in its cancellation. Nevertheless, the evidence shows that Stefansson was not guilty of deceiving the Canadian government as to his real intentions, and he was quite sincere in his expressed wish to continue serving Canada in the North. Even Harkin admitted that he was "convinced that Stefansson is playing the game absolutely loyally to Canada"[229] and that there was "every evidence" that he had "preserved absolute confidence in connection with this subject."[230] Both Stefansson and his biographer suggest strongly that "the Anderson faction" (his detractors following the Canadian Arctic Expedition) had a good deal to do with the cancellation of the expedition,[231] but there is little direct evidence of this, at least in government records.

Certain documents in departmental and other archival files throw additional light on the cancellation and related matters. Harkin wrote a memo for Cory on 13 May 1921, a few days before the cancellation, for the minister to use in Cabinet deliberations. In it Harkin summarized the situation to date, his comments revealing an attitude that placed most of the blame for complicating matters upon Shackleton. For example:

> The programme approved by Council in the Autumn of 1920 was being carried out without a hitch until the early part of March when Sir Ernest Shackleton seeking aid for an exploration trip into the Beaufort Sea approached the Canadian Government.... In this connection the question was also raised as to the amount of expenditure involved in the original Arctic scheme.

> So many questions concerning Shackleton and concerning the question of economy have been raised since the early part of March that to date the whole question of the Northern expedition has been largely up in the air.[232]

When Cory informed Craig on 18 May that the expedition had been cancelled, he added the request that Craig consult with Harkin and prepare a "historical statement" of the action the department had taken throughout the affair so that "the Minister's record on the subject may be clear."[233] This statement went through several drafts before Lougheed received and signed it on 15 June. The final page reads as follows:

> The outfitting of the ship and preparations generally for the expedition proceeded satisfactorily until about the middle of February when Sir Ernest Shackleton, seeking aid for an exploratory trip into the northern regions, and more particularly Beaufort Sea, approached the Government with a request for a substantial grant. Being informed of the expedition already arranged for and its purposes, and being advised that for reasons of economy it was impossible for the Government to support two expeditions, he made a counter proposition that was considered favourably by some Members of the Government, although I did not approve of it, thinking that the arrangements already entered upon by the Government were much more satisfactory.
>
> The matter came up for consideration from time to time until finally Council was doubtful if the expedition should be proceeded with this year. Finally on May 18th last I indicated to Council that, owing to the preparations which we had made, the ship or the expedition would be ready to sail about the first of June, [*and*] it was absolutely necessary that a decision should be arrived at as to whether we should not carry out our original plan.
>
> Council declared against the expedition being proceeded with during the present year.[234]

This revealing statement gives additional information about the matter, notably Lougheed's attitude. As might be expected, it discloses no details about the division of opinion within Cabinet.

In his long memo to Cory on 26 May, Harkin commented, "It is assumed that the abandonment of the Arctic expedition is not the result of any doubt as to the worth-whileness of the Northern Islands but due to a feeling that there is no danger of any challenge of Canadian sovereignty." He also detailed his fears of Danish or American occupation.[235] The forthright Danish denial of any designs upon Ellesmere or any other Canadian Arctic island in early June brought about a change in the Canadian view of the sovereignty problem and of the function of any government expedition which might be sent north. In a letter to Cory on 29 June 1921, dealing with a Danish proposal to protect muskox on Ellesmere Island, Harkin remarked that even though the program appeared adequate and even though Denmark was admitting British sovereignty there, it nevertheless "does not seem to me to be good policy for Canada to be dependent upon the actions of a foreign country for the observance of Canadian law upon Canadian territory."[236] In a long memo written on 16 February 1922, Craig said that, even though the Danish admission was "somewhat reassuring ... it did not dispose of the existing doubt as to the validity of Canada's title, and in fact the incident emphasized the weakness of Canada's case."[237] These comments reflect the continuing feeling that, even though the Danes evidently no longer posed a serious threat, Canada needed to take positive action.

Finnie brought up the matter in a memo of 18 January 1922. "I think we are all agreed that the proper course to insure sovereignty over the various Islands in the Arctic is to have Government officials stationed, permanently, on the larger Islands," he wrote. "Just as soon as the Minister returns this matter will be revived." Finnie added that if the minister would not approve sending out the *Arctic*, an alternative might be to accept the offer of a trader to establish a trading station on the south coast of Ellesmere Island, and to appoint him a government agent.[238] Harkin replied on 25 January, indicating his strong agreement that action should be taken. "On account of the solution of the Danish question there is perhaps not now the same necessity for rushing action," he added. "Nevertheless the fact remains that Canada has not established its sovereignty in the Northern islands." He firmly advocated that government officers should take action, rather than traders holding delegated powers.[239]

In a memo to Cory on 31 January, Finnie put forward the alternative propositions of sending out the *Arctic* to establish posts on the northern islands or contracting the HBC to perform the same duties. He indicated his preference for the first alternative and suggested that it should be made an annual patrol.[240] Cory requested that Finnie, in consultation with Craig and Harkin, prepare a detailed memorandum on the subject for the minister.[241] The response was a ten-page document, written mainly by Craig,[242] which in revised form became the memorandum of 16 February.[243] After a lengthy résumé of the entire background of the case, Craig presented the following three basic alternatives: first, to do nothing further; second, to commission officers of trading companies to perform the desired duties; or third, to establish an annual government patrol and set up RCMP posts on the islands. The officials expressed clear preference for the third alternative which "would, in a short time, certainly establish Canada's title beyond any doubt." They strongly recommended sending out the first such patrol expedition in 1922. By this time, fear of what Denmark might do – which still figured prominently in the thinking of officials at the time of the cancellation – had been replaced by concern for the future status of the Arctic islands if Canada continued to do nothing.

On the other key matter, the real or supposed Danish challenge, other archival sources may contain further explanatory detail.[244] What remains unclear can be summarized in this way. Because of several Danish statements – a letter written by Rasmussen on 8 March 1920, in an official communication from the Danish government to the British government on 12 April 1920, and in a letter from Rasmussen to Stefansson on 11 May 1920, as reported by Stefansson in his talk to the Advisory Technical Board on 1 October 1920 – Canadian authorities got the impression that both Rasmussen and the Danish government denied Canadian sovereignty over Ellesmere Island and intended to establish their own sovereignty there. They clung to this suspicious view thereafter, and they felt that subsequent Danish behaviour gave it substance. When Canadian suspicions threatened to create difficulties for them in this region, however, the Danes took steps to remove them, and in June 1921, they categorically denied any intention of challenging Canadian sovereignty or attempting to acquire new territory themselves in the archipelago claimed by Canada. If one can take all this at face value, it amounts to a categorical Danish denial of Canadian sovereignty in 1920 and a categorical denial of any intention to interfere with it in 1921. But is this the whole story, and is it entirely correct? There are at least two possibilities of additional complications.

The first of these, put in blunt terms, is that the Danish denial of Canadian sovereignty in 1920 was genuine, but the Danish denial of any intention to interfere with Canadian sovereignty in 1921 was not genuine. This would imply that, even after the undertaking in 1921, the Danes still cherished hopes that in some way they could establish a foothold in the Canadian archipelago and, presumably, only gave up these hopes when it became obvious they could not do so. All the available evidence is against this possibility, and in all probability it can be discounted.

The other, more interesting possibility is that the Danish guarantee in 1921 was perfectly straightforward and genuine, but the suspected Danish challenge in 1920 was grossly exaggerated, if indeed it existed at all. This would suggest that Canadian authorities permitted themselves to become obsessed with a morbid, neurotic, unreasoning fear, which had little basis in reality and which caused them to see, figuratively, burglars under every bed, even though there were none. Dr. Édouard-Gaston Deville said his colleagues were being misled in this way when he refused to associate himself with the resolution of the Advisory Technical Board on 27 October 1920.[245]

If Denmark had no acquisitive inclinations in Ellesmere Island in 1920, it seems likely that there was a parallel between this situation and that involving the developing Danish-Norwegian dispute over Eastern Greenland, which might offer at least a partial explanation of Danish behaviour. In the Eastern Greenland dispute, Denmark attempted to draw a distinction between the possession of sovereignty and the exercise of sovereignty, and held that even though she had not in earlier years exercised sovereignty throughout all parts of Greenland, she possessed this sovereignty nonetheless.[246] Thus certain activities by other states or by private individuals in areas where she was not actively exercising her own jurisdiction might be unobjectionable, but they would become objectionable if they constituted a direct challenge to her ultimate sovereignty. In the somewhat similar Ellesmere Island situation, but with the roles changed so that Canada occupied Denmark's position and Denmark found herself in Norway's, a consistent Danish attitude would have held that certain Danish activities (such as killing muskox) in regions where Canada was not asserting her own jurisdiction were unobjectionable, even though ultimate sovereignty in the region was Canadian.

In connection with Canadian fears of the supposed Danish threat, and indeed with Canadian handling of the whole affair, the woeful lack of knowledge of international law amongst responsible government personnel in Ottawa stands out clearly. Stefansson, who was largely responsible for initiating Canadian worries, had only an elementary knowledge of international law. What is surprising, however, is that most of the senior people he had to deal with in Ottawa had even less, and they showed a distinct tendency to take his pronouncements at face value and defer to his opinions. The rather naïve performances of Legal Adviser Christie in his memo of 28 October 1920 and of Assistant Deputy Minister of Justice Edwards in his memo of 10 January 1921, as well as the disinclination of the Department of Justice to commit itself on the matter, are obvious examples. Harkin emphasized this general weakness in international law in a couple of memos to Craig early in 1922. In the first, written on 7 February in reply to Craig's proposal to try to secure authoritative opinion from the Department of Justice, Harkin said:

> I quite agree with you that it is desirable that there should be an authoritative statement from the Justice Department regarding the question of sovereignty. My recollection of the situation last year when we had this matter up personally with the Department of Justice is that that Department had not had any special occasion to specialize on International Law. You will remember that we largely looked the matter up ourselves in consultation with Sir Joseph Pope and Mr. L. C. Christie.[247]

In the second, dated 13 February and commenting on Craig's long draft memo of 11 February about the northern expedition, Harkin wrote in similar vein:

> I am also inclined to think that there should be a section inserted explaining the application of International Law, so far as we could get it, to situations such as exist in the north. I think you may take it for granted that the Minister, like nearly everyone else in Canada, is practically unfamiliar with International Law.[248]

What effect a sophisticated knowledge of international law in appropriate circles in Ottawa would have had upon the handling of this matter is indiscernible, but it is at least safe to say that the course of events would not have been the same.

Once the excitement had died down, a blanket of silence fell over this strange affair, and the inside story of it has never been made public. It is almost as if those who participated in it had conspired to consign it as inconspicuously as possible to the graveyard. It is difficult, for example, to find in Canadian sources any published acknowledgement of or comment on the official Danish denial in 1921 of any predatory intentions towards Ellesmere Island, and yet one would have thought that this important news would have been made public property at an early stage. The conspicuous exception among the leading participants to the generally observed silence was Stefansson, who wanted the story to be made public, feeling that on balance it would help his reputation rather than hurt it. In this he was probably correct. Yet even Stefansson said little publicly and did not divulge many inside details about which he was in a better position to speak than anyone else. He believed that Harkin retained the real story and that Harkin's refusal to release his information maintained the veil of secrecy. For example, Stefansson suggested in his autobiography:

> I never knew why Harkin was brought in, but I do know that he came to be the best-informed man in Ottawa, or anywhere, on both overt and secret matters connected with our plans. I was told that the only files our project ever had were in either Harkin's private apartment in Ottawa or his office....
>
> The one man who knew all sides of the official Canadian government

> position, or at least a great deal more than I did, was James Harkin. At first I felt sure that he would eventually release his information, but the last time I saw him his position still was that Borden had trusted him to keep certain matters secret. He had not been released from that pledge during Borden's lifetime. With the Prime Minister's death, Harkin felt, the secret became inviolate.[249]

It is unsurprising, given the circumstances, that negotiations and preparations for the expedition were hushed up as much as possible and that they proceeded in a sort of cloak-and-dagger atmosphere, replete with suspected spies, traitors, predators, invaders, and villains. But why was this secrecy maintained, especially after Denmark had made it clear that she had no designs on the Canadian archipelago? Several possible answers may be suggested, all of them speculative, each containing probably a modicum of truth, but some more than others.

First, fear about what Denmark might do in the archipelago was gradually replaced by concern over what Canada herself ought to do – hence the decision to institute regular patrol voyages and establish RCMP posts to establish a tangible form of Canadian sovereignty. It may well have been thought that this effort would proceed more efficiently, and with less opposition, with minimal publicity of what had already happened and particularly to the Danish commitments of June 1921.

Second, the affair was handled mainly by senior civil servants and senior cabinet officials. Civil servants are normally, by virtue of their calling, unable to speak freely and openly; Cabinet ministers are not likely to do so, in a muddled and unsatisfactory affair such as this one, if it can be avoided. There seems to have been a marked and understandable reluctance on the part of both elements to draw any unnecessary publicity to the affair.

Third, there may have been an accidental or circumstantial aspect, in that even if the affair was not deliberately withheld from public view, it gradually receded into the background regardless. Nobody was given the responsibility of telling the full story in detail, and those who could have done so gradually passed from the scene.

Fourth, even though certain issues which had occupied the centre of the stage in 1920, 1921, and 1922 had apparently been settled, they were so bound up with others that remained (or were likely to arise) that continued silence seemed advisable. One need think only of Wrangel Island, the Sverdrup Islands, and the expeditions of MacMillan (the subjects of subsequent chapters) to appreciate the likelihood of this attitude and the weight it would have.

Fifth, there may have been an aftermath of feeling among senior officials that they had botched the whole affair and that silence would spare them the embarrassment that would result if their ineptness were publicized. That is to say, they had made a big issue out of what had turned out to be a very small one, and then they had mishandled it by overreacting to presumed threats posed by Stefansson, Danes, and Americans. Regarding Stefansson in particular, senior officials in the civil service had been determined that they would not follow his lead, yet in some respects they had done so, naïvely if only temporarily, and had, as they saw it afterwards, been led down the garden path. So far as the political leaders were concerned, any inhibition of this sort would attach itself mainly to the Meighen administration, which gave up office in December 1921. This might help to account for the silence until that time.

Mackenzie King's administration, taking office immediately afterwards, presumably was not subject to such inhibitions, at least at the outset. In such circumstances, it is known for an incoming administration to point to the failings of its predecessor with considerable relish. There seems to be little evidence of this, however, which in turn suggests that the King government either found itself in accord with Arctic policy as developed during the preceding Conservative years or, if it disagreed, chose to remain discreetly silent.

Whatever the reason or reasons for the deep silence, the records of the projected expedition of 1921 were left to gather dust in government files. Thus the Canadian public remained in almost total ignorance of this extraordinary affair, even though it embodies what is in many ways the key story concerning Canada's Arctic territories in the immediate years after the First World War. More than that, it established certain broad lines of policy and basic patterns of thought and behaviour respecting the North, which became almost self-perpetuating, and thus it went a long way to determining the kind of administration the Canadian government applied to its northern territories for years to come.

11

The Wrangel Island Affair of the Early 1920s

The Wrangel Island scheme of the early 1920s was Vilhjalmur Stefansson's personal project. He promoted it and remained the central figure in it until its disastrous end.[1] To Stefansson it was just one aspect, although a very important one, of his many-faceted plans for northern exploration and northern development generally. He believed that Wrangel Island, in common with other Arctic islands, had genuine intrinsic value in mammals, birds, and marine life, as well as undiscovered mineral wealth. The island would also be useful as a multipurpose base for airplanes and submarines in the approaching age of transpolar traffic and transportation, for weather reports and forecasts, and for further exploration. As far as exploration was concerned, Stefansson was particularly interested in the island as a suitable potential take-off point for investigation of what he termed the "region of maximum inaccessibility" in the Arctic, directly north of Alaska and eastern Siberia and centring upon a pole of maximum inaccessibility several hundred miles south of the geographical North Pole. The island was even more appealing to Stefansson because, although located only 110 miles north of the Siberian coast, it was evidently still unoccupied and, in his own interpretation of the information available to him, not subject to the sovereignty of any state – although a claim of British sovereignty would probably be stronger than any other.

Uncertainty about the discovery and early exploration of Wrangel Island seemed to support Stefansson's contention that the island was open for appropriation. During his Siberian explorations between 1820 and 1824, the German-Russian explorer Ferdinand von Wrangel, then a lieutenant in the Russian navy, made several sledge journeys over the winter sea ice northwards from the mouth of the Kolyma in a search for land that was rumoured to be in this region. Evidence indicates that none of his sledge parties got far enough to see Wrangel Island.[2] So far as can be ascertained, the European discoverer of the island was Captain Henry Kellett of the Royal Navy. Commanding HMS *Herald* on a search for the lost Franklin expedition in 1849, Kellett cruised in the waters north of Bering Strait, landed on and took possession of Herald Island, saw "Plover Island," and also saw what seemed to be a larger land still farther to the southwest.[3] In 1867, Captain Thomas Long entered these waters in his whaling bark *Nile* and, not realizing that the mysterious land had already been christened "Kellett's Land," named it "Wrangel Land" in honour of Ferdinand von Wrangel, who had become a distinguished figure as Baron Wrangel and Governor of Alaska in his later life.[4] At the same time, Long and other American whalers established that in reality

"Plover Island was only a headland of Wrangel Land."[5] When the USS *Jeannette* of George DeLong's ill-fated expedition drifted across the Arctic Ocean a short distance north of Wrangel Land in 1879–81, it demonstrated with near certainty that the territory in question was actually a medium-sized island rather than the continent-sized mass which some had hitherto thought it to be.[6]

The first known landing on the island was that of the American Captain Calvin L. Hooper of *Corwin* on 12 August 1881, during a search for the lost DeLong expedition.[7] Two weeks later, Captain Robert M. Berry of USS *Rodgers* made a more thorough search of the island, spending nearly three weeks there.[8] Although Hooper claimed the island and Berry made a fairly detailed map of it,[9] nothing was done to cement the claim, and it remained unoccupied thereafter for about thirty years. (Unrecorded landings, perhaps by American whalers, are probable.) In the summer of 1911, a landing was made from the Russian icebreaker *Vaigach*, then engaged in a hydrographic expedition, and a tall beacon was erected near the southwestern extremity of the island.[10] Whether the Russians performed any deliberate act to take possession of the island does not seem to be authoritatively recorded, at least in any publication in English.

This was the situation when the party from the wrecked *Karluk* of Stefansson's Canadian Arctic Expedition landed on the island on 12 March 1914 and remained in a sort of enforced occupation of it until picked up by *King* and *Winge* almost six months later. Of the twenty-five human beings who left *Karluk*, only seventeen reached Wrangel Island in safety. Allowing for three who died on the island and two who went to the Siberian mainland for help, only twelve remained in occupation of the island when the rescue ship arrived on 7 September.[11]

After the departure of the party from *Karluk*, Wrangel Island reverted to its unoccupied state. In a note of 4 September 1916, sent by Russian Minister of Foreign Affairs Boris Vladimirovich Stürmer to the Allied and Associated Powers, the Imperial Russian government declared that the islands north of the Russian mainland were to be regarded as Russian territory. The note specifically named various new islands which had been discovered by Commander Boris Vilkitsky in 1913–14 and others (including Wrangel Island) which had already been known.[12]

Stefansson's idea for the Wrangel Island enterprise was derived largely from Captain Jack Hadley. An Arctic resident and traveller of long experience who accompanied *Karluk*, Hadley survived the sojourn on Wrangel Island and later rejoined Stefansson in the Canadian archipelago for the last two or three years of Stefansson's own part of the expedition. Hadley told Stefansson a great deal about the island, which Stefansson himself had never seen, and described it as a place well-suited to Stefanssonian concepts of living off the country and self-support, and also to the sort of economic enterprise the explorer had in mind. In Stefansson's own words, "It was these conversations with Captain Hadley that led to the first tentative formulation of the plans of the Wrangel Island Expedition which eventually sailed north."[13]

Stefansson's plans for an expedition to Wrangel Island took shape during his last year in the Arctic, while he was wintering at his temporary headquarters on Barter Island just off the north coast of Alaska in 1917–18. Entries in his diary show that he envisaged a trip northwards from the Alaskan coast and then an ice drift westwards to the vicinity of Wrangel Island. He worried that the trip might be

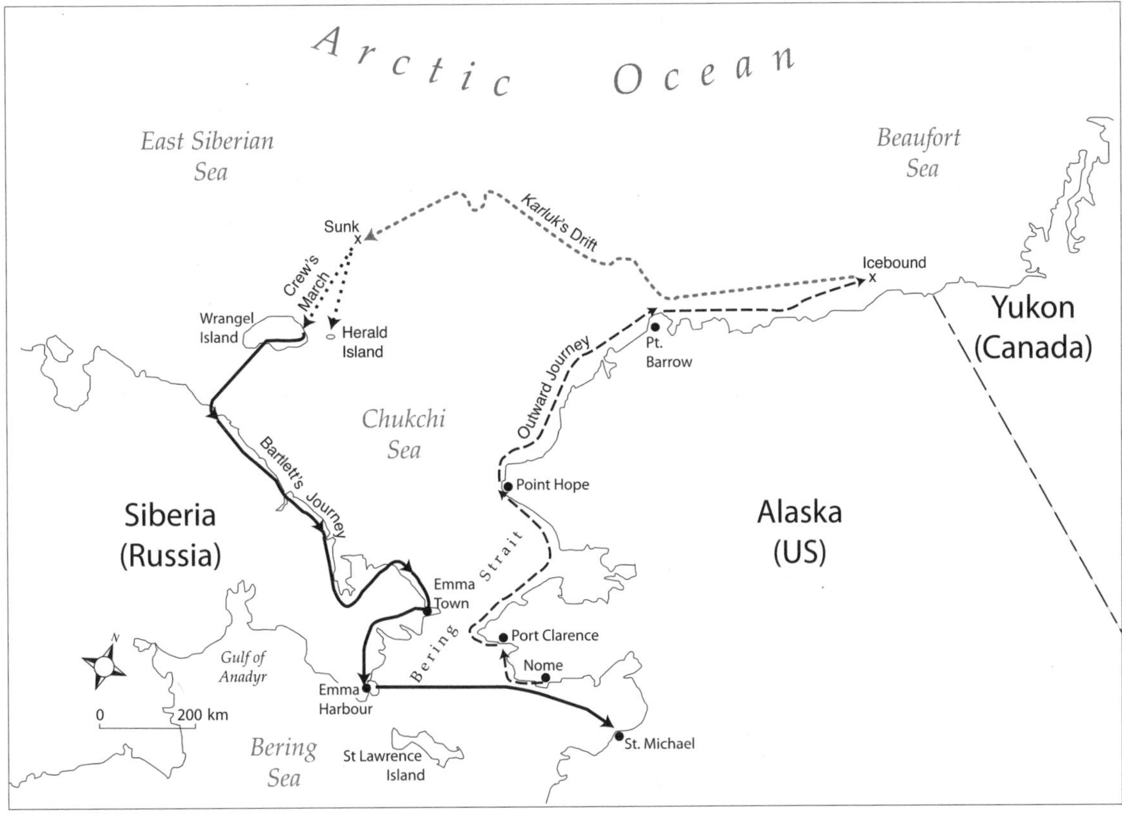

FIGURE 11-1: THE VOYAGE OF THE *KARLUK*, *1914*. *JENNIFER ARTHUR-LACKENBAUER*.

forbidden and he would then have nothing to show for the extra year in the North:

> *Oct. 20*: ....I explained to the men about our proposed 1918 ice trip. The trip is to be northerly from Halkett if possible to 75° N. Lat. then west and south to Wrangell [sic] Island where the *Polar Bear* is to pick us up ....
>
> *Nov. 13*: ....If on the very eve of an ice trip we should receive instructions not to make the trip, we would by not making the trip save only a small percentage of the year's expenses and have nothing to show for the work done and money spent during a whole year ....
>
> *Dec. 18*: ....It is evidently up to us to do something this winter if our country is to be first in this field .... I only wish our trip could be made from First Land or NW Banks Island even instead of Alaska.[14]

Stefansson's diaries do not reveal any intention to establish a territorial claim to Wrangel Island, and it may be that this developed only afterwards. In any event, the illness that struck Stefansson at this time prevented him from making the trip himself, and the attempt was carried out by a small party under the command of his associate Storker Storkerson. Although they reached a point more than 200 miles north of the mainland and spent more than six months on the ice, they were eventually compelled to return to Alaska without getting close to Wrangel Island.[15]

Some time after the return of Stefansson from his expedition in the autumn of 1918, he again took up the Wrangel Island idea as one of his many projects for northern enterprise and development. By now it was clearly connected with a plan to take possession of the island and make it Canadian territory. In adopting this plan, Stefansson was either unaware of, or else chose to ignore, both the Russian-American treaty of 1867 establishing a line between the territories of the two states which proceeded from Bering Strait "due north, without limitation, into the same Frozen Ocean" and the Russian notification of 1916 that Wrangel Island was Russian territory. In his view, occupation should be the decisive factor, and since Wrangel Island was not occupied, it was open to appropriation. His emphasis on occupation meant a corresponding downgrading of other principles or factors, such as contiguity, which would obviously favour Russia, as well as the sector principle, which Canadians had frequently invoked in regard to the North American Arctic Archipelago.

Having resolved to persuade the Canadian government to take official steps to occupy and claim Wrangel Island, Stefansson carried on his campaign with persistence and determination. His many commitments and involvements, including a great deal of lecturing, writing, and travelling, seem to have inhibited action during 1919 and the early part of 1920, but by autumn of the latter year he was ready. As was his custom, he tried to enlist the interest and support of the most influential and potentially most helpful people he could find (see chapter 10). On 16 September, he wrote to Arthur Meighen, soliciting an interview with the new Prime Minister in order to tell him about "two very important matters." The first of these, covered in the previous chapter, had to do with his fears of a Danish attempt to appropriate the islands north of Lancaster Sound. The second concerned "certain islands in the Arctic Sea discovered by Great Britain and not remote from Canada, to which Canada might logically lay claim," and obviously included Wrangel Island.[16] Meighen was leaving for the Eastern Townships and then Western Canada, but on his advice his private secretary referred Stefansson to Loring Christie, legal adviser to the Department of External Affairs.[17] Stefansson promptly dashed off two long letters to Christie, both dated 25 September, the first dealing with various matters including what Stefansson dubiously referred to as the "Canadian" islands,[18] and the second concentrating solely upon Wrangel Island. In the second letter, he recounted briefly the history of Wrangel and noted frequent statements "that there is a treaty between the United States and Russia by which the United States relinquishes all claims it may have to Wrangel Island in favor of Russia." Nevertheless, Stefansson said, "Professor William Frederick Badè has gone into all the documents in the case and has published the statement that there is no such provision in any treaty between the United States and Russia, nor any provision from which an abandonment of claims to Wrangel Island can be logically deduced."[19] The British discovery in 1849 plus the occupation by the Canadian Arctic Expedition in 1914, if followed up by some exploration and commercial development, would give Canada the best claim to the island. Stefansson concluded:

> A further consideration is that there may very well be other undiscovered lands north of Wrangel Island. We are the country most

> logically situated for the development both of lands now known to exist and of others that may be discovered to the north of us. It is no more inevitable that every land north of Alaska shall belong to Alaska than it is that the strip of coast from the vicinity of Skagway to the vicinity of Prince Rupert shall belong to us, which it does not.
>
> The countries to the north will belong to whoever appreciates their value and cultivates them.[20]

Stefansson had an opportunity to present his case for the occupation of Wrangel Island to the Advisory Technical Board, in his appearance before that body at its special meeting on 1 October, and he put forward in summarized form essentially the same arguments he had placed before Christie. Stefansson's views were clearly influential. Dr. Otto Klotz asked, "You consider Wrangel Isle a British possession?" Christie replied, "Not necessarily. It seems that any land goes to the country that values it enough to take it.... That seems to be the whole thing; that whosoever occupies the country holds it."[21]

Stefansson continued to press his case in long letters to Meighen, William W. Cory, and Borden, the first two being written on 30 October and the third at about the same time. The Prime Minister had summoned Christie, Dr. Rutherford, and Stefansson to a conference on 2 October, and at the end of the conference he had asked Stefansson to submit a brief outline of his proposals. In this response, Stefansson referred to Wrangel Island as one of two regions "of main strategic importance" (the other being Ellesmere Island) and said that it would provide one of two main bases for further exploration (the other being Prince Patrick Island). Indeed, he looked upon an "exploratory expedition in Wrangel Island and to the north as most pressing." The claim to Ellesmere Island should be asserted "openly and decisively," but for Wrangel Island the situation was "just the opposite." He suggested that perhaps "our ends would be better served by the establishment of a commercial enterprise ... and exploration by a scientific expedition."[22] Stefansson told Cory that the letter to him was written at the request of Sir James Lougheed and, recounting briefly the history of exploration of Wrangel Island and the superior grounds for a Canadian claim to it, he emphasized that the need for haste was underlined by recent newspaper announcements that the Soviet government had leased about 400,000 square miles of the northeastern corner of mainland Siberia to a syndicate of American capitalists, who might take steps to occupy Wrangel Island.[23] The letter to Borden was in similar vein. After stressing the need to make good Canada's claim to the islands west of Greenland, Stefansson said, "I want to urge the equal importance of an occupation of Wrangel Island and an exploration of the ocean to the north." Borden was sufficiently impressed to write in a note to his successor (as quoted in the previous chapter): "I feel that a good deal of importance should be attached to these observations and that such steps as are reasonably necessary to attain the object suggested ought to be taken."[24]

Another influential person who took a favourable view of Stefansson's proposals, at least at this stage, was Loring Christie. He wrote a secret memorandum to Meighen on 28 October in which he discussed various matters relating to the Arctic islands in terms that Stefansson himself might have used and ended with recommendations for the settlement of Wrangel Island:

Figure 11-2: Loring C. Christie. *Yousuf Karsh / Library and Archives Canada / PA-174532.*

11. A further question that might with advantage be referred at the same time to the technical departments concerned is the feasibility of encouraging the quiet, unostentatious settlement of Wrangel Island by some Canadian development company, such as the Hudson's Bay Company. This if done would establish a basis for a subsequent assertion of Canadian title to the island; an asset that might prove of value in the future.

12. It is also submitted that in the future we should refrain in official or public documents from admitting that the 141st meridian north of Alaska constitutes the Western boundary of the Canadian domain. Official documents in the past have implied such an admission. There is no need for this. The treaty defining the Alaska boundary carries the 141st meridian only "to the frozen ocean."[25]

In due course, Christie's opinion regarding Wrangel Island underwent a complete turnabout, and he made a complete retraction of his recommendation. By contrast, Sir Joseph Pope was completely against the proposition from the start. In a memo to Meighen dated 25 November, Pope remarked that he had been attending some meetings of the Advisory Technical Board at Lougheed's suggestion and made it clear that, although he was in favour of action to cement Canada's claim to the islands north of her mainland, he was completely against any attempt to take possession of Wrangel Island. That island, to quote further from a memo excerpted in the previous chapter:

> is far removed from the Dominion – in fact, is not even wholly in the western hemisphere, as the 180th meridian of longitude falls upon it. Essentially, it is an Asiatic island. The idea of Canada laying claim to it was originally suggested by Mr. Steffanson [*sic*] as a convenient base for exploration in the Arctic Ocean, but the proposal did not find favour with the members of the Advisory Board. It was generally considered that any pretensions we might have to this

> island must be of a very unsubstantial character, and could only result in weakening our legitimate claims to the Arctic islands contiguous to our own territory, for if we can go so far afield as Wrangel to take possession of islands, unconnected with Canada, what is there to prevent the United States, Denmark, or any other power, laying claim to islands far from their shores but adjacent to our own.[26]

The meetings of the Advisory Technical Board to which Pope referred do not seem to be recorded in complete detail, but enough can be gleaned from surviving documents to get an idea of what transpired. In November, Cory sent a note to Deville and Harkin, enclosing copies of Stefansson's letter of 30 October about Wrangel Island, and asking that it be brought up at "tomorrow's meeting" of the Advisory Technical Board.[27] The précis of the minutes of the meeting records that Cory's note was read, but it is unclear whether the attendees discussed Stefansson's letter.[28] It was discussed in detail at the next regular meeting of the board on 10 November, however, and secretary F.C.C. Lynch noted that the board had recognized the potential value of Wrangel Island as a base for exploration and fur trade. Accordingly, the board passed a resolution that "the question of perfecting such claim as Great Britain may have to Wrangel Island should be referred to the Imperial Government with the suggestion that the Imperial Government take such further steps as they may see fit to make good the sovereignty of Great Britain."[29] Cory replied on 18 November, saying that he had read Lynch's memo to the minister and the minister took the view that the matter was for Canada's consideration, not Great Britain's. Consequently, he would like the opinion of the board as to what should be done.[30] At a special meeting of the board on 25 November, Dr. Deville "explained at length to the Minister the position of the Board with respect to Wrangel Island," but the brief record of the meeting does not indicate what decision, if any, was taken.[31]

Most official attention at this time was being given to the proposed expedition to Ellesmere Island documented in the previous chapter. After a lull, Stefansson returned to the attack in early January 1921, with a batch of letters to Meighen, Borden, and Lougheed. In most of these he was pushing his campaign for continued Arctic activity in general and his own participation in it, but in a letter of 8 January to Lougheed, he dealt specifically with Wrangel Island, referring to "our conversation of a few days ago when I urged the importance of following up British discovery of Wrangel Island by occupation." He elaborated:

> I know of a Canadian fur company who are anxious to put a post on Wrangel Island if they have reason to believe that it is to be claimed and occupied as Canadian or British territory. That this company is willing to establish a post not only shows their opinion of the value of the island for one of the several purposes which I urged upon you, but it also indicates a means by which our claim to the island can be made good without expense to the Government.[32]

The "company" referred to was the Hudson's Bay Company (HBC), which Stefansson had connections with at the time through his Baffin Island reindeer scheme and which he was trying to interest in Wrangel Island.[33]

FIGURE 11-3 SIR JAMES LOUGHEED. *GLENBOW / PA-3834-4.*

The developments and documents summarized thus far show the basic division of opinion respecting Stefansson's Wrangel Island project. Borden, given his habitual regard for Stefansson and his ideas, was for it. So was Christie, at least in the early stages. Pope was strongly against it. The Advisory Technical Board was lukewarm about it or, at least according to Pope's report, against it. The attitudes of Meighen and Lougheed do not come through as clearly, but it seems likely, in view of what was about to transpire, that they had a measure of sympathy for it.

The question of whether Wrangel Island was open for appropriation, as Stefansson argued, has already been mentioned. Two other questions, both relating to the events of 1914, were also very much in the background: were the survivors of the *Karluk* disaster authorized to claim Wrangel Island, and had they actually done so? Stefansson's consistent answer to both these questions was a firm "Yes." In *The Adventure of Wrangel Island*, for example, he wrote: "Meantime the crew of the *Karluk* had spent the summer on Wrangel Island, formally reaffirming possession of it for the British Empire according to our instructions from the Canadian government, and keeping the flag flying for more than six months."[34]

By order in council on 2 June 1913, the Cabinet had provided Stefansson "authority to take possession of and annex to His Majesty's Dominions any lands lying to the north of Canadian territory which are not within the jurisdiction of any civilized Power."[35] This authority was given to Stefansson individually rather than to the expedition collectively; however, Stefansson himself had never set foot on Wrangel Island. Furthermore, any such lands were to lie "north" of Canadian territory – and it would obviously require a rather strange interpretation of the meaning of "north" to include Wrangel Island, except in the sense that it actually lay farther north than any part of the Canadian mainland with the exception of the northern tip of Boothia Peninsula.[36]

Regarding the alleged claim, Stefansson quoted a statement by Chief Engineer John Munro, commander of the party after the departure of Captain Bartlett, in a letter written on 17 April 1924. "At this time Maurer, Templeman and I were located at Rodgers Harbor," Munro claimed. "On Dominion Day, July 1st, 1914, we raised a Canadian red ensign about twenty feet from the tent, claiming the island as British."[37] Stefansson also reproduced photos showing the flag being raised, flown, and also flying at half mast by the grave of George Malloch, one of the members of the expedition who died on the island.[38] A statement by another survivor, however, was completely at variance with Munro's. In a memorandum of 15 June 1922, William L. McKinlay wrote as follows:

> I consider that it is only my duty under the present circumstances to state most emphatically that, never, to the best of my knowledge, was the Canadian flag raised on Wrangell [*sic*] Island, with the object of taking formal possession of that island in the name of Canada. The only camp at which a flag was raised after leaving Shipwreck Camp was at Rodgers Harbour, where it was flown at half mast for the reason previously mentioned; and to me it savours of sacrilege to attempt to ascribe to this last act, of homage to our brave dead, a political motive.[39]

The party had another camp at Cape Waring, however, and from Munro's text and McKinlay's memo it is evident that McKinlay was there (or at least absent from Rodgers Harbour) when the formal claim was supposed to have been made.

As discussed at length in the previous chapter, the Canadian government made a tentative agreement in February 1921 for Stefansson to go on an Arctic expedition to Ellesmere and nearby islands. This, of course, could have precluded Stefansson's participation in anything relating to Wrangel Island. In a long letter to Harkin on 7 February, he strongly recommended that there should be "a quiet, entirely unostentatious taking possession of Wrangel Island," which might be carried out by a Canadian fur trader during the upcoming summer.[40] Stefansson hoped to head to Axel Heiberg Island in 1922 and explore north, west, and southwest of this main base, returning in 1925, perhaps by way of Alaska or Siberia.[41] Thus, if Stefansson were to go himself to Wrangel Island, presumably this is how it would be done.

During this visit to Ottawa, Stefansson was also in touch with Meighen, and he succeeded in winning government approval of his plan for a Canadian claim to sovereignty over Wrangel Island. The Prime Minister wrote him the following brief letter on 19 February:

> I have discussed the matters which you laid before me today and desire to advise you that this Government purposes to assert the right of Canada to Wrangel Island, based upon the discoveries and explorations of your expedition.
>
> I believe this is all that is necessary for your purposes now.[42]

Stefansson received this news with jubilation. As soon as he received Meighen's note of 19 February, he told the HBC of the government's decision to claim Wrangel Island and said that unofficially it would welcome the establishment of a company post there.[43] He also sent Sir James Lougheed a copy of his letter to Cory from 30 October 1920, in response to Lougheed's request for a memo on the subject, and added the statement that members of his expedition had formally claimed Wrangel Island in 1914.[44]

Stefansson's delight was short-lived. On 1 March, Meighen's private secretary wrote him a brief note which said simply: "The Prime Minister asks that pending further advice you make no use of his letter to you of February 19th about Wrangel Island."[45] According to Stefansson, he never received any "further advice," except, some time later, word that all Arctic expeditions were cancelled for 1921.[46]

FIGURE 11-4: RT. HON. ARTHUR MEIGHEN. *LIBRARY AND ARCHIVES CANADA / C-005799.*

What accounts for Meighen's abrupt change of mind? On the surface there is no adequate explanation, but it would certainly appear that a memo by Christie, dated 28 February, provides a large part of the answer. As discussed previously, Christie had written a long memo dated 17 February that dealt with various subjects, including Wrangel Island. For some reason, he withdrew the memo immediately and resubmitted all parts except that dealing with Wrangel Island the same day; he resubmitted the Wrangel Island portion on 28 February.[47] In his memo of 28 October, Christie had recommended the occupation of Wrangel Island; now he completely reversed his stand and strongly advised that nothing should be done:

> On further reflection it is submitted that this would be very unwise. The British Empire is already so large, the burden of development upon our white population so great, and the envy and suspicions of foreign powers on account of our great possessions are so active, that it seems clearly in our interest to be careful to refrain from further acquisitions unless in any given case there are compelling practical reasons for the addition. It is difficult to discover any such reasons in this case. Wrangel Island does not naturally fall into what may be regarded as the Canadian regional system. It does not appear that our naval or military authorities have ever recommended its acquisition or worth on strategical grounds. Its commercial value is speculative and apparently no detailed study of this point has been presented to support the case for acquisition.... Again by attempting to occupy the Island we should run the risk of arousing the susceptibilities of both Japan and Russia. Finally by wandering outside our own hemisphere and region we would inevitably detract from the strength of our case for the ownership of the islands immediately north of Canada which we really need and desire. It is submitted that on the present showing the disadvantages far outweigh any possible advantages and that nothing should accordingly be done.[48]

Receipt of the countermanding note of 1 March from Meighen's office did not stop

Stefansson completely. On 7 March, he wrote to the Prime Minister's private secretary, saying that he had heard from the Canadian office of the HBC that they were urging the head office in England to have a post established on Wrangel Island. He said that he would arrive in Ottawa almost as soon as his letter to discuss the matter, and he added cryptically:

> I have some further information about the intentions of the Americans with regard to Wrangel Island. The question will not be whether Wrangel Island shall be British or No-man's Land; neither will it be whether it is to be British or Russian. It will become American unless it remains British.[49]

One highly placed official who apparently was not informed immediately about the adverse decision communicated to Stefansson was Cory. On 5 March, Cory sent Harkin Stefansson's letter to Lougheed of 26 February, observing that "if the Hudson's Bay Company should establish a post on Wrangle [*sic*] Island, I am sure that the Government could vest them with sufficient power to perform those acts that would establish British occupancy. You might advise Mr. Stefansson privately to this effect over your own signature and then send the papers to Mr. Craig to file confidentially."[50] On 17 May, the Department of the Naval Service sent Cory, who had consulted them on the subject, a copy of a report on Wrangel Island that members of the department had recently prepared. The report spoke in disparaging terms of the island's terrain, natural resources, and accessibility, but it noted that both the HBC and Liebe and Company of San Francisco were planning to establish posts there. No nation presently exercised sovereignty over the island, but if necessary, it would "be preferable that Russia should be recognized as the owner rather than the United States." Wrangel Island had no present or potential value in war as a base for ships, although it might have some value as a site for an air station.[51] Obviously the naval authorities did not take the glowing view of the island's possibilities that Stefansson did.

The note from the Prime Minister's Office on 1 March had been mainly a setback to Stefansson's hopes that the Canadian government would take official action to appropriate Wrangel Island. It did not affect greatly the plan for Stefansson's own commitment to the government in the immediate future, since this called for him to carry on exploratory work from a base on Axel Heiberg Island. While carrying out a lecture tour in the United States, he tried to make preliminary arrangements for his part of the expedition, described in the previous chapter. All plans in this framework or context ended when the projected expedition was cancelled on 18 May 1921.[52] When a disappointed Stefansson learned of the cancellation about twelve days later,[53] he faced the hard alternatives of abandoning his ideas for northern work or of making new arrangements.

The unexpected arrival of an old friend, Alfred J. T. Taylor of Vancouver, in Nevada on the same day Stefansson received the telegram from Ottawa enabled him to construct the framework of a new plan within an hour.[54] Briefly, under this new plan he would organize a private expedition of his own to take possession of and occupy Wrangel Island on behalf of Canada, hoping that eventually the Canadian government would confirm the occupation and assume sovereignty over the island. With the help of Taylor and his attorney, a limited liability company, the Stefansson Arctic Exploration and Development Company Ltd., was organized under the laws of Canada and incorporated at Vancouver on 23 June 1921. Fred Maurer, a member of the shipwrecked Wrangel Island party in 1914, and Lorne Knight, both of whom wanted to return to the Arctic, were engaged as members of the occupying group, as was Milton Galle, a young Texan who had been acting as Stefansson's secretary. Allan Crawford was hired as the fourth member of the party; since the other three were all Americans and it was considered necessary to underline that the expedition was officially Canadian, Crawford was made the nominal commander.

The expedition was prepared with as much secrecy as possible during the summer of 1921, but news of it leaked out and reached Ottawa sometime in June.[55] The outfit was purchased partly in Seattle and partly in Nome, Alaska, and was so modest that it prompted speculation that the destination must be near an established trading post where more supplies could be obtained. Stefansson, who did not accompany the expedition, provided most of the limited amount of money that was allotted to the venture and pledged himself for more;[56] at least three members of the party, Knight, Maurer, and Crawford, purchased a small number of shares in the new company.[57] When the party arrived at Nome near the end of August, it chartered the little schooner *Silver Wave* for the voyage to Wrangel Island. The owner, Captain Jack Hammer, insisted on being told in confidence the intended destination before agreeing to make the trip. It had been planned to hire Inuit to stay with the occupying group, but when the time came to sail, only one, a middle-aged woman named Ada Blackjack, was ready to go. This was the party of five which, with seven dogs and one kitten, made up the living contingent that set forth to occupy Wrangel Island. Departing from Nome on 9 September, *Silver Wave* deposited them on the island on 16 September and left them to their own devices.

Immediately after landing on Wrangel, the party raised the British flag and read in ceremonial fashion the following proclamation of sovereignty:

> A PROCLAMATION
> KNOW ALL BY THESE PRESENTS;
>
> That I, Allan Rudyard Crawford, a native of CANADA and a British subject and those men whose names appear below, members of the Wrangel Island Detachment of the Stefansson Arctic Expedition of 1921–, on the advice and council of Vilhjalmur Stefansson, a British subject, have this day, in consideration of lapses of foreign claims and the occupancy from March 12th 1914 to September 7th 1914 of this island by the survivors of the brigantine *Karluk*, Captain R. A. Bartlett commanding, the property of the Government of CANADA chartered to operate in the Canadian Arctic Expedition of 1913–1918 of which survivors Chief Engineer Munro, a native of SCOTLAND and a British subject, raised the Canadian flag, raised the British flag and declared this land known as WRANGEL Island to be the just possession of His Majesty GEORGE, King of GREAT BRITAIN and IRELAND and the Dominions beyond the Seas, Emperor of INDIA, etc., and a part of the BRITISH EMPIRE.
>
> Signed and deposited in this monument this sixteenth day of September in the year of our Lord one

thousand nine hundred and twenty one.

Allan R. Crawford Commander
E. Lorne Knight Second in command
F. W. Maurer
Milton Galle

WRANGEL ISLAND, Sept. 16th, 1921.
GOD SAVE THE KING[58]

In taking this step, the party were only carrying out their instructions,[59] but in one sense the consequences were unpleasant. The crew of *Silver Wave* felt that they had been duped into aiding and abetting a British or Canadian move to take over an island that the United States might have had. Their complaints when they got back to Nome were picked up by many Alaskans, and eventually a protest was sent to Washington. The *New York Times*, hearing of the protest, published a statement on 20 March 1922, which was essentially provided by Stefansson himself and thus not critical of the project. Other newspapers in the United States, Great Britain, and Canada were not so friendly, and the result was a good deal of unfavourable publicity.[60] The matter was brought up in the US Senate on 22 March and 25 March, and the Congressional Record printed, on the first date, two *New York Times* articles on the subject[61] and, on the second date, a letter written by Captain William F. Reynolds, Commandant of the US Coast Guard, telling how he landed on Wrangel Island in 1881 as a junior officer of *Corwin* and took possession for the United States.[62] An account of an interview with Reynolds was published in the *Washington Star* on 26 March, where he told the story in greater detail.

In the meantime, Sir Joseph Pope in Ottawa had reacted very quickly to the newspaper statements, and on 21 March he sent the newly elected Prime Minister William Lyon Mackenzie King a copy of the memorandum he had written on 25 November 1920, strongly criticizing the idea of a Canadian claim to Wrangel Island. In the accompanying note, he reiterated his view that "no more far-fetched claim could well be imagined, and any attempt to associate Canada with such fantastic pretensions could scarcely fail to prejudice us in the eyes of the world, besides weakening our legitimate claim to certain Arctic islands adjacent to our own territory, in respect of which we have a strong case."[63]

Stefansson already had written a long letter to the new Prime Minister on 11 March 1922, urging the adoption of "a definite policy" towards the polar regions in general and Wrangel Island in particular. He reiterated his well-known views about the future value of these lands and summarized briefly the history of Wrangel Island. On the strange and obviously unwarranted assumption that under "a general principle of international law" discovery rights lapse after precisely five years, he stated that British rights to Wrangel Island gained in 1849 had lapsed in 1854, American rights gained in 1881 had lapsed in 1886, and British (Canadian) rights gained in 1914 had lapsed in 1919. He seemed to assume that no other rights had ever been established, thus showing unawareness or ignorance of the Russian landing in 1911 and the Russian claim of 1916. He recounted in detail the story of his current effort to reoccupy the island, observing that he had spent all his savings ($15,000) on the project and had borrowed more ($5,000). He did not ask for a refund of this money but rather for Canadian government support of his actions and maintenance of Canadian rights, particularly to forestall a Japanese occupation of the island which he believed likely. Through a personal friendship with the managing editor of the *New York Times*, Stefansson had been able to persuade that newspaper to postpone publication of the story about American demands for an American claim, at least until he could get in touch with Prime Minister King and give him time to consider what attitude the Canadian government should take.[64] Stefansson followed up this letter with a shorter communiqué on 14 March in which he stressed that although Arthur Meighen had told him that he looked upon these matters as being of Imperial rather than of Canadian concern, British Ambassador Sir Auckland Geddes in Washington, Sir Arthur Balfour, and Sir Robert Borden all considered them to be of primarily Canadian concern.[65]

King declined to commit himself or the government promptly, but on 2 May Stefansson had an opportunity to plead his case in person in Ottawa. He succeeded in meeting with Prime Minister King, with Minister of the Interior Charles Stewart, and with W. W. Cory, O. S. Finnie, and J. D. Craig of Stewart's department. Consequently, he wrote a letter to Finnie on 3 May, proposing that either the Stefansson Arctic Exploration and Development Company or he personally should be granted a long-term lease to Wrangel and Herald Islands, on terms similar to those of the Baffin Island lease he had already received. He emphasized that instead of the lease, his company would really prefer a refund without interest of the money spent to date on the enterprise, which he estimated to be about $20,000. It was only "upon the Government's expressed preference of giving a lease rather than refunding the money" that he had requested the lease. In a handwritten postscript, he urged the need for haste, since he wanted to raise money on the lease to send a ship to Wrangel Island that summer.[66]

Stefansson's letter gives a fairly optimistic view of the situation, but a letter from Finnie to Cory on 3 May, reporting a conversation with Stefansson a day earlier, puts the explorer's chances in a less favourable light. According to Finnie, Stefansson had told him that the minister had refused to consider the return of the money spent, which Stefansson on this occasion had estimated at $17,000, and therefore Stefansson had asked for the less satisfactory lease. Finnie concluded with the question that obviously would be the chief determinant for him and other officials: whether the Canadian or British government "claim or acknowledge a proprietary interest in this Island because of the Stefansson Expedition."[67] J. D. Craig raised the same question in a note to Finnie on 10 May, adding that if Canada effectively occupied the island then the issuing of a lease would be perfectly legal, but "if we are not prepared to stand behind the act [i.e., raising of the flag by Stefansson's party] in every way, we should ignore it."[68]

In spite of the widespread and long-standing reservations held by both political leaders and public servants respecting endorsement of Stefansson's project, the government stumbled into – or was manoeuvred into – a public declaration of support for it in a bizarre exchange in the House of Commons on 12 May. The subject under discussion was a supply item in the Naval Service estimates for patrol of the northern waters of Canada.

> *Arthur Meighen*: Will the minister state what is the policy of the Government towards the northern islands, with particular reference to those covered by the Stefansson

expedition, laid claim to on behalf of Canada, and to Wrangel island.

George Graham: It is a delicate matter to state the policy of the Government on that question.

Meighen: Has the Government any policy?

William Fielding: What we have we hold.

Meighen: I would recommend the Government never to fall away from that principle.

Graham: Some people have failed to do that.

Meighen: The Government failed once, but I think if they had the same thing to do over again they would act differently.

Graham: The old government.

Meighen: Yes, the old government my hon. friend was in. It is well known that there is a dispute as to Wrangel island. The question of the proper attitude of Canada towards that island is doubtless before the Government. This vote has to do with these matters, and I am asking if the Government is in a position to say what its views are with relation to the retention of Wrangel island or the continuance of Canada's claim thereto; and the same words apply to the other islands covered by the expedition.

Graham: The policy of the Government, as I understand it, is as just expressed by the Minister of Finance – what we have we hold.

Meighen: Well, have we Wrangel island?

Graham: Yes, as I understand it, and we propose to retain it.

Fielding: We had it in December, and we have not let it go.[69]

It is unclear whether the commitment embodied in these statements was premeditated, but it was unlikely a deliberately planned expression of policy. In any case, Prime Minister King made the commitment firmer a moment or two later, in a statement categorically supporting the position his ministers had taken:

> The Government has had interviews with Mr. Stefansson. I do not know that it is in the public interest to disclose the full nature of those interviews, but I might say that at the present time the Canadian flag is flying on Wrangel island, and there are Canadians on the island, members of a previous expedition of Stefansson's. Mr. Stefansson is about to take a ship up to Wrangel island with some of his men, and has recently had it fitted out with supplies. The Government certainly maintains the position that Wrangel island is part of the property of this country.[70]

Stefansson received word of this pronouncement with delight, and he began to write letters urging haste in granting him his Wrangel Island lease.[71] The government was obviously having second thoughts about its offhand endorsement of Stefansson's claim, however, and was hesitant to rush into compliance. On 24 May, the assistant official agent of the Soviet government in London sent a note to Foreign Secretary Lord Curzon, asserting that Ferdinand von Wrangel had discovered Wrangel Island during his expedition of 1821–24, that the hydrographic expedition of 1910–15 had raised the Russian flag there, and that there had "never been any question as to Wrangel Island being a Russian possession."[72] Colonial Secretary Winston Churchill cabled word of this disturbing note to Governor General Sir Julian Byng on 2 June, and a copy of the note itself was sent by post.[73] Civil servants continued to express opinions that were generally against the project and sometimes against Stefansson himself. On 5 June, Sir Joseph Pope wrote a memo to Minister of Finance Fielding reiterating his own firm view that Canada should have nothing to do with a claim to Wrangel Island;[74] on 9 June, Finnie advised Cory in a written memo that although Stefansson's claim was in all probability "a just and complete one," it was for diplomatic reasons doubtful whether Canada should support it;[75] and on 15 June, Cory was advised by his son T. L. Cory, a departmental solicitor, that Stefansson had apparently undertaken the venture "for his own commercial benefit" and the government should be very cautious about supporting it.[76] Loring Christie, upon receipt of a 9 June letter from Stefansson saying that a friend had told him Christie had said it was unfortunate for Canada to raise the issue about ownership of Arctic islands, replied angrily in a curt note that he did not admit the truth of the allegation.[77]

There is little mystery about the change in Christie's attitude. He had become quite disillusioned with Stefansson, and then he committed to file a memo explaining why he felt it necessary to renounce Stefansson completely:

> Attached hereto is a letter of June 9th from Mr. Vilhjalmur Stefansson to myself together with a copy of my reply.
>
> Until the receipt of this letter I have had no communication or relations with Mr. Stefansson for more than a year. This letter is so typical of such experiences as I have had with him that I think it worth while putting the matter on file. I first met Mr. Stefansson in the fall of 1920 – September or October I think – and for some months thereafter I saw him several times in connection with the discussions then going on about the status of the Arctic Archipelago. The circumstances in which he was introduced to me were such as to suggest that he was a person with a sense of discretion and responsibility. As the result however of a number of incidents I felt bound to doubt that; and finally, so far as I myself was concerned, I was forced to the conclusion that it would be best to have no relations whatever with him. More than once I discovered that he had, in conversation with officials of other departments, misrepresented what I had said to him. On the last occasion on which I saw him he made to me what I could only regard as a suggestion that I should change a legal opinion I had already given in such a way as to induce an alteration in the plans of one of the other Departments (the Interior Department). It so happened that such an alteration would have been advantageous to Mr. Stefansson's own personal interests. Our interview developed in such a way that I finally put this aspect to Mr. Stefansson. His reply did not seem to me satisfactory and we have never met since.[78]

Two months later, when the Prime Minister asked Christie for advice about any action in the matter, Christie replied that his earlier view remained unchanged because the proposal had no real advantages and many disadvantages. Consequently he advised again "that the matter should be dropped altogether, and that the Government should decline to give either support or recognition to Mr. Stefansson's venture," which appeared to be "an attempt to force the hand of the Government in circumstances that render it not audacious but merely impudent."[79]

On 15 July, Churchill wrote to Byng bringing up the question of the Russian protest and enclosing a copy of the Hydrographer of the Navy's notes on Wrangel Island. These notes asserted that Wrangel's own account showed that, contrary to the Russian claim, he had not discovered the island, and its mixed history showed that in reality Russian title to it rested "on very slender foundations." Stefansson's views about its commercial value appeared to be "somewhat oversanguine," however, and from a naval point of view its ownership was not a matter of much importance. Churchill observed that the Air Council had expressed the view that the island would probably not have any value as an air base for military or civil aviation, and the Foreign Secretary had given his opinion that no country had an indisputable claim to it. In the circumstances, the British government would "await the views of the Canadian government before replying to the Soviet Government's note."[80]

By this time, Stefansson was becoming increasingly worried about the safety of the party on Wrangel Island and the need to make contact with them, not so much because he feared they might be running short of food as because of the danger of sickness or accident. Failing to get prompt action from the Canadian government, and having exhausted his own funds, he successfully appealed to an American friend for help and then completed an arrangement by cable with Captain Joseph Bernard at Nome whereby Bernard would try to get to Wrangel Island later that summer.[81] He also approached the Canadian government again, making the following urgent appeal to Cory on 8 August. "Attached is the brief statement you asked for to be presented to Council on Friday," he noted. "Please urge upon Council that there are on Wrangel Island four men in Canadian service whose lives are in danger. The Arctic summer is nearly over." In the accompanying statement, he emphasized that his own financial means were exhausted, that he believed his claim was good and should be supported, and that he had undertaken the enterprise as a service for Canada. He specifically requested $5,000 for the relief expedition, with details of repayment to be settled later.[82]

Cory's minister (Stewart) had left for the West, but he took prompt action himself, sending copies of Stefansson's communiqués directly to the Prime Minister with the suggestion that if the government responded, it should be for the humanitarian purpose of rescuing the Wrangel Island party rather than to support any of Stefansson's occupation schemes.[83] Cabinet quickly decided to provide help. Although an order in council formally authorizing this help was not issued until 21 August,[84] Cory informed Stefansson by telegram on 12 August that it was coming.[85] The amount was reduced from $5,000 to $3,000, however, because Stefansson's associate Alfred Taylor, wiring urgently for help from Vancouver on 9 August, had said that the cost would not exceed $3,000.[86]

Captain Bernard sailed from Nome in his schooner *Teddy Bear* on 20 August and did his best to reach the island. Unfortunately the 1922 season was exceptionally bad for navigation because of abnormally large quantities of drifting ice. Bernard was obliged to turn back and returned to Nome on 23 September reporting failure.[87] The party would be isolated for another year, unless they left the island and travelled over ice to a settlement on the Siberian coast.

The Wrangel Island venture continued to attract attention in the United States, and on 27 September, the American embassy in London sent a memo on the subject to the British government. The memo outlined briefly the history of the island, and, although it did not state any American claim, it did emphasize American activities there. It also said that the status of the island might now require consideration, especially in view of Minister of the Naval Service George Graham's "reported" statement in the Canadian House of Commons on 12 May 1922. Colonial Secretary the Duke of Devonshire sent a copy of the memo, without comment, to Lord Byng on 4 November.[88]

Evidently the Canadian government was reluctant to take any further public stance on the issue. Doing so offered the equally embarrassing alternatives of supporting or withdrawing from the position they had stumbled into on 12 May. About the beginning of October, the Prime Minister asked Pope to prepare a reply to Churchill's dispatch of 15 July,[89] but nothing was done immediately, although numerous officials expressed or reiterated their opposition to Stefansson's scheme. In communicating with Stewart on the matter, as he was directed to do, Pope remarked that neither he nor Christie considered that the government should go on with the claim, and he had "not yet met with anybody who thought differently."[90] In reply, Stewart sent T. L. Cory's memorandum of 15 June 1922, saying that he agreed with the opinion expressed therein that Canada should not press her claim to Wrangel Island.[91]

It was becoming increasingly difficult to maintain a state of indecision and inaction. On 24 February 1923, Devonshire sent a confidential note to Byng informing him that Britain had received a communication from the US Embassy asking about British and Canadian views and intentions respecting Wrangel Island. Before replying, Devonshire said the British government "would be glad to learn the views of the Canadian government on the question."[92] This request provoked another series of memoranda and notes from government officials opposing any claim,[93] and on 22 March, Pope wrote a memo to the Prime Minister asking whether it would be agreeable that he prepare a dispatch embodying this united view.[94] In a later memo of 5 April, he noted that no answer to any of the British communiqués had yet been sent.[95]

At this stage, things looked very dark for Stefansson's project, but a strange turn of events gave it a new lease of life. He had been engaged in an involved and voluminous correspondence with Ottawa regarding the $3,000 which had been advanced to him in August 1922 and which, from the government's point of view, was returnable. Although Cory's telegram on 12 August had clearly identified that the money was given for the relief of the Wrangel Island party, Stefansson insisted that he had understood it was to help continue the occupation.[96] He hoped that by now the government would see the wisdom of holding the island, would take it over officially, and would return to him and his friends the money they had put into the enterprise.[97] If the government refused, he would try to get private support to continue the occupation, because he remained convinced that the project was sound.[98] In this situation, Stefansson went to Ottawa early in April 1923 to plead his case in person, with rather surprising results.

The correspondence for this period includes two revealing and surprising documents, both damaging to Stefansson and his cause. He had on various occasions expressed his approval of Captain Bernard's role in the attempt to reach Wrangel Island in 1922, but these cordial feelings were not reciprocated. Bernard wrote a letter to Mackenzie King on 21 March regarding Stefansson's reported chartering of the *Teddy Bear* again in 1923, saying that he would not accept any such proposition. Bernard added that he would not "have anything to do whatsoever with him. I have many good and sufficient reasons for this decision."[99] Much more important, in the context of the whole affair, is a statement by J. D. Craig in a letter to Hensley Holmden on 5 April. Speaking of Stefansson's Wrangel Island project, Craig said:

> I … may tell you confidentially that everyone in this Branch who has had a chance to make any sort of report or recommendation regarding this question has been strongly against it. We realize particularly that if Canada makes any attempt to dispute Stefansson's so called occupation of Wrangel Island we may open up questions regarding the islands in our own Archipelago which may get us into great difficulty.[100]

It may well be that the second sentence in this passage goes a long way towards explaining the Canadian government's extremely cautious and uncertain handling of the affair, practically from start to finish.

Stefansson appeared before Cabinet in Ottawa on 7 April, and in a lengthy interview, he succeeded in winning a sort of reprieve for his scheme. According to his own account, the ministers were courteous and attentive, and gave him plenty of time to make a thorough statement of his case.[101] It may well be that his impressive knowledge of Arctic affairs generally and his persuasive manner had a good deal to do with the relatively favourable verdict. Another factor may have been the Prime Minister's evident concern for the Imperial aspects of the matter, although whether this was genuine or simply a device for renouncing Canadian responsibility is debatable.[102] In any case, Cabinet firmly decided upon the question of a Canadian claim to Wrangel Island, and because of Imperial considerations, Stefansson should be authorized to go to England to present his views to the British government – with the Canadian government paying travelling and living expenses for the trip.[103] The Governor General sent the Colonial Secretary a letter, the text of which had been drafted by Sir Joseph Pope in what must have been a rather embarrassing exercise, informing him that Stefansson was proceeding on this mission and asking that he "be afforded an opportunity of expressing his views to the appropriate officials promptly after his arrival."[104]

Understandably, the senior civil servants who had opposed government involvement in the project were not pleased with this turn of events. On 9 April, Craig wrote a memo to Finnie containing the following:

> If it is true … that the Cabinet will probably support Mr. Stefansson, in his claims regarding Wrangel Island or in his overtures to the British Government regarding the Island, I think it should again be drawn to the attention of our Government that in supporting this claim, they are weakening, by a very considerable amount, our claim to some of the islands of the Northern Archipelago and by publicly drawing attention to the undoubted value of Wrangel Island as a future air base,

> they are emphasizing the desirability for similar purposes of some of the islands of the Arctic Archipelago, and are practically inviting some other nation to come in and take possession there.
>
> If this is their policy, we should certainly be provided with funds sufficient to complete immediately our program for maintaining our sovereignty in the north instead of spreading it over a number of years as is the present intention.
>
> Otherwise the Government must be prepared to accept the responsibility when some other nation attempts to establish air bases on some of our islands.[105]

Finnie had evidently decided that further opposition was useless, however, and in a memo to Assistant Deputy Minister Roy A. Gibson, he wrote resignedly, "We have already expressed our views on this question and I hardly think it would be proper for us to make any further representations to the Minister."[106]

Stefansson sailed to England in May, and he was soon involved in official meetings with government representatives and unofficial meetings with other people. His scheme attracted significant attention, although the response to it was mixed. He was fortunate to win the support of two influential figures: First Lord of the Admiralty L. S. (Leo) Amery and Secretary of State for Air Sir Samuel Hoare.[107] A confidential Foreign Office memorandum on Wrangel Island, dated 2 July 1923, reflects this support in its summary of the stated views of the Admiralty and Air Ministry. The Admiralty said that, strictly from its own point of view, the island probably had little immediate value but then, after referring to likely developments in wireless and air traffic, concluded that "the island is the only territory in a vast area to which Great Britain has any claim, and the Admiralty consider that it would be short-sighted policy to surrender our claims to it."[108] The Air Ministry detailed the potential value of the island in connection with shorter Arctic air routes, refuelling facilities, weather forecasting, and wireless, and concluded with cautious optimism: "From a service point of view, the Air Staff do not consider that Wrangel Island can be of value at present, but from the point of view outlined in this memorandum, they feel that its retention would prove a valuable adjunct to the development of British air policy."[109] The Foreign Office reached the conclusion that there were three possible claimants to the island – Russia, the United States, and Great Britain (Canada) – but none had an incontrovertible claim.[110]

During the summer, Stefansson had talks on Wrangel Island and other matters with technical experts, such as the submarine authority Commander J. G. Bower, and with editors of such papers as the *Times*, the *Spectator*, the *Observer*, and the *Manchester Guardian*, for which he wrote articles. Things moved slowly, however, so far as his main business was concerned. He gradually realized that the British government, particularly the Foreign Office, which had principal responsibility in the matter, was not inclined to take positive action on his behalf. He gathered the impression that, although there was considerable sympathy for his efforts, the most the government would do, at least for the time being, was to extend moral support for a continued occupation of the island on a private basis.[111] This meant, in practical terms, that so far as the British government was concerned, Stefansson was on his own. This, in turn, made it highly unlikely that he would get any more help from the Canadian government.

Figure 11-5: Vilhjalmur Stefansson. *Boston Public Library, Leslie Jones Collection.*

Stefansson had already tried to interest influential Americans in Wrangel Island and to prepare the way for a turnover of his project to the United States if both Canada and Great Britain ultimately refused to support him. Among the Americans who expressed interest in or enthusiasm for his enterprise were Assistant Secretary of the Navy Theodore Roosevelt Jr., Chief of the US Bureau of Aeronautics Admiral William A. Moffett, General Billy Mitchell, and co-inventor of the airplane Orville Wright. Moffett, for example, wrote, "I am in entire agreement as to the importance of Wrangel Island and its future use." Stefansson had appeared before a general board of the US Navy on 7 May 1923, before leaving for England, and promised that he would do his best to make Wrangel Island American territory should the British fail to capitalize on their prior right. This commitment is indicative of his view as to the priority of rights to the island – that the British right was best, the American second best, and the Russian a distant third.[112] This order of priority also accorded well with his own personal interest. If Britain or the United States established sovereignty over the island, he might secure a lease or otherwise recover some of the money he had sunk in his scheme, whereas if the Soviet Union made good its title, such possibilities would be almost nonexistent.

While Stefansson was carrying on his various attempts to win support for his project, the question of the status of Wrangel Island was raised at official levels by the governments concerned. On 25 May 1923, M. Krassin, the head of the Soviet trade delegation in London, wrote a note to Lord Curzon reminding him that the British government had already been notified that the island was a Russian possession. Krassin asked that the British government "use its good services with the Canadian government" to put a stop to Stefansson's "raids."[113] On 16 July, William Peters reported to Curzon from the British Commercial Mission in Moscow that *Izvestia* had published an article on 10 July setting forth the grounds for Russia's claim to the island and asserting that the Soviet government would not "countenance this attempt of an agent of British imperialism to seize property which belongs to others."[114] On 25 August, the Soviet government's assistant official agent in Britain sent Lord Curzon a copy of a note which, although making inaccurate claims (such as Lieutenant Wrangel raising the Russian flag on Wrangel Island in 1821–24), nevertheless repeated in firm language that the island was Russian territory.[115] There is no direct British reply to these messages on file.

On 4 June 1923, the American Chargé d'Affaires in London sent a note to Lord Curzon in which he referred to the earlier memo of 27 September 1922. Noting that no reply had been received to this and other informal inquiries, he asked again what position the British government intended to assume regarding Wrangel Island.[116] The Foreign Office simply replied that the matter was being considered in consultation with other departments, and it would send an answer as soon as possible.[117] This was, of course, shortly after Stefansson's arrival in England, when a great deal of such consultation was in progress. On 10 August, Curzon cabled Henry Chilton, the British Chargé d'Affaires in Washington, asking for his views on the likely American reaction to a British claim to the island.[118] Chilton replied that the US government would almost certainly contest such a claim, but he feared he would arouse suspicion if he tried to sound out the State Department about it.[119] About a month later, at Chilton's request, Air Attaché Captain M. Christie engaged in conversations with American army and navy officers, and reported that he had gathered the impression that the United States would contest a British-Canadian claim, would not press its own case, but would probably support Russian sovereignty. He suggested that a British occupation of Wrangel Island might be followed by an American occupation of one of the Canadian Arctic islands.[120] The British government kept Ottawa informed of developments with frequent communiqués.[121]

Whether Stefansson's campaign for official support succeeded or not, it was essential to make contact with the party on Wrangel Island in the summer of 1923. Accordingly, he had tried to arrange a relief expedition. On his instructions, his associate Alfred Taylor, now located in Toronto, sought interviews with the Cabinet and senior government officials in Ottawa to discuss the subject, but he was given scant consideration.[122] The government was still concerned about the $3,000 advance it had made to Stefansson; now there was the further matter of his living allowance of $15 per day while in England, since his stay there had already far exceeded what had originally been anticipated. On 6 September, W. W. Cory informed the Prime Minister that he instructed his government colleagues that if Stefansson asked for further advances on account of his trip to England, the matter was to be referred to him (Cory).[123]

Stefansson thus failed to get any response in Ottawa, but he had better luck in London. Largely through the initiative of Griffith Brewer, London representative of the Wright interests, a sum of more than £2,360 was raised to pay for an expedition to Wrangel Island.[124] With this money, Stefansson was able to arrange by cable to charter the motor schooner *Donaldson* at Nome, Alaska, and to engage Harold Noice, who had been with him during part of his 1913–18 expedition, to take command of it for the trip. There were some alarming reports about action that Russia might take, and on 1 September, the British government instructed

Figure 11-6: Ada Blackjack. *Courtesy of Dartmouth College Library.*

Peters in Moscow to inform the Soviet government that the expedition was a private one organized by Stefansson to rescue the Crawford party, that the question of sovereignty thereby was not raised, and that any attempt to interfere with the expedition would be viewed "most seriously" by His Majesty's Government.[125] Otherwise the British government remained officially a nonparticipant in the affair.

Noice sailed from Nome in *Donaldson* on 3 August, reached Wrangel Island on 20 August, and returned to Nome at the end of the month with disastrous news. Of the party, only the Inuk woman, Ada Blackjack, had been found alive. Knight had died in his tent on 22 June 1923. Crawford, Maurer, and Galle had set out for Siberia the preceding January, but since they had neither returned nor been heard from, it could only be presumed they had perished. In accordance with Stefansson's instructions, Noice left on the island a new occupying party, comprising twelve Alaskan Inuit and Charles Wells, an American citizen from Nome.[126]

News of the disaster decisively ended any remaining chance that Stefansson might get official support from either Canada or Great Britain. He returned to the United States in the autumn, and before long Canadian officials noted that they had received no report from him regarding his negotiations with the British government.[127] In spite of all that had happened, however, Stefansson was still not willing to admit defeat. On 2 January 1924, he wrote to Mackenzie King, raising or reviving various points to uphold his case for the occupation of Wrangel Island and stressing the possibility of American intervention there. He hoped that the Prime Minister would "get someone to go into these matters thoroughly again and see if there is not something which Canada can yet do to prevent her being set back too far by the enterprise and foresight of the Americans."[128] The attitude voiced here, however, does not seem to square very well with the action that Stefansson actually took soon afterwards. He proposed to Carl Lomen that "one day early in the spring of 1924" the "reindeer king" should take Wrangel Island off his hands.[129] The deal was carried through that May. Lomen arranged with his associates "to buy out the Wrangel Island holdings of the Stefansson Arctic Exploration and Development Company, Limited, and to take over the employment of the party then on Wrangel Island."[130] This transfer must have meant, in Stefansson's view, that the occupying authority was now American rather than Canadian or British, since the leader of the occupation group and his followers were American, and Lomen and his associates were also American. Stefansson accounts for the change with the statement, "I was anxious that America should profit by our work if Britain did not care to do so."[131] He was also, by his own admission,[132] in desperate financial straits through having sunk so much money into the enterprise.

Stefansson made still further approaches to both Canadian and British governments, in each case by mail from Sydney, Australia, on 2 June 1924. The letter to Canada was evidently occasioned by a request made of him by the Minister of the Interior when Stefansson was in Ottawa in March. Stewart had asked, Stefansson said, that he set down what he thought the government should do about Wrangel Island, and in his letter he put forward two basic alternative proposals. The first was that Canada or Great Britain should announce the intention, subject to international adjudication, to retain Wrangel Island and, if an investigating committee recommended it, should refund the money that various people (including Stefansson) had put into the venture. His "proposal" to sell out to the Lomen concern would be no barrier if either Canada or Great Britain should decide to go on with the occupation, but if neither did, the next best legal claimant would be the United States. The second proposition, which he said he did not really favour, was that since he had served the Canadian government in Arctic field work for approximately eleven and a half years without pay, the government might pay him back salary which, according to one calculation, would be a little more than $20,000.[133] The files indicate that the Canadian government did not favour Stefansson with a direct reply, and neither the British nor Canadian government made any move to pay him the compensation he requested.[134]

To the extent that the question of Wrangel Island was an issue involving British, Canadian, and Soviet governments, it was decisively settled through diplomatic channels during the summer of 1924. On 18 June, Colonial Secretary James Henry Thomas wrote to Governor General Byng advising him that, since he anticipated that the Soviet government might bring up the question of Wrangel Island at a conference in London, the British government had considered further the possibility of a formal claim. He noted that the United States had "a strong, if not an indisputable, claim to the Island" (a surprising admission), Russia had made a definite claim, and the United States would probably contest a British claim but would not make one itself. In these circumstances, the British government "would be unwilling to adopt an attitude calculated to create difficulties with the Soviet Government, unless substantial interests were at stake." The several ministries consulted by the Secretary of State for Foreign Affairs had paid some heed to the island's future value, but they had generally downgraded its importance. On the whole, the British government "would be disposed not to lay claim to the Island," but before taking a final decision, they asked the Canadian government for its comment.[135]

By this time, the Canadian government was thoroughly fed up with Wrangel Island, the consistent opposition of senior civil servants having gradually influenced and prevailed over the more opportunistic views of some of the political leaders. Accordingly, Canadian agreement with the British stand was a foregone conclusion.[136] In response to Thomas's letter, it issued an order in council on 17 July, declaring that "the view taken by the Imperial Authorities as to the undesirability of laying claim to

Wrangel Island is shared in by the Government of Canada."[137]

The Russians did bring up the question of Wrangel Island at the conference in London. On 6 August, M. Rakovski, the spokesman for the Soviet delegation, asked if he "might receive a reply regarding Wrangel Island," and Arthur Ponsonby replied on behalf of the British delegation that "His Britannic Majesty's Government lay no claim to the Island of Wrangel." Rakovski responded that he was "glad that one of the points, although a small point, which caused misunderstanding between the Soviet Union and Great Britain has been removed, and I would suggest that this should be recorded in the minutes of the Conference."[138]

The issue was thus authoritatively settled as far as British, Canadian, and Soviet governments were concerned. The Foreign Office sent the news to Stefansson on 8 August in a brief letter mailed to his New York address:

> With reference to your letter of June 2nd last, I am directed by Mr. Secretary Ramsay MacDonald to inform you that after due consideration and consultation with the Canadian Government, His Majesty's Government do not propose to take any initiative in advancing a claim to Wrangel Island or to contest any claim preferred by the United States or Soviet Government.[139]

When Carl Lomen bought out the Stefansson interests in Wrangel Island in the spring of 1924, some sort of arrangement was evidently made that Lomen would send an expedition that summer to relieve the occupying party which had been left on the island in 1923.[140] Lomen sailed to Nome in June and was able to make an arrangement with Louis Lane, a veteran Arctic sea captain, to the effect that he would carry out the relief expedition with his motor schooner *Herman* later in the season. Stefansson's associate Donat Marc LeBourdais, who accompanied the expedition and became its chronicler, recounts in detail how they cruised back and forth in the ice-filled waters northwest of Bering Strait but found it impossible to reach the island.[141] They landed upon Herald Island, found the remains of one of the lost *Karluk* parties there, and, "subject to the ratification of this act," claimed the island for the United States.[142] They similarly intended to claim Wrangel Island for the United States, but their inability to land frustrated their plans.[143]

They returned to Nome on 11 October to hear the astounding news that on 20 August, before they had even left on their own trip, the armed Soviet ship *Red October* had reached Wrangel Island, removed Wells and his Inuit companions, raised the Red flag, and taken possession of the island for the Soviet government. Wells and the Inuit were taken as prisoners to Vladivostok, where Wells died. The surviving Inuit (two of them had also died), including a baby born on Wrangel Island, were deported and gradually made their way to Manchuria, Seattle, and back to Alaska.[144]

The decisive action of the Russians thus brought "the Adventure of Wrangel Island" to a disastrous and humiliating end. To underline that such "adventures" would not be tolerated in the future, the People's Commissariat for Foreign Affairs of the USSR sent a special memorandum on 4 November 1924 to the governments of other states, repeating the notification of September 1916.[145] On 15 April 1926, the Soviet Union went a step further, when the Presidium of the Central Executive Committee issued a decree which in effect incorporated the sector principle in Soviet law, by declaring that all islands north of the USSR were Russian territory. The decree claimed for the USSR:

> all lands and islands already discovered, as well as those which are to be discovered in the future, which at the time of the publication of the present decree are not recognized by the Union of Socialist Soviet Republics as the territory of any foreign state, and which lie in the Arctic north of the coast of the Union of Socialist Soviet Republics up to the North Pole, within the limits between the meridian longitude 32°-4'-35' east from Greenwich passing along the eastern side of Vaida Bay through the triangular mark on the Cape Kekurski, and the meridian longitude 168°-49'-36' west from Greenwich passing along the middle of the strait separating Ratmanov and Kruzenshtern Islands of the Diomede Archipelago lying in Bering Strait.[146]

The Soviet government maintained its occupation of Wrangel Island and, at an interdepartmental conference in December 1924, decided to colonize it with Chukchis from northeastern Siberia.[147] The colonization was actually carried out in the summer of 1926.[148] The Soviets were angered by the raising of the American flag on Herald Island in 1924, which (according to a Russian statement) the US State Department refused to explain.[149] They were equally indignant over American involvement in the final stages of the Wrangel Island venture. In the Russian view, the dividing line established by the Alaska treaty in 1867 authoritatively forbade such incursions. Statements in Green Hackworth's authoritative work, however, indicate that the Department of State took the attitude that Russia had no rights over Herald Island because no Russian had ever landed there and the United States had "not relinquished its claim" to Wrangel by 1940 (when Hackworth's book was published).[150] Whether correct or not, it would appear that any American claim had been nullified by 1940 in view of the firm Russian attitude and action respecting sovereignty over the two islands.

Thus ended Stefansson's bold, injudicious Wrangel Island "adventure." In retrospect, it is difficult to comprehend how he or anyone else could ever have believed that it would end otherwise. Apart from all other considerations, Soviet Russia – given the climate of the times and her attitude towards the rest of the world – would not remain passive indefinitely in the face of a Canadian, British, American, or any other "capitalistic" attempt to appropriate island territory so close to its Arctic coast. Even if Stefansson was unaware at the beginning of the Russian landing in 1911, the Russian claim in 1916, and the barrier imposed (at least by implication) by the Alaska convention of 1867 on American claims west of the treaty line, it is virtually impossible that he remained ignorant of them for long. This makes Stefansson's evident assumption that Russia would permit seizure of the island appear the more naïve. That Canadian, British, and American governments all did more than merely toy with the same idea is more surprising still. In so doing, all three were responding positively (at least in part and perhaps unconsciously) to Stefansson's determined campaign. This alone speaks volumes about the influence he was able to exert at the time.

So far as the Canadian government was concerned, it seems evident that it fell into a more or less unpremeditated commitment to support Stefansson's project on 12 May 1922 and then experienced considerable embarrassment and difficulty wriggling out of the commitment. It is also clear, however, that there was for a time a measure of enthusiasm for the scheme, particularly among political figures. The higher echelons of the civil service, however, were almost unanimous in their opposition to it, and in the end the "Nays" won out over the more acquisitive "Yeas." The idea of sending Stefansson to London at Canadian government expense to present his own case to the British government provided a beautiful escape hatch for the Canadian authorities, enabling them to renounce responsibility themselves and, at the same time, to espouse the view that this really was a matter of Imperial and Empire concern. Whether they were mainly anxious to free themselves of the burden, or whether the major consideration was that Great Britain (with her much larger Imperial and Empire responsibilities to look after) might have a genuinely greater interest in the matter than Canada had and should therefore have an opportunity to exercise her own judgment and make her own decision, is unclear.[151] At any rate, in the end Canada had no difficulty in associating herself with the British decision to avoid trying to establish a claim.

One of the important sequels of the Wrangel Island affair was the Soviet government's decision in 1926 to incorporate the sector principle in Soviet law. There is no doubt that there was a cause-and-effect relationship between the two. Another important sequel was the resumption of emphasis upon the sector concept, although in less formal fashion, by the Canadian government following the virtual denial of it during the government's temporary endorsement of Stefansson's plans. By June 1925, Minister of the Interior Stewart was proclaiming officially a Canadian sector extending "right up to the North Pole."[152] Stefansson willingly avowed his responsibility for these fluctuations in Canadian policy. Referring specifically to the cancelled expedition of 1921 rather than to the Wrangel Island venture, he wrote:

> During the time when I had the ear of the Government, between 1919 and 1922 some maps which were printed omitted these lines, on the view that the doctrine would not be in the favor of Canada. For back of our expedition plan was the hope we might discover land outside our sector which would be ours by ordinary international law but would not be ours if the sector principle applied. When it was decided that the expedition would not go after all, the practice of indicating a Canadian Arctic sector on Canadian maps was restored to favor.[153]

Stefansson attacked the validity of the sector principle and endorsed the more traditional discovery and occupation as means of gaining sovereignty over polar territories. Quite apart from whatever his views may have been about the legal principles involved, it is apparent that application of the sector principle would be harmful to his own interests, since under the sector principle sovereignty within the sector is automatic and acquisition beyond the sector is presumably excluded. On the other hand, relying upon discovery and occupation would place high priority upon the very kinds of activities he wanted to carry on and would not necessarily confine them to any particular area. In the end, the Canadian government rejected Stefansson's contentions because adventures like that in Wrangel Island would expose Canada's Arctic islands to similar incursions by other states, and, given the state of insecurity and uncertainty respecting the Canadian archipelago that existed at the time, there is little doubt that the government's final decision to stay inside its own Arctic bailiwick was a wise one. Looked at from this point of view, Stefansson's Wrangel Island "adventure" was remarkably ill-considered and dangerous to Canada's real interests, in spite of his own contrary convictions, and the government's temporary support of it was nothing but an unpremeditated and equally ill-considered aberration.

12

The Question of Sovereignty over the Sverdrup Islands, 1925–30

The Sverdrup Islands were a principal source of worry for Canada in connection with the security of her northern frontier, from the time of their discovery by the Norwegian Otto Sverdrup during his expedition of 1898–1902 until the problem was finally disposed of in 1930. Sverdrup's expedition was privately sponsored by the consul Axel Heiberg and Amund and Ellef Ringnes of the Ringnes brothers brewing firm, each of whom assumed responsibility for one-third of the expenses. The Norwegian government loaned them the little steamer *Fram*, however, and the Storting provided 20,000 Kroner for necessary alteration and repair of the vessel. From bases on the east coast of Ellesmere Island in 1898–99 and the south coast of the same island in 1899–1900, 1900–1901, and 1901–1902, Sverdrup and his small crew carried out remarkable journeys of exploration. They traced almost all of the hitherto unknown western coast of Ellesmere, discovered and explored Alex Heiberg and the two Ringnes Islands, as well as the hitherto untravelled northern coasts of Cornwall, Graham, and Devon Islands, and sighted King Christian Island. Comments in Sverdrup's narrative indicate that he considered he was operating in a region not only unknown but also unclaimed,[1] and the narrative ends with the flat assertion that "An approximate area of one hundred thousand square miles had been explored, and, in the name of the Norwegian King, taken possession of."[2] It was this unofficial claim which aroused Canadian anxiety and led to the complications that followed.

Sverdrup maintained the view that he had established certain Norwegian rights in this part of the North American Arctic, and that later Canadian efforts to establish sovereignty over the islands he had discovered, without reference to Norway, were unjustified. For example, in the autumn on 1902, after Sverdrup had returned to Norway, he reportedly notified King Oscar that he had claimed these territories for the Norwegian Crown.[3] Norway was still united with (and dominated by) Sweden, however, and there seems to have been little inclination in Stockholm to take the matter seriously.

Sverdrup probably derived encouragement from British explorers' generous and accommodating attitude towards his achievements. In April 1903, he went to London to receive the gold medal of the Royal Geographical Society, and to present a paper of his expedition, which was actually read by the society's president Sir Clements R. Markham. The remarks of some members were such that Sverdrup could be excused for concluding, as he must have done, that they were willing to concede to him the lands he had discovered. Admiral Sir Leopold McClintock, who had become renowned as a matter of the technique of sledging while serving as a junior officer during the Franklin search, said:

> We looked upon that part of the arctic regions as so peculiarly our own that we spoke of it as if the Queen's writ was free to run through it even to the North Pole. But we can no longer make that boast; Captain Sverdrup has been there, and he has discovered other lands farther north, so that we cannot look for any immediate increase to the British Empire in that direction.[4]

In his closing remarks, Markham said:

> There are those who believe, as I am inclined to do, that the great cairns discovered on Washington Irving Island are not wholly unconnected with the discoveries of the Norsemen. If that is the case, we must feel that Captain Sverdrup and his companions when near that island in Hayes sound, were on their own land. I do not venture to say that the round towers mentioned up Jones sound had anything to do with the Normans; but I do feel that we may rejoice in finding that the Norwegian explorers have filled up this gap which we have long wished to have filled up, more than if it had been filled by explorers from any other country. I rejoice to see those names which we used to study in the old maps now appearing as a sort of wedge between our eastern and western discoveries.[5]

Historian T. C. Fairley noted that when Norway separated from Sweden and became completely independent in 1905, Sverdrup made fresh inquiries in Oslo (Christiania) about his islands, but again received an indefinite answer. Fairley suggests that Sverdrup and other Norwegians felt, nonetheless, that since the country was now independent the claim on behalf of Norway would be taken care of.[6] Little if anything was done, however, and the years slipped by.

In Canada, officials noted Sverdrup's claim, of course, and it aroused some comment. But it does not seem to have caused alarm on a scale comparable with that aroused by concurrent American activities in the Arctic. The region where the islands were located had presumably been included in the British transfer of 31 July 1880, and if this was insufficient, it must surely have been included in the Canadian orders in council of 2 October 1895 and 18 December 1897. At the same time, it could not be denied that the islands had been unknown until Sverdrup discovered them, and that no Canadian or Britisher had ever set foot on them.

Captain J.-E. Bernier manifested concern over Sverdrup's discoveries at an early stage, but he was also eager to use them as a means of promoting his own hoped-for Arctic voyage. In a February 1903 letter to Sir Wilfrid Laurier, he wrote:

> Je vous envoie une carte géographique faisant voir les bornes du Canada septentrional, telles que je les comprends, et désignant plusieurs iles très – riches en charbon sur un étendu de douze cents milles, qui ont été découvertes de 1898 à 1902 par M. le capitaine Otto Sverdrup et

Figure 12-1. Portrait of Otto Sverdrup on the *Fram*, 1895. *Fridjof Nansen / National Library of Norway /* bldsa_q3c055.

> plusieurs autres explorateurs, et dont je voudrais prendre possession au nom du Canada, auquel elles doivent appartenir.[7]

The Toronto Branch of the Navy League made representations about Sverdrup's claim to the Canadian government, which were forwarded to the Colonial Office in London and came under observation when both the Colonial Office and the Foreign Office were examining W. F. King's *Report* on Canada's Arctic islands. In a confidential letter to the Foreign Office, written on 30 July 1904, H. Bertram Cox of the Colonial Office remarked, *inter alia*:

> I am to take this opportunity of acknowledging the receipt of your letter of the 1st of July, enclosing copy of a letter from the Toronto Branch of the Navy League to the Canadian Government, on the subject of the reported action of Captain Sverdrup in claiming to take possession of Ellesmere Land in the name of the King of Sweden and Norway.
>
> In Mr. King's memorandum there are several references to the territory in question; and it will be noted that Commander Nares is stated to have hoisted the British colours on Ellesmere Land in 1876, in four different places.[8]

If one may judge from this communiqué, the British harboured no great cause for alarm.

The patrol voyages of Low and Bernier began just after Sverdrup had completed his expedition. Again, the evidence suggests that in instituting them Canadian authorities were more worried about Americans than about Norwegians. Nevertheless, both Low and

Bernier, in their acts of taking possession, were careful to include the territories discovered by Sverdrup. When Low took possession on the east coast of Ellesmere Island on 11 August 1904, his proclamation specified that he had taken possession not only of the island itself but also "all the smaller islands adjoining it."[9] Similarly Bernier, when taking possession at King Edward VII Point on the southern extremity of Ellesmere Island on 12 August 1907, named specifically the various parts of Ellesmere Island as they were then designated, the other large islands nearby including those discovered by Sverdrup, and "all adjacent islands" as being annexed to Canada.[10] Bernier's sweeping sector claim at Winter Harbour, Melville Island, on 1 July 1909, named "all islands and territory within the degrees 141 and 60 west longitude" as being Canadian territory,[11] thus including the Sverdrup Islands along with all other land.[12]

Fairley remarked that Sverdrup heard of Bernier's August 1907 appropriation later that year and immediately wrote to the Norwegian Foreign Office asking what it was going to do. Apparently he suggested that Norwegian police should be stationed on the islands. He never received a formal reply, but gathered that Norway was not inclined to take any action until the Canadian government openly endorsed Bernier's activities or challenged Sverdrup's claim.[13]

American expeditions led by Peary, Cook, and MacMillan explored parts of Sverdrup's new land in the early years of the twentieth century (see chapter 6), but no British or Canadian expedition appeared until Vilhjalmur Stefansson's Canadian Arctic Expedition of 1913–18 reached the same area. Stefansson explored parts of Ellef Ringnes, Amund Ringnes, and King Christian Islands, but he did not land upon the largest island of the group, Axel Heiberg. This meant that until after the First World War no British subject had set foot upon this island and the entire group was still unoccupied, facts which Stefansson was not slow to impress upon the Canadian government as part of his campaign for greater activity in the north.[14] As chapter 10 revealed, Canadian officials were less concerned about Norway than about Denmark and the United States, particularly because the Norwegian government was evidently disinclined to take any definite stand respecting Sverdrup's discoveries. In the absence of official Norwegian action, any possible Norwegian claim would presumably deteriorate with the passage of time.[15] Nevertheless, Canadian authorities took the matter seriously enough that one of the main features of the Stefansson expedition planned in 1921 (but which never materialized) was the establishment of a principal base upon Axel Heiberg Island.[16] Even though this plan fell through it was recognized that ultimately some action of this kind would be necessary.[17]

Evidently Sverdrup continued to badger the Norwegian government during these years. According to Fairley, the explorer visited the Norwegian Foreign Office in Oslo "periodically to make sure his islands were not completely forgotten."[18] When the Danish government became involved in April 1920 by endorsing Rasmussen's statement that the entire region was a "No Man's Land" and there was no authority in Ellesmere Island except his own, "in Oslo Sverdrup renewed his old complaint, again asking for Norwegian police to be sent."[19] There was no official contact between Norwegian and Canadian governments about the matter until 1925.

The Norwegian government broached the question in 1924, when it sent a semi-official communiqué to the British Foreign Office, the substance of which Colonial Secretary James

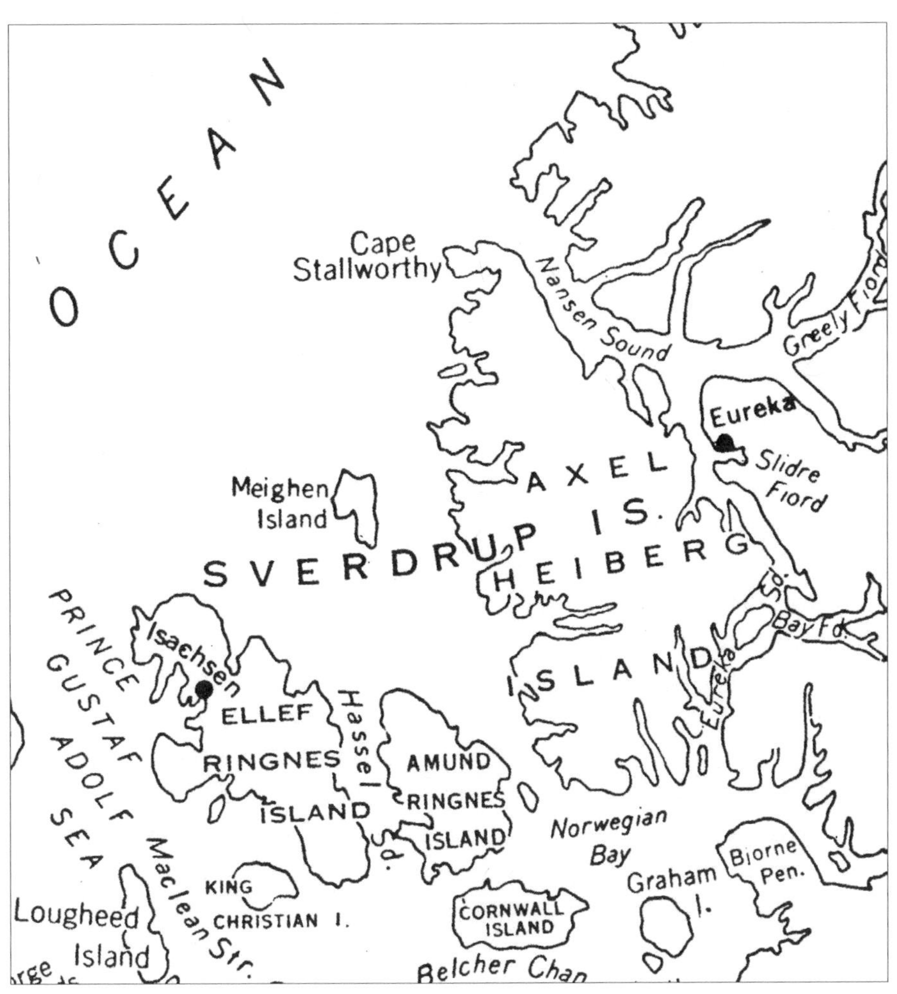

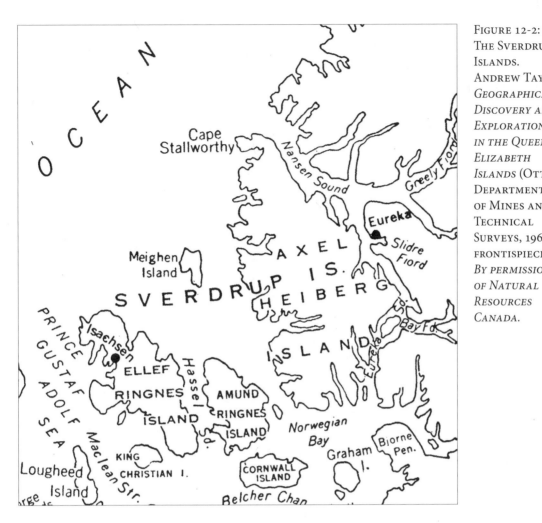

Figure 12-2: The Sverdrup Islands. Andrew Taylor, *Geographical Discovery and Exploration in the Queen Elizabeth Islands* (Ottawa: Department of Mines and Technical Surveys, 1964), frontispiece. *By permission of Natural Resources Canada.*

Henry Thomas initially relayed to Ottawa on 29 October. Thomas's dispatch said that the Norwegian minister:

> states that in May 1900 the Norwegian explorer Captain Sverdrup took possession, in the name of the King of Norway, of the so-called Otto Sverdrup Islands (comprising Ellef Ringnes, Amund Ringnes, Axel Heiberg, Kong Christian and North Cornwall Islands). These islands had been discovered and mapped out by Captain Sverdrup, and a cairn was built at 80° 55′ and the necessary documents place there in a metal box....
>
> The Norwegian minister states that it is not the intention of his Government to claim sovereignty over these islands, but that they probably would like to be informed by Canada on what basis they base their rights... Should Canada maintain their special right he thinks his Government would desire to point out

> that in regard to the discovery and work of Captain Sverdrup, Norwegians should meet with no difficulty in the future if they might desire to pursue some material interest in these islands.[20]

For some reason Thomas cancelled this dispatch by cable to Ottawa on 8 November.[21] The dispatch had noted Norway's intention to have its Consul General in Montreal put Norway's point of view before the Canadian government, and in due course, on 12 March 1925, this was done in a letter written by acting Consul General Sigurd Steckmest. After some remarks about the Norwegian discovery of the islands and their inclusion as Canadian in the report of the Canadian Arctic expedition of 1922, Steckmest said that he had been instructed by his government "to apply to the usual kind assistance of the Canadian Department of External Affairs at Ottawa in order to be informed whether the Canadian government contend that said islands belong to the Dominion of Canada, and, if so, on what basis such claim of sovereignty is founded."[22]

The letter elicited comment in Ottawa as well as interdepartmental memoranda. On one of the latter, a cryptic note in longhand observed that there was more involved here than a mere request for information.[23] No reply was sent. On 16 April, Oswald Finnie, Director of the Northwest Territories and Yukon Branch of the Department of the Interior, wrote a memo to W. W. Cory, remarking that the Norwegians "are mildly questioning our right to Axel Heiberg and the Ringnes Islands." He mentioned also the projected Arctic expeditions by MacMillan, Amundsen, and Krüger, observing that MacMillan planned to use Axel Heiberg as a base for airplane flights, that Amundsen was attempting to fly to the North Pole by way of Spitsbergen and northern Greenland, and that Krüger, who was also going to the Axel Heiberg region, might kill all the muskox in his planned four-year stay. He thought that MacMillan and Krüger should ask the Canadian government for permission before using Canadian territory.[24]

As the memo indicates, this was a time when Canadian authorities were worried about the security of Canada's Arctic territories, and they had Americans and Germans as well as Norwegians to fret about. Largely in response to this situation, an interdepartmental committee was set up to keep an eye on Canada's interests and territorial rights in the Arctic,[25] and Minister of the Interior Stewart made his proclamation claiming for Canada in categorical terms all land within the Canadian sector to the North Pole.[26] The circumstances surrounding these actions (and others which were taken at about the same time) show clearly that Canada was much more concerned over the possibility of trouble with the United States than with Norway.[27]

Stewart's proclamation stirred up a good deal of comment in the American press. The *Washington Sunday Star* published a lengthy article on the subject on 7 June, saying, *inter alia*, that the Canadian claim might derive some support from the precedent of the Sverdrup Islands, since after Sverdrup had discovered and claimed them the Norwegian government had taken no action and had left them for Canada to appropriate. What happened here might inform the right of the United States to claim any Arctic lands that MacMillan might discover. The article concluded that under accepted principles of international law Canada's claim would fall down, but "the Axel Heiberg land case remains to bother all who try to get a clear understanding of the problem."

On 12 June, Henry Chilton, the British chargé d'affaires in Washington, suggested to Ottawa that since Canada feared the MacMillan expedition might end in an American attempt to claim Axel Heiberg and possibly Ellesmere Island, it "would be well to lose no time in intimating to the Government of the United States that Canada regards both these islands as being her territory." Accordingly a note was drafted in Ottawa, sent to Washington,[28] and in substance sent by the chargé d'affaires to American Secretary of State Frank B. Kellogg on 15 June. In his note, Chilton observed that the MacMillan expedition was reported to have the purpose "of exploring and flying over Baffin, Ellesmere, Axel Heiberg, and certain other islands within the northern territories of the Dominion." Drawing attention to the RCMP and HBC posts in the region, he said that although the Canadian government had received no information from the American government regarding the proposed route or intentions of the expedition, they were nevertheless willing to furnish the permits for an exploring and scientific expedition required under Canadian law, and to provide other assistance.[29]

When the Norwegian chargé d'affaires, Daniel Steen, asked at the British Embassy in Washington if the Canadian government had addressed the American government officially on the question of sovereignty in the North, he was told that this was not the case. He replied that if the subject were raised Norway would be interested because of Norwegian discoveries. Chilton communicated this information to the acting Governor General in Ottawa in a note written on 4 August 1925:

> With reference to my dispatch No. 313 of the 24th ultimo, and to previous correspondence regarding the MacMillan expedition to the Arctic regions, I have the honour to inform you that the Norwegian chargé d'affaires called at his Majesty's Embassy in Washington on July 31st and enquired of a Resident Secretary whether any reliance could be placed upon reports which had reached him through the Norwegian Consul in Montreal and the Associated press that the Dominion Government had addressed an official communication to the United States Government setting out their views as regards the sovereignty of territory which might be traversed or discovered by the expedition in question in the far north.[30]

Steen was informed that the governments of Canada and the United States had not discussed the question of sovereignty over these regions. If it was raised, he replied, the Norwegian government would be interested as Norwegian explorers had originally discovered Axel Heiberg and Ellesmere islands.[31]

Fairley suggests that the Canadian government may have feared that the Americans had asked for Norwegian rather than Canadian permission to use Axel Heiberg as a base.[32] Although this fear may have existed, there is no concrete evidence of it. The Canadian government did recognize, however, that American authorities were inclined to question Canadian sovereignty over Axel Heiberg. In a letter on 10 June 1925, to Foreign Secretary Austen Chamberlain, Chilton highlighted that the *New York Times* of 9 June had announced that the State Department were considering two points about the MacMillan expedition: first, whether Axel Heiberg was Canadian territory, so that a Canadian permit would have to be obtained to land there, and, second, whether any discoveries should be claimed as American territory. Chilton sent a copy of the letter to the Governor General of Canada.[33]

Whatever the official Norwegian attitude at the time may have been, there were certainly prominent Norwegians besides Sverdrup who had no reservations about making a forthright claim to the islands. On 15 June 1925, Stefansson's former associate Dr. R. M. Anderson wrote a letter to O. D. Skelton, noting that the *New York Times* had quoted Conservative Carl Joachim Hambro, of the Foreign Affairs Committee of the Norwegian Parliament, saying that Norway claimed Axel Heiberg and the two Ringnes Islands.[34] Skelton replied on 20 June that Hambro had been "reiterating" this claim. He added that Canada had never replied to Norway's inquiry about these islands, but he thought the matter would be taken up "at the next meeting of the Advisory Committee."[35]

For two or three years afterwards the question of Norwegian interest in the Sverdrup Islands apparently aroused little public comment in Ottawa or official discussion with the Norwegian government. On several occasions, however, Norway made inquiries similar to that of 12 March 1925. On 6 February 1926, Ludvig Aubert, the Norwegian Consul General in Montreal, wrote a letter to the Secretary of State for External Affairs, drawing attention to the fact that no reply to this inquiry had been received. Accordingly, he had been instructed "to express to you that the Norwegian government with interest is looking forward to receive the Canadian government's reply to the request for information contained in the above mentioned note."[36] Aubert sent a further note, similar in import to the preceding ones, on 27 September 1926, again observing that no reply had been received. He referred to the Canadian government's regulations for the protection of game "in the Northwest Territories and the Arctic Islands north of Canada," which had been published in the *Canada Gazette* on 31 July 1926, and which he evidently assumed were to apply to the Sverdrup Islands.[37]

The Canadian authorities doubtless felt that their position had been strengthened by the promulgation of this and other regulations applicable to the northern islands and, more particularly, by RCMP Staff Sergeant Alfred Herbert Joy's long patrol from Ellesmere Island to Axel Heiberg in early 1926. The following year, he made an even longer patrol that took him to all the major islands of this group. The Canadian government could now claim that a Canadian had landed upon all these islands for official purposes. On 9 October 1926, Skelton acknowledged Aubert's note of 27 September but only to say that he had left with the Prime Minister for the Imperial Conference and they would consider the matter when they returned from England.[38]

On 27 April 1927, Aubert wrote again, referring to this Canadian note, and asking if the Canadian authorities were now prepared to furnish any information.[39] His note went unanswered, so he wrote again on 26 March 1928, summarizing the background of events and drawing attention to the various unanswered Norwegian letters, as well as a conversation he had had with Skelton on 25 January 1928. Noting that Captain Sverdrup had taken possession of the islands in question for the Norwegian Crown, he concluded, "I am now instructed by my Government to inform you that they reserve to Norway all rights coming to my country under International Law in connection with the said areas."[40] A copy of this note was sent by the Norwegian minister to the British Government, and on 29 June 1928, Dominion Secretary L. S. Amery wrote to Ottawa asking for copies of the relevant correspondence, which, he said, would be of special interest because of

Norwegian claims in the Antarctic.[41] The Canadian government did not answer Aubert until 18 August, when Skelton's secretary sent an interim acknowledgment of Norwegian communications, again noting only that Skelton himself had just gone to Europe and had left word that the matter would receive immediate attention on his return.[42]

In the meantime Aubert had learned certain details about the appointment and responsibilities of James Colebrooke Patterson as a commissioner "to investigate titles of Great Britain (Canada) to lands in the Arctic Seas." The Norwegian Consul General mentioned in particular a reference in the Canadian House of Commons Debates to the provision of Patterson's salary,[43] and asked for copies of two orders in council setting forth certain stipulations about his activities.[44] After discussion in Ottawa, Canadian officials agreed that although the orders in council had not hitherto been made public there was no reason why they should not be and sent copies to him.[45] There was no specific reference either in the cited passage in Hansard or in the orders in council to the Sverdrup Islands.

Sverdrup himself remained as firm as ever in his view that he had established certain rights for Norway and that these rights should be respected. He wrote to the Norwegian Foreign Ministry on 8 February and 10 March 1928:

> I now request the Norwegian Government to declare to the Canadian Government the priority of the Norwegian claim, in a clear and unambiguous way.... I suggest urgently to the Ministry that they do not take a middle course but assert the Norwegian claim to the limit. Failing this, I reserve the right personally to ask the Canadian Government to refund all the expenses of my expedition of 1898–1902.[46]

The ministry answered Sverdrup on 12 March, saying that the Norwegian Consul in Montreal had received no reply to the several inquiries he had made since 12 March 1925, but that he now had instructions "to present a new Note to the Canadian government making reservations with respect to the rights Norway has in those areas, according to intentional law."[47] This resulted, as seen, in Aubert's note on 26 March 1928.

According to Fairley's account, the Norwegian government early in April 1929 gave Sverdrup permission to relinquish Norwegian rights in the Sverdrup Islands, provided he claimed a refund for others who had contributed to the cost of the expedition as well as for himself.[48] Negotiations to this end were formally initiated by a letter written on 3 April to William C. Noxon, Agent General for Ontario in the British Isles, to Prime Minister Mackenzie King. The letter introduced Eivind Bordewick, the Canadian Pacific Railroad representative at Oslo, who had "some matters to settle in which the Government of Canada is concerned."[49] Bordewick became the principal go-between in the bargaining that followed. On 20 April, the veteran explorer Fridtjof Nansen sent King his "warmest recommendation" for his "good friend Capt. Otto Sverdrup,"[50] and on 22 April Sverdrup himself wrote to King, setting down his own case in a lengthy communiqué. Mentioning his awareness that the Canadian government desired to obtain full and undisputed possession of all territories in the region under consideration, he continued:

> I venture, however, to point out that the Norwegian Government

> have laid claim to the sovereign rights of the territories above-mentioned, but I would state that as a result of negotiations with the Norwegian Government these rights will be definitely relinquished should I at any time so desire. As no claim in this connection can be made other than by myself it follows that Canada will enter into full and undisputed possession the moment my claim is dropped, in which case, I am precluded from seeking compensation from the Norwegian Government for my services rendered in connection with the expedition.
>
> As soon as the amount of compensation has been agreed upon I bind myself to obtain by telegraph a satisfactory declaration from the Norwegian Government that the Kingdom of Norway waives all claim to the territories aforesaid.

Noting that he had with the approval of the Norwegian Government entrusted his case to the care of Bordewick, Sverdrup added that Bordewick had his power of attorney to negotiate on his behalf and decide upon the amount of compensation he should receive "to settle the matter finally." An invoice, evidently attached to the letter but dated 15 April 1929, put the total cost of the expedition at $200,900.[51]

The involved pattern of bargaining and fencing which was set off by these communiqués went on during the remainder of 1929 and throughout almost all of 1930. The records, or at least a large portion of them, have survived in External Affairs files, but they are so detailed that they can only be summarized here.

On 7 May 1929, Bordewick wrote a memo about Sverdrup's letter, which in his view contained statements "which might have been worded in another way." He underlined in particular his understanding that although Norway had approached Canada about the matter, "the Norwegian government has not up to the present time laid any official claim to the sovereign rights to the islands discovered by Commander Sverdrup." Nevertheless, he emphasized that he did not want Sverdrup's language in his letter to "prejudice his claim."[52]

An official Norwegian government cable sent from Oslo on 22 May to Bordewick (then in Ottawa) stated cryptically: "Present government willing cede sovereignty but new unwilling therefore definite arrangement payment soonest necessary."[53] This introduced an intangible factor into the situation which hovered over negotiations, but whether this was in reality a source of gratification or of worry to the Norwegian negotiators would appear to be uncertain. A note to Prime Minister King on 3 June, unsigned but evidently written by Skelton, explained that the present Liberal government in Norway was willing to relinquish any title it might have to the islands if Canada would reimburse Sverdrup for the expense of his expedition, but the government was in a minority. The Labour Party, however, which was the strongest and might soon replace it, was averse to cession; hence the alleged need for speed, to prevent renunciation of the proposal.[54] Bordewick made his own explanations in a note to Skelton on 4 June,[55] and brought up the matter repeatedly thereafter, either because of genuine fear of the anticipated change or as a means of putting pressure upon the Canadian government.

Skelton answered Bordewick's note the following day, observing that the proposal to pay compensation to Sverdrup had "not yet received the consideration of the government." Referring to certain proposals Bordewick had

Figure 12-3: Dr. Oscar D. Skelton. *Library and Archives Canada / C-000079.*

made, one being that the final settlement should take place in London not later than 1 October 1929, he said that Bordewick was mistaken in suggesting that the proposal had emanated from a meeting of the Northern Advisory Committee a few days earlier, which both had attended.[56] Prime Minister King also wrote to Bordewick a day later, his letter being a tactful and politely phrased appreciation of Sverdrup's achievements in his expedition, compensation for which the Canadian government would carefully consider.[57] As Skelton observed in another note to Bordewick, however, King's letter dealt essentially with the personal aspect of the matter, and "made no reference to any of the political considerations involved."[58] Bordewick wrote to Skelton from Oslo on 13 September, saying that he was still without information about what was being done.[59] Many other such communiqués followed, by letter or cable, complaining about the lack of information and requesting – and in some case virtually demanding – payment of Sverdrup's compensation.

At Skelton's request, Lester B. Pearson, the first secretary in the Department of External Affairs, had prepared a lengthy report titled "The Question of Ownership of the Sverdrup Islands." During three interviews with Bordewick in June, Pearson noted, Skelton had informed the Norwegian that the Canadian government considered that this territory was already in Canada's possession and therefore any discussion of the matter would be without prejudice to this understanding. He observed also that in the dispute with Britain over Bouvet Island (an uninhabited subantarctic volcanic island in the south Atlantic), Norway had offered as a *quid pro quo* to abandon her claim to the Sverdrup Islands. The British representatives had "sheered off from this suggestion," however, thus foregoing an excellent opportunity to settle the whole matter. Regarding a Norwegian claim to the islands, Norway had apparently never made a public assertion of ownership, and any rights she might have acquired through Sverdrup's discoveries had disappeared. Therefore, Pearson concluded, "there would seem to be no reason why we should pay Captain Sverdrup $200,000 on condition that Norway waive all rights to the islands in question, when those rights have already lapsed." On the other hand it might be wise to pay the money and avoid a long controversy. Interestingly, he suggested as an alternative that "a grant might be made to Captain Sverdrup of grace, not of right, in return for which, though not as a *quid pro quo.* Norway might acknowledge the disputed islands as Canadian territories."[60] This solution was eventually adopted.

On 28 October, while on a visit to England, Skelton attended a meeting of the British Interdepartmental Committee on the Antarctic, where Jan Mayen and the Sverdrup Islands were among the subjects for discussion. The committee took the view that Great Britain should recognize the Norwegian claim to Jan Mayen Island in the Arctic and perhaps to Peter I Island in the Antarctic, and that in return Norway might abandon all claim to the Sverdrup Islands.[61] Skelton had this information sent to Ottawa by cable on 30 October, adding that he still adhered to the opinion of the Northern Advisory Committee that "it would be advisable in view of important Canadian interests concerned to offer some compensation," and asking what amount might be considered.[62] Skelton finally received a reply cable on 30 November, informing him that the Canadian government was prepared to consider paying $25,000 to Sverdrup as compensation, and that Skelton could take up negotiations with Bordewick on this basis.[63]

In a widely publicized speech at Bergen on 10 November about Norwegian policy in the polar regions, Norwegian Prime Minister Johan Ludwig Mowinekel refused to recognize British and Canadian sector claims in the Antarctic and Arctic, saying that these territories could be claimed only through occupation and that the claimant nations had not as yet fulfilled this requirement. Norway had played an important part in the polar regions, he said, and had special interests in both. The speech caused a flurry of excited comment in the Canadian press, and Canadian government officials hastened to reassert Canada's sector claim, which, they said, was official and had now been generally recognized – except, apparently, by Norway.[64]

After various efforts to arrange a meeting Skelton and Minister of Justice Ernest Lapointe met with Bordewick and Sverdrup in Paris on 5 and 6 December. The proposal Skelton put before the Norwegians was essentially that suggested by the Northern Advisory Board: an annuity for Sverdrup of $2,400 for life or a lump sum of $25,000. This disappointing offer was not well received, and on 13 December Bordewick wrote letters to both Prime Minister King and Skelton, objecting to the terms and putting forward his case for more generous treatment. He suggested $100,000 as an appropriate sum for Sverdrup, on the basis of an annuity of $2,400 for approximately forty years (from 1902 till the estimated end of Sverdrup's life). He also asked for $200,900 to refund the cost of the expedition.[65]

After Lapointe and Skelton returned to Canada, and after receipt of the urgent message from the British High Commissioner's office in Ottawa saying that a settlement with the Norwegian government of Arctic and Antarctic was essential,[66] the Canadian government reconsidered the question and adjusted their offer. They would now pay Sverdrup $25,000 cash plus a life annuity of $2,400 for his past service and for the delivery of the original maps, record, diaries, and other material in his possession, along with any other information he might be able to give them if and when required. Simultaneously Norway would recognize Canadian claims, and, the Canadian government assumed, Britain would acknowledge Norwegian sovereignty over Jan Mayen Island and possibly also Peter I Island.[67]

Soon after word of this offer had been received in Oslo, Bordewick sent a confidential cable to Premier Howard Ferguson of Ontario, with whom he was well acquainted personally, saying that he was "absolutely unable" to make Sverdrup accept the offer and asking

Ferguson's advice.[68] When Ferguson sent a copy of the cable to the Prime Minister (incidentally paying scant heed to Bordewick's instruction that it was strictly confidential),[69] King stated the government's refusal to make any further changes.[70] The Canadian authorities were strengthened in their stand by receipt of information through British diplomatic channels that the Norwegian Prime Minister was personally satisfied with their proposals, provided they were satisfactory to Sverdrup.[71] Evidently Sverdrup had some second thoughts, because Bordewick sent a cable to Ottawa on 11 February indicating an unwilling acceptance of the Canadian offer, provided the annuity were estimated at a lump sum of $42,000 for a total cash payment of $67,000.[72] The Canadian government considered and decided to accept this modification, on condition that Sverdrup would furnish the materials already requested, and that the undertaking set forth in his letter of 22 April 1929 (the relinquishment of Norwegian rights) would be carried out. This decision was communicated by cable to Bordewick on 26 February.[73] A note from Skelton to the British High Commissioner's office on 25 February, however, reiterated that any official Norwegian statement should not take the form of a relinquishment of Norwegian sovereignty, which Canada had never accepted, but rather recognition of the Canadian title.[74]

The basic framework of the arrangement had now been established, yet a succession of complications, misunderstandings, and disagreements prevented it from being finalized for eight months. In accepting the Canadian offer, Sverdrup initially attempted to attach the condition that arrangements to pay the $67,000 should be made within one month.[75] Later, he resorted again to the argument that speed was essential because a change in the Norwegian government might mean a change in policy.[76] He was informed that the payment would be provided for in a supplementary estimate, and that the House of Commons would have to approve all estimates, which in this instance could only be done towards the end of the current session.[77] When Bordewick continued to emphasize the need for speed,[78] Canadian officials inquired through the British High Commissioner whether an immediate political change was likely in Norway.[79] The British did not anticipate changes before the coming general election, deducing that the present government would probably remain in power until the end of 1930.[80] The Norwegian Prime Minister attempted to attach two conditions to Norway's recognition: first, that Norwegian subjects should retain fishing and landing rights in the islands and surrounding waters and, second, that no recognition of any sector should be implied.[81] The Canadian government agreed to the second without question, but refused the first on grounds that the fishing would probably be of no value and the proposition involved an objectionable servitude.[82]

A Canadian order in council was promulgated on 14 June 1930, authorizing payment of $67,000 to Sverdrup under the conditions agreed upon, and the Canadian government put forward suggestions about an exchange of notes to bring matters to a conclusion.[83] After Bordewick cabled on 2 July that "Formal release Sovereign rights notified British minister June tenth,"[84] it remained vague whether the Norwegian recognition had been granted in acceptable form; or that it had been granted at all.[85]

On 8 August, the Department of the Interior sent Skelton a sterling exchange draft in favour of Sverdrup for the equivalent of $67,000.[86] Delays ensued owing to the illness of the Norwegian Prime Minister,[87] and then by a further attempt by the Norwegian government to attach conditions, in this instance that the Canadian government should "declare themselves willing not to interpose any obstacles to Norwegian fishing, hunting or industrial and trading activities in the area which the recognition comprises."[88] The Canadian government refused,[89] and a good deal of haggling followed, including suggestions that Norway should be granted most-favoured-nation status in respect of these activities[90] and that Norwegians should be placed in the same position as British subjects except Aboriginal people.[91] In the meantime, Sverdrup was ill in Copenhagen[92] and Bordewick's frequent communiqués took on an increasingly urgent tone. While trying to bring matters to a satisfactory and formal conclusion, Canadian authorities held to their stand that the money should not be paid until the full deal was done – and said little more than this when replying to Bordewick's rather testy cables.[93] In the meantime the sterling draft was sent to the British minister in Oslo on 23 September, with instructions that it was not to be paid until negotiations had been concluded.[94]

A further snag was encountered when Skelton informed Bordewick by cable on 14 October that the draft had been forwarded, and that the Canadians understood that Sverdrup would now be prepared to deliver the materials mentioned in earlier telegrams.[95] Bordewick's answering cable a day later said rather abruptly that, apart from some specified documents that had already been disposed of, "Commander Sverdrup had no additional data maps diaries documents of service whatever."[96] The Canadian reply on 16 October asserted with equal bluntness:

> Have noted with surprise your statement Commander Sverdrup has no additional data (stop) You will recall in our telegram of January twenty-fourth and February twenty-sixth we stated our understanding that Commander Sverdrup would be prepared to furnish any additional data not published including maps, notes, diaries and other documents of service and that in your reply of February stated (stop) We cannot understand why position was not made clear at that time (stop).

The cable concluded with the firm statement that payment could not be made until negotiations had been completed.[97] Bordewick's cable the next day regretted the "misunderstanding," but observed that the agreement "stated precisely not published material considered unnecessary repeat what verbally stated Ottawa that all material of expedition had been published." Sverdrup would deliver six copies of sketches of charts and thirteen handwritten private diaries in Norwegian which he still had in his possession.[98] Canadian officials decided to accept these as the most obtainable in the circumstances, along with an additional copy of a report which had already been published by the Nansen fund.[99]

All remaining obstacles to a settlement having now been removed, matters were brought to a conclusion on 5 November. The essential documents comprise two Norwegian notes respecting the recognition which had already been presented to the British government in London on 8 August, an exchange of notes in Oslo on 5 November respecting the privileges which Norway had asked for and Canada had refused, and Sverdrup's acknowledgment of receipt of the $67,000, also dated 5 November. These documents are reproduced below.

> 1. From the Norwegian Chargé d'affaires, London, to the Secretary of

State for Foreign Affairs, London. Royal Norwegian Legation, No. 95/1930 London, August 8th, 1930.

Sir, – Acting on instructions from my Government I have the honour to request you to be good enough to inform His Majesty's Government in Canada that the Norwegian Government, who do not as far as they are concerned claim sovereignty over the Sverdrup Islands, formally recognise the sovereignty of His Britannic Majesty over these islands.

At the same time my Government is anxious to emphasize that their recognisance of the sovereignty of His Britannic Majesty over these islands is in no way based on any sanction whatever of what is named "the sector principle."

I have the honour to be, etc., Daniel Steen Chargé d'affaires a.i.

The Right Honourable Arthur Henderson, P. C., M. P., etc., etc., etc.

2. From the Norwegian Chargé d'Affaire, London, to the Secretary of State for Foreign Affairs, London. Royal Norwegian Legation, No. 96/1930. London, August 8th, 1930.

Sir. – With reference to my note of to-day in regard to my Government's recognition of the sovereignty of His Britannic Majesty over the Sverdrup Islands, I have the honour, under the instructions from my Government, to inform you that the said note has been despatched on the assumption on the part of the Norwegian Government that His Britannic Majesty's Government in Canada will declare themselves willing not to interpose any obstacles to Norwegian fishing, hunting or industrial and trading activities in the area which the recognition comprises. I have the honour to be, etc., Daniel Steen, Chargé d'Affaires a.i.

The Right Honourable Arthur Henderson P. C., M. P., etc., etc., etc.

3. From the British Chargé d'Affaires, Oslo, to the Norwegian Minister for Foreign Affairs, Oslo. No 122 British Legation, Oslo, 5th November, 1930.

Monsieur le Ministre d'Etat, – At the instance of His Majesty's Government in Canada and under the instructions of His Majesty's Principal Secretary of State for Foreign Affairs, I have the honour to invite reference to the two notes addressed to His Majesty's Secretary of State for Foreign Affairs by the Norwegian Chargé d'Affaires in London on August 8th last, in regard to the recognition by the Norwegian Government by the sovereignty of His Britannic Majesty over the Otto Sverdrup Islands, and to inform you that His Majesty's Government in Canada has noted the desire on the part of the Norwegian Government that no obstacle should be interposed to Norwegian fishing, hunting, or industrial and trading activities in the area which the recognition comprises, and wishes to assure the Norwegian Government that it would have pleasure in according any possible facilities. It wishes, however, to draw attention to the fact that it is the established policy of the Government of Canada, as set forth in an Order in Council of July 19, 1926, and subsequent Orders, to protect the Arctic areas as hunting and trapping preserves for the sole use of the aboriginal population of the Northwest Territories, in order to avert the danger of want and starvation through the exploitation of the wild life by white hunters and traders. Except with the permission of the Commissioner of the Northwest Territories, no person other than native Indians or Eskimos is allowed to hunt, trap, trade, or traffic for any purpose whatsoever in a large area of the mainland and in the whole Arctic Island area, with the exception of the southern portion of Baffin Island. It is further provided that no person may hunt or kill or traffic in the skins of the musk-ox, buffalo, wapiti, or elk. These prohibitions apply to all persons, including Canadian nationals. Should, however, the regulations be altered at any time in the future, His Majesty's Government in Canada would treat with the most friendly consideration any application by Norwegians to share in any fishing, hunting, industrial, or trading activities in the area which the recognition comprises.

I avail myself of this opportunity to assure you, Monsieur le Ministre d'Etat, of my highest consideration.

Kenneth Johnstone.

Son Excellence Monsieur J. L. Mowinckel. Etc., etc., etc.

4. From the Norwegian Minister for Foreign Affairs, Oslo, to the British Chargé d'Affaires, Oslo, 5th November, 1930. (Translation)

Monsieur le Chargé d'Affaires, – I have the honour to acknowledge the receipt of your note of the 5th instant in reply to the two notes from the Norwegian Chargé d'Affaires in London to the British Foreign Minister of the 8th August last regarding Norway's recognition of His Britannic Majesty's sovereignty over the Otto Sverdrup Islands.

The Norwegian Government has noted that the Canadian Government would willingly have granted every possible facility to Norwegian fishing, hunting or industrial and trading activities in these regions, but that it is a leading principle in the policy of the Canadian Government to preserve the Arctic regions as hunting and trapping preserves for the sole use of the aboriginal population of the Northwest Territories, in order to prevent their being in want as a consequence of the exploitation of the wild life by white hunters and trappers, and that they have drawn up more definite regulations to this end by means of several Orders in Council.

The Norwegian Government has further noted that should these regulations be altered in the future, the Canadian Government will treat in the most friendly manner any applications from Norwegians for facilities to carry on fishing, hunting, industrial or trading activities in the areas which the Norwegian Government's recognition comprises.

I beg to inform you that in these circumstances the Norwegians' Government find themselves able to concur in this reply to the above-mentioned notes of 8th August last.

I avail myself, etc, (for the Minister for Foreign Affairs) Aug. Esmarch.

Kenneth Johnstone Esq., The British Government's Chargé d'Affaires, etc., etc.[100]

5. Acknowledgement of Receipt of Draft for 13,767.2.£ by Otto Sverdrup.

I hereby acknowledge of receipt of draft for – 13,767.2.£ from the Government of Canada in recognition of my contributions of the knowledge of the Arctic Archipelago in the Sverdrup Islands area and in full payment for maps, notes and other material bearing on the said region, which I have delivered for transmission to the Government of Canada. I am prepared to offer my services to the Government of Canada for consultation in regard to this region any time that may be desired.

(Signed) *Alex Nansen* on behalf of Commander Otto Sverdrup.

Date November 5, 1930.[101]

By prearrangement, news of the completion of the settlement was communicated to the press on 11 November, and published as close to simultaneously as possible in Ottawa and Oslo the following day.[102] A wave of announcements, newspaper articles, and comments followed. The official Canadian communications to the press maintained the same separation between the Norwegian recognition and the award to Sverdrup that Canada had insisted upon throughout the negotiations, and took the form of two releases, one titled " Canadian Sovereignty in the Arctic" and the other "Norwegian Explorer Rewarded by Canada."[103] Unfortunately, Sverdrup did not live long enough to get any real satisfaction or enjoyment from the money he had received, as he died of cancer (which according to Bordewick had been discovered only in July of that year and had developed very rapidly) on 26 November.[104] In due course, after they had been photostatted in Ottawa, Sverdrup's original diaries were returned to his widow, in accordance with a request she made through Bordewick.[105]

The negotiations took a long time to complete, but in the circumstances an earlier settlement would probably have done little for Sverdrup except to give him peace of mind. It is not easy to affix responsibility for the excessive delay, but it would certainly appear that both sides could have done more to expedite matters had they been so inclined. The Canadian authorities were determined to have their pound of flesh, and to insist upon the most formal processes of obtaining it before releasing the money to Sverdrup. They were also not disturbed about the passage of time, especially in the early stages of the proceedings. On the other hand, the Norwegian authorities, although not particularly worried over the matter, were inclined if possible to avoid a clear-cut recognition with no strings attached. As far as Bordewick himself was concerned, he obviously cared little about Canadian wishes or the form of protocol, and would have been happy to get the money for Sverdrup without paying particular heed to what was expected of Norway in return. The Canadian authorities were unaware of the seriousness of Sverdrup's illness and that he was actually on his deathbed. It is to be hoped that this was so, at any rate, otherwise some of their communiqués become remarkably crude, and insensitive. For example, the form prescribed for his acceptance of the money had him say, "I am prepared to offer my services to the Government of Canada for consultation in regard to this region at any time that may be desired," and the cable to Bordewick on 12 November advising him about transmission of the draft asked him to convey to Sverdrup "best wishes for health and happiness."[106] It may be assumed, however, that Bordewick and the Norwegian government were reluctant to tell the Canadians the true state of affairs, since in calculating the amount of the fee payable to Sverdrup a considerable additional life span had been taken for granted. This circumstance also accounts in large part for Bordewick's anxiousness to obtain the money as quickly as possible.

The settlement of 1930 effectively ended all questions relating to the official status of the Sverdrup Islands, as far as the Canadian and Norwegian governments were concerned.[107] After the Second World War, however, Bordewick attempted privately to reopen negotiations to secure more money for Sverdrup's son Otto Jr., who, like most of his countrymen, was in financial difficulty after the German occupation. He tried to make the point that Norway had ceded the Sverdrup Islands but the cession had not been completed, and to make the cession complete a further payment would be in order.[108] The Canadian government answered sympathetically, but at the same time made it clear that there was no prospect of a second grant. It was pointed out to Bordewick that in 1930 Norway had denied any claim to the Sverdrup Islands and had formally recognized Canadian sovereignty over them, so that no cession was involved, and that in any case the payment to Sverdrup was not connected with the alleged "cession." In addition the words "in full payment" in the receipt which Sverdrup's authorized representative had signed led the Canadian government to consider the payment of 1930 as final.[109] Evidently Bordewick dropped the matter, and it is important only as apparently the sole instant of an attempt emanating from Norway to question the finality of the settlement of 1930.

13

The Eastern Greenland Case and Its Implications for the Canadian North

The dispute over Eastern Greenland between Denmark and Norway, which was decided by the Permanent Court of International Justice on 5 April 1933,[1] was not directly connected with the Canadian Arctic, but it nevertheless had important implications for Canada's claims to sovereignty over the entire archipelago north of the Canadian mainland. The case was one of the most involved of all those settled by the court, and even though the territories in dispute were not considered to be of great value, it was evident that by analogy the judgment might have far-reaching consequences in other parts of the world. The roots of the dispute lay in the remote past, and to find its real origins, it is necessary to go back to the very beginning of European experience in the western hemisphere. As the case developed, it came to involve practically the entire history of Norwegian and Danish activity in Greenland and also many aspects of their relations with each other.[2]

During the nineteenth and early twentieth centuries, Denmark gradually extended her activity and control in Greenland.[3] In 1894, the first Danish settlement on the east coast was made at Angmagssalik at latitude 65° 36' N, and a Danish station was established in Scoresby Sound, at about 70° 30' N, in 1925.[4] Norwegians also undertook a good deal of important exploratory and scientific work in and near Greenland, with their interests gradually focusing upon Eastern Greenland, much of which was unoccupied and, from Norway's point of view, open to exploitation. Norwegians began the hunting of fur-bearing animals in Eastern Greenland, and they wintered there for the first time in 1893–94, at Kulusuk at approximately 65° 30' N latitude. In or about 1910, the practice of wintering on the scene was temporarily abandoned, but it was resumed in the early 1920s and was accompanied by increasing activity in fishing, whaling, and even the building of permanent posts and meteorological and wireless stations. This activity, and the implications that went with it, brought the disagreement with Denmark over Eastern Greenland to crisis.[5]

In the meantime, Denmark's effort to bring all Greenland under her sovereignty continued, and gradually took on a more comprehensive and official aspect than that indicated by explorers' claims and the establishment of mostly private settlements. While attempting to consolidate her sovereignty over Greenland, Denmark also undertook to obtain recognition of this sovereignty from other states which might be interested.[6] When Denmark endeavoured to obtain this by approaching the delegates who were meeting at the Paris peace conference,[7] the delegates – preoccupied with problems arising directly out of the war – were not favourable.[8] The Danish government therefore

Figure 13-1: Norway's claim to Eastern Greenland. *Jennifer Arthur-Lackenbauer.*

decided to submit the matter to each of the principal Allied powers separately,[9] whose replies, taken collectively, did little to remove the ambiguity.[10] For its part, Britain's definitive response was delayed because its government believed that Britain's recognition should be qualified by a right of pre-emption granted by the Danish government in case Denmark should ever decide to dispose of Greenland (see chapter 10). As discussed, on 6 September 1920, after consultations with Canada, the Foreign Office sent a note to the Danish government, recognizing Danish sovereignty over Greenland but stating that Britain reserved her right to be consulted if Denmark should ever consider the "alienation" of the territory.

Having thus obtained recognition of a sort from the five principal Allied powers, Denmark undertook to obtain recognition from Sweden and Norway. The Swedish response was prompt and favourable. The response from the Norwegian government turned out to be an entirely different matter. When the Danish Minister of the Interior issued a proclamation on 10 May 1921, announcing that henceforth all Greenland was to be under Danish sovereignty,[11] the new Norwegian Foreign Minister stated that his government could not accept an extension of Danish sovereignty over Greenland that would entail a corresponding extension of the monopoly to the detriment of Norwegian interests.[12] Denmark insisted that it would not accept the Norwegian concept that hunting and fishing by Norwegian subjects close to Greenland should be related to the question of Danish sovereignty over the island.[13]

This exchange of notes established the basic position of the two states in the matter and brought the dispute into the open. The passage of time failed to provide a settlement, and the differences of view became sharper in the years ahead. Denmark contended that in spite of the wording of some of her own documents and those of other states, she actually had full sovereignty over all Greenland for some time, and she had only asked Norway for written acknowledgment of an existing fact. Norway contended that Denmark had sovereignty over only those parts of Greenland which she genuinely occupied and administered, that this was all Norway had acknowledged, and that an extension of this occupation and administration was necessary before Denmark's full sovereignty over all Greenland could be recognized.[14] Although a convention agreed to in 1924 brought a *modus vivendi*, and open controversy over Eastern Greenland remained at a lower ebb for about half a dozen years, neither side forgot the dispute and both endeavoured to improve their positions. The Danish government, determined not to yield in its contention that it had sovereignty over Eastern Greenland, enacted laws to regulate hunting and fishing in Greenland waters, set up new administrative arrangements, and reserved all commercial activity to the Danish state.[15] The Norwegian government registered formal protests against laws that it believed applied "to regions where the sovereignty of Denmark has not yet been demonstrated"[16] and did its best to counter Danish moves and advance its own interests.

Like Denmark, Norway also tried to increase its own activity in Eastern Greenland. The Foldvik Expedition was sent to this region in 1926, the Hird Expedition in 1927, the Norwegian East Greenland Expedition in 1928, an expedition of the company Arktisk Naeringsdrift A/S in 1929, and a Norwegian scientific expedition that same year. Most of these expeditions erected houses and other establishments, some of them scientific. By 1930, it was apparent that Norway had done much more to actually occupy the central part of Eastern Greenland than Denmark had.[17]

The dispute was brought into the open again in the summer of 1930. The Norwegian government conferred police powers upon some Norwegian subjects to enable them to inspect Norwegian hunting stations in Eastern Greenland, and Denmark refused to accept the granting of such authority to Norwegians in territories under Danish sovereignty.[18] When the Norwegian Foreign Office replied that it considered its action justified because Eastern Greenland was, in its view, *terrra nullius*,[19] the Danish government instructed its embassy in Oslo to inform the Norwegian government that police authority over all persons in Eastern Greenland was being conferred upon a large Danish expedition which was being sent out.[20] Both parties later indicated their willingness to withdraw or abstain from such measures.[21]

When the Norwegian government proposed on 30 June 1931, however, that during the life of the 1924 convention neither side should establish any police authority in Eastern Greenland or carry out any acts of sovereignty there,[22] the Danish government refused to agree because this would have exceeded the limits in the 1924 convention and would recognize the Norwegian point of view.[23] In the meantime, Denmark inaugurated a comprehensive three-year plan for scientific research in the central part of Eastern Greenland. The Norwegian government objected to this plan because its focus was precisely where Norway had concentrated her own enterprise and contemplated establishing a colony.[24]

The Norwegian government took decisive action. On 28 June 1931, some Norwegian nationals raised the flag of their country in Mackenzie Bay in Eastern Greenland and proclaimed occupation of the surrounding area.[25] On 10 July, Norway issued a royal proclamation confirming this occupation and proclaiming Norwegian sovereignty over the territory from 71° 30' N to 75° 40' N.[26] On the following day, Denmark submitted the dispute to the Permanent Court of International Justice,[27] in accordance with the previous agreement between the two and also in conformity with the "optional clause" of article 36 of the court's statute, which both had accepted.[28] The oral arguments began on 21 November 1932 and ended on 7 February 1933.[29]

In the arguments, both written and oral, both sides held firmly to the basic positions which had already been established. These were well stated in a brief summary by the court in its judgment:

> The Danish submission in the written pleading, that the Norwegian occupation of July 10th, 1931, is invalid, is founded upon the contention that the area occupied was at the time of the occupation subject to Danish sovereignty; that the area is part of Greenland, and at the time of the occupation Danish sovereignty existed over all Greenland; consequently it could not be occupied by another Power.
>
> In support of this contention, the Danish Government advances two propositions. The first is that the sovereignty which Denmark now enjoys over Greenland had existed for a long time, had been continuously and peacefully exercised and, until the present dispute, has not been contested by any Power. This proposition Denmark sets out to establish as a fact. The second proposition is that Norway has by treaty or otherwise herself recognized Danish sovereignty over Greenland as a whole and therefore cannot now dispute it.
>
> The Norwegian submissions are that Denmark possesses no sovereignty over the area which Norway occupied on July 10, 1931, and that at the time of the occupation the area was *terra nullius*. Her contention is that the area lay outside the limits of the Danish colonies in Greenland and that Danish sovereignty extended no further than the limits of these colonies.
>
> Other contentions were also developed in the course of the proceedings.
>
> On the Danish side it was maintained that the promise which in 1919 the Norwegian Minister for

> Foreign Affairs, speaking on behalf of his Government, gave to the diplomatic representative of the Danish Government at Christiania debarred Norway from proceeding to any occupation of territory in Greenland, even if she had not by other acts recognized an existing Danish sovereignty there.
>
> In this connection Denmark has adduced certain other undertakings by Norway, e.g. the international undertakings entered into by that country for the pacific settlement of her disputes with other countries in general, and with Denmark in particular.
>
> On the Norwegian side it was maintained that the attitude which Denmark adopted between 1915 and 1921, when she addressed herself to various Powers in order to obtain a recognition of her position in Greenland, was inconsistent with a claim to be already in possession of the sovereignty over all Greenland, and that in the circumstances she is now estopped from alleging a long established sovereignty over the whole country.[30]

The award of the court, generally favourable to Denmark, was given on 5 April 1933. The lengthy written judgment, besides summarizing the main arguments in the form quoted above, set forth the historical background of the case in detail and then proceeded to comment upon the principal propositions which had been advanced.

The court pointed out that although Denmark's case was based essentially upon the claim that it had exercised sovereignty over Greenland as a whole for many years, the validation of its case did not require that this sovereignty should have existed throughout the entire period. On the other hand, it was necessary that it should have existed at the time when the Norwegian occupation took place (10 July 1931), which thus became the critical date. Since Denmark's claim to sovereignty was founded basically upon historical rights, however, it was also necessary to consider both the existence and the extent of these rights.[31]

The court went on to observe that a claim to sovereignty "based not upon some particular act or title such as a treaty of cession but merely upon continued display of authority, involves two elements, each of which must be shown to exist: the intention and will to act as sovereign, and some actual exercise or display of such authority."[32] Another important matter was that of competing claims, which, although present in most such cases, were absent in the case at hand until 1931. In fact, "up till 1921, no Power disputed the Danish claim to sovereignty." The court then made what was undoubtedly one of the key observations in the entire judgment:

> It is impossible to read the records of the decisions in cases as to territorial sovereignty without observing that in many cases the tribunal has been satisfied with very little in the way of the actual exercise of sovereign rights, provided that the other State could not make out a superior claim. This is particularly true in the case of claims to sovereignty over areas in thinly populated or unsettled countries.[33]

On the question of historical rights, the court held that insofar as it was possible to apply modern terminology to the rights and pretensions of the kings of Norway in Greenland during the time of the ancient Norse settlements, these rights amounted to sovereignty and were not limited to the two settlements. Although Norway had argued that Norwegian sovereignty was lost in Greenland because of *terra nullius* when these settlements disappeared, and put forward conquest and voluntary abandonment as the reason thereof, the court maintained that "conquest" was not an appropriate expression to describe the massacre of the inhabitants by the Aboriginal population, even if this could be established as fact, and there was no evidence of voluntary abandonment. On the contrary, the tradition of the king's rights lived on.[34]

Considering the early period of resettlement, from the founding of Hans Egede's colonies in 1721 to the Treaty of Kiel in 1814, the court found that both elements necessary to establish sovereignty – intention and exercise – were present, but the question arose as to how far these elements operated. Norway had maintained that the word "Greenland" as used in contemporary legislative and administrative acts had meant only the colonized area on the west coast, but the court rejected this argument, holding that the ordinary geographical connotation of "Greenland" as designating the entire island must be accepted in the absence of proof to the contrary. In the words of the judgment:

> The conclusion to which the Court is led is that, bearing in mind the absence of any claim to sovereignty by another Power, and the Arctic and inaccessible character of the uncolonized parts of the country, the King of Denmark and Norway displayed during the period from the founding of the colonies by Hans Egede in 1721 up to 1814 his authority to an extent sufficient to give his country a valid claim to sovereignty, and that his rights over Greenland were not limited to the colonized area.[35]

The court underlined that where prior to 1814 the rights possessed by the king of Denmark-Norway over Greenland were enjoyed by him as king of Norway, the effect of the Treaty of Kiel was that what had been a Norwegian possession was left with the king of Denmark and became a Danish possession. Thus Denmark became full inheritor of Norway's rights in and over Greenland.[36] Looking at the period of one hundred years following, and considering all the evidence, the court took the view that "Denmark must be regarded as having displayed during this period of 1814 to 1915 her authority over the uncolonized part of the country to a degree sufficient to confer a valid title to the sovereignty."[37]

The judgment went into considerable detail discussing Danish applications to other governments between 1915 and 1921 which sought recognition of Denmark's position in Greenland. Noting that the dispute was between Denmark's contention that it was seeking recognition of an existing sovereignty extending over all Greenland, and Norway's that it was trying to get the powers to accept an extension of its sovereignty over territory which did not as yet belong to it, the court observed that the correspondence did not make the matter entirely clear.

Nevertheless, and in spite of the fact that certain expressions in the documents such as "extension of sovereignty" obviously did not support the Danish argument, "the conclusion which the Court had reached is that the view upheld by the Danish government in the present case is right."[38] In coming to this verdict, the court relied heavily upon various official Danish statements claiming that full sovereignty already existed over all Greenland, even though Danish administration had not yet been extended over all of it. The court judged that during the previous decade Denmark had met the two necessary elements (intention and exercise) to establish a valid title to sovereignty, and even if this period were completely isolated from all the preceding ones and taken by itself, this would still be true. Accordingly, the court was satisfied "that Denmark has succeeded in establishing her contention that at the critical date, namely, 10 July 1931, she possessed a valid title to the sovereignty over all Greenland" and that the Norwegian government's steps to occupy it "were illegal and invalid."[39] Norway accepted the majority award of the court without quibbling. On 7 April 1933, only two days after the judgment was given, the Norwegian government revoked the declaration of sovereignty over Eastern Greenland it had made on 10 July 1931.[40]

The greatest significance of the *Eastern Greenland Case* lies in the definition it helped to give to the requirements for sovereignty over thinly settled or uninhabited lands, and particularly those in the polar regions. This was, in fact, the first occasion when an international tribunal was called upon to adjudicate a dispute about sovereignty over polar territories, and it was one of the few instances of serious disagreement regarding the ownership of such lands. Thus, the case had implications of an importance out of proportion to the value of the territories involved, which, at least in the context of the time, was rather small.

What the case really accomplished was to suggest, in fairly clear terms, that requirements for sovereignty over territory might be reduced if the circumstances of the situation warranted such reduction. Requirements for sovereignty have undergone a considerable evolution over the centuries, the main trend being a lessening emphasis upon certain things formerly considered important (such as papal grants, discovery, and symbolic acts of appropriation) in favour of genuine occupation. Contrary to what has sometimes been said on the subject, occupation has always been considered a matter of significance, but nonetheless it is also true that the stress upon occupation gradually increased as the age of discovery changed to and merged with the age of appropriation and exploitation (colonization). The Conference of Berlin on Africa in 1884–85 laid down effective occupation as a requirement for possession of any territories claimed by the participating powers in that continent,[41] and since then, effective occupation has been considered applicable as a general principle, although discovery has retained its traditional value in conferring an inchoate title. A counter-trend also set in, applicable to territories which were so inaccessible, intemperate, unproductive, or miniscule that they could not be occupied in a normal way, if at all, and yet could or should be identified as the property of particular states. This counter-trend is illustrated by the cases of *Bouvet Island* in 1928, *Palmas Island* in 1928, and *Clipperton Island* in 1931.[42]

The *Eastern Greenland Case* continued and enhanced the trend towards acceptance of a lesser degree of "effective occupation" in cases involving remote, insignificant, and largely unexploitable lands. Here, however, the territory involved was not a tiny island but an enormous land of almost continental size, about nine-tenths of which is permanently covered with ice and thus uninhabited and unexploitable. In accepting Denmark's rather shaky case for sovereignty over the entire island, in spite of this limited circumstance, the court placed its stamp of approval upon a minimum requirement of effective occupation for acquisition of sovereignty over lands of a similar kind, and thus set a potent precedent which in all probability would be applied to polar territories generally.

This is a significant feature of the judgment. It shows not only how very small a part, if any, actual control or possession played in the creation of what was deemed to be an ancient and basic right of sovereignty but also how small an amount of control, measured geographically or otherwise, sufficed under the circumstances to yield a vast and unoccupied and unclaimed island to the modern inheritor and existing possessor of the right of sovereignty.[43]

The outcome of the *Eastern Greenland Case* was of vital importance to Canada. Like Denmark, Canada had fretted over the security of its Arctic territories for many years, although in Canada's case there had not been a challenge to its sovereignty as open, deliberate, and official as there was in the case of Denmark. The analogy between Danish and Canadian Arctic territories, although by no means exact, is close, the main difference being that Greenland is essentially one enormous island encompassed closely by many small islands, while the insular part of Canada's Arctic territories comprises a huge archipelago of many islands both large and small, no single one being dominant. If they were faced with challenges to their sovereignty, Denmark would likely assert the principle of continuity and Canada that of contiguity (for whatever benefit might be derived from these two inconclusive and much-debated doctrines). There is the further important difference that whereas most of Greenland is covered with a permanent ice cap, the Canadian archipelago is mostly free of such ice, with the exception of parts of Baffin and Ellesmere Islands. Otherwise, the Arctic lands of the two states have characteristics that are quite similar, both being very large, essentially Arctic in climate, difficult to access by surface transportation throughout much of their extent, very thinly inhabited with large areas not inhabited at all, and with few known resources that can be exploited on any considerable scale. Both Canada and Denmark would have great difficulty in demonstrating a satisfactory degree of effective occupation if the same standards were expected here as in more equable and populated parts of the world. For this reason, the decision in the *Eastern Greenland Case*, obviously gratifying to Denmark, could be greeted with almost equal satisfaction by Canada.[44] Canada's case for sovereignty over the archipelago has been in most respects similar and not inferior to Denmark's case for sovereignty over all Greenland. For this reason, if at any time after 1933 Canada's title had been formally challenged in law, the precedent then established would almost certainly have been sufficient to decide the case in her favour.

14

American Explorers in the Canadian Arctic and Related Matters, 1918–39

Earlier chapters have dealt with Canadian and American involvement in the North up to 1918 and have shown that fear of what the United States might do in this region was always a matter of concern – and sometimes a source of real worry – to the Canadian government. At the end of the First World War, the Canadian government had virtually no official activity in the remotest parts of its North. Although its initial concerns were connected specifically with Denmark, the Canadian government was more anxious about the role the United States might wish to play in the North American Arctic; in a situation of real stress, the United States would obviously be much more difficult to handle than Denmark. Canadian fears about the possibilities of trouble with the United States during these years were, for the most part, rather vague and ill-defined. Insofar as they took concrete form, however, they were concerned chiefly with the activities of the American explorer Donald B. MacMillan.

Although there was an impression among Canadian officialdom that MacMillan was actually a former Canadian who had been born in Nova Scotia or Newfoundland and had become American by naturalization,[1] this was not the case. According to the authoritative biography of him, he was born and raised in Provincetown, Massachusetts.[2] It does not appear that his earlier expeditions in the Canadian North, notably the Crocker Land Expedition of 1913–17, aroused much comment or concern in Canadian government circles, and he made a favourable impression when he testified before the Reindeer-Muskox Commission in May 1920, stating firmly his view that foreign expeditions should operate in the Canadian Arctic only with the permission of the Canadian government and under Canadian law. "I think all expeditions should be prohibited from going into that country, unless on permission obtained from the Dominion of Canada," he noted on one occasion. "If I were coming into Canada, as I had hoped to, I would expect to get permission from the Canadian government, and if they said No, I could not expect to come."[3] The attitude of the Canadian authorities towards MacMillan soon changed.

There is plenty of evidence that after the First World War, when Canadian officials were so worried about the presumed Danish threat to Ellesmere Island, they did not lose sight of the possibility of complications of some kind with the United States. In his secret memo of 28 October 1920 for Prime Minister Arthur Meighen, Loring Christie observed that Denmark had had nothing to do with the discovery and exploration of Canada's Arctic islands and that the "rivals" in

FIGURE 14-1: DONALD B. MACMILLAN AT THE WHEEL, 1928. *COURTESY OF THE BOSTON PUBLIC LIBRARY, LESLIE JONES COLLECTION 08_06_009321.*

these activities were Norwegians and Americans – but that so far neither Norway nor the United States had shown any official intention of making an effective occupation.[4] The Advisory Technical Board's report of November 1920 on the Arctic islands said that the American attitude towards Britain's desire for a right of pre-exemption in the acquisition of Greenland emphasized the necessity for Canada to take prompt action regarding her own Arctic claims. "The longer these claims are allowed to remain in the present inchoate condition," it noted, "the greater opportunity there will be for the United States to raise objections later on."[5] Remarks such as these do not appear to have been focused upon any specific matter, however, until a new dispatch, emanating from New York on 3 January 1921 and published in the *Montreal Gazette* the following day, announced that sixteen exploratory expeditions were being planned for different parts of the world, including an expedition by MacMillan to the Canadian Arctic islands.[6]

The report aroused some concern in Ottawa government circles, with Acting Deputy Minister of the Interior Roy A. Gibson suggesting that the Home Office in London (evidently he meant the Secretary of State for the Colonies) might be able to obtain information. Sir Joseph Pope replied that the Secretary of State for the Colonies was usually too slow in such matters and that he would therefore prefer to ask the High Commissioner.[7] Having received some further information about MacMillan's projected expedition from Dr. Wilfred Grenfell, Gibson wrote back on 22 January, asking that Pope "ascertain through confidential channels the real object of this expedition and particularly whether it is a private expedition or one backed by the United States Government."

Pope passed this request on to Merchant M. Mahoney, Secretary of the Canadian Mission in Washington, on 25 January, eliciting the reply on 15 February that Mahoney had not been able to find any official American support for the expedition, which appeared to be privately sponsored and for scientific purposes only. Acting on Mahoney's suggestion, the British Embassy in Washington made further inquiries through the British consul at Boston, but it obtained little additional information and none to indicate that the expedition was other than privately sponsored.[8]

In connection with Canadian worries at this time over possible American rivalry in the northern archipelago, the figure of Vilhjalmur Stefansson also looms large. As recounted in previous chapters, it was precisely at this time that the Canadian government was planning an expedition to the Arctic principally for sovereignty purposes in which Stefansson was eager to take a leading role. Canadian officials were instructing him to maintain absolute secrecy in the matter while carrying out his American lecture tour,[9] and at the same time, they were plotting how they might retain his loyalty, at least temporarily, so that he would not desert to either the United States or Denmark.[10] There was little likelihood, of course, that Stefansson would have had much enthusiasm or sympathy for MacMillan's proposed expedition, especially since its major field of activity was to be Baffin Island – an area in which Stefansson himself was already interested.[11] After the projected Canadian expedition of 1921 had been cancelled, William W. Cory wrote a letter to Sir Joseph Pope noting that the British Admiralty had indicated they had no reason to believe the MacMillan expedition had "any other than a purely scientific object in view." Nevertheless, Cory continued, "in this connection I would be very much obliged if you could ask the British authorities at Washington to pay special attention to the organization and aims of any United States expeditions that may be sent into the northern regions, and to keep us advised in this regard."[12] This request was passed on through the usual channels.[13]

For the 1921 expedition, MacMillan had his newly constructed *Bowdoin*, a little 60-ton schooner equipped with an auxiliary 40-horsepower engine. On 15 July, Mahoney wrote to Sir Joseph Pope to inform him that the *Bowdoin* was to sail from Wiscasset, Maine, the following day and that she would comply with customs formalities at Sydney, Nova Scotia, and again at Port Burwell at the entrance to Hudson Strait.[14] James Harkin had already pointed out in a note to Cory that MacMillan had applied for licences, and he suggested that it would be wise to issue the licences at once.[15] The Canadian authorities, however, were obviously determined not to overlook any detail that might be a possible source of future trouble. In a confidential note to Pope on 29 July, Cory observed that although MacMillan had taken out permits under the Northwest Game Act and had thus acknowledged Canadian sovereignty, it could be argued "that these permits apply only to the recognized Canadian area and not to the unexplored portions." An article in the *Halifax Herald* on 20 July, saying that the expedition was being financed completely by MacMillan and his friends "save a couple of thousand which the U.S. Government allows him," had attracted official attention. Cory suggested "the possibility that this may be covering a salary of some nature, such as for a Commissionership," and he asked that Pope "again request the British authorities at Washington to … ascertain confidentially to what extent the United States Government is interested in the expedition, and particularly whether a Commissionership of any kind has been given to MacMillan."[16]

The inquiries indicated that MacMillan was not receiving a grant from the American government, was "not intrusted [sic] with any special mission of a political nature," and therefore it "would appear that there are no grounds for the uneasiness entertained by the Department of the Interior."[17] The venerable Captain Bernier's suspicions also had been aroused by MacMillan's expedition, and he wrote a vigorously worded letter to Prime Minister Meighen on 29 July 1921. "I wish to stand on record very strongly in this matter," he stated, and, with reference to the imposition of dues upon Americans entering Franklin District, "I am at your disposition to see that this is carried out."[18]

MacMillan wintered at Schooner Harbour on the southwestern coast of Baffin Island in 1921–22, returned to the United States in the summer of 1922, and then took *Bowdoin* back north the following year. Oswald Finnie, Director of the Northwest Territories and Yukon Branch of the Department of the Interior, wrote to him on 16 June 1923, mentioning press reports that he was starting another expedition to the Canadian Arctic and saying that he had approved a permit for him to take scientific specimens during the years 1923 and 1924. Finnie also pointed out that MacMillan could obtain licences to hunt and trap from any Royal Canadian Mounted Police (RCMP) post in the north, enclosed a copy of the Northwest Game Act for his guidance, and asked him for information about his expedition and its work.[19]

MacMillan left without acknowledging this letter. On 22 October 1924, after he had returned, Finnie wrote him a rather stiffly worded note reminding him of the fact. The Canadian authorities were aware, Finnie said, that he had permits to take scientific specimens but none to hunt, trap, or trade. Yet reports indicated that he had killed muskox and trapped fur animals. Since the department checked returning expeditions closely, Finnie said, and since questions might be asked in Parliament, he sought a full statement from MacMillan about the matter and an assurance that the expedition was purely scientific.[20] This time MacMillan replied promptly:

> Amid the rush of getting away for the Arctic in 1923, I failed to notify you on the receipt of the Northwest Game Act and regulations, for which I thank you.
>
> The main objects of my expedition were purely scientific....
>
> The expedition, as you know, wintered not in Canadian waters but in Refuge Harbour, North Greenland. Nothing in Canadian Territory was trapped or killed or traded for by me or a single member of my personnel, else you would have received notice immediately upon my return and check forwarded for hunting and trading licence.[21]

Finnie replied briefly on 4 November, expressing his pleasure at the assurance and saying that MacMillan's statement would be used, if needed, in the House of Commons.[22]

The proposed flight of the American navy dirigible *Shenandoah* to the North Pole also caused worry in Ottawa at this time.[23] The project was brought to the attention of official circles through news dispatches of 4 December 1923, notably one appearing in the *Washington Post*. On 20 November, President Calvin Coolidge had formally authorized Secretary of the Navy Edwin Denby to organize the expedition. Bob Bartlett, now a lieutenant commander in the US naval reserve, had apparently made the suggestion that initiated planning for the expedition, which was to explore unknown regions adjacent to the North Pole. The date, route, and procedure remained to be decided.[24]

W. W. Cory drew the attention of Sir Joseph Pope to the project in a note dated 7 December, "in order that Council may consider the propriety of consulting the United States to ascertain their intentions and whether they expect to utilize Canadian territory as a base of operations."[25] Pope sent a copy of Cory's note with a memorandum to Prime Minister King on 11 December, inquiring whether the British chargé d'affaires in Washington should be asked to look into the matter. King did not respond until 22 January 1924; when he did, in a handwritten note on Pope's memo, his answer was: "By all means." Stefansson also wrote to King about the proposed flight, saying that "the announcements from Washington … read almost as if they had been copied from my 'Northward Course of Empire.'" He hoped that King would "get someone to go into these matters thoroughly again and see if there is not something which Canada can yet do to prevent her being set back too far by the enterprise and foresight of the Americans."[26] The Prime Minister's private secretary, following instructions, wrote a polite but rather noncommittal reply.[27]

Secretary Denby went before the House of Representatives Naval Committee on 19 January 1924 to stir up Congressional support for the project, and his remarks emphasized that there was a large unknown region north of Alaska, quite possibly containing undiscovered land which he declared should be made American territory. In the course of his statement, he said:

> The polar flight is undertaken by the United States Navy partly because of the known fact that there is an unexplored area directly north of Alaska in the polar region of 1000000 square miles.… I think it must be perfectly clear to everybody that it is at least highly desirable that the United States should know what is in that region.
>
> And, furthermore, in my opinion, it is highly desirable that if there is in that region land, either habitable or not, it should be the property of the United States… And, for myself, I cannot view with equanimity any territory of that kind being in the hands of another Power.…
>
> One object of this proposed flight is to make sure whether or not there is land, and if there is, what its character is and, if possible, should there be land there, to add it to the sovereignty of the United States.
>
> We go quickly upon this expedition, because if we do not go this year, it will not be any use to go at all. If we do not go, that entire region will be photographed and mapped and probably controlled by another Power within two years.[28]

Denby's statement was widely publicized in the American press[29] and immediately attracted official attention in Ottawa. On 24 January, Governor General Byng sent a telegram to the British ambassador in Washington, asking that his ministers "be informed as to what basis of fact it [Denby's statement] may possess, and also, if it be well founded, to what extent the United States Government would propose to use Canadian territory as base of operations in the coming expedition."[30] The ambassador did not reply directly, but on the same day, the Embassy wrote a report on the matter to British Foreign Secretary Ramsay MacDonald, and

FIGURE 14-2: AIRSHIP USS *SHENANDOAH* (ZR-1) AND USS *PATOKA* OFF NEWPORT, RHODE ISLAND, C.1924–25. *BOSTON PUBLIC LIBRARY, LESLIE JONES COLLECTION, 08_06_001984.*

two days later a copy of the report was sent to Ottawa.[31]

While memos were flying back and forth from department to department in Ottawa, the *New York Times* published an editorial on 6 February, saying that the projected flight of the *Shenandoah* had hastened the preparations of the Canadian government to send Captain Bernier on another cruise to the northern islands and that he would "be instructed to establish posts on their shores." The United States had no designs upon any of the islands to which Great Britain had a title by discovery, the editorial went on, but "when it comes to land between the Pole and the Alaskan coast which may be discovered by the American exploration party on the *Shenandoah*, the United States would certainly put in a claim of title."[32] The *Washington Post* carried a report on 13 February which said that orders had been given which "completed the preparatory steps for the flight and set at rest rumors that the trip might not be carried through."[33] Two days later, the *Washington Herald* published an article titled "Canadians May Ban Shenandoah Relief," which suggested that plans to use another airship to aid the *Shenandoah* in case she got into difficulties might be jeopardized if Canada refused to permit flight over Canadian territory.[34]

Canadian worries were relieved unexpectedly on 15 February when President Coolidge ordered suspension of preparations for the *Shenandoah* flight. The official explanation was that the President had been made aware of considerable opposition in Congress to the project, and he was anxious to have congressional approval of the proposed expenditure of $350,000 on it before letting plans proceed.[35] Since the project faced a tight time schedule, and since (given the prevailing circumstances in the Arctic) any considerable delay would nullify plans for that season, the suspension turned out to be the equivalent of cancellation. The British Embassy in Washington sent word of the suspension to Ottawa on 16 February in a brief, factual note accompanied by newspaper clippings.[36] (It does not appear that any action had been taken on Governor General Byng's request of 24 January.)

Two oft-quoted statements of official policy by American Secretary of State Charles Evans Hughes around this time have been widely interpreted as clear indications of the American government's attitude towards the requirements for sovereignty over polar territories. The first, in connection with Roald Amundsen's projected transarctic flight, was in reply to a statement by the Norwegian ambassador that any land Amundsen might discover would be claimed on behalf of the Norwegian Crown. In his answering note, Hughes declared:

> In my opinion rights similar to those which in earlier centuries were based upon the acts of a discoverer, followed by occupation or settlement consummated at long and uncertain periods thereafter, are not capable of being acquired at the present time. To-day, if an explorer is able to ascertain the existence of lands still unknown to civilization, his act of so-called discovery, coupled with a formal taking of possession, would have no significance, save as he might herald the advent of the settler; and where for climatic or other reasons actual settlement would be an impossibility, as in the case of the Polar regions, such conduct on his part would afford frail support for a reasonable claim of sovereignty. I am therefore compelled to state, without now adverting to other considerations, that this Government cannot admit that such taking of possession as a discoverer by Mr. Amundsen of areas explored by him could establish the basis of rights of sovereignty in the Polar regions, to which, it is understood, he is about to depart.[37]

Hughes's second statement answered a private inquiry about a suggested American declaration of sovereignty over Wilkes Land in the Antarctic:

> It is the opinion of the Department that the discovery of lands unknown to civilization, even when coupled with a formal taking of possession, does not support a valid claim of sovereignty unless the discovery is followed by an actual settlement of the discovered country. In the absence of an act of Congress assertative in a domestic sense of dominion over Wilkes Land this Department would be reluctant to declare that the United States possessed a right of sovereignty over that territory.[38]

These statements suggest that the Canadian authorities may have had less reason to worry than they assumed over the possibility that discoveries such as those that MacMillan or *Shenandoah* might have made would lead to authoritative claims of sovereignty by the United States. On the other hand, they suggest that the American government would take a hard look at Canada's performance in the Arctic before recognizing Canadian claims and that, consequently, Canadian authorities would be wise to question the adequacy of their own measures and to try to improve them.

Press reports about a new MacMillan expedition prompted Finnie to renew the correspondence with him on 14 January 1925 in a letter similar to that of 16 June 1923. Observing, perhaps with tongue in cheek, that the 1923 letter had "reached you too late to be answered," Finnie said he would now provide the requisite information in good time, and he again asked for "some particulars regarding the expedition and its objects." On this occasion, instead of approving in advance a permit for MacMillan to collect scientific specimens, Finnie asked him to apply for it to the National Parks Branch of the Department of the Interior.[39]

Undoubtedly MacMillan's expedition of 1925 caused more anxiety to Canadian authorities – and more discussion in Ottawa, Washington, and London – than any other issue connected with Canadian-American relations in the Arctic at this time. MacMillan's aim was to explore the still unknown portion of the polar sea northwest of the Canadian archipelago and between Alaska and the North Pole, where there was still a possibility that new land might be discovered. His expedition, which was to be sponsored by the National Geographic Society, would comprise two ships – *Peary* and his own *Bowdoin* – while the US Navy would provide two or three planes and personnel to operate them under Lieutenant Commander Richard E. Byrd. MacMillan's intention to operate in Canadian Arctic territory and claim any new territories he discovered for the United States, combined with the involvement of the US Navy and the use of planes, worried officialdom in Ottawa.

On 30 March 1925, MacMillan had an interview with President Coolidge in which he reportedly urged the American government to try to claim additional territory near the North Pole. The interview was covered in the *Washington Star* of 31 March, but the announcement did not make clear precisely where this territory would be.[40] If it lay outside the Canadian sector, obviously Canada would not be greatly concerned. If it were either previously discovered land or new land within the Canadian sector, Canada's known views on the subject would make it impossible for her not to react. A news article in the *Washington Post* on 6 April said that the expedition would be undertaken as a private enterprise financed by the National Geographic Society, but it gave details about the US Navy's intention to provide planes and volunteer pilots and about the plan to establish an advance base. Other statements about the preparation of the expedition also appeared in the press from time to time.

On 16 April 1925, Finnie wrote a memo about various subjects connected with the Arctic to Cory, who was on the point of leaving for Washington. Finnie paid particular attention to the MacMillan expedition, and he suggested that if it should winter on or use any Canadian Arctic island as an air base, it should first secure permission from the Canadian government. He suggested further that Undersecretary of State for External Affairs O.D. Skelton might inform the Secretary of State in Washington that Canada would be glad to grant this permission, on condition that a Canadian pilot should accompany exploratory flights.[41] In a memo to R. A. Gibson four days later, Finnie observed that although MacMillan had applied to the Danish authorities for permission to explore in Greenland, neither he nor Krüger, the German who was also planning an expedition, had made an application to the Canadian government. He suggested that a small committee should be appointed to look after sovereignty problems in the North, with the following members: Skelton, James White (technical adviser to the

Department of Justice), Commissioner Cartlandt Starnes of the RCMP, J. B. Harkin, J. D. Craig, W. M. Cory (a son of W. W. Cory and legal adviser to the Department of the Interior), and Finnie himself.[42]

An order in council was issued on 23 April, creating a committee – the Northern Advisory Board – similar to that which Finnie had recommended. All the men he had suggested became members, as well as several others. According to the order, the specific function of the committee would be to draft a document "to place on record with all interested Governments a statement indicating the extent of territory claimed by Canada for the British Empire" in the Arctic.[43] Under the authority of this order in council, the committee held a meeting on 24 April. The members noted that MacMillan had declared himself to be strongly in favour of Canadian control of foreign expeditions in the Canadian North during his appearance before the Reindeer-Muskox Commission in May 1920. This information formed the subject of several communiqués among interested officials, who intended to use the information as advantageously as possible.[44]

On 28 April, MacMillan answered a letter from Harkin about pemmican for use in the North, saying that his expedition would take place in summer only and would use airplanes based at Etah, North Greenland. He remarked that the pemmican would be invaluable as emergency rations "in case our planes fail to function at four or five hundred miles from the ship."[45] Skelton's rather sarcastic comment when he received a copy of the letter is indicative of the suspicious view the Canadian government took of the expedition: "It will be interesting to note whether the four or five hundred miles radius from Etah is what he really expects to cover."[46]

On 13 May, the Northern Advisory Board met and chose a subcommittee to draft a letter to the British ambassador in Washington asking for information about the MacMillan expedition and intimating that it should comply with Canadian laws and regulations. The same subcommittee was to prepare as rapidly as possible a memorandum justifying Canada's claim to Arctic territories.[47] The subcommittee comprised Skelton, George Joseph Desbarats, Finnie, and White; nevertheless, when the memo appeared about twelve days later, it was evidently the handiwork of White alone.[48] Under the authority of an order in council of 5 June,[49] Governor General Byng sent the above-mentioned documents to the British ambassador in Washington with supporting materials.[50]

On 23 May, Finnie wrote a note to Skelton setting forth briefly the case against MacMillan. He said that MacMillan's reply of 27 October 1924 was "decidedly ambiguous and evasive," since, among other things, he had stated that he had killed or trapped no animals on Canadian territory, yet advice from the RCMP "was that beyond question he had killed some muskoxen on Ellesmere Island." As to the letter written to him on 14 January 1925, "Dr. MacMillan has not favoured us with a reply and, although his boat will sail within the next month, there is nothing to indicate that he intends to secure any licenses or permits from us." Finnie suggested that MacMillan possibly did not admit that Ellesmere Island was Canadian territory.[51]

In this context, and with this background, Minister of the Interior Charles Stewart made his oft-quoted statements in the House of Commons in June 1925. On 1 June, he moved the second reading of a bill to amend the Northwest Territories Act, and in dealing in committee with the issuing of licences to scientists or explorers, he spoke as follows:

> This amendment is to provide for the issuing of licenses and permits to scientists and explorers who wish to enter the Northwest Territories. We are having visits from representatives of various foreign countries who go into the northern sections of Canada, and in some cases they have voluntarily come to us and secured permits, and we have examined their outfits going in, as well as coming out. But this has not been done in every case by the explorers who are going into this territory, and we are asking for this amendment in order that we may have authority to notify parties going into that country that they must obtain a permit of entry, thereby asserting our ownership over the whole northern archipelago….
>
> …. Here we are getting after men like MacMillan and Doctor Amundsen, men who are going in presumably for exploration purposes, but possibly there may arise a question as to the sovereignty over some land they may discover in the northern portion of Canada, and we claim all that portion.
>
> *John Livingstone Brown (Lisgar)*: We claim right up to the North Pole.
>
> *Mr. Stewart (Argenteuil)*: Yes, right up to the North Pole…. What we want to do is to assert our sovereignty. We want to make it clear that this is Canadian territory and that if foreigners want to go in there they must have permission in the form of a license.[52]

Stewart's remarks aroused a great deal of comment in Washington. The *Washington Star* reported them on 2 June, saying that MacMillan had already made clear his intention of claiming the mysterious "Crocker Land" for the United States if he found it.[53] A day later, the *Washington Post* said that American officials were "somewhat perplexed" at the news from Ottawa that Canada would claim any new lands discovered and were not aware that any such claim had ever been asserted before.[54] The *Washington Star* of 4 June asserted that Canada had informed the American government that the MacMillan-Byrd expedition should ask permission to cross Ellesmere Land, but the Navy Department had referred the matter to the Department of State because to ask permission would constitute recognition of Canada's claim to Ellesmere Island. Deputy Minister of the Interior W. W. Cory had made a special trip to Washington to discuss the matter, and Minister of the Interior Stewart had written a formal note about it. Nevertheless, American authorities asserted that if MacMillan found new territory, the United States would be entitled to claim it.[55] The *Star* took a slightly different tack on 7 June, saying that Canada's Arctic claim might "be valid on fine point," although the precise nature of this point was not clarified.[56] The *Washington Post* in an editorial two days later spoke favourably of an American acquisition of newly discovered Arctic territories, saying: "Having planted our flag on the shore of Alaska and the North Pole, it will be fitting for the same ensign to fly over all the lands that lie between the two."[57] Henry Chilton, the British chargé d'affaires in Washington, took note of the reaction by the press to Stewart's remarks in a letter of 10 June to Foreign Secretary Austen Chamberlain, explaining that the State Department was considering two main questions: first, whether Axel Heiberg Island was Canadian, thus necessitating Canadian permission for naval aviators with the MacMillan expedition to land there; and, second, whether the United States should claim any newly discovered land.[58]

Stewart made his second important pronouncement in the House of Commons on 10 June. Referring to a Washington newspaper report that Canadian authorities had not yet discussed Canada's claim to "all land between Canada and the pole" with the American government but had asked Lieutenant Commander Byrd if he had obtained a permit to land on Axel Heiberg Island, the Hon. Henry Herbert Stevens asked if the governor had taken the matter up with the American government. The Minister of the Interior replied:

> Mr. Speaker, this government has been very much alive to what we claim to be the possessions of Canada in the northern territory adjacent to the Dominion. Indeed, I made the statement in the House the other evening that we claimed all the territory lying between meridians 60 and 141. This afternoon when dealing with the estimates of the Department of the Interior I propose to bring down a map to make it clear what precautions we are taking to establish ourselves in that territory and to notify the nationals of foreign countries passing over it that we think Canada should be advised of their plans and that they should ask for permits from the Canadian Government. That is the extent to which we have gone at the moment. I might say further to my hon. friend from Vancouver Centre that some considerable time ago a despatch dealing with the subject was sent to Washington, to which we have had no reply.[59]

Stewart went into further detail on the question of Canada's Arctic claims in a press conference on 12 June, which had obviously been carefully arranged.[60] He stated with greater precision the limits claimed by Canada, as the following report indicates:

> He stated that Canada's northern territory includes the area bounded on the east by a line passing midway between Greenland and Baffin, Devon and Ellesmere Islands to the 60th meridian of longitude, following this meridian to the Pole; and on the west by the 141st meridian of longitude following this meridian to the Pole, as indicated for example by the official map published in 1904, showing "Explorations in Northern Canada." Mr. Stewart emphasized the fact that no new claims are being advanced on Canada's behalf, and that the present policy of the Government was simply a continuation of methods followed for many years past in administering the northern territories of the Dominion.

In the remainder of his statement, Stewart summarized the bases, both historical and contemporary, for Canada's claim to the northern territories within these limits.[61]

On the same day, Governor General Byng transmitted the statement verbatim by code telegram to the British chargé d'affaires in Washington, asking him to inform the American secretary of state that no official American communication about the MacMillan expedition had been received but that the Canadian

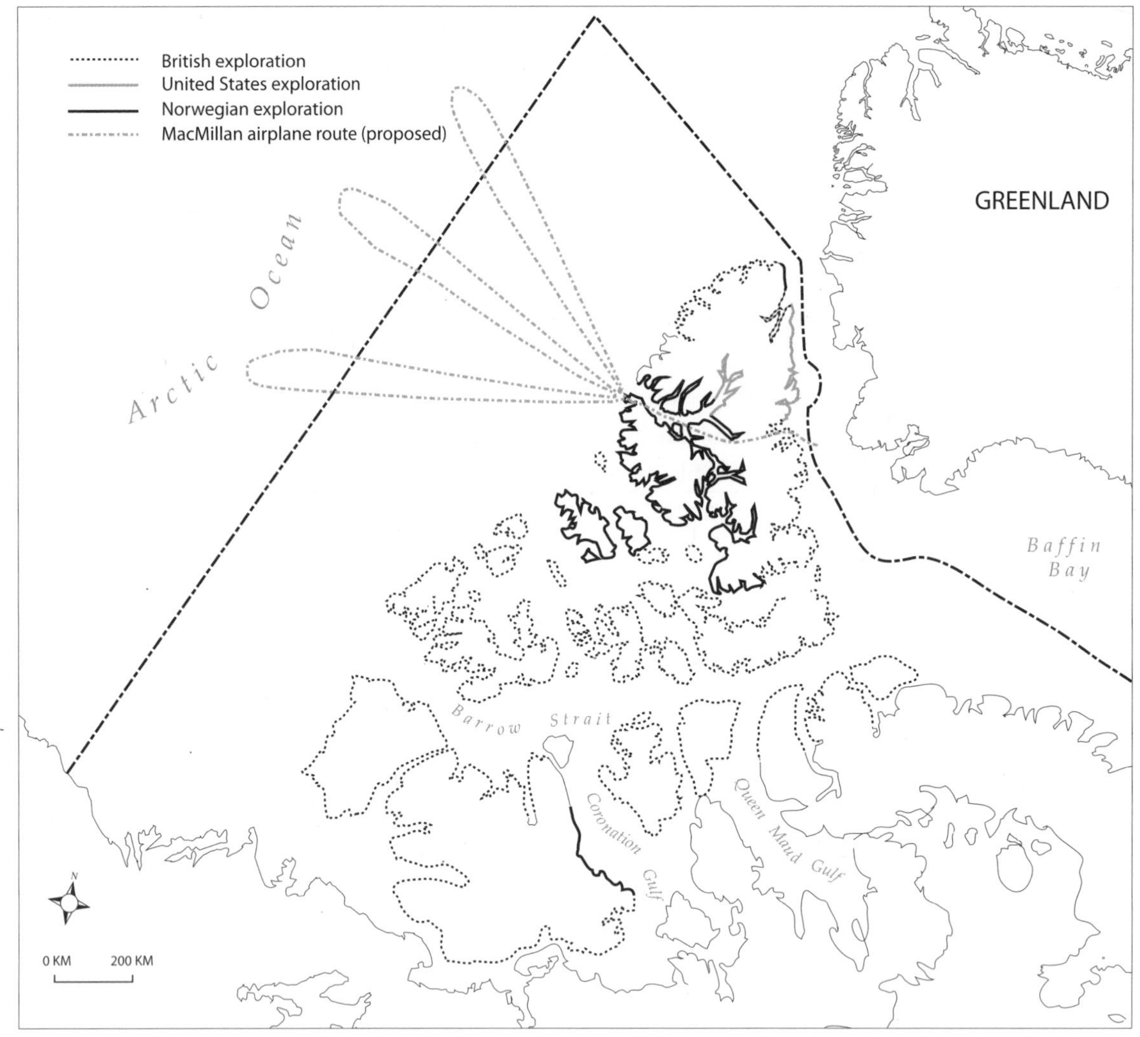

Figure 14-3: Map of the Northwest Territories showing the areas of British, American and Norwegian exploration in the Arctic, projected aeroplane routes from MacMillan's supply base on Axel Heiberg Island and the boundaries of Canadian sovereignty in the north. *Library and Archives Canada, RG10, vol. 3237, file 600352-1. Jennifer Arthur-Lackenbauer.*

government was ready to furnish all permits required and render any assistance.[62]

A Washington news item of 12 June announced that, according to Secretary of the Navy Curtis D. Wilbur, MacMillan was leaving without any official instructions about flying over disputed territories or claiming lands he might discover. Although MacMillan had requested instructions from the State Department, he expected no reply. The article closed with the interesting remark that "no foreign government has raised a question as to the right of the planes to fly over Ellesmere land or establish an advance base on Axel Heiberg land."[63] Possibly because of this report, and because of evident Canadian fears that the United States might claim Axel Heiberg and Ellesmere Islands, Chilton suggested in a cypher telegram to Byng that "it would be well to lose no time in intimating to the Government of the United States that Canada regards both these islands as being her territory."[64] This suggestion was taken promptly in Ottawa, and on 13 June, Byng sent an answering telegram stating the Canadian government's agreement that "a more explicit statement should now be conveyed to the United States Government." He was inclined to dodge the issue of Axel Heiberg, however, saying that no Canadian posts had ever been established there and suggesting that reference to air permits should be limited initially to a phrase such as "flying over Ellesmere, Baffin and other islands within Canadian Boundaries."[65]

The result was one of the more important and better-known exchanges of communiqués with the American government. On 15 June, Chilton wrote the following note to Secretary of State Frank B. Kellogg:

> I have the honour to inform you that the Government of Canada have reason to believe, from statements which have lately appeared in the press, that a scientific expedition, commonly referred to as the MacMillan expedition, organised under the auspices of the National Geographical [*sic*] Society with the co-operation of the United States Navy, will shortly be leaving for the far North for the purpose of exploring and flying over Baffin, Ellesmere, Axel Heiberg and certain other islands within the northern territories of the Dominion.
>
> As you are doubtless aware, posts of the Royal Canadian Mounted Police have been established in Baffin and Ellesmere islands and other sections of the Canadian northern territories, in addition to which Police patrols through the Arctic islands have created depots of provisions at various centres. There are also a number of Hudson Bay Company posts in existence at island and mainland points.
>
> In these circumstances, and although the Dominion Government have received no intimation from the Government of the United States regarding the route of the MacMillan expedition or of the intention of the members thereof to carry our explorations through and over Canadian territory, they have requested me to inform you of their readiness to furnish the expedition with the necessary permits for an exploring and scientific expedition entering Canadian northern territories, and possibly desiring to fly over Baffin, Ellesmere and the adjoining islands within the boundaries of the Dominion. Legislation formally requiring scientific or exploring expeditions to secure such permits before entering any part of the Canadian northern territories was enacted by both Houses of Parliament this month.
>
> I would also take this opportunity of assuring you of the Canadian Government's readiness to afford the MacMillan expedition any assistance within the power on the Royal Canadian Mounted Police and the other Canadian officers in the north. In the connection, I would add that the Dominion Government S. S. *Arctic* will sail at an early date on her customary northern patrol, and

> will carry Royal Canadian Mounted Police details and reliefs. This vessel will touch at various points and will visit the police and trading posts on Ellesmere Island.[66]

Secretary Kellogg answered this carefully worded note on 19 June, in a note phrased with equal care:

> I beg to acknowledge the receipt of your note No. 627, dated June 15, 1925, concerning the proposed MacMillan Exploring Expedition. It is the understanding of this Department that the Expedition in question will sail from Wiscasset, Maine, on June 20, directly to Etah, Greenland, and that no flights over Baffin Island are contemplated. The planes attached to the Expedition are expected to fly from Etah across Ellesmere Island to Axel Heiberg Land, and to establish a base there from which exploration flights to the northward and westward may be made.
>
> A copy of your note has been forwarded to the other interested departments of this Government and, upon receipt of further information, I shall address a communication to you dealing with the other questions raised in your note.
>
> In order that full information may be available for use in studying these questions, I shall be grateful if you will inform me what constitutes a post of the Royal Mounted Police mentioned in the second paragraph of your note and the establishment thereof; where such posts have been established; how frequently they are visited; and whether they are permanently occupied, and, if so, by whom.
>
> I desire to thank you for the offer of cooperation by any Canadian agency which may temporarily be in the same territory with the MacMillan Expedition and I am sure that the persons responsible for the Expedition will also appreciate the kind offer of the Canadian Government. The scientific character of the Expedition and the experience of those participating in it give assurance that useful data and information of value to the world will unquestionably result from their efforts.[67]

Upon receipt of information from Ottawa about the points raised in the third paragraph of Kellogg's note, Chilton replied in detail on 2 July, describing the locations and characteristics of the RCMP posts in the eastern Arctic and the duties of the personnel stationed there.[68] On 18 July, Kellogg wrote a brief, formal, and probably unintentionally humorous acknowledgement of this note "concerning certain laws of the Arctic Ocean and posts of the Royal Canadian Mounted Police established therein." He added that, after study, he would forward a reply, but apparently this was not done.[69]

A Washington news report which announced the departure of MacMillan from Boston on 17 June said that if he discovered any new land he would raise the American flag over it, but the question of formal claims would be left to the American government. The report added that the State Department had not given any special instructions to MacMillan, even though he had asked for them.[70] Later reports told of a serious dispute over the US Navy's insistence that its own radio equipment should be installed on the navy planes, the dispute being resolved in decisive fashion by the navy's blunt order that either this should be done or the navy personnel and planes should be set ashore at Sydney, Nova Scotia. Secretary of the Navy Wilbur made it clear that the navy part of the expedition was only co-operating with MacMillan and remained under the complete control of the Navy Department.[71] Such reports were closely observed in Ottawa.

A minor incident occurred during the expedition's voyage north when some of its personnel were apprehended by the chief federal migratory bird officer for Ontario and Quebec while taking (or preparing to take) specimens of wild birds and eggs on Perroquet Island on the Quebec side of the Strait of Belle Isle. The expedition's ornithologist, Walter Koelz of the University of Michigan, said that he had been given a permit to make such collections, but later examination showed that his permit was good for the provinces of Ontario and Manitoba only.[72] Officials in Ottawa decided not to make a particular issue of this little incident, however, since there were extenuating circumstances, and senior authorities felt that the expedition's activities in the Arctic were of greater concern.[73]

The flights of the US Navy planes under Lieutenant Commander Richard E. Byrd from the base at Etah over Ellesmere Island in the direction of Axel Heiberg caused more serious complications. Several flights had already occurred when the CGS *Arctic* called at Etah in the course of its annual eastern Arctic Patrol. Learning of the flights, and being reasonably sure that no permits to fly over Canadian Arctic territory had either been requested by or granted to any member of the American expedition, Canadian patrol commander George P. Mackenzie sent his secretary to inform Byrd that he would be glad to issue such a permit if it had not already been obtained. After initially stating his impression that the expedition lacked a permit, Byrd shortly thereafter came aboard the *Arctic* to say that he had consulted with MacMillan and had been informed that the permit had been granted to the expedition after it had set sail. Although doubtful, Mackenzie conceded the possibility that this might have happened; nevertheless, he got First Officer L. D. Morin of the *Arctic* to act as witness and make note of the conversation.[74] An odd coincidence is that these events took place on 20 August; on this same date, Byrd received instructions by radio from Secretary of the Navy Wilbur to stop trying to fly to Axel Heiberg Island, and MacMillan ordered commencement of the return voyage southwards.[75] After the *Arctic* had arrived back at Quebec, the Canadian press reported that the visit of the Canadian patrol was responsible for the cessation of the flights,[76] but leading American accounts say that bad weather and the approaching freeze-up were the main reasons. (Indeed, some of the latter do not even mention the Canadian visit.)[77]

The matter was sufficiently serious to generate an official protest to the American government. In a note to the British ambassador in Washington, Governor General Byng summarized the episode (including MacMillan's reported statement to Byrd that a permit for flights over the archipelago had been obtained) and explained:

> The Government of Canada has never received an application by the MacMillan Expedition or any person attached thereto for permission to carry on flying operations over the Canadian Arctic Archipelago, as provided by the Air Board Act, and no such permit has ever been issued, nor has an application been received or permit or licence been issued to

Figure 14-4: Byrd ready for South Pole expedition, 1928. *Boston Public Library, Leslie Jones Collection, 08_06_002249.*

> enter said archipelago for scientific purposes as provided by the Northwest Territories Act.
>
> Neither the steamship "Peary" nor the auxiliary schooner "Bowdoin" when reported outwards from the port of Sydney, Nova Scotia, on the 26th of June, 1925, indicated any intention of landing goods on Canadian territory, nor on the inward report at the same port on the 3rd day of October, 1925, did they report having landed any goods in Canadian territory, as provided by the Customs regulations.
>
> I would request Your Excellency to have the goodness to draw the attention of the United States Secretary of State to the apparent failure on the part of the Expedition to observe the requirements of the Canadian laws.[78]

The substance of Byng's note, together with some relevant documents, was transmitted to the Department of State on 21 December 1925. Joseph C. Grew's acknowledgement on 11 January 1926 included the following: "I have been pleased to bring these statements and affidavits to the attention of the authorities responsible for the MacMillan Expedition, including Commander MacMillan himself, and thank you for calling the attention of the Government to the matters in question."[79]

The 1925 incident was brought up again in Canadian government circles in 1927 and 1928. On 25 January 1927, Colonel Wilfrid Bovey of McGill University wrote a letter to Major General James Howden MacBrien, Chief of the General Staff, informing him that MacMillan had visited Montreal the previous day. Bovey and MacMillan, who belonged to the same college fraternity, were together during the visit, and MacMillan brought up the 1925 incident by saying that he feared it had put him in the bad books of the Canadian government. Nonetheless, he claimed that he had asked the Bureau of Aeronautics in Washington to get him a permit from the Canadian government, and the bureau had refused on grounds that to ask for a permit would constitute recognition of Canadian sovereignty, which they refused to give. He said that he learned of the incident at Etah only some time after it had happened, and he suggested that Byrd knew his statement that MacMillan had been granted a permit was false. In Bovey's words, MacMillan explained that "he felt very badly about the whole affair, that he did not want to be party to anything unfriendly to Canada, the more so as he was born in Canada himself." Bovey stated his own conviction that MacMillan was telling "an absolutely correct story" and that he had no unfriendly motives whatever.[80]

On 28 January, MacBrien sent a copy of Bovey's letter to Skelton, whose reaction to MacMillan's story was considerably more skeptical. "I note that MacMillan denies that he said that the Government of Canada had given him a flying permit, and throws the responsibility for this statement wholly upon Byrd," Skelton quoted at length from Byng's dispatch of 9 December 1925 to Washington. "I have no personal acquaintance with either Commander Byrd or Commander MacMillan, though the members of the Canadian Arctic Committee, who know them both, seem inclined to have much more faith in Commander Byrd's veracity."[81] When he saw Skelton's letter, Bovey wrote to MacBrien that he could not believe Byrd's statement about the permit since it was "perfectly incredible … that a man actually in charge of flying operations should not know whether a permit had been granted or not." In any case, "the American government was certainly well aware that no permit had been granted."[82] Finnie's reaction to the correspondence was that the whole affair was "a nasty mess." He suggested to W. W. Cory that Byrd might be given a chance to reply. Cory decided that they should be guided by Skelton's advice, and he added, "My own view is that no good purpose can be attained by further discussion just now."[83]

The MacMillan-Byrd expedition of 1925 was largely responsible for provoking a Canadian reaction of a rather different kind. Major Robert A. Logan, the Canadian airman who had accompanied the 1922 Eastern Arctic Patrol to locate sites for landing fields in the Arctic islands, had afterwards become an employee of the Fairchild Aerial Camera Corporation in New York City. For some time, he had been warning the Canadian government that many Americans interested in the North, including MacMillan, took Canada's Arctic claims rather lightly. On 17 March 1924, for example, Logan wrote to Finnie saying that Stefansson "claims that Canada has little or no real title to any of the Arctic Islands not occupied by Canadians and that anybody could go there and hunt etc. without being subject to Canadian laws and I gather that MacMillan has the same idea." In another letter to Finnie on 12 April 1925, commenting on his connections with the Explorer Club in New York, Logan wrote that "I have met and talked with quite a few men well known in Arctic Exploration and the general belief seems to be that Arctic islands are 'no man's lands.'"[84]

Logan was anxious to "help the Canadian cause along" and came up with an interesting idea. On 5 June 1925, he wrote a letter to the Prime Minister of Canada asking to lease four small tracts of land, about 640 acres each, in the Far North to establish and operate air bases. One of these tracts would be located near the northern extremity of Ellesmere Island, one near the northern extremity of Axel Heiberg, one at Craig Harbour on the south coast of Ellesmere Island, and the remaining one less precisely located on the "so far uncharted land" east of the 141st meridian and near the 83rd parallel. (There are no islands near this last location, but at the time MacMillan and others were hoping to find new land there.) Under the terms, Logan proposed that the leases would have to remain Canadian, they would be of twenty-one years' duration after survey, and the fees and charges would total not more than one cent per acre. In his letter, Logan explained his belief that "if the Canadian Government were to lease certain areas of land in the far north and to issue licenses for Air Harbours (or Air Stations) such action would materially strengthen the claims of Canada regarding that region between Greenland and the 141st Meridian."[85]

Logan's application was referred to the Departments of External Affairs, National Defence, and the Interior. On 19 June, Deputy Minister of National Defence G. J. Desbarats wrote him a letter saying that his department was "prepared to grant temporary permission for you to use all or any of the sites for the operation of aircraft." His plan was favourably received overall, but Logan explained in correspondence that he had "no desire for the land" and did not see how he could actually put it to use. His idea was simply that the action by the government which he invited would "help in confirming Canada's intention of holding and developing the Arctic Islands."[86] In these circumstances, nothing further seems to have been done. This little project of Logan's was publicized in the United States but, ironically, not in Canada. This seems unfortunate, because it would have given the Canadian government an opportunity to demonstrate that it had full administrative control in the Far North.[87]

R. M. Anderson wrote a memo to W. W. Cory telling of a chance meeting with MacMillan at Sydney, Nova Scotia, on 4 September 1925. On this occasion, MacMillan spoke again of the incident earlier that year, which seemed to worry him, and gave Anderson essentially the same explanation he had given Bovey. Referring to Byrd's statement about the permit, Anderson's memo said that "the statement was 'diplomacy' on Byrd's part, but MacMillan would call it a lie which had put MacMillan in the wrong light with the Canadian authorities." Anderson added that MacMillan "argues that it is foolish of the United States officials to protest Canadian jurisdiction in the Arctic, since by occupation Canada has so firmly established her title, and said he would argue the matter in Washington every chance he had."[88] Anderson's memo seems to have aroused less interest in Ottawa than Bovey's, however, probably because by this time MacMillan was going through the required formalities.[89]

MacMillan went on a summer cruise to Labrador, Baffin Island, and Greenland in 1926, and according to records, he obtained an explorer's permit from the Canadian government for that year.[90] This requirement had been formalized by an ordinance passed by the Northwest Territories Council on 23 June 1926, which specified that no one should enter the Northwest Territories for scientific or exploratory purposes without obtaining a licence and that the activities carried on should be scientific or exploratory only (not commercial or political).[91] MacMillan's longer expedition to the same region in 1927–28, during which he wintered on the Labrador coast, prompted some anxious comments by Canadian newspapermen, one of which Vincent Massey at the Canadian Legation in Washington referred to Skelton.[92] When Skelton asked W. W. Cory whether MacMillan had complied satisfactorily with all requirements for explorers entering Canadian Arctic territory,[93] he received assurance that MacMillan had applied for, and been granted, permits for his crew and himself to carry on exploratory and scientific work in both 1927 and 1928.[94]

Complications arose again over MacMillan's summer cruise in 1929, at first because of an unfounded suspicion that he was trying to enter Canadian Arctic territory without permission,[95] and later over reports that the expedition had killed large numbers of eider ducks in Labrador and Baffin Island.[96] Vincent Massey observed, in a note to Secretary of State Henry L. Stimson, that this admission had been made by S. C. Palmer, a member of the expedition,[97] and that eider ducks were protected by both Canada and the United States under a treaty of 16 August 1916.[98] After bringing the matter to the attention of MacMillan, the Department of State returned an answer incorporating his statement that the expedition had killed "not less than five and not more than ten eider ducks" and that this had happened only because their ship had been locked in an ice pack and they had not had any fresh meat for several weeks. MacMillan explained:

> I am indeed sorry if our act of securing this one meal of eider ducks was resented by the Canadian Government.... However, I am very happy to assure Mr. Massey and the Canadian Government that no member of my future expeditions, if I can prevent it, will ever kill animal or bird outside of the law unless for the actual preservation of life, or for scientific purposes, and then only when permits have been granted.[99]

For MacMillan's 1931 expedition, the American minister in Ottawa requested permission for MacMillan and his pilot to fly over Labrador on their way to Greenland, Iceland, and England.[100] John T. Crowell, Jr., master of the *Bowdoin*, submitted a detailed application to the RCMP at Port Burwell for permission to enter the Northern Territories.[101] At the end of his cruise, Crowell sent a report of the expedition's activities in Baffin Island and adjacent waters to the Department of the Interior in Ottawa.[102]

On 4 May 1934, some time before MacMillan was scheduled to sail on his planned expedition to Labrador and Baffin Island, the Northwest Territories Council passed a resolution that henceforth all scientific expeditions to the Canadian Arctic, other than British, should be required to take with them a member of the RCMP.[103] This resolution was watered down, either by the council or by Cabinet, so that the person accompanying the expedition simply had to be a representative of the Canadian government. In a letter of 17 May, Minister of the Interior Thomas Gerow Murphy remarked to Minister of Justice Hugh Guthrie that the representative might be "a scientist of good judgment, otherwise a Royal Canadian Mounted Policeman should act."[104] There was some confusion and delay over MacMillan's application for permits for his expedition when a letter he wrote was sent by mistake to Fort Smith, NWT, instead of Ottawa,[105] but as soon as this had been discovered, the Canadian authorities were willing to grant him the permits, especially since he indicated his complete willingness to observe Canadian regulations. In the letter that went astray, MacMillan wrote: "I am very happy to carry with me on the *Bowdoin* a representative of the Canadian Government.... I heartily approve of the action of the Council."[106] Later, he added in another letter that "I have always endeavored to respect the laws of the Canadian Government whenever I entered the waters of the Northwest Territories."[107]

In the same year, the Canadian authorities also had Captain Bob Bartlett on the carpet. Bartlett, a Newfoundlander who had become an American citizen, had already conducted several expeditions in the Canadian Arctic and had formerly complied with Canadian regulations.[108] In 1933, however, he took his ship *Effie M. Morrissey* on an extensive expedition in the Hudson Bay region without getting permits or observing customs formalities, and then he failed to answer wireless signals or to stop when communicated with. Bartlett went to Ottawa and appeared before a special session of the Northwest Territories Council on 23 January

1934, where his explanations were accepted and he was granted, retroactively, permits for 1933.[109] It was later decided to give him permits for 1934 on condition that he, like MacMillan, should be accompanied by a representative of the Canadian government.[110]

In summary, it would appear that during the 1920s and early 1930s the Canadian government gradually succeeded in imposing its wishes and its regulations upon American explorers who wanted to conduct their operations on and among the Canadian Arctic islands. There do not seem to have been any provocative or embarrassing incidents in the later 1930s. This was a period of lessened activity in Arctic exploration and, apart from a select few including MacMillan and Bartlett, American explorers were not active in the region. So far as the American government was concerned, however, it seemed obvious that it had declined to recognize in expressed terms all that Canada claimed.[111] To this extent, Canadian worries were understandable. Otherwise, judging by the events summarized here, the Canadian attitude was excessively suspicious and exacting. The outbreak of the Second World War in 1939 soon put Canadian-American relations respecting the North, and accompanying problems, on a completely different footing.

15

The Eastern Arctic Patrol, the Royal Canadian Mounted Police, and Other Government Activities, 1922–39

The background of the institution of an annual patrol voyage in the eastern Arctic after the First World War has already been provided in chapter 10. To recapitulate briefly, it involved a combination of circumstances and events which developed after the war, including Vilhjalmur Stefansson's campaign for more activity in the North; the unwillingness of Knud Rasmussen to acknowledge Canadian authority in Ellesmere Island and the Danish government's apparent support of his stand; the fear of Danish, American, and Norwegian infiltrations and claims in the Arctic islands; information emerging from the Reindeer-Muskox Commission's investigation and report; and a growing feeling in official circles that it had become absolutely essential to take steps to establish Canada's authority and sovereignty in these outlying territories. In this atmosphere of stress and worry, consideration was at first given to a plan that involved sending an emergency expedition to the northern islands in the autumn of 1920.

This plan was soon abandoned as impractical, and subsequent efforts concentrated on preparing an expedition for the summer of 1921. John Davidson Craig of the Dominion Lands Surveys and the International Boundary Commission was given overall command of the planning and of the expedition itself. Captain H. C. Pickels of Mahone Bay, Nova Scotia, was appointed ship's captain; the CGS *Arctic*, which for several years had been in the lightship service in the lower St. Lawrence River, was transferred from the Department of Marine and Fisheries to the Department of the Interior, and negotiations were carried on with Vilhjalmur Stefansson, who wanted to command the expedition. Doubts and disagreements in official circles about Stefansson and his role, coupled with the entry of English explorer Sir Ernest Shackleton as a rival to Stefansson, led the Canadian government to drop its plans for a 1921 expedition in May of that year. The work of repairing and outfitting the *Arctic* continued at a slower pace, but Captain Pickels, who had immediate charge of this work, died on 1 October 1921, and the ship was left in winter quarters at Quebec until June 1922. This was approximately the situation when the Northwest Territories and Yukon Branch of the Department of the Interior received instructions on 9 June 1922 to prepare as quickly as possible for an Arctic voyage, which Ottawa officials had decided upon for that summer.

FIGURE 15-1: CGS *ARCTIC* NEAR PORT BURWELL, QUEBEC. *GEORGE R. LANCEFIELD / LIBRARY AND ARCHIVES CANADA / PA-096482.*

The Eastern Arctic Patrol (1922)

The lateness of the decision to send out the expedition, and the shortness of the navigation season in northern waters, made it necessary to complete preparations in a hurry. John Craig documented the bustle and confusion that occurred between 9 June and the date of sailing.[1] Captain Joseph-Elzéar Bernier, who had already offered his services,[2] was appointed in June to succeed Captain Pickels as ship's captain, thus reuniting this seventy-year-old veteran and the ship he had already commanded on four northern expeditions. A total of 950 tons of cargo were loaded in great haste, including 500 tons of coal for the ship and 150 for the police posts that were to be built, 225 tons of lumber for the police buildings, and 75 tons of food and other supplies. The expedition totalled forty-three men, including Craig, Bernier, and the crew of five officers and twenty men; the Royal Canadian Mounted Police (RCMP) detachment of Inspector C. E. Wilcox and nine others; and six additional members with scientific, technical, and administrative responsibilities. The last group comprised the expedition's medical officer Dr. Leslie D. Livingstone, the Air Board's representative Major Robert A. Logan, the surveyor and meteorologist L. O. Brown, the assistant surveyor T. P. Reilly, the cinematographer G. H. Valiquette, and the commanding officer's secretary W. H. Grant. Plans to send a larger and more varied group of scientists were abandoned, mainly because they would have little time ashore to do their work.

After five weeks of "feverish activity," all was ready aboard the *Arctic* on the evening of 17 July, "the engines turned over under their own steam for the first time in several years,"[3] and the expedition sailed early the next morning. Some minor engine problems caused short delays, but after these were overcome, the ship passed through the Strait of Belle Isle and northwards along the Greenland coast without much difficulty. It reached Bylot Island on 15 August, but ice prevented landing at Pond Inlet as anticipated to establish a police post there, so the expedition proceeded north to Ellesmere Island. Sverdrup's Fram Fiord on the south coast had been tentatively selected as the site of the police post on Ellesmere, but the approaches were still completely blocked by ice, and a small harbour close to King Edward VII Point at the extreme southeastern tip of the island was chosen instead. Eight days of "feverish haste and almost unceasing work" followed at Craig Harbour, as the place was christened, unloading two years' equipment and supplies for the police and getting their buildings sufficiently advanced so that they could safely be left behind. Plane table and photographic surveys were made of the area; observations for latitude, longitude, and azimuth were taken; and a bronze tablet marked "Canada, N.W.T. 1" was set in solid rock, "signifying the first tablet set in Franklin District under the direction of the North West Territories Branch" of the Department of the Interior. Major Logan succeeded in finding a suitable site for an air landing strip on the opposite side of the valley. With freeze-up already starting, the *Arctic* departed on 29 August, leaving behind Inspector Wilcox, six of the RCMP constables, and a family of Pond Inlet Inuit who had agreed to accompany the Mounties and stay with them for one year.

On the way south, the expedition stopped to examine Dundas Harbour, near Cape Warrender and the southeastern extremity of Devon Island, to ascertain its suitability as the site for another police post in the future. The harbour was large and almost completely landlocked, with a sheltered spot suitable for a post at one side, not far from a good anchorage. Returning to Pond Inlet on 6 September, the men discovered that the harbour was still blocked by ice; however, the ship got close enough to land the supplies and equipment for the second RCMP post that the expedition established. The ship made contact with Staff Sergeant Alfred Herbert Joy of the RCMP, who had come to Pond Inlet in September 1921 to investigate the murder of a white trader named Robert Janes, the second officer on Bernier's 1910–11 expedition. Joy, who had been living at the recently established Hudson's Bay Company (HBC) post, was to be left in charge of the new RCMP post with the three remaining members of the RCMP (a corporal and two constables) assigned to serve with him.[4] As at Craig Harbour, a bronze tablet, No. 2, was set in a large boulder as a survey marker, but a shortage of time meant that only preliminary survey work was accomplished. As the HBC was already located here and there were local Inuit to provide any needed help, it was not considered necessary to stay any longer than was required to complete unloading, and the *Arctic* left on 7 September. It made a call at Godhavn, Greenland, on the way home,

FIGURE 15-2: INUIT WITH MEMBERS OF THE CGS *ARCTIC* EXPEDITION, 1922. *WILLIAM H. GRANT / LIBRARY AND ARCHIVES CANADA / E002282921.*

permission to land having been obtained previously by Inspector Wilcox.[5] The Canadians showed no inclination to try to ignore or circumvent formalities and regulations in Greenland, as they suspected the Danes themselves had done in Ellesmere. After an uneventful trip south, the *Arctic* arrived back at Quebec on 2 October.

The main accomplishment of the expedition was the establishment of Craig Harbour and Pond Inlet, each of which was to serve triple duty as RCMP post, post office, and customs house. Craig summarized this and the other achievements of the expedition in his published report.[6] He observed that the Janes murder case, the presence of traders, and the entry almost every season of expeditions from outside warranted the maintenance of RCMP posts, and he already envisaged the establishment of several others. In a brief report, Major Logan gave details about the potential landing fields he had found at Craig Harbour and Pond Inlet, as well as general flying conditions in the Arctic. He advised that use of airplanes in the region should be feasible during most of the year (employing wheels in summer and skis in winter) and that conditions were also favourable for other work connected with flying, such as wireless and photography. He also recommended that Canada should establish an experimental air station at some central point in the archipelago and maintain it throughout the year as an observation post.[7]

The Eastern Arctic Patrol (1923)

The Canadian government made plans to send two ships on the 1923 patrol: *Arctic* and another vessel which was to be obtained in England and renamed *Franklin*. Captain Bernier went to England to take over the command of the new vessel, leaving L. D. Morin as captain of *Arctic*, but delays in finishing repairs to *Franklin* nullified the plan. Thus, *Arctic* went north unaccompanied in 1923, again with

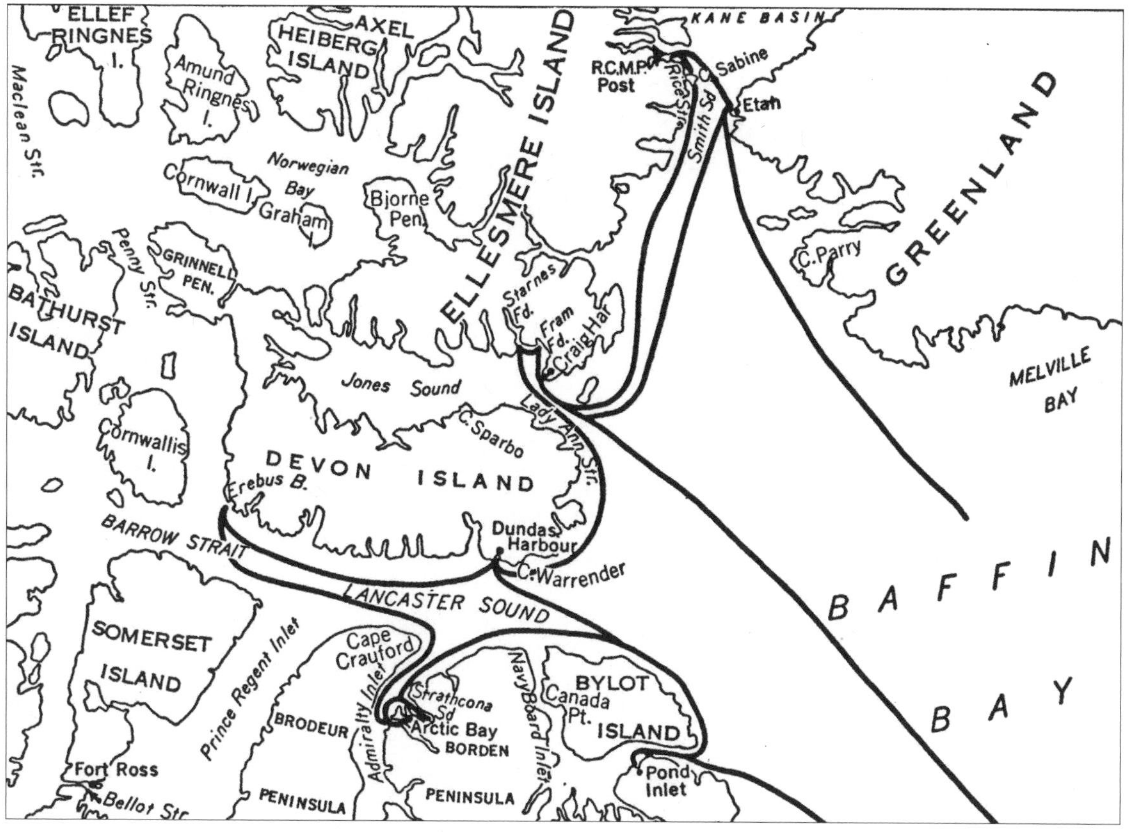

Figure 15-3: Eastern Arctic Patrols, 1922–24. Andrew Taylor, *Geographical Discovery and Exploration in the Queen Elizabeth Islands* (Ottawa: Department of Mines and Technical Surveys, 1964), 125. *By permission of Natural Resources Canada.*

Bernier as ship's captain and J. D. Craig as expedition commander. The expedition's principal purpose was to establish one or two new RCMP posts, but there was some uncertainty as to where these should be. Officials had decided that one should be established at or near Cape Sabine in the southern part of Kane Basin if weather and ice conditions permitted. The sovereignty aspect was uppermost in the selection of this site, and also in some officials' preference for Dundas Harbour as the site for the second post in Cumberland Sound, to maintain surveillance over Inuit and traders there.[8]

Arctic departed from Quebec on 9 July. Besides Craig and his personal secretary, Bernier and the ship's officers and crew, and the RCMP relief force of two constables, *Arctic* carried a considerably larger group of scientific, technical, and other officials than the year before. These included the medical officer Dr. Livingstone, the surveyor Frank D. Henderson, the naturalist J. Dewey Soper from the Victoria Memorial Museum, a hydrographer from the Department of Marine and Fisheries, the engineer Major Lachlin Taylor Burwash from the Northwest Territories and Yukon Branch, the wireless operator William George Earl, and a cinematographer. There was also a five-man court, which was to try the Inuit accused of murdering the trader Janes and which comprised the stipendiary magistrate Louis-Alfred-Adhémar Rivet, prosecuting attorney Adrien Falardeau, attorney for the defence Leopold Tellier, registrar François Biron, and interpreter William (Sivutiksaq) Duval.[9] The ship called at Godhavn to pick up some dogs and kamiks (native boots), which had been ordered the year before for the RCMP serving in the North. As soon as Craig landed, he was approached by an officer of the Royal Danish Navy inspection ship *Islands Falk* with a "polite but firm request" for papers showing the right to land in Greenland. This requirement had been foreseen and provided for, and the documents presented "satisfied the officer fully."[10]

The ship reached Craig Harbour on 5 August, and all RCMP and Inuit there came aboard to help set up the new post at Cape Sabine. MacMillan and his expedition were found at Etah, and through him arrangements were made with the two Inuit families remaining at Etah who agreed to accompany the Canadian police and stay with them. Thick ice made it impossible to get to Cape Sabine, however, so the police, Inuit, and supplies that had been destined for the projected new post were all landed at Craig Harbour. During the short stay there, the new "post office" was officially opened, and wireless operator Earl was able to set up equipment and receive messages broadcast in code from Europe. A short exploratory trip was made along the south coast of Ellesmere, a call was made at Dundas Harbour where Inspector Wilcox selected a site for a future police post, and a memorial ceremony was performed on Beechey Island at the Franklin cenotaph. At Pond Inlet, a formal trial was conducted of the three Inuit charged with the 1920 murder of Janes. One Inuk was found guilty of manslaughter and sentenced to ten years' imprisonment in Stony Mountain Penitentiary, the second was found guilty but with clemency recommended and sentenced to two years' close confinement at Pond Inlet, and the third was found not guilty and set free.[11]

The expedition left Pond Inlet on 3 September and made the last major stop at Pangnirtung in Cumberland Sound, where officials finally decided to establish the new RCMP post. All hands helped with the construction, and by the time the expedition departed on 22 September, the buildings for the RCMP detachment under Inspector Wilcox, who was to spend the winter there, were almost completed. By 4 October, *Arctic* was back at Quebec. Subsidiary results of the expedition were Henderson's completion of surveys for the police posts at Craig Harbour, Dundas Harbour, Pond Inlet, and Pangnirtung, and for HBC posts at Cape Strathcona, Pond Inlet, and Pangnirtung; other results were Dr. Livingstone's medical examinations of Inuit, especially at Pond Inlet and Pangnirtung.[12]

The Eastern Arctic Patrol (1924)

For 1924, plans were again made to send two ships to the north, but once again these plans had to be cancelled and only *Arctic* was used. Craig was unable to go, so the command fell to Frank Henderson, who had been surveyor on the 1923 patrol. Bernier was the ship's captain once again, and the ship's company included the officers and crew, scientific and technical personnel, and six RCMP who were to relieve others and man a new post. One of the technicians was Richard Sterling Finnie, son of the director of the Northwest Territories and Yukon Branch, who served as assistant wireless operator. Extra quantities of food, supplies, and building materials caused the ship to be

FIGURE 15-4: INSPECTOR C. E. WILCOX, RCMP, AND INUIT, KEKERTEN ISLAND, NWT, 1924. *L.T. BURWASH / LIBRARY AND ARCHIVES CANADA / E002344291.*

overloaded, and a fatal accident was narrowly avoided in a storm north of the Strait of Belle Isle when it was found necessary to jettison the deck load of coal and lumber.

Calls were made at Blacklead Island and then at Pangnirtung, where the naturalist J. D. Soper left the expedition to carry on a one-year study of plant and animal life around Cumberland Gulf. After a stop at Godhavn, *Arctic* proceeded to Pond Inlet and then to Craig Harbour, where it was discovered that the main building erected in 1922 had burned down during the winter. All personnel were removed from Craig Harbour and taken to Fram Havn near Cape Sabine, where a new police post was to be established. The Inuit families who had come with the expedition to assist and remain with the police refused to stay, however, so only a supply post (christened Kane Basin) was erected, and all police and Inuit intended for the new post were taken back and left at Craig Harbour. (The police at Craig Harbour planned to make a patrol to the Kane Basin supply post and occupy it for part of the year.) On the return trip, the ship made a ten-day stop from 17 to 26 August at Dundas Harbour to construct buildings for the new post "Dundas," which was formally opened just before *Arctic* departed. Three RCMP members were left to occupy it. Other stops were made at Pond Inlet (28 August), Clyde (6 September), and Home Bay (7 September), after which *Arctic* proceeded without interruption to Quebec, arriving on 24 September.[13]

The Eastern Arctic Patrol (1925)

The expedition of 1925 was under the command of George Patton MacKenzie, who had been Gold Commissioner of the Yukon before his appointment. Again the ship's company included scientific and technical personnel and several RCMP members who were going north as replacements, this having become a regular feature of the cruise and one continued thereafter. Also on board the *Arctic* was the Inuk who had been sentenced in 1923 to a prison term in Stony Mountain Penitentiary and who, because of ill health, was now being returned on parole to his home at Pond Inlet. (He died in December 1925.)

As in 1924, the ship was heavily loaded and got into difficulties in the stormy Atlantic waters north of the Strait of Belle Isle. Heavy ice frustrated an attempt to call at Pangnirtung, and twenty days were lost first trying to get through it and then trying to escape from it. After a short stop at Godhavn, *Arctic* proceeded to Etah, where it made contact with *Bowdoin* and *Peary* of MacMillan's Arctic expedition (see chapter 14). The meeting was cordial, but MacMillan's activities in the Arctic Archipelago had been a matter of concern to the Canadian government for some time, and MacKenzie took up with the American leaders the question of Lieutenant Commander Byrd's airplane flights over Ellesmere Island and whether permits had been obtained for such flights. Byrd passed on to Mackenzie the alleged statement by MacMillan that permits had been secured, but it was later established that they had not.[14] The next stop was the Kane Basin subpost, where the expedition found a record saying that Corporal T. R. Michelson had visited the post on 24 April 1925 while on patrol from Craig Harbour. Although the expedition had intended to establish a post still farther north at Bache Peninsula, the lateness of the season, shortage of coal, and the leaky condition of *Arctic* compelled it to abandon the idea. After restocking the storehouse at Kane Basin and leaving other supplies at nearby Fram Havn, the expedition proceeded south to Craig Harbour. Here the work of unloading supplies was completed as quickly as possible, Staff Sergeant Joy was left in charge, the two Inuit families obtained at Etah for the planned Bache Peninsula post remained with the RCMP, and the Inuit families already at Craig Harbour were taken aboard to be transferred to Dundas Harbour. The ship made hasty calls at Dundas Harbour, Pond Inlet, Albert Harbour, and Pangnirtung, and the expedition arrived back at Quebec somewhat later than usual on 10 October.[15]

This was the last cruise of the famous old *Arctic*, which became the property of ship breakers and was left to become a hulk.[16] It was also Captain Bernier's last voyage to the northern islands.[17]

The Eastern Arctic Patrol (1926)

The Canadian government now decided that a larger and faster ship than the *Arctic* was necessary to handle the increasing cargoes and growing responsibilities of the annual summer patrol. For the 1926 voyage, the government chartered the SS *Beothic*, a 2,700-ton, 10-knot steel ship owned by the Job's Sealfishery Company of St. John's, Newfoundland. Under the terms of the charter, the owners provided the ship's captain, Enoch Falk, and the officers and crew (with the exception of Captain L. D. Morin, who had formerly been first officer on the *Arctic* and was taken as pilot because of his knowledge of northern waters). George Mackenzie was again the officer in charge, and the ship's company totalled forty-two, including the expedition's physician Dr. Livingstone, Dr. Lud Weeks and Dr. Maurice Fall Haycock of the Geological Survey, and Corporal H. P. Friel and seven constables of the RCMP.

Leaving North Sydney, Nova Scotia, on 15 July, the expedition called in turn at Godhavn, Pond Inlet, Dundas, Craig Harbour, and Etah.

FIGURE 15-5: INUIT ON SS *BEOTHIC* AT POND INLET (MITTIMATALIK/TUNUNIQ), 1926. *RICHARD S. FINNIE / LIBRARY AND ARCHIVES CANADA / PA-207912.*

At Fram Havn, it picked up the goods left the year before and, after the expedition had succeeded in crossing Buchanan Bay, the expedition members established an RCMP post at Bache Peninsula in accordance with the plan that had to be abandoned in 1925. Staff Sergeant Joy was left in charge of the new post, with two constables and three Inuit families. On the return voyage, *Beothic* made calls in succession at Etah, Dundas, Arctic Bay, Pond Inlet, Clyde River, and Pangnirtung. Weeks and Haycock were left at Pangnirtung to carry on geological investigations, and Livingstone also remained there to investigate the health and living conditions of local Inuit. Thanks largely to radio operator S. J. Mead, the ship was in daily contact with Ottawa throughout the voyage. *Beothic* arrived back at North Sydney on 29 August.[18]

The Eastern Arctic Patrol (1927)

The expedition left North Sydney in *Beothic* on 16 July 1927, again with MacKenzie in charge. Among the ship's company were Dr. Frederick Banting of the University of Toronto, the artist A. Y. Jackson, and Inspector C. E. Wilcox and seven other RCMP members. Calls were made in succession at Godhavn, Dundas Harbour, Craig Harbour, Etah, Fram Havn, Bache Peninsula, Craig Harbour, Dundas Harbour, Beechey Island, Port Leopold, Arctic Bay, Pond Inlet, River Clyde, Pangnirtung, Lake Harbour, Wakeham Bay, and Port Burwell, and *Beothic* arrived back at North Sydney on 5 September. Drs. Weeks, Haycock, and Livingstone, who had been left at Pangnirtung the year before, all returned with the expedition, while Inspector Wilcox remained at Pond Inlet. The patrol, which was routine in most respects, was stated in the annual report of the Department of the Interior to have "fully accomplished" its purposes.[19] It did not, however, succeed in getting farther west than Beechey Island and Port Leopold in the planned reconnaissance west of Lancaster Sound.

The Eastern Arctic Patrol (1928)

Again *Beothic* was used for the patrol, its company totalling forty-eight, including MacKenzie in command, thirty-four officers and crew under Captain Falk, medical officer Dr. Livingstone, moving picture operator and commander's secretary R. S. Finnie, assistant secretary R. T. Bowman, and Inspector Joy and eight other RCMP members. Dr. Rudolph Martin Anderson, Chief of the Biological Division, Department of Mines, also accompanied the expedition. Leaving North Sydney on 19 July, *Beothic* proceeded in turn to Godhavn, Pond Inlet, Dundas Harbour, Fram Havn, the Greenland settlement of Nerke, Craig Harbour, Cape Sparbo, Dundas Harbour, Beechey Island, Pond Inlet, River Clyde, Pangnirtung, Lake Harbour, Port Burwell, and then back to North Sydney, arriving on 2 September. The Greenland Inuit who had been with the RCMP at Dundas Harbour were left at Nerke; a supply base was established at Beechey Island for Inspector Joy, who was making his headquarters for the coming year at Dundas Harbour and expected to go on a long patrol westwards; and a residence was built at Pangnirtung for Dr. Livingstone, who remained to establish his headquarters there.[20]

The Eastern Arctic Patrol (1929)

Beothic departed from North Sydney on 20 July 1929, under the command of G. P. Mackenzie. The ship's company of forty-four included thirty-six officers and crew, with Captain Falk as a master and Captain L. D. Morin as ice pilot, medical officer Dr. Hugh Stuart, ornithologist Percy Algernon Taverner, secretary R. S. Finnie, and four RCMP constables. Calls were made at Godhavn, Dundas Harbour, Cape Sparbo, Craig Harbour, Fram Havn, Etah, the Nerke settlement, Dundas Harbour again, Pond Inlet, River Clyde, Pangnirtung, Lake Harbour, Chesterfield Inlet, Coats Island, Resolution Island, and Port Burwell, in that order, before returning to North Sydney, the home port being reached on 3 September. At Fram Havn, the expedition met the Backe Peninsula detachment and also Inspector Joy, who had recently completed a long patrol from Dundas Harbour to Melville Island and back to Bache Peninsula. The German scientist Dr. Hans Krüger and his assistant Åge Rose Bjare, who were on their way to northwestern Greenland, were picked up at Godhavn and taken to the Nerke settlement. Dr. Stuart was left at Pangnirtung to replace Dr. Livingstone as health officer. Contact was made with SS *Armore* and SS *Sambro* at Resolution Island, where the Marine Department was setting up a direction finding station.[21]

The Eastern Arctic Patrol (1930)

The patrol was again carried out by *Beothic* under MacKenzie's command. The ship's company totalled fifty-six, including thirty-five officers and crew members and twenty-one other personnel. Among the latter were the ship's doctor D. S. Bruce, the Canadian artists Lawren Harris and A. Y. Jackson, the Danish scientist Dr. Morten Porsild and his little granddaughter, and three American scientists, as well as ten constables and Inspector Joy of the RCMP. The itinerary included Godhavn, Alexander Haven and Cape Rutherford near Bache Peninsula, Dundas Harbour, Cornwallis Island, Bathurst Island, Pond Inlet, River Clyde, Pangnirtung, Lake Harbour, Chesterfield Inlet, Coats Island, and Port Burwell. The expedition was later than usual this year, departing from North Sydney on 31 July and returning on 27 September. Heavy ice conditions in Kane Basin made it necessary to land the Bache Peninsula supplies at Cape Rutherford rather than at the police post, and similar conditions in Viscount Melville Sound compelled abandonment of a plan to reach Melville Island. Dr. Stuart was picked up at Pond Inlet, having made a patrol of this point from Pangnirtung the previous winter, and taken back to his post; Dr. Bruce replaced Dr. Livingstone as medical officer at Chesterfield Inlet; and Dr. Livingstone returned to North Sydney with the ship. Building materials and equipment were taken to Pangnirtung for the construction of a hospital there.[22]

The Eastern Arctic Patrol (1931)

Under a reorganization of the Department of the Interior, arising out of the transfer of natural resources to the Prairie provinces in 1930, the administration of the Northwest Territories and Yukon (including the Eastern Arctic Patrol) became the responsibility of the Dominion Lands Administration. For the patrol in 1931, *Beothic* was chartered as usual, with Captain Falk serving as master as he had done on previous voyages of this ship, but with L. T. Burwash as expedition commander. Besides the usual complement of ship's officers, crew, and RCMP replacements, *Beothic* carried the medical officer Dr. Livingstone, the American physician and medical researcher Dr. Peter Heinbecker, and two representatives of Canadian newspapers. Leaving North Sydney on 30 July, the expedition called in turn at Godhavn, Fram Havn, Bache Peninsula, Fram Havn, Robertson Bay and Thule (Greenland), Craig Harbour, Cape Sparbo, Dundas Harbour, Pond Inlet, Dundas Harbour, Pond Inlet, River Clyde, Pangnirtung, Cape Hopes Advance, Lake Harbour, Chesterfield Inlet, and Port Burwell, and it was back at North Sydney by 17 September. At Fram Havn, the expedition members learned that Krüger and Bjare, who had left Bache Peninsula on their expedition westwards about seventeen months earlier, had not been heard from. Burwash thus cancelled a projected move of the Bache Peninsula detachment to Craig Harbour and arranged search expeditions and other emergency measures. As the itinerary indicates, short additional trips were made for various unscheduled purposes. At Pangnirtung, where the new hospital had just been completed, Dr. Livingstone replaced Dr. Stuart, who went back south with the ship. *Beothic* rendezvoused with CGS *N. B. McLean* east of Nottingham Island and transferred some passengers and mail.[23]

The Eastern Arctic Patrol (1932)

Several important changes were instituted for the patrol of 1932. To save money, the government entered into a contract with the HBC for joint use of SS *Ungava*, which would not only carry out its annual supply voyage to company posts but would carry the Eastern Arctic Patrol as well.[24] The HBC chartered *Ungava*, the 2,000-ton sister ship of the *Beothic*, from Job's Sealfishery Company. The new officer in charge of the expedition was Major David Livingstone McKeand, Secretary of the Northwest Territories Council of the Department of the Interior, who received his appointment and commission on 12 May 1932. Other orders in council appointed him a Justice of the Peace in and for the Northwest Territories and authorized him to receive applications during the expedition for aliens wishing to be naturalized.[25]

The ship's company of sixty-three included Captain Thomas Farrar Smellie and the crew of thirty-five, Inspector T. V. Sandys-Wunsch and twelve other RCMP members, medical officer Dr. J. S. Douglas, veterinarian Dr. J. R. West, secretary and historian Garnet A. Woonton, and several others including two HBC officials. The route followed was longer than in earlier years, mainly because of the need to call at HBC posts in Hudson Bay. Leaving Montreal on 9 July, the *Ungava* proceeded in turn to Cartwright, Port Burwell, Lake Harbour, Wakeham Bay, Sugluk West, Wolstenholme, Cape Smith, Port Harrison, Southampton Island, Wolstenholme, Dorset, Lake Harbour, Port Burwell, Pangnirtung, River Clyde, Pond Inlet, Kane Basin, Craig Harbour, Dundas Harbour, Pond Inlet, Godhavn, and Port Burwell, ending the cruise at St. John's, Newfoundland, on 16 September. As the itinerary shows, the ship visited some posts a second and even a third time. Bad ice conditions defeated an attempt to call at Bache Peninsula, the only post not reached. This was an unfortunate failure, given the government's intention to transfer the personnel at this post to Craig Harbour. At Godhavn, the expedition learned that a Greenland party had visited Bache Peninsula in early spring and found the police in good health. Neither the police nor the Greenlanders had been able to find any trace of Krüger, Bjare, or Akqioq (the Polar Inuk who joined them on the expedition), and officials now concluded that there was little possibility of their safe return.[26]

The Eastern Arctic Patrol (1933)

For the year 1933, further significant changes were made in the patrol, which was steadily becoming larger because of the increasing scope of the responsibilities assumed. The Canadian government again made a contract with the HBC for joint use of the ship that the company was using for its own patrol, in this case SS *Nascopie*, a vessel specially designed for use in Arctic waters (and generally superior to *Ungava*). The larger party aboard the ship reflected the increasing scale of the work undertaken and included, besides the ship's captain and crew, the commanding officer D. L. McKeand, assistant officer in charge W. C. Bethune, medical officer Dr. Jon Bildfell, geologist Dr. Henry C. Gunning, botanist Dr. Oscar Malte, meteorologist William Edgar Knowles Middleton, parasitologist Dr. Ivan W. Parnell, secretary and historian A. P. Norton, and Inspector T. V. Sandys-Wunsch and four other RCMP members. The *Nascopie* sailed from Montreal on 8 July and returned to St. John's, Newfoundland, on 27 September; in between these dates, the itinerary included successive calls at Cartwright, Port Burwell, Lake Harbour, Wakeham Bay, Sugluk, Wolstenholme, Cape Smith, Port Harrison, Charlton Island, Churchill, Southampton Island, Wolstenholme, Cape Dorset, Lake Harbour, Port Burwell, Dundas Harbour, Craig Harbour, Robertson Bay, Pond Inlet, River Clyde, Pangnirtung, Port Burwell, and Cartwright.

During the expedition, as much scientific work as time permitted was carried on, although botanical research was unfortunately terminated at Charlton Island by the sudden illness and subsequent death of Dr. Malte. During the second call at Wolstenholme, a preliminary hearing was held in connection with the murder of an Inuk at Mansel Island the preceding winter. The police temporarily closed posts at Bache Peninsula and Dundas Harbour and reopened the post at Craig Harbour (which had been closed). A patrol party from Bache

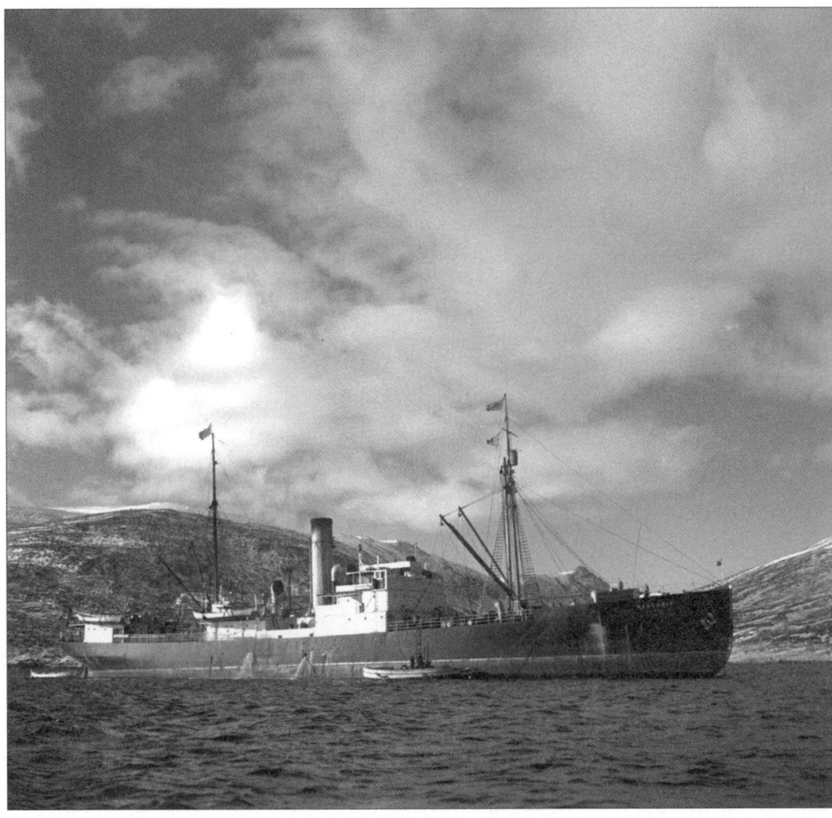

FIGURE 15-6: THE SS *NASCOPIE* ANCHORED IN PANGNIRTUNG FIORD. *GEORGE HUNTER/ NATIONAL FILM BOARD OF CANADA /LIBRARY AND ARCHIVES CANADA / E010692597.*

Peninsula found a message left by Krüger in a cairn on the northern coast of Axel Heiberg Island but was unable to find any further trace of him. The Inuit who had aided the police in their search were returned to Robertson Bay. Dr. Bildfell was left at Pangnirtung to replace Dr. Livingstone, who returned to Ottawa with the expedition.[27]

The Eastern Arctic Patrol (1934)

The patrol of 1934 again used *Nascopie*, and again D. L. McKeand was officer in charge, with T. F. Smellie as ship's captain. Among the large ship's company were medical officer Dr. A. G. MacKinnon, anthropologist Douglas Leechman, veterinarian Dr. Seymour Hadwen, magnetician R. Glenn Madill, ornithologist E.F.G. White, secretary and postal representative F. Gilbert, and Superintendent T. H. Irvine and eight other RCMP members. Starting from Montreal on 7 July and returning to Halifax on 30 September, *Nascopie* made successive calls at Cartwright, Port Burwell, Lake Harbour, Wakeham Bay, Wolstenholme, Cape Smith, Port Harrison, Charlton Island, Churchill, Coral Harbour (Southampton Island), Wolstenholme, Cape Dorset, Lake Harbour, Port Burwell, Pangnirtung, River Clyde, Pond Inlet, Dundas Harbour, Craig Harbour, Pond Inlet, Port Burwell, and Cartwright.

At Port Burwell on the outward trip, contact was made with D. B. MacMillan's expedition (see chapter 14), which was awaiting the arrival of Sergeant Frederick Anderton of the RCMP, who had been specially detailed as the Canadian government representative with the expedition while it was in Canadian waters. At Churchill, the supplies for Chesterfield were transferred to the motor ship *Fort Severn*, and Dr. Livingstone took passage on the same ship to resume his duties as medical officer at this port. A new HBC trading post, the most northerly in Canada, was opened at Dundas Harbour. At Pangnirtung, Dr. MacKinnon replaced Dr. Bildfell, who returned south with the ship.[28]

The Eastern Arctic Patrol (1935)

The patrol of 1935 sailed from Montreal on 13 July in *Nascopie*, again with Major McKeand in command, and returned to Halifax on 28 September. Among the ship's company were medical doctors A. L. Richard, Charles Birchard, and Israel Mordecai Rabinowitch; anthropologist Douglas Leechman; physiographer David A. Nichols; geodetic surveyor Charles Herman "Marsh" Ney; entomologist W. J. Brown; historian and observer Hon. William George Martin; secretary and postal representative W. M. MacLean; naval commander C. T. Beard of the Department of National Defence; and Superintendent T. V. Sandys-Wunsch and twelve other RCMP members. The itinerary included calls, in succession, at Cartwright, Port Burwell, Lake Harbour, Wakeham Bay, Sugluk West, Wolstenholme, Cape Smith, Port Harrison, Churchill, Chesterfield, Southampton Island, Wolstenholme, Cape Dorset, Lake Harbour, Port Burwell, Craig Harbour, Dundas Harbour, Pond Inlet, River Clyde, Pangnirtung, and Port Burwell.

As much scientific and technical work was carried on as circumstances permitted. The three medical doctors investigated problems concerning the health of Inuit. Leechman left the ship on the outward call at Port Burwell and excavated some Inuit ruins on the Button Islands. Ney's function with the expedition was to establish geodetic astronomical stations at the various points of call, and he also made precise latitude and longitude determinations at most of the stops. Commander Beard examined and collected information on Canada's northern harbours. The RCMP closed their detachment at Port Burwell, planning to have a constable in charge there for the summer months only, and opened a new detachment at Port Harrison on the east coast of Hudson Bay.[29]

The Eastern Arctic Patrol (1936)

The patrol of 1936 was made in *Nascopie*, again with Major McKeand in command. The government party comprised medical officer Dr. N. A. MacArthur, anthropologist Douglas Leechman, geodetic surveyors C. H. Ney and Joseph Courtright, physiographer David Nichols, botanists Dr. Nicholas Polunin and Rev. Father Arthème Dutilly, historians and parliamentary press reporters Lloyd Roberts and Thomas Wayling, post office representative G. H. Lawrence, and Inspector Keith Duncan and six other members of the RCMP. Leaving Montreal on 14 July, the expedition proceeded in turn to Hebron, Port Burwell, Lake Harbour, Wakeham Bay, Sugluk West, Wolstenholme, Cape Smith, Port Harrison,

Churchill, Chesterfield, Southampton Island, Wolstenholme, Cape Dorset, Lake Harbour, Port Burwell, Pond Inlet, Craig Harbour, Dundas Harbour, Arctic Bay, Pond Inlet, Clyde River, Pangnirtung, and Port Burwell, ending at Halifax on 1 October.

Dr. MacArthur left the ship at Churchill and was replaced by Dr. T. J. Orford, who later relieved Dr. MacKinnon at Pangnirtung. The RCMP also investigated a few instances of crimes among Inuit. Leechman and Nichols spent about three weeks on investigations in the Wolstenholme area between calls of the ship at that point. Similarly, Ney left the ship at Port Burwell and carried on an investigation along the coast of Ungava Bay before being picked up when the ship returned. Polunin and Dutilly made an extensive collection of botanical specimens.[30]

The Eastern Arctic Patrol (1937)

The patrol of 1937 left Montreal on 10 July on *Nascopie*, with Major McKeand in charge, and returned to Halifax on 28 September. The government party included medical officer Dr. L. D. Livingstone; geodetic surveyors C. H. Ney and K. Gladstone; physiographer D. A. Nichols; astronomer R. G. Madill; ichthyologist H. M. Rogers; biologist V. C. Wynne-Edwards; radio engineers J.H.T. Arial, A. F. Crowell, and A. Tamblin; Canadian Broadcasting Corporation representatives Frank Willis and Roy Cahoon; cinematographer Richard Finnie; post office representative E. Gravel; historian and press reporter R. K. (Andy) Carnegie; and Superintendent G. F. Fletcher and nine other RCMP members. The steadily increasing number of scientific and technical personnel accompanying the cruise indicates the increasing scope and complexity of the work being done. Others aboard the ship during part of the voyage included Dr. George F. Crile of Cleveland, Ohio, and Dr. C. Stuart McEwen of the Royal Victoria Hospital, Montreal.

Stops were made in succession at Hebron, Port Burwell, Lake Harbour, Wakeham Bay, Sugluk West, Dorset, Wolstenholme, Southampton Island, Cape Smith, Port Harrison, Churchill, Chesterfield Inlet, Wolstenholme, Lake Harbour, Craig Harbour, Arctic Bay, Fort Ross, Pond Inlet, Clyde River, Pangnirtung, and Port Burwell.

Perhaps the most notable feature of the 1937 patrol was the meeting in Bellot Strait of *Nascopie*, coming from the east, and *Aklavik*, coming from the west. This was, in a sense, a Canadian negotiation of the Northwest Passage, although it was accomplished by two vessels rather than one. A similar completion of the Northwest Passage had occurred a few years earlier, when *Fort James*, sailing from the east, met *Fort MacPherson*, sailing from the west, at Gjoa Haven. A new HBC trading post, Fort Ross, was established at the eastern extremity of Bellot Strait. The visit to the new post at Arctic Bay, which had been established the year before by transferring some Inuit from Dundas Harbour to this site, found the resident party apparently satisfied with their new home. During the expedition, efforts were made to expand the use of radio communication in the regions visited, and direct radio contact with Ottawa was maintained throughout the voyage. Finnie also took motion pictures illustrating various features of Inuit life.[31]

The Eastern Arctic Patrol (1938)

The 1938 patrol sailed from Montreal on *Nascopie* on 9 July and returned to Halifax on 19 September, again with Major McKeand in charge. Among the ship's company were medical officer Dr. Keith Rogers, physiographer D. A. Nichols, ornithologist T. M. Shortt, artist Frederick H. Varley, special researcher Jon Bildfell, historian Marion Grange, post office representative F.R.E. Sparks, and Superintendent Thomas B. Caulkin and five other RCMP members, two of whom were accompanied by their wives. The ports of call were, in order, Hebron, Port Burwell, Lake Harbour, Wakeham Bay, Sugluk West, Dorset, Wolstenholme, Southampton, Cape Smith, Port Harrison, Churchill, Chesterfield Inlet, Wolstenholme, Lake Harbour, Port Burwell, Thule, Craig Harbour, Arctic Bay, Fort Ross, Pond Inlet, Clyde River, Pangnirtung, and Hebron.

For the second successive year, contact was made at Fort Ross with *Aklavik*, coming from the western Arctic. At Cape Dorset, arrangements were made to transport several Inuit families to Arctic Bay and Fort Ross so that they could join relatives who were already at these points. After the traditional exchange of courtesies with Danish officials at Thule, a small party of Greenland Inuit was hired to serve two years with the RCMP at Craig Harbour. Shortt made a large collection of bird specimens, and Bildfell made a special study of the nesting grounds of the eider duck. The scientific work done during this expedition was on a smaller scale than usual, however, largely because of the smaller number of scientific personnel accompanying the cruise.[32]

The Eastern Arctic Patrol (1939)

Again the patrol was on *Nascopie*, with David McKeand in charge. Among the ship's company were medical officer Dr. John Melling; physiographer D. A. Nichols; zoologist John G. Oughton; biologists Maxwell John Dunbar, Dennis Chitty, and Harold S. Peters; parasitologist Lynden Laird Lyster; dentist Charles H. M. Williams; barristers J. A. McLean and F. G. Whitaker; historian Richard Marriott; post office representative R. A. Perkins; secretary J. Lambert; and Inspector D. J. Martin and five other members of the RCMP. Leaving Montreal on 8 July and returning to Halifax on 23 September, *Nascopie* called in turn at Hebron, Port Burwell, Lake Harbour, Wakeham Bay, Sugluk West, Cape Dorset, Wolstenholme, Southampton Island, Cape Smith, Port Harrison, Churchill, Chesterfield Inlet, Wolstenholme, Lake Harbour, Port Burwell, Craig Harbour, Fort Ross, Arctic Bay, Pond Inlet, Clyde River, Pangnirtung, and Hebron.

At Chesterfield, Dr. John Melling replaced his brother Dr. Thomas Melling, who became ship's doctor for the rest of the cruise. An unusual feature of the trip was the trial at Pangnirtung of an Inuk murderer, with McLean and Whitaker acting as Crown prosecutor and defence counsel, respectively. He was found insane and taken south for treatment. The large number of scientific personnel among the ship's company gives an indication of the size and scope of the scientific work attempted, which covered a wider range of subjects than on any previous expedition. The post at Port Burwell, which had been a regular port of call since the government and HBC cruises were joined, was closed after the second visit. On 4 September, after the outbreak of war, *Nascopie* was put under war regulations and camouflaged with paint as much as possible.[33]

The Royal Canadian Mounted Police, 1922–39

Perhaps the most significant step in the gradual extension of the RCMP's surveillance of Canada's Arctic regions and maintenance of law and order therein was taken in 1922, when Inspector Wilcox and nine other ranks accompanied the first annual Eastern Arctic Patrol and established a new detachment at Craig Harbour. This formed part of the Canadian government's larger policy aimed at taking such steps as seemed possible, practicable, and necessary to assert and consolidate sovereignty over the Arctic regions that Canada claimed.

By 1924, the RCMP had twenty detachments grouped in four subdistricts in the Arctic and subarctic parts of the North, not counting the Yukon and the several detachments there. The so-called Ellesmere Island subdistrict had Pond Inlet and Pangnirtung on Baffin Island, Dundas Harbour on Devon Island, and Craig Harbour, with the subpost at Kane Basin, on Ellesmere Island itself. Hudson Bay subdistrict had Port Nelson and Chesterfield Inlet; the Arctic subdistrict had Aklavik, Herschel Island, Tree River, and Baillie Island; and the Mackenzie River subdistrict had Fitzgerald, Fort Smith, Chipewyan, Resolution, Rae, Providence, Simpson, Norman, and Good Hope. Port Burwell in Hudson Strait was administered from Ottawa.[34] Changes to the RCMP's northern footprint, as well as the overarching administration, occurred on an annual basis and are beyond the scope of this study but did represent effective Canadian occupation through the interwar period.[35]

Investigating and prosecuting serious crimes took up a large portion of the RCMP's time in northern detachments. In the early 1920s, police were kept occupied by an unusually large number of murders among the Inuit. During the year after his arrival at Pond Inlet, Staff Sergeant A. H. Joy succeeded in arresting three Inuit for the murder of Robert Janes and then found himself obliged to make another investigation when he received reports of several more Inuit murders near Home Bay on the east coast of Baffin Island. The murders at Kent Peninsula in 1921 had been followed by more violence and at least one more murder; when one of the suspects, Alikomiak, was arrested by Corporal William Andrew Doak, he shot and killed both Doak and Otto Binder, the manager of the HBC post at Tree River. Three other separate Inuit murders of Hav-oo-Ogak, Hiktak, and Kapolak, all in the region looked after by the Tree River detachment, were under investigation, and still another was reported to have occurred in the Repulse Bay region of Hudson Bay. In connection with all these murders and also in the normal course of duty, many long patrols were made, notably from Rampart House, Tree River, Chesterfield Inlet, Port Burwell, and Pond Inlet.[36] From Chesterfield Inlet, post visits were exchanged with Knud Rasmussen's Fifth Thule Expedition, which was wintering on an island off Lyon Inlet, southeast of Melville Peninsula.[37]

The main feature of the RCMP's work in the North in 1923 was their participation in two full-fledged murder trials, one at Pond Inlet for the three Inuit accused of murdering Janes and one at Herschel Island for the several Inuit who had been arrested in connection with the murders of Doak, Binder, and two of their own people. The trial at Pond Inlet, resulting in two convictions and one acquittal, has already been described in the section on

FIGURE 15-7: POLICE POSTS IN THE NORTHWEST TERRITORIES, 1925. *JENNIFER ARTHUR-LACKENBAUER BASED ON WILLIAM MORRISON, SHOWING THE FLAG: THE MOUNTED POLICE AND CANADIAN SOVEREIGNTY IN THE NORTH, 1894-1925* (VANCOUVER: UBC PRESS, 1985), XVI-XVII, AND *ANNUAL REPORT FOR THE ROYAL CANADIAN MOUNTED POLICE FOR THE YEAR ENDED SEPTEMBER 30, 1926.*

the Eastern Arctic Patrol. For the trial at Herschel Island, the judicial party travelled north from Edmonton and by boat down the Mackenzie River. Alikomiak and Tatamigana were found guilty of murder and sentenced to death, Ekootuk was found guilty of manslaughter and sentenced to one year's imprisonment at Herschel Island, and Olepsekak and Amokuk were acquitted.[38] Staff Sergeant Joy's responsibilities in connection with the Janes case had prevented him from going to Home Bay to investigate the reported murders there, but he learned from Inuit that a man named Neakuteuk had gone insane and then, after prevailing upon members of his tribe to kill two men, had been put to death himself. In the spring of 1923, Staff Sergeant Walter Munday travelled from Chesterfield Inlet to a point about seventy-five miles north of Baker Lake to investigate the murder of an Inuk named Ook-pa-tow-yuk, but he was unable to investigate the reported murder of another Inuk in the remote region north of Repulse Bay.

Another murder trial took place at Herschel Island in 1924, when a judicial party found Ik-a-luk-piak guilty of the murder of Hav-ou-gach south of Tree River in 1921 and sentenced him to five years' imprisonment in Stony Mountain penitentiary. Corporal Finley McInnes and Constable William MacGregor travelled from Pangnirtung to Home Bay in early 1924 to investigate three reported murders there, and several more murders were under investigation. A member of the Tree River detachment arrested I-ter-goo-yuk, accused of the murder of Ook-pa-tow-yuk north of Baker Lake about two years earlier, on King William Island during the winter of 1924–25. In accordance with instructions from Ottawa, I-ter-goo-yuk was released with only a severe warning because of the practical impossibility of obtaining a legal conviction. The Tree River detachment also arrested I-ka-yena, accused of the murder of Uluksak (who had himself been convicted of murder several years earlier), near Queen Maud Gulf early in 1925. He was tried before Judge Lucien Dubuc at Aklavik in June 1926 and found not guilty because of extenuating circumstances and released. The RCMP also investigated another reported Inuit murder of Puyerack by Tekack on Adelaide Peninsula about 1921. Tekack voluntarily surrendered at Tree River after Sergeant F. A. Barnes had made a futile trip to King William Island in 1925 to arrest him. He also was tried before Judge Dubuc at Aklavik in June 1926, pleading guilty of manslaughter and receiving a sentence of one year's imprisonment at Herschel Island. Cases of accidental deaths, missing persons, infanticide, and starvation were also investigated.[39]

These general patterns continued in the years ahead. No serious criminal cases had come to light in the Northwest Territories in 1927,[40] suggesting strongly that the RCMP were making their presence felt, but in the Yukon, an Indian named Jackie MacIntosh was found guilty of manslaughter and sentenced to three years' imprisonment for the murder of Pelly Jim.[41] In 1929, the RCMP investigated a large number of deaths, both violent and accidental, including a multiple murder case in the interior of Baffin Island and another murder near Bathurst Inlet. In the first case, the murderer himself had been put to death in what was obviously self-defence, so no prosecution was undertaken, but in the second case, a court from Edmonton held a trial at Aklavik and sentenced the murderer, Okchina, to one year's imprisonment – a light punishment owing to extenuating circumstances.[42] The most spectacular event of the 1930s was the RCMP's greatest manhunt, for the "Mad Trapper" Albert Johnson, who killed one Mountie and wounded several others before he was finally tracked down and shot on the Eagle River in February 1932.[43]

Pursuant to these investigations and the Canadian government's general sovereignty assertion policy, the RCMP also undertook an active patrolling program throughout the Arctic. Commissioner Cortlandt Starnes noted in his 1925 report that these long patrols, especially in the Arctic, were often not made in connection with "cases" but were nevertheless a special tradition of the RCMP; their real purpose was supervision of remote areas and isolated settlements rather than to search for infractions of the law.[44] In reference to these patrols, Starnes wrote two years later that "perhaps even here there is a slight decrease in the romantic side of the northern work, for, while long pioneer journeys still are made, nevertheless practice in patrolling has brought facilities, and our men now as a matter of routine traverse regions which not long ago were the objects of difficult and tedious discovery."[45]

Among the many patrols in 1922 and 1923, Corporal Finley McInnes and William B. MacGregor completed an arduous trek from Pond Inlet to the Fury and Hecla Strait Inuit settlement of Igloolik; Sergeant H. Thorne from Edmonton ventured to Herschel Island (by way of Alaska and Rampart House) in connection with the two hangings there; Staff Sergeant Joy travelled from Pond Inlet to Lancaster Sound in a bold but futile attempt to reach Ellesmere Island; and Inspector H. L. Fraser went from Fort Smith towards Great Bear Lake.[46] In April and May 1925, Corporal T. R. Michelson patrolled from Craig Harbour to the subpost at Kane Basin and back.

Among the many patrols in early 1926, Inspector C. E. Wilcox went from Pond Inlet to Home Bay; Sergeant J.E.F. Wight and Constable T. H. Tredgold from Pangnirtung to Lake Harbour and back; Staff Sergeant Joy from Craig Harbour to Axel Heiberg Island and back; and Corporal Petty from Chesterfield Inlet to Wager Bay and Back River, and back.[47] Some of these patrols disclosed appalling conditions of hardship among Inuit in remote settlements, and the Mounties did what they could to give immediate help and make arrangements for more. The most spectacular of the many northern patrols in 1927 was newly promoted Inspector Joy's foray westwards of Ellesmere Island, in this case from Bache Peninsula to several of the Sverdrup Islands and back.[48] The following year, Constable E. (Ted) Anstead patrolled from Bache Peninsula to Axel Heiberg Island and back, and Inspector Wilcox patrolled from Pond Inlet to Fury and Hecla Strait, Foxe Basin, and Igloolik, and back. Corporal R. A. Williams, in charge of the Reliance detachment, made several patrols eastwards in search of the missing party led by the English adventurer John Hornby.[49] By this point, Commissioner Starnes commented on the comprehensiveness of the RCMP's northern patrols in these terms:

> The Arctic coast-line from the Alaska boundary to the neighbourhood of the magnetic pole now is under regular observation and control; so are Hudson strait, Baffin island, North Devon island, and the southern half of Ellesmere island; while the western coast of Hudson bay and James bay also are policed. The mineral developments in northwestern Manitoba are causing our patrols to go further north in that region and in northern Saskatchewan, while we are steadily working into the Barren Lands from the eastern ends of the great lakes of the north.[50]

The extension of the RCMP's posts into the Arctic islands facilitated long patrols into even the most remote parts of the archipelago. In the spring of 1929, for example, Inspector Joy made a record-breaking patrol of 1,700 miles from Dundas Harbour to Winter Harbour in Melville Island, and then back to Bache Peninsula by way of Lougheed, King Christian, Ellef Ringnes, and Axel Heiberg Islands.[51] Concurrently, Corporal Anstead, in charge of the Bache Peninsula post, was making a patrol of 1,084 miles in Axel Heiberg Island and along the west coast of Ellesmere, while Constable S.H.C. (Hugh) Margetts travelled from Pond Inlet to Foxe Basin and back, a distance of 970 miles.[52] Many other patrols were made, both in the islands and on the northern mainland, an unusual and sad one being that of Inspector Charles Trundle from Great Slave Lake to the cabin on the Thelon River where the Hornby party had perished to bury the bodies, recover the records, and make any other dispositions necessary.[53] Among the more arduous patrols in 1930 were by Constables N. M. McLean and W. C. (Bill) Beatty from Bache Peninsula to the western and southern coasts of Ellesmere Island, discovering a new route on the trip; by Corporal Maurice Mason Timbury and Constable R. W. Hamilton from Dundas Harbour to Cornwallis Island and back; by Corporal Hugh A. McBeth from Pond Inlet to Foxe Basin

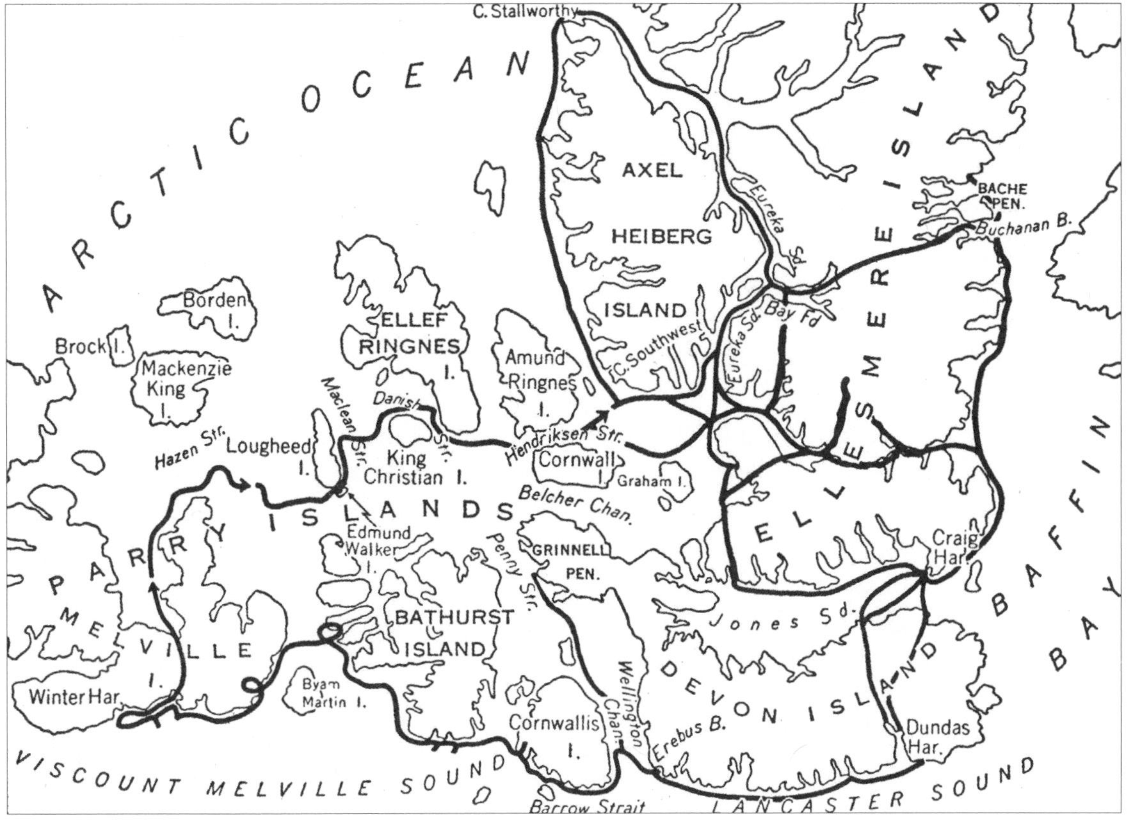

Figure 15-8: RCMP patrols in the High Arctic, 1929. Andrew Taylor, *Geographical Discovery and Exploration in the Queen Elizabeth Islands* (Ottawa: Department of Mines and Technical Surveys, 1964), 128. *By permission of Natural Resources Canada.*

and back; and by Constable F. W. Ashe from Pond Inlet to Home Bay and back.[54] By this point, Commissioner Starnes referred to the last two as "habitual" and "customary."[55]

Land patrolling continued through the 1930s. Corporal Harry Stallworthy made a long patrol in the spring of 1931 from Bache Peninsula to Craig Harbour and other points in a futile search for Dr. Krüger and his two companions (Bjare and Akqioq).[56] The following year, his detachment made two more long patrols in search of the lost Krüger expedition, with Corporal Stallworthy circling Axel Heiberg Island and Constable Hamilton travelling west as far as Amund Ringnes and Cornwall Islands. (Nothing was found except a written record left by Dr. Krüger at the northern extremity of Axel Heiberg Island on 24 April 1930, and it could only be concluded that he and his party had perished.)[57] In March 1934, Constable L.W.L. White led a patrol from Cambridge Bay to King William Island to investigate the murder of an Eskimo named Anaruak two years earlier,[58] and Corporal McInnes completed one from Pangnirtung to Frobisher Bay and Lake Harbour, and back.[59] The following year the longest patrol was led by Constable Albert "Frenchie" Chartrand, who travelled from Coppermine to several points in Victoria Island and Coronation Gulf, and back again.[60] In the early months of 1936, Acting Lance Corporal R. C. Gray and several others (including Alex Stevenson of the HBC) made a long patrol from Pond Inlet to Pingitkalik on the east coast of Melville Peninsula and back. Another long patrol that season was led by Acting Sergeant G. T. Makinson, which went from the *St. Roch* at Cambridge Bay to King William Island and on to Matty Island near Boothia Peninsula before returning, with the primary objective of investigating two Inuit murders.[61]

Maritime patrols, dealt with at length in the discussion of the Eastern Arctic Patrol, also facilitated RCMP coverage of the Arctic. In 1925, the motor launch *Lady Borden* was transferred from Chesterfield Inlet to Pangnirtung and helped the police visit settlements along the eastern coast of Baffin Island. The most striking addition to the force's facilities was the 200-ton motor schooner *St. Roch* in 1928. Classed as a "floating detachment," the ship would patrol Arctic waters and help maintain contact among the detachments on the coast and in the islands.[62] The following year, Commissioner Starnes noted that the force had twenty-five boats of various sorts for service in the North, the largest being *St. Roch*.[63] By the early 1930s, it wintered regularly at Tree River, giving the police another base in the area,[64] and it also served as a hub for long patrols. Constable S. E. Alexander of *St. Roch* spent almost the entire winter of 1936–37 on patrol in the Cambridge Bay–Coppermine region, travelling a total of 1,583 miles, and Sergeant Henry Asbjorn Larsen, the venerable skipper of the *St. Roch*, made a 900-mile patrol from Cambridge Bay, where the vessel was wintering, to King William Island and back.[65]

Other Canadian Government Expeditions, Surveys, Investigations, and Patrols in the North

There were other Canadian government expeditions, surveys, investigations, and patrols of various kinds during these years. Some of those in the eastern Arctic were connected with the Eastern Arctic Patrol, and others in the Yukon, the Mackenzie Valley region, and the western Arctic islands also played a role in Canada's effort to occupy, administer, and develop the North.[66]

The Eastern Arctic Patrol certainly facilitated research into health conditions among Inuit. Dr. Leslie Livingstone, who had been appointed medical health officer for the District of Franklin in 1925, went north on *Beothic* in 1926 and established his base for the following year at Pangnirtung, returning south with the same ship in 1927. During the winter and spring, he made two long trips to southwestern and northern Baffin Island to investigate and treat Inuit illnesses, and he was picked up at Pond Inlet by *Beothic* for the return voyage.[67] In 1928 and 1929, he returned to begin establishing a medical headquarters and hospital at Pangnirtung, and undertook a similar project at Chesterfield Inlet in 1930. Travelling by rail to Churchill in April and then by dog team to Chesterfield, he opened the medical post and helped to plan the projected hospital, before returning to Ottawa in the autumn.[68] Another medical officer active in the Arctic was Dr. James A. Urquhart at Aklavik, who went on an investigative tour of health conditions in 1932 through the Northwest that took him to Herschel Island, Coronation Gulf, and Great Bear Lake.[69]

Figure 15-9: Major L. T. Burwash, 1926. *Library and Archives Canada / Indian and Northern Affairs, Department Library Albums.*

Other officials conducted surveys of economic and local conditions. Major L. T. Burwash, an exploratory engineer with the Department of the Interior, was particularly active in the eastern and central Arctic during these years. In the summer of 1923, he left the Eastern Arctic Patrol at Pangnirtung and spent a year making an economic survey and general reconnaissance of southwestern Baffin Island, returning south on HBC vessels in 1924.[70] The following year, he was instructed to conduct a comprehensive investigation of the Arctic coast and travelled eastwards from the Mackenzie delta, wintered on King William Island, and continued in the spring of 1926 to Chesterfield Inlet, where he took passage on an HBC boat back to Ottawa.[71] In the summer of 1927, he completed an economic survey of Inuit conditions and a geographical reconnaissance along the eastern coast of James and Hudson Bays from Rupert House to Richmond Gulf, including the adjacent islands.[72]

Major Burwash spent the summers of 1928 and 1929 investigating the Arctic coast and offshore islands between Coronation Gulf and Boothia Peninsula. Travelling via the Mackenzie River and then eastwards from Aklavik in the government's gasoline boat *Ptarmigan*, he wintered at Gjoa Haven on King William Island, made three trips to the vicinity of the North Magnetic Pole on Boothia Peninsula, and investigated Inuit stories about the fate of the Franklin expedition. Uncertainty as to the fate of the Dominion Explorers air expedition headed by Colonel C.D.H. MacAlpine caused a long wait at this party's base near the entry of the Burnside River into Bathurst Inlet, and it was not until mid-November, when the safety of the expedition had been ascertained, that Burwash was able to set off on the first of several plane hops that took him south to Winnipeg.[73] He spent the summer of 1930 in the same region, travelling by boat and plane, with instructions to continue his investigations of the mineral resources of the Coppermine area and to examine further the correctness of various reports and rumours about the Franklin expedition. Accompanied by Richard Finnie, Burwash flew around King William Island and searched the ground along the west coast but found no new, conclusive evidence about the Franklin party.[74]

Other Canadians carried out official inspections in the western Arctic during the interwar years. Chief Inspector John Francis Moran visited the Mackenzie District, travelling down the Mackenzie River to the delta in 1922, 1924, 1926, and 1928, in the latter case continuing eastwards along the Arctic coast in SS *Baychimo* as far as Queen Maud Gulf.[75] In

1927, J. A. McDougal, the district agent at Fort Smith, carried out an inspection and investigated Inuit conditions in the region between Fort Smith and Cambridge Bay.[76] In the summer of 1929, Oswald S. Finnie, Director of the Northwest Territories and Yukon Branch, made a field inspection of posts and settlements in the Mackenzie District and Yukon Territory to secure first-hand information about conditions from local spokesmen and to advise government about desirable change and development. His route was by train from Ottawa to Waterways, Alberta; by steamboat down the Athabasca, Slave, and Mackenzie Rivers; by plane from Aklavik to Dawson (this being a pioneering flight); by ship along the Pacific coast to Vancouver; and then by train back to Ottawa. In the course of his journey through the North, he made as many stops and visits to outlying points as possible.[77]

The expansion of the mining frontier also elicited direct attention. A. L. Cumming, Chief Mining Inspector (and later a member of the Northwest Territories Council), flew from Fitzgerald in August 1931 to make a field investigation of stakings and claims in promising ore bodies in the Great Bear Lake–Coppermine River region, notably at Echo Bay and the Dismal Lakes.[78] The following summer he travelled by canoe from Fort Smith to the Mackenzie delta, inspecting schools, hospitals, radio stations and public utilities, generally in the settlements en route, and also the reindeer camp east of the delta. On the return trip, he went up Bear River and visited several mining locations, including some he had seen in 1931.[79] Dr. Charles Camsell, the Deputy Minister of Mines, and Dr. Harold W. McGill, the Deputy Superintendent General of Indian Affairs, made inspection trips in the Northwest Territories during the summer of 1935 and submitted reports to the Northwest Territories Council (of which both were members).[80] Three years later, Camsell followed this up with an inspection trip to Fort Smith and the Yellowknife mining district, and Roy A. Gibson, Director of the Lands, Parks, and Forests Branch, inspected a number of settlements and mining sites in the Mackenzie District.[81]

Government officials also were involved in extensive geological and geographical survey work. For example, Dr. Lud Weeks of the Geological Survey, accompanied by Maurice Haycock, wintered at Pangnirtung in 1926–27 and carried on extensive investigations in southern Baffin Island.[82] Guy Houghton Blanchet of the Department of the Interior Topographical Survey, who earlier in the 1920s had made important investigations in Wood Buffalo Park[83] and in the regions around and to the north and east of Great Slave Lake,[84] spent the working seasons of 1928 and 1929 carrying out similar duties in Keewatin District. Acting as a government representative with several private companies which were prospecting for minerals, he went into the region by ship through Hudson Bay, wintered at Tavani on the west coast of the bay south of Chesterfield Inlet, and during the two seasons participated in various prospecting trips by airplane. Although this method of travel was in its infancy in the North and obviously had many problems to overcome, he was optimistic about its future utility for prospecting and for other purposes.[85] Blanchet took charge of the search for the MacAlpine party and continued to make flights under difficult circumstances until he received news in early November that the lost party was safe at Cambridge Bay.[86]

A large proportion of the scientific expeditions which were made during these years were carried on in conjunction with the Eastern Arctic Patrol. For example, in 1936 David Nichols of the Geological Survey, Douglas Leechman

Figure 15-10: J. D. Soper and party on a survey of Parketuk Bay, 1929. *J.D. Soper / Library and Archives Canada / e002342694.*

of the National Museum, and C. H. Ney of the Geodetic Service of Canada went north on the *Nascopie* and left the ship to carry on periods of research in their own disciplines, Nichols and Leechman at Wolstenholme and Ney at Port Burwell. This was common practice at the time. Nichols, for example, accompanied the *Nascopie* and made geological studies in this way each year from 1935 to 1939.[87]

Similarly, studies of Arctic flora and fauna took Canadian scientists to the Far North. In August 1924, the naturalist J. D. Soper followed Burwash's example by leaving the *Arctic* at Pangnirtung, establishing his base at the RCMP post, and carrying on investigations in the Nettilling and Amadjuak Lakes region before boarding *Nascopie* at Amadjuak in August 1926 and heading home.[88] In the summer of 1928, he returned to Baffin Island to carry out research on Inuit and wildlife (particularly to determine the breeding grounds of the blue goose) and established his headquarters at Cape Dorset until 1929.[89] He returned to Baffin Island the following year to continue his investigations of wildlife in the southern part of the island, but illness forced him to return to Ottawa in August 1931.[90] In 1932 and 1933, he was occupied with a comprehensive investigation of flora and fauna in Wood Buffalo Park.[91]

W.H.B. Hoare, an investigator for the Northwest Territories and Yukon Branch of the Department of the Interior, also spent extensive time in the field. In 1924, 1925, and 1926, he made a comprehensive investigation of wildlife, especially caribou, along a large portion of the Yukon and Mackenzie coast and in the interior.[92] He following this with fieldwork in the Thelon Game Sanctuary (created by a federal order in council on 15 June 1927) from January 1928 to August 1929. Building a cabin on the Thelon River to serve as his headquarters, he examined the southern part of the sanctuary in the summer of 1928 and the northern part in 1929, primarily to ascertain the number

Figure 15-11: Bob Porsild feeding the dogs, Eskimo Lakes, NWT, 1927. *AEP / Library and Archives Canada / e010933876.*

and general condition of muskox there. Later in the summer of 1929, he descended the Thelon River to Chesterfield and returned home on the Eastern Arctic Patrol vessel *Beothic*.[93] Hoare returned to Thelon the following summer to continue his faunal investigations, overwintering in the field near the eastern extremity of the sanctuary before returning to Ottawa in August 1931.[94] He also assisted Dr. Charles Henry Douglas Clarke of the University of Toronto with biological surveys of the sanctuary in 1936 and 1937.[95] The same pair returned for further investigations in 1937.

As discussed in chapter 9, the Danish brothers Alf and Robert Porsild investigated the possibility of introducing the reindeer industry in parts of the Canadian North, covering the coastal region as far east as Coronation Gulf and the interior east of the Mackenzie delta and around Great Bear Lake in 1927–28.[96] Alf made a botanical investigation of some of the islands in James Bay during the summer of 1929[97] and then made a botanical investigation in Keewatin the following year in a further search for reindeer grazing grounds.[98] In 1931, he conducted three Saami (Lapp) herders down the Mackenzie River to Kittigazuit and then continued from there on a patrol into Alaska.[99] Robert had also been sent to the Mackenzie delta in connection with the reindeer project in the summer of 1930.[100] Other researchers followed on inspection tours of the region, supervising fieldwork and conducting detailed studies on the reindeer herd.[101]

Canadian researchers also completed important hydrographic work during the interwar years. The Canadian government decided in the mid-1920s to complete the Hudson Bay railway and terminals, and an order in council of 22 January 1927 provided for the appointment of an advisory board under the chairmanship of the representative of the Department of Marine and Fisheries, N. B. McLean, to organize an investigation into ice conditions, navigation, and related matters in Hudson Strait.[102] Using the CGS *Stanley* and the freighter *Larch* to transport men, materials, and supplies, McLean's party established three bases in the Hudson Strait during the summer and fall of 1927: at Port Burwell at the eastern extremity, Nottingham Island at the western extremity, and

Wakeham Bay halfway between the two. From these bases, they made detailed observations by airplane, by boat, and from the ground. The CGS *Montcalm* and *Larch* withdrew the expedition in the autumn of 1928 according to the original plan, but the expedition left direction finding stations in operation at Port Burwell, Nottingham Island, and Cape Hopes Advance. Insofar as conclusions could be drawn from weather and ice observations during the two seasons, McLean anticipated a possible navigation period of about four months: from about 20 July to 20 November.[103]

Other hydrographic surveys followed in the late 1920s and 1930s. For example, N. Wilson of the Canadian Hydrographic Service travelled down the Mackenzie River from Fort Smith in 1930 in the hydrographic launch *Pilot I* and surveyed the Richards Island channel in the delta, some of the passages among the outer islands, and the offshore waters westwards to Shingle Point on the Arctic coast and northwards to Hooper Island. His main objective was to try to locate a navigable channel for seagoing vessels between open water and the Mackenzie River. He continued the survey in 1933 in the vicinity of Port Brabant, Kittigazuit, and the eastern part of the delta.[104] Hydrographic operations also continued in connection with the development of the Hudson Bay route during eight consecutive seasons from 1928 through 1935. F.C.G. Smith and then J. U. Beauchemin surveyed the west coast of Hudson Bay in the vicinity of Churchill in 1928, 1929, 1930, and 1931. Smith carried on yearly surveys in Hudson Strait, on the Quebec side in 1931, 1932, and 1935, and on the Baffin Island side in 1933 and 1934. Using the DGS icebreaker and patrol ship *N. B. McLean*, Smith completed his survey for the most important parts of the route.[105]

Finally, in connection with the International Polar Year in 1932–33, three Canadian stations were put into operation in the Arctic, at Cape Hopes Advance, Chesterfield Inlet, and Coppermine. Frank Davies, Balfour Currie, Stuart McVeigh, and John Rae were stationed at Chesterfield Inlet; R. C. Jacobsen at Coppermine; J. R. Lilly at Cape Hopes Advance; and E. H. Vestine at Meanook, Alberta. John Patterson was Director of the Meteorological Service, W.E.W. Jackson was the Assistant Director, and Andrew Thomson was in charge of meteorological planning. "Some of the future giants of Canadian science received thorough practical education during the Second International Polar Year," a subsequent report noted. "Although not all the data from the Second International Polar Year could be analyzed because of the interruption of the world war, it has been estimated that the information gathered was worth 'hundreds of millions of dollars' worldwide for telecommunications alone."[106]

16

Epilogue: Henry Larsen, the St. Roch, and the Northwest Passage Voyage of 1940–42

The voyage of the Royal Canadian Mounted Police (RCMP) vessel *St. Roch* through the Northwest Passage in 1940–42 is forever associated with the name of the famous skipper of the *St. Roch*, Henry Asbjørn Larsen[1] – and with the assertion of Canadian sovereignty. The common assumption that the transit served sovereignty purposes is often asserted in popular writing but seldom grounded in evidence. Larsen's writing, coupled with RCMP files, suggests that this motivation factored heavily into the planning and execution of the voyage.

Larsen was a native of Norway, having been born at Fredrikstad, a village only a few miles distant from Roald Amundsen's birthplace at Sarpsborg, on 30 September 1899. His boyhood fancies were inevitably captivated by the exploits of Amundsen and the galaxy of other great Nordic explorers and adventurers, both contemporary and historical; in 1914, at barely fifteen years of age, he went to sea to begin his own nautical career. His first voyage was on a cargo sloop owned by two of his uncles, which sailed to Norwegian, Swedish, and Danish ports transporting lumber and other goods. After about a year of this, he was hired by Captain H. Olsen, who took him along with the rest of his crew to Brest, France, to man the sailing ship *Baunen*, which left for Barbados, Gulfport (Mississippi), and Buenos Aires in early 1916. During the next three years, Larsen sailed continuously on several ships to US and South American ports. To get home from New York in 1919, he embarked on a long roundabout voyage which took him to Cape Town, the East Indies, Ceylon, and the Suez Canal en route to Christiania (Oslo). There he attended the Norwegian State Navigation School, graduating as a fully qualified navigator in the summer of 1920; he then put in a period of compulsory service in the Norwegian navy. In 1922, he became a mate on the Norwegian motor ship *Theodore Roosevelt*, and during the next two years, he sailed between Norway and Pacific Ocean ports, including San Francisco, Seattle, Vancouver, Honolulu, and Japan. While in Seattle on one occasion, he met Amundsen and his pilot Oscar Omdahl, and through them his long-held desire for a career in the North received new impetus and encouragement.

In Seattle during the spring of 1924, Danish-born Arctic trader Charlie Klengenberg hired Larsen as navigator. On Klengenberg's schooner *Maid of Orleans*, he made two trips to the Beaufort Sea region in 1924–25 and the summer of 1926. Wintering at Herschel Island during the first voyage, he became acquainted with the inhabitants of the region, Inuit and white alike, and he also took advantage of the opportunity to become familiar with (and even expert in) Inuit modes of

Figure 16-1: Inspector Henry Larsen aboard the RCMP vessel *St. Roch*. *Library and Archives Canada / C-070771.*

hunting, sealing, fishing, and travelling, which were necessary to anyone wishing to be even passably self-reliant in the North. He spoke to Inspector T. B. Caulkin, officer commanding at Herschel Island, of his desire to join the RCMP, and meeting with an encouraging response, he applied for Canadian citizenship on a later visit to Vancouver. This was granted on 18 November 1927, and several months later he was sworn in as a member of the police force at the Fairmont Barracks in Vancouver, on 16 April 1928.[2]

The idea of the *St. Roch* apparently originated with serving Mounties in the North. Larsen first learned of it during the winter of 1924–25 from Inspector Caulkin, who

> was of the opinion that the Force should have a little schooner of its own which could sail everywhere in this enormous area to act as a floating detachment in the summer and a permanent station during the winter. The idea had originated with his predecessor, Inspector S. T. Wood, who had left for the South a short while earlier after five years' service in the Arctic, mostly on Herschel Island. Both of these police officers were experienced men who knew the Arctic well, and realized that the RCMP was suffering by being dependent on civilian trading ships for transportation and supplies.[3]

Needless to say, this prospect provided further incentive to Larsen to join the force.

Commissioner Cortlandt Starnes presented the suggestion to Minister of Marine and Fisheries Arthur Cardin in a letter on 23 October 1924. "The Officer Commanding the Mounted Police at Herschel Island," Starnes noted, "has … recommended that an auxiliary schooner be purchased for the purpose of carrying Police freight to our detachments at Baillie Island and Tree River from Herschel or the mouth of the Mackenzie, and also as a movable Detachment, such a vessel to move to any point and remain for the freeze-up, if necessary."[4] The minister approved the suggestion in January 1925,[5] the initial plan being to purchase a vessel.[6] All efforts to find a suitable vessel failed, however, so another order in council was issued on 29 September 1927 to contract the Burrard Dry Dock Company, of North Vancouver, to build a schooner for $80,200.[7] Construction proceeded during the early months of 1928, with Corporal Ed Pasley of the RCMP as supervisor or "overseer," and the ship was ready for service before the end of June. She was named the *St. Roch* – "guardian of the poor" – after a parish in the Quebec East constituency of Ernest Lapointe, whose Ministry of Justice was responsible for the RCMP at the time.

The *St. Roch* was 104 feet in length, 25 feet in beam, with draft when loaded of 12½ feet and net tonnage of 80 tons. Designed especially for Arctic service, she had a saucer-shaped cross section, which enabled her to rise above the crushing pressure of surrounding ice rather than being squeezed in it. For greater strength, the ship was built solidly of heavy Douglas fir, with a complete outside sheeting of Australian ironbark. She had schooner rigging and was equipped with a 150-horsepower diesel engine.[8]

According to the original plan, the ship would sail north in 1928 with an elderly Newfoundland skipper, Captain William Hugh Gillen, in command, and when it arrived at Herschel Island, he would leave and be replaced by Corporal Pasley. Pasley, however, withdrew from service on the *St. Roch* and shortly afterwards from the RCMP when he was refused permission to take his new wife along. Thus, the ship sailed on 28 June without him, with Gillen as skipper and Constable Larsen as first mate. When Gillen was about to leave following the arrival at Herschel Island in August, Inspector Vernon A. M. Kemp, who was then officer commanding in the western Arctic, appointed Larsen skipper and chief navigator in spite of his short police service and low rank. Sergeant Frederick Anderton was simultaneously appointed to take charge of the floating detachment for all police purposes. Thus, within six months of joining the RCMP, Larsen found himself commander of a ship and holder of one of the most interesting and challenging positions in the force.[9] He remained as commander of the *St. Roch* during her entire career of northern service, from 1928–48.[10]

Just how and with whom the idea originated of taking the *St. Roch* through the Northwest Passage appears uncertain. It is likely that the idea began with Larsen himself; it may well be that this was a dream he had cherished practically from the time his service with the ship began. There is clear evidence that he was putting the suggestion before his superiors years before an attempt was actually made and that some of them were not impressed with it. On 27 November 1934, back in Vancouver after four consecutive years in the Arctic, Larsen wrote a letter to Assistant Commissioner J. W. Phillips, officer commanding "E" Division in Vancouver, suggesting: "In summer, from any of these places [in the western Arctic], I believe the 'St. Roch' could proceed right through and connect with the East Arctic, via Viscount Melville Sound, Barrows Straight [*sic*] and Lancaster Sound, should such a trip be considered."[11] In a note two weeks later, Superintendent T. H. Irvine of "G" Division commented that "Sergeant Larsen makes reference to the possibility of connecting with the Eastern Arctic through Viscount Melville Sound, Barrow Straits [*sic*], and Lancaster Sound; the possibility of this route has not yet been established, and it does not appear that anything can be gained by doing this."[12] Inspector A. T. Belcher, who had served in the North but was then at the Adjutant's Branch at Ottawa Headquarters, similarly disapproved. "I do not agree with the suggestion that the boat attempt to make the North West Passage as suggested by Sergt Larsen and connect up with the Eastern Detachments," he noted on 17 December, "as I think this too risky."[13]

On 9 May 1936, still icebound after wintering at Cambridge Bay, Larsen wrote to Inspector G. M. Curleigh, officer commanding the Western Arctic subdivision at Aklavik that "from Gwoa [*sic*] Haven I am of the opinion St.

Roch would have no difficulty to connect with Eastern Arctic supply ship at any place along Lancaster Sound if it should be desired."[14] Curleigh sent the suggestion on to Ottawa, but his comment met with the response that "the suggestion advanced by Sgt. Larsen, that the 'St. Roch' proceed north to Lancaster Sound and connect with the Eastern Arctic Supply Ship, appears to be a trifle ambitious at this time."[15]

In July of that year, Commissioner James Howden MacBrien visited the *St. Roch* at Cambridge Bay while on a flying tour of northern detachments. Larsen again broached the subject of a Northwest Passage trip, again with rather negative results. He recorded the event in the original manuscript of his autobiography as follows:

> I had opportunity to mention, that I would like to at some time proceed right through the North-West Passage with the St. Roch, pointing out, that since it was decided we should spend the winter of 1936–7 in the King William Isl. area, the logical thing to do, would be to proceed East from there, instead of treading the narrow ice infested channels back Westward, and possibly be late to get back out past Point Barrow, to which he replied, that our Role in the Arctic was not to be Explorers, but to carry out the various duties and administrations on behalf of the various departments of the Federal Government, but also that he hoped that in the future an opportunity to Navigate from one side of the Arctic would present itself.[16]

The matter of primary concern in the present context, however, is the purpose of the Northwest Passage voyages. It has been commonly stated that the voyages were primarily for sovereignty purposes, but little concrete evidence has been given. Such evidence is not easy to find, but some is available which throws at least modest light on the subject. For example, Larsen noted in his autobiography that, after arriving in Ottawa in early January 1940:

> One morning in February I was sent for by Assistant-Commissioner T. B. Caulkin, who was then the Officer Comm[anding] "G" Division in Ottawa, and whom I had last seen at Herschel Island in 1926, prior to joining the force. He was now my commanding officer and I was glad to see him again and to give him first hand information about his many Arctic friends, both Inuits [*sic*] and whites. A/C Caulking informed that Commissioner S. T. Wood wanted to see me and to discuss personally the next Voyage for the St. Roch. I had not previously meet Comm. Wood. He had succeeded Sir James MacBrien as senior Officer of the Force, upon the latter's death in 1938. As will be recalled, the St. Roch had been built as a result of Wood's far-seeing recommendations and its doings were of great personal interest to him. On arrival at his office I was both astounded and surprised to learn that as soon as the season permitted I was to take the "St. Roch" into the Western Arctic with a full load of Supplies for the Detachments there, retain 18 months supplies for ourselves, and when our duties in the Western Arctic were finished, I was to take her into the Eastern Arctic

FIGURE 16-2: THE *ST ROCH* IN VANCOUVER AFTER HER NORTHWEST PASSAGE. *COURTESY ARCTIC INSTITUTE OF NORTH AMERICA. AINA 51-124.*

> and endeavour to reach Halifax, and if not, to winter somewhere in Eastern Arctic Waters of the Lancaster Sound area. In simple language, I was to complete the North-West Passage, and did I think I could do it he asked, to which I replied I foresaw no great difficulty if the season was anywhere normal as far as weather and ice conditions, also that the 1939 season had been perfect with no ice whatever, should we however experience ice seasons like the two last ones of 1936–37 it would be difficult to make it in one season and I would then have to winter somewhere handy. The place agreed upon in such a case was Banks Island, or close to it, so that patrols could cover this large Island, previously not visited by police patrols owing to distance from nearest detachment at Coppermine. It was a great moment for me. Canada was at War and the Government realizing the need to demonstrate sovereignty over the Arctic Islands, was continuing to entrust the discharge of that responsibility to the Royal Canadian Mounted Police as it had done for decades, ever since the first detachment was built at Cape Fullerton on the West side of Hudson Bay in 1903.[17]

No written orders dealing with the purpose or purposes of the first voyage have come to light. Larsen himself committed to paper, years afterwards, his own understanding of what lay behind the voyage:

> The "Nascopie" did however take some fuel oil to Pond Inlet for us in 1940. The reason for this, I believe, was that prior to the "St. Roch" leaving Vancouver on its eastward journey through the Arctic, Denmark had been invaded and Greenland was more or less left on its own. Had the "St. Roch" managed to navigate the Northwest Passage that year it is my understanding that our Government was planning to send her to Greenland. I believe also that a Canadian Consulate was established in Greenland about that time, and I understand this was one of the reasons

why the "St. Roch" was instructed to proceed eastward in 1940.

However owing to our delays in having to carry cargo etc., plans had changed by the time we reached Pond Inlet in 1942 and we did not proceed to Greenland. The Americans had by this time pretty well taken over in Greenland and the "St. Roch" trip was cancelled.

It was the object of the Government and our Department to ensure that the "St. Roch" could be kept in operation in the Eastern Arctic after she arrived there, and the fuel oil delivered to Pond Inlet by the "Nascopie" was not to assist the "St. Roch" through the Northwest Passage. It was taken there solely for the proposed trip to Greenland.... I know for a fact that she was asked to take fuel oil to Pond Inlet only because we expected the "St. Roch" would be sent to Greenland.[18]

Larsen wrote another letter to the commissioner on the same subject a couple of days later, and he included some additional detail.

> During the summer of 1940 the "Nascopie" took 3500 gallons of fuel oil to Pond Inlet as a cache to be left for us there, as the plans then were that we might be requested to spend the winter at some designated spot in the Eastern Arctic, also for a possible trip to Greenland. Captain Smellie seems to be under the impression that the Northwest Passage trip was something of a stunt or else a trip to compete with the "Nascopie."
>
> Had it not been for the war we would never have had the occasion or opportunity to make this passage. As previously mentioned the plans were that perhaps the "St. Roch" could be utilized to advantage in the Eastern Arctic and perhaps have to winter at some designated spot, bearing in mind that we had closed three of our Eastern Arctic detachments prior to the war, namely Dundas Harbour, Craig Harbour and Bache Peninsula. These detachments had as you know been established for Sovereignty purposes and that was also one of the reasons for our passage. Owing to our delay by adverse ice and weather conditions, also because we had to supply our Western Arctic posts in 1940 and 1941, we did not manage to reach the Eastern Arctic before 1942, and then it was felt there was no particular need to keep the "St. Roch" in these waters after 1943. We then received instructions to proceed back West by a different route.[19]

It was true, as Larsen suggests, that if the *St. Roch* had succeeded in getting through the Northwest Passage in 1940, the Canadian government had planned to send her on to Greenland, which had been placed in a very insecure position by the German invasion of Denmark. This could not have had anything to do with the original plans for completion of the Northwest Passage, however, since Larsen was told of these in February 1940 and the invasion of Denmark came (without much warning) in April. Furthermore, although both Dundas Harbour and Bache Peninsula were closed before the war, Craig Harbour was not closed until the summer of 1940. Plans were being made at least as early as January and February 1940 to close Craig Harbour,[20] however, so Larsen was right to anticipate that if he got through the passage, he would find no police posts on the northernmost islands.

RCMP officials were hesitant about what to do with the *St. Roch* if she did not get through the passage in 1940. On 20 August of that year, Adjutant F. A. Blake wrote to the officer commanding "G" Division that "the Commissioner further directs that if Sgt. Larsen decides later that he cannot get through to Ponds Inlet, he be instructed to winter the vessel on Banks Island." Blake also noted that "the Commissioner has not given his decision regarding the vessel continuing to the Eastern Arctic next summer."[21] On 8 March 1941, Inspector D. J. Martin wrote to the officer commanding at Aklavik, repeating an earlier message that the commissioner had ordered that the *St. Roch* should undertake the voyage to the eastern Arctic "in accordance with the plans arranged for last year."[22] By this time, the RCMP clearly had decided to stick with the original plan.

Larsen seemed clear about the purpose for the voyage in his diary entry just before the ship set out to sea:

> Well, we are set and ready for the great adventure of trying again to make the Northwest Passage. We must do all in our power to uphold Canada's claim to this section of the Arctic. I feel very proud that this important mission has been assigned to me again and I hope that I will be able to fulfil the task before me, to uphold Canada's claim to these valuable islands and the bulwark of our northern frontier. Canada and its people have adopted me as one of their own sons and it is up to me to be worthy of such an honour.[23]

This was not public knowledge, however, and press reports of the voyage reveal an aspect of secrecy. For example, an article in the *Globe and Mail* on 10 October 1942 stated that "the purpose of the trip remained secret." In the same issue, referring to a scroll which had been made for "Frenchie" Chartrand (who had died at Pasley Bay during the voyage), the report noted that "on this scroll is only a hint of the purpose of the voyage, not yet known to any newspaperman in Canada." The day before, the *New York Sun* also said that "details of the Mounties' voyage were cloaked by official secrecy, the members of the expedition declining to disclose their purpose in undertaking the hazardous journey." Larsen also spoke to the requirement of secrecy in his book *The Big Ship*, explaining:

> When I returned to the *St. Roch* after the completion of my course in late March, I was full of enthusiasm over what was ahead of us. Our destination was to be kept a secret until we reached the North, as no undue publicity was wanted. Only two crew members – the engineer, Corporal Jack Foster, and the Mate, Constable Farrar – were informed of the project, but I was under orders not to tell even them until we had reached Arctic waters several weeks later.[24]

An account by one of these crew members, however, indicates that Larsen was more casual about the matter of secrecy than the above passage would indicate. Constable Fred Farrar (whose narrative, it should be noted, was completed by another after his sudden death in

February 1955) indicated that Larsen told him of their destination on 8 June 1940, before the voyage had even begun. He told the rest of the crew on 24 June – their first night at sea. "It was back in the Naval Dockyard at Esquimalt, B. C., where I first heard of our assignment. That day, June 8th, 1940, had broken clear and warm," Farrar wrote. He quoted Larsen disclosing that "I've just received orders from Headquarters to take the *St. Roch* through the Northwest Passage." Farrar also recounts a conversation on the evening of 24 June 1940, as the ship "passed out of the narrow neck of water between Vancouver Island and the mainland and into the Pacific":

> "What's your opinion Mate," Frenchie asked, "do you think we'll make the Northwest Passage this year?"
>
> Larsen had told the boys at supper that night.[25]

Whatever the case, the ship set out for the North on 21 June 1940. It is apparent that Larsen had initially intended to take a more northerly route through Prince of Wales Strait and Viscount Melville Sound, which he referred to as "the one which should be used for any future enterprise among the Arctic Islands, or in yearly negotiation of the North-West Passage for any purpose that might occur."[26] He spent the winter of 1940–41 at Walker Bay on the west coast of Victoria Island and that of 1941–42 at Pasley Bay on the west coast of Boothia Peninsula.[27] Writing from the latter location on 31 December 1941, Larsen remarked that "my original intention was to return westward from Cambridge Bay, proceed Northward through Prince of Wales Strait then into Melville and Lancaster Sound, as this is no doubt the best route in an average year, but owing to heavy ice encountered leaving Walker Bay, also in Amundsen Gulf, it was not practical to do so this year."[28] He eventually took the southern route below King William Island and through Bellot Strait, heading out into Baffin Bay, and thus completing the first transit of the Northwest Passage from west to east before reaching Halifax on 11 October 1942.

All told, the information presented in the preceding pages paints a clearer general picture that matters relating to sovereignty loomed large in planning and carrying out Larsen's transit of the Northwest Passage during 1940–42. Other contextual factors also help to explain the decision: the worrisome Greenland situation, the temporary abandonment of the most northerly RCMP detachments, the question of supplying existing and possibly future police detachments along the route, the search for a usable route, and the RCMP's desire to focus attention upon its northern activities by capitalizing upon the inevitable publicity and prestige that would result from successful transit of the passage. Nevertheless, RCMP documents themselves indicate that sovereignty was a primary factor, if not the primary one. If Larsen did not himself initiate the idea of taking the *St. Roch* through the Northwest Passage, certainly he was promoting the project long before it had any appeal to his superiors. Probably he was not thinking in terms of sovereignty at the beginning, but this aspect of the voyages obviously appealed to his fancy or judgment. Based on what he wrote on the subject, ultimately he came to view the sovereignty aspect as the most important of all.[29]

There is no reason to fear that Canada's legal position has deteriorated since this time. On the contrary, it has probably improved. No new foreign claims have been made. Canada's own program of governmental and other activity has steadily expanded since the Second World

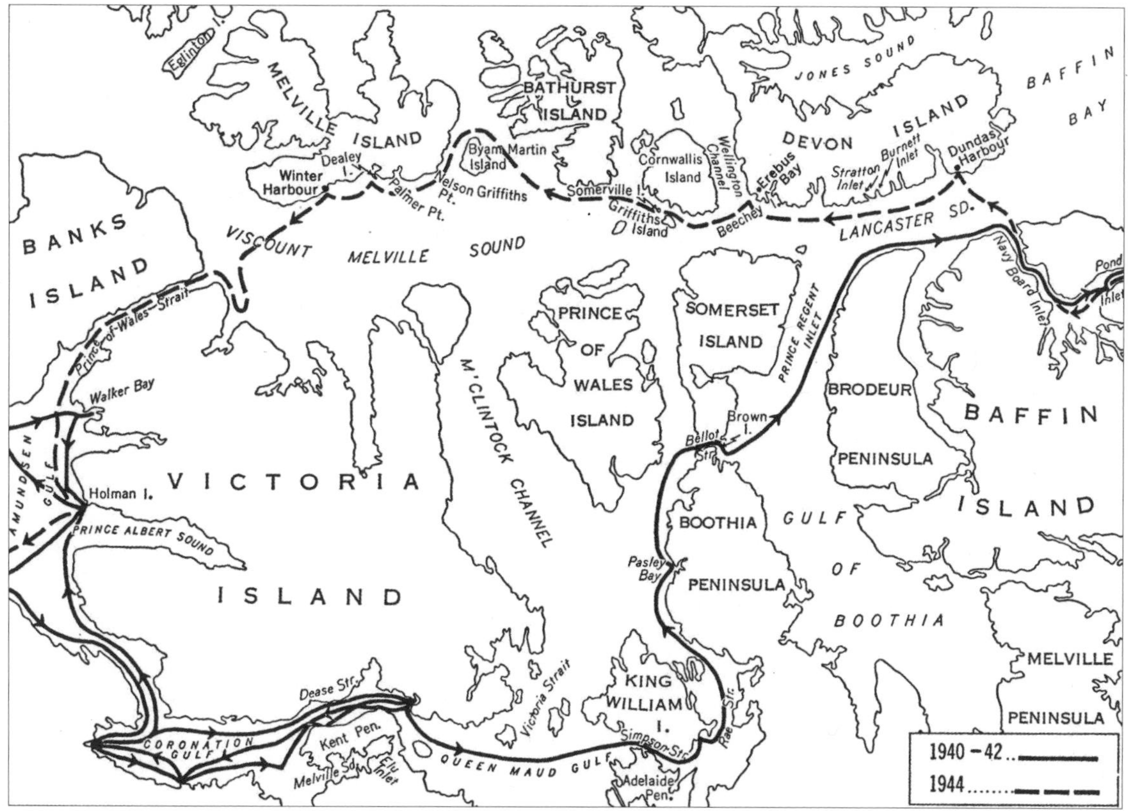

16-3: Voyages of the *St. Roch*, 1940–44. Andrew Taylor, *Geographical Discovery and Exploration in the Queen Elizabeth Islands* (Ottawa: Department of Mines and Technical Surveys, 1964), 130. *By permission of Natural Resources Canada.*

War. The moderating trend in the legal requirements for territorial sovereignty, as highlighted by the *Eastern Greenland Case*, does not appear to have been reversed. The United States played a leading role in joint defence projects during and after the Second World War, but successive Canadian administrations have been careful to maintain Canada's sovereign rights, and the United States has apparently shown no unwillingness to meet Canadian wishes. This attitude has applied consistently to wartime projects, such as the Alaska Highway and the Canol Pipeline, and to postwar and Cold War projects, such as the Joint Arctic Weather Stations and the Distant Early Warning (DEW) Line. In these circumstances, it may be asserted with confidence that Canada's legal title to her northern territories, particularly to the archipelago, is secure today and has been at least since the 1930s.[30]

Editor's Note

1 Prime Minister's Office, "Prime Minister Stephen Harper announces new Arctic offshore patrol vessels," 9 July 2007. http://pm.gc.ca/eng/media.asp?id=1742.

2 On this theme, see Ron Macnab, "'Use it or Lose it' in Arctic Canada: Action Agenda or Election Hype?" *Vermont Law Review* 34/3 (2009), 3–14.

3 Rob Huebert, "Canada and the Changing International Arctic: At the Crossroads of Cooperation and Conflict," in *Northern Exposure: Peoples, Powers and Prospects for Canada's North*, eds. Frances Abele, Thomas J. Courchene, F. Leslie Seidle, and France St-Hilaire (Ottawa: Institute for Research on Public Policy).

Introduction

1 F. L. Oppenheim, *International Law*, ed. H. Lauterpacht, 8th ed. (London: Longmans, Green, 1955), vol. 1, 546.

2 A. S. Hershey, *The Essentials of International Public Law and Organization*, rev. ed. (New York: Macmillan, 1935), 285.

3 F.A.F. von der Heydte, "Discovery, Symbolic Annexation and Virtual Effectiveness in International Law," *American Journal of International Law* 29, no. 3 (July 1935): 448–71.

4 *American Journal of International Law, Supplement*, 3, no. 1 (January 1909): 7–25; also *British and Foreign State Papers 1884–1885*, vol. 76, 4–20.

5 *Editor's Note*: This conclusion, which some readers might consider dismissive of Aboriginal rights, is contentious today in light of s. 35 of the *Canada Act* (1982), which enshrines Aboriginal and treaty rights; comprehensive land claim settlement agreements; and international declarations such as the United Nations Declaration on the Rights of Indigenous Peoples (UNCRIP).

6 See Helge Ingstad, "Discovery of Vinland," *The Arctic Circular* 15, no. 1 (January 1963): 2–6, where the author locates the long-sought Vinland of the Norsemen at the northern tip of Newfoundland. The article also brings out the uncertainties that still persist regarding many aspects of the Norse voyages.

7 H. P. Biggar, ed., *The Precursors of Jacques Cartier 1497–1534* (Ottawa: Government Printing Bureau, 1911), 8–10.

8 Richard Hakluyt, *The Principal Navigations, Voyages, Traffiques, and Discoveries of the English Nation*, 12 vols. (Glasgow: J. MacLehose and Sons , 1903), vol. 7, 282.

9 A. S. Keller, O. J. Lissitzyn, and F. J. Mann, *Creation of Rights of Sovereignty Through Symbolic Acts 1400–1800* (New York: Columbia University Press, 1938), esp. 148–51.

10 C.C.A. Gosch, ed., *Danish Arctic Expeditions 1605 to 1620* (London: Hakluyt Society, 1897), vol. II, 15, 19, 23, 83.

11 Hakluyt, *Principal Navigations*, vol. VII, 326.

12 W. Ellis, *An Authentic Narrative of a Voyage Performed by Captain Cook and Captain Clerke* (London: Robinson et al., 1783), vol. 1, 262–63.

13 Thomas Simpson, *Narrative of the Discoveries on the North Coast of America ... etc.* (London: R. Bentley, 1843), 8, 153.

14 *Arctic Papers*, vol. 2, no. 97 (7 March 1851), 33.

15 *Treaties and Conventions Between Great Britain and Foreign Powers*, vol. 3, 362–66.

16 C. F. Hall, *Life with the Esquimaux* (London: S. Low, Son, and Marston, 1864), vol. 2, 111, 118, 119.

17 George Chalmers, ed., *A Collection of Treaties Between Great Britain and Other Powers* (London, 1790), vol. 1, 340–90.

18 Chalmers, *A Collection of Treaties*, vol. 1, 467–94 (The Peace of Paris).

19 *Statutes of Great Britain*, 1–2 Geo. IV, c. 66, 2 July 1821.

20 Chester Martin, "The Royal Charter," *The Beaver*, Outfit 276 (June 1945), 26.

21 On whaling in the North American Arctic, see A. P. Low, *The Cruise of the Neptune 1903–04* (Ottawa: Government Printing Bureau, 1906), 248–82, which gives a good deal of information about whaling in Hudson Bay and Davis Strait during the nineteenth century and up to 1904. See also B. Lubbock, *The Arctic Whalers* (Glasgow: Brown, Son, and Ferguson, 1937 and 1955); and for an earlier classic, W. Scoresby, *An Account of The Arctic Regions and of the Whale-Fishery*, 2 vols. (Edinburgh: Constable and Co., 1820). *Editor's note*: Smith noted that "Missionary activity in the North, of little importance here, was divided among Moravians on the northern Labrador coast and Anglicans and Roman Catholics elsewhere in the northern mainland; but prior to the 1870s none of these sects had any permanent missions in the archipelago."

1 | The Transfers of Arctic Territories

1 Gordon W. Smith, "Sovereignty in the North: The Canadian Aspect of an International Problem," in *The Arctic Frontier*, ed. R. St. J. Macdonald (Toronto: University of Toronto Press, 1966), 194–255, esp. 198–204. I have tried here to summarize briefly the background of the two transfers and the most vital details about them.

2 See *The Beaver*, Outfit 276 (June 1945), 26–35, for an accurate reproduction of the original charter, with a foreword by Chester Martin.

3 For detailed accounts of the transfer and its background, see A. S. Morton, *A History of the Canadian West to 1870–71* (London: T. Nelson and Sons, 1939), esp. 802–920; E. E. Rich, *The History of the Hudson's Bay Company 1670–1870* (2 vols.; London: Hudson's Bay Record Society, 1958–59), esp. chaps. 30–31; and J. S. Galbraith, *The Hudson's Bay Company as an Imperial Factor 1821–1869* (Toronto: University of Toronto Press, 1957), esp. pt. IV.

4 *Statutes of Great Britain*, 30–31 Vict., c. 3 (British North America Act, 1867), s. 146.

5 *Statutes of Great Britain*, 31–32 Vict., c. 105 (Rupert's Land Act, 31 July 1868).

6 Joint Addresses of 16–17 December 1867, and 29–31 May 1869. See *Statutes of Canada*, 35 Vict. (1872), lxvii–lxxvii.

7 Deed of Surrender, 19 November 1869. See in ibid., lxxvii–lxxxiii.

8 Imperial Order in Council, 23 June 1870. See in ibid., lxiii–lxvii.

9 *Statutes of Canada*, 33 Vict., c. 3 (Manitoba Act, 12 May 1870).

10 *Report from the Select Committee on the Hudson's Bay Company, with Proceedings, Minutes of Evidence, Appendix, and Index* (July–August 1857), 46.

11 *Statutes of Great Britain*, 34–35 Vict., c. 28 (British North America Act, 29 June 1871). *Editor's note*: Smith did not refer to indigenous rights, focusing his attention on international questions related to sovereignty. Accordingly, he does not engage issues related to the Métis Resistance around Red River in 1869 and subsequent developments. For general overviews of the historiography, see J. R. Miller, "From Riel to the Metis," *Canadian Historical Review* 69 (1988): 1–20, and Brad Milne, "The Historiography of Métis Land Dispersal," *Manitoba History* 30 (Autumn 1995). Scholars have also produced an extensive body of literature on First Nations land rights and the numbered treaties. The best general survey is J. R. Miller, *Compact, Contract, Covenant: Aboriginal Treaty-Making in Canada* (Toronto: University of Toronto Press, 2009).

12 National Archives, Kew, United Kingdom [hereafter NA], Colonial Office Papers, Series No. 42 [hereafter CO 42], vol. 734, 419. Harvey to Colonial Office, 3 January 1874.

13 NA, CO 42, vol. 734, 421–22. Harvey to Colonial Office, 15 January 1874.

14 NA, CO 42, vol. 734, 423–44. Holland to Harvey, 16 January 1874. Draft copy.

15 NA, CO 42, vol. 734, 420. Lampson to Holland, 12 January 1874.

16 NA, CO 42, vol. 732, 178–79. Mintzer to Crump, 10 February 1874. The close relationship of the Harvey and Mintzer applications in respect of time, place, and purpose is evident, and arouses curiosity as to whether there had been any contact, friendly or otherwise, between the two men.

17 NA, CO 42, vol. 732, 177. Crump to Granville, 20 February 1874.

18 NA, CO 42, vol. 732, 176. Foreign Office to Colonial Office, 28 March 1874.

19 NA, CO 42, vol. 731, 51. W. D. (?) to Sir H. T. Holland, 22 April 1874.

20 NA, CO 42, vol. 731, 52, 25 April 1874. Signature illegible.

21 NA, CO 42, vol. 731, 58–60. Carnarvon to Dufferin, 30 April 1874. Draft copy.

22 NA, CO 42, vol. 731, 55–57.

23 NA, CO 42, vol. 732, 180–81. Holland to Secretary of the Admiralty, 13 April 1874. Draft copy.

24 Carnarvon to Dufferin, 26 August 1874. *Editor's Note*: Smith noted that this was "from handwritten copy in case Arctic Islands Documents" held at External Affairs.

25 Library and Archives Canada [hereafter LAC], Record Group 85, Northern Affairs Program [hereafter RG 85], vol. 584, file 571, pt. 5, H. R. Holmden to A.G. Doughty, "Memo re the Arctic Islands," 26 April 1921, 3–4 [hereafter Holmden, "Memo re the Arctic Islands"]. Smith was unable to locate Herbert's letter in the archives documents, but Holmden must have seen it because he quotes from it verbatim. Nor did Smith see any record of a reply to Mintzer.

26 NA, CO 42, vol. 730, 5–6. Dufferin to Carnarvon, 4 November 1874.

27 Canada, Order in Council, PC No. 1248, 10 October 1874.

28 NA, CO 42, vol. 731, 196–99. Carnarvon to Dufferin, 6 January 1875. Draft copy.

29 NA, CO 42, vol. 731, 189–95, 2 December 1874.

30 NA, CO 42, vol. 731, 179–85, 19 December 1874.

31 NA, CO 42, vol. 731, 200. Carnarvon to Dufferin, 27 March 1875. Draft copy.

32 NA, CO 42, vol. 736, 393. Dufferin to Carnarvon, 1 May 1875.

33 Canada, Order in Council PC No. 46D, 30 April 1875.

34 NA, CO 42, vol. 736, 396. Carnarvon to "The Officer Adm. the Govt," 1 June 1875. Draft copy.

35 NA, CO 42, vol. 747, 476–77. Blake to Carnarvon, 15 August 1876.

36 NA, CO 42, vol. 747, 479–80. Colonial Office to Blake, 22 August 1876. Draft copy.

37 NA, CO 42, vol. 747, 369. Blake to Colonial Office, 23 August 1876.

38 NA, CO 42, vol. 747, 371. Carnarvon to O.A.G., 13 September 1876. Draft copy.

39 NA, CO 42, vol. 747, 373. Carnarvon to Dufferin, 1 November 1876, Dispatch No. 324. Draft copy.

40 Holmden, "Memo re the Arctic Islands," 10, draws attention to a statement by Donald Smith (afterwards Lord Strathcona) in Canada, House of Commons *Debates*, 3 May 1878, 2392, to the effect that the cargo was worth $120,000. Smith did not identify the Mintzer expedition by name, but there is little doubt it was the one to which he referred.

41 NA, CO 42, vol. 747. Dispatch No. 297, 23 Oct. 1877.

42 NA, CO 42, vol. 747. Dispatch of 23 Oct. 1877.

43 NA, CO 42, vol. 749, 788–89. Dufferin to Carnarvon, 1 December 1877.

44 Canada, Order in Council, PC No. 922D, 29 November 1877.

45 NA, CO 42, vol. 749, 793–95. Malcolm to attorney general and solicitor general, 22 February 1878. Draft copy.

46 This doubt is now raised in the correspondence for the first time, so far as I can tell. Holmden, "Memo re the Arctic Islands," 14, is obviously in error when he asserts that it was first brought up in Hicks-Beach's letter of 17 July 1878.

47 NA, CO 42, vol. 753, 391–94. See the text of the joint address also in Canada, Senate *Debates*, 3 May 1878, 903; and in W. F. King, *Report upon the Title of Canada to the Islands North of the Mainland of Canada* (Ottawa: Government Printing Bureau, 1905), 9–10. King was Chief Astronomer of the Dominion.

48 Canada, House of Commons *Debates*, 3 May 1878, 2386–94. Holmden, "Memo re the Arctic Islands," 11, says that some of the official correspondence on the subject had been secretly shown to Macdonald the day before.

49 NA, CO 42, vol. 753, 395–97. Hicks-Beach to Dufferin, 17 July 1878, Dispatch No. 184. Draft copy.

50 See NA, CO 42, vol. 754, 531–33. Law Officers to Hicks-Beach, 28 May 1878.

51 NA, CO 42, vol. 754, 142. Dufferin to Hicks-Beach, 8 October 1878. Dispatch No. 247.

52 NA, CO 42, vol. 754, 145–51, 30 August 1878.

53 NA, CO 42, vol. 754, 143–44. Canada, Order in Council, PC No. 1162D, 2 October 1878.

54 Imperial Order in Council, 23 June 1870 (above, note 8).

55 *Statutes of Great Britain*, 34–35 Vict., c. 28 (British North America Act, 29 June 1871).

56 NA, CO 42, vol. 754, 156–59.

57 NA, CO 42, vol. 754, 152–55. Colonial Office to Secretary of the Admiralty, 18 January 1879. Draft copy.

58 NA, CO 42, vol. 759, 24–25. Admiralty to Colonial Office, 28 January 1879.

59 NA, CO 42, vol. 759, 26–32. Hydrographer's Report, 23 January 1879.

60 NA, CO 42, vol. 759, 19–23.

61 NA, CO 42, vol. 759, 20, 6 February 1879.

62 NA, CO 42, vol. 759, 19, 29 January 1879.

63 NA, CO 42, vol. 759, 22, 10 February 1879.

64 NA, CO 42, vol. 759, 22, 20 February 1879.

65 NA, CO 42, vol. 759, 33–39. Colonial Office to Law Officers of the Crown, 26 February 1879. Draft copy.

66 NA, CO 42, vol. 759, 195–98. Law Officers to Hicks-Beach, 3 April 1879.

67 NA, CO 42, vol. 759, 199–201. Hicks-Beach to Marquis of Lorne, 18 April 1879, Dispatch No. 106. Draft copy.

68 NA, CO 42, vol. 759, 202–3. Hicks-Beach to Marquis of Lorne, 19 April 1879. Draft copy.

69 NA, CO 42, vol. 758, 11–12. Marquis of Lome to Hicks-Beach, 5 November 1879. Dispatch No. 315.

70 NA, CO 42, vol. 758, 13–14. Canada, Order in Council, PC No. 88E, 4 November 1879.

71 NA, CO 42, vol. 758, 8–10, 15. Colonial Office to Law Officers of the Crown, 6 February 1880. Draft copy.

72 NA, CO 42, vol. 765. A. S. Dennis to Colonial Office, 28 July 1880. Acknowledged in NA, CO 42, vol. 765, Colonial Office to Macdonald, 31 July 1880.

73 NA, CO 42, vol. 765, Lord Kimberley to Lord President of the Council, 28 July 1880.

74 Imperial Order in Council (31 July 1880). See in NA, CO 42, vol. 764, 329; also *Canada Gazette*, vol. XIV, no. 15, 9 October 1880, 389; and King, *Report upon the Title*, 10.

75 NA, CO 42, vol. 764, 330. Kimberley to Marquis of Lorne, 16 August 1880, Dispatch No. 131. Draft copy.

76 More evident, in the case of the Canadians, during the later stages of the negotiations. For example, see the remarks about the need for speedy action by Mackenzie, Mills, and Macdonald in the House of Commons on 3 May 1878.

77 See, for example, King, *Report upon the Title*, 4–8; Holmden, "Memo re the Arctic Islands," 11–13, 17fn; A. E. Millward, *Southern Baffin Island* (Ottawa: King's Printer, 1930), 12–13.

78 If taken at face value this would presumably include British Honduras, Bermuda, the Bahamas, and the British West Indies. So far as I know no one has ever raised the question as to whether all these possessions were inadvertently handed over to Canada at the time of the transfer!

79 King, *Report upon the Title*, 6.

80 Holmden, "Memo re the Arctic Islands," 11–12.

81 See Colonial Office minute of 19 December 1874 (above). In this connection it is perhaps worth recalling that the Nares expedition had been active in northwest Greenland in 1875–76, and had explored farther along the northern coast than any other expedition up till that time. Lt. Greely of the US Army did not begin his expedition to the same region until 1881.

82 King, *Report upon the Title*, 5.

83 Holmden, "Memo re the Arctic Islands," 14ff.

84 NA, Law Office, [hereafter L.O.] 10568/66 Cape, 8 November 1866, and NA, L.O., 4558/71 Cape, 8 May 1871. The first advised that the annexation of "Nomansland" to Natal, which had been brought about in 1863–64 by means of letters patent and a local ordinance, had been lawful, and that the proposed annexation of the Penguin Islands to Cape Colony could also be effected by the Crown. The second advised that the annexation of Chief Waterboer's territory to Cape Colony could similarly be effected by the Crown. In each of the proposed annexations, according to the law officers, Her Majesty's action should be accompanied by an act of the local legislature.

85 Both the order in council cited below and the attached report by Macdonald say that the question was raised "during the last Session of the Canadian Parliament." I do not see any direct reference to it in the debates, except that on 4 May Mr. Mills asked "if the Government intended to ask the Imperial confirmation of the power of this Bill," and Macdonald replied that there was

"some doubt in this respect about the appointment of Senators." Mr. Wood thought that "with the exception of Senators the provisions of the Bill would be embraced under an Imperial Order in Council." House of Commons *Debates*, 4 May 1870, cols. 1361–62.

86 NA, CO 42, vol. 696, 2–4. Lisgar to Kimberley, 3 January 1871. Dispatch No. 1.

87 Canada, Order in Council, PC No. 503, 2 January 1871. See, with Macdonald's report, in NA, CO 42, vol. 696, 8–13.

88 NA, CO 42, vol. 696, 5–6. Kimberley to Lisgar, 26 January 1871. Dispatch No. 341.

89 Canada, Order in Council, PC No. 416B, 27 February 1871.

90 NA, CO 42, vol. 697, 18–19. Lisgar to Kimberley, 2 March 1871. Dispatch No. 53.

91 Canada, *Journals of the Senate* (13 April 1871), 154–55, gives the complete text. See also House of Commons *Debates*, 13 April 1871, cols. 1081–82.

92 NA, CO 42, vol. 697, 516–17. Lisgar to Kimberley, 18 April 1871. Dispatch No. 86.

93 *Statutes of Great Britain*, 34–35 Vict., c. 28, 29 June 1871.

94 Holmden, "Memo re the Arctic Islands," 20–22, emphasizes the differences between the Canadian draft or drafts and the final act, and says that the Imperial authorities, refusing to accept the former, composed the latter themselves. It is true that there are differences, but most of them are of minor importance, and essentially the Kimberley draft, the Canadian drafts of 27 February and 13 April, and the final act are similar in import if not in structure. Note also that the Kimberley draft, which Holmden does not mention, set the pattern for the Canadian drafts. Holmden did not see the joint address of 13 April, nor, apparently, did he see a note from the Colonial Office to the Secretary to the Treasury (NA, CO 42, vol. 697, 22–24, 2 May 1871), which shows clearly that the British authorities were in fact trying to meet the wishes of the Canadian government.

95 Holmden, "Memo re the Arctic Islands," 12–13.

96 See Blake of the Colonial Office to Bramston in NA, CO 42, vol. 759, 19, 29 January 1879: "The object in annexing these unexplored territories to Canada is, I apprehend, to prevent the United States from claiming them, and not from the likelihood of their proving of any value to Canada."

97 Holmden, "Memo re the Arctic Islands," 12. See also V. Kenneth Johnston, "Canada's Title to the Arctic Islands," *Canadian Historical Review* 14, no. 1 (March 1933): 24–41, esp. 29. Johnston questions that Britain's title to all the islands was perfect by the end of the nineteenth century; nevertheless he seems to consider that the transfer as such had been valid. E.g., "the British government, by order-in-council in 1880, transferred to Canada all British territories in North America except Newfoundland and its dependencies." He then adds, evidently following King, that the order "was confirmed by imperial statute in 1895." Yvon Beriault, "Les problèmes politiques du Nord canadien," University of Ottawa doctoral thesis (Montreal: Bernard Valiquette, 1942), makes several references to the transfer (e.g., 100, 101, 111, 112, 113) and raises questions about it, but otherwise does not go into detail.

2 | Period of Relative Inactivity and Unconcern

1 W. F. King, *Report upon the Title of Canada to the Islands North of the Mainland of Canada* (Ottawa: Government Printing Bureau, 1905).

2 Library and Archives Canada [hereafter LAC], Record Group 85, Northern Affairs Program [hereafter RG 85], vol. 584, file 571, pt. 5, H. R. Holmden to A. G. Doughty, "Memo re the Arctic Islands," 26 April 1921, esp. 12–31 [hereafter Holmden, "Memo re the Arctic Islands"].

3 *Editor's note*: Hudson's Bay Company regulations forbade specific citation or quotation of such correspondence at the time Smith was conducting his research. Smith was unable to locate it in government sources.

4 National Archives, Kew, United Kingdom [hereafter NA], Colonial Office Papers, Series No. 42 [hereafter CO 42], vol. 772, 182–83. Sir W. J. Ritchie (Administrator) to Kimberley, 25 September 1882. Dispatch No. 28.

5 Canada, Order in Council, PC No. 1839, 23 September 1882.

6 A. E. Millward, *Southern Baffin Island* (Ottawa: King's Printer, 1930), 13, interprets Lt. A. R. Gordon's three voyages in 1884, 1885, and 1886 as being connected with Canada's assumption of responsibility in the newly transferred territories. I can find little to justify this supposition since, as Gordon's narratives and Millward's own quotations and comments make clear, the voyages were

designed primarily to gather information about navigation in Hudson Strait, and they penetrated no farther north. See Gordon's three reports, for 1884, 1885, and 1886, issued under the authority of the Minister of Marine and Fisheries, in the departmental annual reports [hereafter Gordon, *Report(s)*].

7 *Statutes of Great Britain*, 58–59 Vict., c. 34 (Colonial Boundaries Act, 6 July 1895).

8 NA, CO 42, Chamberlain to Officer Administering the Government, 26 July 1895.

9 King, *Report upon the Title of Canada*, 5, 8.

10 Holmden, "Memo re the Arctic Islands," 23–26. See also Millward, *Southern Baffin Island*, 12.

11 See Great Britain, *Parliamentary Debates*, 4th Series, 58–59 Vict., vol. xxxv, 25 June–6 July 1895, cols. 46–47, 195. Speaking in the House of Lords on 1 July, the Marquess of Ripon, outgoing Secretary of State for the Colonies in the defeated Rosebery administration, said in reference to the proposed measure: "Some small islands have been added to New Zealand; and the boundaries of some Australian colonies have been altered. The doubts relate to cases of that kind." Three days later the following exchange took place in the House of Commons: "Dr. Clark asked whether under this Bill Cape Colony and Natal would be able to extend their borders without reference to that House. The Secretary of State for the Colonies (Mr. J. Chamberlain, Birmingham W.) replied in the negative."

12 LAC, Record Group 15, Department of the Interior [hereafter RG 15], vol. 722, reel T-12450, file 384996, H. Jenkyns, memorandum, 21 May 1895.

13 See *Statutes of Canada*, 47 Vict., c. 18, 19 April 1884. This act divided the former Department of Marine and Fisheries into two departments, the Department of Marine and the Department of Fisheries, but the Minister of Marine and Fisheries remained in charge of both.

14 "Report of the Select Committee of the House of Commons to Enquire into the Question of the Navigation of Hudson's Bay," in *Journals of the House of Commons*, vol. XVIII, appendix 2 (Ottawa, 1884), iv–viii. See also Canada, Senate *Debates*, 6 May 1879, 455–59.

15 See Gordon, *Reports*. Gordon was accompanied in 1885 by Mr. D. G. Beaton, editor of the *Winnipeg Times*, and in 1886 by Capt. A. H. Markham, RN, both of whom were representatives of a concern entitled *The Winnipeg and Hudson Bay Railway Company*, which already was promoting the idea of a railway from Winnipeg to Hudson Bay. See Gordon, *Reports*, 1885, 2; 1886, 4, 9; and M. E. and F. A. Markham, *The Life of Sir Albert Hastings Markham* (Cambridge: University Press, 1927), 188–203.

16 *Report*, 1886, 8–11. The Hudson Bay railway was a much-discussed subject at this time. See, for example, Canada, Senate *Debates*, 11 Feb. 1890, 65–82, 868–72, 876–80.

17 Gordon, *Report*, 1886, 42–43. See also Canada, Department of Marine, *Nineteenth Annual Report* (1886), 197–215, where preliminary reports on the 1886 expedition by Gordon are included as appendices 27 and 28. See esp. 206–7, 214–15.

18 Millward, *Southern Baffin Island*, 13.

19 Gordon, *Report*, 1884, 3.

20 Gordon, *Report*, 1884, 20.

21 Gordon, *Report*, 1886, 4.

22 Canada, House of Commons *Debates*, 19 May 1886, II, 1378. It is perhaps worth noting that the Canadian government had evidently tried, without success, to involve Great Britain in the expeditions. See Canada, House of Commons *Debates*, 5 April 1884, 1380, where the following exchange is recorded: "Mr. Blake. Has the hon. Gentleman any communication from the Imperial authorities on this subject at all? Mr. McLelan. They have declined to take any part in the expedition." (McLelan was Foster's predecessor as Minister of Marine and Fisheries).

23 Gordon, *Report*, 1884, 14–15.

24 Gordon, *Report*, 1884, 13–17, passim.

25 Gordon, *Report*, 1885, 54. See also Canada, House of Commons *Debates*, 27 June 1892, cols. 4262–4263, where the same question was brought up. Mr. McMullen referred to a recent report to the Minister of the Interior by Lt. Gov. Schultz of Manitoba and Keewatin, which complained about the uncontrolled activities of American whalers in the waters off the Keewatin coast. In reply to McMullen's query as to whether the matter would be referred to the Bering Sea arbitrators, Sir John Thompson, speaking for the government, suggested that the time was not opportune to announce any action contemplated, and the question was not suitable for the Bering Sea arbitrators in any case. Mr. Mills (Bothwell) asserted, "The whole of Hudson Bay is Canadian water."

26 Gordon, *Report*, 1886, 60–67, esp. 66–67, also 92.

27 J. W. Tyrrell, *Across the Sub-Arctics of Canada*, 3rd ed. (Toronto: Wm. Briggs, 1908), 72, 82.

28 See G. M. Dawson, *Report on an Exploration in the Yukon District, N.W.T., and Adjacent Northern Portion of British Columbia 1887, Report B in Geological and Natural History Survey of Canada Annual Report 1887–88* (Montreal: Dawson Bros., 1888), 6B. For further information about the work of J. B. Tyrrell, R. G. McConnell, Dr. Bell, A. P. Low, and others who were active in the North during these years, see Capt. Ernest J. Chambers, ed., *Canada's Fertile Northland: Evidence Heard Before a Select Committee of the Senate of Canada During the Parliamentary Session of 1906–7, and the Report Based Thereon* (Ottawa: Government Printing Bureau, 1908).

29 *Statutes of Canada*, 36 Vict., c. 35, 23 May 1873. See esp. s. 10. "The Governor in Council may constitute a Police Force in and for the North West Territories...."

30 Canada, Order in Council, PC No. 1134, 30 August 1873.

31 Government of Canada, Report of the Commissioner of the Northwest Mounted Police Force 1890, Sessional Paper No. 19 (1891), "Report of Inspector Bégin," 126–36. See also R. C. Fetherstonhaugh, *The Royal Canadian Mounted Police* (New York: Carrick and Evans, 1938), 94–95; Harwood Steele, *Policing the Arctic* (London: Jarrolds Publishers, 1936), 23–24.

32 Fetherstonhaugh, *Royal Canadian Mounted Police*, 96; Steele, *Policing the Arctic*, 24; *Report of the Commissioner of the North-West Mounted Police Force* 1893, appendix E, 93. In 1894 what Harwood Steele called the "northern battle-line" included Cumberland, Prince Albert, Battleford, Fort Saskatchewan, and St. Albert, counting only the permanent posts – none of them farther north than 54°. Of the summer detachments the most northerly, Grand Rapids, was only at 56°. Steele, *Policing the Arctic*, 24.

33 Holmden, "Memo re the Arctic Islands," 24–25. Holmden's failure to uncover any evidence of activity accords with the similar failure of Dr. King almost twenty years earlier, except that King, unaware of Canadian Order in Council No. 1839 of 23 September 1882 (and its implications), considers the period of inactivity to have lasted right from the transfer of 1880 to 1895. King remarks: "For light upon the understanding by Canada of the effect of this document (i.e., the Imperial Order in Council of July 31, 1880, making the transfer) we have to wait for fifteen years. A search through the Canadian Statutes and Orders in Council fails to show any recognition even of the fact that these lands had been transferred to Canada, until 1895." King, *Report upon the Title of Canada*, 6.

34 As King put it in 1904, "the North-west Territories, by the revised statutes of 1886, comprise Rupert's Land and the North-west Territories [*sic*], excluding Manitoba and Keewatin. No amendment to this North-west Territories Act, so as to include the northern territories, appears to have been enacted up to the present time." King, *Report upon the Title of Canada*, 6. The Manitoba Act of 1870 provided for the withdrawal of Manitoba, and defined the remaining "North-West Territories" as "such portion of Rupert's Land and the North-Western Territory, as is not included in the Province of Manitoba." *Statutes of Canada*, 33 Vict., c. 3, 12 May 1870. See s. 35. This definition was retained, essentially, in the North-West Territories Act of 1875. *Statutes of Canada*, 38 Vict., c. 49, 8 April 1875. See s. 1. The Keewatin Act of 1876 did not actually withdraw Keewatin from the Northwest Territories, but rather set it apart "as a separate district for the said North-West Territories." *Statutes of Canada*, 39 Vict., c. 21, 12 April 1876. See Preamble and s. 1. It is apparent that the act of 1876 did not specify clearly what Canada's northern limits were at the time, but the most reasonable interpretation of the quoted passage would appear to be that the boundary of Keewatin would run due north from the stated point until it reached the Arctic Ocean, and then follow the continental coastline eastward to the northern extremity of Hudson Bay. It is obvious, at any rate, that it was not the intention in the act of 1876 to include the Arctic Islands within the District of Keewatin; the fact that the same wording was retained in the Revised Statutes of 1886 would suggest, in itself, that these islands were still regarded as being beyond "the northerly limits of Canada." *Revised Statutes of Canada*, 1886, c. 53, s. 3.

3 | Organization and Administration of the NWT

1 Canada, Order in Council, PC No. 2640, 2 October 1895.

2 W. F. King, *Report upon the Title of Canada to the Islands North of the Mainland of Canada* (Ottawa: Government Printing Bureau, 1905), 6, 8.

3 Library and Archives Canada [hereafter LAC], Record Group 85, Northern Affairs Program [hereafter RG 85], vol. 584, file 571, pt. 5, H. R. Holmden to A. G. Doughty, "Memo re the Arctic Islands," 26 April 1921, 26–31, esp. 26, 30 [hereafter Holmden, "Memo re the Arctic Islands"]. See

also LAC, Record Group 15, Department of the Interior [hereafter RG 15], vol. 722, file 384,996. The Marquis of Ripon's letter of 28 May 1895, enclosed a draft of the Colonial Boundaries Bill, which was received in the Department of the Interior on 17 July 1895. Thus, so far as the time factor is concerned, Daly's report could have been affected by this draft of the bill.

4 House of Commons *Debates*, 28 May 1894, col. 3276.

5 Holmden, "Memo re the Arctic Islands," 26, 30–31.

6 Holmden, "Memo re the Arctic Islands," 27.

7 Canada, House of Commons *Debates*, 28 May 1894, cols. 3276–3278. See LAC, RG 15, vol. 707, file 357602, A/D.M. of Marine J. Hardin to Under Secretary of State L. A. Catellier, 26 June 1894, and D.M. of Interior A. M. Burgess to Catellier, 4 July 1894, each saying that there was no correspondence in his department regarding the Majesty's sovereignty over Hudson Bay.

8 Canada, Department of the Interior, *Annual Report for 1890* (Ottawa: Queen's Printer, 1891), VI, 4; Canada, Department of the Interior, *Annual Report for 1891*, IV, 4.

9 Canada, Department of the Interior, *Annual Report for 1894*, VI, 4–5. I have not been able to find either Schultz's first warning of "seventeen years ago," i.e., in or about 1877, regarding American activities in Hudson Bay, or his reports "from time to time" about American activities in the Arctic Ocean east of Bering Strait. For further discussion of Schultz's reports, see chapter 4.

10 Canada, Department of the Interior, *Annual Report for 1894*, xxxvii.

11 Canada, Department of the Interior, *Annual Report for 1894*, xix–xx.

12 Canada, Department of the Interior, *Annual Report for 1892*, xxxiii–xxxv.

13 Canada, Department of the Interior, *Annual Report for 1895*, xxxviii.

14 Canada, Department of the Interior, *Annual Report for 1895*, xxxvi–xxxix, also VI, 10.

15 There were certain other matters, for example the Bering Sea fur seals controversy, which, although not directly related to the region in question, may have helped to arouse Canadian anxiety as to its security. On 6 May 1890, Senator Girard of Manitoba moved in the Senate: "That in the opinion of this House, the time has arrived to organize that north-western part of the Dominion known as the Great Mackenzie Basin, and the attention of the Government is specially called to necessity for adopting a scheme for the better protection of its people, its valuable mines, fisheries and hunting grounds." In the course of his remarks supporting his motion, Mr. Gerard said, "My intention in moving this resolution is to call the attention of the Government to the necessity for constituted authority in this country – but that is not all. The great object is to keep the country for ourselves." Government Senate Leader J.J.C. Abbott in his reply referred to a senate committee which had investigated the "merits and capabilities of the great Mackenzie Basin" during the two preceding years, and to an expedition which was being sent as soon as possible to the region for the same purpose, and then added that "we confidently expect that next Session we shall be able to state formally what measures we shall take for the protection and development of this Territory." On his request Mr. Girard withdrew his motion. See Canada, Senate *Debates*, 6 May 1890, 695–702, and 29 May 1891, 58–60.

16 Canada, Order in Council, PC No. 2640, 2 October 1895. See in Canada, Department of the Interior, Orders in Council 1895, 603–4; also King, *Report upon the Title of Canada*, 11–13.

17 Canada, Order in Council, PC No. 3388, 18 December 1897. See in Canada, Department of the Interior, Orders in Council 1897, pp. 739–42 and map; also King, *Report upon the Title of Canada*, 14–16.

18 See King, *Report upon the Title of Canada*, 6–7, 16–17, for a discussion of these deficiencies, except those relating to the islands in Hudson Bay and Strait, as shown on the attached map, and the islands north of Keewatin.

19 It is worth noting that where the 1895 order spoke of "the unorganized and unnamed districts of the North West Territories," the 1897 order substituted instead the description "the portions of Canada not comprised within any Province." This change was probably not accidental.

20 L. J. Burpee, *An Historical Atlas of Canada* (Toronto: T. Nelson and Sons, 1927), 22.

21 *Statutes of Canada*, 61 Vict., c. 6, 13 June 1898.

22 Canada, Order in Council, PC No. 2406, 16 August 1897. See in *Canada Gazette*, XXXI, No. 8 (21 August 1897), 350; and as Sched. to 61 Vict., c. 6 (cited above).

23 King, *Report upon the Title of Canada*, 7, 17–19.

24 King, *Report upon the Title of Canada*, 19. King also observed (p. 18) that a rather odd Yukon

Provisional District might have been left after the Yukon Territory had been created in 1898, comprising only a seventeen-mile strip of water and islands between the three- and twenty-mile limits.

25 *Statutes of Canada*, 1 Edw. VII, c. 41, 23 May 1901.

26 King, *Report upon the Title of Canada*, 17–19. See also Canada, House of Commons *Debates*, 16 April 1901, cols. 3091–3094. Other aspects of the boundaries of the Yukon, on the east and southwest, were discussed, but the exchange in the northern boundary was passed over.

27 The Keewatin Act of 1876 provided (s. 1) that the governor in council might at any time re-annex portions of Keewatin to the Northwest Territories, but said nothing about adding territories to it.

28 *Statutes of Canada*, 4–5 Edw. VII, c. 3 and c. 42, 20 July 1905.

29 This subject is dealt with in considerable detail in C. C. Lingard, *Territorial Government in Canada: The Autonomy Question in the Old North-West Territories* (Toronto: University of Toronto Press, 1946), esp. chap. 6; N. L. Nicholson, *The Boundaries of Canada, Its Provinces and Territories*, Memoir 2 of Geographical Branch, Department of Mines and Technical Surveys (Ottawa: Queen's Printer, 1954), esp. pp. 79–85. See also L. H. Thomas, *The Struggle for Responsible Government in the North-West Territories 1870–97* (Toronto: University of Toronto Press, 1956), 256–58.

30 See Sir Wilfrid Laurier's remarks in House of Commons *Debates*, 21 February 1905, cols. 1427–1428; 15 March 1905, cols. 2505–2506.

31 I have not seen any act or order in council specifically making this addition, or the further addition to Keewatin, north of the 60th parallel, of the territory between the 100th and 102nd meridians. Yet some maps show these territories as part of Keewatin after 1905, e.g., L. J. Burpee, *Historical Atlas of Canada*, 21, map 59.

32 Canada, Order in Council, PC No. 1438, 24 July 1905. It was evidently intended that the order should make the additions of territory mentioned in the preceding footnote, as it stated that "it is advisable that all the said area should be first brought under one administration." However, although the order re-annexed the whole of Keewatin to the Northwest Territories, it did not specifically annex the territories in question to Keewatin. It was later argued in the House of Commons that the order was probably illegal, because the Keewatin Act gave authority only to re-annex part of Keewatin to the Northwest Territories, not all of it. See House of Commons *Debates*, 5 March 1912, cols. 4402, 4413–4415, 4445–4446.

33 *Statutes of Canada*, 4–5 Edw. VII, c. 27, 20 July 1905. When the second reading of this bill (No. 160) took place in the House of Commons on 4 July 1905, the following discussion on the quoted section occurred (col. 8765):

Mr. R. L. Borden. These are all embraced in the Dominion?

Mt. Fitzpatrick. We are taking in a part of territory about which there may be some doubt – the part, lying between the height of land in Ungava and the Labrador coast. It would appear at first sight as if Rupert's Land included all the territory watered by the rivers that run from the height of land in the Hudson Bay, but between the height of land in Ungava and the Labrador coast there is a small strip of territory which is apparently no man's land at present.

Mr. R. L. Borden. Is there any danger of this expression taking in all the British West India Islands?

Mr. Fielding. If they are in North America.

Mr. R. L. Borden. The section says 'adjacent to.' I think there is a piece of British territory on the mainland in Central America.

Mr. Fielding. The hon. gentleman refers to British Guiana?

Mr. R. L. Borden. No; near Honduras, on the mainland of Central America. I confess I do not know the names of all the British West Indies.

Mr. Fitzpatrick. As far as a declaration of this parliament can affect it, we might bring it in; but I think a declaration of this sort would be exceedingly useful to us, because there are islands in the north that belong to Canada, and already two foreign states have entered into possession of a portion of our territory. In order to make my position closer, I may say that this is taken from the Order in Council which was passed July 1st, 1880 – it is an adaptation of that description.

34 *Revised Statutes of Canada* (RSC) 1906, c. 62, s. 2 (a). This definition was repeated verbatim in *RSC* 1927, c. 142, s. 2 (k).

35 The Hon. F. D. Monk later remarked that this appeared to be a contradiction between *R.S.C.* 1906, c. 62, s. 2, and 4–5 Edw. VII, c. 27. See House of Commons *Debates*, 5 March 1912, cols. 4413–4415.

36 *Statutes of Canada*, 2 Geo V, c. 32, c. 40, c. 45, 1 April 1912. See also Nicholson, *Boundaries of Canada*, 85–90.

37 *Statutes of Canada*, 61 Vict., c. 3, 13 June 1898. See also Nicholson, *Boundaries of Canada*, 64–66.

38 All three of the 1912 acts were modelled upon a resolution introduced by former Prime Minister Laurier and passed by the House of Commons on 13 July 1908. See House of Commons *Debates*, 13 July 1908, cols. 12776–12777, 12836.

39 House of Commons *Debates*, 13 July 1908, col. 12779; 4 March 1912, col. 4264.

40 House of Commons *Debates*, 18 March 1912, col. 5270.

41 For the entire case, see Great Britain, in the Privy Council, *In the Matter of the Boundary Between the Dominion of Canada and the Colony of Newfoundland in the Labrador Peninsula*, 12 vols. (London: Wm. Clowes and Sons, 1927). For the Report only, see *Dominion Law Reports* (1927), II, 401–29. *Editor's note*: The text of Smith's chapter on the Labrador boundary dispute will eventually be made available on a permanent website.

42 Unless the islands in Hudson and James Bays and Hudson Strait, formerly part of Ungava and not given to Quebec in 1912, still constituted an Ungava District. See Canada, Department of Mines and Technical Surveys Geographical Branch, *Atlas of Canada* (Ottawa: Queen's Printer, 1957), Plate No. 109 (1912).

43 Canada, Order in Council, PC No. 655, 16 March 1918. See also in Canada, Department of the Interior, Orders in Council 1918, 225–26, and map.

44 The map accompanying the order in council bears out these suppositions, except that, so far as one can tell, the islands within twenty miles of the Yukon coast were included in Franklin District. This could hardly have been the case, since the order in council could not have changed specific provisions of the act of 1901. Also, although the order says nothing about sector lines, such lines are shown marking the limits of Franklin on both west and east. The western line simply follows the 141st meridian; the eastern one runs in irregular fashion through Baffin Bay and Davis Strait to the northeastern extremity of Quebec near Cape Chidley.

45 Burpee, *Historical Atlas of Canada*, 22.

4 | Whaling and the Yukon Gold Rush

1 Captain W. Scoresby, *The Northern Whale-Fishery* (London: Religious Tract Society, n.d.), 25; Basil Lubbock, *The Arctic Whalers* (Glasgow: Brown, Son, and Ferguson, 1955), 82, 85ff., passim; E. Keble Chatterton, *Whalers and Whaling* (London: P. Allan, 1925), 39.

2 *An Act for the further Support and Encouragement of the Fisheries carried on in the Greenland Seas and Davis's Streights*, 1786, 26 Geo. III, c. 41; and Scoresby, *Northern Whale-Fishery*, 27.

3 Clements R. Markham, ed., *The Voyages of William Baffin 1612–1622* (London: Hakluyt Society, 1881), 145, 151–53.

4 Lubbock, *The Arctic Whalers*, 346, 356–57; Alexander Starbuck, *History of the American Whale Fishery from its Earliest Inception to the Year 1876* (New York: Argosy-Antiquarian, 1964), 1:24–25, 168; 2:440–41; A. P. Low, *Cruise of the Neptune 1903–04* (Ottawa: Government Printing Bureau, 1906), 250.

5 E. E. Rich, "Letters Outward 1679–1694," in *The Publications of the Hudson's Bay Record Society* (London: Hudson's Bay Record Society, 1948), 1:234–35, 440, 448, and 11:236–340.

6 Rich, "Letters Outward 1679–94," 1:539–40, 621–22; S. Hearne, "A Journey from Prince of Wales's Fort in Hudson's Bay to the Northern Ocean in the Years 1769, 1770, 1771, and 1772," in *The Publications of The Champlain Society*, ed. J. B. Tyrell (Toronto: Champlain Society, 1911), 6:363–65.

7 John Rae, *Narrative of an Expedition to the Shores of the Arctic Sea in 1846 and 1847* (London: T. and W. Boone, 1850), 13, 27, 32, 190.

8 Starbuck, *History of the American Whale Fishery*, 1:139–40, 148; 2:580–83, 596–603. According to Lubbock (Lubbock, *The Arctic Whalers*, 103), ships from the American colonies engaged successfully in whaling in Hudson Bay as early as 1764.

9 Chatterton, *Whalers and Whaling*, 231–32.

10 William Wakeham, *Report of the Expedition to Hudson Bay and Cumberland Gulf in the Steamship "Diana"* (Ottawa: Queen's Printer, 1898), 74, 54–61.

11 Low, *Cruise of the Neptune 1903–04*, 252.

12 Starbuck, *History of the American Whale Fishery*, 1:98–99; A. Hyatt Verrill, *The Real Story of the Whaler* (New York: Appleton and Co., 1931), 288; C. L. Andrews, *The Story of Alaska* (Caldwell, Idaho: Caxton Printers, 1947), 113; H. W. Clark,

History of Alaska (New York: Macmillan, 1930), 57, 62.

13 Lloyd C. M. Hare, *Salted Tories: The Story of the Whaling Fleets of San Francisco* (Mystic, CT: Marine Historical Association, 1960), passim, 12, 33, 56, 64; Starbuck, *History of the American Whale Fishery*, 1:100.

14 Andrews, *Story of Alaska*, 113; Hare, *Salted Tories*, 86ff.

15 Andrews, *Story of Alaska*, 144–45; Hare, *Salted Tories*, 90ff.

16 Lt. A. R. Gordon, *Report*, 1884, 13–17; Gordon, *Report*, 1885, 54–55; Gordon, *Report*, 1886, 60–67, 92.

17 Canada, House of Commons *Debates* (16 April 1888), 826 (Mr. Amyot, MP, and Mr. Foster, MP).

18 Gordon, *Report*, 1886, 66–67.

19 Canada, Department of the Interior, *Annual Report for 1890* (Ottawa: Queen's Printer, 1891), 6:4.

20 Canada, Department of the Interior, *Annual Report for 1891* (Ottawa: Queen's Printer, 1892), 4:4. The passage from Lt.-Gov. Schultz's reports for 1891 was brought up in the House of Commons by J. McMullen (North Wellington) on 27 June 1892. Quoting the passage himself, he asked if the government had considered the matter, and if it intended to refer it to the Bering Sea arbitrators, or "take other steps to prevent a continuance of the alleged poaching and smuggling by United States vessels in Canadian waters in Hudson Bay?" Replying for the government, Justice Minister Sir John Thompson said that whatever steps seemed necessary would be taken, but the time was not opportune to announce any action contemplated, and in any case the question did not fall within the responsibility of the Bering Sea arbitrators. Mr. Mills (Bothwell) asserted that "the whole of Hudson Bay is Canadian water." Canada, House of Commons *Debates*, 27 June 1892, cols. 4262–4263 (Mr. McMullen, MP and Mr. Thompson, MP).

21 Canada, Department of the Interior, *Annual Report for 1891*, xxix.

22 Canada, Order in Council, PC No. 457H, 29 April 1891. In Library and Archives Canada, with accompanying documents, newspaper clipping, 29 November 1890, Gray to Graham, 5 December 1890, Secretary for Scotland to Colonial Office, 12 January 1891, and Knutsford to Stanley, 16 January 1891.

23 *Canada Gazette*, 25 July 1891. See also *Revised Statutes of Canada* 1886.

24 Canada, Order in Council, PC No. 2034, 12 September 1892. The Order further noted that replies had been sent by the HBC Commissioner on 17 August 1891, and 19 September 1891, saying that the officer in charge of the Mackenzie River District had been instructed to distribute the posters.

25 Canada, Senate *Debates*, 11 April 1894, 208 (Mr. Ferguson, Senator).

26 Canada, House of Commons *Debates*, 28 May 1894, cols. 3276–3278 (Mr. Mills, MP, and Mr. Tupper MP).

27 Canada, Department of the Interior, *Annual Report for 1894* (Ottawa: Queen's Printer, 1895), 6:4–5.

28 Canada, Department of the Interior, *Annual Report for 1894*, xxxvii.

29 Canada, Department of the Interior, *Annual Report for 1896* (Ottawa: Queen's Printer, 1895), 6:4.

30 Canada, Department of the Interior, *Annual Report for 1896*, xli.

31 Canada, House of Commons *Debates*, 12 April 1897, col. 794 (Mr. Davis, MP).

32 Canada, House of Commons *Debates*, 21 June 1897, col. 4735 (Mr. Oliver, MP).

33 Canada, Sessional Papers, 1897, No. 15, Report of the Commissioner of the North-West Mounted Police Force in 1896. See Constantine's report in appendix DD, 232–39, esp. 238.

34 International Boundary Commission, *Joint Report upon the Survey and Demarcation of the International Boundary between the United States and Canada along the 141st Meridian from the Arctic Ocean to Mount St. Elias* (Ottawa, 1918), 212; Frederick Whymper, *Travel and Adventure in the Territory of Alaska* (New York: Harper and Bros., 1871), 193.

35 W. H. Dall, "Travels on the Yukon and in the Yukon Territory in 1866–1868," in *The Yukon Territory*, ed. F. M. Trimmer (London: Downey and Co, 1898).

36 Dall, "Travels on the Yukon," 63, 85, 110; Whymper, *Travel and Adventure*, 258–59.

37 Whymper, *Travel and Adventure*, 239.

38 International Boundary commission, *Joint Report upon the Survey and Demarcation*, 212–13; William Ogilvie, *Early Days on the Yukon* (London: John Lane, The Bodley Head, 1913), 22–24; G. M. Dawson, *Report on an Exploration in the Yukon District, N.W.T., and Adjacent Northern Portion of British Columbia 1887, issued by the Geological and Natural History Survey of Canada* (Montreal:

Dawson Bros., 1888), 14, 136–38. See also the long and informative speech on the Yukon and its early history by Yukon Territory M.P. Dr. A. Thompson in Canada, House of Commons *Debates*, 7 June 1905, cols. 7021–7067, esp. 7021–7026.

39 International Boundary Commission, *Joint Report upon the Survey and Demarcation*, 213; Dawson, *Report on an Exploration*, 14, 138; Ogilvie, *Early Days on the Yukon*, 24; Whymper, *Travel and Adventure*, 253.

40 Dawson, *Report on an Exploration*, 139. *Editor's note*: I updated the reference to the attackers using Ken Coates, "Robert Campbell (1808–1894)," *Arctic* 38, no. 3 (1985): 249.

41 C. W. Raymond, Report of a Reconnaissance of the Yukon River, Alaska Territory, July to September, 1869, U.S. Senate, 42nd Congress, 1st Session, Ex. Doc. No. 12 (Washington, DC: Government Printing Office, 1871), 16. See also Dawson, *Report on an Exploration*, 140.

42 Ogilvie, *Early Days on the Yukon*, 26, 62; International Boundary Commission, *Joint Report upon the Survey and Demarcation*, 227. See also R. G. McConnell, *Report of an Exploration in the Yukon and Mackenzie Basins, N.W.T., issued by the Geological and Natural History Survey of Canada* (Montreal: W. F. Brown and Co., 1891), 131, where he observed, "As a fur post it barely pays expenses … and is kept up mainly as a protection against the encroachments of traders from the west."

43 Dawson, *Report on an Exploration*, 142, 179. See also International Boundary Commission, *Joint Report upon the Survey and Demarcation*, 214.

44 F. Schwatka, *Along Alaska's Great River* (New York: Cassell and Co., 1885), e.g., 117–18, 179–80, 187–88.

45 Report of Deputy Minister A. M. Burgess to Minister of the Interior Thomas White, in Canada, Department of the Interior, *Annual Report for the Year 1886*, xxxiv.

46 Dawson, *Report on an Exploration*; also his summary in Canada, Department of the Interior, *Annual Report for the Year 1887*, Part III, 5–10.

47 McConnell, *Report of an Exploration*; also his summaries in Canada, Department of the Interior, *Annual Report for the Year 1887*, Part III, 10–11, and *1888*, Part III, 10–12.

48 William Ogilvie, "Exploratory Survey of Part of the Lewes, Tat-On-Duc, Porcupine, Bell, Trout, Peel, and Mackenzie Rivers, in Canada," Department of the Interior, *Annual Report for the Year 1889*, Part VIII, 1–101; also his preliminary report in *Annual Report for the Year 1887*, Part II, 64–69; and Deputy Minister Burgess's brief comment in *Annual Report for the Year 1888*, xix–xx. See also International Boundary Commission, *Joint Report upon the Survey and Demarcation*, 218–25.

49 Canada, Department of the Interior, *Annual Report for the Year 1887*, xxiv.

50 Canada, Department of the Interior, *Annual Report for the Year 1888*, xix–xx.

51 Whymper, *Travel and Adventure*, 258.

52 G. M. Dawson, *Annual Report for the Year 1887*, 179.

53 Pierre Berton, *The Klondike Fever* (New York: A. A. Knopf, 1959), 5.

54 Dawson, *Annual Report for the Year 1887*, 26; also Dawson in Department of the Interior *Annual Report for the Year 1887*, Part III, 8–9.

55 Ogilvie in Department of the Interior *Annual Report for the Year 1887*, Part II, 68; Dawson, *Annual Report for the Year 1887*, 182.

56 Canada, Department of the Interior, *Annual Report for the Year 1895*, xxxvi–xxxix.

57 Canada, Department of the Interior, *Annual Report for the Year 1895*, xxxviii. See *Annual Report for the Year 1896*, Part II, 48, for Ogilvie's note written at Fort Cudahy on 6 Sept. 1896, informing the authorities in Ottawa of the great strike on the Klondike. This was perhaps the first message to be sent "outside" about the discovery.

58 International Boundary commission, *Joint Report upon the Survey and Demarcation*, 225–36, also 25. See also Ogilvie, *Early Days on the Yukon*, 60–61.

59 A very large literature, both fact and fiction, has been produced on the Yukon Gold Rush. See the comprehensive bibliographies in Berton, *Klondike Fever*, 446–57; and in J. R. Lotz, *Yukon Bibliography, Preliminary Edition*, Yukon Research Project Report No. 1, issued by the Northern Co-ordination and Research Centre, Department of Northern Affairs and National Resources (Ottawa, 1964), esp. 67–83. A few of the more important works, besides those by Berton and Ogilvie already cited, are T. Adney, *The Klondike Stampede of 1897–1898* (New York and London: Harper and Bros., 1900); P. Berton, *The Golden Trail: The Story of the Klondike Rush* (Toronto: Macmillan, 1954); K. Winslow, *Big Pan-Out* (New York: Norton and Co., 1951); A. T. Walden, *A Dog-Puncher on the Yukon* (Boston: Houghton Mifflin, 1928); Mrs. G. Black, *My Seventy Years* (London: T. Nelson and Sons, 1938); J. Lynch, *Three Years in the Klondike*,

ed. D. L. Morgan (Chicago: Lakeside Press, 1967); W. R. Hamilton, *The Yukon Story* (Vancouver: Mitchell Press, 1964); F. Palmer, *In the Klondyke* (New York: Scribner's Sons, 1899); and W. B. Haskell, *Two Years in the Klondyke and Alaskan Gold-Fields* (Hartford: Hartford Publishing, 1898).

60 Canada, Department of the Interior, *Annual Report for the Year 1898*, Part IV, 326 (Report of Major J. M. Walsh, Commissioner of Yukon District.). See also Berton, *Klondike Fever*, 300, 417.

61 An unidentified writer in the *Review of Reviews*, cited in Adney, *Klondike Stampede*, 385.

62 Adney, *Klondike Stampede*, 432.

63 Canada, Department of the Interior, *Annual Report for the Year 1902–1903*, xlviii (Report of the Deputy Minister J. A. Smart, dated 5 December 1903). It can safely be assumed that the value figure was too low, since many would conceal their gold in order to avoid having to pay royalties on it. Dr. Thompson, in the above-mentioned speech in the House of Commons on 7 June 1905, said that since 1896 the Yukon had produced over $120,000,000 worth of gold (col. 7025).

64 See Appendix by Dr. Thompson in Ogilvie, *Early Days on the Yukon*, 302ff.

65 Canada, Order in Council, PC No. 1638, 28 May 1894, appointed Constantine "a Commissioner of Police within the North-West Territories of Canada." See also Pierre Berton, *Klondike* (Toronto: McClelland and Stewart, 1958), 26–27.

66 See Constantine's report in Canada, Sessional Papers (1895), No. 15; *Report of the Commissioner of the North-West Mounted Police Force 1894*, 69–85.

67 H. T. Steele, *Policing the Arctic* (London: Jarrolds Publishers, 1936), 27–28; D. A. Young, *The Mounties* (London: Hodder and Stoughton, 1968), 61–62; R. C. Fetherstonhaugh, *The Royal Canadian Mounted Police* (New York: Carrick and Evans, 1938), 69–71; Canada, Sessional Papers (1896), No. 15; *Report of the Commissioner of the North-West Mounted Police Force 1895*, 21–22.

68 See Constantine's report for 1896 in Canada, Sessional Papers (1897), No. 15; *Report of the Commissioner of the North-West Mounted Police Force 1896*, 232–39; also excerpts from Constantine's letters to the commissioner in T. M. Longstreth, *The Silent Force* (New York: Century, 1927), 196–97.

69 See extracts from Ogilvie's reports in Canada, Sessional Papers (1897), No. 13, Part II, pp. 40–54. For example, in that of 6 September 1896, written at Fort Cudahy: "I am very much pleased to be able to inform you that a most important discovery of gold has been made on creek called Bonanza creek.... You can fancy the excitement here.... Already on Bonanza creek they are disputing about the size of claims.... A continuation of this state of affairs is most undesirable in the interests of our country."

70 Canada, Order in Council, PC No. 2468, 17 August 1897, appointed Walsh Commissioner of the Yukon Territory, and gave him astonishing powers: "Chief executive officer of the Government in that district ... vested with the fullest authority over all the officials of the various Departments of the Government ... power to remove, suspend or supersede any official except the Judge of the Supreme Court .... In full command of the North West Mounted Police Force .... power to vary, alter or amend any mining regulations issued under authority of Your Excellency in Council ...." Walsh's powers and responsibilities were further detailed in later orders in council, PC No. 2500, 26 August 1897, appointing him "Commissioner of Police within the North West Territories"; PC No. 2501 (26 Aug. 1897), appointing him "a Superintendent, without salary, in the North West Mounted Police," with precedence in rank in the Yukon District and relieving the Commissioner of the North West Mounted Police of responsibility and command there; and PC No. 2697, 20 September 1897, giving him authority which had previously been held by Constantine, to control the cutting and disposal of timber in the Yukon.

71 Canada, Sessional Papers (1899), No. 15, Part III, 16–17; Part IV, 7.

72 Canada, Order in Council, PC No. 1775, 4 July 1898; also PC No. 1901, 3 Aug. 1898, appointing Ogilvie Inspector of Customs. See also S. B. Steele, *Forty Years in Canada* (Toronto: McClelland et al., 1918), 318; Major J. M Walsh, *Report Respecting the Yukon District*, pamphlet issued by the Department of the Interior (Ottawa: Government Printing Bureau, 1898).

73 Steele, *Policing the Arctic*, 38.

74 Canada, Order in Council, PC No. 1796, 7 July 1898, also PC No. 1813, 7 July 1898, appointing Steele a member of the newly created Yukon Council. See also Steele, *Forty Years in Canada*, 291, 317.

75 Canada, Sessional Papers (1899), No. 15, Part III, 1–139; (1900), No. 15, Part II, 1–79; Fetherstonhaugh, *Royal Canadian Mounted Police*, 69–84; Steele, *Forty Years in Canada*, 288–337; Steele, *Policing the Arctic*, 17–96; Young, *The Mounties*, 61–69; Longstreth, *Silent Force*, 193–207; T. M. Longstreth, *In Scarlet and Plain Clothes* (Toronto:

Macmillan, 1933), 198–234; A. L. Haydon, *The Riders of the Plains* (London: A. Melrose, 1910), 188–228; and E. J. Chambers, *The Royal North-West Mounted Police* (Montreal: Mortimer Press, 1906), 119ff.

76 Canada, Sessional Papers (1898), No. 15, Appendix N, 183–96, also Report of Commissioner L. W. Herchmer, 3; (1899), No. 15, Appendix C, 42–44, also Part II, 3–82, 83–101, also Report of Commissioner Herchmer, 1–2.

77 *Foreign Relations of the United States* (hereafter cited as *FRUS*) *1897*, 327, Adam to Sherman, 23 July 1897.

78 *FRUS 1897*, 327, Adee to Adam, 28 July 1897.

79 H. G. Classen, *Thrust and Counterthrust: The Genesis of the Canada–United States Boundary* (Don Mills: Longmans Canada, 1965), 319.

80 *FRUS 1897*, 327–28, Adam to Sherman, 11 August 1897.

81 *FRUS 1897*, 329, Sherman to Adam, 14 September 1897.

82 *FRUS 1897*, 325–26, Sherman to Pauncefote, 20 December 1897, and enclosure.

83 *FRUS 1897*, 326, Pauncefote to Sherman, 27 December 1897.

84 Canada, Department of the Interior, *Annual Report for the Year 1898*, Part IV, 317–18.

85 *British and Foreign State Papers* (1870–1871), LXI, 51 (Washington Treaty, 8 May 1871).

86 J. B. Moore, *A Digest of International Law*, I, 635–36, citing Mr. Adee, Second Assist. Sec. of State, to Mr. Woodbury, 6 Jan. 1898, 224 MS Dom. Let. 229. See *British and Foreign State Papers (1897–1898)*, XC, 434–41, for US "Regulations governing the Entry and Transportation of Merchandize destined for the Klondike Region and North-west Territory of British Columbia…," 2 February 1898, Canadian "Regulations issued by the Commissioner of Customs…," 17 December 1897, and 8 January 1898, and US "Regulations respecting the Navigation of the Yukon and Porcupine Rivers and their Tributaries…," 2 February 1898.

87 See *American Journal of International Law*, VII, Part 2 (1913), 885–90. American and British Claims Arbitration, Award of the Tribunal in the Matter of Yukon Lumber, Claim No. 5, 18 June 1913.

5 | The Alaska Boundary Dispute

1 Hubert H. Bancroft, *History of Alaska, vol. 33 of The Works of Hubert Howe Bancroft* (San Francisco: A. L. Bancroft, 1886), 20.

2 Gerhard F. Muller, *Voyages from Asia to America*, trans. T. Jefferys (London: T. Jefferys, 1764), esp. 4–14. Muller, a German historian who was attached to Bering's second expedition, discovered Dezhnev's original account of his expedition in the archives at Yakutsk in 1736. The actuality of Dezhnev's achievement, and the validity of Muller's interpretation of his story, have been strongly attacked in Frank A. Golder, *Russian Expansion on the Pacific 1641–1850* (Cleveland: A. H. Clark, 1914), 67–95. See appendices A and B in Golder's book for Muller's account of Dezhnev's voyage and Dezhnev's own report. See also Bancroft, *History of Alaska*, 22–24; and Terence E. Armstrong, *Russian Settlement in the North* (Cambridge: Cambridge University Press, 1965), 23–24. Both of these accept Dezhnev's report and Muller's interpretation of it.

3 Frank A. Golder, ed., *Bering's Voyages*, American Geographical Society Research Series 1 and 2, ed. W.L.G. Joerg (New York: American Geographical Society, 1922, 1925). See also Bancroft, *History of Alaska*, 35–98.

4 Bancroft, *History of Alaska*, passim; Clarence L. Andrews, *The Story of Alaska* (Caldwell, ID: Caxton Printers, 1947); Ernest Gruening, *The State of Alaska* (New York: Random House, 1954); Stepan P. Karsheninnikov, *The History of Kamtschatka And the Kurilski Islands, with the Countries Adjacent*, trans. James Grieve (St. Petersburg, 1754; London, 1764; Chicago: Quadrangle Books, 1962); Henry W. Clark, *History of Alaska* (New York: Macmillan, 1930); William Coxe, *Account of the Russian Discoveries between Asia and America* (London: T. Cadell, 1787); William H. Dall, "The Discovery and Exploration of Alaska," in *Alaska*, ed. C. Hart Merriam (London: J. Murray, 1902), 2:185–204.

5 See summaries of these expeditions in *Fur Seal Arbitration*, 2:26–33, 4:14–19; Alaska Boundary Tribunal, *British Case*, 6–13; also Bancroft, *History of Alaska*, 49–56.

6 The text of the ukase may be seen in Alaska Boundary Tribunal, *Appendix to the Case of His Majesty's Government*, 1:5–6; Fur Seal Arbitration, 2: Appendix, 14–15; 4:22–23; also Bancroft, *History of Alaska*, 379–90. For a detailed treatment of the Russian American Company, with a strongly Marxist viewpoint, see Semen B. Okun,

The Russian-American Company, ed. B. D. Grekov, trans. Carl Ginsburg (Cambridge, MA: Harvard University Press, 1951).

7 *Fur Seal Arbitration*, 4:21–22, 24–25, citing *American State Papers*: Foreign Relations, 5:461.

8 See Count Romanzoff to Harris, 17 May 1808 in *Memorandum for Counsel, Various Documents Bearing on the Question of the Alaska Boundary*, Alaska Boundary Tribunal (London: McCorquodale, 1903), 2:20–30; Daschkoff to Smith, January 4, 1810, in *Memorandum for Counsel*, Alaska Boundary Tribunal, 2:20–30; and Daschkoff to Smith, 24 April 1810, in *Memorandum for Counsel*, Alaska Boundary Tribunal, 2:20–30.

9 British and Foreign State Papers (1821–22), 9:472–82; Alaska Boundary Tribunal, *Appendix to the Case of His Majesty's Government*, I:7–14; Alaska Boundary Tribunal, *Reports, Treaties, etc.*, no. 1, 136–42; Alaska Boundary Tribunal, *Memorandum for Counsel*, 2:7–11; *Fur Seal Arbitration*, 2: Appendix, 16–24; 4:30–33. See especially parts 1, 2.

10 *Fur Seal Arbitration*, 2: Appendix, 24–27.

11 Alaska Boundary Tribunal, *Memorandum for Counsel*, 2:11.

12 Alaska Boundary Tribunal, *Memorandum for Counsel*, 2:11–12.

13 Alaska Boundary Tribunal, *Memorandum for Counsel*, 2:13. See also *Fur Seal Arbitration*, 4:38–41.

14 *American State Papers*: Foreign Relations, 5:246. See ibid., 432–71, for correspondence between the United States and Russia on the Russian regulations of 1824.

15 William M. Malloy, ed., *Treaties, Conventions, International Acts, Protocols and Agreements between the United States of America and Other Powers 1776–1909* (Washington, DC: Government Printing Office, 1910), 2:1512–14; British and Foreign State Papers (1824–25), 12:595–600. See also Alaska Boundary Tribunal, *Memorandum for Counsel*, 2:13–55; *Fur Seal Arbitration*, 2: pt. 1, 51ff.; Appendix, 35–37; 4:38–42.

16 Alaska Boundary Tribunal, *Appendix to British Case*, 1:14–15.

17 Robinson to Londonderry, 20 November 1821, in *Appendix to British Case*, Alaska Boundary Tribunal, 1:16.

18 Bagot to Londonderry, 17 November 1821, in *Appendix to British Case*, Alaska Boundary Tribunal, 1:18–19. Article 12 of the Treaty of Utrecht stated that "the subjects of the most Christian King shall hereafter be excluded from all kind of fishing in the said seas, bays, and other places, on the coasts of Nova Scotia, that is today, on those which lie towards the east, within 30 leagues." See George Chalmers, *A Collection of Treaties between Great Britain and Other Powers* (London: J. Stockdale, 1790), 1:380–81.

19 Londonderry to Lieven, 18 January 1822, in *Appendix to British Case*, Alaska Boundary Tribunal, 1:20–21.

20 For details about the coalition, see E. E. Rich, *The History of the Hudson's Bay Company 1670–1870* (London: Hudson's Bay Record Society, 1958–59), 2: chaps. 16, 17; Arthur S. Morton, *A History of the Canadian West to 1870–71* (London: T. Nelson and Sons, 1939), 623–43; John S. Galbraith, *The Hudson's Bay Company as an Imperial Factor 1821–1869* (Toronto: University of Toronto Press, 1957), 3–13.

21 An Act for Regulating the Fur Trade, and Establishing a Criminal and Civil Jurisdiction within certain Parts of North America, 1821, 1 & 2 Geo. IV, c. 66. For both act and royal licence (5 Dec. 1821), see Hudson's Bay Company, Charters, Statutes, Orders in Council, etc., Relating to the Hudson's Bay Company (London: HBC, 1960), 93–102, 217. For complete text of royal licence, see House of Commons, "Report from the Select Committee on the Hudson's Bay Company together with the proceedings of the committee, minutes of evidence, appendix and index," *Sessional Papers, 1857–1858, Hudson's Bay Company*, 2:425–27.

22 Pelly to Londonderry, 27 March 1822, in *Appendix to British Case*, Alaska Boundary Tribunal, 1:22–23.

23 Pelly to Canning, 25 September 1822, in *Appendix to British Case*, Alaska Boundary Tribunal, 1:24–25; Pelly to Canning, 8 January 1824, in *Appendix to British Case*, Alaska Boundary Tribunal, 1:63–64.

24 Bathurst to Wellington, 14 September 1822, in *Appendix to British Case*, Alaska Boundary Tribunal, 1:23.

25 Memorandum by Wellington, 11 September 1822, in *Appendix to British Case*, Alaska Boundary Tribunal, 1:23–24.

26 Canning to Wellington, 27 September 1822, in *Appendix to British Case*, Alaska Boundary Tribunal, 1:28–29.

27 Wellington to Nesselrode, 17 October 1822, in *Appendix to British Case*, Alaska Boundary Tribunal, 1:29–30.

28 Nesselrode to Wellington, 23 November 1822, in *Appendix to British Case*, Alaska Boundary Tribunal, 1:30–32.

29 Wellington to Lieven, 28 November 1822, in *Appendix to British Case*, Alaska Boundary Tribunal, 1:32.

30 Wellington to Canning, 29 November 1822, in *Appendix to British Case*, Alaska Boundary Tribunal, 1:32.

31 Canning to Bagot, 12 July 1823, in *Appendix to British Case*, Alaska Boundary Tribunal, 1:40; Nesselrode to Lieven, 26 June 1823, in *Appendix to British Case*, Alaska Boundary Tribunal, 1:42.

32 Canning to Bagot, 5 February 1823, 25 February 1823, in *Appendix to British Case*, Alaska Boundary Tribunal, 1:34–25.

33 Canning to Bagot, 12 July 1823, in *Appendix to British Case*, Alaska Boundary Tribunal, 1:41.

34 Tuyll to Nesselrode, 2 November 1822, in *Appendix to British Case*, Alaska Boundary Tribunal, 1:33. This would be just south of the 55th parallel.

35 Bagot to Canning, 31 August 1823, in *Appendix to British Case*, Alaska Boundary Tribunal, 1:45; Bagot to Canning, 29 October 1823, in *Appendix to British Case*, Alaska Boundary Tribunal, 1:48.

36 Bagot to Canning, 29 October 1823, in *Appendix to British Case*, Alaska Boundary Tribunal, 1:48. Poletica to Nesselrode, 3 November 1823, in *Appendix to British Case*, Alaska Boundary Tribunal, 1:53, 55.

37 Poletica to Nesselrode, 3 November 1823, in *Appendix to British Case*, Alaska Boundary Tribunal, 1:53, 55.

38 Bagot to Canning, 29 March 1824, in *Appendix to British Case*, Alaska Boundary Tribunal, 1:66–75 and Enclosures 2, 4. See also James White, "Henry Cabot Lodge and the Alaska Boundary Award," *Canadian Historical Review* 6, no. 4 (Dec. 1925): 920–23, and map facing 938.

39 Bagot to Canning, 29 March 1824, in *Appendix to British Case*, Alaska Boundary Tribunal, 1:66–75 and Enclosures 1, 3; See also Nesselrode to Lieven, 17 April 1824, in *Appendix to British Case*, Alaska Boundary Tribunal, 1:75–78. This letter indicates the determination of the Russian government to stand by its proposal, which Nesselrode justified on grounds that "we desire to keep and the English Companies want to acquire."

40 Alaska Boundary Tribunal, *Appendix to British Case*, 1:66–67. I cannot agree with the statement in Galbraith, *The Hudson's Bay Company as an Imperial Factor*, 130, that the hypothesis that the Russo-American treaty of 17 April 1824 was a serious embarrassment to the British and a factor in their eventual "surrender" of the Russian case "bears no relationship to fact." It may be true, as he suggests, that Canning had decided to agree substantially to the Russian proposals before the news of the treaty reached him. But this is not the whole story. All three governments knew what was in the offing well before the treaty was signed, and, as the correspondence shows clearly, this knowledge did embarrass the British and stiffen the resolution of the Russians. See Alaska Boundary Tribunal, *Appendix to British Case*, 1:60–61, where Canning, in ạ letter of 15 January 1824 to Bagot, writes, "Your Excellency's despatch No. 48 describes latitude 50° as the point at which M. Poletica appeared to wish that the line of demarcation between Russia and Great Britain should be drawn. By a Memorandum which I have received from Mr. Rush of what his Government would propose as a general settlement, it appears that latitude 55° is the point at which the United States likewise have proposed fork that same line of demarcation. This coincidence certainly argues either a foregone understanding between Russia and the United States, or a disposition on the part of the United States to countenance and promote what they know to be the desire of Russia." See also Nesselrode to Lieven, 17 April 1824, in *Appendix to British Case*, Alaska Boundary Tribunal, 1:77: "However, the Washington Cabinet has admitted that our frontier should extend south as far as the 54th degree 40'. They have admitted it by a formal transaction which we have just initialed with its Plenipotentiary; this acknowledgment does not only strengthen our pretensions; but it entails other results which we considered with reason of the utmost interest to us."

41 Pelly to Canning, 19 April 1824, 26 May 1824, in *Appendix to British Case*, Alaska Boundary Tribunal, 1:78–79, 80–81.

42 Canning to Bagot, 24 April 1824, in *Appendix to British Case*, Alaska Boundary Tribunal, 1:81, 85–86; Canning to Lieven, 29 May 1824, in *Appendix to British Case*, Alaska Boundary Tribunal, 1:81, 85–86; Canning to Bagot, 12 July 1824, in *Appendix to British Case*, Alaska Boundary Tribunal, 1:81, 85–86; Canning to Lieven, 29 May 1824, in *Appendix to British Case*, Alaska Boundary Tribunal, 1:81,85–86; Canning to Bagot, 12 July 1824, in Appendix to British Case, Alaska Boundary Tribunal, 1:81, 85–86.

43 Bagot to Canning, 24 August 1824, in *Appendix to British Case*, Alaska Boundary Tribunal, 1:92–94.

It should be noted that Canning's letter of 12 July to Bagot instructed him to make approximately these demands. There appears to have been a certain difference, however, in that where he was directed to demand perpetual right to use the rivers, creeks, etc., on the continent, he demanded perpetual right to navigate and trade along the coast of the *lisière* and islands adjacent. See also Nesselrode to Liven, 31 August 1824, in *Appendix to British Case*, Alaska Boundary Tribunal, 1:103–7.

44 G. Canning to S. Canning, 8 December 1824, in *Appendix to British Case*, Alaska Boundary Tribunal, 1:112–15.

45 Bagot to Canning, 12 August 1824, 26 August 1824, in *Appendix to British Case*, Alaska Boundary Tribunal, 93–94, 95 and Enclosure, art. 6. See also G. Canning to S. Canning, 8 December 1824, in *Appendix to British Case*, Alaska Boundary Tribunal, 1:113.

46 Alaska Boundary Tribunal, *Appendix to British Case*, 1:37–39. See text of treaty also in British and Foreign State Papers (1824–25), 12:38–43; *Fur Seal Arbitration*, 2: Appendix, 39–43; 4:42–44. For an able treatment of the negotiations leading up to the 1824 and 1825 treaties, see Stuart R. Tompkins, "Drawing the Alaskan Boundary," *Canadian Historical Review* 26, no. 1 (March 1945): 1–24.

47 Malloy, ed., *Treaties, Conventions, International Acts, Protocols and Agreements between the United States of America and Other Powers 1776–1909*, 2:1651–58; also British and Foreign State Papers (1820–21), 8:524–40. See esp. art. 3.

48 Malloy, ed., *Treaties, Conventions, International Acts, Protocols and Agreements between the United States of America and Other Powers 1776–1909*, 1:631–33; British and Foreign State Papers (1818–19), 6:3–5. See esp. art. 3.

49 Malloy, ed., *Treaties, Conventions, International Acts, Protocols and Agreements between the United States of America and Other Powers 1776–1909*, 1:643–44; British and Foreign State Papers (1826–27), 14:975–76. See esp. arts. 1, 2, 3.

50 Malloy, ed., *Treaties, Conventions, International Acts, Protocols and Agreements between the United States of America and Other Powers 1776–1909*, 1:643–44; British and Foreign State Papers (1845–46), 34:14–15. See esp. art. 1. For a detailed treatment of the Oregon boundary dispute, see Frederic W. Howay, Walter N. Sage, and H. F. Angus, *British Columbia and the United States: The North Pacific Slope from Fur Trade to Aviation* (Toronto: Ryerson Press, 1942), passim, esp. chap. 6. See also H. G. Classen, *Thrust and Counterthrust: The Genesis of the Canada-United States Boundary* (Don Mills: Longmans Canada, 1965), 148–216; White, "Henry Cabot Lodge and the Alaska Boundary Award," 838–71; Galbraith, *The Hudson's Bay Company as an Imperial Factor*, 177–250.

51 Alaska Boundary Tribunal, *The Case of the United States*, Appendix, 265ff.; Pelly to Palmerston, 24 October 1835, in *Appendix to British Case*, Alaska Boundary Tribunal, 1:155–56.

52 Alaska Boundary Tribunal, *The Case of the United States*, Appendix, 285–308.

53 Alaska Boundary Tribunal, *Appendix to British Case*, 1:150–52. See also Galbraith, *Hudson's Bay Company*, 156–74, passim.

54 Alaska Boundary Tribunal, *Appendix to British Case*, 1:87. See also Galbraith, Hudson's Bay Company, 156–74, passim.

55 See Charles C. Tansill, *Canadian-American Relations*, 1875–1911 (New Haven, CT: Yale University Press, 1943), 129–30, and references. See also Wrangell to Board of Directors of Russian American Company, 30 April 1835, in *Appendix to British Case*, Alaska Boundary Tribunal, 1:274–79; and Pelly to –, 24 Oct. 1835, in *Appendix to British Case*, Alaska Boundary Tribunal, 1:274–379.

56 Galbraith, *Hudson's Bay Company*, 163–69; Bancroft, *History of Alaska*, 570–72; Okun, *The Russian-American Company*, 234–42; Alaska Boundary Tribunal, *The Counter Case of the United States*, Appendix, 12–21.

57 Board of Directors of Russian American Company to Minister of Finance, 9 January 1863, in *The Counter Case of the United States*, Alaska Boundary Tribunal, Appendix, 27–28.

58 Minister of Finance to Board of Directors of Russian American Company, 23 February 1863, in *The Counter Case of the United States*, Alaska Boundary Tribunal, 32.

59 Bancroft, *History of Alaska*, 590–96; Okun, *The Russian-American Company*, 234ff.; Alaska Boundary Tribunal, *The Case of the United States*, Appendix, 324–33. Both Russia and the United States were motivated by a desire to prevent Alaska's falling into the hands of the British. See J. Moore, "Alaska's First American Century: The View Ahead," *Polar Record* 14, no. 88 (Jan. 1968): 3–13, esp. 4–6.

60 Malloy, ed., *Treaties, Conventions, International Acts, Protocols and Agreements between the United States of America and Other Powers 1776–1909*, 2:1521–24; British and Foreign State Papers

(1866–67), 57:452–55; International Boundary Commission, *Joint Report upon the Survey and Demarcation of the International Boundary between the United States and Canada along the 141st Meridian from the Arctic Ocean to Mount St. Elias* (Ottawa, 1918), 208–11; see also Alaska Boundary Tribunal, *The Case of the United States*, Appendix, 17–22; and Alaska Boundary Tribunal, *Appendix to British Case*, 1:136–38.

61 General J. C. Davis, 12 November 1867, in *The Case of the United States*, Alaska Boundary Tribunal, Appendix, 334–36. Special Correspondent of the Alta, San Francisco, 18 October 1867, in *The Case of the United States*, Alaska Boundary Tribunal, Appendix, 334–36.

62 Bancroft, *History of Alaska*, 590. See also Okun, *Russian-American Company*, 253.

63 Bancroft, *History of Alaska*, 579–80; Galbraith, *Hudson's Bay Company*, 173.

64 Russian Minister of Finance to Vice Chancellor Gortchakov, 16 March 1867, and Enclosed Memorandum, in *The Counter Case of the United States*, Alaska Boundary Tribunal, Appendix, 32–35.

65 Hudson's Bay Company Archives [hereafter HBC Archives], A. 8/12, 19–22. Lord Kimberley to T. F. Elliot (June 11, 1868), and Enclosure Chief Factor Tolmey to Secretary W. G. Smith (29 Apr. 1868); Adderley to Kimberley (4 July 1868). See also Galbraith, *Hudson's Bay Company*, 173–74, and 453nn53, 54. And see Alaska Boundary Tribunal, *The Case of the United States*, Appendix, 448–53.

66 Alaska Boundary Tribunal, *Appendix to British Case*, 1:162–63.

67 Thornton to Granville, 18 November 1872, in *Appendix to British Case*, Alaska Boundary Tribunal, 164–65, 168; and Thornton to Granville, 15 February 1873, in *Appendix to British Case*, Alaska Boundary Tribunal, 164–65, 168.

68 Alaska Boundary Tribunal, *The Counter Case of the United States*, Appendix, 49–50. The address spoke of "the boundary of the 30 mile belt of American territory running along a part of the seaboard," and this may account for the fact that it and some related documents were not included in the British case.

69 Alaska Boundary Tribunal, *Appendix to British Case*, 1:173.

70 Alaska Boundary Tribunal, *Appendix to British Case*, 1:179–82.

71 Dennis to Minister of the Interior, 17 February 1874, in *Appendix to British Case*, Alaska Boundary Tribunal, 1:177–78.

72 Thornton to the Earl of Derby, 27 September 1875, in *Appendix to British Case*, Alaska Boundary Tribunal, 1:183.

73 Secretary of the Treasury to Customs Collectory at Sitka, 14 July 1876, in *The Counter Case of the United States*, Alaska Boundary Tribunal, 69–72; Collector at Sitka to Choquette, 19 September 1876, in *The Counter Case of the United States*, Alaska Boundary Tribunal, 69–72; Choquette to Brodie, 29 September 1876, in *The Counter Case of the United States*, Alaska Boundary Tribunal, 69–72; Collector at Sitka to Secretary of the Treasury, 29 March 1877, in *The Counter Case of the United States*, Alaska Boundary Tribunal, 69–72; Secretary of the Treasury to Collector at Sitka, 23 April 1877, in *The Counter Case of the United States*, Alaska Boundary Tribunal, 69–72; Collector at Sitka to Secretary of the Treasury, 15 June 1876, in *The Counter Case of the United States*, Alaska Boundary Tribunal, 69–72. See also Justice Gray to P. M. Mackenzie, 16 October 1876, in *Appendix to British Case*, Alaska Boundary Tribunal, 1:191–93; Colonial Office to Foreign Office, 22 December 1876, in *Appendix to British Case*, Alaska Boundary Tribunal, 1:191–93.

74 Alaska Boundary Tribunal, *Appendix to British Case*, 1:186–235, passim. See esp. Fish to Thornton, 2 November 1876, in *Appendix to British Case*, Alaska Boundary Tribunal, 1:186; Fish to Thornton, 10 January 1877, in *Appendix to British Case*, Alaska Boundary Tribunal, 1:198–99; Thornton to Fish, 15 January 1877, in *Appendix to British Case*, Alaska Boundary Tribunal, 1:202–3.

75 Surveyor General Dennis to Hunter, in *Appendix to British Case*, Alaska Boundary Tribunal, 3 March 1877, 1:224–25.

76 Alaska Boundary Tribunal, *Appendix to British Case*, 1:226–31.

77 Alaska Boundary Tribunal, *Appendix to British Case*, 1:231.

78 Carnarvon to Dufferin, 16 August 1877, in *Appendix to British Case*, Alaska Boundary Tribunal, 1:231–32.

79 Richards to Plunkett, 20 September 1877, in *Appendix to British Case*, Alaska Boundary Tribunal, 1:232 and Enclosure. See also Plunkett to Seward, 25 September 1877, in *The Counter Case of the United States*, Alaska Boundary Tribunal, Appendix, 87. For a good account of the Martin affair, see Classen, *Thrust and Counterthrust*, 284–88, 304–6.

80 Thornton to Evarts, 19 January 1878, in *Appendix to British Case*, Alaska Boundary Tribunal,

1:241–42; Evarts to Thornton, 20 February 1878, in *Appendix to British Case*, Alaska Boundary Tribunal, 1:241–42.

81 Thornton to Davis, 31 July 1873, in *The Counter Case of the United States*, Alaska Boundary Tribunal, Appendix, 53–57; Thornton to Fish, 1 December 1873, in *The Counter Case of the United States*, Alaska Boundary Tribunal, Appendix, 53–57 and Enclosures.

82 Fish to Thornton, 2 January 1874, in *The Counter Case of the United States*, Alaska Boundary Tribunal, 58.

83 Report by Canadian Minister of Justice R. Laflamme, 19 September 1877, in *Appendix to British Case*, Alaska Boundary Tribunal, 1:232–33. The report quotes despatch from Secretary of State for the Colonies.

84 Report by Canadian Minister of Justice Edward Blake, 5 February 1877, in *Appendix to British Case*, Alaska Boundary Tribunal, 1:210–11, esp. arts. 25–33. See also Canada, House of Commons *Debates* (10 March 1879), 230–32 (Mr. Blake, MP).

85 "Treaty of Saint Petersburg," 1825, art. 6; "Treaty of Washington," 1871, art. 26.

86 Carnarvon to Dufferin, 16 August 1877, in *Appendix to British Case*, Alaska Boundary Tribunal, 1:231–32.

87 Dall to Dawson, 24 April 1884, in *Appendix to British Case*, Alaska Boundary Tribunal, 1:248.

88 Bayard to Phelps, 20 November 1885, in *Appendix to British Case*, Alaska Boundary Tribunal, 248–55; Phelps to Salisbury, 19 January 1886, in *Appendix to British Case*, Alaska Boundary Tribunal, 248–55.

89 Tansill, *Canadian-American Relations, 1875–1911*, 142–43; John B. Moore, *A Digest of International Law*, 1:471. Cleveland brought the matter up again in later annual messages, of 6 Dec. 1886, and 3 Dec. 1888. See Moore, *A Digest of International Law*, 1:471.

90 Salisbury to Phelps, 26 January 1886, in *The Counter Case of the United States*, Alaska Boundary Tribunal, Appendix, 91.

91 Helyar to Bayard, 12 March 1886, in *The Counter Case of the United States*, Alaska Boundary Tribunal, 91–92; Rosebery to Phelps, 15 April 1886, in *The Counter Case of the United States*, Alaska Boundary Tribunal, 91–92.

92 Salisbury to West, 20 August 1887, in *Appendix to British Case*, Alaska Boundary Tribunal, 1:256–57; West to Bayard, and Enclosure, 14 September 1887, in *Appendix to British Case*, Alaska Boundary Tribunal, 1:257.

93 This expression has been used to describe Cameron's thesis, e.g., in Classen, *Thrust and Counterthrust*, 308ff.

94 Alaska Boundary Tribunal, *Reports, Treaties, etc.*, no. 1, 3–30.

95 Alaska Boundary Tribunal, *Reports, Treaties, etc.*, no. 1, 21–22.

96 Classen, *Thrust and Counterthrust*, 309.

97 Alaska Boundary Tribunal, *The Counter Case of the United States*, Appendix, 110.

98 Alaska Boundary Tribunal, *The Counter Case of the United States*, 111.

99 Congress, US Senate Executive Document, 50th Cong., 2d sess., no. 146, cited in Alaska Boundary Tribunal, *The Counter Case of the United States*, 94.

100 Memorandum of 3 February 1890, by G. M Dawson, in *Reports, Treaties, etc.*, Alaska Boundary Tribunal, 104; Unsigned Memorandum of 10 October 1892, in Reports, Treaties, etc., Alaska Boundary Tribunal, 125. See also British Columbia, Executive Council of British Columbia, *Report of a Committee of the Honourable Executive Council of British Columbia on the Question of the Boundary between Canada and Alaska* (1884), 1–11, in Tansill, *Canadian-American Relations, 1875–1911*, 139–41. See also Tansill, *Canadian-American Relations, 1875–1911*, 151–52, 154–55. Gray's 1884 report may be seen in British Columbia, *Sessional Papers*, 3rd sess., 4th Parliament (1885), 451–60.

101 Burgess to Macdonald, 19 June 1888, in *Appendix to British Case*, Alaska Boundary Tribunal, 1:263–66; Tupper to Colonial Office, 1 August 1888, with Memorandum by Maj. Gen. D. R. Cameron, in *Appendix to British Case*, Alaska Boundary Tribunal, 1:263–66; Salisbury to West, 31 August 1888, in *Appendix to British Case*, Alaska Boundary Tribunal, 1:263–66; and West to Bayard, 10 September 1888, in *Appendix to British Case*, Alaska Boundary Tribunal, 1:263–66.

102 Bayard to West, 15 September 1888, in *Appendix to British Case*, Alaska Boundary Tribunal, 1:266. See also Alaska Boundary Tribunal, *British Case*, 37–38, 94; also Alaska Boundary Tribunal, *The Argument of the United States*, 187–90.

103 Alaska Boundary Tribunal, *Appendix to British Case*, I:268. Pauncefote to Blaine (5 June 1891). See also ibid., 38, 98; also Alaska Boundary Tribunal, *The Argument of the United States*, 190–92.

104 Canada, *Sessional Papers* (1893), 26, vol. 11, no. 52, 1–8, esp. 1, 8; Foster to Hay, 7 November 1899, in *The Counter Case of the United States*, Alaska Boundary Tribunal, Appendix, 122–23. See also Tansill, *Canadian-American Relations, 1875–1911*, 158–59.

105 Canada, *Sessional Papers* (1893), 26, vol. 11, no. 52, 1–8, esp. 1, 8; Foster to Hay, 7 November 1899, in *The Counter Case of the United States*, Alaska Boundary Tribunal, Appendix, 122–23.

106 Alaska Boundary Tribunal, *Appendix to British Case*, 1:271; British and Foreign State Papers (1893–94), 86:12–13; Malloy, ed., *Treaties, Conventions, International Acts, Protocols and Agreements between the United States of America and Other Powers 1776-1909*, 1:765–66.

107 Rosebery to W. F. King, 8 March 1893, in *Appendix to British Case*, Alaska Boundary Tribunal, 1. This appointment had been recommended by the Canadian government in an order in council (PC No. 1396H) of 12 Sept. 1892.

108 Foster to Mendenhall, 8 September 1892, in *The Counter Case of the United States*, Alaska Boundary Tribunal, Appendix, 268–69.

109 Olney to Gough, 25 June 1895, in *Appendix to British Case*, Alaska Boundary Tribunal, 1:281.

110 Alaska Boundary Tribunal, *Appendix to British Case*, 1:282–86. See also report by Deputy Minister A. M. Burgess in Canada, Department of the Interior, *Annual Report for 1896*, xx–xxiii.

111 Canada, Order in Council, P. C. No. 1492, 1 June 1895. See also Deputy Minister of the Interior A. M. Burgess's Report of 28 Dec. 1895, in Canada, Department of the Interior, *Annual Report for 1895*, xxxvi–xxxix, where the substance of the order in council is repeated in approximately the same form.

112 Gough to Olney, 20 August 1895, in *Canadian Correspondence, Russian Monuments, etc.*, section entitled "Canadian Correspondence, February, 1886, to February, 1896," Alaskan Boundary, 49–50. A summary of this letter is given in Moore, *A Digest of International Law*, 1:472. President Cleveland recommended strongly that the US should participate in a joint survey in his annual message on 2 December 1895. See Moore, *A Digest of International Law*, 1:472, and Tansill, *Canadian-American Relations, 1875–1911*, 162n81.

113 Canada, Order in Council, PC No. 1620J, 28 September 1896, referring to American proposal in letter from Olney to British ambassador, 11 March 1896.

114 Alaska Boundary Tribunal, *Appendix to British Case*, 1:287–88; also International Boundary Commission, *Joint Report upon the Survey and Demarcation*, 238–40.

115 McDougald to Howell, 22 July 1897, in *Appendix to British Case*, Alaska Boundary Tribunal, 1:289.

116 Howell to McDougald, 22 July 1897, in *Appendix to British Case*, Alaska Boundary Tribunal, 1:289.

117 Howell to McDougald, 22 July 1897, in *Appendix to British Case*, Alaska Boundary Tribunal, 1:289.

118 Scott to Howell, 19 August 1897, in *Appendix to British Case*, Alaska Boundary Tribunal, 1:290.

119 Howell to Scott, 20 August 1897, in *Appendix to British Case*, Alaska Boundary Tribunal, 1:290.

120 Alaska Boundary Tribunal, *The Argument of the United States*, 196–201, disputing the argument in Alaska Boundary Tribunal, *British Case*, 92–97. See the customs regulations published by the American and Canadian governments in late 1897 and early 1898, in British and Foreign State Papers (1897–98), 90:434–41.

121 Pauncefote to Sherman, 23 February 1898, in *Appendix to British Case*, Alaska Boundary Tribunal, 1:291.

122 Pauncefote to Sherman, 23 February 1898, in *Appendix to British Case*, Alaska Boundary Tribunal, 1:291.

123 Day to Pauncefote, 9 May 1898, in *Appendix to British Case*, Alaska Boundary Tribunal, 1:292.

124 Alaska Boundary Tribunal, *Appendix to British Case*, 1:297–99. The protocol may be seen in Malloy, ed., Treaties, Conventions, International Acts, *Protocols and Agreements between the United States of America and Other Powers 1776–1909*, 1:770–73. It listed eleven subjects for settlement, the Alaska boundary being Number 3.

125 See Classen, *Thrust and Counterthrust*, 326, and his undocumented quotation from a letter Herschell wrote in September.

126 See Canada, Order in Council, PC No. 490, 28 February 1898, with accompanying letter and memorandum by Sifton setting forth these claims, and map lithographed in the Department of the Interior illustration of them. All the foregoing except the map may be seen in "Canadian Correspondence 1896 to 1902," 3–5, in Alaska Boundary, *Canadian Correspondence, Russian Monuments, etc.*

127 See Alaska Boundary Tribunal, *Reports, Treaties, etc.*, 160–63, for some of the proposals and counter-proposals exchanged by Lord Herschell

and Senator Fairbanks, the chairman of the American delegation. The same documents, e.g., an American memorandum of 20 Dec. 1898, and a British of 2 Feb. 1899, show that the British-Canadian delegation had abandoned the British Columbia claim.

128 Alaska Boundary Tribunal, *Reports, Treaties, etc.*, 161, 163–69.

129 British and Foreign State Papers (1900–1901), 94:46–48. Treaty between Great Britain and the United States, relative to the Establishment of a Communication by Ship Canal between the Atlantic and Pacific Oceans (18 Nov. 1901). See also ibid., 468–70, for unratified convention of 5 Feb. 1900, and 470–73, for the Clayton-Bulwer Treaty of 19 April 1850, which may also be seen in ibid. (1849–50), 38:4–8. And see ibid. (1900–1901), 94:478–79, for an explanation by the Marquis of Lansdowne for Britain's reluctance to concede an advantageous arrangement to the United States respecting a Panama Canal, without a satisfactory settlement of the Alaska boundary problem.

130 Secretary Hay to Henry White, 3 December 1898, quoted in Tansill, *Canadian-American Relations, 1875–1911*, 174.

131 See the excellent account of the 1898–99 conference in Tansill, *Canadian-American Relations, 1875–1911*, 169–89; also Classen, *Thrust and Counterthrust*, 325–35. President McKinley made the following comment on the failure of the conference, in his annual message to Congress on 5 December 1899. "Much progress had been made by the Commission toward the adjustment of many of these questions, when it became apparent that an irreconcilable difference of views was entertained respecting the delimitation of the Alaskan boundary. In the failure of an agreement as to the meaning of articles 3 and 4 of the treaty of 1825 between Russia and Great Britain, which defined the boundary between Alaska and Canada, the American Commissioners proposed that the subject of the boundary be laid aside and that the remaining questions of difference be proceeded with, some of which were so far advanced as to assure the probability of a settlement. This being declined by the British Commissioners, an adjournment was taken until the boundary should be adjusted by the two Governments." Moore, *A Digest of International Law*, 1:474; British and Foreign State Papers (1898–99), 91:1267.

132 Hay to Pauncefote, 20 March 1899, "Canadian Correspondence 1896 to 1902," Alaska Boundary, in *Canadian Correspondence, Russian Monuments, etc.*, 16.

133 Alaska Boundary, "Canadian Correspondence 1896 to 1902," in *Canadian Correspondence, Russian Monuments, etc.*, 15–16. Canada, Order in Council, PC No. 1306K, 20 March 1899.

134 Villiers to Choate, 13 May 1899, in *The Counter Case of the United States*, Alaska Boundary Tribunal, Appendix, 124–25.

135 Salisbury to Choate, 1 July 1899, in *The Counter Case of the United States*, Alaska Boundary Tribunal, 128–29.

136 Choate to Salisbury, 9 August 1899, in *The Counter Case of the United States*, Alaska Boundary Tribunal, 129–32. See British and Foreign State Papers (1896–97), 89:57–65, for the Venezuela–British Guiana boundary arbitration treaty (2 Feb. 1897); ibid. (1899–1900), 92:466–69, for the rules of procedure adopted by the arbitration tribunal (14 June 1899); ibid., 160–62, for the tribunal's award (3 Oct. 1899).

137 Canada, Order in Council, PC No. 1525K, 19 August 1899, with accompanying memorandum by Laurier dated 17 Aug.

138 Alaska Boundary Tribunal, *Appendix to British Case*, 1:305; "Canadian Correspondence 1896 to 1902," Alaska Boundary, *Canadian Correspondence, Russian Monuments, etc.*, 16–49; British and Foreign State Papers (1898–99), 91:116–18; Malloy, ed., *Treaties, Conventions, International Acts, Protocols and Agreements between the United States of America and Other Powers 1776–1909*, 1:777–78; Moore, *A Digest of International Law*, 1:468–69.

139 Pauncefote to Sherman, 23 February 1898, in *Appendix to British Case*, Alaska Boundary Tribunal, 1:291.

140 Alaska Boundary Tribunal, *Reports, Treaties, etc.*, 161 (two British memoranda given to Senator Fairbanks 16 Dec. 1898).

141 Alaska Boundary Tribunal, *Reports, Treaties, etc.*, 164–65. (British memorandum presented 9 Feb. 1899, and British draft arbitration treaty submitted 16 Feb. 1899).

142 Alaska Boundary Tribunal, *Reports, Treaties, etc.*, 163 (memorandum received from US commissioners 9 Feb. 1899).

143 Alaska Boundary Tribunal, *Reports, Treaties, etc.*, 167–69 (counter project submitted by US commissioners 18 Feb. 1899).

144 Philip C. Jessup, *Elihu Root* (New York: Dodd, Mead, 1938), 1:389–90; O. D. Skelton, *Life and Letters of Sir Wilfrid Laurier* (Toronto: Oxford University Press, 1921), 2:136–38; O. D. Skelton,

"The Day of Sir Wilfrid Laurier," in *Chronicles of Canada*, eds. George M. Wrong and H. H. Langton (Toronto: Glasgow, Brook, 1922), 30:211–12; J. W. Dafoe, *Clifford Sifton in Relation to His Times* (Toronto: Macmillan, 1931), 215–17.

145 George B. Cortelyou to Secretary Elihu Root, 27 March 1902, in Tansill, *Canadian-American Relations, 1875–1911*, 224. See also Jessup, *Elihu Root*, 1:391–92, where the point is made that in ordering this action to be taken Roosevelt was concerned mainly with preventing disturbances along the disputed boundary line.

146 Tansill, *Canadian-American Relations, 1875–1911*, 224–26, and references.

147 Dafoe, *Clifford Sifton in Relation to His Times*, 217.

148 Sir M. Herbert to the Marquis of Lansdowne, 17 October 1902, in Great Britain, *Parliamentary Papers*, Correspondence Respecting the Alaska Boundary, 1877 (London: His Majesty's Stationery Office, 1904), 33.

149 Minto to Chamberlain, 18 November 1902, in Great Britain, *Parliamentary Papers*, Correspondence Respecting the Alaska Boundary, 1877 (London: His Majesty's Stationery Office, 1904), 34.

150 Herbert to Lansdowne by cable and by letter, 8 December 1902, in Great Britain, *Parliamentary Papers*, Correspondence Respecting the Alaska Boundary, 1877 (London: His Majesty's Stationery Office, 1904), 34–35.

151 Lansdowne to Herbert, 23 January 1903, in Great Britain, *Parliamentary Papers*, Correspondence Respecting the Alaska Boundary, 1877 (London: His Majesty's Stationery Office, 1904), 40.

152 Herbert to Lansdowne, 24 January 1903, in Great Britain, *Parliamentary Papers*, Correspondence Respecting the Alaska Boundary, 1877 (London: His Majesty's Stationery Office, 1904), 40.

153 The text of the treaty may be seen in Great Britain, *Parliamentary Papers*, Correspondence Respecting the Alaska Boundary, 1877 (London: His Majesty's Stationery Office, 1904), 41–44; Alaska Boundary Tribunal, *Appendix to British Case*, 1:1–4; Alaska Boundary Tribunal, *The Case of the United States*, Appendix, 1–6; British and Foreign State Papers (1902–1903), 96:84–89; Malloy, ed., *Treaties, Conventions, International Acts, Protocols and Agreements between the United States of America and Other Powers 1776–1909*, 1:787–92.

154 Herbert to Lansdowne, 14 February 1903, in Great Britain, *Parliamentary Papers*, Correspondence Respecting the Alaska Boundary, 1877 (London: His Majesty's Stationery Office, 1904), 44.

155 Earl of Onslow to Governor General Minto, 18 February 1903, in Great Britain, *Parliamentary Papers*, Correspondence Respecting the Alaska Boundary, 1877 (London: His Majesty's Stationery Office, 1904), 45.

156 Minto to Onslow, 21 February 1903, in Great Britain, *Parliamentary Papers*, Correspondence Respecting the Alaska Boundary, 1877 (London: His Majesty's Stationery Office, 1904), 45.

157 Onslow to Minto, 26 February 1903, in Great Britain, *Parliamentary Papers*, Correspondence Respecting the Alaska Boundary, 1877 (London: His Majesty's Stationery Office, 1904), 45–46.

158 Great Britain, *Parliamentary Papers*, Correspondence Respecting the Alaska Boundary, 1877 (London: His Majesty's Stationery Office, 1904), 46–47. See also Skelton, *Life and Letters of Sir Wilfrid Laurier*, 2:144–45; also British and Foreign State Papers (1902–1903), 96:1, where the Speech from the Throne on 17 February is reproduced, containing the following statement: "A Treaty providing for the reference of these questions to an Arbitral Tribunal has been signed and ratified." Obviously the word "ratified" was incorrect at the time.

159 Roosevelt to Arthur Lee, 7 December 1903, Roosevelt Papers cited in Thomas A. Bailey, "Theodore Roosevelt and the Alaska Boundary Settlement," *Canadian Historical Review* 18, no. 2 (June 1937): 125; Jessup, *Elihu Root*, 1:393.

160 Herbert to Lansdowne, 14 February 1903, in Great Britain, *Parliamentary Papers*, Correspondence Respecting the Alaska Boundary, 1877 (London: His Majesty's Stationery Office, 1904), 44. See also Skelton, *Life and Letters of Sir Wilfrid Laurier*, 2:145.

161 White, "Henry Cabot Lodge and the Alaska Boundary Award," 334.

162 Dafoe, *Clifford Sifton in Relation to His Times*, 221–22.

163 Onslow to Minto, 26 February 1903, in Great Britain, *Parliamentary Papers*, Correspondence Respecting the Alaska Boundary, 1877 (London: His Majesty's Stationery Office, 1904), 45–46.

164 Minto to Onslow, 6 March 1903, in Great Britain, *Parliamentary Papers*, Correspondence Respecting the Alaska Boundary, 1877 (London: His Majesty's Stationery Office, 1904), 46–47.

165 Onslow to Minto, 7 March 1903, in Great Britain, *Parliamentary Papers*, Correspondence Respecting the Alaska Boundary, 1877 (London: His Majesty's Stationery Office, 1904), 47–48; Minto

to Onslow, 7 March 1903, in Great Britain, *Parliamentary Papers*, Correspondence Respecting the Alaska Boundary, 1877 (London: His Majesty's Stationery Office, 1904); Minto to Chamberlain, 17 March 1903, in Great Britain, *Parliamentary Papers*, Correspondence Respecting the Alaska Boundary, 1877 (London: His Majesty's Stationery Office, 1904).

166 Minto to Chamberlain, 23 July 1903, in Great Britain, *Parliamentary Papers*, Correspondence Respecting the Alaska Boundary, 1877 (London: His Majesty's Stationery Office, 1904), 49.

167 Alaska Boundary Tribunal, *Protocols, Oral Arguments, with Index, Award of the Tribunal, and Opinions of Its Members* (London: Harrison and Sons, 1903), v–vi, 1–2; Skelton, *Life and Letters of Sir Wilfrid Laurier*, 2:148; Dafoe, *Clifford Sifton in Relation to His Times*, 222; Tansill, *Canadian-American Relations, 1875–1911*, 247n67. In London, Joseph Pope became one of the secretaries of the tribunal and A. P. Collier served as a member of the British agent's staff.

168 Hay to Roosevelt, 2 July 1903, quoted in Tyler Dennett, *John Hay: From Poetry to Politics* (Port Washington, NY: Kennikat Press, 1963), 359–60.

169 Foster MS, Hay to Foster, 2 July 1903: "I have a vehement letter from the President, stated by one from Lodge, protesting against any delay in the Alaska Tribunal," quoted in Tansill, *Canadian-American Relations, 1875–1911*, 242n45.

170 Dennett, *John Hay*, 360.

171 Lodge to White, 8 May 1903 quoted in Tansill, *Canadian-American Relations, 1875–1911*, 239–40; Alaska Boundary Tribunal, *Protocols, Oral Arguments, etc.*, 2.

172 Jessup, *Elihu Root*, 1:395.

173 Dafoe, *Clifford Sifton in Relation to His Times*, 224–25; William R. Thayer, *The Life and Letters of John Hay* (Boston: Houghton Mifflin, 1915), 2:208–11; Bailey, "Theodore Roosevelt and the Alaska Boundary Settlement," 128. The full text of the letter is given in Joseph B. Bishop, *Theodore Roosevelt and His Time Shown in His Own Letters* (New York: Scribner's Sons, 1920), 1:259–61. Chamberlain's reaction may be gathered from the following confidential memo in his papers, obviously written by Chamberlain himself, although neither writer nor recipient is identified:

Colonial Office,

Aug. 8, 1903.

Mr. Justice Holmes called upon me today and read to me a private letter from President Roosevelt to himself....

I told Mr. Justice Holmes that I had heard the letter with the greatest regret, as the spirit it showed seemed to me unworthy of the head of a great country. No doubt everybody who engaged in litigation believed in the justice of his own claim and no one was impartial in his own case. But arbitration implied a readiness to allow impartial judges to decide between claims, and while I made no complaint that President Roosevelt should take a strong view on the matter in dispute, exactly as we did in the dispute with regard to the boundary in Venezuela, it seemed to me impossible to preserve friendship if one side accompanied his assent to arbitration by saying that if the arbitration went against him he would take the matter into his own hands.

Mr. Holmes is returning to America but said he thought he should let the matter drop. He evidently did not sympathize with the extreme views expressed by President Roosevelt.

This memo is followed immediately by a brief note, dated 8 Oct. 1903, which says simply, "I propose, if there is no objection, to send copy of this to the Lord Chief Justice." Thus, for whatever reason, Chamberlain evidently decided that Alverstone should be informed. See the Joseph Chamberlain Papers, Library and Archives Canada (hereafter LAC), MG27, 2:A2, vol. 2.

174 Lord Newton, *Lord Lansdowne: A Biography* (London: Macmillan, 1929), 264–65; Dafoe, *Clifford Sifton in Relation to His Times*, 225–26; Bailey, "Theodore Roosevelt and the Alaska Boundary Settlement," 128–29; Alfred L. P. Dennis, *Adventures in American Diplomacy 1896–1906* (New York: E. P. Dutton, 1928), 154–55.

175 Jessup, *Elihu Root*, 1:396.

176 Jessup, *Elihu Root*, 1:400.

177 Alaska Boundary Tribunal, *British Case*, 45–49.

178 Capt. George Vancouver, *A Voyage of Discovery to the North Pacific Ocean and Round the World* (London: Robinson and Edwards, 1798), 2:371.

179 Vancouver, *A Voyage of Discovery*, 2:379.

180 Alaska Boundary Tribunal, *British Case*, 49–63; Alaska Boundary Tribunal, *British Counter-Case*, 6–12; Alaska Boundary Tribunal, *British*

Argument, 1–10; Arguments of Sir Robert Finlay, in Protocols, Oral Arguments, etc., Alaska Boundary Tribunal, 67–167; Arguments of Christopher Robinson, in *Protocols, Oral Arguments, etc.*, Alaska Boundary Tribunal, 454; Sir Edward Carson, in *Protocols, Oral Arguments, etc.*, Alaska Boundary Tribunal, 559–69.

181 Alaska Boundary Tribunal, *The Case of the United States*, 103–4; Alaska Boundary Tribunal, *The Counter Case of the United States*, 11–28; Alaska Boundary Tribunal, *The Argument of the United States*, 19–54; Arguments of Mr. Taylor, in *Protocols, Oral Arguments, etc.*, Alaska Boundary Tribunal, 520–35; Arguments of Mr. Dickinson, in *Protocols, Oral Arguments, etc.*, Alaska Boundary Tribunal, 660–711.

182 Alaska Boundary Tribunal, *Protocols, Oral Arguments, etc.*, 77–82, 564–65. This point should be emphasized because in the end the majority of the tribunal voted for Tongass Passage as the entrance of Portland Canal.

183 Alaska Boundary Tribunal, *British Case*, 64–68; Alaska Boundary Tribunal, *British Counter-Case*, 12–17; Alaska Boundary Tribunal, *British Argument*, 10–17; Arguments of Sir Robert Finlay, in *Protocols, Oral Arguments, etc.*, Alaska Boundary Tribunal, 67–167, esp. 11–124; Arguments of Mr. Robinson, in *Protocols, Oral Arguments, etc.*, Alaska Boundary Tribunal, 453–54; Arguments of Sir Edward Carson, in *Protocols, Oral Arguments, etc.*, Alaska Boundary Tribunal, 569–71.

184 Alaska Boundary Tribunal, *The Case of the United States*, 103–4; Alaska Boundary Tribunal, *The Counter Case of the United States*, 11, 13–28; Alaska Boundary Tribunal, *The Argument of the United States*, 54–56; Arguments of Mr. Watson, in *Protocols, Oral Arguments, etc.*, Alaska Boundary Tribunal, 387–92; Arguments of Mr. Taylor, in *Protocols, Oral Arguments, etc.*, Alaska Boundary Tribunal, 535–37; Arguments of Mr. Dickinson, in *Protocols, Oral Arguments, etc.*, Alaska Boundary Tribunal, 710–11.

185 Alaska Boundary Tribunal, *British Case*, 69. See also Alaska Boundary Tribunal, *British Counter-Case*, 17–21; Alaska Boundary Tribunal, *British Arguments*, 17–23; Arguments of Sir Robert Finlay, in *Protocols, Oral Arguments, etc.*, Alaska Boundary Tribunal, 167–82; Arguments of Mr. Robinson, in *Protocols, Oral Arguments, etc.*, Alaska Boundary Tribunal, 454–55; Arguments of Sir Edward Carson, in *Protocols, Oral Arguments, etc.*, Alaska Boundary Tribunal, 571–75.

186 Alaska Boundary Tribunal, *The Case of the United States*, 103–4; Alaska Boundary Tribunal, *The Counter Case of the United States*, 28–31, esp. 29; Alaska Boundary Tribunal, *The Argument of the United States*, 56–61; Arguments of Mr. Watson, in *Protocols, Oral Arguments, etc.*, Alaska Boundary Tribunal, 392–96; Arguments of Mr. Taylor, in *Protocols, Oral Arguments, etc.*, Alaska Boundary Tribunal, 537–39; Arguments of Mr. Dickinson, in *Protocols, Oral Arguments, etc.*, Alaska Boundary Tribunal, 711–18, esp. 712, 715, 718.

187 Alaska Boundary Tribunal, *British Case*, 71–76; Alaska Boundary Tribunal, *British Counter-Case*, 21–56; Alaska Boundary Tribunal, *British Argument*, 24–61; Arguments of Sir Robert Finlay, in *Protocols, Oral Arguments, etc.*, Alaska Boundary Tribunal, 182–326; Arguments of Mr. Robinson, in *Protocols, Oral Arguments, etc.*, Alaska Boundary Tribunal, 455–99; Arguments of Sir Edward Carson, in *Protocols, Oral Arguments, etc.*, Alaska Boundary Tribunal, 575–656. As noted in the text, some of the arguments treated the last three questions together, and even when separated they tended to merge to some extent. See esp. Finlay's summary, 323–26.

188 Argument of Mr. Taylor, in *Protocols, Oral Arguments, etc.*, Alaska Boundary Tribunal, 543.

189 Alaska Boundary Tribunal, *The Case of the United States*, 102–5; Alaska Boundary Tribunal, *The Counter Case of the United States*, 31–92; Alaska Boundary Tribunal, *The Argument of the United States*, 61–204; Arguments of Mr. Watson, in *Protocols, Oral Arguments, etc.*, Alaska Boundary Tribunal, 394–441; Arguments of Mr. Taylor, in *Protocols, Oral Arguments, etc.*, Alaska Boundary Tribunal, 539–57; Arguments of Mr. Dickingson, in *Protocols, Oral Arguments, etc.*, Alaska Boundary Tribunal, 718–835.

190 Alaska Boundary Tribunal, *British Case*, 76–79; Alaska Boundary Tribunal, *British Argument*, 61–63; Argument of Sir Robert Finlay, in *Protocols, Oral Arguments, etc.*, Alaska Boundary Tribunal, 183–84.

191 Alaska Boundary Tribunal, *The Case of the United States*, 102–6; Alaska Boundary Tribunal, *The Counter Case of the United States*, 31–42, 90–92; Argument of Mr. Dickinson, in *Protocols, Oral Arguments, etc.*, Alaska Boundary Tribunal, 718–22, 762.

192 Alaska Boundary Tribunal, *British Case*, 80–83; Alaska Boundary Tribunal, *British Counter-Case*, 56–64; Alaska Boundary Tribunal, *British Argument*, 63–109; Arguments of Sir Robert Finlay, in *Protocols, Oral Arguments, etc.*, Alaska Boundary Tribunal, 238–39, 268–71, 287–88, 325; Arguments of Mr. Robinson, in *Protocols*,

Oral Arguments, etc., Alaska Boundary Tribunal, 462–64.

193 Alaska Boundary Tribunal, *The Case of the United States*, 102–6; Alaska Boundary Tribunal, *The Counter Case of the United States*, 38–42, 90–92; Alaska Boundary Tribunal, *The Argument of the United States*, 99–123, 135–39; Arguments of Mr. Watson, in *Protocols, Oral Arguments, etc.*, Alaska Boundary Tribunal, 416; Arguments of Mr. Dickinson, in *Protocols, Oral Arguments, etc.*, Alaska Boundary Tribunal, 763–71.

194 Alaska Boundary Tribunal, *British Case*, 31–32; Alaska Boundary Tribunal, *Appendix to British Case*, 1:226–31.

195 Alaska Boundary Tribunal, *British Case*, 36–37; Alaska Boundary Tribunal, *Appendix to British Case*, 256–57.

196 Alaska Boundary Tribunal, *British Case*, 37.

197 Alaska Boundary Tribunal, *British Case*, 37–38; Alaska Boundary Tribunal, *Appendix to British Case*, 1:263–66.

198 Alaska Boundary Tribunal, *British Case*, 40.

199 Alaska Boundary Tribunal, 41–42; Alaska Boundary Tribunal, *Appendix to British Case*, 1:297–99.

200 Congress, *U.S. Senate Executive Document*, 50th Cong., 2d sess., no. 146, cited in Alaska Boundary Tribunal, *British Case*, 37.

201 Congress, *Congressional Records*, 3 January 1896, cited in Alaska Boundary Tribunal, *British Argument*, 57–58.

202 Congress, *Congressional Records*, 12 February 1896, cited in Alaska Boundary Tribunal, *British Argument*, 58.

203 Alaska Boundary Tribunal, *The Counter Case of the United States*, 61–74; Alaska Boundary Tribunal, *The Argument of the United States*, 165–204; Argument of Mr. Dickinson, in *Protocols, Oral Arguments, etc.*, Alaska Boundary Tribunal, 803–20. See also Choate to Salisbury, 22 January 1900, in *The Counter Case of the United States*, Alaska Boundary Tribunal, Appendix, 153–54, where the point is made that Salisbury's claim was forwarded to the American government on 1 August 1898, and received on 3 August.

204 Canada, House of Commons *Debates*, 10 March 1879, 1:230–31 (Mr. Mills, MP), quoted in Alaska Boundary Tribunal, *The Counter Case of the United States*, Appendix, 165.

205 Canada, Senate *Debates*, 29 February 1892, 14–15 (Mr. Scott, Senator), quoted in Alaska Boundary Tribunal, *The Counter Case of the United States*, 70; Appendix, 167–68.

206 Canada, House of Commons *Debates*, 11 February 1898, 1:405 (see cols. 407–8) (Mr. Laurier, MP), quoted in Alaska Boundary Tribunal, Appendix, 168–69.

207 Canada, House of Commons *Debates*, 16 February 1898, 1:619, quoted in Alaska Boundary Tribunal, Appendix, 170.

208 Canada, House of Commons *Debates*, 7 March 1898, 1:1274 (see col. 1277), quoted in Alaska Boundary Tribunal, Appendix, 170–72.

209 See above, at n173ff.

210 Roosevelt-Lodge Correspondence, Roosevelt Papers, 2:61, quoted in Jessup, *Elihu Root*, 1:398–99.

211 E.g., see Dennett, *John Hay*, 360–61, giving Hay's letter of 25 September to Roosevelt.

212 Ibid.

213 Allan Nevins, *Henry White: Thirty Years of American Diplomacy* (New York: Harper and Brothers, 1930), 198, giving Hay's letter to White.

214 Quoted in Tansill, *Canadian-American Relations, 1875–1911*, 257–58.

215 For example, Lodge to Roosevelt, 24 September 1903, in Jessup, *Elihu Root*, 1:397–98, from *Roosevelt-Lodge Correspondence*, 2:59: "We went over after the session yesterday and had a long talk with Choate on the situation. We all agreed that if Alverstone decided in our favor on the main contention, namely, the heads of the inlets, that we could afford, with a slight modification to accept their Portland Channel."

216 White to Hay, 20 October 1903, quoted in Tansill, *Canadian-American Relations, 1875–1911*, 261. See also Nevins, *Henry White*, 201.

217 White, "Henry Cabot Lodge and the Alaska Boundary Award," 332–36.

218 Lodge to White, 2 October 1903, in Tansill, *Canadian-American Relations, 1875–1911*, 254, quoting Confidential, White MS.

219 Root to White. 2 October 1903, in Tansill, *Canadian-American Relations, 1875–1911*, 254–55, quoting White MS.

220 Nevins, Henry White, 200–201; Dennis, *Adventures in American Diplomacy 1896–1906*, 154–55.

221 Nevins, Henry White, 200; White, "Henry Cabot Lodge and the Alaska Boundary Award," 335–36.

222 Choate to Hay, 20 October 1903, in Dennis, *Adventures in American Diplomacy 1896–1906*,

154; also Tansill, *Canadian-American Relations, 1875–1911*, 258–59n98.

223 Lodge to Roosevelt, 30 July 1903, quoted in Tansill, *Canadian-American Relations, 1875–1911*, 244, from *Selections from the Correspondence of Theodore Roosevelt and Henry Cabot Lodge, 1884–1918*, 2:41–43.

224 White, "Henry Cabot Lodge and the Alaska Boundary Award," 335, 336.

225 Lodge to Roosevelt, 13 September 1903, Tansill, *Canadian-American Relations, 1875–1911*, 250, from *Correspondence of Theodore Roosevelt and Henry Cabot Lodge*, 2:55–57.

226 Hay to White, 20 September 1903, in Nevins, *Henry White*, 198.

227 Nevins, *Henry White*, 199.

228 Lodge to White, 2 October 1903, in Tansill, *Canadian-American Relations, 1875–1911*, 254.

229 Dafoe, *Clifford Sifton in Relation to His Times*, 228; also Skelton, *Life and Letters of Sir Wilfrid Laurier*, 2:149.

230 Dafoe, *Clifford Sifton in Relation to His Times*, 228–29; also Skelton, *Life and Letters of Sir Wilfrid Laurier*, 2:149. In reproducing this message Skelton omits the sentence, "Shame Chief Justice and carry that point." See typewritten copy of these two cables in LAC, Laurier Papers, MG 26 G, (hereafter Laurier Papers), vol. 284, 77602.

231 Dafoe, *Clifford Sifton in Relation to His Times*, 233. See also Laurier Papers, vol. 286, 77891–97.

232 Dafoe, *Clifford Sifton in Relation to His Times*, 232.

233 Maurice Pope, ed., *Public Servant: The Memoirs of Sir Joseph Pope* (Toronto: Oxford University Press, 1960), 297, 151–52. H. G. Classen is apparently mistaken in assuming (*Thrust and Counterthrust*, 345) that Alverstone on this occasion proposed a division of the four disputed islands, with Canada getting the two larger and the United States the two smaller. It is true that according to Pope's record Alverstone named only Wales and Pearse Islands when asking what would satisfy Canada, but it may well be that he simply did not bother to mention the two smaller islands. Elsewhere Pope wrote, "I desire to record here that Lord Alverstone never, at any time, suggested to me in the most remote manner that he thought Tongass Passage was Portland Channel, or hinted that our case for Wales and Pearse Islands did not cover Sitklan and Kannaghunut Islands." Pope, *Public Servant*, 153.

234 White, "Henry Cabot Lodge and the Alaska Boundary Award," 335.

235 White to Hay, 19 September 1903, quoted in Nevins, *Henry White*, 197.

236 White to Roosevelt, 19 September 1903, White MS quoted in Tansill, *Canadian-American Relations, 1875–1911*, 249.

237 Lodge to Roosevelt, 24 September 1903, quoted in Tansill, *Canadian-American Relations, 1875–1911*, 250–51, from *Correspondence of Theodore Roosevelt and Henry Cabot Lodge*, 2:57–59. See also Jessup, *Elihu Root*, 1:397–98. In the same letter Lodge said that Alverstone had "opened himself pretty well now" to him and Root.

238 Lodge to White, 2 October 1903, Confidential, White MS quoted in Tansill, *Canadian-American Relations, 1875–1911*, 254.

239 Canada, House of Commons *Debates*, 12 October 1903, 6:13671 (Mr. Bell, MP).

240 Canada, House of Commons *Debates*, 13 October 1903, 6:13806 (Mr. Laurier, MP).

241 Canada, House of Commons *Debates*, 12 October 1903, 6:13667–68 (Mr. Borden, MP and Mr. Laurier, MP); 13 October 1903, 13806; 14 October 1903, 13957–64. Sir Mackenzie Bowell asked about Aylesworth's alleged indiscretion in the Senate. Canada, Senate *Debates*, 13 October 1903, 1367–68 (Mr. Bowell, MP).

242 Alaska Boundary Tribunal, *Protocols, Oral Arguments, etc.*, 939–41; Great Britain, Parliamentary Papers, Correspondence Respecting the Alaska Boundary, 1877 (London: His Majesty's Stationery Office, 1904), 49–51; British and Foreign State Papers (1904–1905), 98:152–55; Malloy, ed., *Treaties, Conventions, International Acts, Protocols and Agreements between the United States of America and Other Powers 1776–1909*, 1:792–94.

243 Alaska Boundary Tribunal, *Protocols, Oral Arguments, etc.*, 950.

244 Alaska Boundary Tribunal, *Protocols, Oral Arguments, etc.*, 970.

245 Alaska Boundary Tribunal, *Protocols, Oral Arguments, etc.*, 977, 978.

246 Alaska Boundary Tribunal, *Protocols, Oral Arguments, etc.*, 956–57.

247 Alaska Boundary Tribunal, *Protocols, Oral Arguments, etc.*, 958–67.

248 Alaska Boundary Tribunal, *Protocols, Oral Arguments, etc.*, 945–48.

249 Dafoe, *Clifford Sifton in Relation to His Times*, 230; Skelton, *Life and Letters of Sir Wilfrid Laurier*, 2:151–52.

250 Dafoe, *Clifford Sifton in Relation to His Times*, 232.

251 Quoted in Dafoe, *Clifford Sifton in Relation to His Times*, 232–33.

252 Quoted in Skelton, *Life and Letters of Sir Wilfrid Laurier*, 2:157.

253 Quoted in George W. Smalley, *Anglo-American Memories* (London: Duckworth, 1911), 238.

254 Rt. Hon. Viscount Alverstone, *Recollections of Bar and Bench* (London: E. Arnold, 1914), 240–41.

255 Skelton, *Life and Letters of Sir Wilfrid Laurier*, 2:152.

256 John S. Ewart, *The Kingdom of Canada, Imperial Federation, The Colonial Conferences, The Alaska Boundary, and Other Essays* (Toronto: Morang, 1908), 322.

257 F. C. Wade, *Treaties Affecting the North Pacific Coast* (Vancouver, 1914), 16ff. In this connection Alverston's opinion as given here, in the tribunal award, and in Ewart, *The Kingdom of Canada*, should be compared.

258 Alaska Boundary Tribunal, *Protocols, Oral Arguments, etc.*, 950.

259 Ewart, *The Kingdom of Canada*, 343.

260 Alaska Boundary Tribunal, *Protocols, Oral Arguments, etc.*, 77–82, 564–65.

261 See Aylesworth's Opinion in the case proceedings, 949, 950, 955.

262 James White, "Boundary disputes and treaties," in A. Shortt and A. G. Doughty, eds., *Canada and Its Provinces*, vol. 8 (Toronto, 1914), 940.

263 Pope, ed., *Public Servant*, 153. See also 299. See also Dafoe, *Clifford Sifton*, 231.

264 Ewart, *Kingdom of Canada*, 320, 322.

265 Ewart, *Kingdom of Canada*, 321.

266 Alaska Boundary Tribunal, *Protocols, Oral Arguments, etc.*, 950. It is apparent that Aylesworth here introduced non-judicial considerations rather similar to those both he and Laurier accused Alverstone of taking into account. See Alaska Boundary Tribunal, *Protocols, Oral Arguments, etc.*, 971, for a similar statement in Jetté's Opinion.

267 Hay to Choate, 16 October 1903 quoted in Tansill, *Canadian-American Relations, 1875–1911*, 257–58. See also Hugh L. Keenleyside, *Canada and the United States: Some Aspects of Their Historical Relations*, rev. ed. (New York: A. A. Knopf, 1952), 185.

268 Award of Tribunal, Answer to Question 7.

269 Memorandum from Count Lieven, 24 July 1824: "It is to be observed that, as a general principle, when a chain (chaîne) of mountains serves to define any boundary, it is always the top (cime) of these mountains which forms the line of demarcation. In the case now under consideration the word base ... would appear hardly suitable to secure the delimitation against subsequent disputes, for it would not be impossible ... that the mountains designated as the boundary should extend, by and insensible slope, down to the very border of the coast." See Award of Tribunal, 113–14, for British acceptance of, indeed insistence upon, this proposition. G. Canning to S. Canning (8 Dec. 1824): "The Russian Plenipotentiaries propose to withdraw entirely the limit of the lisière on the coast which they were themselves the first to propose, viz., the summit of the mountains which run parallel to the coast.... We cannot agree to this change.... Where the mountains are the boundary, we are content to take the summit instead of the "'seaward base' as the line of demarcation." In the end the proposal, mutually accepted, was written into art. 3 of the 1825 convention: "the line of demarcation shall follow the summit of the mountains situated parallel to the coast" (in Alaska Boundary Tribunal, *Appendix to British Case*, 1:91).

270 Alaska Boundary Tribunal, *Protocols, Oral Argument, etc.*, 238. On this see also Ewart, *Kingdom of Canada*, 313–18.

271 See Pope, *Public Servant*, 297, for the following comment in Joseph Pope's record of his conversation on 13 September 1903, with Lord Alverstone: "He told me he thought we had a convincing case on the Portland Channel and also for a mountain boundary. Adding that he feared our case for the heads of inlets was correspondingly weak. All this agreed quite with my own opinion."

272 Classen, *Thrust and Counterthrust*, 350–51.

273 From Aylesworth's Opinion. Whether Aylesworth himself was politically inclined at the time is perhaps doubtful, but at any rate he became a political person not long afterwards, campaigning unsuccessfully as a Liberal candidate in the general election of 1904, winning a seat in a by-election in 1905, and serving successively as Postmaster General, Minister of Labour, and Minister of Justice. This is well known, of course, but what is not so well known is that Laurier had tried unsuccessfully to get him to run in the general election of 1900. See LAC, Laurier Papers, MG 26 G, vol. 289, 78658, for the following in a letter Laurier wrote on 10 November 1903, to Charles Murphy, and Ottawa barrister: "If you can prevail

upon Aylesworth to accept a candidature at the next general elections, whenever they take place, and carry a county, you will have done a great service to the party and the country. Aylesworth ought to have been in Parliament long ago. Before the election of 1900, I begged of him almost on my bended knees, to enter into public life; I could not move him. If you can do now what I failed to do then, I will be first to thank you." See Canada, House of Commons *Debates*, 16 March 1906, col. 258 (Mr. Laurier, MP), for a rather similar statement by Laurier. Evidently some British officials were not so impressed with Aylesworth. See LAC, Sifton Papers, MG 27, II, D15, vol. 274, 650, for the following in a letter Sir John Anderson of the Colonial Office wrote on 1 Aug. 1903, to Sifton, after the death of Armour: "Armour will be a great loss to our side. Aylesworth I have not yet met, but I am told he has nothing like the force of character which marked Armour."

274 Canada, House of Commons *Debates*, 19 February 1902, col. 151 (Mr. Gourley, MP).

275 Canada, House of Commons *Debates*, 23 October 1903, cols. 14842–14843 (Mr. Hughes, MP, Mr. Gourley, MP).

276 Canada, House of Commons *Debates*, 23 October 1903, cols. 14814–14817 (Mr. Laurier, MP).

277 Canada, House of Commons *Debates*, 23 October 1903, cols. 14774, 14782 (Mr. Bourassa, MP).

278 For example, see White, "Boundary Disputes and Treaties," 957–58.

279 Smith noted that "it will be apparent that my conclusions about the Alaska Boundary Case are very different from those of most other Canadians who have written about the subject." The works that he cited in 1973 were Norman Penlington, *The Alaska Boundary Dispute: A Critical Reappraisal* (Toronto: McGraw-Hill Ryerson, 1972), and John A. Munro, ed., *The Alaska Boundary Dispute* (Toronto: Copp Clark, 1970).

6 | Foreign Explorers in the Canadian North

1 George E. Tyson, *The Cruise of the Florence*, ed. Capt. Henry W. Howgate (Washington: J. J. Chapman, 1879).

2 Tyson, *Cruise of the Florence*, 5–15.

3 E.g., Tyson, *Cruise of the Florence*, 33: "We soon cleared the decks of all the rubbish, Esquimaux and all."

4 Tyson, *Cruise of the Florence*, 12.

5 Tyson, *Cruise of the Florence*, 7–8.

6 William H. Gilder, *Schwatka's Search* (New York: Scribner's Sons, 1881).

7 Gilder, *Schwatka's Search*, xi, 220, 238–39.

8 Gilder, *Schwatka's Search*, 133.

9 V. Kenneth Johnston, "Canada's Title to the Arctic Islands," *Canadian Historical Review* 14, no. 1 (March 1933): 26, 28, assumed that this was the intention.

10 Gilder, *Schwatka's Search*, 239–40.

11 Julius Payer, *New Lands within the Arctic Circle* (New York: Appleton, 1877).

12 See summary of Weyprecht's address, and favourable report thereon by the German Commission on Arctic Exploration, in *Nature* 13 (April 1876): 32–34.

13 Patrick H. Ray, *Report of the International Polar Expedition to Point Barrow, Alaska* (Washington: Government Printing Office, 1885).

14 For good brief summaries of the background of the First International Polar Year and the work of the fifteen stations, see Adolphus W. Greely, *A Handbook of Polar Discoveries*, 3rd ed. (Boston: Little, Brown, 1907), 221–40; and Greely, *The Polar Regions in the Twentieth Century* (London: Harrap, 1929), 174–82.

15 The principal accounts are Adolphus W. Greely, *Three Years of Arctic Service* (New York: Scribner's Sons, 1886); and Greely, *Report on the Proceedings of the United States Expedition to Lady Franklin Bay, Grinnell Land* (Washington: Government Printing Office, 1888).

16 Henry W. Howgate, *Polar Colonization* (Washington: Beresford, 1879).

17 For references to attempts to get bills through Congress see *Cong. Rec.*, 44th Cong., 1st sess., 1877, 5, pt. 3:1823; *Cong. Rec.*, 44th Cong., 1st sess., 1877, 5, pt. 6:184; *Cong. Rec.*, 44th Cong., 1st sess., 1878, 7, pt. 11:1417; *Cong. Rec.*, 44th Cong., 1st sess., 1878, 7, pt. 5:392–97.

18 *Cong. Rec.*, 44th Cong., 2d sess., 1879, 9, pt. 1:34; *Cong. Rec.*, 44th Cong., 2d sess., 1879, 9, pt. 1:1091.

19 *Cong. Rec.*, 46th Cong., 2d sess., 1880, 10, pt. 3:2417–18. Reading of Bill H. R. No. 3534, passed later and approved 1 May.

20 For details of the background of the expedition, see Nellis M. Crouse, *The Search for the North Pole* (New York: R. R. Smith, 1947), 148–54, and references therein; also Alden L. Todd, *Abandoned: The Story of the Greely Arctic Expedition 1880–1884*

(New York: McGraw-Hill, 1961), 5–16. It is ironic that the original promoter Capt. Howgate ended up a fugitive from justice for embezzlement of army funds. See Todd, *Abandoned*, 22–23, 66–67, 157, 313.

21 Journals of the sledging trips may be seen in Greely, *Report on the Proceedings of the United States Expedition to Lady Franklin Bay*, 1:Appendices. See esp. Lockwood's for his record-breaking trip in 1882, 185–232.

22 See, for example, Greely, *Report on the Proceedings of the United States Expedition to Lady Franklin Bay*, 1:208 (Lockwood's farthest in 1882), and 1:290 (Lockwood's farthest in Greely Fiord in 1883). See also Greely, *Three Years of Arctic Service*, 1:403: "Our flag was displayed from the summit of Mount Arthur" (Greely's farthest southwest of Lake Hazen on 4 July 1882).

23 Greely, *Three Years of Arctic Service*, 1:viii–xiii; Greely, *Report on the Proceedings of the United States Expedition to Lady Franklin Bay*, 1:97–107. It is true that some Americans interested in the enterprise took a rather different view. For example, R.W.D. Bryan of the US Naval Observatory wrote, "The United States has the right to consider the Smith's Sound route as peculiarly its own." (Howgate, *Polar Colonization*, 99). I have seen no evidence that the Canadian government showed any particular concern over this aspect of the Greely expedition at the time.

24 A vast literature on the Greely expedition has grown up, especially in connection with the dramatic rescue of the survivors. Besides the works already cited, see the following: David L. Brainard, *The Outpost of the Lost* (Indianapolis: Bobbs-Merrill, 1929); Winfield S. Schley and James R. Soley, *The Rescue of the Greely* (London: Low et al., n.d.); Bessie R. James, ed., *Six Came Back: The Arctic Adventure of David L. Brainard* (Indianapolis: Bobbs-Merrill, 1940); Charles Lanman, *Farthest North: The Life and Explorations of Lieutenant James Booth Lockwood* (New York: Appleton, 1885); and Theodore Powell, *The Long Rescue* (New York: Doubleday, 1960).

25 Franz Boas, "A Journey in Cumberland Sound and on the West Shore of Davis Strait in 1883 and 1884," *Journal of the American Geographical Society* 16 (1884): 241–72; Franz Boas, "The Central Eskimo," in *Smithsonian Institution Bureau of Ethnology Sixth Annual Report 1884-1885* (Washington: Government Printing Office, 1888), 399–669.

26 Otto Sverdrup, *New Land: Four Years in the Arctic Regions* (London: Longmans, Green, 1904), 1:1.

27 Sverdrup, *New Land*, 1:1–2.

28 See, for example, Laurence P. Kirwan, *The White Road: A Survey of Polar Exploration* (London: Hollis and Carter, 1959), 206–8.

29 Fram Expedition, *Report of the Second Norwegian Arctic Expedition in the "Fram," 1898–1902* (Kristiania: Videnskals-Selskabet, 1904–30).

30 Sverdrup, *New Land*, 1:144–48, 318, 404–5, 490; 2:11, 370, 381. See also *Summary of Reports of Commander Otto Sverdrup's Explorations in 1898–1902* (Oslo: Wittusen and Jensen, 1928), in Library and Archives Canada [hereafter LAC], Record Group 85, Northern Affairs Program [hereafter RG 85], vol. 350, file 200-2, "Maps, Memoranda, & Reports on Canada's Claim to Sovereignty in the Arctic Archipelago." On pp. 6 and 7, in a summary of the expeditions of spring 1900, the following passage occurs: "The Expeditions had … rounded West coast of Axel Heiberg Land, on which, on the North-West coast at 80° 55' North latitude, [they] erected a cairn and into same deposited a record of the journey and a declaration that the Expedition took possession of this land and all the lands discovered in the name of the Kingdom of Norway." Also, on p. 12, in a summary of the expedition of Sverdrup and Schei in the spring of 1902, there is the following passage: "The party … reached the nothernmost [*sic*] point, which they called Lands Lokk, at 81° 40' Lat. N. A cairn was built there, in which a report of the journey was deposited, as also a declaration that the Expedition had taken and hereby took possession of this land and all the lands discovered in the name of the Kingdom of Norway." The passages in *New Land* telling of these events (1:404; 2:370) do not mention taking possession.

31 See, for example, Sverdrup, *New Land*, 1:227: "There are no game laws to be respected in these happy regions."

32 Sverdrup, *New Land*, 2:449–50. See also Sverdrup, *New Land*, 1:1, for his comment regarding the offer to him of the leadership of the expedition: "There were still many white spaces on the map which I was glad of an opportunity of colouring with the Norwegian colours." See also T. C. Fairley, *Sverdrup's Arctic Adventures* (London: Longmans, 1959), 273–93.

33 Roald Amundsen, *The North West Passage* (London: Constable, 1908), 1:5; Roald Amundsen, *My Life as an Explorer* (London: W. Heinemann, 1927), 33–34.

34 Amundsen, *North West Passage*, 1:6, 13; 2:365–68; Amundsen, *My Life as an Explorer*, 35–36.

35 Amundsen, *North West Passage*, 1:247, 263–68; 2:69–76. Amundsen does not give the texts of these letters here, and I have not seen them anywhere else.

36 Amundsen, *North West Passage*, 2:296–364, esp. 355. Hansen's narrative is included here as a supplement.

37 The five Greenland expeditions are described in detail in Robert E. Peary, *Northward over the "Great Ice"* (London: Methuen, 1898). The first three are well summarized in Nellis M. Crouse, *The Search for the North Pole* (New York: Richard R. Smith, 1947), 293–306. See also Josephine D. Peary, *My Arctic Journal* (New York: Contemporary Publishing, 1897).

38 Robert E. Peary, "Expedition of 1898–1902," in *Nearest the Pole* (London: Hutchinson, 1907), 295–352, esp. 295–96; Peary, *Northward over the "Great Ice,"* xlixff.; Peary, "Four Years' Arctic Exploration, 1898–1902," *Geographical Journal* 22, no. 1 (July 1903): 646–72, esp. 646–47; Peary, "Report of R. E. Peary, C. E., U.S.N., on Work Done in the Arctic in 1898–1902," *Bulletin of the American Geographical Society* 35, no. 5 (1903): 496–534.

39 Peary, *Nearest the Pole*, see 355–72 for details about the *Roosevelt* and her construction, 3–282 for the narrative of the expedition.

40 Peary, *Nearest the Pole*, 134–35.

41 Peary, *Nearest the Pole*, 190–209.

42 Peary, *Nearest the Pole*, 190, 192, 212.

43 Peary, *Nearest the Pole*, x, xi, 101, 182. This is the aspect he stressed perhaps most of all in his attempts to raise funds. See Robert E. Peary, "The Value of Arctic Exploration," *National Geographic Magazine* 16, no. 12 (December, 1903): 429–36.

44 Robert E. Peary, *The North Pole* (London: Hodder and Stoughton, 1910), 26–30.

45 Peary, *The North Pole*, 19–21, 185–87.

46 See Matthew A. Henson, *A Negro Explorer at the North Pole* (New York: F. A. Stokes, 1912), for Henson's account of the trip.

47 Andrew Croft, *Polar Exploration* (London: A and C. Black, 1939), 32–33. A more detailed explanation of this strange affair is given in George P. Putnam, *Mariner of the North: The Life of Captain Bob Bartlett* (New York: Duell, Sloan and Pearce, 1947), 187–94.

48 Peary, *The North Pole*, 257–69, esp. 266. Peary's assertion that he had reached the Pole, and in fact his entire record as an explorer and a man, became matters of violent controversy. Fitzhugh Green, *Peary: The Man Who Refused to Fail* (New York: Putnam's Sons, 1926), and William H. Hobbs, *Peary* (New York: Macmillan, 1936), give generally favourable views; J. Gordon Hayes, *Robert Edwin Peary* (London: Richards and Toulmin, 1929) is bitterly antagonistic throughout. When Peary informed President Taft of the claim made in his behalf, the president commented that he would have difficulty "in finding any application for such an interesting and generous present." Reported in T. A. Taracouzio, *Soviets in the Arctic* (New York: Macmillan, 1938), 326; and in Rene Waultrin, "Le problème de la souveraineté des poles," *Revue générale de droit international public* 16 (1909): 653.

49 Frederick A. Cook, *My Attainment of the Pole* (New York: M. Kennerley, 1912), esp. 284. See also Cook, *Return from the Pole*, ed. F. J. Pohl (New York: Pellegrini and Cudahy, 1951). In his introduction Pohl argues against Peary's claim to have reached the Pole and, less convincingly, in favour of Cook's.

50 Cook, *My Attainment of the Pole*, 191.

51 Cook, *My Attainment of the Pole*, 449.

52 Cook, *My Attainment of the Pole*, 439. See also Cook, *Return from the Pole*, 88. See also V. Stefanson, *The Problem of Meighen Island*, limited edition privately printed for Mr. Joseph Robinson (New York, 1939).

53 A. E. Millward, *Southern Baffin Island* (Ottawa: King's Printer, 1930), 39–40, appendix, 103–30. The account given in the appendix was prepared from Hantzsch's diaries and notes by Dr. M. Rosenmüller, and translated by M.B.A. Anderson.

54 D. B. MacMillan, *Four Years in the White North* (New York: Harper and Brothers, 1918), introduction.

55 See MacMillan, *Four Years in the White North*, 321–22, for MacMillan's brief summary of the achievements of the expedition.

56 MacMillan, *Four Years in the White North*, 276.

57 MacMillan, *Four Years in the White North*, 305. For a briefer treatment of this expedition, see Everett S. Allen, *Arctic Odyssey: The Life of Rear Admiral Donald B. MacMillan* (New York: Dodd, Mead, 1962), 165–218.

7 | Canadian Government Expeditions

1 The Department of Marine and Fisheries had been divided into two separate departments, the Department of Marine and the Department of Fisheries, by the statute 47 Vict., c. 18, in 1884. The

two were reconstituted as a single department in 1892. See *Statutes of Canada*, 55–56 Vict., c. 17, 12 April 1892.

2 Canada, House of Commons *Debates*, 2 October 1896, col. 2498.

3 Canada, House of Commons *Debates*, 2 October 1896, cols. 2498, 2500.

4 W. Wakeham, *Report of the Expedition to Hudson Bay and Cumberland Gulf in the Steamship "Diana"* (Ottawa: Queen's Printer, 1898), 1, 3–4. The report was published separately, but was also published in Canada, *Sessional Papers* (1898), vol. 9, no. 11B, 1–83.

5 Wakeham, *Report of the Expedition to Hudson Bay*, 3.

6 Wakeham, *Report of the Expedition to Hudson Bay*, 67, 69.

7 Canada, Senate *Debates*, 10 March 1896, 280. See also 6 May 1897, 288–89.

8 Canada, House of Commons *Debates*, 6 May 1897, col. 1816. See also Library and Archives Canada [hereafter LAC], Record Group 15, Department of the Interior [hereafter RG 15], vol. 742, file 448,926, for a letter G. M. Dawson, Deputy Head of the Geological Survey, wrote to Minister of Marine and Fisheries Dr. L. Davies on 12 July 1897, enclosing a clipping from the *New York Evening Post* of 8 July which showed Peary's interest in Baffin Island, and noting that he had sent a copy of the clipping to Wakeham, who was already on his way, via Sydney. Davies passed on Dawson's suggestion that the British government itself send a ship to Colonial Minister Chamberlain in a letter on 30 July, observing that although Wakeham was concerned mainly with navigation he had also been instructed to plan the *[illegible]* in Cumberland Sound. In a letter of 20 November 1897, the Deputy Minister of the Interior, James Smart, now expressed the view that further action was necessary.

9 Wakeham, *Report of the Expedition*, 1, 4. I have not been able to find an order in council setting forth plans for the expedition.

10 Wakeham, *Report of the Expedition*, 71–78.

11 Wakeham, *Report of the Expedition*, 24, and photograph.

12 Canada, House of Commons *Debates*, 18 May 1899, col. 3337. However, another question asked by Mr. Roche at the time indicates that the information he referred to was concerned more with the question of navigability than with sovereignty.

13 It will be remembered that A. R. Gordon had recommended this step (e.g., see his report in the *Department of Marine and Fisheries Report 1885*, 54). Wakeham had not been so impressed with the need for it. (Wakeham, *Report of the Expedition*, 77–78.) LAC, RG 15, vol. 707, 357602, and vol. 742, file 448926, give a good deal of information about the expedition and its background. On 15 November 1902, J. A. Allen, Curator of the American Museum of Natural History in New York, wrote a letter to Madison Grant, of New York, saying that a whaling master whom he did not wish to identify reported that so many muskoxen were being killed in the region west of Hudson Bay that soon they would all be exterminated. Somehow this letter got into the hands of Clifford Sifton, and in response to his request for information, replies were written by Fred White (27 November) and Robert Bell (1 December) recommending that Canada assert her sovereignty in these northern regions. White emphasized the northern waters, Bell the northern lands. On 15 December 1902, Deputy Minister Smart reported to Sifton that White, Bell, Commissioner of Customs John McDougall, Deputy Minister of Marine and Fisheries Gourdeau, Commander Asprey Spain of the same department, and he himself had attended two meetings in his office; in consequence they jointly recommended the appointment of two commissioners for the north, with a dividing line at about the 100th meridian, and the dispatch of two expeditions, one via the Atlantic and one via the Pacific, to the regions in question. A great deal of correspondence and planning followed. In a letter to Smart written from London on 31 March 1903, Sifton underlined his view that the necessary appropriation should be put through the House speedily and without publicity, and that the two expeditions should sail with sealed orders to preserve secrecy. On Sifton's suggestion, because of his absence in London in connection with the Alaska Boundary Case, Smart put the matter in the hands of Minister of Finance W. S. Fielding, by a letter written on 24 April, noting that it had not been possible to find a ship on the west coast and so that voyage would have to be postponed for that year, with the dispatch of Supt. Constantine of the NWMP down the Mackenzie River as temporary substitute. Ostensibly the appropriation was to be for "an extension of the Coast Service of the Marine Department."

14 A. P. Low, *Report of the Dominion Government Expedition to Hudson Bay and the Arctic Islands on board the C.G.S. Neptune 1903–1904* (Ottawa: Government Printing Bureau, 1906), 4.

15 Canada, Order in Council, PC No. 1379, 13 August 1903.

16 See in Low, *Report of the Dominion Government Expedition to Hudson Bay*, ix–x.

17 See in LAC, Fred Cook Papers, MG 30 C12, "Memos and Articles." Gourdeau was the Deputy Minister of Marine and Fisheries; Dr. Bell was the Acting Deputy Head and Director of the Geological Survey.

18 LAC, Cook Papers. I have reproduced these documents as they appear, without taking note of the numerous errors, e.g., "Chief" for "chief."

19 See in A. E. Millward, *Southern Baffin Island* (Ottawa: King's Printer, 1930), 14–15. See also LAC, RG 15, vol. 707, file 357602, White's memo, 2 January 1904, in recommending that the government "make this a permanent service, and extend it to the whole of the extreme northerly portion of the Dominion." Commander Spain had already made the same recommendation in a memo written on 11 August 1903.

20 I do not know if Low had detailed written instructions; at any rate, if he had, I have not seen them. H. R. Holmden says that most of his instructions were given verbally (LAC, Record Group 85, Northern Affairs Program [hereafter RG 85], vol. 584, file 571, pt. 5, Holmden to A. G. Doughty, "Memo re the Arctic Islands," 26 April 1921), but A. E. Millward quotes from what would appear to have been written instructions (*Southern Baffin Island*, 14). In LAC, RG 85, vol. 601, no. 2502, pt.1, "Explorations C.G.S. Arctic 1922," written instructions from Deputy Minister of Marine and Fisheries F. Gourdeau to Low, dated 8 August 1903, Gourdeau writes, *inter alia*, "I have to instruct you that you have been appointed by the Honourable the Minister of Marine and Fisheries to the command of the S. S. "NEPTUNE", taking the Hudson Bay Expedition to the Northward.... In all cases of doubt as to the course to pursue, you will consult with Captain Bartlett and Major Moodie, and in that manner arrive at a decision." See the same file for written instructions given Low by Acting Director Robert Bell of the Geological Survey of Canada, dated 25 July 1903. Bell's instructions dealt only with geological work. See also LAC, RG 15, vol. 707, file 357602, for Commissioner of Customs John McDougald's letter of 1 August 1903, to Moodie appointing him as Inspector of Customs and giving him instruction and also a memorandum dated 11 August 1903, which Commander Spain wrote for Gourdeau, setting down in some detail information about the voyage. Regarding Low's appointment see LAC, RG 15, vol. 742, file 448926, for the following letters or names: Bell to Smart, 16 June 1903, recommending Low as commander of the expedition; Smart to Sifton, 24 July 1903, saying that White does not seem to think the NWMP has an available man suitable for the command and so someone from "outside" might be better; Bell to Smart, 5 August 1903, saying "I have always understood that Mr. Low was appointed as commander of the expedition."; and Low to Goudeau, from Halifax, 3 August 1903, saying "It is absolutely necessary that my commission be sent.... It is apparent that there was much confusion over the appointment."

21 Canada, House of Commons *Debates*, 15 May 1906, col. 3361.

22 Canada, House of Commons *Debates*, 15 May 1906, cols. 3372–3373.

23 Canada, House of Commons *Debates*, 15 May 1906, col. 3394. See also Canada, House of Commons *Debates*, 28 June 1906, col. 6441, where Mr. F. B. Carvell (Carleton, NB), said: "It is no harm to say now that it was the policy of the government, and it was a policy adhered to by members of the opposition, that an expedition should be sent up there not only for the purpose of exploring the country but for the purpose of asserting rights of Canada to that country, for the purpose of getting acquainted with the natives, learning their traditions and placing it beyond doubt that that portion of the American continent was within the jurisdiction of Canada so that no matter what should happen we never should be placed in the same position as we were in respect to the Alaskan territory."

24 Canada, House of Commons *Debates*, 30 September 1903, col. 12821.

25 Low, *Report of the Dominion Government Expedition to Hudson Bay*, xvii.

26 Low, *Report of the Dominion Government Expedition to Hudson Bay*, 8.

27 Low, *Report of the Dominion Government Expedition to Hudson Bay*, 10–12.

28 Low, *Report of the Dominion Government Expedition to Hudson Bay*, 20ff. But see note 34 below for necessary qualification.

29 Low, *Report of the Dominion Government Expedition to Hudson Bay*, 25, 69.

30 Low, *Report of the Dominion Government Expedition to Hudson Bay*, 48.

31 See in LAC, Cook Papers, "Memos and Articles"; also in K. Ethel Borden, "Northward 1903–04," *Canadian Geographical Journal* 62, no. 1 (Jan.

1961): 32–39, at 38. These two versions of the proclamation differ slightly. The one I have taken is from the Cook Papers. Dr. L. E. Borden, surgeon and botanist of the expedition, was the husband of Ethel Borden. It will be noted that in his narrative Low says that the ceremony was at Cape Herschel, but his proclamation says that the document was deposited at Cape Isabella, about twenty miles to the south. A copy of the proclamation, presented to the Archives by Dr. Borden, is in LAC, MG 30 B33-4, A. P. Low Papers. See also Dr. Borden's diary in LAC, MG 30 B46, Dr. Lorris Elijah Borden Papers, where the ceremony is mentioned. And see Canada, House of Commons *Debates*, 5 July 1956, 5691–95; 11 August 1956, 7433; 20 August 1958, 3833–34; as well as LAC, Borden Papers, Borden's memoirs, pt. VI, 2ff., for information about his presentation of his copy of the proclamation to the Archives. Borden, by this time in his declining years and probably the sole surviving member of the expedition, had the assistance of H. W. Herridge, MP for Kootenay West, in arranging for the presentation.

32 The document left at Beechey Island is quoted in J. E. Bernier, *Cruise of the "Arctic" 1906–07* (Ottawa: King's Printer, 1909), 22. Low himself does not mention it in his narrative. He does refer (53–54) to a record left there by the Amundsen expedition in August 1903, and says that the Norwegians were aware of the whaling and police establishments in the northwestern part of Hudson Bay. See the A. P. Low Papers for a copy of a proclamation, dated 15 August 1904.

33 See text of document in Bernier, *Cruise of the "Arctic,"* 13. Low refers to the taking of possession but does not reproduce the document. The documents left at Beechey Island and Port Leopold were almost identical in wording to the one for Ellesmere Island.

34 Low, *Report of the Dominion Government Expedition to Hudson Bay*, 54; Borden, "Northward 1903–04," 37, and Dr. Borden in his diary, 136, says that on 23 June 1904, while still in Hudson Bay, Low took formal possession of Southampton Island at Cape Kendall. Low mentions the trip to Southampton Island but not the ceremony (*Report of the Dominion Government Expedition to Hudson Bay*, 31–34). Mrs. Borden also says in "Northward 1903–04," 36, that Captain Comer deeply resented the presence of the Mounted Police in Hudson Bay and their introduction of Canadian regulations. In his report Major Moodie does not say openly that this was the case; but that it was so, at least in some degree, may be inferred front his remarks. See Canada, Sessional Papers (1905), vol. 12, no. 28, pt. 4, "Report of Superintendent J. D. Moodie on Service in Hudson Bay, per SS Neptune, 1903–4," 8, regarding the intervention of the police in trouble on Corner's ship: "The police have only been called upon once, viz., in a complaint made by one of the crew of the Era ... had the protection of our flag not been asked for, no notice would have been taken of the matter, but it was brought before me officially and I was compelled to act"; also 12, regarding Moodie's prohibition of the export of muskox hides: "Knowing the wish of the government in this matter, I took the only method which would be of practical use, and issued, on 8 November 1903, a notice prohibiting the export, &c. The Era was on the point of dispatching a large party of natives to hunt those animals, and any action to be effective, had to be taken at once. The natives did not go." Moodie observes (3) that the Scottish whalers and the missionary in Baffin Island expressed pleasure that the Canadian government was taking steps to introduce law and order into the region. Dr. Borden is less reserved and more informative in his diary. For example, on p. 18, "Sept. 24th. The Capt of the schooner 'Era' was very much puzzled yesterday when he saw the Canadian Ensign & did not know how to take us." 58: "Nov. 14th .... A huge repast was served ... Capt. Comer could not see his way clear to come after the Proclamation which was lately issued regarding the sale & export of musk ox heads & skins." 60: "Nov. 19th .... Capt Comer has not been on board for some time. Would not speak to Mr. Low & Capt. yesterday." 63: "27th [Nov.] .... Capt Comer trying to make overtures." 69: "Dec 14th .... Capt. Comer apologized today for his treatment a few weeks ago." 74: "Jan 4th .... Custom house opened & Capt Comer entered what stuff he had." 97: "Mar 26th .... Comer has had considerable trouble with his men the last two days for some dispute between them he ironed one yesterday & confined him in the hold. The men complained to the major & Comer ironed more & came to the major to tell him that he was captain & not to interfere. Matters were settled but according to what Comer told Caldwell & myself this morning he bears a fearful enmity for the major & will certainly get even with him if ever the opportunity offers itself." 150: "July 18th ....at last after 9 long mos. made a start .... Capt Comer & his men cheered us which was returned 2 salutes of flags interchanged." See also Dr. Borden's Memoirs of a Pioneer Doctor (unpublished), LAC, Dr Lorris E. Borden's Papers, III, 35, 68, 70–71, for relations with Capt. Comer, and for acts of possession, III, 91, 107, 112.

35 J. E. Bernier, *Master Mariner and Arctic Explorer* (Ottawa: Le Droit, 1939), 5–304. This is Bernier's autobiography, unfinished and published posthumously. See also T. C. Fairley and C. E. Israel, *The True North: The Story of Captain Joseph Bernier* (Toronto: Macmillan, 1957), 9–66.

36 Bernier, *Master Mariner*, 264–67.

37 See the J. E. Bernier Papers, LAC, MG 30 B 6, vol. 2, for a reproduction from *Canadian Life and Resources* (Jan. 1896) of a polar map by Bernier, dated 1896, and showing the route of the *Fram*, the assumed route of the *Jeannette* relics, and Bernier's projected route, approximating the latter. The map bears the caption: "The only feasible way to reach the Pole."

38 Bernier, *Master Mariner*, 265–304; also Fairley and Israel, *True North*, 30–36, 47–66.

39 LAC, Laurier Papers, MG 26 G, vol. 68, 21269–91.

40 LAC, Laurier Papers, vol. 72, 22393–95. C. Baillairgé to Laurier, 9 April 1898, saying the society has heard Bernier, supports his efforts, and suggests that he be given a grant. Also vol. 108, 32584–86, president of the society to Laurier, 15 April 1899; vol. 109, 32853–57, C. Baillairgé to Laurier, 21 April 1899 and 12 February 1901.

41 LAC, Laurier Papers, vol. 189, 53904, 53976–78. At its meeting on 2 March 1901, the Canadian Institute passed a unanimous resolution asking the government to support Bernier's enterprise.

42 LAC, Laurier Papers, vol. 234, 65430–31, Bender to Laurier, 29 May 1902, enclosing resolution of support unanimously adopted by the Royal Society of Canada on 28 May at Toronto. About a year earlier, on 23 May 1901, Bernier had addressed a meeting of the Royal Society of Canada in Ottawa, and a motion of support, moved by Senator P. Poirier and seconded by Dr. Robert Ben, was unanimously carried (clipping in author's possession).

43 LAC, Laurier Papers, vol. 187, 53412–37. Bernier to Laurier, 13 February 1901, enclosing a copy of a speech he gave before the Royal Colonial Institute on 17 January 1901, with Sir Clements Markham in the chair and Lord Strathcona and the Antarctic explorer Robert Scott among those present. It is apparent from his speech that Bernier had by now practically abandoned his Franz Joseph Land plan, since be barely mentioned it and concentrated instead upon the Bering Strait route.

44 LAC, Laurier Papers, vol. 190, 54343–51, Bernier to Laurier, 22 March 1901; also vol. 191, 54625; regarding a speech to members of both Commons and Senate on 21 March 1901, See also vol. 229, 64244–51, Bernier to Laurier, 12 April 1902, enclosing supporting statement signed by a large number of the members of Parliament.

45 LAC, Laurier Papers, vol. 109, 32853–57.

46 LAC, Laurier Papers, vol. 187, 53437.

47 LAC, Laurier Papers, vol. 252, 70352–54.

48 LAC, Laurier Papers, vol. 194, 55351.

49 LAC, Laurier Papers, vol. 210, 59552.

50 LAC, Laurier Papers, vol. 201, 57314–16.

51 LAC, Laurier Papers, vol. 208, 59245–47.

52 Canada House of Commons *Debates*, 21 March 1901, col. 1798.

53 Canada House of Commons *Debates*, 14 May 1901, cols. 5191–5194, and 21 May 1901, col. 5790, where Laurier, answering another question, said, "The government has not thought it advisable to ask parliament to vote any appropriation this session."

54 Canada House of Commons *Debates*, 1 May 1902, cols, 3951–3980, at 3952–3964.

55 Canada House of Commons *Debates*, 1 May 1902, col. 3971.

56 Canada House of Commons *Debates*, 30 September 1903, cols. 12805–12822, at 12806, 12811–12812, 12814.

57 LAC, Laurier Papers, vol. 288, 78415–18. Edwards to Laurier, 28 October 1903; Laurier to Edwards, 29 October 1903.

58 Bernier, *Master Mariner*, 305. Fairley and Israel, evidently following Bernier, make the same statement, although without identifying the sponsors, and they also say the money was voted early in 1904. *True North*, 63.

59 Canada, House of Commons *Debates*, 30 September 1903, cols. 12820–12822.

60 Canada, House of Commons *Debates*, 12 October 1903, col. 13760.

61 Canada, House of Commons *Debates*, 15 May 1906, col. 3361 et passim. See also my text to note 23, above.

62 Canada, House of Commons *Debates*, 29 July 1904, cols. 7968–7969.

63 Canada, House of Commons *Debates*, 21 June 1904, cols. 5210–5218, esp. 5210. Possibly the $100,000 voted on 12 October 1903 was not only for Low's expedition but also for the purchase of a ship. A year later, on 23 May 1905, when explaining how the expedition of the *Arctic* in 1904–5

had been financed, Préfontaine said that $170,000 had been transferred from the NWMP to the Department of Marine and Fisheries for the "Hudson bay expedition," of which $29,018 had been paid as the balance due on the total of $70,000 which the *Gauss* had cost, $40,982 having already been paid from the appropriation for 1903–4. On the same date, 23 May 1905, a further sum of $65,000 was allotted for the expedition, or, as it was expressed, "for the extension of the coast service and surveys on the north and northwest coasts of Canada." Canada, House of Commons *Debates*, 23 May 1905, cols. 6468–6473. See also Canada, Order in Council, PC No. 1563, 17 Aug. 1904, which recommended "that the item of $200,000 XX .... voted in the Supplementary Estimates for the fiscal year 1904–05, be apportioned for the purposes of expenditure $170,000 XX to the Department of Marine and Fisheries and $30,000 XX to the North West Mounted Police." This must be authoritative, but it certainly does not tally with Préfontaine's explanation. It may be that all these seemingly discordant elements actually do fit into a simple, cohesive pattern, but on the face of it this does not appear to be the case.

64 Bernier said that the ship cost $75,000. *Master Mariner*, 305. Préfontaine said that the price would be $75,000 if the ship went seven knots per hour, $70,000 if it did not, that it did not, and so the price paid was $70,000. House of Commons *Debates*, 21 June 1904, col. 5210.

65 Bernier, *Master Mariner*, 305. This statement, as Bernier gives it, hardly rings true, since the captain (obviously Comer) had been under the observation of Moodie and Low during the entire preceding winter, and the *Neptune* was still in northern waters.

66 Bernier, *Master Mariner*, 305–6.

67 Canada, House of Commons *Debates*, 30 September 1903, cols. 12820–12822.

68 Canada, House of Commons *Debates*, 21 June 1904, col. 5210.

69 Canada, House of Commons *Debates*, 11 May 1906, cols. 3218, 3222.

70 Fairley and Israel, *True North*, 69.

71 Bernier, *Master Mariner*, 305–6.

72 Bernier, *Master Mariner*, 307.

73 The only detailed report of this expedition is by Major Moodie. See Canada, *Sessional Papers* (1906), vol. 13, "Report of Superintendent J. D. Moodie on Service in Hudson Bay," 30 December 1905, pt. 4, in Report of the Royal North-West Mounted Police 1905, 1–16. Bernier himself gives only a brief summary of it in *Cruise of the "Arctic,"* 330–31. Neither says anything specifically about the suspected sale of liquor to the natives which, according to Bernier, had been the prime cause of the voyage.

74 Canada House of Commons *Debates*, 28 June 1906, col. 6391.

75 "Report of Superintendent J. D. Moodie," 3.

76 Bernier, *Cruise of the "Arctic,"* 330, 331. There is no doubt that on this point Moodie was right and Bernier was wrong. See Canada, Order in Council, PC No. 1755, 16 September 1904, giving Moodie his appointment and his commission. By this order he was appointed "Officer in Charge of the Dominion Government Ship 'Arctic'," and also "a Fishery Officer for Canada, with authority to exercise therein during his term of office as such Fishery Officer, the powers of a Justice of the Peace for all the purposes of the Fishery Laws and Regulations." So far as the reports show, this expedition annexed no land to Canada. See also Canada, House of Commons *Debates*, 28 June 1906, cols. 6524–6525, for statement by the chief engineer of the Neptune, who at Moodie's request examined the *Arctic* at Chateau Bay on 21 September 1905, to see if she was in fit condition to continue the voyage.

77 See "Report of Superintendent J. D. Moodie," 10–15.

78 Canada, House of Commons *Debates*, 11 May 1904, col. 3201.

79 Canada, House of Commons *Debates*, 11 May 1906, cols. 3201–3233; 15 May 1904, cols. 3350–3399; 18 May 1906, cols. 3620–3672; 28 June 1906, 6371–6537. See also Canada, Senate *Debates* 31 May 1906, 516–17.

80 Canada, House of Commons *Debates*, 11 May 1906, col. 3207.

81 Canada, House of Commons *Debates*, 11 May 1906, col. 3208.

82 Canada, House of Commons *Debates*, 11 May 1906, col. 3232.

83 Canada, House of Commons *Debates*, 15 May 1906, col. 3352.

84 Canada, House of Commons *Debates*, 15 May 1906, cols. 3383–3384.

85 Canada, House of Commons *Debates*, 28 June 1906, cols. 6489–6491.

86 Canada, House of Commons *Debates*, 18 May 1906, cols. 3620–3621.

87 Canada, House of Commons *Debates*, 18 May 1906, cols. 3628–3629, 3669–3671.

88 Canada, House of Commons *Debates*, 28 June 1906, cols. 6498–6505.

89 Canada, House of Commons *Debates*, 28 June 1906, cols. 6535–6537. See Canada, House of Commons *Debates*, 4 December 1907, cols. 184–185, for a tabulation of expenditure on the Arctic, year by year, from 1903–4 to 1907–8.

90 One other leading figure who did not come out of the affair nearly so well was Brodeur, who had assumed the post of Minister of Marine and Fisheries in December 1905 and was continually embarrassed by his obvious lack of knowledge about various details respecting the department and the expedition. Apart from this, his belligerent and abrasive manner unnecessarily antagonized the opposition, and, combined with his deficient grasp of factual information, sometimes got him into embarrassing situations from which extrication was difficult.

91 Canada, House of Commons *Debates*, 11 May 1904, col. 3232.

92 Canada, Order in Council, PC No. 1547, 23 July 1906.

93 See both of these commissions in Bernier, *Cruise of the Arctic*, xxvii–xxix. The commission as fishery officer, but not as officer in charge, is given on p. 5.

94 Bernier, *Master Mariner*, 307. In a letter of 18 October 1907, to Mr. Brodeur, given in *Cruise of the "Arctic,"* 3, Bernier makes a similar statement: "In accordance with the instructions contained in the above mentioned commissions I proceeded northward, with a view of asserting Canadian sovereignty in the Arctic regions which are territory of this Dominion by right of cession made to Canada by the Imperial government." But see note from O. S. Finnie (Director, NWT and Yukon Branch, Dept. of the Interior) to W. W. Cory (Deputy Minister of the Interior), dated 31 March 1926, in LAC, RG 85, vol. 5. After noting Bernier's commissions, Finnie continues: "I am unable to find, however, any evidence that he was authorized to hoist the British flag on any of our Northern Islands, or to claim them on behalf of the British Crown. Captain Bernier himself has been unable to produce any such authority." Nevertheless, as Finnie observes, Prime Minister Laurier himself said that Bernier "was commissioned to assert Canada's Dominion over the northern islands." See the same volume for Laurier's remarks to the Canadian Club, Ottawa, on 16 October 1909, following an address by Bernier, where the Prime Minister actually made this statement. See also Canada, Sessional Papers (1909), vol. 12, no. 21, *Report of the Department of Marine and Fisheries (Marine) for 1908*, "Report of Deputy Minister F. Gourdeau," 26: "The most important work accomplished by Captain Bernier was the annexing of a number of islands to the Dominion of Canada, raising the Dominion flag, building cairns and depositing documents proclaiming the fact that the land was taken possession of in the name of Canada and in accordance with the granting of the northern islands and lands, the possessions of Great Britain, to Canada." See LAC, RG 85, vol. 601, file 2502, pt. 1, "Explorations C.G.S. Arctic 1922," for instructions from Deputy Minister Gourdeau to Bernier, dated 23 June 1906, which in all probability account for the discrepancy. Gourdeau writes, *inter alia*, "It will be your duty to formally annex all new lands at which you may call, leaving proclamations in cairns at all points of call.... By the Minister's instructions I am to impress upon you the necessity of being most careful in all your actions not to take any course which might result in international complications with any Foreign country. When action on your part would seem likely to give rise to any such contingency, you will hold your hand but fully report the facts on your return." Obviously, to carry out these instructions, Bernier would have to know what was meant by "all new lands," and he may have interpreted the expression to suit himself. Oddly, Gourdeau tells Bernier, "You should be off the mouth of Hudson Strait not later than the 20th September," so he apparently did not intend that the expedition should winter in the North.

95 Bernier, *Master Mariner*, 306.

96 Bernier, *Cruise of the "Arctic,"* 12, 14–21, 29–31, 48–50.

97 Bernier, *Cruise of the "Arctic,"* 18, 50.

98 Bernier, *Cruise of the "Arctic,"* 12.

99 Bernier, *Cruise of the "Arctic,"* 50.

100 Bernier, *Cruise of the "Arctic,"* 11, 27, 28, 43.

101 Bernier, *Cruise of the "Arctic,"* 43, 72.

102 Bernier, *Cruise of the "Arctic,"* 71.

103 Bernier, *Cruise of the "Arctic,"* 27, 28, 39, 40–41, 42, 43, 44.

104 Bernier, *Cruise of the "Arctic,"* 62.

105 Bernier, *Cruise of the "Arctic,"* 30, 34.

106 Bernier, *Cruise of the "Arctic,"* 13–14, 22–23.

107 Bernier, *Cruise of the "Arctic,"* e.g., 14–15, 16, 22, 23.

108 Canada, House of Commons *Debates*, 27 February 1908, col. 3985.

109 Canada, House of Commons *Debates*, 27 February 1908, cols. 4011–4012.

110 Canada, House of Commons *Debates*, 27 February 1908, col. 4159.

111 Canada, House of Commons *Debates*, 27 February 1908, cols. 3985–4218.

112 Canada, House of Commons *Debates*, 10 March 1908, cols. 4747–4751.

113 Canada, House of Commons *Debates*, 20 May 1908, cols. 8863–8866. From the naivete of his remark about Skagway, one would judge that even at this date Sir Wilfrid did not appreciate fully the hard realities of the Alaska Boundary Case.

114 Bernier, *Cruise of the Arctic*, xix.

115 Bernier, *Cruise of the "Arctic,"* 1.

116 Bernier, *Master Mariner*, 325.

117 See Morin's report in Bernier, *Cruise of the "Arctic,"* 126–38, esp. 135. Their record claimed not only Banks and Victoria Islands but also King William Island, although they were about 500 miles from it.

118 Bernier, *Cruise of the "Arctic,"* 145–61 (Green's report).

119 Bernier, *Cruise of the "Arctic,"* 167–77, esp. 177 (Morin's report).

120 Bernier, *Cruise of the "Arctic,"* 167. See also Fairley and Israel, *True North*, 120–22. They are evidently mistaken in saying (122) that Morin's second expedition built cairns on both Banks and Victoria Islands.

121 Bernier, *Cruise of the "Arctic,"* 112–14.

122 Bernier was mistaken here. The British grant mentioned no specific boundaries of latitude or longitude.

123 Bernier, *Cruise of the "Arctic,"* 192.

124 Bernier, *Cruise of the "Arctic,"* 195–97. Shortly after the return of the expedition, an exact copy of the tablet, made on board the *Arctic*, was placed in the vestibule of the Library of Parliament, in conformity with instructions from the Speaker of the House of Commons. See Canada, House of Commons *Debates*, 12 January 1910, col. 1730.

125 See Canada, House of Commons *Debates*, 12 January 1910, 321: "There are numerous small islands on the coasts of the large islands, all of which were annexed at the same time as the large divisions."

126 See LAC, Laurier Papers, vol. 288, 78415–18.

127 Bernier, *Cruise of the "Arctic,"* 269, 281.

128 Bernier, *Cruise of the "Arctic,"* 273, also 277, 281. See also H. Whitney, *Hunting with the Eskimos* (New York: Century, 1911), 441–43, for Whitney's version of the meeting: "Canada lays claim to pretty much all of the Arctic region in general, and to the islands lying between her continental possessions and the Pole specifically, and requires a license to hunt or fish in these regions, or trade with the natives inhabiting them. One of the duties imposed upon Captain Bernier was a strict enforcement of this law. I was a poacher, therefore, in the eyes of Canada, though I had known nothing of this far-reaching law until Captain Bernier informed me of its existence. Never have I willingly poached, and so in exchange for fifty dollars I received the requisite license from the Captain, permitting me to hunt, chase, kill and obtain, anything from hares or trout to bears or whales; and to exchange, barter and trade with the said and aforesaid natives of the wide and limitless Arctic dominions of Canada with a free and law-abiding hand. I was very glad to get this document, and I felt now, at least, that I was breaking no law of any nation, empire, kingdom, or principality, for Canada had clothed me with authority."

129 Bernier, *Cruise of the "Arctic,"* 17.

130 Bernier, *Cruise of the "Arctic,"* 143.

131 See these instructions in W. W. Stumbles et al., *The Arctic Expedition 1910* (Ottawa: Department of Marine and Fisheries, n.d.), 3. Stumbles also helped to produce the report of the expedition of 1908–9. For this expedition also, as for the expedition of 1908–9, the commissions given to Bernier in 1906 were evidently considered still valid. See also Canada, Sessional Papers (1911), vol. 13, no. 21, *Report of the Department of Marine and Fisheries (Marine) for 1910*, appendix no. 23, 269–70, where the 1906 commissions are reproduced as applicable to the expedition of 1908–9.

132 *Arctic Expedition of 1910*, 3. See also 2, where Johnston, in a letter to the new Minister of Marine and Fisheries J. D. Hazen, says that the purposes of the expedition were those "of making the Northwest passage and for patrolling waters where whaling is prosecuted."

133 *Arctic Expedition of 1910*, 85–89, 89–106 (Reports of Lavoie's two expeditions), and 42, 88. See also W. T. Larmour, "Symbol of Sovereignty," *Canadian Geographical Journal* 49, no. 2 (August 1954): 82–86, telling of a cairn built by the expedition.

134 *Arctic Expedition of 1910*, 15, 80, 81, 83–84.

135 *Arctic Expedition of 1910*, 79.

136 *Arctic Expedition of 1910*, 143–44.

137 A. Tremblay, *Cruise of the Minnie Maud*, trans. A. B. Reader (Quebec: Arctic Exchange, 1921). Bernier's autobiography *Master Mariner and Arctic Explorer* does not even mention his role at the point where it would logically appear (c. page 371), although a brief summary of his appointments at the end of the book (408) contains the following notation: "Maintaining possession of Northern Territories of Canada, by cruising and visiting these parts with Schooner 'Minnie Maud' during 1912–1913." Evidently Bernier felt that he was continuing to act in at least an unofficial capacity as guardian of Canada's interests in the North.

138 Tremblay, *Cruise of the Minnie Maud*, 51–259, 262–63.

139 Tremblay, *Cruise of the Minnie Maud*, xi–xii, 181, 192–93.

140 See V. Stefansson, *Discovery: The Autobiography of Vilhjalmur Stefansson* (New York: McGraw-Hill, 1964), for the author's own account of his early life and experiences, including these two summer expeditions.

141 V. Stefansson, *Hunters of the Great North* (London: G. G. Harrap, 1923).

142 V. Stefansson, *My Life with the Eskimos* (New York: Macmillan, 1927).

143 For details see Stefansson, *Discovery*, 45, 51–52, 61–62, 101–2; *Hunters of the Great North*, 19; *My Life with the Eskimos*, ix–xvi, 1–3.

144 Stefansson, *Discovery*, 145–47; *The Friendly Arctic: The Story of Five Years in Polar Regions*, rev. ed. (New York: Macmillan, 1943), xiii–xvi, xxi–xxiii, xxvii. See also LAC, R. L. Borden Papers, vol. 234, RLB2117, 130238–130241, for a letter Stefansson wrote to Borden on 4 February 1913, enclosing an outline plan of his proposed expedition. The first two paragraphs, quoted below, show clearly that in Stefansson's own thinking the main object of the expedition was to discover and explore new lands, and scientific work was secondary:

> Main object: To discover new land, if any exists, in the million or so square miles of unknown area north of the continent of North America and West of the Parry Islands.
>
> Secondary objects: To gather scientific information and collections in the departments of oceanography, geography, geology, zoology, botany, ethnology and archaeology, and to take meteorological and magnetic observations.

See also the same file, page 130245, for a report by a Sub-Committee of Council, dated 7 February which records that Stefansson was asked to become a naturalized British subject as a condition for Canada paying the entire cost of the expedition:

> The Sub-Committee of Council appointed to talk matters over with Mr. Stefansson met him this afternoon. We decided that if it could be arranged we thought it advisable for the Dominion to pay the whole cost of the proposed expedition, on condition that Mr. Stefansson would become a naturalized British subject before leaving and that the expedition would fly the British flag. In this way we would get the entire benefit of the expedition and Canada would have any land that might be discovered. Mr. Stefansson would not say definitely whether he would agree to this arrangement or not but stated that he thought it would be very satisfactory to have the whole cost paid from one source. He did not seem to have any particular objection to taking the oat [*sic*] of naturalization although he did not say definitely that he would do so.

I have not seen anywhere any authoritative statement as to whether Stefansson did or did not take the oath.

145 Stefansson, *Friendly Arctic*, xxvii (introduction by Sir Robert Borden). See also Borden's letter of 21 February 1913, to G. H. Grosvenor, Director and Editor of the National Geographic Society, Washington, DC, in *Friendly Arctic*, xxii–xxiii, which contains the following passage: "The Government of Canada feels, however, with regard to the present exploration, that it would be more suitable if the expenses are borne by the Government more immediately interested, and if the expedition sails under the flag of the country which is to be explored."

146 Canada, Order in Council, PC No. 406, 22 February 1913.

147 LAC, Record Group 25, Department of External Affairs [hereafter RG 25], vol. 2668, file 9058-E-40C, pt. 1, Connaught to Harcourt (1 March 1913).

148 LAC, RG 25, vol. 2668, file 9058-E-40C, pt. 1, Harcourt to C.A.G., 10 May 1913. See also in

LAC, R. L. Borden Papers, vol. 234, RLB2117, 130279–130281.

149 Canada, Order in Council, PC No. 1316, 2 June 1913.

150 LAC, Record Group 42, Department of Marine fonds [hereafter RG 42], vol. 464, file 84-2-2. See Morris Zaslow, *The Opening of the Canadian North 1870–1914* (Toronto: McClelland and Stewart, 1971), 272–77; and Zaslow, *Reading the Rocks: The Story of the Geological Survey of Canada, 1842–1972* (Toronto: Macmillan, 1975), 319–25.

151 Chipman did not act in this capacity, although Stefansson wanted him to, because he found that the RNWMP were already doing so. Chipman Diaries, 10 March and 4 April 1914, also verbal statement to author by Chipman. It seems to me that Zaslow gives too much credence to the claim that the southern party in reality constituted a quite separate unit under the authority of Geological Survey Director R. W. Broch.

152 Government of Canada, *Report of the Canadian Arctic Expedition 1913–18*, several volumes (Ottawa: King's Printer, various dates). See also Stefansson, *Friendly Arctic*, 763–83, for Stefansson's summary of Dr. Anderson's "Report of the Southern Division of the Canadian Arctic Expedition of 1913."

153 R. A. Bartlett and R. T. Hale, *The Last Voyage of the Karluk* (Boston: Small, Maynard, 1916); R. A. Bartlett, *The Log of Bob Bartlett: The True Story of Forty Years of Seafaring and Exploration* (New York: Putnam's Sons, 1928), 254–79; C. P. Putnam, *Mariner of the North: The Life of Captain Bob Bartlett* (New York: Duelle, Sloan and Pearce, 1947), 108–31; J. Hadley, *Hadley's Narrative of the Wreck of the "Karluk,"* unpublished typewritten manuscript, and also photostat copy of original, in the Aboriginal Affairs and Northern Development Canada (AANDC) Library, Gatineau; LAC, William Liard McKinlay Papers, MG 30 B25, containing the diary of W. L. McKinlay from 15 July 1913, to 6 September 1914; LAC, Robert J. Williamson Papers, MG 30 B44; B. M. McConnell et al., *The Karluk Chronicle, a journal written aboard the Karluk, with misc. papers*, typewritten copy in the AANDC Library, Gatineau. See also W. L. McKinlay, *Karluk* (London: Weidenfeld and Nelson, 1976).

154 The literature on Stefansson's part of the expedition is very extensive. The main reference is Stefansson, *Friendly Arctic*, but see also Stefansson, *Discovery*, 145–213; E. P. Hanson, *Stefansson; Prophet of the North* (New York: Harper and Bros., 1941), 102–72; D. M. LeBourdais, *Stefansson: Ambassador of the North* (Montreal: Harvest House, 1963), 61–142. For Stokerson's exploration of northeastern Victoria Island, see *Friendly Arctic*, 657–58, also map at 594; for his drift see *Friendly Arctic*, appendix I, 715–29 (reprinted from *MacLean's Magazine*, 15 March, 1 April 1920). See also D. M. LeNourdais, "Vilhjalmur Stefansson," *Canadian Geographical Journal* 61, no. 2 (Aug. 1960): 62–67; V. Stefansson, "The Activities of the Canadian Arctic Expedition from October, 1916 to April, 1918," *Geographical Review* (Oct. 1918): 354–69; and Stefansson, "The Canadian Arctic Expedition of 1913 to 1918," *Geographical Journal* 62, no. 4 (Oct. 1921): 283–305.

155 Stefansson, *Discovery*, 193.

156 Stefansson, *Friendly Arctic*, 330.

157 Stefansson, *Friendly Arctic*, 497.

158 Stefansson, *Discovery*, 193. Since Stefansson's travels it has been found that Borden Island is divided by a strait, and that there is actually a constellation of islands, large and small, the largest of which now bears the name of Mackenzie King Island.

159 Stefansson, *Friendly Arctic*, 520, 546–47. Initially Stefansson designated the new islands simply "First Land" (Brock and Borden), "Second Land" (Meighen) and "Third Land" (Lougheed). See Stefansson, *Friendly Arctic*, 450, 522, 542.

160 LAC, R. L. Borden Papers, MG 36 H, 1(c), vol. 185, R.L.B. 529, 101610. For additional general information on the expedition, see Canada, Sessional Papers, *Reports of the Department of the Naval Service*, vol. 26 (1915), no. 38, 12–14; vol. 27 (1916), no. 38, 12–18, 22–54; vol. 21 (1917), no. 38, 16–19, 71–80; vol. 13 (1918), no. 38, xiv–xviii, 22–70; vol. 10 (1919), no. 38, 18–31; vol. 10 (1920), no. 39, 36–41.

8 | The Sector Principle

1 A possible exception might be northeastern Ellesmere Island, which lies immediately north of Greenland, rather than any part of the Canadian mainland.

2 Gustav Smedal, *Skrifter om Svalbard og Ishavet*, trans. C. Meyer as *Acquisition of Sovereignty over Polar Areas* (Oslo: J. Dybwad, 1931), 54.

3 Canada, Senate *Debates*, 20 February 1907, 266–73 (Mr. Poirier, MP).

4 F. G. Davenport, *European Treaties Bearing on the History of the United States* (1917), 1:71–78, esp. 77. See also Samuel E. Dawson, *The Line of*

Demarcation of Pope Alexander VI, in A. D. 1493 and that of the Treaty of Tordesillas in A. D. 1494: with an inquiry concerning the Metrology of Ancient and Mediaeval Times (Toronto: Copp Clark, 1899), *Proceedings and Transactions of the Royal Society of Canada*, 2nd Ser., vol. 5, 26 May 1899, 467–546. See esp. 484–89, 532–34.

5 Davenport, *European Treaties*, 1:84–100, esp. 95; Dawson, *Line of Demarcation*, 496–500.

6 Davenport, *European Treaties*, 1:146–98, esp. 188.

7 The treaty of 17 April 1824, between the United States and Russia, is not relevant in this respect, since it simply established the parallel of 54° 40' N latitude as the future dividing line between Russian and American settlements on the northwestern coast of North America and adjacent islands. Malloy, ed., *Treaties, Conventions, International Acts, Protocols and Agreements between the United States of America and Other Powers 1776–1909*, 2:1512–14; *British and Foreign State Papers (1824–1825)*, 12:595–600. See art. 3.

8 *British and Foreign State Papers (1824–1825)*, 12:38–43. See art. 3.

9 For a detailed discussion of the interpretation of the expression "jusqu'à" see Elmer Plischke, "Jurisdiction in the Polar Regions" (PhD diss., Clark University, 1943), 356–64.

10 Malloy, ed., *Treaties, Conventions, International Acts*, 2:1521–24. See esp. art. 1.

11 David H. Miller, "Political Rights in the Polar Regions," in *Problems of Polar Research*, ed. W.L.G. Joerg (New York: American Geographical Society, 1928), 247.

12 Miller, "Political Rights," 244, 247.

13 W. L. Lakhtine, "Rights over the Arctic," *American Journal of International Law* 24, no. 4 (Oct. 1930): 705, 710.

14 T.E.M. McKitterick, "The Validity of Territorial and Other Claims in Polar Regions," *Journal of Comparative Legislation and International Law* 21 (1939): 91, 95. M. F. Lindley has taken a similar view. *The Acquisition and Government of Backward Territory in International Law* (London: Longmans, Green, 1926), 4–6, 235.

15 Smedal, *Skrifter om Svalbard og Ishavet*, 60–64.

16 Friedrich A. F. von der Heydte, "Discovery, Symbolic Annexation and Virtual Effectiveness in International Law," *American Journal of International Law* 29, no. 3 (July 1935): 470–71.

17 Oscar Svarlien, "The Legal Status of the Arctic," *Proceedings of the American Society of International Law* 52 (1958): 138–39.

18 L. M. Gould, "Antarctica in World Affairs," Headline Series 128 (New York: Foreign Policy Association, Inc., March–April 1958): 19.

19 Howard J. Taubenfeld, "A Treaty for Antarctica," *International Conciliation* 531 (New York: Carnegie Endowment for International Peace, January 1961): 253–54.

20 See in Henry S. Commager, ed., *Documents of American History,* 8th ed. (New York: Appleton-Century-Crofts, 1968), 11.

21 See in Commager, *Documents of American History*, 17.

22 McKitterick, "Validity of Territorial and Other Claims," 91.

23 Bibliothèque Nationale, Margry Papers, 9284, ff. 10–25, cited in Grace L. Nute, *Caesars of the Wilderness* (New York: Appleton-Century, 1943), 108, 121–22, 124–29. See also E. E. Rich, *The History of the Hudson's Bay Company 1670–1870* (London: Hudson's Bay Record Society, 1958–59), 1:73–74.

24 Reproductions of the Charter may be seen in E. E. Rich ed., *Minutes of the Hudson's Bay Company 1671–1674*, Hudson's Bay Record Society Publications 5 (London: Champlain Society for the Hudson's Bay Record Society, 1942), appendix A, 129–48; and in Chester Martin, ed., "The Royal Charter," *The Beaver*, Outfit 276 (June 1945): 26–35.

25 Charles Hay, Secretary of Hudson's Bay Company to Lords Commissioners of Trade and Plantations, 3 October 1750, in CO 323, vol. 12, 317. See also on microfilm, Library and Archives Canada [hereafter LAC], reel B. 3497, 256.

26 Great Britain, House of Commons, "Report from the Select Committee on the Hudson's Bay Company, with Proceedings, Minutes of Evidence, Appendix, and Index" (July–August 1857), 46. See esp. Questions 737, 738.

27 Abel Holmes, *Annals of America, from the Discovery by Columbus in the Year 1492 to the Year 1826* (Cambridge: Hilliard and Brown, 1829), 1:211–12.

28 *Rapport de l'Archiviste de la Province de Québec pour 1930–1931*, 157–58; Marie de l'Incarnation, *Lettres*, 2:670–71; Nute, *Caesars of the Wilderness*, 146–48.

29 For a detailed treatment of explorers' claims, see Arthur S. Keller, Oliver J. Lissitzyn, and Frederick J. Mann, *Creation of Rights of Sovereignty through Symbolic Acts 1400–1800* (New York: Columbia

University Press, 1938). See, for example, p. 43, recounting the Spanish claims of Balboa and Dávila to the Pacific Ocean and all islands and lands in and adjoining it, and of Quiros to all lands, including those still undiscovered, to the South Pole. See also Government of Ontario, Statutes, *Documents, and Papers .... etc.* 53, for extract from M. de Mofras, California, which contains the following: "L'Escarbot, who wrote in 1617, among others, states as follows: - Thus our New France has for its limits ... on the north that land called unknown, towards the icy sea as far as the Arctic pole."

30 British and Foreign State Papers (1817–18), 5:327–28, Pinchney and Monroe to Don Pedro Cevallos (April 20, 1805). See also Lindley, *Acquisition and Government of Backward Territory*, 277–82. The same two principles were matters of debate during the British Guiana Boundary Arbitration.

31 French-Portuguese Convention, 12 May 1886, in Sir E. Hertslet, ed., *The Map of Africa by Treaty* (London: Her Majesty's Stationary Office, 1894), 1:298–300. See especially art. 4.

32 German-Portuguese Agreement, 30 December 1886 in Hertslet, *Map of Africa*, 1:323–25, see esp. art. 3.

33 Memorandum transmitted by British Chargé d'Affaires at Lisbon to Portuguese Minister for Foreign Affairs, 13 August 1887, in Hertslet, *Map of Africa*, 1:325–26.

34 British-Portuguese Convention, 11 June 1891, in Hertslet, *Map of Africa*, 2:731–42. See also British and Foreign State Papers (1885–86), 77:517–20, 603–5; British and Foreign State Papers (1887–88), 79:1062–65; British and Foreign State Papers (1890–91), 83:27–41.

35 See in Canada, Senate *Debates*, 3 May 1878, 903; Canada, House of Commons *Debates*, 3 May 1878, 2386.

36 Canada, Order in Council, PC no. 3388, 18 December 1897. The map did not show the sector lines running all the way to the Pole.

37 See in map pocket attached to W. F. King, *Report upon the Title of Canada to the Islands North of the Mainland of Canada* (Ottawa: Gov't. Printing Bureau, 1905).

38 LAC, Laurier Papers, MG 26 G, vol. 109, 32853–57.

39 LAC, Laurier Papers, vol. 187, 53437.

40 Canada, House of Commons *Debates*, 1 May 1902, col. 3952 (Mr. Charlton, MP).

41 Canada, House of Commons *Debates*, 1 May 1902, col. 3964 (Mr. Flint, MP).

42 Canada, House of Commons *Debates*, 30 September 1903, col. 12806 (Mr. Charlton, MP).

43 Canada, House of Commons *Debates*, 30 September 1903, col. 12811–12812 (Mr. Bell, MP).

44 Canada, House of Commons *Debates*, 30 September 1903, col. 12814 (Mr. Henderson, MP).

45 Canada, House of Commons *Debates*, 30 September 1903, col. 12818 (Mr. Gourley, MP).

46 Canada, Senate *Debates*, 18 July 1905, 872 (Mr. Landry, MP, Mr. Templeman, MP, and Mr. Scott, MP).

47 Canada, Senate *Debates*, 20 October 1903, 1662–63 (Mr. Poirier, Senator).

48 See, for example, Smedal, *Skrifter om Svalbard og Ishavet*, 54: "Generally credited with having called attention to this principle for the first time"; Lakhtine, "Rights over the Arctic," 706: "for the first time"; Plischke, "Jurisdiction in the Polar Regions," 409: "earliest Canadian reference"; Gould, "Antarctica in World Affairs," 19: "first proposed"; Svarlien, "Legal Status of the Arctic," 139: "generally regarded as the first advocate of this principle"; and Ivan L. Head, "Canadian Claims to Territorial Sovereignty in the Arctic Regions," *McGill Law Journal* 9 (1963): 203: "first publicly propounded."

49 Canada, Senate *Debates*, 20 February 1907, 266 (Mr. Poirier, Senator). The speech, a lengthy one, runs from pages 266 to 273.

50 Canada, Senate *Debates*, 20 February 1907, 271.

51 Smedal, *Skrifter om Svalbard og Ishavet*, 55.

52 Poirier was an opposition senator, having been appointed by the Conservative administration of Sir John A. Macdonald in 1885. See Canada, Senate *Debates*, 10 March 1885, 239, and 12 March 1885, 269.

53 Canada, Senate *Debates*, 20 February 1907, 273–74.

54 Canada, Senate *Debates*, February 20, 1907, 274.

55 I do not recall having seen any other reference to a conference or negotiations on the subject at this time.

56 I have seen no genuine evidence that this was the case.

57 Joseph E. Bernier, *Cruise of the Arctic 1908–9* (Ottawa: Government Printing Bureau, 1910), 1:1.

58 As I noted in the chapter on Canadian government expeditions, Bernier did have at least some such authorization. See LAC, RG85, vol. 601, no.

2502, "Explorations Arctic," vol. 1 (1922–23), and Goudreau to Bernier, 23 June 1906.

59 Again, I know of no such evidence.

60 Canada, House of Commons *Debates*, 31 January 1910, cols. 2711–2712 (Mr. Laurier, MP, and Mr. Foster, MP). See also Canada, Senate *Debates*, 1 February 1910, 179–85, for speech by Senator Poirier and comments by Senators Cartwright and Lougheed. Poirier asked if the government intended to appoint a commissioner to take charge of all Canada's Arctic lands and islands, to which undisputed English right could be claimed, "between Hudson bay and the newly discovered pole," and, citing what he termed the Russian acquisition of Alaska "by fraud," he urged the appointment of such a commissioner to patrol and "assert the undoubted jurisdiction of Canada" over the Arctic territories, Cartwright assured him that the government was asserting jurisdiction and considering the matter of a commissioner, and, when Lougheed complained of Bernier's alleged loose talk in New York, Cartwright said that care would be taken to prevent repetition of such indiscretions.

61 LAC, Laurier Papers, vol. 613, 166359–166367. The memo as it appears here does not identify the deputy minister to whom it was addressed.

62 LAC, Laurier Papers, vol. 614, 166829–166830.

63 LAC, Laurier Papers, vol. 614, 166832–166833.

64 Great Britain, House of Commons *Debates*, 8 September 1909, col. 1308 (Mr. Parker, MP, and Mr. Asquith, MP).

65 LAC, Record Group 25, Department of External Affairs [hereafter RG 25], vol. 1095, file 1909-238-C, Crewe to Grey, 10 September 1909. The despatch of 22 April 1907, mentioned in the cable contained a report of Senator Pairier's speech of 20 Feb. 1907.

66 LAC, RG 25, vol. 1095, file 1909-238-C, Murphy to Grey, 11 September 1909.

67 LAC, RG 25, vol. 1095, file 1909-238-C, Pope to Deputy Minister of the Interior, 11 September 1909.

68 Great Britain, House of Commons *Debates*, 15 September 1909, col. 2128 (Mr. Balearres, MP, and Mr. Seely, MP). Col. J.E.B. Seely was Undersecretary for the Colonies.

69 Canada, House of Commons *Debates*, 1 June 1925, 3772–73 (Mr. Stewart, MP), and 10 June 1925, 4069–84 (Mr. Stewart, MP).

9 | Vilhjalmur Stefansson and His Plans

1 Library and Archives Canada [hereafter LAC], R6113-0-X-F, Robert L. Borden fonds, vol. 185, 101514–101520, V. Stefansson to R. L. Borden, 8 January 1914.

2 LAC, R6113-0-X-F, Robert L. Borden fonds, vol. 185, 101560–101570.

3 LAC, R6113-0-X-F, Robert L. Borden fonds, vol. 185, 101610. See section above on the Canadian Arctic Expedition.

4 Vilhjalmur Stefansson, *Discovery: The Autobiography of Vilhjalmur Stefansson* (New York: McGraw-Hill, 1964), 229–31. I have not been able to find this letter.

5 Canada, Sessional Papers, *Reports of the Department of the Naval Service*, e.g., (1915), vol. 26, no. 38, 12–14; (1917), vol. 21, no. 38, 16–19, 71–75; (1918), vol. 13, no. 38, xiv–xvi, 22–27; (1919), vol. 10, no. 38, 18–31.

6 See, for example, Vilhjalmur Stefansson, *The Friendly Arctic: The Story of Five Years in Polar Regions* (New York: Macmillan, 1943), 1–16, 688–713; Vilhjalmur Stefansson, *The Northward Course of Empire* (New York: Macmillan, 1924), passim; Vilhjalmur Stefansson, *The Adventure of Wrangel Island* (New York: Macmillan, 1925), 64–90; D. M. LeBourdais, *Stefansson: Ambassador of the North* (Montreal: Harvest House, 1963), 143–72; Stefansson, *Discovery: The Autobiography of Vilhjalmur Stefansson*, 214–68.

7 Stefansson, *The Friendly Arctic*, 688.

8 See LAC, MG 26 I, Arthur Meighen fonds, vol. 13, series 2, folder 7, "Arctic Island Exploration," Stefansson to Prime Minister Meighen, 30 October 1920, 007391–007394. In this letter, written at Meighen's request, Stefansson outlined his suggestions for projects in the North, as follows: (1) Announce plan to continue explorations; (2) Revenue cutter service; (3) Police posts; (4) Mapping of known lands; (5) Economic survey of the known lands; (6) Discovery of new lands; (7) Policy to encourage development. Enlarging on the question of Canada's territorial rights, he maintained that the two regions of greatest strategic importance were Ellesmere Island and Wrangel Island.

9 See LAC, R6113-0-X-F, Robert L. Borden fonds, vol. 185, 100683, for a memorandum of 12 July 1919, by Desbarats, in which he stressed that the order in council of 22 February 1913 had given Stefansson complete command of the expedition. He added, "As the full responsibility for the Expedition was placed on Mr. Stefansson, he should

certainly have a say as to the preparation of the report, and possibly he should be appointed editor to supervise the work." Also see LAC, R6113-0-X-F, Robert L. Borden fonds, vol. 185, 101684–101687, for a memo of the same kind by Dr. Prince of Desbarats's department.

10 For information in detail, see S. Jackson, *Report on Introduction of Domestic Reindeer into Alaska, with Maps and Illustrations* (Washington: Government Printing Office, 1893), and Jackson's annual reports for some years thereafter. For a good brief summary, see Canada, *Report of the Royal Commission to Investigate the Possibilities of the Reindeer and Musk-Ox Industries in the Arctic and Sub-Arctic Regions of Canada* (Ottawa: King's Printer, 1922), appendix 2. See also G. H. Grosvenor, "Reindeer in Alaska," *The National Geographic Magazine*, vol. 14, no. 4 (April 1903): 127–49.

11 Sir Wilfred Grenfell, *Forty Years for Labrador* (Boston: Houghton Mifflin, 1919, 1932), 188–200; Sir Wilfred Grenfell, *A Labrador Doctor* (London: Hodder and Stoughton, 1920, 1940), 214–25; J. L. Kerr, *Wilfred Grenfell: His Life and Work* (Toronto: Ryerson Press, 1959), 169–70, 180–81, 224–25.

12 Canada, *Report of the Royal Commission to Investigate the Possibilities of the Reindeer and Musk-Ox Industries in the Arctic and Sub-Arctic Regions of Canada*, appendix 7, 66–67. See also George Inglis, "And Then There Were None —," *North*, vol. 16, no. 2 (Mar.–Apr. 1969): 6–11.

13 Canada, *Report of the Royal Commission to Investigate the Possibilities of the Reindeer and Musk-Ox Industries in the Arctic and Sub-Arctic Regions of Canada*, appendix 3, 52–54. Report by W. T. Hornaday.

14 Canada, *Report of the Royal Commission to Investigate the Possibilities of the Reindeer and Musk-Ox Industries in the Arctic and Sub-Arctic Regions of Canada*, Proceedings Testimony of Capt. Bernier, 243; D. B. MacMillan also had kept young muskox as pets. Canada, *Report of the Royal Commission to Investigate the Possibilities of the Reindeer and Musk-Ox Industries in the Arctic and Sub-Arctic Regions of Canada*, 481.

15 LAC, R5254-0-9-E, Vilhjalmur Stefansson fonds, vol. 1, Diary vol. 4, 70–71.

16 Stefansson, *The Northward Course of Empire*, 141.

17 Stefansson, *The Northward Course of Empire*, 163–65.

18 LAC, R1644-0-7-E, John D. Craig fonds, vol. I, pt. 3, "Reports and Memoranda 1905–1923."

19 Stefansson, *Discovery: The Autobiography of Vilhjalmur Stefansson*, 264–65; Stefansson, *The Northward Course of Empire*, 42–43; LeBourdais, *Stefansson: Ambassador of the North*; *Ottawa Citizen*, 7 May 1919. I have not seen a verbatim transcript of Stefansson's speech. It does not seem to have occasioned much comment in the parliamentary debates, except that Mr. John A. Campbell (Nelson) referred to it in some detail more than a month afterwards. Canada, House of Commons *Debates*, 17 June 1919, 3561–3562. Mr. Alfred Thompson (Yukon) evidently had Stefansson in mind on 7 March 1919, when he spoke favourably of putting caribou and muskox resources to use, but this was, of course, before Stefansson spoke to the members of Parliament. Canada, House of Common *Debates*, 7 March 1919, 304–5.

20 LAC, MG 26 I, Arthur Meighen fonds, vol. 7, folder 43, "Northern Canada," 004122–004123.

21 Canada, Order in Council, PC No. 1079, 20 May 1919. The order mentioned Stefansson several times, and its wording indicates that it was based essentially upon his recommendations. One statement therein, i.e., "the Minister considers that there are good grounds for believing that the Canadian North may become a great permanent meat and wool producing area," suggests that at this time Meighen was becoming a convert to Stefansson's views on the subject.

22 Canada, *Report of the Royal Commission to Investigate the Possibilities of the Reindeer and Musk-Ox Industries in the Arctic and Sub-Arctic Regions of Canada*, Transcript of Evidence. See also LAC, Record Group 25, Department of External Affairs [hereafter RG 25], vol. 2668, file 9057-C-40, Canadian Sovereignty Over Hudson Bay, for undated memo by Mr. James White dealing, *inter alia*, with reindeer herding.

23 Canada, *Report of the Royal Commission to Investigate the Possibilities of the Reindeer and Musk-Ox Industries in the Arctic and Sub-Arctic Regions of Canada*, Transcript of Evidence, 545, 532–33.

24 Canada, *Report of the Royal Commission to Investigate the Possibilities of the Reindeer and Musk-Ox Industries in the Arctic and Sub-Arctic Regions of Canada*, 36.

25 Canada, *Report of the Royal Commission to Investigate the Possibilities of the Reindeer and Musk-Ox Industries in the Arctic and Sub-Arctic Regions of Canada*, 14–15, 31–32.

26 Canada, *Report of the Royal Commission to Investigate the Possibilities of the Reindeer and Musk-Ox Industries in the Arctic and Sub-Arctic Regions of Canada*, 498, 500, 510. See also p. 478: "We found

musk-oxen in that north country, and found them in the middle of the winter night at the most northern part of Canadian land, at Cape Columbia." Thus MacMillan admitted that Ellesmere Island was Canadian territory.

27 On 8 June 1920, answering a question by the Hon. Rodolphe Lemieux, Minister of the Interior, Arthur Meighen gave a brief description of the commission and its work. Canada, House of Commons *Debates*, 8 June 1920, 3284–85. See also Canada, House of Commons *Debates*, 14 March 1921, 841, 871–72. The Senate took greater note of the matter, in discussing the report of a special committee on the Hudson Bay route. See Canada, Senate *Debates*, 15 June 1920, 530–50; Canada, Senate *Debates*, 17 June 1920, 600–607; Canada, Senate *Debates*, 18 June 1920, 629–34. The report said, *inter alia* (Canada, Senate *Debates*, 18 June 1920, 533): "Your Committee feel that they cannot too strongly endorse the valuable suggestion of Mr. Stefansson as to the cultivation of the reindeer and muskox ...." Senator Casgrain, for one, disagreed strongly (Canada, Senate *Debates*, 18 June 1920, 536): "I have no faith whatever in Mr. Stefansson when he comes along with his 30,000,000 reindeer and 10,000,000 muskox down here."

28 Canada, House of Commons *Debates*, 4 June 1921, 4543. The report was presented to the House of Commons on 4 May 1921, by Mr. Meighen. See Canada, House of Commons *Debates*, 4 May 1921, 2940. See Canada, *Report of the Royal Commission to Investigate the Possibilities of the Reindeer and Musk-Ox Industries in the Arctic and Sub-Arctic Regions of Canada*, 36–38, for a summary of the Commission's recommendations.

29 Canada, *Report of the Royal Commission to Investigate the Possibilities of the Reindeer and Musk-Ox Industries in the Arctic and Sub-Arctic Regions of Canada*, 11. Incidentally, Stefansson applied later that year for a lease at the mouth of the Mackenzie. See LAC, R2033-0-7-E, James Bernard Harkin fonds, vol. 2, folder "Canadian Sovereignty of Arctic Islands re V. O. Stefansson," Stefansson to Harkin, 21 Nov. 1920. Evidently nothing came of this application. Stefansson's resignation was formally accepted by Canada, Order in Council, PC No. 785, 14 April 1920.

30 For details see Stefansson, *The Northward Course of Empire*, 131–33, Stefansson, *Discovery: The Autobiography of Vilhjalmur Stefansson*, 265–66; LeBourdais, *Stefansson: Ambassador of the North*, 153–55.

31 Canada, Order in Council, PC No. 1229, 29 May 1920, with accompanying indenture.

32 Stefansson, *Discovery: The Autobiography of Vilhjalmur Stefansson*, 266–68; Stefansson, *The Northward Course of Empire*, 133–34; Le Bourdais, *Stefansson: Ambassador of the North*, 155–57. The cancellation of the lease was brought about by Canada, Order in Council P. C. No. 1010, 27 May 1927.

33 Canada, *Report of the Royal Commission to Investigate the Possibilities of the Reindeer and Musk-Ox Industries in the Arctic and Sub-Arctic Regions of Canada*, 36–37.

34 C. J. Lomon, *Fifty Years in Alaska* (New York: D. McKay, 1954), 247–48.

35 A. E. Porsild, Northwest Territories and Yukon Branch, Department of the Interior, *Reindeer Grazing in Northwest Canada* (Ottawa: King's Printer, 1929); A. E. Porsild, *Report on the Reindeer and the Mackenzie Delta Reindeer Grazing Reserve 1947* (Ottawa: National Museum, 1947), 1–2; Canada, *Canada's Reindeer* (Ottawa, Department of Mines and Resources, Lands, Parks and Forests Branch, 1940), 1–2; Bureau of Northwest Territories and Yukon Affairs, *Reindeer Manual* (Ottawa, Department of Mines and Resources, Lands, Parks and Forests Branch, 1942), 3–4; C.H.D. Clarke, *Report on Development of Reindeer Industry-Mackenzie District 1942* (Ottawa, Department of Mines and Resources, Lands, Parks and Forests Branch, 1942); O. S. Finnie, "Reindeer for the Canadian Eskimo," *Natural History* 31, no. 4 (1931): 409–16.

36 A. E. Porsild, *Report on the Reindeer and the Mackenzie Delta Reindeer Grazing Reserve 1947*, 2. Another northerner of some distinction, where strong views on the subject were expressed at a fairly early stage and turned out to be quite prophetic, was Capt. Henry Lake Munn. He was quoted in an editorial in the *St. John Telegraph-Journal*, 17 June 1925, as follows: "Let the Canadian Government declare all the islands lying to the north of the American Continent, over which Canada holds sovereignty, and a deep fringe of the northern part of the continent itself, from the Mackenzie River, eastward to Hudson Bay, a Crown Reserve, operated solely by the Government, along the same lines as the Danes administer. Greenland .... Simultaneously with the creation of this Crown Reserve, arrangements could be made with an Alaskan reindeer company for the delivery of from 2,000 to 3,000 reindeer at the Mackenzie River delta, together with trained Alaskan herders

to teach the Canadian Esquimaux the art of herding."

37 Canada, Order in Council, PC No. 745, 1 May 1929. The contract was made in New York on 8 May, between Carl Lomen as president of the reindeer corporation and Deputy Minister of the Interior W. W. Cory as representative of the Canadian government. Lomen, *Fifty Years in Alaska*, 248–49. The text of the contract is given in M. Miller, *The Great Trek* (New York: Doubleday, Doran, 1935), 25–27.

38 Lomen, *Fifty Years in Alaska*, 249–73. See also A. R. Evans, *Reindeer Trek* (Toronto: McClelland and Stewart, 1935).

39 By 1967, however, the total was about 8,000, all in one herd.

40 Canada, Order in Council, PC No. 2554, 14 December 1933.

41 In 1952 the Canadian government decided to enlarge the reserve by adding an adjacent tract extending south and east as far as the Anderson River, thus making a total area of about 18,000 square miles. R. M. Hill, *Mackenzie Reindeer Operations, Report NCRC 67-1* (Ottawa, Northern Co-ordination and Research Centre, Department of Indian Affairs and Northern Development, 1967), 5, 2. The addition was made by Order in Council, PC No. 1188, 29 February 1952. This order in council was replaced by another, PC No. 329, 8 March 1955, but the boundary and area of the reserve were left unchanged.

42 "The Reindeer Protection Ordinance," Northwest Territories Ordinance, 18 October 1933.

43 R. M. Hill, *Mackenzie Reindeer Operations, Report NCRC 67-1*, 8; G. Abrahamson, "Canada's Reindeer," *Canadian Geographical Journal* 56, no. 6 (June 1963): 188–93. In its stead grew an essentially commercial operation handled by private enterprise, which, it was hoped, would in due course become self-supporting. A five-year contract, to begin in October 1960, was made with John Teal of Burlington, Vermont, and game farmer Al Oeming of Edmonton, Alberta. However, this quickly proved unworkable and was terminated in December 1961. After a short period of renewed government operation, however, a new contract for two years was made with Oeming in March 1963. When this contract expired in March 1965 it was not renewed; but a further contract, for one year only, was made with Sven Johansson, an immigrant reindeer expert from Sweden who had served as Oeming's project manager. His contract was renewed annually for two or three years. The transfer of the industry to contractors resulted in a number of beneficial changes. A modernization program was undertaken, with improvements in transportation, communication, housing and living conditions, and operations. Aircraft, powered boats and canoes, high frequency radio service with portable radios, oil heating, and security fences were either introduced or improved and used more extensively, as the case might be. To improve housing and to avoid the frightfully cold tents which were the herders' customary homes in winter time, some attention was given to the use of semi-permanent cabins, prefabricated huts, trailers, and, as H. J. Hargrave suggested in 1947, "some adaptation of the sheep camp used on all sheep ranches." H. J. Hargrave, "The Canadian Reindeer Industry" (Department of Indian Affairs and Northern Development, 1947), 3. Mimeographed article in AANDC Library, Gatineau. Presumably trailers or "sheep camps" would have to be transported by caterpillar tractor, and only in the wintertime, since throughout most of the area wheels cannot be used in any season. However, the double-walled winter tent, with an insulating layer of air between the two walls, was found very serviceable. Such changes resulted in more efficient operation with fewer personnel, but the reduction in personnel, whatever its advantages may have been from a business point of view, also meant smaller opportunities for employment. Another fundamental change came on 1 April 1968, when the Canadian Wildlife Service took over management of the herd for an initial period of five years. R. F. Nowasad, "The Canada Reindeer Project" (unpublished manuscript, 1971), 1–2.

44 Some of the more obvious alternatives are: (1) the contract under government supervision; (2) the government corporation; (3) private privileges enterprise; (4) reserve grazing privileges hold under fee or licence; (5) the co-operative; (6) exclusive native ownership, enterprise, and participation; and (7) outright government control and direction. Which of these, or which combination of these, would be best in the long run is still uncertain, since each has both pluses and minuses, but this is perhaps the most fundamental question which must be answered before the future of the industry is assured. R. M. Hill, *Mackenzie Reindeer Operations, Report NCRC 67*, 9–10, 146–55. For good summaries of developments up to 1967, see E. Treude, "The Development of Reindeer Husbandry in Canada," *Polar Record* 14, no. 88 (Jan. 1968): 15–19; R. M. Hill, "The Canadian Reindeer Project," *Polar Record* 14, no. 88 (Jan. 1968): 21–24.

10 | Danish Sovereignty, Greenland, and the Ellesmere Island Affair

1 British and Foreign State Papers (1812–14), I, pt. 1, 194–204. See esp. art. 4.

2 For a good summary of the history of Greenland and the acquisition by Denmark of sovereignty over it, see Permanent Court of International Justice, *Legal Status of Eastern Greenland*, Series A/B, Fascicule No. 53, 5 April 1933, 22–75. See also O. Svarlien, *The Eastern Greenland Case in Historical Perspective* (Gainesville: University of Florida Press, 1964).

3 U.S. Treaty Series, No. 629, 14.

4 See these declarations in Gustav Smedal, *Skrifter om Svalbard og Ishavet.* Translated by C. Meyer as *Acquisition of Sovereignty over Polar Areas.* (Oslo: J. Dybwad, 1931), 84–85.

5 Library and Archives Canada [hereafter LAC], Record Group 25, Department of External Affairs [hereafter RG 25], vol. 3278, file 6732-40, Gov. Genn. Minto to Colonial Minister Lyttelton, 3 December 1903; LAC, RG 25, vol. 3278, file 6732-40, memo from Canadian Government, 3 December 1903; LAC, RG 25, vol. 3278, file 6732-40, Lyttelton to Minto, 18 March 1904; LAC, RG 25, vol. 3278, file 6732-40, H. B. Cox to Under Secretary of State Foreign Office, 1 January 1904; LAC, RG 25, vol. 3278, file 6732-40, Hardings to Under Secretary of State Colonial Office, 9 Mar. 1904; LAC, RG 25, vol. 3278, file 6732-40, Gaschan to Marquis of Lansdowne, 18 Feb. 1904. See also LAC, RG 25, vol. 3278, file 6732-40, R. A. MacKay, "Canada's Relations With Greenland," April–May 1944, Section II, 7.

6 LAC, RG 25, vol. 3278, file 6732-40 pt. 1, paper by J. D. Hazen, 20 April 1917; LAC, RG 25, vol. 1343, file 1923-138, Paraphrase of Governor General to Secretary of State for the Colonies, 27 September 1919.

7 LAC, RG 25, vol. 1343, file 1923-138, Milner to Devonshire, 10 September 1919. See also Colonial Office, Dominions No. 79, Greenland, May 1921.

8 LAC, RG 25, vol. 1343, file 1923-138; also C.O., Dominions No. 79, Devonshire to Milner, 27 September 1919.

9 LAC, RG 25, vol. 1343, file 1923-138; also C.O., Dominions No. 79, L. D. Amery (for Secretary of State) to Devonshire, 28 January 1920.

10 LAC, RG 25, vol. 1343, file 1923-138; also C.O., Dominions No. 79, Foreign Office to Grevenkop-Castenskold, 11 December 1919.

11 LAC, RG 25, vol. 1343, file 1923-138; also C.O., Dominions No. 79, Danish minister to Curzon, 16 March 1920.

12 LAC, RG 25, vol. 1343, file 1923-138; also C.O., Dominions No. 79, Foreign Office to Grevenkop-Castenskiold, 19 May 1920.

13 LAC, RG 25, vol. 1343, file 1923-138; also C.O., Dominions No. 79, Davis to Curzon, 8 June 1920.

14 LAC, RG 25, vol. 1343, file 1923-138; also C.O., Dominions No. 79, Milner to Devonshire, 7 July 1920, with Enclosures.

15 LAC, RG 25, vol. 1343, file 1923-138; also C.O., Dominions No. 79, Grevenkop-Castenskiold to Curzon, 20 July 1920.

16 LAC, RG 25, vol. 1343, file 1923-138; also C.O., Dominions No. 79, Milner to Devonshire, 5 August 1920.

17 LAC, RG 25, vol. 1343, file 1923-138; also C.O., Dominions No. 79, Devonshire to Milner, 20 August 1920.

18 LAC, RG 25, vol. 1343, file 1923-138; also C.O., Dominions No. 79, J. D. Gregory (for Secretary of State) to Grevenkop-Castenskiold, 6 September 1920. LAC, RG 25, vol. 3278, file 6732-40, R. A. MacKay, "Canada's Relations With Greenland," April–May 1944, 7–9.

19 LAC, R2033-0-7-E, James Bernard Harkin fonds, vol. I, folder, July 1919–October 1920. This copy does not identify the writer of the letter, but presumably it was Harkin himself.

20 LAC, R2033-0-7-E, James Bernard Harkin fonds, vol. I, folder, July 1919–October 1920, W. W. Cory to Pope, 23 July 1919. Many of the documents in this collection have been numbered. This one is no. 1.

21 LAC, R2033-0-7-E, James Bernard Harkin fonds, vol. I, folder, July 1919–October 1920, Rasmussen to Administration of the Colonies of Greenland, 8 March 1920. Copy in English translation (no. 3).

22 LAC, R2033-0-7-E, James Bernard Harkin fonds, vol. I, folder, July 1919–October 1920 (no. 3), Danish minister to Lord Curzon, 12 April 1920. Additional copies of these letters, and of other documents relating to this subject, may be seen in LAC, R1644-0-7-E, John D. Craig fonds. It should be stated that many of the documents I refer to hereafter may be seen in several of the sources frequently cited in this section, rather than in one only. See also J. Lloyd, "Knud Rasmussen and the Arctic Islands Preserve," *The Musk-Ox*, no. 25 (1979), 85–90. Lloyd says that part of the translation of Rasmussen's letter which go to the

Department of the Interior was misread there, but he does not reproduce what was misread or give further details about it. See p. 86.

23 LAC, R2033-0-7-E, James Bernard Harkin fonds, vol. I, folder, July 1919–October 1920 (no. 3), noted in Pope to Cory, 12 May 1920.

24 LAC, R2033-0-7-E, James Bernard Harkin fonds, vol. I, folder, July 1919–October 1920 (no. 2), Harkin to Cory, 4 May 1920 (no. 2).

25 LAC, R2033-0-7-E, James Bernard Harkin fonds, vol. I, folder, July 1919–October 1920 (no. 1), Stefansson to Harkin, 15 May 1920. LAC, R2033-0-7-E, James Bernard Harkin fonds, vol. I, folder, July 1919–October 1920 (no. 30), copy of a letter Rasmussen wrote to Stefansson from Denmark on 11 May 1920, telling about the founding and work of his Cape York Station.

26 LAC, R2033-0-7-E, James Bernard Harkin fonds, vol. I, folder, July 1919–October 1920 (no. 7), Harkin to Cory, 16 June 1920. LAC, R2033-0-7-E, James Bernard Harkin fonds, vol. I, folder, July 1919–October 1920 (no. 10), see for a further memo from Harkin to Cory, dated 29 June 1920, on the same subject.

27 LAC, R2033-0-7-E, James Bernard Harkin fonds, vol. I, folder, July 1919–October 1920 (no. 9), Cory to Sir Joseph Pope, 23 June 1920.

28 LAC, R1644-0-7-E, John D. Craig fonds, pt. I, "Correspondence 1903–1922," Devonshire to Milner, 13 July 1920.

29 LAC, MG 26 I, Arthur Meighen fonds, vol. 13, folder 7, "Arctic Island Exploration," 007389. In the same letter Borden quoted from a memorandum Stefansson had written to him, in part as follows: "I am sorry to say that no step has so far been taken by Canadian Government to recognize our work in any way; possibly Government routine is such that this cannot be done." Borden commented, "There is no recognition which the Government of Canada could give to Mr. Stefansson so far as I am aware except through the medium of an Order in Council containing an appreciation of his work. Perhaps you will be good enough to consider whether this would be practicable." This is, of course, what was eventually done, and on 21 January 1921, on the recommendation of the Prime Minister Meighen himself, an order in council (P. C. No. 2887) was promulgated extending the formal thanks of the Canadian government to Stefansson for his "distinguished services."

30 LAC, MG 26 I, Arthur Meighen fonds, vol. 13, folder 7, "Arctic Island Exploration," 07395.

31 See the minutes of this meeting, with Stefansson's lengthy speech, LAC, R2033-0-7-E, James Bernard Harkin fonds, vol. I, folder, July 1919–October 1920; LAC, R1644-0-7-E, John D. Craig fonds, folder 3. *Editor's Note*: On the Advisory Technical Board's mandate, see Janice Cavell and Jeff Noakes, *Acts of Occupation* (Vancouver: UBC Press, 2010), 57, 274–75 (en. 73).

32 LAC, R2033-0-7-E, James Bernard Harkin fonds, vol. I, folder, July 1919–October 1920, Minutes, 7.

33 LAC, R2033-0-7-E, James Bernard Harkin fonds, vol. I, folder, July 1919–October 1920, Minutes, 1–2.

34 LAC, R2033-0-7-E, James Bernard Harkin fonds, vol. I, folder, July 1919–October 1920, Minutes, 7.

35 LAC, R2033-0-7-E, James Bernard Harkin fonds, vol. I, folder, July 1919–October 1920, Minutes, 8.

36 LAC, R2033-0-7-E, James Bernard Harkin fonds, vol. I, folder, July 1919–October 1920, Minutes, 9.

37 LAC, Record Group 85, Surveys and Mapping Branch [hereafter RG 85], Surveys Mapping and Remote Sensing, vol. 5, file 17435, Advisory Technical Board subcommittee report, 13 October 1920.

38 See these memos in LAC, R1644-0-7-E, John D. Craig fonds, vol. I, pt. 1, "Correspondence 1903–1922."

39 LAC, RG 88, vol. 5, file 17435.

40 LAC, R2033-0-7-E, James Bernard Harkin fonds, vol. I, folder, July 1919–October 1920 (no. 15). See there also Harkin's letter of 14 October 1920 to C. C. Camsell about Malcolm's "very complete" memorandum.

41 LAC, RG 88, vol. 5, file 17435.

42 LAC, R2033-0-7-E, James Bernard Harkin fonds, vol. I, folder, July 1919–October 1920 (no. 32).

43 LAC, R2033-0-7-E, James Bernard Harkin fonds, vol. I, folder, July 1919–October 1920 (no. 27), Rasmussen (signed by Carlaillollr) to Governor of Canada, 8 August 1920; Carlaillollr to Secretary of Governor of Canada, 15 September 1920.

44 LAC, R2033-0-7-E, James Bernard Harkin fonds, vol. I, folder, July 1919–October 1920 (no. 18). The writer evidently was Harkin, although the copy of the memo in the *Harkin Papers* is unsigned. Harkin was wrong about Bartlett who, although a Newfoundlander by birth, had become an American citizen before 1920.

45 LAC, R2033-0-7-E, James Bernard Harkin fonds, vol. I, folder, July 1919–October 1920 (no. 20),

Harkin to Cory, 22 October 1920. Captain Bernier's name was conspicuously absent.

46 LAC, R2033-0-7-E, James Bernard Harkin fonds, vol. I, folder, July 1919–October 1920 (no. 21), Cory to W. H. Sullivan, 23 October 1920.

47 LAC, R2033-0-7-E, James Bernard Harkin fonds, vol. I, folder, July 1919–October 1920, Harkin to Cory, 3 November 1920; LAC, R2033-0-7-E, James Bernard Harkin fonds, vol. I, folder, July 1919–October 1920, Harkin to Dr. Grenfell, 27 November 1920; LAC, R2033-0-7-E, James Bernard Harkin fonds, vol. I, folder, July 1919–October 1920, Dr. Grenfell to Harkin, 27 November 1920; LAC, R2033-0-7-E, James Bernard Harkin fonds, vol. I, folder, July 1919–October 1920, LAC, RG 85, vol. 583, file 570, Deville to Cory, 30 November 1920. And see, in LAC, RG 85, vol. 583, file 570, Cory to Pickels, 1 December 1920, and a copy of Pickels' contract, 16 December 1920.

48 LAC, R2033-0-7-E, James Bernard Harkin fonds, vol. I, folder, July 1919–October 1920 (no. 31). Of the members of the board previously unidentified, J. B. Challies was Superintendent of the Water Power Branch. T. W. Dwight was Assistant Director of Forestry, and Chalifour was Chief Geographer of the Department of the Interior.

49 LAC, RG 88, vol. 5, file 17435.

50 See in LAC, R1644-0-7-E, John D. Craig fonds, vol. I, folder 3, "Reports & Memoranda 1905–1923," L. C. Christie to Prime Minister Meighen, 28 October 1920.

51 LAC, R2033-0-7-E, James Bernard Harkin fonds, vol. I, folder, July 1919–October 1920 (no. 24).

52 LAC, R2033-0-7-E, James Bernard Harkin fonds, vol. I, folder, July 1919–October 1920.

53 LAC, RG 88, vol. 5, file 17435.

54 LAC, RG 88, vol. 5, file 17435.

55 LAC, R2033-0-7-E, James Bernard Harkin fonds, vol. 2, folder "Canadian Sovereignty of Arctic Islands re V. O. Stefansson." The note was written from Fort William, Ontario. Harkin sent the requested information on 13 November.

56 LAC, RG 88, vol. 5, file 17435. See V. Stefansson, "The Region of Maximum Inaccessibility in the Arctic," *Geographical Review* 9, no. 9 (September 1920): 167–72.

57 LAC, RG 88, vol. 5, file 17435.

58 LAC, R2033-0-7-E, James Bernard Harkin fonds, vol. I, folder, July 1919–October 1920 (no. 40), précis of minutes of 18th regular meeting of Advisory Technical Board, 3 November 1920.

59 LAC, R2033-0-7-E, James Bernard Harkin fonds, vol. I, folder, July 1919–October 1920, 12-page memo "Title to Northern Islands;" LAC, R2033-0-7-E, James Bernard Harkin fonds, vol. I, folder, July 1919–October 1920, 2-page memo "Peculiarities in connection with Danish action re Ellesmere Land; ibid., several short untitled drafts on the subject, one marked "Confidential"; LAC, R2033-0-7-E, James Bernard Harkin fonds, vol. I, folder, July 1919–October 1920, 29-page untitled draft marked "Strictly Confidential."

60 LAC, RG 15, series A-2, vol. 5–6, "Memo re Northern Islands." It also is unsigned, but related documentary evidence clearly identifies it as Harkin's work. LAC, RG 88, vol. 5, file 17435, Harkin to Deville, 16 November 1920. "The report which I prepared was transmitted to the Minister from the Committee"; also Pope to Deville, 2 December 1920. "I have to thank you for … the copy of Mr. Harkin's report on the Arctic Islands." See also LAC, R2033-0-7-E, James Bernard Harkin fonds, vol. I, folder, November–December, 1920, for note from Cory to Harkin, 24 November 1920, saying that a copy of his report is being returned to him and that the minister would like him to shorten it.

61 LAC, R2033-0-7-E, James Bernard Harkin fonds, vol. I, folder, July 1919–October 1920. These "peculiar" features are similar to those mentioned in the memo "Peculiarities in connection with Danish action re Ellesmere Land." Reading them, one cannot help but feel that Harkin's attitude was excessively suspicious and quite irrational, and that he was, in fact, living in a dream world all his own. Undoubtedly the influence upon him of Stefansson at this time was very great.

62 LAC, R2033-0-7-E, James Bernard Harkin fonds, vol. I, folder, November–December, 1920 (no. 60). There seems to be little record of any direct or immediate reaction to Harkin's report, except that Cory wrote to him on 24 November saying that the minister would like him to condense the report for presentation to Council, and that this should be done immediately, because the minister was going to see the Advisory Technical Board "tomorrow morning."

63 LAC, R2033-0-7-E, James Bernard Harkin fonds, vol. I, folder, November–December, 1920 (no. 78). See also in LAC, RG 85, vol. 584, file 573 (1920–1929). Col. Henderson was correctly identified with the Governor General's office, but he was not Secretary of State for External Affairs.

64 LAC, RG 25, vol. 4252, file 9057-40 pt. 1. See also in LAC, Arthur Meighen Papers, MG 26 I, vol. 13, folder 7, 007381.

65 LAC, RG 88, vol. 5, file 17435.; also LAC, R2033-0-7-E, James Bernard Harkin fonds, vol. I, folder, November–December 1920 (no. 65).

66 LAC, R2033-0-7-E, James Bernard Harkin fonds, vol. I, folder, November–December 1920 (no. 67). See also LAC, R1644-0-7-E, John D. Craig fonds, vol. I, folder 1, "Correspondence 1903–1922," for the Advisory Technical Board for its preparatory work and remarking that Craig had now been given charge of the expedition.

67 LAC, R2033-0-7-E, James Bernard Harkin fonds, vol. I, folder, November–December 1920 (no. 73).

68 LAC, R2033-0-7-E, James Bernard Harkin fonds, vol. I, folder, November–December 1920 (no. 68).

69 LAC, R2033-0-7-E, James Bernard Harkin fonds, vol. I, folder, November–December 1920 (no. 69), Harkin to Orr, 2 December 1920.

70 LAC, R2033-0-7-E, James Bernard Harkin fonds, vol. I, folder, November–December 1920 (no. 70), Harkin to Cory, 2 December 1920.

71 LAC, R2033-0-7-E, James Bernard Harkin fonds, vol. I, folder, November–December 1920 (no. 75), Cory to Harkin, 6 December 1920.

72 LAC, R2033-0-7-E, James Bernard Harkin fonds, vol. I, folder, November–December 1920 (no. 76), Harkin to Cory, 6 December 1920.

73 LAC, MG 26 I, Arthur Meighen fonds, vol. 13, folder 7, 007400.

74 LAC, MG 26 I, Arthur Meighen fonds, vol. 13, folder 7, 007400.

75 LAC, R2033-0-7-E, James Bernard Harkin fonds, vol. I, folder, January–March 1921 (no. 85).

76 LAC, MG 26 I, Arthur Meighen fonds, vol. 13, folder 7, 007399.

77 LAC, MG 26 I, Arthur Meighen fonds, vol. 13, folder 7, 007398, Borden to Meighen, 11 January 1921.

78 LAC, RG 88, vol. 5, file 17435.

79 Also see LAC, R1644-0-7-E, John D. Craig fonds, pt. I, "Correspondence 1903–1922."

80 LAC, R1644-0-7-E, John D. Craig fonds, pt. I, "Correspondence 1903–1922." The note was evidently sent under the signature of Acting Deputy Minister R. A. Gibson, and Pope replied to Gibson.

81 LAC, R1644-0-7-E, John D. Craig fonds, pt. I, "Correspondence 1903–1922"; also LAC, R2033-0-7-E, James Bernard Harkin fonds, vol. I, folder, January–March 1921.

82 LAC, R2033-0-7-E, James Bernard Harkin fonds, vol. I, folder, January–March 1921 (no. 87).

83 LAC, R2033-0-7-E, James Bernard Harkin fonds, vol. I, folder, January–March 1921 (no. 85).

84 LAC, R2033-0-7-E, James Bernard Harkin fonds, vol. I, folder, January–March 1921 (no. 83).

85 LAC, R2033-0-7-E, James Bernard Harkin fonds, vol. I, folder, January–March 1921 (no. 91).

86 LAC, R2033-0-7-E, James Bernard Harkin fonds, vol. I, folder, January–March 1921 (no. 92).

87 LAC, R2033-0-7-E, James Bernard Harkin fonds, vol. I, folder, January–March 1921 (no. 95).

88 LAC, R2033-0-7-E, James Bernard Harkin fonds, vol. I, folder, January–March 1921 (no. 99).

89 LAC, R2033-0-7-E, James Bernard Harkin fonds, vol. I, folder, January–March 1921 (nos. 96, 97, 100).

90 LAC, R2033-0-7-E, James Bernard Harkin fonds, vol. I, folder, January–March 1921 (no. 103).

91 LAC, R2033-0-7-E, James Bernard Harkin fonds, vol. I, folder, January–March 1921. The letter to Harkin is no. 141.

92 LAC, R2033-0-7-E, James Bernard Harkin fonds, vol. I, folder, January–March 1921 (no. 146).

93 LAC, MG 26 I, Arthur Meighen fonds, vol. 13, no. 7, 007412. I have not been able to find a copy of Shackleton's memo.

94 LAC, R2033-0-7-E, James Bernard Harkin fonds, vol. I, folder, January–March 1921 (no. 98).

95 LAC, MG 26 I, Arthur Meighen fonds, vol. 13, no. 7, 007415. See also LAC, RG 85, vol. 583, file 571 pt. 2, for an undated clipping from the *Ottawa Citizen*, telling of a lecture given by Shackleton in that city "last night." The clipping is stamped 24 February 1921, but may have been a week or two old when stamped. The lecture was presided over by Prime Minister Meighen, and Leader of the Opposition W. L. Mackenzie King proposed a vote of thanks afterwards. The subject was Shackleton's latest Antarctic expedition, but Meighen in his remarks drew attention to the fact that the explorer was in Ottawa in connection with his proposed Arctic expedition.

96 LAC, R2033-0-7-E, James Bernard Harkin fonds, vol. I, folder, January–March 1921 (no. 139).

97 LAC, R2033-0-7-E, James Bernard Harkin fonds, vol. I, folder, January–March 1921 (no. 138).

98 LAC, R2033-0-7-E, James Bernard Harkin fonds, vol. I, folder, January–March 1921 (no. 137).

99 LAC, R2033-0-7-E, James Bernard Harkin fonds, vol. I, folder, January–March 1921 (no. 144).

100 LAC, R2033-0-7-E, James Bernard Harkin fonds, vol. I, folder, January–March 1921 (no. 145).

101 LAC, R2033-0-7-E, James Bernard Harkin fonds, vol. I, folder, January–March 1921 (nos. 142, 110).

102 LAC, R2033-0-7-E, James Bernard Harkin fonds, vol. I, folder, January–March 1921 (no. 227).

103 LAC, R2033-0-7-E, James Bernard Harkin fonds, vol. I, folder, January–March 1921 (no. 118).

104 LAC, R2033-0-7-E, James Bernard Harkin fonds, vol. I, folder, January–March 1921.

105 LAC, R2033-0-7-E, James Bernard Harkin fonds, vol. I, folder, January–March 1921.

106 LAC, R2033-0-7-E, James Bernard Harkin fonds, vol. I, folder, January–March 1921.

107 LAC, R2033-0-7-E, James Bernard Harkin fonds, vol. I, folder, January–March 1921 (no. 120).

108 LAC, R2033-0-7-E, James Bernard Harkin fonds, vol. I, folder, January–March 1921 (no. 121).

109 LAC, R2033-0-7-E, James Bernard Harkin fonds, vol. I, folder, January–March 1921 (no. 122).

110 LAC, R2033-0-7-E, James Bernard Harkin fonds, vol. I, folder, January–March 1921 (no. 123).

111 LAC, R2033-0-7-E, James Bernard Harkin fonds, vol. I, folder, January–March 1921 (no. 140).

112 LAC, R2033-0-7-E, James Bernard Harkin fonds, vol. I, folder, January–March 1921 (no. 129).

113 LAC, R2033-0-7-E, James Bernard Harkin fonds, vol. I, folder, January–March 1921 (no. 226). The letter was written from Louisville, Kentucky.

114 LAC, R2033-0-7-E, James Bernard Harkin fonds, vol. I, folder, January–March 1921 (no. 136). Folder April 1921.

115 LAC, R2033-0-7-E, James Bernard Harkin fonds, vol. I, folder, January–March 1921 (no. 149).

116 LAC, R2033-0-7-E, James Bernard Harkin fonds, vol. I, folder, January–March 1921, Harkin to Cory, 12 April 1921.

117 LAC, R2033-0-7-E, James Bernard Harkin fonds, vol. I, folder, January–March 1921 (no. 157).

118 LAC, R2033-0-7-E, James Bernard Harkin fonds, vol. I, folder, January–March 1921 (no. 158), Harkin to Cory, 18 April 1921.

119 LAC, R2033-0-7-E, James Bernard Harkin fonds, vol. I, folder, January–March 1921 (nos. 160, 163).

120 LAC, R2033-0-7-E, James Bernard Harkin fonds, vol. I, folder, January–March 1921 (no. 163), Harkin to Cory, 19 April 1921.

121 LAC, R2033-0-7-E, James Bernard Harkin fonds, vol. I, folder, January–March 1921 (no. 164).

122 LAC, R2033-0-7-E, James Bernard Harkin fonds, vol. I, folder, January–March 1921 (no. 173).

123 LAC, R2033-0-7-E, James Bernard Harkin fonds, vol. I, folder, January–March 1921 (no. 171).

124 LAC, R2033-0-7-E, James Bernard Harkin fonds, vol. I, folder, January–March 1921 (no. 172), Harkin to Cory, 25 April 1921.

125 LAC, R2033-0-7-E, James Bernard Harkin fonds, vol. I, folder, May–December 1921 (no. 176). This wire was sent from San Bernardino, California.

126 LAC, R2033-0-7-E, James Bernard Harkin fonds, vol. I, folder, May–December 1921 (no. 177), Harkin to Cory, 4 May 1921.

127 LAC, R2033-0-7-E, James Bernard Harkin fonds, vol. I, folder, May–December 1921 (no. 186).

128 LAC, R2033-0-7-E, James Bernard Harkin fonds, vol. I, folder, May–December 1921, Harkin to Cory, 11 May 1921.

129 LAC, R2033-0-7-E, James Bernard Harkin fonds, vol. I, folder, May–December 1921 (no. 215).

130 LAC, R2033-0-7-E, James Bernard Harkin fonds, vol. I, folder, May–December 1921 (no. 191).

131 LAC, R2033-0-7-E, James Bernard Harkin fonds, vol. I, folder, May–December 1921 (no. 198).

132 LAC, R2033-0-7-E, James Bernard Harkin fonds, vol. I, folder, May–December 1921 (no. 204), Harkin to Cory, 26 May 1921.

133 LAC, R2033-0-7-E, James Bernard Harkin fonds, vol. I, folder, May–December 1921 (no. 212).

134 LAC, R2033-0-7-E, James Bernard Harkin fonds, vol. I, folder, May–December 1921 (no. 229).

135 LAC, R2033-0-7-E, James Bernard Harkin fonds, vol. I, folder, May–December 1921, Harkin to Stefansson, at Lakeport, California, 30 May 1921.

136 LAC, R2033-0-7-E, James Bernard Harkin fonds, vol. I, folder, May–December 1921 (no. 214), Harkin to Stefansson, at Reno, Nevada, 31 May 1921.

137 On 7 March 1921, Cory wrote a brief note to Harkin to accompany some memoranda relating to Shackleton's proposed expedition which he was returning, and which he had discussed with the minister. LAC, R2033-0-7-E, James Bernard Harkin fonds, vol. I, folder, January–March 1921. On the same day Stefansson wrote a letter to Captain

Armstrong, Prime Minister Meighen's secretary, denying the truth of Shackleton's statement to Meighen that "he had a letter from me to the effect that I was not going North and that I voluntarily conceded to him the preference in that field." Stefansson added that he understood from the Prime Minister that the matter "might possibly be of some importance." LAC, MG 26 I, Arthur Meighen fonds, vol. 13, folder 7, 007423–007424. He also enclosed a copy of what he claimed was the letter in question, which he had written to Shackleton on 15 April 1920. In it he had offered advice and assistance to Shackleton in connection with his projected Arctic expedition, but had certainly not stated his own withdrawal from the field. LAC, MG 26 I, Arthur Meighen fonds, vol. 13, folder 7, 007429–007430. It will be recalled that Shackleton had attempted to convince Meighen that Stefansson was not interested in going north, in a personal interview at Montreal on 5 February. See M. and J. Fishen, *Shackleton* (London: J. Barrie Books, 1957), 441–45, for an account of Shackleton's negotiations in connection with this expedition. See also Vilhjalmur Stefansson, *Discovery: The Autobiography of Vilhjalmur Stefansson* (New York: McGraw-Hill, 1964), 238–39, where in commenting on the matter he seems to have forgotten completely that he did offer help to Shackleton.

138 LAC, MG 26 I, Arthur Meighen fonds, vol. 13, folder 7, 007425–007435.

139 LAC, MG 26 I, Arthur Meighen fonds, vol. 13, folder 7, 007444, 007447; also LAC, R2033-0-7-E, James Bernard Harkin fonds, vol. I, folder, April 1921 (nos. 135, 181).

140 LAC, MG 26 I, Arthur Meighen fonds, vol. 13, folder 7, 007439–007441.

141 LAC, MG 26 I, Arthur Meighen fonds, vol. 13, folder 7, 007442.

142 LAC, MG 26 I, Arthur Meighen fonds, vol. 13, folder 7, 007443.

143 LAC, MG 26 I, Arthur Meighen fonds, vol. 13, folder 7, 007448, Shackleton to Bassett, 20 April 1921.

144 LAC, MG 26 I, Arthur Meighen fonds, vol. 13, folder 7, 007465.

145 LAC, MG 26 I, Arthur Meighen fonds, vol. 13, folder 7, 007464, Bassett to Meighen, 3 May 1921.

146 LAC, R2033-0-7-E, James Bernard Harkin fonds, vol. I, folder, May–December 1921, Cory to Harkin, 4 May 1921.

147 LAC, R2033-0-7-E, James Bernard Harkin fonds, vol. I, folder, May–December 1921, Harkin to Cory, 6 May 1921.

148 LAC, MG 26 I, Arthur Meighen fonds, vol. 13, folder 7, 007471–007476.

149 LAC, MG 26 I, Arthur Meighen fonds, vol. 13, folder 7, 007479, Meighen to Shackleton, 9 May 1921.

150 LAC, MG 26 I, Arthur Meighen fonds, vol. 13, folder 7, 007480–007482.

151 LAC, MG 26 I, Arthur Meighen fonds, vol. 13, folder 7, 007484, Meighen to Shackleton, 16 May 1921.

152 Fishen, *Shackleton*, 444. Ottawa knew of Shackleton's projected Antarctic expedition by 29 June 1921, at the latest, as on that day the *Ottawa Citizen* printed a news report about it.

153 LAC, RG 85, vol. 582, file 566, Craig to Cory, 4 January 1921.

154 The memorandum from the Department of Justice, which actually took the form of a letter from Assistant Deputy Minister W. Stuart Edwards to Craig on 10 January, comprised various suggestions, some of less merit than others. LAC, R1644-0-7-E, John D. Craig fonds, vol. I, pt. I, Edwards to Craig, 10 January 1921.

155 LAC, RG 85, vol. 582, file 566, Craig to Gibson, 13 January 1921. See also LAC, RG 85, vol. 583, file 571 pt. 1, for a note from Desbarats to Craig, 13 January 1921, saying Patterson had turned in no report. Craig saw Mr. Buskard of the Prime Minister's Office about Christie, and Buskard suggested that the Minister of the Interior should formally ask the Prime Minister for his services, upon which the Prime Minister would send instructions to Christie in London. LAC, R2033-0-7-E, James Bernard Harkin fonds, vol. I, folder January–March 1921 (no. 89), Craig to Gibson, copy to Harkin, 14 January 1921. This suggestion was acted upon without delay; Lougheed made the request by letter on 14 January, and Meighen replied the next day saying, "I have no objection to Mr. Christie performing the services you desire provided it does not take too long. If you will submit the questions to me I will transmit them to him in London." LAC, R1644-0-7-E, John D. Craig fonds, vol. I, pt. I, Meighen to Lougheed, 15 January 1921.

156 LAC, R2033-0-7-E, James Bernard Harkin fonds, vol. I, folder January–March 1921 (no. 84), Craig to Harkin, 17 January 1921.

157 LAC, RG 85, vol. 583, file 571 pt. 1, "Northern Archipelago," Craig to Gibson, 19 January 1921.

158 LAC, R1644-0-7-E, John D. Craig fonds, vol. I, pt. I, Memo to Deputy Minister, 19 January 1921.

159 LAC, R1644-0-7-E, John D. Craig fonds, vol. I, pt. I. The *Montreal Gazette* dispatch referred to was that of 4 January 1921, telling of MacMillan's plans to explore Baffin Island.

160 LAC, RG 85, vol. 582, file 566, Craig to Cory, 8 February 1921.

161 LAC, RG 85, vol. 582, file 566, Craig to Gibson, 22 January 1921; See also LAC, RG 85, vol. 583, file 571 pt. 1, Craig to Gibson, 21 January 1921.

162 LAC, RG 85, vol. 582, file 566, Craig to Cory, 15 February, 24 February, 8 March 1921; LAC, RG 85, vol. 583, no. 571, pt. 2, Craig to Cory, 14 April, 15 April 1921.

163 LAC, RG 85, vol. 583, file 571 pt. 2.

164 LAC, RG 85, vol. 583, file 571 pt. 2. A handwritten note on the memo says, "Mr. Christie's copy returned to him at his request for revision," and the Wrangel Island section is struck out. See the separated versions in LAC, Arthur Meighen Papers, MG 26 I, vol. 13, folder 7, 007418, 007421.

165 LAC, R2033-0-7-E, James Bernard Harkin fonds, vol. I, folder January–March 1921, Craig to Cory, 24 February 1921.

166 LAC, RG 85, vol. 583, file 571 pt. 2, Christie to Craig, 25 February 1921.

167 LAC, RG 85, vol. 583, file 571 pt. 2, Craig to Cory, 26 February 1921.

168 LAC, RG 85, vol. 583, file 571 pt. 2, Cory to Doughty, 3 March 1921.

169 LAC, RG 15, A-2, vol. 5–6, Office of the Deputy Minister, Interior Department, Arctic Islands Documents, Reports on Sovereignty, Memoranda, Maps. See Craig's letter of 21 January to Doughty in booklet *Arctic Islands 1920*, and Holmden's comment about using it in booklet *The Arctic Islands: Canada's Title*.

170 LAC, R2033-0-7-E, James Bernard Harkin fonds, vol. I, folder, April 1921, Craig to Cory, 14 April 1921, enclosing Holmden's preliminary draft.

171 LAC, RG 15, A-2, vol. 5–6, in booklet *The Arctic Islands: Canada's Title*, signed by Holmden and dated 26 April 1921, on p. 48. A number of other copies of this version are extant.

172 LAC, RG 85, vol. 583, file 571, folder 3, Doughty to Cory, 16 November 1921. See also LAC, R1644-0-7-E, John D. Craig fonds, vol. I, folder 3. Memo by Craig, 16 February 1922: "A lengthy memorandum was prepared by the Archives summarizing such material as was available, but it was not possible to complete it owing to the non-arrival of certain papers bearing on the question, which had to be procured from London. These arrived only comparatively recently …."

173 LAC, RG 15, A-2, vol. 5–6, H. R. Holmden, *The Arctic Islands*, 11–14.

174 This work had never been done previously. See LAC, RG 15, A-2, vol. 5–6, H. R. Holmden, *The Arctic Islands*, 48.

175 A. E. Millward, *Southern Baffin Island* (Ottawa: King's Printer, 1930), 9–13.

176 I do not deal with the substance of Holmden's memo in greater detail here, since I have discussed it in the earlier part of this book. For the background of the transfer of 1880, see chapter 1.

177 LAC, RG 85, vol. 583, file 571, folder 3, Memo by Lougheed, 15 June 1921.

178 *Ottawa Citizen*, 22 December 1920.

179 LAC, R1644-0-7-E, John D. Craig fonds, vol. I, folder 1, Pickels to Craig, 5 January 1921. But see handwritten original, dated 3 January, in LAC, RG 85, vol. 583, file 570, folder 1.

180 LAC, RG 85, vol. 582, file 566, Craig to Cory, 4 January 1921.

181 LAC, RG 85, vol. 583, file 570, folder 1, Lougheed to Ballantyne, 5 January 1921. A return memo from deputy minister to deputy minister made the transfer effective. LAC, RG 85, vol. 583, file 570, folder 1, Acting Deputy Minister E. A. Hawken to Cory, 11 January 1921. Marine and Fisheries was better able than Interior to make the necessary repairs and alterations to the ship so, following a request from the Minister of the Interior, an order in council was issued on 21 January providing that the Department of Marine and Fisheries should provide the facilities for this work, the Department of the Interior to pay for it at cost. LAC, RG 85, vol. 583, file 570, folder 1, Minister of the Interior to Governor General in Council, 14 January 1921; Canada, Order in Council, PC No. 118, 21 January 1921. A few days earlier, on 18 January, another order in council had been issued for a Governor General's warrant to authorize the expenditure of $30,000 in connection with the "unforeseen contingency" which had arisen, this sum to be covered by a supplementary estimate at the next session of parliament. Canada, Order in Council, PC No. 79, 18 January 1921.

182 LAC, RG 85, vol. 583, file 571, folder 3, Memo by Lougheed, 15 June 1921. Also LAC, RG 85, vol. 582, file 566, Craig to Cory, 8 March 1921. LAC, RG 85, vol. 583, no. 571, folder 2. Craig to Cory, 8 March 1921; Cory to Craig, 11 March 1921. Also Canada, House of Commons *Debates*, 3 June 1921, 4494.

183 LAC, RG 85, vol. 583, file 568, Craig to Cory, 10 March 1921.

184 LAC, RG 85, vol. 583, file 568, Cory to Craig, 12 March 1921.

185 LAC, RG 85, vol. 582, file 566, Craig to Cory, 22 March 1921.

186 LAC, RG 85, vol. 582, file 567, Craig to Perry, 17 and 20 January 1921.

187 LAC, RG 85, vol. 582, file 570 pt. 3, Pickels to Craig, 4 May 1921, with enclosure Chief Engineer Patterson to Pickels, 4 May 1921.

188 LAC, RG 85, vol. 582, file 570 pt. 3, Pickels to Craig, 18 and 20 May 1921.

189 LAC, RG 85, vol. 582, file 570 pt. 3, Craig to Pickels, 20 May 1921.

190 LAC, RG 85, vol. 582, file 570 pt. 3, Cory to Craig, 20 May 1921.

191 LAC, RG 85, vol. 582, file 570 pt. 3, Ballantyne to Lougheed, 26 May 1921.

192 LAC, RG 85, vol. 582, file 570 pt. 3, Cory to Craig, 11 June 1921; and draft letter, unsigned, to Ballantyne (n.d.).

193 LAC, RG 85, vol. 582, file 570 pt. 3, Pickels to Craig, 27 May, 9 June 1921.

194 LAC, RG 85, vol. 582, file 570 pt. 3, Craig to Cory, 15 June 1921; also draft letter, unsigned, to Sir Joseph Pope (n.d.).

195 LAC, R2033-0-7-E, James Bernard Harkin fonds, vol. I, folder, April 1921 (no. 133), Harkin to Cory, 1 April 1921.

196 See clippings in LAC, R2033-0-7-E, James Bernard Harkin fonds, vol. I, folder, April 1921 (no. 133).

197 LAC, RG 85, vol. 583, file 571 pt. 3, Griffith to Cory, 28 April 1921, enclosing a copy of Lambert to Griffith, 16 March 1921; Churchill to the Duke of Devonshire, 29 April 1921. Churchill said that the interview was on 15 March, Lambert that it was on 16 March.

198 LAC, RG 85, vol. 583, file 571 pt. 3, Marling to Curzon, 30 April 1921.

199 LAC, RG 85, vol. 583, file 571 pt. 3, Craig to Cory, 12 May 1921.

200 LAC, RG 85, vol. 583, file 571 pt. 3, Harkin to Cory, 26 May 1921.

201 LAC, RG 85, vol. 583, file 571 pt. 3, Harkin to Cory, 30 May 1921.

202 LAC, RG 85, vol. 583, file 571 pt. 3, Fitzgerald to Lougheed, by telegram, 4 June 1921. This telegram refers to the cable from Winnipeg on 20 May, which apparently has not been preserved in the files. See LAC, RG 85, vol. 584, file 573, pt. 1, for Rasmussen's plan of his expedition, submitted to Lambert on 4 June, with a covering note claiming the expedition was "of a purely scientific character."

203 LAC, RG 85, vol. 583, file 571 pt. 3, Lougheed to Fitzgerald, by telegram, 8 June 1921.

204 LAC, MG 26 I, Arthur Meighen fonds, series 2, vol. 13, folder 7, 007496, Churchill to Devonshire, 8 June 1921.

205 LAC, MG 26 I, Arthur Meighen fonds, series 2, vol. 13, folder 7, Churchill to Devonshire, 9 June 1921.

206 LAC, MG 26 I, Arthur Meighen fonds, series 2, vol. 13, folder 7, 007500, Churchill to Devonshire, 10 June 1921.

207 LAC, MG 26 I, Arthur Meighen fonds, series 2, vol. 13, folder 7, 007501–007502, Danish memorandum, 8 June 1921.

208 LAC, RG 85, vol. 583, file 571 pt. 3, Fitzgerald to Lougheed, 11 June 1921, copying messages mentioned in text.

209 LAC, RG 85, vol. 583, file 571 pt. 3, Fitzgerald to Lougheed, by telegram, 13 June 1921.

210 LAC, RG 85, vol. 584, file 573 pt. 1, Griffith to Pope, 21 June 1921.

211 LAC, RG 85, vol. 584, file 573 pt. 1, Harkin to Cory, 4 January 1922.

212 LAC, RG 85, vol. 584, file 573 pt. 1, Finnie to Perry, 23 January 1922.

213 LAC, RG 85, vol. 584, file 573 pt. 1, Sgt. Douglas to Officer Commanding H.Q. Division R.C.M.P., 2 October 1922.

214 LAC, RG 85, vol. 584, file 573 pt. 1, W. C. Caron to Finnie, 5 December 1922.

215 LAC, RG 85, vol. 584, file 573 pt. 1, Fitzgerald (H.B.C.) to Finnie, 27 March 1923.

216 LAC, RG 85, vol. 584, file 573 pt. 1, Inspector Wilcox to Officer Commanding H.Q. Division R.C.M.P., 8 September 1923.

217 LAC, RG 85, vol. 584, file 573 pt. 1, Douglas to O. C., 2 October 1922. See note 211.

218 LAC, RG 85, vol. 584, file 573 pt. 1, Finnie to Fitzgerald, 31 March, 11 October 1923; also Fitzgerald to Finnie, 31 October 1923.

219 LAC, RG 85, vol. 584, file 573 pt. 1, Rasmussen to Commissioner, N.W.T., 28 August 1922.

220 LAC, RG 85, vol. 584, file 573 pt. 1, Finnie to Fitzgerald, 1 May 1923; Insp. Munday to O. C., R.C.M.P., Prince Albert, 31 December 1923.

221 LAC, RG 85, vol. 584, file 573 pt. 1, Rasmussen to Finnie, 19 April 1925.

222 LAC, RG 85, vol. 584, file 573 pt. 1, see also Finnie's memo of 24 April 1925, to the newly created Northern Advisory Board, in which, while discussing foreign explorers generally, he observed that although MacMillan had apparently applied to the Danish authorities for permission to explore in Greenland he had made no such application to the Canadian government for permission to explore in the Canadian Arctic islands. Finnie suggested that the NWT Act should be amended to give the Commissioner authority to issue licences or permits to scientists or explorers wishing to enter the NWT.

223 LAC, RG 85, vol. 584, file 573 pt. 1, Rasmussen to O. D. Skelton, 5 May 1925. LAC, RG 25, vol. 4252, file 9057-40 pt. 1.

224 Vilhjalmur Stefansson, *The Friendly Arctic: The Story of Five Years in Polar Regions* (New York: Macmillan, 1943), 690–91; Vilhjalmur Stefansson, *Discovery: The Autobiography of Vilhjalmur Stefansson* (New York: McGraw-Hill, 1964), 237–40.

225 LAC, R2033-0-7-E, James Bernard Harkin fonds, vol. I, folder, May–December 1921 (no. 229); LAC, R2033-0-7-E, James Bernard Harkin fonds, vol. I, folder, May–December 1921, Harkin to Stefansson, at Lakeport, Cal., 30 May 1921; LAC, R2033-0-7-E, James Bernard Harkin fonds, vol. I, folder, May–December 1921 (no. 214), Harkin to Stefansson, at Reno, Nevada, 31 May 1921.

226 LAC, R2033-0-7-E, James Bernard Harkin fonds, vol. I, folder, November–December 1920 (no. 70), Harkin to Cory, 2 December 1920.

227 LAC, R1644-0-7-E, John D. Craig fonds, vol. I, pt. 1.

228 LAC, Arthur Meighen Papers, MG 26 I, vol. 13, folder 7, 007400.

229 LAC, R2033-0-7-E, James Bernard Harkin fonds, vol. I, folder, January–March 1921 (no. 118), Harkin to Cory, 15 March 1921.

230 LAC, R2033-0-7-E, James Bernard Harkin fonds, vol. I, folder, May–December 1921 (no. 191), Memo by Harkin, 17 May 1921.

231 Stefansson, *Discovery: The Autobiography of Vilhjalmur Stefansson*, 239–40; Donat Marc LeBourdais, *Stefansson: Ambassador of the North* (Montreal: Harvest House, 1963), 160.

232 LAC, RG 85, vol. 583, file 571 pt. 3, Harkin to Cory, 13 May 1921.

233 LAC, RG 85, vol. 583, file 571 pt. 3, Cory to Craig, 18 May 1921.

234 LAC, RG 85, vol. 583, file 571 pt. 3, memo signed by Lougheed, 15 June 1921. See also LAC, RG 85, vol. 583, file 571 pt. 3, Craig to Christie, 6 June 1921, a handwritten note saying that Mr. Cory would like to know if the memo "contains any compromising statements or any which might later be quoted against us," and Craig to Cory, 8 June 1921, noting that by request the statement had been made "in the first person." Obviously what was wanted was a "safe" statement for the record, for which the minister would take responsibility.

235 LAC, RG 85, vol. 583, file 571 pt. 3, Harkin to Cory, 26 May 1921. This was written before receipt of the official Danish disavowals of such intentions in early June. Harkin was by no means reconciled to the cancellation of the expedition, and argued that *Arctic* was practically ready to sail, that the $55,000 already spent was gone in any case, that a patrol voyage would cost only about $26,000 more, and therefore the expedition should be sent out without delay.

236 LAC, R2033-0-7-E, James Bernard Harkin fonds, vol. I, folder, May–December 1921 (no. 233), Harkin to Cory, 29 June 1921.

237 LAC, R1644-0-7-E, John D. Craig fonds, vol. I, folder 3, memo by Craig, 16 February 1922. In the same memo Craig makes the rather surprising statement that the Department of Justice had declined, at least temporarily, to give a formal expression of opinion as to the validity of Canada's title and as to the actual territory covered by it.

238 LAC, RG85, vol. 583, file 571 pt. 3, Finnie to Harkin, 18 January 1922. The "Minister" referred to was presumably Charles Stewart, Minister of the Interior in the new King government.

239 LAC, RG85, vol. 583, file 571 pt. 3, Harkin to Finnie, 25 January 1922.

240 LAC, RG85, vol. 583, file 571 pt. 3, Finnie to Cory, 31 January 1922.

241 LAC, RG85, vol. 583, file 571 pt. 3, Cory to Finnie, 3 February 1922.

242 LAC, RG85, vol. 583, file 571 pt. 3, memo by Craig, 11 February 1922.

243 LAC, RG85, vol. 583, file 571 pt. 3, revised memo by Craig, 16 February 1922.

244 *Editor's Note*: Janice Cavell, a historian with the Department of Foreign Affairs, has noted that Trevor Lloyd read Smith's draft manuscript in 1974 and wrote a seven-page commentary on it which is held in the Lloyd papers at Trent University (87-014-8-7). "Lloyd offered both praise and some fairly sharp criticism," she observes. For example, Lloyd says that Smith's section on the Rasmussen episode "elaborates on previously known facts and draws traditional conclusions. He misses the real point." Furthermore, Lloyd provided Smith with information from his own research, including material from the Stefansson Collection and Rasmussen's personal papers (obtained from the Rasmussen family and later deposited in the Arktisk Institut). A letter from Smith dated 12 September 1975 (87-014-10-2) thanks Lloyd for the historical information and comments in some detail about the Rasmussen episode, referring to a recent conversation between the two researchers. "Smith was obviously reluctant to accept Lloyd's conclusion about the lack of a real Danish threat," Cavell notes. "He admits that Stefansson 'muddied the waters' in 1920, but adds: 'whether deliberately or not I'm sure I can't say.' He also raises the possibility that there might have been 'something in the wind that no non-Danes have learned about to this day.'" In Cavell's book with Jeff Noakes, *Acts of Occupation*, they conclude based upon their readings of the Lloyd and Harkin papers that the whole Danish threat "was a fake." Email from Cavell, 6 August 2013.

245 See the minutes of this meeting, with Stefansson's lengthy speech, LAC, R2033-0-7-E, James Bernard Harkin fonds, vol. I, folder, July 1919–October 1920; LAC, R1644-0-7-E, John D. Craig fonds, folder 3.

246 Permanent Court of International Justice, *Legal Status of Eastern Greenland*, Fascicule No. 53, 107.

247 LAC, RG 85, vol. 583, file 571 pt. 3, Harkin to Craig, 7 February 1922.

248 LAC, RG 85, vol. 583, file 571 pt. 3, Harkin to Craig, 13 February 1922.

249 Stefansson, *Discovery: The Autobiography of Vilhjalmur Stefansson*, 232, 239. It is apparent that Stefansson's suppositions were only partly correct. Harkin did not have the only files on the project, and Borden could hardly have bound Harkin to secrecy, even had he wished to do so. Stefansson might have been closer to the truth if he had said that Harkin had been "putting him on." In the same passage he says that probably Christie could also have written "an adequate account." If Christie had done so, one may hazard the guess that the Stefansson part of the story would not have received very generous treatment! See also LAC, R2033-0-7-E, James Bernard Harkin fonds, vol. 2, folder "Canadian Sovereignty of Arctic Islands re. V. O. Stefansson," for a copy of a letter Stefansson wrote to Deputy Minister of Mines and Resources H. L. Keenleyside on 3 November 1949, containing the following:

We talked about J. B. Harkin, who used to be at the head of the parks service, and we said I was to write you about him. I had a feeling that he had been up in our correspondence before and I discover a paragraph about him buried in a long letter to you of May 16, 1944. The length of the letter and the cares of the War probably combined against action then. I quote the paragraph by itself now:

"You speak of sovereignty questions, and that I use as an entering wedge for bringing up what has long been to me an important matter. J. B. Harkin is, according to my belief and also according to what he has told me, in possession of a good deal of information that has a bearing on the history of sovereignty proposals and acts in Canada which is not available in any records, even secret ones. When last I talked with him, about ten years ago, he still held strongly an idea which has baffled me, that it is his duty to let certain secrets die with him. Since they cannot be wholly secret, but must be partially known, it is a disservice, I think, to history and maybe to Canada, in relation to its sovereignty problems, if Harkin does not place on record (in secret archives if you like) everything that he has in his memory or can dig up from memoranda which he perhaps intends to destroy."

.... There were so many remifications [*sic*] from these superficial issues that I feel sure a study of the entire collection of documents will throw an interesting and perhaps an important light on the development of Canadian policy with regard to the Arctic.

Hugh Keenleyside sent this to Harkin on 27 February 1950, with a request for any information on the subject that he could send to the Department of External Affairs, and whether any part of it should be made available to Stefansson. Harkin, who was now seventy-five years of age, either did not write a reply or, if he did, apparently did not leave a copy of the reply in his papers. He attempted to frame a reply, however, and in his random jottings appear such revealing comments as the following:

> There is only one issue & that is whether certain information should be made available to Dr. Stef. The plea for history winds up in a plea for information re an incident concerning himself.
>
> .... What I always said was that I considered information I had should be kept secret till all persons who were concerned in the affair were dead and that it then should be made available for the Canadian Archives.
>
> I am as much convinced today as I ever was that it would be contrary to the National interest to follow any other course.

Harkin did, of course, eventually turn over his information, or at least some of it, to the Public Archives (now Library and Archives Canada).

11 | The Wrangel Island Affair of the Early 1920s

1 The main reference is Vilhjalmur Stefansson, *The Adventure of Wrangel Island* (New York: Macmillan, 1925; London: Jonathon Cape, 1926). See also Richard J. Diubaldo, "Wrangling over Wrangel Island," *Canadian Historical Review* 48, no. 3 (September 1967): 201–26; Elmer Plishchke, "Jurisdiction in the Polar Regions" (PhD diss., Clark University, 1943), 295–309; A. Stevenson, "Wrangel Island Wrangle," *North* 13, no. 3 (September–October 1966): 20–29.

2 Ferdinand von Wrangel, *Narrative of an Expedition to the Polar Sea in the Years 1820, 1821, 1822, and 1823*, trans. and ed. Edward and Mrs. Sabine (London: J. Madden, 1840, 1844), 348, 380 (1840 ed.), 334, 364–65 (1844 ed.). 344 (1844 ed.): "our last hope vanished of discovering the land, which we yet believed to exist." 364–65 (1844 ed.): "Our return to Nijnei Kolymsk closed the series of attempts made by us to discover a northern land; which though not seen by us, may possibly exist."

3 *Arctic Papers*, 1, no. 107 (March 5, 1950): 9–22, esp. 18; Berthold Seemann, *Narrative of the Voyage of H. M. S. Herald* (London: Reeve, 1853), 2:114–16.

4 John Muir, *The Cruise of the Corwin* (Boston: Houghton Mifflin, 1917), xv–xvi.

5 Stefansson, *The Adventure of Wrangel Island*, 19.

6 Muir, *The Cruise of the Corwin*, xvi–xvii. The main account of the expedition is George W. DeLong, *The Voyage of the Jeannette* (Boston: Houghton, Mifflin, 1884). See also Emma W. DeLong, *Explorer's Wife* (New York: Dodd, Mead, 1938), esp. map facing 200, showing the drift of the Jeannette.

7 Muir, *The Cruise of the Corwin*, xvii, 169, 174.

8 Muir, *The Cruise of the Corwin*, 223 and fn.; also *Proceedings of the Royal Geographical Society* (1881), 3:733–34. See also the preceding note, 731–33, on Hooper's visit to Wrangel Island.

9 Muir, *The Cruise of the Corwin*, 169, 180.

10 *The Geographical Journal* 62, no. 6 (December 1923): 440–44. The article is reproduced in Stefansson, *The Adventure of Wrangel Island*, appendix 6, 393–98.

11 See Robert A. Bartlett and Ralph T. Hale, *The Last Voyage of the Karluk* (Toronto: McClelland, 1916); Robert Bartlett, *The Log of Bob Bartlett: The True Story of Forty Years of Seafaring and Exploration* (New York: G.P. Putnam's Sons, 1929), 254–79; George P. Putnam, *Mariner of the North: The Life of Captain Bob Bartlett* (New York: Duell, Sloan and Pearce, 1947), 108–31; J. Hadley, *Hadley's Narrative of the Wreck of the "Karluk,"* unpublished typewritten manuscript, and also photostat copy of original, in the Aboriginal Affairs and Northern Development Library, Gatineau; LAC, R2288-0-X-E, William Laird McKinlay fonds; Library and Archives Canada [hereafter LAC], R1633-0-1-E, Robert J. Williamson fonds.

12 The key part of the note has been translated as follows:

> The Imperial Russian Government has the honor to notify herewith the Governments of the Allied and Associated Powers that these islands [i.e., the new islands] are included in the territory of the Russian Empire. The Imperial Government takes this occasion to set forth that it considers as constituting an integral part of the Empire the islands Henriette, Jeanette, Bennett, Herald, and Uedinenie, which, with the Novosibirski Islands, Vrangel and others situated near the Asiatic coast of the Empire, form an extension toward the north of the

continental shelf of Siberia. The Imperial Government has not judged it necessary to include in this notification the islands Novaia Zemlia, Kalguev, Vaigach, and others of smaller dimensions situated near the European coast of the Empire, it being granted that their appurtenance to the territories of the Empire has been recognized for centuries.

As given in T. A. Taracouzio, *Soviets in the Arctic* (New York: Macmillan, 1938), 69. See also V. Lakhtine, "Rights over the Arctic," *American Journal of International Law* 24 no. 4 (October 1930): 708.

13 Stefansson, *The Adventure of Wrangel Island*, 66.

14 LAC, R5254-0-9-E, Vilhjalmur Stefansson fonds. The quoted excerpts are in vol. 7 of his diary. See also Vilhjalmur Stefansson, *Discovery: The Autobiography of Vilhjalmur Stefansson* (Toronto: McGraw-Hill, 1964), 206–7.

15 See Vilhjalmur Stefansson, *The Friendly Arctic* (New York: MacMillan, 1921), appendix 1, 715–29, for Storkerson's own account of the ice drift. See also Stefansson, *The Adventure of Wrangel Island*, 72–74.

16 LAC, R2065-0-6-E, Loring Christie fonds, vol. 6, folder 19, 5835.

17 LAC, R2065-0-6-E, Loring Christie fonds, vol. 6, folder 19, 5835–36.

18 LAC, R2065-0-6-E, Loring Christie fonds, vol. 6, folder 19, 5835–42.

19 Thus Stefansson accepted the denial of the obvious implications of the Russian-American treaty of 1867. The view of David Hunter Miller, expressed a few years later, was undoubtedly sounder. Speaking of the relevant passage in the treaty, he said, "These words 'without limitation' are pretty strong words. They come very near to fixing the territorial rights of Russia and the United States, so far as those two countries could then fix them, up to the Pole." David Hunter Miller, "Political Rights in the Arctic," *Foreign Affairs* 4, no. 1 (October 1925): 59. See also Muir, *The Cruise of the Corwin* (Boston: Houghton Mifflin, 1917), xxiii (Introduction by W. F. Badè).

20 LAC, R2065-0-6-E, Loring Christie fonds, vol. 6, folder 19, 5843–45.

21 LAC, R2033-0-7-E, James Bernard Harkin fonds, vol. 1, folder, July 1919–October 1920.

22 LAC, MG 26 I, Arthur Meighen fonds, vol. 13, folder 7, 007391–007394, Stefansson to Meighen, 30 October 1920.

23 LAC, Record Group 88, Surveys and Mapping Branch [hereafter RG 88], Surveys Mapping and Remote Sensing, vol. 5, file 17435, Stefansson to Cory, 30 October 1920.

24 LAC, MG 26 I, Arthur Meighen fonds, vol. 13, folder 7, 007391–007394, 007395, Borden to Meighen, 3 November 1920. Quoting from a "recent" letter from Stefansson.

25 LAC, R1644-0-7-E, John D. Craig fonds, vol. 1, folder 3; also LAC, Record Group 25, Department of External Affairs [hereafter RG 25], vol. 4252, file 9057-40 pt. 1, Christie to Meighen, 28 October 1920. See also in LAC, MG 26 I, Arthur Meighen fonds, vol. 13, folder 7, 007383–007388.

26 LAC, RG 25, vol. 2667, file 9057-B-40 pt. 1, Pope to Meighen, 25 November 1920. See also LAC, MG 26 I, Arthur Meighen fonds, vol. 13, folder 7, 007381.

27 LAC, R2033-0-7-E, James Bernard Harkin fonds, vol. 1, folder, November–December 1920 (no. 39).

28 LAC, R2033-0-7-E, James Bernard Harkin fonds, vol. 1, folder, November–December 1920 (no. 40), Précis of minutes of 18th regular meeting of Advisory Technical Board, 3 November 1920.

29 LAC, RG 88, vol. 5, file 17435, Lynch to Cory, 12 November 1920.

30 LAC, RG 88, vol. 5, file 17435, Cory to Lynch, 18 November 1920.

31 LAC, R2033-0-7-E, James Bernard Harkin fonds, vol. 1, folder, November–December 1920 (no. 40), Minutes of 3rd special meeting of Advisory Technical Board, 25 November 1920.

32 LAC, R2033-0-7-E, James Bernard Harkin fonds, vol. 1, folder, January–March 1921 (no. 85), Stefansson to Lougheed, 8 January 1921.

33 Diubaldo, "Wrangling over Wrangel Island," 206 and references; D. M. LeBourdais, *Stefansson: Ambassador of the North* (Eugene: Harvest House, 1963), 159–60.

34 Stefansson, *The Adventure of Wrangel Island*, 25–26.

35 Canada, Order in Council, PC No. 1316, 2 June 1913.

36 See Diubaldo, "Wrangling over Wrangel Island," 205. It is true, however, that Deputy Minister Debarats' instructions of 29 May 1913 to Stefansson said that any lands discovered in the Beaufort Sea should be claimed.

37 Stefansson, *The Adventure of Wrangel Island*, 60.

38 Stefansson, *The Adventure of Wrangel Island*, 60, 290, 61.

39 LAC, MG 30, R. M. Anderson fonds, vol. 21, folder 22, Wm. L. McKinlay Memoranda, 15 June 1922. Received by M.B.A. (Mrs. R. M.) Anderson in Ottawa, 27 June 1922. See also LAC, R2288-0-X-E, William Laird McKinlay fonds.

40 LAC, R2033-0-7-E, James Bernard Harkin fonds, vol. 1, folder, January–March 1921 (no. 99), Stefansson to Harkin, 7 February 1921.

41 LAC, R2033-0-7-E, James Bernard Harkin fonds, vol. 1, folder, January–March 1921 (no. 103), Harkin to Cory, 17 February 1921.

42 LAC, MG 26 I, Arthur Meighen fonds, vol. 13, folder 7, 007416, Meighen to Stefansson, 19 February 1921.

43 Stefansson to C. V. Sale, 23 February 1921, cited in Diubaldo, "Wrangling over Wrangel Island," 206, fns. 19, 20; also LAC, Arthur Meighen Papers, MG 26 I, vol. 13, folder 7, 007422, Stefansson to Armstrong, 7 March 1921.

44 LAC, R2033-0-7-E, James Bernard Harkin fonds, vol. 1, folder, January–March 1921 (no. 137), Stefansson to Lougheed, 26 February 1921.

45 LAC, MG 26 I, Arthur Meighen fonds, vol. 13, folder 7, 007419, Meighen's private secretary to Stefansson, 1 March 1921.

46 Stefansson, *The Adventure of Wrangel Island*, 80.

47 LAC, Record Group 85, Northern Affairs Program [hereafter RG 85], vol. 583, file 571 pt. 2; LAC, MG 26 I, Arthur Meighen fonds, vol. 13, folder 7, 007418, 007421; LAC, RG 25, vol. 2667, file 9057-B-40 pt. 1.

48 LAC, RG 25, vol. 2667, file 9057-B-40 pt. 1, Memo by Christie for Prime Minister, 28 February 1921.

49 LAC, R2033-0-7-E, James Bernard Harkin fonds, vol. 1, folder, January–March 1921 (no. 137), Stefansson to Armstrong, 7 March 1921.

50 LAC, R2033-0-7-E, James Bernard Harkin fonds, vol. 1, folder, January–March 1921 (no. 137), Cory to Harkin, 5 March 1921.

51 LAC, RG 85, vol. 583, file 571, R. Stephens (Department of the Naval Service) to Cory, 17 May 1921. Enclosed copy of Occasional Paper No. 30, "Wrangel Island," prepared by Naval War Staff, Ottawa, 13 April 1921.

52 LAC, R2033-0-7-E, James Bernard Harkin fonds, vol. 1, folder, May–December 1921 (no. 229), Cory to Harkin, 18 May 1921.

53 LAC, R2033-0-7-E, James Bernard Harkin fonds, vol. 1, folder, May–December 1921 (no. 229), Harkin to Stefansson at Lakeport, California, 30 May 1921.

54 Stefansson, *The Adventure of Wrangel Island*, 76 and ff.

55 LAC, RG 85, vol. 582, file 565, News Clippings June and July 1921.

56 LeBourdais, *Stefansson: Ambassador of the North*, 164.

57 Stefansson, *The Adventure of Wrangel Island*, 89–90.

58 See photograph of this proclamation in Stefansson, *The Adventure of Wrangel Island*, facing 119.

59 Stefansson to Crawford, 15 August 1922, cited in Diubaldo, "Wrangling over Wrangel Island," 210.

60 Stefansson, *The Adventure of Wrangel Island*, 119–24; Stefansson, *Discovery: The Autobiography of Vilhjalmur Stefansson*, 257–58.

61 *Cong. Rec.*, 67th Cong., 2nd sess., 1922, 4737–39.

62 *Cong. Rec.*, 67th Cong., 2nd sess., 1922, 4963–64. These excerpts, and many newspaper clippings, may be seen in LAC, RG 25, vol. 2667, file 9057-B-40 pt. 1.

63 LAC, RG 25, vol. 2667, file 9057-B-40 pt. 1, Christie to King, 21 March 1922.

64 LAC, R10383-0-6-E, William Lyon Mackenzie King fonds, vol. 82, 69270–75, Stefansson to King, 11 March 1922.

65 LAC, R10383-0-6-E, William Lyon Mackenzie King fonds, vol. 82, 69276, Stefansson to King, 14 March 1922. Handwritten notes by Stefansson on both these letters show that he had had a personal interview with King at this time, and wrote the letters mainly as memoranda of the conversation.

66 LAC, RG 85, vol. 1124, file 1005-5-1 pt. 1, Stefansson to Finnie, 3 May 1922. Diubaldo is obviously mistaken in asserting that Stefansson's letter made "no mention of compensation or a cash settlement." Diubaldo, "Wrangling over Wrangel Island," 211. See also LAC, RG 85, vol. 584, file 571 pt. 5, for three letters Stefansson wrote to Minister of the Interior Stewart about Wrangel Island on 3 May 1922, with an enclosure.

67 LAC, RG 85, vol. 1124, file 1005-5-1 pt. 1, Finnie to Cory, 3 May 1922. See also LAC, RG 85, vol. 1124, file 1005-5-1 pt. 1, Finnie to Cory, 12 May 1922.

68 LAC, RG 85, vol. 1124, file 1005-5-1 pt. 1, Craig to Finnie, 10 May 1922.

69 Canada, House of Commons *Debates*, 12 May 1922, 1750–51, Mr. Meighen, MP, and Mr. Graham, MP. Graham was the Minister of Militia and Defence.

70 Canada, House of Commons *Debates*, 12 May 1922, 1751. See also Diubaldo, "Wrangling over Wrangel Island," 212–13.

71 LAC, RG 85, vol. 1124, file 1005-5-1 pt. 1, Stefansson to Finnie, 15 May 1922 and 31 May 1922.

72 LAC, RG 25, vol. 2667, file 9057-B-40 pt. 1, Klishko to Curzon, 24 May 1922.

73 LAC, RG 25, vol. 2667, file 9057-B-40 pt. 1, Churchill to Byng, 2 June 1922.

74 LAC, RG 25, vol. 2667, file 9057-B-40 pt. 1, Pope to Fielding, 5 June 1922.

75 LAC, RG 85, vol. 1124, file 1005-5-1 pt. 1, Finnie to W. W. Cory, 9 June 1922.

76 LAC, RG 85, vol. 1124, file 1005-5-1 pt. 1, T. L. Cory to W. W. Cory, 15 June 1922. See T. L. Cory's memo also in LAC, R10383-0-6-E, William Lyon Mackenzie King fonds, vol. 147, file 1205.

77 LAC, RG 25, vol. 2667, file 9057-B-40 pt. 1, Stefansson to Christie, 9 June 1922; LAC, RG 25, vol. 2667, file 9057-B-40 pt. 1, Christie to Stefansson, 12 June 1922.

78 LAC, RG 25, vol. 2667, file 9057-B-40 pt. 1, Memo to file by Christie, 12 June 1922.

79 LAC, RG 25, vol. 2667, file 9057-B-40 pt. 1, Memo by Christie for Prime Minister, 9 August 1922. Sir Joseph Pope also reiterated his view that Canada should have nothing to do with a claim to Wrangel Island. LAC, RG 25, vol. 2667, file 9057-B-40 pt. 1, Pope to Stewart, 16 October 1922.

80 LAC, RG 25, vol. 2667, file 9057-B-40 pt. 1, Churchill to Byng, 15 July 1922, with enclosure Admiralty H. 3618/22, 17 June 1922. See also LAC, R1644-0-7-E, John D. Craig fonds, vol. 1, folder 3.

81 Stefansson, *The Adventure of Wrangel Island*, 132–36.

82 Stefansson, *The Adventure of Wrangel Island*, 136–37; also LAC, RG 85, vol. 1124, file 1005-5-1 pt. 1, Stefansson to Cory, 8 August 1922.

83 LAC, RG 85, vol. 1124, file 1005-5-1 pt. 1, Cory to King, 9 August 1922.

84 Canada, Order in Council, P. C. No. 1735, 21 August 1922.

85 LAC, RG 85, vol. 1124, file 1005-5-1 pt. 1, Cory to Stefansson, by telegram, 12 August 1922.

86 LAC, RG 85, vol. 1124, file 1005-5-1 pt. 1, Taylor to Minister of Public Works J. H. King, by telegram, 9 August 1922.

87 Stefansson, *The Adventure of Wrangel Island*, 136–40, also Capt. Bernard's report, appendix III, 351–54. In a letter to Cory, Stefansson attributed the failure to the late sailing date, but apparently he changed his mind. LAC, RG 85, vol. 1124, file 1005-5-1 pt. 1, Stefansson to Cory, 27 December 1922.

88 LAC, RG 25, vol. 2667, file 9057-B-40 pt. 1, Devonshire to Byng, 4 November 1922, with enclosure from American embassy, 27 September 1922.

89 LAC, RG 25, vol. 2667, file 9057-B-40 pt. 1, Pope to Stewart, 16 October 1922.

90 LAC, RG 25, vol. 2667, file 9057-B-40 pt. 1, Pope to Stewart, 16 October 1922.

91 LAC, RG 25, vol. 2667, file 9057-B-40 pt. 1, Stewart to Pope, 1 December 1922.

92 LAC, RG 25, vol. 4252, file 9057-40, pt. 1, Devonshire to Byng, 24 February 1923.

93 LAC, RG 25, vol. 2667, file 9057-B-40 pt. 1, E.g., Stewart to Pope, 19 March 1923; LAC, RG 25, vol. 2667, file 9057-B-40 pt. 1, Pope to King, 22 March 1923, 5 April 1923.

94 LAC, RG 25, vol. 2667, file 9057-B-40 pt. 1, Pope to King, 22 March 1923.

95 LAC, RG 25, vol. 2667, file 9057-B-40 pt. 1, Pope to King, 5 April 1923. See also LAC, R10383-0-6-E, William Lyon Mackenzie King fonds, vol. 147, no. 1205, for another memo from Pope to King, dated 28 Aug. 1923, again opposing Canadian concern with Wrangel Island except from an Imperial point of view.

96 LAC, RG 85, vol. 1124, file 1005-5-1 pt. 2, Stefansson to Finnie, 14 March 1923.

97 LAC, RG 85, vol. 1124, file 1005-5-1 pt. 2, Stefansson to Cory, 14 March 1923.

98 LAC, RG 85, vol. 1124, file 1005-5-1 pt. 2, Stefansson to Finnie, 24 March 1923.

99 LAC, RG 85, vol. 1124, file 1005-5-1 pt. 2, Bernard to King, 21 March 1923.

100 LAC, RG 85, vol. 1124, file 1005-5-1 pt. 2, Craig to Holmden, 5 April 1923.

101 Stefansson, *Discovery: The Autobiography of Vilhjalmur Stefansson*, 259; Stefansson, *The Adventure of Wrangel Island*, 143–44.

102 LAC, RG 25, vol. 2667, file 9057-B-40 pt. 1, L. C. Moyer (Private Secretary to President of the Privy Council) to Walker, 9 April 1923.

103 LAC, RG 25, vol. 2667, file 9057-B-40 pt. 1, Moyer to Stewart, 9 April 1923. See also LAC, R10383-0-6-E, William Lyon Mackenzie King fonds, vol. 134, Memoranda & Notes, no. 1075. This decision was taken the same afternoon, and was formalized by an order in council on April 21. Canada, Order in Council, PC No. 714, 21 April 1923.

104 LAC, RG 25, vol. 2667, file 9057-B-40 pt. 1, Pope to Governor General's Secretary, 19 April 1923; LAC, RG 25, vol. 2667, file 9057-B-40 pt. 1, Byng to Devonshire, 23 April 1923.

105 LAC, RG 85, vol. 1124, file 1005-5-1 pt. 2, Craig to Finnie, 9 April 1923.

106 LAC, RG 85, vol. 1124, file 1005-5-1 pt. 2, Finnie to Gibson, 9 April 1923.

107 Stefansson, *The Adventure of Wrangel Island*, 145-150; Stefansson, *The Friendly Arctic*, 692–93.

108 LAC, RG 85, vol. 1124, file 1005-5-1 pt. 2, "Foreign Office Confidential Memorandum on the History, Value and Ownership of Wrangel Island," no. A 3956/750/45, 2-3, 2 July 1923.

109 LAC, RG 85, vol. 1124, file 1005-5-1 pt. 2, "Foreign Office Confidential Memorandum on the History, Value and Ownership of Wrangel Island," no. A 3956/750/45, 3-4, 2 July 1923.

110 LAC, RG 85, vol. 1124, file 1005-5-1 pt. 2, "Foreign Office Confidential Memorandum on the History, Value and Ownership of Wrangel Island," no. A 3956/750/45, 4-5, 2 July 1923.

111 Stefansson, *The Adventure of Wrangel Island*, 144–56; Stefansson, *Discovery: The Autobiography of Vilhjalmur Stefansson*, 260; Diubaldo, "Wrangling over Wrangel Island," 220.

112 Diubaldo, "Wrangling over Wrangel Island," 216–18, and references.

113 LAC, RG 85, vol. 1124, file 1005-5-1 pt. 2, Krassin to Curzon, 25 May 1923.

114 LAC, RG 85, vol. 1124, file 1005-5-1 pt. 2, Peters to Curzon, 16 July 1923.

115 LAC, RG 85, vol. 1124, file 1005-5-1 pt. 2, Berzin to Curzon, 25 August 1923.

116 LAC, RG 85, vol. 1124, file 1005-5-1 pt. 2, American Chargé d'Affaires to British Secretary of State for Foreign Affairs, 4 June 1923.

117 LAC, RG 85, vol. 1124, file 1005-5-1 pt. 2, Warner to Post Wheeler, 11 June 1923.

118 LAC, RG 85, vol. 1124, file 1005-5-1 pt. 2, Curzon to Chilton, 10 August 1923.

119 LAC, RG 85, vol. 1124, file 1005-5-1 pt. 2, Chilton to Curzon, 15 August 1923.

120 LAC, RG 85, vol. 1124, file 1005-5-1 pt. 2, Christie to Chilton, 21 September 1923.

121 LAC, RG 85, vol. 1124, file 1005-5-1 pt. 2, e.g., Devonshire to Byng, 20 August 1923, 25 August 1923, 13 September 1923, 17 September 1923.

122 LAC, RG 85, vol. 1124, file 1005-5-1 pt. 2, Taylor to Prime Minister's secretary, 30 June 1923; LAC, RG 85, vol. 1124, file 1005-5-1 pt. 2, McGregor to Taylor, 3 July 1923; LAC, RG 85, vol. 1124, file 1005-5-1 pt. 2, Taylor to Cory, 5 July 1923; LAC, RG 85, vol. 1124, file 1005-5-1 pt. 2, Gibson to Taylor, 6 July 1923; LAC, RG 85, vol. 1124, file 1005-5-1 pt. 2, Gibson to Finnie, 7 July 1923; LAC, RG 85, vol. 1124, file 1005-5-1 pt. 2, Finnie to Cory, 17 August 1923.

123 LAC, RG 85, vol. 1124, file 1005-5-1 pt. 2, Cory to King, 6 September 1923. See LAC, RG 85, vol. 764, file 5064 for correspondence relating to Stefansson's trip to England, his living allowance, and the time limit for it. Department of the Interior officials insisted that a time limit of 30 days had been agreed upon (e.g., Cory to Finnie, 26 April 1923). Stefansson said that there had been no firm time limit, noting that none had been specified in the order in council providing for the trip, and maintained that he had been delayed unavoidably in England because the British Government took so long to give him their decision (e.g., Stefansson to Finnie, 8 December 1925). It would appear from the correspondence that both Prime Minister King and O. D. Skelton were willing to make some allowance for the extra time (e.g., King's secretary to Stewart, 18 January 1926, and Skelton to Finnie, 25 February 1926), but the senior officials of the Department of the Interior were not. On 14 September 1925, a cheque for $330.20 – the balance for 30 days – was sent to Stefansson (Finnie to Stefansson, 14 September 1925), which Stefansson characterized as "at least $330.20 more than nothing" (Stefansson to Finnie, 19 September 1925).

124 Stefansson, *The Adventure of Wrangel Island*, 156–65, also appendix 11, 419–24.

125 LAC, RG 85, vol. 1124, file 1005-5-1 pt. 2, Foreign Office to Peters, code telegram, 1 September 1923.

126 Stefansson, *The Adventure of Wrangel Island*, 165–69.

127 LAC, RG 25, vol. 2667, file 9057-B-40 pt. 2, Cory to Pope, 24 November 1923; LAC, RG 25, vol. 2667, file 9057-B-40 pt. 2, Pope to Cory, 27 November 1923.

128 LAC, RG 85, vol. 1124, file 1005-5-1 pt. 2, Stefansson to Mackenzie King, 2 January 1924.

129 D. M. LeBourdais, *Northward on the New Frontier* (Ottawa: Graphic Publishers, 1931), 15. See also 16, 38.

130 Stefansson, *The Adventure of Wrangel Island*, 300.

131 Stefansson, *The Adventure of Wrangel Island*, 299.

132 Stefansson, *The Adventure of Wrangel Island*, 299.

133 LAC, RG 85, vol. 1124, file 1005-5-1 pt. 2, Stefansson to Stewart, 2 June 1924, with two enclosures.

134 Stefansson's letter to the British government stressed his view that Britain had a clear legal claim to Wrangel Island and should maintain it, offering to submit the case to arbitration by the League of Nations if the need arose. He was unable to continue and would "be forced to try to sell our interests ... to an American company." He also suggested reimbursement of money contributed. LAC, RG 25, vol. 2667, file 9057-B-40 pt. 2, Stefansson to Foreign Office, 2 June 1924.

135 LAC, RG 85, vol. 1124, file 1005-5-1 pt. 2, Thomas to Byng, 18 June 1924.

136 The gradual retreat from the categorical assertion of sovereignty over Wrangel Island is well illustrated by statements the House of Commons.

Debates, 31 May 1923, 3360:

Hanson: I would like the minister to tell us who owns Wrangel island.

Lapointe: I should like to know myself.

Debates, 14 June 1923, 3948

Shaw: Do we own it or not?

Stewart (Argenteuil): I do not think we own it.

Debates, 7 April 1924, 1110:

McQuarrie: Will the minister explain what is the situation with respect to Wrangel island?

Stewart (Argenteuil): ...So far as Canada is concerned we do not intend to set up any claim to the island.

On 16 May 1923, Conservative Senator George William Fowler had been prepared to introduce a resolution to the effect that "in the opinion of the Senate it is desirable that the Canadian Government shall forthwith take such steps as are necessary to protect the rights of Canada to Wrangel Island." He had learned, however, the government had just sent Stefansson to London to meet with the Imperial authorities, so he did not move his resolution. Canada, Senate *Debates*, 16 May 1923, 548–49.

137 Canada, Order in Council, PC No. 1227, 17 July 1924. The substance of this order was sent by cable to Thomas on 18 July, and copies of it were sent by mail six days later. LAC, RG 25, vol. 2667, file 9057-B-40 pt. 2, Byng to Thomas, by code telegram, 18 July 1924; Byng to Thomas, with enclosures, 24 July 1924.

138 LAC, RG 85, vol. 1124, file 1005-5-1 pt. 2, Extract from Anglo-Soviet Conference, 6 August 1924.

139 LAC, RG 85, vol. 1124, file 1005-5-1 pt. 2, G. R. Warner to Stefansson, 8 August 1924. In his account of this phase of the affair Stefansson does not acknowledge receipt of this letter. He says, "We would like to tell all we know of the rest of the story down to January, 1925. But we are so uncertain of essential facts that we are not commit ourselves as to several of them." Apparently, in his view, one of the "essential facts" he was uncertain of was whether the new Conservative Government in Great Britain would "reverse the Labor policy with regard to Wrangel." See Stefansson, *The Adventure of Wrangel Island*, 300–301.

140 LeBourdais, *Northward on the New Frontier*, 16.

141 LeBourdais, *Northward on the New Frontier*, 233–308.

142 LeBourdais, *Northward on the New Frontier*, 271–72.

143 LeBourdais, *Northward on the New Frontier*, 55–56, 61, 262.

144 LeBourdais, *Northward on the New Frontier*, 309–11. See also Stefansson, *The Adventure of Wrangel Island*, 302–12, for a collection of contemporary newspaper reports, and also a letter to him from Carl Lomen, dated 29 January 1925, giving information about the final disastrous phase. See also LAC, RG 85, vol. 1124, file 1005-5-1 pt. 1, for a copy of a letter written on 31 October 1924, by J. C. Hill of the British commercial mission at Vladivostok to British chargé d'affaires P. H. Hodgson in Moscow. Hill gives an account of the episode which is based largely on his attendance on 30 October at an examination and questioning of Wells by Russian officials. The impression gathered from his account differs in certain details from that conveyed by North American newspaper articles and the reports of Stefansson, LeBourdais, Noice, and others connected with the affair. According to Hill's account Wells had not understood he was claiming the island; Noice had told him all was settled between British and Soviet governments and he needed no passports or documents; the Russians treated him and his party with consideration and they were satisfied with this treatment.

145 Lakhtine, "Rights over the Arctic," 708. See LAC, RG 85, vol. 1124, file 1005-5-1 pt. 2, communication of 4 November 1924, in both French and English.

146 As translated in Taracouzio, *Soviets in the Arctic* appendix 2, 381. His translation on 320 has an obvious error in the last dozen words, i.e., "middle of the strait separating Ratmanoff and Krutzenshtern Islands from the group of Diomede Islands in Bering Strait." The same error is in the translation in Lakhtine, "Rights over the Arctic," 709.

147 LAC, RG 85, vol. 1124, file 1005-5-1 pt. 2, Hill to British chargé d'affaires, Moscow, 7 February 1925. Includes an enclosed translation of article "The Colonisation of Wrangel Island," by Soviet local agent M. Fonshtein.

148 LAC, RG 25, vol. 2667, file 9057-B-40 pt. 2, H. A. MacRae of British vice consulate at Hakodate to British ambassador to Japan the Rt. Hon. Sir J. Tilley, 30 September 1926.

149 LAC, RG 85, vol. 1124, file 1005-5-1 pt. 2, "The Colonisation of Wrangel Island," by Soviet local agent M. Fonshtein.

150 Green Haywood Hackworth, *Digest of International Law*, vol. 1 (Washington: US Government Printing Office, 1940), 465, 464. Diubaldo, "Wrangling over Wrangel Island:" 224, fn. 95, says that Carl Lomen, acting on advice from the State Department, made a formal private complaint to the Soviet government about the Red October, and when the Russians refused to pay him any compensation, received $46,630 from the American Government. Lomen claimed that Secretary of State Hughes had urged him to hold the island.

151 Diubaldo, "Wrangling over Wrangel Island," 225, after referring to the King government's stand in the Chanak affair that "the dominion could pass judgment on just what was or was not a Canadian interest," goes on to say, "The Wrangel Island controversy extended this principle for the dominion attempted to dictate the course of action Imperial authorities should take." I can see little evidence to justify this view, and, it seems to me, the general tenor and development of the author's own well-researched article show, in fact, that this was not the case.

152 Canada, House of Commons *Debates*, 1 June 1925, 3773, Mr. Stewart, MP.

153 Stefansson, *The Friendly Arctic*, 691. See also LAC, RG 85, vol. 437, file 4457, for a collection of newspaper articles and clippings giving a variety of opinions on the Wrangel Island affair, including a letter written by Crawford's parents on 28 April 1925, and published in the *Ottawa Evening Journal* on 30 April. They were not in the least inclined to accept Stefansson's accounting for the tragedy.

12 | The Question of Sovereignty over the Sverdrup Islands

1 Otto Sverdrup, *New Land: Four Years in the Arctic Region* (London: Longmans, Green, 1904), e.g., 1:1: "There were still many white spaces on the map which I was glad of an opportunity of colouring with the Norwegian colours."

2 Sverdrup, *New Land: Four Years in the Arctic Region*, 449–50. In his narrative Sverdrup does not record any instance where he actually took possession "on the ground." However, see Library and Archives Canada [hereafter LAC], Record Group 85, Northern Affairs Program [hereafter RG 85], vol. 347, file 201-1, *Summary of Reports of Commander Otto Sverdrup's Explorations in 1898–1904* (Oslo: Wittusen and Jensen, 1928). For the following passages recording claims: 6–7. [On spring expeditions 1900.] "The Expeditions had ... rounded West coast of Axel Heiberg Land, on which, on the North-West coast at 80[0] 55' North latitude, erected a cairn and into same deposited a record of the journey and a declaration that the Expedition took possession of this land and all the lands discovered in the name of the Kingdom of Norway." 12. [On spring expedition 1902.] "The party ... reached the northernmost [*sic*] point, which they called Lands Lokk, at 81[0], 40' Lat. N. A cairn was built there, in which a report of the journey was deposited, as also a declaration that the Expedition had taken and hereby took possession of the land and all the lands discovered in the name of the Kingdom of Norway." This little booklet does not identify its author, but from internal evidence one would judge that it was Sverdrup himself.

3 T. C. Fairley, *Sverdrup's Arctic Adventures* (London: Longmans, 1959), 263, 274. Fairley gives a very good account of these matters but unfortunately includes very little precise identification of sources.

4 Otto Sverdrup, "The Second Norwegian Polar Expedition in the 'Fram,' 1898–1902," *Geographical Journal* 22, no. 1 (July 1903): 38–55; also P. Schei, "Summary of Geographical Results," *Geographical Journal* 22, no. 1 (July 1903): 56–65; also the subsequent discussion. *Geographical Journal* 22, no. 1 (July 1903): 65–69. The quoted passage is on 65.

5 Schei, "Summary of Geographical Results," 68–69. See also Fairley, *Sverdrup's Arctic Adventures*, 263–65.

6 Fairley, *Sverdrup's Arctic Adventures*, 274.

7 LAC, R10811-0-X-F, Wilfrid Laurier fonds, vol. 252, 70352–54.

8 Canada, Order in Council, PC no. 261M, 12 September 1904, and enclosures. Cox's letter is Enclosed No. 2.

9 A. P. Low, *Cruise of the Neptune 1903–04* (Ottawa: Government Printing Bureau, 1906), 48; LAC, R1681-0-8-E, Frederick Cook Papers, "Memos and Articles."

10 Joseph E. Bernier, *Cruise of the "Arctic": Report of the Dominion of Canada Government Expedition to the Arctic Islands and Hudson Strait on Board the D.G.S. Arctic* (Ottawa: Government Printing Bureau, 1910), 50.

11 Bernier, *Cruise of the "Arctic,"* 192.

12 Pascal Poirier's famous pronouncement in the Canadian Senate on 20 February 1907, specified some limits. Canada, Senate *Debates*, 20 February 1907, 271, Mr. Poirier, Senator.

13 Fairley, *Sverdrup's Arctic Adventures*, 277.

14 E.g., see LAC, MG 26 I, Arthur Meighen fonds, vol. 13, folder 7, 007393, Stefansson to Meighen, 30 October 1920: "It will be important to explore and occupy the Ringnes Islands and Heiberg Island. To Heiberg Island we have as yet no claim at all, for no British subject has ever set foot upon it."

15 E.g. see LAC, R2033-0-7-E, James Bernard Harkin fonds, Harkin "Memo re Northern Islands," p. 4a: "As these islands lie entirely to the west of the islands on which it is suggested mounted police stations should be established and as the Norwegians have not established or validated their claims by occupation and administration there would not appear to be any pressing necessity for action in regard to them for the present."

16 LAC, R2033-0-7-E, James Bernard Harkin Fonds, vol. I, folder January–March 1931, file 103, Harkin to Cory, 17 February 1921. "It is considered that when the Arctic makes her second trip in 1922 for the purpose of carrying supplies to the various police stations Mr. Stefansson should proceed on her to the head of one of the Fiords near Cape Sabine and then travel on to his main base, located by the advance party on Axel Heiberg Island."

17 E.g., LAC, R2033-0-7-E, James Bernard Harkin fonds, Harkin "Memo re Northern Islands," p. 4a: "However, it is suggested that the Mounted Police should gradually extend their administration acts to cover these areas."

18 Fairley, *Sverdrup's Arctic Adventures*, 278. I think Fairley is mistaken in suggesting (279) that Sverdrup was the main cause of Canadian activity in the North in 1903 and again in 1922. It was the US the first time, and Denmark and the US the second.

19 Fairley, *Sverdrup's Arctic Adventures*, 278.

20 LAC, Record Group 25, Department of External Affairs [hereafter RG 25], vol. 1386, file 1924-1339-C, Thomas to Governor General Byng, 29 October 1924.

21 LAC, RG 25, vol. 1386, file 1924-1339-C, Thomas to Governor General Byng, 29 October 1924.

22 LAC, RG 25, vol. 2667, file 9057-A-40 pt. 1, Steckmest to Secretary of State for External Affairs, 12 March 1925.

23 LAC, RG 25, vol. 2667, file 9057-A-40 pt. 1, Cory to Pope, 14 March 1925.

24 LAC, RG 25, vol. 4252, file 9057-40, pt. 1, O. S. Finnie, Director of the Northwest Territories and Yukon Branch of the Department of the Interior, to Cory, 16 April 1925.

25 Canada, Order in Council, PC no. 603, 23 April 1925. This was the Northern Advisory Board.

26 Canada, House of Commons *Debates*, 1 June 1925, 3773, Mr. Stewart, MP; Canada, House of Commons *Debates*, 10 June 1925, 4069, Mr. Stewart, MP.

27 It seems to me that Fairley goes too far in trying to relate American and Danish activities in the North to Norwegian and make a single, connected story. *Sverdrup's Arctic Adventures*, 279–85. The net effect is to convey the impression that the Norwegian aspect had a greater importance at the time than was actually the case. He is also in error in suggesting on p. 278 that during the years 1911–1922 Captain Bernier was the only one to show any concern on behalf of Canada about the Sverdrup Islands. It was Stefansson, much more than Bernier, who, especially in the post-war years, brought home to the Canadian government the weakness of Canada's position respecting the Sverdrup Islands and in the North generally.

28 These documents are in LAC, RG 25, vol. 4252, file 9057-40, pt. 1. A note of 13 June from Under Secretary of State Skelton to the Governor General's secretary says, "While Canada considers this island [i.e., Axel Heiberg] as being her territory, it is probably the area most open to question, though

open to question only from the Norwegian and not from the United States Government."

29 See in L. C. Clark, ed., *Documents on Canadian External Relations*, 1919–1925 (Ottawa: Department of External Affairs, 1970) [hereafter *DCER*], 3:577–78. Kellogg replied to this note on 19 June, and there was some further correspondence. *DCER*, 1919–1925, 578–81.

30 *DCER*, 1919–1925, 581. See also LAC, RG 25, vol. 4252, file 9057-40, pt. 1, Chilton to Anglin, 4 August 1925.

31 LAC, RG 25, vol. 4252, file 9057-40, pt. 1, Chilton to Anglin, 4 August 1925.

32 Fairley, *Sverdrup's Arctic Adventures*, 283.

33 LAC, RG 25, vol. 4252, file 9057-40, pt. 1, Chilton to Foreign Secretary Austen Chamberlain, 10 June 1925.

34 LAC, RG 25, vol. 4252, file 9057-40, pt. 1, Dr. Anderson to Dr. Skelton, 15 June 1925. *Editor's Note*: Hambro was one of the most influential foreign policy decision makers of the interwar period. See Patrick Salmon, *Scandinavia and the Great Powers, 1890-1940* (Cambridge: Cambridge University Press, 1997).

35 LAC, RG 25, vol. 4252, file 9057-40, pt. 1, Skelton to Anderson, 20 June 1925.

36 LAC, RG 25, vol. 2667, file 9057-A-40 pt. 1, Ludvig Aubert, Norwegian Consul General in Montreal, to the Secretary of State for External Affairs, 6 February 1926. Smith noted that suggestions were made that the "Norway Advisory Board" might consider the question at its next meeting and that a draft reply might be prepared, but although it was decided to act on these suggestions apparently no reply was sent. LAC, RG 25, vol. 2667, file 9057-A-40 pt. 1, Skelton to Finnie, 20 February 1926; LAC, RG 25, vol. 2667, file 9057-A-40 pt. 1, Finnie to Skelton, 25 February 1926; LAC, RG 25, vol. 2667, file 9057-A-40 pt. 1, Skelton to Finnie, 25 February 1926.

37 LAC, RG 25, vol. 2667, file 9057-A-40 pt. 1, Note by Mr. Ludwig Aubert.

38 LAC, RG 25, vol. 2667, file 9057-A-40 pt. 1, Acting Under Secretary of State of External Affairs to Consul General of Norway, 9 October 1926. Fairley says that on 2 June 1926, the Canadian government decided to ask the Norwegian government about its claim and the Canadian position was outlined to the Norwegians. The document or documents he mentioned are not in the files I have seen. Fairley, *Sverdrup's Arctic Adventures*, 285.

39 LAC, RG 25, vol. 2667, file 9057-A-40 pt. 1, Ludvig Aubert, Norwegian Consul General in Montreal, to the Secretary of State for External Affairs, 27 April 1927.

40 LAC, RG 25, vol. 2667, file 9057-A-40 pt. 1, Ludvig Aubert, Norwegian Consul General in Montreal, to the Secretary of State for External Affairs, 26 March 1928.

41 LAC, RG 25, vol. 2667, file 9057-A-40 pt. 1, Note from Leopold Amery, 29 June 1928.

42 LAC, RG 25, vol. 2667, file 9057-A-40 pt. 1, Skelton to Aubert, 18 August 1928.

43 Canada, House of Commons *Debates*, 1 June 1928, 3691, Mr. Aubert, MP (not 3867 as in Aubert's letter).

44 LAC, RG 25, vol. 2667, file 9057-A-40 pt. 1, Aubert to Skelton, 7 June 1928. Canada, Order in Council, PC no. 1170, 6 June 1919. This was Patterson's original appointment. Aubert referred to it as PC 1160. Canada, Order in Council, PC no. 1391, 10 June 1913. The long gap in time between Patterson's original appointment in 1910 and the continued provision of salary for him in 1928 is evident. In his remarks in the House of Commons on the date referred to (1 June 1928), the Hon. Pierre Cardin, Minister of Marine and Fisheries, mentioned only the numbers of the orders in council, and not the years when they were promulgated.

45 LAC, RG 25, vol. 2667, file 9057-A-40 pt. 1, Skelton to Aubert, 25 June 1928.

46 Fairley, *Sverdrup's Arctic Adventures*, 286.

47 Quoted in Fairley, *Sverdrup's Arctic Adventures*, 286.

48 Fairley, *Sverdrup's Arctic Adventures*, 287.

49 LAC, RG 25, vol. 2667, file 9057-A-40 pt. 1, Noxon to King, 3 April 1929.

50 LAC, RG 25, vol. 2667, file 9057-A-40 pt. 1, Nansen to King, 20 April 1929.

51 LAC, RG 25, vol. 2667, file 9057-A-40 pt. 1, Sverdrup to King, 22 April 1929.

52 LAC, RG 25, vol. 2667, file 9057-A-40 pt. 1. The addressee of this memo, which was written in Montreal is not here identified.

53 LAC, RG 25, vol. 2667, file 9057-A-40 pt. 1, Oslo to Bordewick, 22 May 1929.

54 LAC, RG 25, vol. 2667, file 9057-A-40 pt. 1, Unsigned memo to King, 3 June 1929.

55 LAC, RG 25, vol. 2667, file 9057-A-40 pt. 1, Bordewick to Skelton, 4 June 1929.

56 LAC, RG 25, vol. 2667, file 9057-A-40 pt. 1, Skelton to Bordewick, 5 June 1929.

57 LAC, RG 25, vol. 2667, file 9057-A-40 pt. 1, King to Bordewick, 6 June 1929.

58 LAC, RG 25, vol. 2667, file 9057-A-40 pt. 1, Skelton to Bordewick, 6 June 1929.

59 LAC, RG 25, vol. 2667, file 9057-A-40 pt. 1, Bordewick to Skelton, 13 September 1929.

60 LAC, RG 25, vol. 2667, file 9057-A-40 pt. 1, The date 23 September 1929 is stamped on the report.

61 Ibid.

62 LAC, RG 25, vol. 2667, file 9057-A-40 pt. 1, Canadian High Commissioner (London) to Secretary of State for external Affairs (Ottawa).

63 LAC, RG 25, vol. 2667, file 9057-A-40 pt. 1, Secretary of State for External Affairs to Canadian High Commissioner. The Northern Advisory Board had recommended a lump sum of $25,000 or an annuity of $2,400. (See preceding cable of 29 November.)

64 LAC, RG 25, vol. 2667, file 9057-A-40 pt. 1, High Commissioner for Canada to Secretary of State for External Affairs, 23 November 1929. See also articles in Canadian newspapers, e.g., *Ottawa Citizen, Toronto Globe, Vancouver Star, Edmonton Journal, Montreal Gazette* (21 November 1929), *Kingston Whig Standard* (23 November 1929).

65 LAC, RG 25, vol. 2667, file 9057-A-40 pt. 1. Evidently Skelton had tried to tie the British renunciation of claims to Bouvet Island with the Norwegian renunciation of claims to the Sverdrup Islands, and Bordewick pointed out that the matter of Bouvet Island had already been settled as an act of grace by Great Britain and without conditions. If Bordewick was correct in his assumption about Skelton's inclusion of Bouvet Island in the discussions, it would seem possible that Skelton had confused Bouvet with Jan Mayen. This would appear to be borne out by the contents of a letter written by R. H. Hadow at the British High Commissioner's office in Ottawa to Skelton on 3 January 1930 (LAC, RG 25, vol. 2667, file 9057-A-40 pt. 1).

66 LAC, RG 25, vol. 2667, file 9057-A-40 pt. 1, Hadow to Skelton, 7 January 1930.

67 LAC, RG 25, vol. 2667, file 9057-A-40 pt. 1, Skelton to Hadow, 7 January 1930; See also LAC, RG 25, vol. 2667, file 9057-A-40 pt. 1, External Affairs to Bordewick, 24 January 1930.

68 LAC, RG 25, vol. 2667, file 9057-A-40 pt. 1, Bordewick to Ferguson, 29 January 1930.

69 LAC, RG 25, vol. 2667, file 9057-A-40 pt. 1, Ferguson to King, 30 January 1930.

70 LAC, RG 25, vol. 2667, file 9057-A-40 pt. 1, King to Ferguson, 3 February 1930.

71 LAC, RG 25, vol. 2667, file 9057-A-40 pt. 1, Hadow to Skelton, 7 February 1930.

72 LAC, RG 25, vol. 2667, file 9057-A-40 pt. 1, Bordewick to External Affairs, 11 February 1930.

73 LAC, RG 25, vol. 2667, file 9057-A-40 pt. 1, External Affairs to Bordewick, 26 February 1930.

74 LAC, RG 25, vol. 2667, file 9057-A-40 pt. 1, Skelton to Hadow, 25 February 1930.

75 LAC, RG 25, vol. 2667, file 9057-A-40 pt. 1, Bordewick to External Affairs, 28 February 1930.

76 LAC, RG 25, vol. 2667, file 9057-A-40 pt. 1, Bordewick to External Affairs, 15 March 1930.

77 LAC, RG 25, vol. 2667, file 9057-A-40 pt. 1, External Affairs to Bordewick, 12 March 1930. See also the memo under Skelton's signature (14 May 1930) setting forth the item for the supplementary estimates.

78 LAC, RG 25, vol. 2667, file 9057-A-40 pt. 1, Bordewick to External Affairs, 30 April 1930.

79 Skelton to Hadow, 2 May 1930, Canada, Department of External Affairs, no. 9057-A-40C, part 1.

80 LAC, RG 25, vol. 2667, file 9057-A-40 pt. 1, Hadow to Skelton, 3 May 1930.

81 LAC, RG 25, vol. 2667, file 9057-A-40 pt. 1, British High Commissioner's office to External Affairs, 2 April 1930.

82 LAC, RG 25, vol. 2667, file 9057-A-40 pt. 1, Skelton to Hadow, 22 May 1930; see also LAC, RG 25, vol. 2667, file 9057-A-40 pt. 1, Finnie to Gibson, 25 April 1930.

83 Canada, Order in Council, PC No. 1371, 14 June 1930.

84 LAC, RG 25, vol. 2667, file 9057-A-40 pt. 1, Bordewick to Skelton, 2 July 1930.

85 LAC, RG 25, vol. 2667, file 9057-A-40 pt. 1, Hadow to Skelton, 2 July 1930, 11 July 1930, and 22 July 1930; also LAC, RG 25, vol. 2667, file 9057-A-40 pt. 1, C. Wingfield of British Legation, Oslo, to Foreign Secretary Arthur Henderson, 11 June, 24 June 1930.

86 LAC, RG 25, vol. 2667, file 9057-A-40 pt. 2, Gibson to Skelton, 8 August 1930.

87 LAC, RG 25, vol. 2667, file 9057-A-40 pt. 2, Hadow to Skelton, 6 August 1930.

88 LAC, RG 25, vol. 2667, file 9057-A-40 pt. 2, Norwegian Chargé d'Affaires Daniel Steen (London) to Henderson, 8 August 1930.

89 LAC, RG 25, vol. 2667, file 9057-A-40 pt. 2, Skelton to Hadow, 14 August 1930. Evidently part of the trouble was caused by a failure of the Norwegian government to consult the British minister in Oslo regarding the terms of the required notes. See LAC, RG 25, vol. 2667, file 9057-A-40 pt. 2, Hadow to Skelton, 11 August 1930. See also LAC, RG 25, vol. 2667, file 9057-A-40 pt. 2, for minutes of a special session of the NWT Council on 19 August 1930, which recommended that Dr. Skelton should draft an official communication pointing out that the former government (i.e., that of Mackenzie King) had authorized the payment only on condition that Norway would completely relinquish her claim, and that the game regulations would not permit anyone, even a Canadian, to hunt and trap in the area.

90 LAC, RG 25, vol. 2667, file 9057-A-40 pt. 1, Hadow to Skelton, 14 August 1930.

91 LAC, RG 25, vol. 2667, file 9057-A-40 pt. 1, Hadow to Skelton, 15 September 1930, passing on this Norwegian suggestion.

92 LAC, RG 25, vol. 2667, file 9057-A-40 pt. 1, Skelton to Liesching at British High Commissioner's office, 2 September 1930, referring to press dispatches. See *New York Times*, 23 August 1930.

93 E.g. LAC, RG 25, vol. 2667, file 9057-A-40 pt. 2, Skelton to Bordewick, 24 September 1930, by cable.

94 LAC, RG 25, vol. 2667, file 9057-A-40 pt. 2, Skelton to British minister in Oslo, 27 September 1930.

95 LAC, RG 25, vol. 2667, file 9057-A-40 pt. 2, Skelton to Bordewick. 14 October 1930.

96 LAC, RG 25, vol. 2667, file 9057-A-40 pt. 2, Bordewick to External Affairs, 15 October 1930.

97 LAC, RG 25, vol. 2667, file 9057-A-40 pt. 2, External Affairs to Bordewick, 16 October 1930.

98 LAC, RG 25, vol. 2667, file 9057-A-40 pt. 2, Bordewick to External Affairs, 17 October 1930. See, however, LAC, RG 25, vol. 2667, file 9057-A-40 pt. 2, Finnie to Skelton, 17 October 1930: "To tell us at this late date, after negotiations had practically been closed, that he has no such maps or records, is an extraordinary and surprising turn in the affair."

99 LAC, RG 25, vol. 2667, file 9057-A-40 pt. 2, External Affairs to Bordewick, 24 October 1930.

100 These four documents may be seen in Dominion of Canada, Treaty Series (1930), no. 17.

101 See in LAC, RG 25, vol. 2667, file 9057-A-40 pt. 2: Skelton had suggested a form of receipt for Sverdrup to use, and Sverdrup followed it precisely. See LAC, RG 25, vol. 2667, file 9057-A-40 pt. 2, Skelton to Hadow, 14 October 1930. Sverdrup had authorized Alexander Nansen of Oslo, the brother of Fridtjof, to act for him in receiving and acknowledging the payment, hence Nansen's signature. LAC, RG 25, vol. 2667, file 9057-A-40 pt. 2, Typewritten note signed by Sverdrup, 16 October 1930.

102 See LAC, RG 25, vol. 2667, file 9057-A-40 pt. 2, Hadow to Skelton, 8 November 1930, regarding synchronization of announcements. There appears to be some doubt as to when the money was actually paid to Sverdrup. According to British documents it was on November 12 (e.g., LAC, RG 25, vol. 2667, file 9057-A-40 pt. 2, British chargé d'affaires at Oslo to Skelton, 2 November 1930); but according to Bordewick it was on 5 November (LAC, RG 25, vol. 2667, file 9057-A-40 pt. 2, Bordewick to Skelton, 19 December 1930).

103 See copies in LAC, RG 25, vol. 2667, file 9057-A-40 pt. 2. Also comment in Fairley, *Sverdrup's Arctic Adventures*, 289–90.

104 LAC, RG 25, vol. 2667, file 9057-A-40 pt. 2, Bordewick to Skelton, 19 December 1930. See also LAC, RG 25, vol. 2667, file 9057-A-40 pt. 2, Bordewick to Skelton, 26 November 1930, by cable: "Commander Otto Sverdrup died this morning."

105 LAC, RG 25, vol. 2667, file 9057-A-40 pt. 2, Bordewick to Skelton, 20 April 1932; acknowledgement of receipt by Alex Nanses, 9 August 1932. See also LAC, RG 85, vol. 584, file 571, pt. 7, for additional information about the diaries and other matters. At a meeting in the Northern Advisory Board on 22 January 1931, it was agreed that the thirteen volumes of diaries Sverdrup had provided should not be only photostatted but also translated. On 27 March 1931, the head translator, Mr. Sylvain, told Finnie that for economy reasons the translation could not be done, and on 2 April he protested to Gibson that the job would take nine to ten months and cost $2400. Nevertheless on 9 April Deputy Minister Rowatt told Finnie to proceed with the translation. On 8 May 1932, Rowatt informed Minister of the Interior T. G. Murphy that the photostatting was finished and the translation partly done, and recommended that the originals be returned to Mrs. Sverdrup. It does not appear that the translation was ever finished; at any rate there seems to be no trace of it.

106 LAC, RG 25, vol. 2667, file 9057-A-40 pt. 2, External Affairs to Bordewick, 12 November 1930.

107 In the Eastern Greenland Case it was categorically denied in the Norwegian Rejoinder that Norway had ever made any claim to the islands. See Permanent Court of International Justice, *Legal Status of Eastern Greenland*, "Duplique du Gouvernement Norvégien," series C, no. 63, 1416: "Le Gouvernement norvégien n'a jamais émis la moindre prétention à la soverainté sur ces iles.... Elles appartenaient indubitablement au Canada lorsque la déclaration norvégienne fut donnée." See also the comment by Danish counsel M. Steglich-Peterson in Permanent Court of International Justice, *Legal Status of Eastern Greenland* no. 66, 2760–61: "The Norwegian Rejoinder, on page 1416, states that with regard to Canada it was only a question of an already existing state of law." Steglich-Peterson was trying to establish that it was "utterly absurd for the Norwegian Rejoinder to maintain that in this case with Canada there was an existing status to recognize any more than in the case of Denmark with regard to the whole of Greenland."

108 LAC, RG 25, vol. 2667, file 9057-A-40 pt. 2, Bordewick to Canadian government, 12 July 1946; LAC, RG 25, vol. 2667, file 9057-A-40 pt. 2, Bordewick to Under Secretary of State for Foreign Affairs, 9 August 1946.

109 LAC, RG 25, vol. 2667, file 9057-A-40 pt. 2, Acting Under Secretary of State for External Affairs H. H. Wrong to Bordewick, 23 July 1946; LAC, RG 25, vol. 2667, file 9057-A-40 pt. 2, Acting Under Secretary of State for External Affairs H. H. Wrong to Bordewick, 26 August 1946.

13 | The Eastern Greenland Case and its Implications

Editor's note: Smith undertook a detailed historical analysis of the case, which is beyond the scope of this particular volume on Canadian sovereignty. Accordingly, his background notes will be posted on a website.

1 Permanent Court of International Justice, Series A/B, *Legal Status of Eastern Greenland Judgements, Orders and Advisory Opinions*, Fascicule No. 53 (5 April 1933), 19–147. See also Series C, *Pleadings, Oral Statements and Documents*, No. 62–67.

2 For a good brief treatment of the history of Greenland after the European discovery, see Permanent Court of International Justice, Fascicule No. 53, 26. There is a very extensive literature on this subject. See, for example, Vilhjalmur Stefansson, *Greenland* (New York: Doubleday, Doran, 1943). For a brief but reasonable comprehensive treatment of the Norwegian-Danish dispute and the judgment of 1933, see O. Svarlien, *The Eastern Greenland Case in Historical Perspective* (Gainsvillle: University of Florida Press, 1964). For the Norwegian background, and also the settlement of Iceland and Greenland, see K. Gjerset, *History of the Norwegian People*, vol. I (New York: Macmillan, 1915), 137–42, 197–204. See also Frede Castberg, "Le conflit entre le Danemark et la Norvège concernant le Groenland," *Revue de droit international et de législation comparée*, 3e série, vol. V (1924): 252–67; F. Castberg, "L'accord sur le Groenland oriental entre le Danemark et la Norvège, " *Revue générale de droit international public* XXXII (1925): 163–93; Gustav Rasmussen, "L'accord dano-norvégien sur le Groenland oriental et son historique," Revue *de droit international et de législation comparée*, 3e série, vol. VIII (1927): 293–321, 656–96; Jens Bull, " La question de la soveraineté sur le Groenland oriental," *Revue de droit international et de législation comparée*, 3e série, vol. X (1929): 572–605.

3 See *Meddelelser om Gronland*, e.g., vols. VI, IX, XVII, XXVII, XXVIII for details of these expeditions, and for a brief summary, Gustav Smedal, *The Acquisition of Sovereignty over Polar Areas* (Oslo: Jacob Dybwal, 1931), 82.

4 Permanent Court of International Justice, *Legal Status of Eastern Greenland*, Fascicule No. 53, 33. See also Library and Archives Canada [hereafter LAC], Record Group 25, Department of External Affairs [hereafter RG 25], vol. 4254, file 9057-40 pt.1, Knud Rasmussen to O. D. Skelton, 5 May 1925. "I establish in the year 1910 together with Mr. N. Nyeboe the Cape York Station Thule in North Star Bay, Woldenholme [*sic*] Sound." According to Rasmussen both he and the Danish Government considered that he was operating in a No Man's Land. A little further on he says, "However, it happened about 1910 that the Eskimos, who lived without the protection of any country, got into a critical position.... I therefore drew the above matter to the attention of the Danish Government and proposed the establishment of a trade station in the Cape York District for the Natives. However, I received an answer to the effect that the land being considered No Man's Land the Danish Government, which had monopoly of the rest of Greenland, did not see its way to establish a station there, as such an act could not be covered by the above mentioned monopoly. The establishment within this district would therefore have to be left to a private initiative. This was the basis

for the establishment of The Cape York Station Thule.'"

5 Svarlien, *The Eastern Greenland Case in Historical Perspective*, 23–25; Smedal, *The Acquisition of Sovereignty over Polar Areas*, 100–128. For Nansen's expedition see F. Nansen, *The First Crossing of Greenland* (London: Longmans, Green, 1896). For a good summary of Danish, Norwegian, and other exploration in Greenland up to 1931, see Skeie, *Greenland: The Dispute Between Norway and Denmark* (London: J. M. Dent and Sons, 1932), 35–44. This little book presents essentially the Norwegian view of the dispute. For a strong counter-expression of the Danish view, see K. Berlin, *Denmark's Right to Greenland* (London: Oxford University Press, 1932).

6 Svarlien, *The Eastern Greenland Case in Historical Perspective*, 40; U.S. Treaty Series, No. 629, 14. For example, while she was carrying on negotiations in 1915 for the cession of her West Indian islands to the United States, the question of Danish sovereignty over Greenland was brought up. When the treaty was signed on 4 August 1916, Secretary Lansing declared in an appendix that the US "will not object to the Danish Government extending their political and economic interests to the whole of Greenland." A conspicuous feature of the Danish request and the American response is that both spoke of an extension of Danish sovereignty to the whole of Greenland. Precisely what meaning was intended in each document is perhaps a bit uncertain, but taken quite literally both obviously suggest that at the time the two parties both took the view that Denmark did not have sovereignty over all Greenland, and that an extension of her sovereignty would be necessary before she did. At any rate this was the attitude taken by a number of writers (e.g., Smedal, *The Acquisition of Sovereignty over Polar Areas*, 83; Lawrence Preuss, "The Dispute Between Denmark and Norway over the Sovereignty of East Greenland," *American Journal of International Law* 26, no. 3 [1932]: 474), naturally including those who took Norway's side on the controversy that developed, and it also became the official position of the Norwegian government. On the other hand some pro-Danish writers, and also the Danish government itself, held that the real implication was simply a renewed recognition, or reconfirmation, of Danish sovereignty over all Greenland. This later became one of the main points argued before the Permanent Court of International Justice.

7 LAC, RG 25, vol. 1343, file 1923-138 pt. 1, Colonial Secretary Milner to Governor General Devonshire, 10 September 1919. See also Colonial Office (CO), Dominions No. 79, Greenland, 1 May 1921.

8 LAC, RG 25, vol. 1343, file 1923-138 pt. 1; also CO, Dominions No. 79, Foreign Office to Grevenkop-Castenskiold, 11 December 1919.

9 LAC, RG 25, vol. 1343, file 1923-138 pt. 1; also CO, Dominions No. 79, Danish minister to Foreign Secretary Lord Curzon, 16 March 1920. See also Permanent Court of International Justice, *Legal Status of Eastern Greenland*, 1821–1824. The requests to these states were made in writing, in each case asking for recognition of Danish sovereignty "over the whole of Greenland" or "sur tout le Groenland." However, an accompanying memorandum contained what could hardly be taken other than as an admission that Danish occupation of Greenland was not complete, and that an extension would be necessary to make it so:

> Danish explorers have visited practically the whole of uninhabited Greenland and made maps of the country, but no formal occupation of the whole of Greenland has actually taken place. In view of Danish sentiments in this matter as well as interests of the Esquimaux population, it would be desirable if the Danish Government could extend its activities by proclaiming its sovereignty over the entire territory of Greenland.

Each note suggested that recognition might take the same form as that granted by the United States in 1916. Permanent Court of International Justice, *Legal Status of Eastern Greenland*, c. 64, 1825–1826.

10 The main point that emerges upon comparing the four notes of recognition is that while the French and Japanese were willing to accept an extension of Danish sovereignty over all Greenland, the Italian and British were willing to recognize Danish sovereignty over all Greenland, without mention of any extension.

11 Permanent Court of International Justice, *Legal Status of Eastern Greenland*, 2163–2164. Text in Danish, with French translation. For an English translation, see *British and Foreign State Papers* (1921), vol. CXIV, 720.

12 Permanent Court of International Justice, *Legal Status of Eastern Greenland*, 1586.

13 Permanent Court of International Justice, *Legal Status of Eastern Greenland*, 1589–1592. Kruse to Raestad, 19 December 1920. See LAC, RG 25, vol.

1343, file 1923-138 pt. 1, for copies of informative reports to London on these matters from the British legations in Christiania and Copenhagen.

14 For comments on these fundamental differences of opinion, see Preuss, "Dispute Between Denmark and Norway," 476–78; G. Smedal, *The Acquisition of Sovereignty over Polar Areas*, 77–100; Svarlien, *The Eastern Greenland Case in Historical Perspective*, 31–37.

15 Permanent Court of International Justice, *Legal Status of Eastern Greenland*, 1541–1545. For English translation see *British and Foreign State Papers* (1925), vol. CXXII, 364–78, arts. 1, 21, 45.

16 Permanent Court of International Justice, *Legal Status of Eastern Greenland*, 1618–1619.

17 Smedal, *The Acquisition of Sovereignty over Polar Areas*, 100–128.

18 Permanent Court of International Justice, *Legal Status of Eastern Greenland*, 1622–1623. Danish Ambassador Oldenburg to Norwegian Foreign Minister Mowinckel, 20 December 1930.

19 Permanent Court of International Justice, *Legal Status of Eastern Greenland*, 1623. Mowinckel to Oldenburg, 6 January 1931.

20 Permanent Court of International Justice, *Legal Status of Eastern Greenland*, 1626–1627. Danish Legation to Norwegian Department of Foreign Affairs, 14 March 1931.

21 Permanent Court of International Justice, *Legal Status of Eastern Greenland*, 1631. Danish Legation to Norwegian Department of Foreign Affairs, 13 June 1931.

22 Permanent Court of International Justice, *Legal Status of Eastern Greenland*, 1634–1635. Norwegian Department of Foreign Affairs to Danish Legation, 30 June 1931.

23 The Danes suggested that if agreement were impossible the question should be submitted to a commission of conciliation or to the Permanent Court of International Justice. The Norwegian government agreed that the question should be submitted to the court; but it asked also that Denmark would not oppose acquisition of sovereignty by Norway over any Eastern Greenland territories which the court might find were not already Danish, but that the court's decision should be based on the factual and legal situation as of 1 July 1931. The Danish government declined to concede these two points. Permanent Court of International Justice, *Legal Status of Eastern Greenland*, 1635–1641, Danish Legation to Norwegian Department of Foreign Affairs, 3 July 1931; Norwegian Department of Foreign Affairs to Danish Legation, 7 July 1931; and Danish Legation to Norwegian Department of Foreign Affairs, 10 July 1931.

24 Permanent Court of International Justice, *Legal Status of Eastern Greenland*, 1623–1625, Norwegian Ambassador Huitfeldt to Danish Foreign Minister Munch, 20 February 1931. The Danish government replied in rather conciliatory fashion on 11 March, pointing out, however, that under the convention Norwegian establishments in the area in question could serve only as dwellings or depots, and not as evidence of taking possession. Permanent Court of International Justice, *Legal Status of Eastern Greenland*, 1625–1626, Munch to Huitfeldt, 11 March 1931.

25 Permanent Court of International Justice, *Legal Status of Eastern Greenland*, 89; Fascicule No. 53, 42.

26 Permanent Court of International Justice, *Legal Status of Eastern Greenland*, 1641; Fascicule No. 53, 43; c. 62, 170.

27 Permanent Court of International Justice, *Legal Status of Eastern Greenland*, c. 64, 1641–1642. Danish Legation to Norwegian Department of Foreign Affairs, 11 July 1931. The text of the Danish application may be seen in M. O. Hudson, *World Court Reports* vols. I–IV (Washington: Carnegie Endowment for International Peace, 1934–1943), 149–50.

28 The Statute of the Permanent Court of International Justice, and the Danish and Norwegian notes of acceptance of the "optional clause," may be seen in Hudson, *World Court Reports*, vol. 1, 17–26, 34, 41.

29 Most of these details are given in the case itself, esp. Fascicule No. 53, 22–26; c. 66, 2592–617. See also Hudson, *World Court Reports*, vol. II, 148–54; O. Svarlien, *The Eastern Greenland Case in Historical Perspective*, 40–41.

30 Permanent Court of International Justice, *Legal Status of Eastern Greenland*, Fascicule No. 53, 44–45. The written arguments are in Permanent Court of International Justice, *Legal Status of Eastern Greenland*, c. 62, c. 63; the oral arguments are in c. 66, c. 67. The supporting documents for the two cases are in c. 64, c. 65.

31 Permanent Court of International Justice, *Legal Status of Eastern Greenland*, Fascicule No. 53, 45.

32 Permanent Court of International Justice, *Legal Status of Eastern Greenland*, Fascicule No. 53, 45–46.

33 Permanent Court of International Justice, *Legal Status of Eastern Greenland*, Fascicule No. 53, 46.

34 Permanent Court of International Justice, *Legal Status of Eastern Greenland*, Fascicule No. 53, 46–48.

35 Permanent Court of International Justice, *Legal Status of Eastern Greenland*, Fascicule No. 53, 50–51.

36 Permanent Court of International Justice, *Legal Status of Eastern Greenland*, Fascicule No. 53, 51.

37 Permanent Court of International Justice, *Legal Status of Eastern Greenland*, Fascicule No. 53, 51–54.

38 Permanent Court of International Justice, *Legal Status of Eastern Greenland*, Fascicule No. 53, 55.

39 Permanent Court of International Justice, *Legal Status of Eastern Greenland*, Fascicule No. 53, 59, 61, 64.

40 Hudson, *World Court Reports*, vol. III, 148.

41 *British and Foreign State Papers* (1884–85), vol. LXXVI, 4–20. An English translation is given in *American Journal of International Law*, Supplement, vol. III, no. 1 (Jan. 1909): 7–25. See arts. 34, 35.

42 G. H. Hackworth, *Digest of International Law*, vol. 1 (Washington: U.S. Government Printing Office, 1940), 468–70.

43 C. C. Hyde, "The Case Concerning the Legal Status of Eastern Greenland," *American Journal of International Law* 27, no. 4 (Oct. 1933): 736–37.

44 See the relevant comment by Lord Asquith of Bishopstone in his award "In the Matter of an Arbitration Between Petroleum Development (Trucial Coast) Ltd. And the Sheikk of Abu Dhabi," published in *International and Comparative Law Quarterly* 1, pt. 2 (April 1952): 247–61, at 257: "The doctrine that occupation is vital in the case of a res nullius has in any case worn thin since the East Greenland Arbitration and more especially since that relating to Clipperton Island."

14 | American Explorers in the Canadian Arctic

1 See, for example, Library and Archives Canada [hereafter LAC], Record Group 25, Department of External Affairs [hereafter RG 25], vol. 2668, file 9058-40, "MacMillan's Arctic Expedition," Col. Wilfrid Bovey to Maj. Gen. J. H. MacBrien, 25 January 1927: "MacMillan himself was born in Canada in the Province of Nova Scotia.... and became an American citizen." See also LAC, RG 25, vol. 2668, file 9058-40, Gov. Gen. Byng to Sir Esme Howard, 4 June 1925: "Dr. MacMillan, a Newfoundlander by birth...."

2 Everett S. Allen, *Arctic Odyssey: The Life of Rear Admiral Donald B. MacMillan* (New York: Dodd, Mead, 1926), 3.

3 Canada, *Report of the Royal Commission to Investigate the Possibilities of the Reindeer and Musk-Ox Industries in the Arctic and Sub-Arctic Regions of Canada* (Ottawa: King's Printer, 1922), Transcript of Evidence, 498, 500.

4 LAC, R1644-0-7-E, John D. Craig fonds, vol. 1, folder 3; see also in LAC, RG 25, vol. 4252, file 9057-40, pt. 1.

5 LAC, R2033-0-7-E, James Bernard Harkin fonds, vol. I, folder Nov.–Dec. 1920.

6 LAC, R1644-0-7-E, John D. Craig fonds, vol. 1; LAC, R2033-0-7-E, James Bernard Harkin fonds, vol. I, folder no. 86, Jan.–Mar. 1921.

7 LAC, R1644-0-7-E, John D. Craig fonds, vol. 1, folder 1, Gibson to Pope, 14 January 1921; LAC, R1644-0-7-E, John D. Craig fonds, vol. 1, folder 1, Pope to Gibson, 15 January 1921. Pope wrote to the High Commissioner's Office in London on 15 January, and a reply was sent back to him on 2 March, enclosing a letter from the Royal Geographic Society, dated 19 February, gave some information about the expeditions of the Danes Rasmussen and Koch, but regarding MacMillan's said only that news about it was " not quite so easy to obtain." LAC, Record Group 85, Northern Affairs Program [hereafter RG 85], vol. 584, file 573 pt. 1, Griffith to Pope, 2 March 1921; LAC, RG 85, vol. 584, file 573 pt. 1, Secretary Hinks of Royal Geographical Society to Under Secretary of State Office, 19 February 1921.

8 LAC, RG 25, vol. 2668, file 9058-40, Pope to Mahoney, 22 February 1921; LAC, RG 25, vol. 2668, file 9058-40, "MacMillan's Arctic Expedition," Mahoney to Pope, 7 March 1921, and 9 March 1921, with enclosures.

9 E.g., LAC, R2033-0-7-E, James Bernard Harkin fonds, vol. 1, folder Jan.–Mar. 1921, Harkin to Stefansson, 21 January 1921.

10 E.g., LAC, R2033-0-7-E, James Bernard Harkin fonds, vol. 1, folder Jan.–Mar. 1921, Harkin to Cory, 2 March 1921, and 15 March 1921.

11 There is on record a letter in which Stefansson wrote to Harkin on 21 January 1921, inquiring anxiously if the Canadian government would discourage MacMillan's expedition, and whether

the lease to his Hudson's Bay Reindeer Company would enable the company to protect the caribou on Baffin Island. LAC, RG 85, vol. 582, file 565.

12 LAC, RG 25, vol. 2668, file 9058-40, "MacMillan's Arctic Expedition," Cory to Pope, 21 June 1921.

13 LAC, RG 25, vol. 2668, file 9058-40, "MacMillan's Arctic Expedition," Pope to Mahoney, 23 June 1921.

14 LAC, RG 25, vol. 2668, file 9058-40, "MacMillan's Arctic Expedition," Mahoney to Pope, 15 July 1921. For an account of MacMillan's expeditions during this period, see Allen, *Arctic Odyssey*, 219ff., also 31ff.

15 LAC, R2033-0-7-E, James Bernard Harkin fonds, vol. I, folder May–Dec. 1921. See also A. E. Millward, *Southern Baffin Island, Report issued by the Department of the Interior* (Ottawa: King's Printer, 1930), 43: "In accordance with Canadian Government regulations Dr. MacMillan applied for a permit, from the Department of the Interior, to undertake certain scientific and ornithological researches in the northern regions. This permit was duly issued, and Dr. MacMillan also paid the necessary fee for a Non-Resident, Non-British Hunting and Trapping license, for five of his men and himself." See also LAC, RG 85, vol. 350, file 203, J. D. Craig's Diary of the 1922 Arctic Expedition, Entry for 5 September 1922: "Captain Munn before leaving stated that according to his estimate the trade done by the ostensible scientific parties under MacMillan and Rasmussen had decreased his year's receipts by not less than three or four thousand dollars. MacMillan is known to have procured trapping and trading licenses costing him in the neighborhood of one thousand dollars and so possibly may be aid to have paid his way; so far as is known, however, Rasmussen has no licenses although Sergeant Joy will collect fees from him if he appears here next year as he promises to."

16 LAC, RG 25, vol. 2668, file 9058-40, "MacMillan's Arctic Expedition," Cory to Pope, 29 July 1921.

17 LAC, RG 25, vol. 2668, file 9058-40, "MacMillan's Arctic Expedition," Mahoney to Walker, 28 September 1921.

18 LAC, RG 25, vol. 2668, file 9058-40, "MacMillan's Arctic Expedition," Bernier to Meighen, 29 July 1921.

19 LAC, RG 25, vol. 2668, file 9058-40, "MacMillan's Arctic Expedition," Finnie to MacMillan, 16 June 1923. MacMillan's expedition was also mentioned in the House of Commons by Minister of the Interior Stewart, who said that the government was anxious to establish a police post at Cape Sabine on the Ellesmere Island coast just across the strait from Greenland, "because Captain MacMillan [*sic*] proposed wintering there with an American expedition ... and we are somewhat fearful of claims being set up to these northern islands." Canada, House of Commons *Debates*, 14 June 1923, 3944. See also LAC, RG 85, vol. 668, file 4107, Craig to Logan, 16 November 1923: speaking of a radio communication by MacMillan: "He says he is at Refuge Harbour, which is on the Greenland side a little north of Cape Sabine, I have no doubt that he or his party will be hunting in Canadian Territory during the winter and I only hope that our boys at Craig Harbour will have an opportunity of checking him up before he leaves for the south."

20 LAC, RG 25, vol. 2668, file 9058-40, "MacMillan's Arctic Expedition," Finnie to MacMillan, 22 October 1924.

21 LAC, RG 25, vol. 2668, file 9058-40, "MacMillan's Arctic Expedition," MacMillan to Finnie, 27 October 1924.

22 LAC, RG 25, vol. 2668, file 9058-40, "MacMillan's Arctic Expedition," Finnie to MacMillan, 4 November 1924.

23 See LAC, RG 25, vol. 2668, file 9058-D-40C, "Arctic Flight of Airship 'Shenandoh' – Proposals."

24 The clipping may be seen in LAC, RG 25, vol. 2668, file 9058-D-40C, "Arctic Flight of Airship 'Shenandoh' – Proposals."

25 LAC, RG 25, vol. 2668, file 9058-D-40C, "Arctic Flight of Airship 'Shenandoh' – Proposals," Cory to Pope, 7 December 1923.

26 LAC, RG 25, vol. 2668, file 9058-D-40C, "Arctic Flight of Airship 'Shenandoh' – Proposals," Stefansson to King, 2 January 1924.

27 LAC, RG 25, vol. 2668, file 9058-D-40C, "Arctic Flight of Airship 'Shenandoh' – Proposals," F. A. McGregor to Stefansson, 5 January 1924.

28 As quoted in Cf. Gustav Smedal, *Skrifter om Svalbard og Ishavet*, trans. C. Meyer as *Acquisition of Sovereignty over Polar Areas* (Oslo: J. Dybwad, 1931), 68. See also remarks in *Cong. Rec.*, 68th Cong., 1st sess., 1924, 1086; *Cong. Rec.*, 68th Cong., 1st sess., 1924, 1190–91; *Cong. Rec.*, 68th Cong., 1st sess., 1924, 1816–19. Senator Dill roundly condemned the project; Representative Rogers of Massachusetts praised it.

29 E.g., see *Washington Herald*, 20 January 1924.

30 LAC, RG 25, vol. 2668, file 9058-D-40C, "Arctic Flight of Airship 'Shenandoh' – Proposals."

31 LAC, RG 25, vol. 2668, file 9058-D-40C, "Arctic Flight of Airship 'Shenandoh' – Proposals," H. W. Brooks to MacDonald, 24 January 1924; LAC, RG 25, vol. 2668, file 9058-D-40C, "Arctic Flight of Airship 'Shenandoh' – Proposals," H. W. Brooks to Byng, 26 January 1924.

32 *New York Times*, 6 February 1924.

33 *Washington Post*, 13 February 1924.

34 *Washington Herald*, 15 February 1924.

35 See Washington press dispatches, e.g., *Washington Post*, 16 February 1924, where the official statement is given. See also the discussion of the subject in E. Plischke's *Jurisdiction in the Polar Regions* (PhD diss., Clark University, 1943), 375–77, where the author rejects the idea that the American inclination to claim any land discovered north of Alaska was based upon the sector principle. V. Lakhtine, "Rights over the Arctic," *American Journal of International Law* 24 no. 4 (Oct. 1930): 706–7, is obviously mistaken in trying to relate the Shenandoah episode to an alleged American relinquishment of "claims" in the Canadian sector and acknowledgement of Canadian rights there.

36 LAC, RG 25, vol. 2668, file 9058-D-40C, "Arctic Flight of Airship 'Shenandoh' – Proposals," Mahoney to Pope, 16 February 1924.

37 *Foreign Relations of the United States* (1924), 2:518–20, Secretary Hughes to the Norwegian Minister, H. H. Byne, 2 April 1924.

38 Secretary Hughes to A. W. Prescott, 13 May 1924, Department of State, file 811.014/101 quoted in Green Haywood Hackworth, *Digest of International Law*, vol. 1 (Washington: US Government Printing Office, 1940), 399. On 3 March 1938, by executive order, President Roosevelt claimed for the United States the Central Pacific islets of Canton and Enderbury, which although claimed previously by Great Britain, were thought to have been discovered by American whalers. Commenting on State and Navy Department efforts to verify these discoveries, B. D. Hulen wrote in *The New York Times* on 6 March 1938, "This implies that the State Department had rejected the thesis informally put forward by Charles Evans Hughes when Secretary of State that discovery alone was not sufficient to lay a basis for a claim of sovereignty but that discovery had to be followed by occupation."

39 LAC, RG 25, vol. 2668, file 9058-40, "MacMillan's Arctic Expedition," Finnie to MacMillan, 14 January 1925.

40 See clipping in LAC, RG 25, vol. 2668, file 9058-40, "MacMillan's Arctic Expedition."

41 LAC, RG 25, vol. 2668, file 9058-40, "MacMillan's Arctic Expedition," Finnie to Cory, 16 April 1925.

42 LAC, RG 25, vol. 2668, file 9058-40, "MacMillan's Arctic Expedition," Finnie to R. A. Gibson, 20 April 1925. See also LAC, RG 85, vol. 668, file 4107, Finnie to Logan, 23 April 1925: "We have not been advised officially by the United States of this expedition."

43 Canada, Order in Council, PC No. 603, 23 April 1925.

44 LAC, RG 25, vol. 2668, file 9058-40, "MacMillan's Arctic Expedition," Finnie to Skelton, 27 April 1925; LAC, RG 25, vol. 2668, file 9058-40, "MacMillan's Arctic Expedition," Skelton to W. W. Cory, 27 April 1925.

45 LAC, RG 25, vol. 2668, file 9058-40, "MacMillan's Arctic Expedition," MacMillan to Harkin, 28 April 1925.

46 LAC, RG 25, vol. 2668, file 9058-40, "MacMillan's Arctic Expedition," Skelton to Harkin, 6 May 1925. In MacMillan's letter the word "Etah" had mistakenly been replaced by "Utah."

47 LAC, RG 25, vol. 2668, file 9058-40, "MacMillan's Arctic Expedition," Finnie to Desbarats, 20 May 1925.

48 See the memo in LAC, RG 25, vol. 4252, file 9057-40, pt. 1, accompanied by a letter from White to Skelton, 25 May 1925, in which he refers to it as "my memo." The memo, fourteen pages in length, was a rather superficial rehash of familiar arguments for Canadian sovereignty in the North.

49 Canada, Order in Council, PC No. 887, 5 June 1925.

50 LAC, RG 25, vol. 2668, file 9058-40, "MacMillan's Arctic Expedition," Byng to Sir Esme Howard, two letters, 4 June 1925.

51 LAC, RG 25, vol. 2668, file 9058-40, "MacMillan's Arctic Expedition," Finnie to Skelton, 23 May 1925.

52 Canada, House of Commons *Debates*, 1 June 1925, 3772–73 (Mr. Stewart, MP and Mr. Brown, MP). See also Canada, House of Commons *Debates*, 27 May 1925, 3593–94 (Mr. Stewart, MP), for earlier remarks by Stewart when introducing the bill.

53 *Washington Star*, 2 June 1925.

54 *Washington Post*, 3 June 1925.

55 *Washington Star*, 4 June 1925. It would appear that the Star had obtained some advanced information,

and some of it, e.g., the formal note by Stewart, may not have been strictly accurate.

56 *Washington Star*, 7 June 1925.

57 *Washington Post*, 9 June 1925.

58 LAC, RG 25, vol. 4252, file 9057-40, pt. 1, Chilton to Chamberlain, 10 June 1925. In this letter Chilton denied that Cory had, as reported in the American press, gone to Washington expressly to discuss the question of sovereignty over any lands MacMillan might discover.

59 Canada, House of Commons *Debates*, 10 June 1925, 4069. See also remarks on 4083, 4084, and 4086. If the dispatch Stewart referred to was the one sent on or about 4 June, the "considerably time ago" was only about six days.

60 In a memo to Skelton on 10 June, Finnie enclosed "a draft statement for the Press purporting to come from the Honourable Charles Stewart," and said that it was to be discussed at a meeting of the Northern Advisory Board on June 11. LAC, RG 25, vol. 4252, file 9057-40, pt. 1, Finnie to Skelton, 10 June 1925.

61 See report in LAC, RG 25, vol. 4252, file 9057-40, pt. 1.

62 LAC, RG 25, vol. 4252, file 9057-40, pt. 1, Byng to Chilton, 12 June 1925.

63 *Washington Star*, 12 June 1925.

64 LAC, RG 25, vol. 4252, file 9057-40, pt. 1, Chilton to Byng, 12 June 1925. On 12 June the *Windsor Star* published a news item emanating from London on the same day as follows: "Great Britain will assist in preparing Canada's claim to Arctic territory and make any representations decided on, if the controversy between and the U.S. develops, it was understood here today, Officials were wary of commenting before knowing all the facts in the situation, but they were beginning to consult maps and examine precedents on the situation."

65 LAC, RG 25, vol. 4252, file 9057-40, pt. 1, Byng to Chilton, 13 June 1925. See also LAC, RG 25, vol. 4252, file 9057-40, pt. 1, Skelton to Governor General's Secretary, 13 June 1925.

66 *Foreign Relations of the United States* (1925), 1:570, Chilton to Kellogg, 15 June 1925.

67 LAC, RG 25, vol. 2668, file 9058-40, "MacMillan's Arctic Expedition," Kellogg to Chilton, 19 June 1925.

68 *Foreign Relations of the United States* (1925), 1:571–73, Chilton to Kellogg, 2 July 1925.

69 *Foreign Relations of the United States* (1925), 1:573, Kellogg to Chilton, 18 July 1925. See also LAC, RG 85, vol. 582, file 565, Stefansson to Harkin, 21 January 1921.

70 *Washington Star*, 17 June 1925. See also D. H. Dinwoodie, "Arctic Controversy: the 1925 Byrd-MacMillan Expedition Example," *Canadian Historical Review* 53, no. 1 (March 1972): 51–65, especially 59, where the author says that the State Department decided that "the expedition should proceed with neither formal comment from the State Department nor specific authorization to proclaim annexation of new land," and 60, for the statement that the American authorities considered, and rejected the idea of "applying the Monroe Doctrine to the issue." According to an editorial the *Ottawa Citizen* of 22 June, Gov. Brewster of Maine was willing to add any new territory to his state. The editorial began as follows: "Governor Brewster of Maine has authorized Captain Donald MacMillan, who is on his way to the Arctic, to claim any new land the latter might discover in the Polar regions for the State of Maine."

71 *Washington Star*, 24 June 1925.

72 LAC, RG 25, vol. 2668, file 9058-40, "MacMillan's Arctic Expedition," H. F. Lewis to Harkin, 11 July 1925.

73 LAC, RG 25, vol. 2668, file 9058-40, "MacMillan's Arctic Expedition," Cory to Skelton, 16 September 1925. LAC, RG 25, vol. 2668, file 9058-40, "MacMillan's Arctic Expedition," Skelton to Cory, 18 September 1925.

74 LAC, RG 25, vol. 2668, file 9058-40, "MacMillan's Arctic Expedition," See the sworn statements by Morin, 3 November 1925, Mackenzie's secretary Harwood Steele, 3 November 1925, and MacKenzie, 6 November 1925.

75 Charles J. V. Murphy, *Struggle: The Life and Exploits of Commander Richard E. Byrd* (New York: F. A. Stokes, 1928), 149–51.

76 *Toronto Globe*, 13 October 1925.

77 See Murphy, *Struggle*, 149–51; Richard E. Byrd, *Skyward* (New York: Blue Ribbon Books, 1928), 162–63; Allen, *Arctic Odyssey*, 261–62; also a series of short articles in *The Beaver* in 1950 and 1951, as follows: Frank H. Ellis, "First Flights in Canada's Arctic," *The Beaver* (Sept. 1950): 16–17; Eugene F. McDonald, "First Short-Wave in the Arctic," *The Beaver* (Dec. 1950): 57; Richard Finnie, "First Short-Wave in the Arctic II," *The Beaver* (March 1951): 23; also Richard E. Byrd, "Flying over the Arctic," *National Geographic Magazine* 48, no. 5 (Nov. 1925): 477–532.

78 LAC, RG 25, vol. 2668, file 9058-40, "MacMillan's Arctic Expedition," Byng to Howard, 9 December 1925.

79 LAC, RG 25, vol. 2668, file 9058-40, "MacMillan's Arctic Expedition," Grew to Howard, 11 January 1926.

80 LAC, RG 25, vol. 2668, file 9058-40, "MacMillan's Arctic Expedition," Bovey to MacBrien, 25 January 1927.

81 LAC, RG 25, vol. 2668, file 9058-40, "MacMillan's Arctic Expedition," Skelton to MacBrien, 1 February 1927.

82 LAC, RG 25, vol. 2668, file 9058-40, "MacMillan's Arctic Expedition," Bovey to MacBrien, 15 February 1927.

83 LAC, RG 25, vol. 2668, file 9058-40, "MacMillan's Arctic Expedition," O. S. Finnie to W. W. Cory, 8 February 1927. A letter for G. P. Mackenzie to Byrd was drafted but not mailed. LAC, RG 25, vol. 2668, file 9058-40, "MacMillan's Arctic Expedition," Mackenzie to Byrd, 11 March 1927. Marked "Draft only not sent O.S.F."

84 LAC, R5025-0-3-E, Robert Archibald Logan fonds, vol. 1, file "Licenses for Air Harbours in Arctic, 1925," 12 April 1925.

85 LAC, R5025-0-3-E, Robert Archibald Logan fonds, vol. 1, file "Licenses for Air Harbours in Arctic, 1925," 12 April 1925, Logan to Prime Minister, 5 June 1925.

86 LAC, R5025-0-3-E, Robert Archibald Logan fonds, vol. 1, file "Licenses for Air Harbours in Arctic, 1925," 12 April 1925, Desbarats to Logan, 19 June 1925.

87 LAC, RG 85, vol. 668, file 4107; personal correspondence between Col. Logan and Gordon W. Smith. It was through Logan's letter to *North* magazine, published in the September–October 1976 issue, that Smith became aware of this interesting little affair.

88 LAC, RG 25, vol. 1513, file 1928-207, Anderson to W. W. Cory.

89 The plan of the Australian George Hubert Wilkins to fly over the North Pole in the 1920s was also kept under observation, but again little of importance developed. Efforts were being made in late 1925 and early 1926 to get the Detroit Arctic Expedition, as it was called, ready for a transpolar flight from Alaska to Spitsbergen the following March, and occasioned some newspaper comments. See, for example, *Washington Sunday Star*, 10 January 1926. In confidential communiqués to, from, and in Ottawa, John Cameron, the British Consul in Detroit, reported that an object of the expedition was to plant the American flag on any land discovered between Point Barrow and the North Pole, but that the sponsors of the flight, especially the Fords, were not very enthusiastic, because they "do not consider that a Fokker plane piloted by an Australian aviator constitutes a valid example of the possibilities of Detroit's newest industry." LAC, RG 25, vol. 1422, file 1925-417A, Cameron to Howard, 25 November 1925, 2 February 1926. By oversight, the substance of these reports was not sent on to Ottawa until some time had elapsed. See LAC, RG 25, vol. 1422, file 1925-417A, Howard to Sir A. Chamberlain, 2 March 1926. As events turned out, Wilkins was unable to make the projected flights in 1926, but in 1928, with his copilot Carl Ben Eielson, he succeeded in flying non-stop from Point Barrow to Spitsbergen. Referring to reports that the expedition had intended to claim for the United States any new land discovered within the Canadian sector, British officials raised with the Canadian government the question of whether there would be any Canadian objection to a British award to Wilkins for this and other feats. LAC, RG 25, vol. 1422, file 1925-417A, Larkin to Premier of Canada, 12 May 1928. Evidently the Canadian authorities were inclined to take the view that the question of the expedition's claims to new lands was no longer important, since no new lands had been sighted, but Finnie felt that Wilkins should be asked to account for his behaviour. Observing that Wilkins' flight had taken him 200 or 300 miles to the right of the direct line from Point Barrow to Spitsbergen, "which brought him into Canadian territory," and that the Italian General Nobile had applied for and been granted Canadian permits for his Arctic flying, he stated that Wilkins had neither asked for nor been given such permits. He advised that before Wilkins was given any honours it should be ascertained whether he was still a British subject, whether he would actually have claimed new land in the Canadian sector for the United States, and why he had not obtained Canadian permits. LAC, RG 25, vol. 1422, file 1925-417A, Finnie to W. W. Cory, 16 May 1928. Departmental records do not indicate that this advice was ever acted upon.

90 LAC, RG 25, vol. 4252, file 9057-40, pt. 2, "List of persons issued with Explorer's Permits-1926," in envelope marked "Enclosures to letter of 4 Oct. 1926, from the Deputy Minister of the Interior." Richard Byrd's polar flight of 1926 caused a certain amount of concern in Ottawa when it was in the planning stages, but little of note developed because in the end he decided to fly from and back to Spitsbergen rather than some point in

the North American Arctic. When news of the projected flight came out in the American press at the end of January 1926, however, reports said that he might use Etah for his base as an alternative to Spitsbergen, and he intended to explore the region north of Greenland, Canada, and Alaska, and that he would plant the American flag upon any new lands discovered. The British Embassy in Washington drew the attention of the Canadian authorities to these reports, observing that the American government had still expressed no definite opinion about Canada's jurisdiction over the northern territories she claimed, or about the permits she exacted from explorers. Nor had any expression of regret been received from the State Department regarding the failure of the MacMillan expedition to comply with Canadian requirements. It was suggested that discussions should be undertaken without delay because they "would be likely to cause less feeling if they were undertaken *before* someone plants the American flag, than afterwards." Furthermore, Minister of the Interior Stewart's press statement of 12 June 1925 had not been communicated officially to the American government. LAC, RG 25, vol. 1422, file 1925-417B, Howard to Byng, 25 February 1926. Evidently Canadian authorities had already taken steps to contact Byrd. See LAC, RG 85, vol. 668, file 4107, Finnie to Logan, 15 February 1926: "Mr. Cory was in Washington last week and saw Lieutenant Commander Byrd." Before long it became definitely known that Byrd was going to use Spitsbergen for his base, and this seems to have allayed worries over the matter, even though messages were sent to Ottawa from both the British embassy in Washington and the Dominions office in London suggesting that it would be advisable to approach the American government with a view to obtaining an understanding. LAC, RG 25, vol. 1422, file 1925-417B, Howard to Byng, 8 March 1926; LAC, RG 25, vol. 1422, file 1925-417B, Secretary of State for Dominion Affairs to Byng, 1 April 1926. The subject was brought up shortly afterwards when James White of the Canadian Department of Justice visited Washington, and was reported by the British embassy as follows: "In the course of this conversation with Mr. Valance of the Legal Division of the State Department, who is concerned with all questions related to claims of all descriptions, some reference was made to the far northern territories above mentioned whereupon Mr. Vallance turned to Mr. White and remarked that the Canadian claims to these were 'not' worth a damn." LAC, RG 25, vol. 1422, file 1925-417B, Chilton to Sir A. Chamberlain, 28 April 1926. Byrd's successful polar flight (which was privately sponsored although the US Navy helped by giving him and other members of the crew leave of absence) was made directly to the North Pole and directly back to Spitsbergen on 9 May 1926. See Richard Byrd, *Skyward: Man's Mastery of Air* (New York: G. P. Putnam's Sons, 1928), 166–206; LAC, RG 85, vol. 764, file 5052. In this file there is a copy of an article written by Byrd which was published in the *New York Times* on 28 March 1926 in which Byrd said, "If I do find new land, I will descend on it, if possible, and hoist the American flag." The context of the article shows that he was talking about the still largely unexplored area between the north coast of Greenland and the North Pole. He did not fly over, or land upon, any of the Canadian Arctic islands.

91 LAC, RG 25, vol. 1513, file 1928-207, Northwest Territories Council Ordinance, "An Ordinance Respecting Scientists and Explorers," 23 June 1926.

92 LAC, RG 25, vol. 1513, file 1928-207, Massey to Skelton, 7 February 1928.

93 LAC, RG 25, vol. 1513, file 1928-207, Skelton to Cory, 11 February 1928.

94 LAC, RG 25, vol. 1513, file 1928-207, Gibson to Skelton, 14 February 1928; also LAC, RG 25, vol. 1513, file 1928-207, Skelton to Massey, 20 February 1928. See also comments in Millward, 100–101, to the effect that MacMillan was granted permits in 1926, 1927, and 1928. For evidence that anything written on the subject of Arctic sovereignty by government officials and employees at this time was carefully appraised, see LAC, RG 25, vol. 4252, file 9057-40, pt. 2, Skelton to Cory, 12 March 1930. Skelton commented on Millward's booklet at Cory's request, wrote: "The only comment which I had thought of making was to question the advisability on page 101, for example, of making such detailed reference to the permit issue to MacMillan, as it might be considered that the very minuteness of reference indicated some uncertainty on the part of the Canadian Government. On further reflection, however, I should be inclined to think the reference is quite all right." In the same file are a number of comments on the Department of the Interior booklet, *Canada's Eastern Arctic*, which appeared in 1934.

95 LAC, RG 25, vol. 1542, file 1929-381, Finnie to Starnes, 1 June 1929: LAC, RG 25, vol. 1542, file 1929-381, Finnie to MacMillan by telegraph, 2 July 1929; LAC, RG 25, vol. 1542, file 1929-381, Mackenzie to Finnie, 19 July 1929.

96 LAC, RG 25, vol. 1542, file 1929-381, W. W. Cory to Skelton, 19 November 1929.

97 LAC, RG 25, vol. 1542, file 1929-381, Massey to Stimson, 29 November 1929.

98 *British and Foreign State Papers* (1916), "Convention between Great Britain and the United States of America for the protection of Migratory Birds in Canada and the United States," 16 August 1916, 110:767–70. For the implementation of the convention in Canada see the Migratory Birds Convention Act of 1917, *Statutes of Canada*, 7–8 Geo. V, c. 18, 1917. Amending acts were passed from time to time.

99 LAC, RG 25, vol. 1542, file 1929-381, G. H. Shaw to Massey, 20 January 1930.

100 LAC, RG 25, vol. 1595, file 1931-207-C, US Minister to Canadian Secretary of State for External Affairs, 6 July 1931.

101 LAC, RG 25, vol. 1595, file 1931-207-C, Crowell to Port Burwell Detachment of RNWMP, 1 August 1931.

102 LAC, RG 25, vol. 1595, file 1931-207-C, Crowell to Department of the Interior, 16 November 1931.

103 LAC, RG 25, vol. 2016, file 1934-463, Minutes of the 52nd Session of the NWT Council, 4 May 1934.

104 LAC, RG 25, vol. 1595, file 1931-207-C, Murphy to Guthrie, 17 May 1934. The copy of the letter here is unsigned, but other evidence shows that it was by Murphy.

105 LAC, RG 25, vol. 1595, file 1931-207-C, Gibson to MacMillan, 14 June 1934.

106 LAC, RG 25, vol. 1595, file 1931-207-C, MacMillan to Gibson, 21 May 1934.

107 LAC, RG 25, vol. 1595, file 1931-207-C, MacMillan to Gibson, 15 June 1934.

108 Earlier, Bartlett's ship had been used by, and Bartlett himself had served as ship's captain for, two expeditions commanded by George Palmer Putnam of the American Museum of Natural History, to Greenland and the Canadian eastern Arctic islands in 1926, and to Hudson Strait and Fort Bassin in 1927. All necessary permits were secured for both expeditions, and Putman's reports indicated that all regulations had been complied with. Trouble arose when Putnam's fourteen-year-old son wrote a book on the second expedition, published in late 1927, which told in uninhibited fashion of the killing of numerous mammals and birds for food and sport. Putnam's excuse, a rather lame one for a man of his undoubtedly high repute, was that he had not read the permits carefully enough to appreciate fully the limits that were imposed. Putnam made a special journey to Ottawa in December 1928, voluntarily but in considerable embarrassment, to appear before the Advisory Board on Wild Life Protection, and his explanation and apologies were accepted. See LAC, RG 85, vol. 776, file 5099 pt. 1–2. Also David Binney Putnam, *David Goes to Baffin Land* (New York: G. P. Putnam's Sons, 1927), 71, 117, 129, 154, et passim.

109 LAC, RG 25, vol. 1595, file 1931-207-C, Minutes of Special Session of the NWT Council, 23 January 1934.

110 LAC, RG 25, vol. 1595, file 1931-207-C, Minutes of 52nd Session of the NWT Council, 4 May 1934. See also LAC, RG 25, vol. 1595, file 1931-207-C, Murphy to Gurthie, 17 May 1934. See also LAC, RG 85, vol. 437, file 4421 for information about expeditions planned in the 1920s by Harold Noice, which did not materialize.

111 When Canada's claim to all the islands between her Arctic coast and the North Pole was asserted at a meeting of the Institute of Politics at Williamstown, Mass., on 4 August 1930, the reaction of Americans present was reported by Louis Stark in the *New York Times*, 5 August 1930 as follows: "From this statement the spokesman of the United States courteously but emphatically dissented, pointing out that on official American maps the islands north of Canada were marked as no man's land and as not belonging to Canada." International affairs authority H. K. Norton asked what international validity a declaration by a Secretary of the Interior (presumably that by Minister of the Interior Stewart in 1925) would have, drawing from Dean Corbett of McGill University the reply, " No more validity than the declaration of President Monroe." Responding to Corbett's statement that Canada would not act as "the dog in the manger" regarding Arctic air routes, the *New York Times* said in an editorial on 6 August, "What more could reasonably be asked?"

15 | The Eastern Arctic Patrol

1 J. D. Craig, *Canada's Arctic Islands: Log of Canadian Expedition 1922* (Ottawa: King's Printer, 1923), 9. For brief accounts of all these patrol expeditions from 1922 to 1949 inclusive, see the annual reports of the Department of the Interior and its successors.

2 Library and Archives Canada [hereafter LAC], MG 26 I, Arthur Meighen fonds, vol. 13, folder 7, 007504–007505, Bernier to Meighen, 29 July 1921. See LAC, Record Group 85, Northern Affairs Program [hereafter RG 85], vol. 601, file 2502 pt. 1, for

a copy of Bernier's commission and his instructions, both dated 1 June 1922. See also Canada, Order in Council, P.C. No. 1465, 10 July 1922, for appointment of Craig as officer in charge and as a fishery officer. Actually, Craig drafted his own instructions and Captain Bernier's, and sent them to Cory to have them rewritten and forwarded to Bernier and himself. See LAC, RG 85, vol. 595, file 758, Craig to Cory, 4 July 1922. And see LAC, RG 85, vol. 595, file 758, for Craig's appointments as a justice of the peace in and for the NWT (5 July), a game officer (6 and 7 July), and, for an unclear reason, a coroner (5 July). His commission, dated 10 July, is also in this file.

3 Craig, *Canada's Arctic Islands: Log of Canadian Expedition 1922*, 11.

4 Joy's instructions, given in a letter of 6 July 1921, from Commissioner Perry of the RCMP, informed him of his appointment as Justice of the Peace in the NWT, Coroner, Special Officer of the Customs, and Postmaster of a post office at Pond Inlet. He was to carry out all responsibilities associated with these appointments; his "general duty" was "to enforce law and order in all the district tributary to Ponds Inlet; and his special duty was to investigate the murder of Janes. Apart from all this the letter said little which would relate directly to sovereignty matters; but an earlier letter from Perry to the President of the Privy Council, recommending the appointment, spoke of "administrative acts to confirm authority and possession over that territory." Joy went to Pond Inlet on the HBC ships *Baychimo* in the summer of 1921. Dr. L. J. Jackman, medical officer of the expedition, said in 1948 that Joy had proclaimed Canadian sovereignty at Pond Inlet on 1 September 1921. See LAC, RG 85, vol. 1515, file 1009-28 pt. 2, Perry to President of the Privy Council, 24 June 1921; LAC, RG 85, vol. 1515, file 1009-28 pt. 2, Perry to Joy, 6 July 1921; LAC, RG 85, vol. 1515, file 1009-28 pt. 2, Jackman to Louis St. Laurent, 21 April 1948; LAC, RG 85, vol. 1515, file 1009-28 pt. 2, Jackman to Marius Barbeau, 30 April 1948.

5 Of this landing Craig wrote as follows: "His [i.e., Inspector Wilcox's] letters from the Danish authorities, granting permission to land and to make purchases, he had handed to us, and … we went ashore in our launch and presented our credentials and letters." Craig, *Canada's Arctic Islands: Log of Canadian Expedition 1922*, 20.

6 Craig, *Canada's Arctic Islands: Log of Canadian Expedition 1922*, 23–24. See also H. P. Lee, *Policing the Top of the World* (London: John Lane The Bodley Head, 1928). Lee was one of the constables stationed at Craig Harbour with Wilcox, and tells of his experiences there during the years 1922–23 and 1923–24. See also LAC, RG 85, vol. 601, file 2502 pt. 1, Craig to Cory from aboard *Arctic*, 19 July 1922:

"The last two or three days in Quebec were rather rushed but I think we have all our supplies on board. The Police however, as I advised you verbally, were unable to get any of the outfit for their last detachment on the boat and from present indications I would say that besides establishing a permanent station at Ponds [*sic*] Inlet where Sergeant Joyce [*sic*] has been for the last year, we will be able to establish only one other detachment, preferably somewhere near the south eastern corner of Ellesmere Island. If it were not so late in the season we would of course attempt to establish this station much further north, probably opposite Etah. I think however for this year the South Eastern corner of Ellesmere will have to answer unless we have reason to believe that some other Nation is attempting to establish a post further north."

See also LAC, RG 85, vol. 587, file 591, for some information about Joy, and his commission as justice of the peace, dated 5 July 1921.

7 Craig, *Canada's Arctic Islands: Log of Canadian Expedition 1922*, 25–27. Logan's report was included at the end of Craig's, as an appendix. Logan wrote a much longer report, of 64 foolscap pages, which may be seen in LAC, RG 85, vol. 601, file 2502 pt. 1, but apparently it was never published. See Craig's diary in LAC, RG 85, vol. 350, file 203. And see F. H. Ellis, "Arctic Airfield Survey," *The Beaver* (Sept. 1945): 22–25.

8 LAC, RG 85, vol. 582, no. 567, "R.C.M.P. Explorations 1921–," especially memo by J. D. Craig, 4 May 1923, Craig to Finnie, 4 May 1923, Starnes to Director N.W.T., 7 March 1923, and clipping from *Montreal Gazette*, 27 June 1923. See LAC, RG 85, vol. 610, file 2706, for details about Capt. Bernier's trip to Britain in early 1923. It was generally agreed that the *Arctic* was now too old and should be either accompanied or replaced.

9 J. D. Craig, "Canadian Arctic Expedition 1923," in *Canada's Arctic Islands: Canadian Expeditions 1922-23-24-25-26* (Ottawa: King's Printer, 1927), 23. For a longer, but unpublished, report of the expedition by Craig see LAC, RG 85, vol. 610, file 2713. Another member of the expedition, evidently unofficial, was Craig's wife. See LAC, RG 85, vol. 668, file 4107, Craig to Logan, 8 November 1923, "Mrs. Craig accompanied in this year as you have surmised and had a most wonderful trip…."

This must have established a "first" of some sort. *Editor's note*: Full names in this section are derived from Shelagh Grant, *Arctic Justice* (Kingston and Montreal: McGill-Queen's University Press, 2002).

10 Craig, "Canadian Arctic Expedition 1923," 13–14.

11 An interested observer at the trial was Dr. Therkel Mathiassen of Rasmussen's expedition, who had come up from Repulse Bay in May. Conscious of the formalities and regulations which the Canadian authorities were now attempting to enforce in the North, Mathiassen reported to the police upon his arrival and presented permits and passports which they found satisfactory. Craig, "Canadian Arctic Expedition 1923," 23. See LAC, RG 85, vol. 602, file 2502 pt. 2, Craig to Finnie, 29 September 1923: "Sergeant Joy stated that the Doctor was absolutely astounded to hear that we had a Police post on Ellesmere Island .... It is anticipate [*sic*] that, with the help of their Etah Eskimos, the Police there will make a patrol to Sabine in the spring, more especially if Freuchen calls as expected, and we will then have absolute knowledge as to MacMillan's activities during the winter." And further on in the letter: "The relations between Mr. Wilcox, Captain Bernier and myself have again been most cordial." See also LAC, RG 85, vol. 602, file 2502 pt. 2, Craig to Finnie, 3 November 1923, where, referring to the scientific achievements of the Danish expedition, Craig recommended strongly that Canada should get involved: "This once more emphasizes the fact that Canada is doing little or nothing along these lines .... It does not seem right that scientists of other nations should be allowed to come in and secure the cream of the evidence regarding the activities of the Eskimos during past centuries. The matter is of quite as much interest to us and we should have men on the ground investigating it on our behalf." For J. D. Soper's reports on his scientific work and other matters, see LAC, RG 85, vol. 350, file 203, "Soper's Reports on the Arctic Expedition 1933."

12 For another official but briefer report of the expedition, see Canada, Department of the Interior, *Annual Report for the Fiscal Year Ended March 31, 1924* (Ottawa: King's Printer, 1924), 134–35. For Finnie's suggestion that Craig again be made commander, for the expedition of 1923, and its approval, see LAC, RG 85, vol. 595, file 758, Finnie to Cory, 31 October 1922, and Finnie to Craig, 3 November 1922.

13 F. D. Henderson, "Canadian Arctic Expedition 1924," in *Canada's Arctic Islands: Canadian Expeditions 1922-23-24-25-26*, 29–41. See also Department of the Interior, *Annual Report for the Fiscal Year Ended March 31, 1925* (Ottawa: King's Printer, 1925), 135–36, and LAC, RG 85, vol. 602, file 2502 pt. 2, for newspaper articles expressing concern over the planned Arctic flight of the American airship *Shenandoah* in 1924. Although Craig did not go, he remained in charge of the patrol. See LAC, RG 85, vol. 668, file 4107, Craig to Logan, 25 June 1924: "You will be surprised to hear that I am not going North this year, although I still remain Departmental Office in Charge. Thus is a very recent development, the Deputy Minister having advised me about ten days ago, that he wanted me in Ottawa this summer."

14 I discuss this affair in greater detail in chapter 14 dealing with Canadian-American relations in the Arctic 1918–39, so say little about it here. See LAC, RG 85, vol. 602, file 2502 pt. 3, Finnie to Commissioner Starnes, 27 June 1925, asking that RCMP in the North watch MacMillan closely.

15 G. P. Mackenzie, "Canadian Arctic Expedition 1925," in *Canada's Arctic Islands: Canadian Expeditions 1922-23-24-25-26*, 43–48. See also Department of the Interior, *Annual Report for the Fiscal Year Ended March 31, 1926* (Ottawa: King's Printer, 1926), 134; LAC, RG 85, vol. 1515, file 1009-28 pt. 2, *Factual Record Supporting Canadian Sovereignty in the Arctic*, 78; LAC, RG 85, vol. 602, file 2502 pt. 3, esp. McKeand to Finnie, 23 October 1925, complaining about loss of contact with the *Arctic* by wireless during the voyage.

16 J. E. Bernier, *Master Mariner and Arctic Explorer* (Ottawa: Le Droit, 1939), 389. See LAC, Record Group 25, Department of External Affairs [hereafter RG 25], vol. 4252, file 9057-40 pt. 2, M.B.A. Anderson to L. Breitfuss, 7 April 1929: "The hull is now lying in the Montreal harbour. The old 'Arctic' is therefore no longer in existence."

17 Bernier made several private trips to Hudson Bay between 1925 and 1929, before dying on 26 December 1934, at the age of almost eighty-three. Bernier, *Master Mariner and Arctic Explorer*, 403–6. It is rather distressing to have to record that Captain Bernier had undoubtedly been a problem for the authorities, especially in his last years of service, largely because of his inability to maintain silence about matters they wished to keep as quiet as possible. For example, when he went to England in early 1924 on an abortive trip to take command of the *Franklin*, he provoked a steady stream of rather excited newspaper articles on both sides of the Atlantic, suggesting that the flight of the *Shenandoah* might result in American Arctic claims which it would be necessary to forestall. A London dispatch of 4 April 1924, in the *Ottawa Journal*, in

which he speaks grandiloquently of "my expeditions," provoked the following exasperated handwritten notations beside a copy of the article now in a Department of the Interior file:

"Mr. Finnie -

X!?!XXO!!

The Captain is impossible so far as publicity is concerned.

OSF."

LAC, RG 85, vol. 602, file 2502 pt. 2.

18 G. P. Mackenzie, "Canadian Arctic Expedition 1926," in *Canada's Arctic Islands: Canadian Expeditions 1922-23-24-25-26*, 49–54. See also Department of the Interior, *Annual Report for the Fiscal year Ended March 31, 1927* (Ottawa: King's Printer, 1927), 16, 121; LAC, RG 85, vol. 1515, file 1009-28 pt. 2, *Factual Record Supporting Canadian Sovereignty in the Arctic*, 79–80; LAC, RG 85, vol. 602, file 2502 pt. 4. See especially Mackenzie's speech about the 1926 expedition to the Canadian Club in Ottawa, 27 November 1926. In it he notes that the wireless troubles of the year before had been overcome, and the ship was in two-way communication with Montreal every day, even when at Bache Peninsula. See also LAC, RG 85, vol. 68, file 201-1 pt. 1, "E. A. Patrol 1926," for a great deal of background information. E.g., see O. S. Finnie's letter to W. W. Cory, 24 December 1925, in which Finnie expressed disapproval of the idea of using a HBC ship, because "it would certainly create, in the minds of the Eskimo, the idea that the Hudson's Bay Co. is more powerful even than the Government." And see Mackenzie to Finnie, 5 November 1926, after the voyage was finished, noting a suggestion that "in the interests of our sovereignty in the North" another detachment of the RCMP should be established farther west in Lancaster Sound or on Melville Island. Finnie spoke of this suggestion favourably in letters to Gibson, 19 November 1926, and Cory, 5 November 1926, but it was not acted upon at the time, mainly because on the 1927 voyage the *Beothic* was prevented by ice from getting any further west than Port Leopold while on a reconnaissance trip in Lancaster Sound. See LAC, RG 85, vol. 68, file 201-1 pt. 2, "E. A. Patrol 1927," Mackenzie to Job's Co., Feb. 3, 1927; LAC, RG 85, vol. 68, file 201-1 pt. 2, Finnie to Job's Co., 12 August 1927.

19 Department of the Interior, *Annual Report for the Fiscal Year Ended March 31, 1928* (Ottawa: King's Printer, 1928), 119–21; LAC, RG 85, vol. 1515, file 1009-28 pt. 2, *Factual Record Supporting Canadian Sovereignty in the Arctic*, 80; F. G. Banting, "With the Arctic Patrol," *Canadian Geographical Journal* 1, no. 1 (May 1930): 19–30; LAC, RG 85, vol. 602, file 2502 pt. 5.

20 Department of the Interior, *Annual Report for the Fiscal Year Ended March 31, 1929* (Ottawa: King's Printer, 1929), 150–52; LAC, RG 85, vol. 1515, file 1009-28 pt. 2, *Factual Record Supporting Canadian Sovereignty in the Arctic*, 80–81. See also *Toronto Daily Star*, 4 Sept. 1928, for a long article by Richard Finnie on the 1928 voyage.

21 Department of the Interior, *Annual Report for the Fiscal Year Ended March 31, 1930* (Ottawa: King's Printer, 1930), 143–45; LAC, RG 85, vol. 1515, file 1009-28 pt. 2, *Factual Record Supporting Canadian Sovereignty in the Arctic*, 81–82; LAC, RG 85, vol. 602, file 2502, pt. 7.

22 Department of the Interior, *Annual Report for the Fiscal Year Ended March 31, 1931* (Ottawa: King's Printer, 1931), 135–37; LAC, RG 85, vol. 1515, file 1009-28 pt. 2, *Factual Record Supporting Canadian Sovereignty in the Arctic*, 82–83; LAC, RG 85, vol. 602, file 2502 pt. 8.

23 Department of the Interior, *Annual Report for the Fiscal Year Ended March 31, 1932* (Ottawa: King's Printer, 1932), 25–26; 39–41; LAC, RG 85, vol. 1515, file 1009-28 pt. 2, *Factual Record Supporting Canadian Sovereignty in the Arctic*, 83–84; L. T. Burwash, *Eastern Arctic Patrol S. S. "Beothic" 1931* (Ottawa: King's Printer,1931), especially Appendix IX, "Charter between the Department of the Interior and Job's Sealfishery Co., Ltd., for use of the Beothic"; *Polar Record* 3 (Jan. 1932): 22–23; LAC, RG 85, vol. 602, file 2502 pt. 9: The transfer of the RCMP from Bache Peninsula to Craig Harbour was in view at least as early as May 1930, the reason being that with the anticipated Norwegian recognition of Canadian sovereignty in the Sverdrup Islands the Bache Peninsula post would no longer be considered necessary. See LAC, RG 85, vol. 69, file 201-1 pt. 5: Finnie writes in a letter of 17 May 1930, to R. A. Gibson, "With the recognition of our rights by Norway it is altogether likely that the Police will be withdrawn from the Bache Peninsula post and re-establish [*sic*] at Craig Harbour." See also report by Burwash in LAC, RG 85, vol. 350, file 201-1.

24 D. L. McKeand, "Eastern Arctic Patrol S. S. 'Ungava' 1932" (Ottawa: King's Printer, 1932), appendix 6. See also appendix 5 for correspondence relating to the agreement, between the government and the HBC, and also appendix 7. And see LAC, RG 85, box 155715, file 7367, for a letter from O. D. Skelton to Deputy Minister of the Interior H. H. Rowatt, containing the following passage, "I am not aware of any international ground at the

present time which would make it unadvisable to utilize a vessel run by a private company. As you state, the Canadian position with regard to the Arctic archipelago is much stronger now than it was a few years ago." The letter is dated 21 January 1932. See LAC, RG 85, vol. 70, file 201-1 pt 7, for a letter of 26 October 1931, from Finnie to Rowatt, saying that the arrangement with Job Sealfisheries Co. and their ship *Beothic* had always been very satisfactory, but only "this morning" Col. Reid of the HBC had proposed that one ship might be used to do both the government's and the HBC's work.

25 McKeand, "Eastern Arctic Patrol S. S. 'Ungava' 1932," appendices 1, 2, 3. Canada, Orders in Council, PC Nos. 1109, 12 May 1932, 1373, 16 June 1932, and 1559, 13 July 1932. See also LAC, RG 85, box 155715, file 7367, for letter of 4 May 1932, from (signature illegible) to Rowatt, suggesting that McKeand should be given the same authority as his predecessors, so that "the continuity of administrative acts for sovereignty purposes may not be broken."

26 McKeand, "Eastern Arctic Patrol S. S. 'Ungava' 1932," esp. appendix 13; Department of the Interior, *Annual Report for the Fiscal Year Ended March 31, 1933* (Ottawa: King's Printer, 1933), 26–27; LAC, RG 85, vol. 1515, file 1009-28 pt. 2, *Factual Record Supporting Canadian Sovereignty in the Arctic*, 84–85; *Polar Record* 5 (Jan. 1933): 45–46; LAC, RG 85, vol. 602, file 2502 pt. 10. *Editor's Note*: I added in the reference to Akqioq based upon Robert W. Park and Douglas R. Stenton, "A Hans Krüger Arctic Expedition Cache on Axel Heiberg Island, Nunavut," *Arctic* 60, no. 1 (Mar. 2007): 1–6.

27 Department of the Interior, *Annual Report for the Fiscal Year Ended March 31, 1934* (Ottawa: King's Printer, 1932), 34–36; LAC, RG 85, vol. 1515, file 1009-28 pt. 2, *Factual Record Supporting Canadian Sovereignty in the Arctic*, 85–86; *Polar Record* 6 (July 1933): 114; *Polar Record* 7 (Jan. 1934): 64–68; W. C. Bethune, *Canada's Eastern Arctic: Its History, Resources, Population and Administration* (Ottawa: King's Printer, 1935), 39–41. See also *Polar Record* 8 (July 1934): 121–29, for an account of the Krüger search expeditions in 1932. And see LAC, RG 85, vol. 602, file 2502 pt. 11, esp. unsigned memo to Deputy Minister Rowatt, 22 August 1933, complaining that Capt. Bob Bartlett, reported in a wireless message from McKeand to be in Hudson Bay, had no permits of any kind to carry on this US-sponsored voyage of exploration. This file has also records of the patrol voyages of 1934 and 1935. See also LAC, RG 85, vol. 155715, file 7367 for a memo dated 6 July 1933, from H. E. Hume, Chairman of the Dominion Lands Board, to McKeand, giving him his instructions for the 1933 patrol. LAC, RG 85, vol. 531, file 7712 contains historian and secretary A. P. Norton's narrative of the voyage and his daily record, among other things.

28 Department of the Interior, *Annual Report for the Fiscal Year Ended March 31, 1935* (Ottawa: King's Printer, 1935), 38–39; LAC, RG 85, vol. 1515, file 1009-28 pt. 2, *Factual Record Supporting Canadian Sovereignty in the Arctic*. 86–87; *Polar Record* 2, no. 9 (Jan. 1935–July 1938): 47–49. See also J. H. MacBrien, "The Mounties in the Arctic," *Canadian Geographical Journal* 10, no. 4 (April 1935): 156–66; and for a report on the patrol by McKeand, dated 17 December 1934, see LAC, RG 85, vol. 155715, file 7367. This file has a great deal of information on the patrols during the years 1932–45. See also LAC, RG 85, vol. 536, file 7819, for the rather routine reports of the meetings aboard the ship, written by Secretary F. Gilbert.

29 Department of the Interior, *Annual Report for the Fiscal Year Ended March 31, 1936* (Ottawa: King's Printer, 1936), 36–37; LAC, RG 85, vol. 1515, file 1009-28 pt. 2, *Factual Record Supporting Canadian Sovereignty in the Arctic*, 87–88; *Polar Record* 2, no. 10 (Jan. 1935–July 1938): 100–102; "The Arctic Patrol," *Canadian Geographical Journal* 11, no. 5 (Nov. 1935): VI; also LAC, RG 85, vol. 155715, file 7637, for McKeand's report.

30 Department of Mines and Resources, *Annual Report for the Fiscal Year Ended March 31, 1937* (Ottawa: King's Printer, 1937), 59–60. The Department of Mines and Resources came into existence on 1 December 1936, amalgamating the former Departments of Mines, Interior, Indian Affairs, and Immigration. See LAC, RG 85, vol. 1515, file 1009-28 pt. 2, *Factual Record Supporting Canadian Sovereignty in the Arctic*, 88–89; *Polar Record* 2, no. 13 (Jan. 1935–July 1938): 49–51; and LAC, RG 85, vol. 155715, file 7367 for a number of reports, including one written by McKeand on the *Nascopie* on 12 August 1936. This file has also the minutes of meetings held by government personnel aboard the *Nascopie* during the 1936 patrol. Such meetings were a regular feature of the patrol during these years, after their inauguration in 1933. See also LAC, RG 85, vol. 536, file 7819, for a very informative report on the voyage from Churchill on by T. Wayling, one of the historians for the patrol.

31 Department of the Interior, *Annual Report for the Fiscal Year Ended March 31, 1938* (Ottawa: King's Printer, 1938), 70; LAC, RG 85, vol. 1515,

file 1009-28 pt. 2, *Factual Record Supporting Canadian Sovereignty in the Arctic*, 89–90; *Polar Record* 2, no. 14 (Jan. 1935–July 1938): 130; see also D. L. McKeand, "The Annual Eastern Arctic Patrol," *Canadian Geographical Journal* 17, no. 1 (July 1938): 36–39; T. Wayling, "Eskimo Exodus," *Canadian Geographical Journal* 13, no. 9 (Jan. 1937): 518–29; J. F. Grant, "Patrol to the Northwest Passage," *Canadian Geographical Journal* 16, no. 5 (May 1938): VI; *Polar Record* 4, no. 27 (Jan. 1944): 134. See also LAC, RG 85, vol. 603, file 2502 pt. 12, telegram McKeand to Gibson, 17 July 1937, telling of a meeting on 16 July with Commander Donald MacMillan at Hebron, Labrador. The telegram reads, in part, "Introduced Wynn Edwards to Commander MacMillan who expressed appreciation for courtesy of Canadian Government in appointing representative to accompany his expedition to Northwest Territories." The irony is evident, and one may guess how appreciative MacMillan really was.

This file also has a good deal of information about the opening of the post at Fort Ross and the meeting with the *Aklavik* in Bellot Strait. See also LAC, RG 85, vol. 536, file 7819, for reports on the voyage by Acting Secretary R. Finnie and Historian R. K. Carnegie. A most unusual feature of the voyage was the imposition of $10 fines upon Anglican missionaries J. Turner and M. Flint, who had deliberately eaten snow goose eggs in contravention of the Migratory Birds Convention Act, to make a test case of the prohibition.

Even though the sovereignty aspect of the Eastern Arctic Patrol had been receding into the background during these years, it was still very much in the minds of government officials. See LAC, RG 85, vol. 73, file No. 201-1 pt. 12, "E. A. Patrol 1937," for the following in a letter from Deputy Minister of Mines and Resources C. Camsell to Deputy Postmaster General J. A. Sullivan, 4 June 1937: "In all our correspondence we are careful to refer to the Eastern Arctic Patrol as being a Governmental affair rather than a trip of the Hudson's Bay Company's boat. As you are aware, it is necessary in the interest of the maintenance of British sovereignty to have it generally known that there is a Governmental Patrol and that Government institutions are maintained in the far North."

32 Department of Mines and Resources, *Annual Report for the Fiscal Year Ended March 31, 1939* (Ottawa: King's Printer, 1939), 79–80; LAC, RG 85, vol. 1515, file 1009-28 pt. 2, *Factual Record Supporting Canadian Sovereignty in the Arctic*, 90–91; *Polar Record* 3, no. 17 (Jan. 1939): 51–52. See also Mrs. Grange's reports in LAC, RG 85, vol. 155715, file 7367, and McKeand's letter of 26 September 1938, to Gibson, criticizing her work in severe terms.

33 Department of Mines and Resources, *Annual Report for the Fiscal Year Ended March 31, 1940* (Ottawa: King's Printer, 1940), 69; LAC, RG 85, vol. 1515, file 1009-28 pt. 2, *Factual Record Supporting Canadian Sovereignty in the Arctic*, 91–92; *Polar Record* 3, no. 18 (July 1939): 137–38; D. L. McKeand, "The Eastern Arctic Patrol," an address to the Empire Club of Canada, 14 March 1940; R. S. Marriott, "Canada's Eastern Arctic Patrol," *Canadian Geographical Journal* 20, no. 3 (March 1940): 154–61; LAC, RG 85, vol. 74, file 201-1 pt. 14, McKeand to Gibson, 9 December 1939.

34 Five new RCMP posts were established in the North in 1924, namely Providence, Rae, and Good Hope in the Mackenzie District, Dundas Harbour on the south coast of Devon Island, and Kane Basin, actually a subdetachment not designed for permanent occupation, on the east coast of Ellesmere Island. Canada, *Report of the Royal Canada Mounted Police for the Year Ended September 30, 1924* (Ottawa: King's Printer, 1924), 26, 35–36.

35 See, for example, the appropriate parts of R. C. Fetherstonhaugh, *The Royal Canadian Mounted Police* (New York: Carrick and Evans, 1938); Harwood Steele, *Policing the Arctic* (London: Jarrolds, 1936); T. M. Longstreth, *The Silent Force* (New York: Century, 1927; and *In Scarlet and Plain Clothes* (Toronto: Macmillan, 1933). On the establishment of new posts, see LAC, RG 85, vol. 601, file 2502 pt. 1. Regarding sovereignty, Craig wrote to Finnie on 7 November 1923: "We had no knowledge of the secret despatch recently forwarded by the Under Secretary of State for External Affairs regarding Wrangel Island, and the possible occupation by the United States of some of our Canadian islands, and this makes even more important and urgent the establishment of a post somewhere west of Lancaster Sound and Barrow Strait." LAC, RG 85, vol. 601, file 2502 pt. 2.

36 Canada, *Report of the Royal Canadian Mounted Police for the Year Ended September 30, 1922*, passim, for details about all these murders, investigations, and patrols.

37 Canada, *Report of the Royal Canadian Mounted Police for the Year Ended September 30, 1922*, 37.

38 Canada, *Report of the Royal Canadian Mounted Police for the Year Ended September 30, 1923* (Ottawa: King's Printer, 1923), 32–34. The two men condemned to death were hanged at Herschel Island in February 1924.

39 See Canada, *Report of the Royal Canada Mounted Police for the Year Ended September 30, 1926* for details on all these matters. The case of Komeuk, suspected of the murder of Hiktak, remained unsettled. Canada, *Report of the Royal Canada Mounted Police for the Year Ended September 30, 1925*, 40–41, 45–48.

40 Canada, *Report of the Royal Canada Mounted Police for the Year Ended September 30, 1927*, 23.

41 Canada, *Report of the Royal Canada Mounted Police for the Year Ended September 30, 1927*, 45–46.

42 Canada, *Report of the Royal Canada Mounted Police for the Year Ended September 30, 1929*, 87, 93.

43 Canada, *Report of the Royal Canada Mounted Police for the Year Ended September 30, 1932*, 106–11. Much has been written about this strange man, whose real identity has never been conclusively established. See Fetherstonhaugh, *Royal Canadian Mounted Police*, 245–49; and Steele, *Policing the Arctic*, 318–26.

44 Canada, *Report of the Royal Canada Mounted Police for the Year Ended September 30, 1925*, 14.

45 Canada, *Report of the Royal Canada Mounted Police for the Year Ended September 30, 1927*, 11. Superintendent J. Ritchie, reporting for "G" Division (Northern Alberta and the western NWT) underlined the surprising fact that many members of the Force liked service in the North so much that they had no wish to come out after as much as thirteen years' continuous service, and added, "What I am trying to convey is that the North is very appealing." Canada, *Report of the Royal Canada Mounted Police for the Year Ended September 30, 1927*, 25.

46 Canada, *Report of the Royal Canada Mounted Police for the Year Ended September 30, 1924*, 5.

47 Canada, *Report of the Royal Canada Mounted Police for the Year Ended September 30, 1926*, 43–85.

48 Canada, *Report of the Royal Canada Mounted Police for the Year Ended September 30, 1927*, 51–59.

49 Canada, *Report of the Royal Canada Mounted Police for the Year Ended September 30, 1928*, 67–70, 73–76, 106–7. A prospector finally found the bodies in this region in July 1928.

50 Canada, *Report of the Royal Canada Mounted Police for the Year Ended September 30, 1928*, 13.

51 Canada, *Report of the Royal Canada Mounted Police for the Year Ended September 30, 1929* (Ottawa: King's Printer, 1929), 62–71. See A/Sup't V.A.M. Kemp, "The Royal Canadian Mounted Police," *Polar Record* 1, no. 7 (Jan. 1934): 75–80, esp. 80, where, speaking of Joy's patrol, he says, "During the course of this patrol no other living soul was seen, but game conditions were observed, and Canada's sovereignty over these remote islands was thus maintained."

52 Canada, *Report of the Royal Canada Mounted Police for the Year Ended September 30, 1929*, 71–78.

53 Canada, *Report of the Royal Canada Mounted Police for the Year Ended September 30, 1929*, 105–7.

54 Canada, *Report of the Royal Canada Mounted Police for the Year Ended September 30, 1930*, 55–57, 58–60, 60–63, 63–64.

55 Canada, *Report of the Royal Canada Mounted Police for the Year Ended September 30, 1930*, 60, 63. Constable J. W. McCormick made a winter trip from Chesterfield Inlet to Churchill to contact the mail train which now travelled over the new railroad to this point. Canada, *Report of the Royal Canada Mounted Police for the Year Ended September 30, 1930*, 76–77.

56 Canada, *Report of the Royal Canada Mounted Police for the Year Ended September 30, 1931*, 67–68, 69–72.

57 Canada, *Report of the Royal Canadian Mounted Police for the Eighteen Months Ended March 31, 1934*, 37. For a general description of Arctic patrols based on his own experience, see A/Sergeant H. W. Stallworthy, "Winter Patrols in the Arctic," *R.C.M.P. Quarterly* 2, no. 2 (Oct. 1934): 17–25. See also Cst. J. H. Bilton, "My First Northern Patrol," *R.C.M.P. Quarterly* 7, no. 2 (Oct. 1939): 126–36, for the author's description of his patrol in the Great Bear Lake region in the winter of 1932–33. For an account of the searches for Krüger, see "Krüger Search Expeditions, 1932," *Polar Record* 1, no. 8 (July 1934): 121–29, also article by J. Montagnes in *The Toronto Star Weekly*, 1 September 1934.

58 Canada, *Report of the Royal Canadian Mounted Police for the Year Ended March 31, 1935*, 59–61. The following August, a judicial party from Edmonton conducted a trial at Coppermine and sentenced the guilty party, Ahigiak, to five years' imprisonment at Aklavik.

59 Canada, *Report of the Royal Canadian Mounted Police for the Year Ended March 31, 1935*, 61. See also Maj. Gen. J. H. MacBrien, "The Mounties in the Arctic," *Canadian Geographical Journal* 10, no. 4 (April 1935): 156–66; "Royal Canadian Mounted Police: Three Patrols Made in the Canadian Arctic in 1934," *Polar Record* 2, no. 10 (Jan. 1935–July 1938): 111–18.

60 Canada, *Report of the Royal Canadian Mounted Police for the Year Ended March 31, 1936*, 83–84.

See "Some Patrols Made by Members of the Royal Canadian Mounted Police in the Canadian Arctic, 1935," *Polar Record* 2, no. 12 (Jan. 1935–July 1938): 149–55. *Polar Record* continued to publish thereafter, with a few lapses, accounts of some of the major patrols performed each year by the RCMP.

61 Canada, *Report of the Royal Canadian Mounted Police for the Year Ended March 31, 1937*, 83–86. See also "Patrol-Cambridge Bay to King William and Matty Islands, N.W.T., 1936," *R.C.M.P. Quarterly* 4, no. 4 (April 1937): 271–73. In 1938, many patrols were made from the northern detachments according to custom, including long journeys in Baffin, Ellesmere, Victoria, and King William Islands. Canada, *Report of the Royal Canadian Mounted Police for the Year Ended March 31, 1939*, 103–8.

62 Canada, *Report of the Royal Canada Mounted Police for the Year Ended September 30, 1928*, 37–38, 56–57, 92.

63 Canada, *Report of the Royal Canada Mounted Police for the Year Ended September 30, 1929*, 110, 93–94.

64 Canada, *Report of the Royal Canada Mounted Police for the Year Ended September 30, 1932*, 89.

65 Canada, *Report of the Royal Canadian Mounted Police for the Year Ended March 31, 1938*, 99–101. In the summer of 1937, *St. Roch* also rescued the crew of the stricken HBC vessel *Fort James*, which sank in the ice-filled water of Dolphin and Union Strait.

66 *Editor's note*: Dr. Smith simply listed material in this section chronologically. I have regrouped it thematically to reduce redundancy and streamline the narrative.

67 A. E. Millward, *Southern Baffin Island* (Ottawa: King's Printer, 1930), 88–95; LAC, RG 85, vol. 1515, file 1009-28 pt. 2, *Factual Record Supporting Canadian Sovereignty in the Arctic*, 212–13; Department of the Interior, *Annual Report for the Fiscal Year Ended March 31, 1928*, 120.

68 D. Copland, *Livingstone of the Arctic* (Ottawa: D. Copland, 1967), 99–105; Department of the Interior, *Annual Report for the Fiscal Year Ended March 31, 1931*, 140.

69 Department of the Interior, *Annual Report for the Fiscal Year Ended March 31, 1933*, 29–30; *Polar Record* 2, no. 5 (Jan. 1933): 47–49.

70 Millward, *Southern Baffin Island*, 50–62.

71 L. T. Burwash, *Canada's Western Arctic: Report on Investigations in 1925–1926, 1928–29, and 1930* (Ottawa: King's Printer, 1931), 11–52. For a detailed account by Burwash of the 1925–1926 expedition, see LAC, RG 85, vol. 347, file 203, "Major Burwash's Report."

72 L. T. Burwash, *The Eskimo, Their Country and Its Resources: Economic Survey of the East Coasts of Hudson Bay and James Bay from Richmond Gulf to Rupert House, Including the Belcher and Other Adjacent Islands 1927* (Ottawa: King's Printer, 1928).

73 Burwash, *Canada's Western Arctic: Report on Investigations in 1925–1926, 1928–29, and 1930*, 53–82.

74 Burwash, *Canada's Western Arctic: Report on Investigations in 1925–1926, 1928–29, and 1930*, 83–116. See also Department of the Interior, *Annual Reports*, 1928–1929, 152; 1929–1930, 145–46; 1930–1931, 137–39; L. T. Burwash, "The Franklin Search," *Canadian Geographical Journal* 1, no. 7 (Nov. 1930): 587–603.

75 J. F. Moran, *Local Conditions in the Mackenzie District 1922* (Ottawa: King's Printer, 1923); Department of the Interior, *Annual Reports*, 1924–1925, 132; 1926–1927, 117; 1928–1929, 150. See also pamphlet entitled *Analysis of Evidence Given Before J. F. Moran May and June 1928 re Administration of Mackenzie District N.W.T.* (no author, no date), pamphlet in Aboriginal Affairs and Northern Development Library, Gatineau.

76 Department of the Interior, *Annual Report for the Fiscal Year Ended March 31, 1928*, 120.

77 Department of the Interior, *Annual Report for the Fiscal Year Ended March 31, 1930*, 8, 17, 141–42. During the same summer F. H. Kitto of Dominion Lands Surveys made a settlement survey on Charlton Island in James Bay. Department of the Interior, *Annual Report for the Fiscal Year Ended March 31, 1930*, 146, 163.

78 Department of the Interior, *Annual Report for the Fiscal Year Ended March 31, 1932*, 35–37.

79 Department of the Interior, *Annual Report for the Fiscal Year Ended March 31, 1933*, 26.

80 Department of the Interior, *Annual Report for the Fiscal Year Ended March 31, 1936*, 30–31. See LAC, R1528-0-0-E, Charles Camsell fonds for information about this trip and others made by Camsell. During the summer of 1925 the Governor General, Lord Byng, had made a trip down the Mackenzie River and along the Arctic coast to Kittigazuit. This was the first visit made by a governor general to this part of the country. Department of the Interior, *Annual Report for the Fiscal year Ended March 31, 1926*, Pt. 5, 131.

81 Department of Mines and Resources, *Annual Report for the Fiscal Year Ended March 31, 1939*, 70. During the fiscal year 1934–1935 the title of the branch of the Department of the Interior mainly responsible for affairs in the North was changed from "Dominion Lands Administration" to "Lands, Northwest Territories and Yukon Branch." The change produced no major innovation or transformation in the functions of the branch, but it was felt that the new title reflected more accurately the nature and scope of its activities. Department of the Interior, *Annual Report for the Fiscal Year Ended March 31, 1935*, 25.

82 L. J. Weeks, *Cumberland Sound Area, Baffin Island* (Ottawa: King's Printer, 1928). See also Millward, *Southern Baffin Island*, 96–97; LAC, RG 85, vol. 1515, file 1009-28 pt. 2, *Factual Record Supporting Canadian Sovereignty in the Arctic*, 159–60. Weeks also made a geological and geographical survey of the Mistake Bay area on the west coast of Hudson Bay, about ninety miles south of Chesterfield Inlet, in 1929. L. J. Weeks, "Mistake Bay Area, West Coast of Hudson Bay, North West Territories," *Summary Report, 1929*, Part B, bulletin issued by the Geological Survey, Department of Mines (Ottawa: King's Printer, 1930), 172–74.

83 G. H. Blanchet, *Preliminary Report on the Fort Smith Wood Buffalo Park, Department of the Interior Topographical Survey mimeographed booklet* (Ottawa, 1927).

84 G. H. Blanchet, *Great Slave Lake Area Northwest Territories*, booklet issued by the NWT and Yukon Branch, Department of the Interior (Ottawa: King's Printer, 1926).

85 G. H. Blanchet, *Keewatin and Northeastern Mackenzie: A General Survey of the Life, Activities, and Natural Resources of this Section of the Northwest Territories, Canada, and Preliminary Report on the Aerial Mineral Exploration of Northern Canada* (Ottawa: King's Printer, 1930).

86 G. H. Blanchet, "Searching the Arctic by Aeroplane," *Canadian Geographical Journal* 1, no. 8 (Dec. 1930): 641–62.

87 Department of Mines and Resources, *Annual Report for the Fiscal Year Ended March 31, 1937*, 26, 34, 60, 169; LAC, RG 85, vol. 1515, file 1009-28 pt. 2, *Factual Record Supporting Canadian Sovereignty in the Arctic*, 160.

88 Millward, 67–83; J. D. Soper, *A Faunal Investigation of Southern Baffin Island, National Museum of Canada Bulletin No. 53* (Ottawa: King's Printer, 1928).

89 In the spring and summer of the following year, Soper succeeded in establishing with certainty that the long-sought nesting area was in the vicinity of Bowman Bay near the southwestern tip of Baffin Island. Making his way with great difficulty by canoe back to Cape Dorset, he was then able to make contact with the government patrol ship *Beothic* at Lake Harbour, and returned home with it in late August 1929. J. D. Soper, "Discovery of the Breeding Grounds of the Blue Goose," *Canadian Field-Naturalist* 44, no. 1 (Jan. 1930): 1–11; J. D. Soper, *The Blue Goose: An Account of its Breeding Ground, Migration, Eggs, Nests, and General Habits*, pamphlet issued by the N.W.T. and Yukon Branch, Department of the Interior (Ottawa: King's Printer, 1930); Department of the Interior, *Annual Reports*, 1928–1929, 152; 1929–1930, 145–46; Millward, *Southern Baffin Island*, 101–2; J. D. Soper, "Adventuring in Baffin Island," *Canadian Geographical Journal* 1, no. 3 (July 1930): 191–206.

90 Department of the Interior, *Annual Report for the Fiscal Year Ended March 31, 1931*, 137; Department of the Interior, *Annual Report for the Fiscal Year Ended March 31, 1932*, 41.

91 Department of the Interior, *Annual Report for the Fiscal Year Ended March 31, 1933*, 29; Department of the Interior, *Annual Report for the Fiscal Year Ended March 31, 1934*, 33. J. D. Soper finished his long investigation in Wood Buffalo Park in 1934, and reported among other things that in his estimation the number of buffalo there was between 8,500 and 9,000. Department of the Interior, *Annual Report for the Fiscal Year Ended March 31, 1936*, 32.

92 Department of the Interior, *Annual Report for the Fiscal year Ended March 31, 1926*, Part V, p. 117; W.H.B. Hoare, *Report of Investigations Affecting Eskimo and Wild Life District of Mackenzie 1924-1925-1926* (Ottawa: King's Printer, 1926).

93 W.H.B. Hoare, *Conserving Canada's Musk-Oxen*, pamphlet issued by the N.W.T. and Yukon Branch, Department of the Interior (Ottawa: King's Printer, 1930); Department of the Interior, *Annual Reports*, 1927–1928, 120–21; 1928–1929, 153; 1929–1930, 146.

94 Department of the Interior, *Annual Report for the Fiscal Year Ended March 31, 1931*, 137; Department of the Interior, *Annual Report for the Fiscal Year Ended March 31, 1932*, 41.

95 Department of Mines and Resources, *Annual Report for the Fiscal Year Ended March 31, 1937*, 34, 56; Department of Mines and Resources, *Annual Report for the Fiscal Year Ended March 31, 1938*,

42, 67. After the 1936 survey, which was conducted partly by air and partly on the ground, Clarke estimated a total of 255 muskox in the Thelon area.

96 A. E. Porsild, *Reindeer Grazing in Northwest Canada* (Ottawa: King's Printer, 1929); Department of the Interior, *Annual Reports*, 1926–1927, 118–19; 1927–1928, 121; 1928–1929, 153–54.

97 Department of the Interior, *Annual Report for the Fiscal Year Ended March 31, 1930*, 146.

98 Department of the Interior, *Annual Report for the Fiscal Year Ended March 31, 1931*, 138.

99 Department of the Interior, *Annual Report for the Fiscal Year Ended March 31, 1932*, 41.

100 Department of the Interior, *Annual Report for the Fiscal Year Ended March 31, 1931*, 137. In 1937, A. E. Porsild accompanied R. A. Bartlett's summer cruise to the North, which went to both Labrador and Greenland and made a collection of vascular plants. Department of Mines and Resources, *Annual Report for the Fiscal Year Ended March 31, 1938*, 42.

101 In the summer of 1937, Mackay Meikle, agent of the Department of Mines and Resources at Fort Smith, made a long tour of inspection in the Mackenzie District, during which he visited the reindeer station and supervised the establishment of various aids to navigation in some of the lakes and rivers of the Mackenzie system. Dr. J. A. Urquhart, medical officer at Aklavik, had also the responsibility of supervising field work in the reindeer station. During the summer of 1939, Dr. Seymour Hadwen, Director of Pathology and Bacteriology at the Ontario Research Foundation in Toronto, inspected the reindeer in the preserve on behalf of the Department of Mines and Resources, and made a detailed study of herd management, diseases, predators, and other aspects of the industry. Department of Mines and Resources, *Annual Report for the Fiscal Year Ended March 31, 1938*, 68–69, 71.

102 Canada, Order in Council, PC No. 85, 22 January 1927.

103 N. B. McLean, *Report of the Hudson Strait Expedition 1927–28* (Ottawa: King's Printer, 1929), 3–20. See also N. B. McLean, *Report of the Hudson Strait Expedition to December 31, 1927* (Ottawa: King's Printer, 1928); F. H. Ellis, "First Flights over Hudson Strait," *The Beaver* (March 1944): 15–19; W/CR. V. Manning, "The Hudson Straight Expedition 1927–8," *Canadian Geographical Journal* 62, no. 2 (Feb. 1961): 40–53.

104 LAC, RG 85, vol. 1515, file 1009-28 pt. 2, *Factual Record Supporting Canadian Sovereignty in the Arctic*, 161–62.

105 LAC, RG 85, vol. 1515, file 1009-28 pt. 2, *Factual Record Supporting Canadian Sovereignty in the Arctic*, 162–63; F.C.G. Smith, "The Canadian Hydrographical Survey of the Hudson Bay Route," *The Geographical Journal* 87, no. 2 (Feb. 1936): 127–40; *Polar Record* 2, no. 9 (Jan. 1935): 52.

106 *Editor's Note*: I added all but the first sentence of this paragraph. The quote is from Balfour W. Currie, "The Polar Years," on University of Saskatchewan Archives, "The Second International Polar Year: Epilogue," http://scaa.usask.ca/gallery/northern/currie/en_epilogue.shtml (last accessed 28 August 2013).

16 | Epilogue

1 Larsen's personal papers have been turned over to Library and Archives Canada [hereafter LAC] by members of the family, and are identified as MG30 B75, Henry A. Larsen fonds [hereafter Larsen fonds], 6 vols. They contain the main source of information about Larsen's life and career: his autobiography in its original typewriting (hereafter "Larsen autobiography manuscript"). I understand that this enormous record, comprising fully 1,000 well-filled foolscap-size pages of typing, was done completely by Larsen himself, in approximately the last two years of his life, and is in its original state. More available to the public is the shorter published version, H. A. Larsen, *The Big Ship*, done in co-operation with F. R. Sheer and E. Omholt-Jensen (Toronto: McClelland and Stewart, 1967).

2 Larsen, *The Big Ship*, 1–2, 27, 34–35; Larsen autobiography manuscript, 230, 304–5.

3 Larsen, *The Big Ship*, 28. See also Larsen autobiography manuscript, 230. It may be that some instructions Wood received from Ottawa at an early stage of his service in this region had something to do with the formation of the idea. These instructions came at the time when officials in Ottawa were uneasy about suspected Danish encroachments in Ellesmere Island, and ran as follows: "Instruct Inspector Wood as follows: – All islands in the Arctic north of the American continent claimed as part of Canada, exercise jurisdiction over them if practicable as hitherto. Send patrol Banks Land but not if you consider it too dangerous stop. Instruct Tree River detachment to make patrols as frequently as possible to Victoria Island to see Canadian Laws observed by traders

and others." LAC, RG 18, accession 1984-85/084, vol. 33, file G-516-37, vol. 1, Commissioner Perry to O. C. at Dawson, 29 December 1920.

4 LAC, RG18, vol. 3475, file S1200-9, vol. 1, Starnes to Cardin, 23 October 1924.

5 Ibid., Assistant Commissioner to Minister in control of RCMP, 14 July 1925.

6 Authority for the purchase was granted by Canada, Order in Council, PC No. 474, 31 March 1926. Attached to the order is a memo, dated 19 March 1926, by Commissioner Starnes.

7 Canada, Order in Council, PC No. 1893, 29 September 1927.

8 This engine served well for years but in 1944 was replaced by a similar but much more powerful 300 hp engine. For details about the *St. Roch*, see Larsen, *The Big Ship*, 36–39; also RCMP booklet *St. Roch Past and Present* (Ottawa: Queen's Printer, 1966).

9 Larsen, *The Big Ship*, 46–47. See also LAC, RG 18, series F-1, vol. 3475, file S1200-9, vol. 5, "Standing Orders" signed by Insp. Kemp, 31 July 1928; Kemp to "G" Div., 7 August 1928; memo signed by Larsen, 27 August 1928.

10 Larsen wintered with her at various locations in the western and central Arctic during the years 1928–29, 1930–34, 1935–37, 1938–39, 1940–42, 1945–46, and 1947–48. He was promoted successively to corporal (1929), sergeant (1929), staff sergeant (1943), sub-inspector (1944), inspector (1946), and superintendent (1953). In 1949 he was appointed commanding officer of the Force's "G" Division, responsible for the Northwest Territories and Yukon, and remained in this position, with his base at Ottawa headquarters, until his retirement in 1961. After his retirement he resided briefly at Lunenburg, Nova Scotia, and then returned to Vancouver, where he died on 29 October 1964. There are many sources for details about the careers of both Larsen and the *St. Roch*, but the best are Larsen's autobiography manuscript and *The Big Ship*.

11 LAC, RG 18, vol. 8139, file "Patrols and Mileage of St Roch Detachment" (formerly RCMP file G567-84), vol. 1, Larsen to O. C. "E" Div., 27 November 1934.

12 Ibid., vol. 2, Irvine to MacBrien, 13 December 1934.

13 Ibid., vol. 1, Belcher to RCMP Adjutant, 17 December 1934.

14 Ibid., vol. 2, Larsen to Curleigh, 9 May 1936.

15 Ibid., Curleigh to O. C. "G" Div., 25 May 1936.

16 Larsen autobiography manuscript, 621; also Larsen, *The Big Ship*, 113. The quotation is given verbatim from the autobiography manuscript.

17 Larsen autobiography manuscript, 745–46, verbatim quotation. See also Larsen, *The Big Ship*, 140–42.

18 LAC, Larsen fonds, vol. 1, file *Smellie Capt. Thomas F*, Larsen to Commissioner L. H. Nicholson, 13 November 1957. This letter was written regarding a controversy the RCMP was having with Captain Smellie, formerly skipper of the HBC ship *Nascopie*, about the achievements, responsibilities, etc., of their two ships.

19 LAC, Larsen fonds, vol. 1, file *Smellie Capt. Thomas F*, Larsen to Commissioner, 15 November 1957.

20 Minutes of 104th session of NWT Council on 30 January 1940, sec. 2(i); minutes of Special Session on 15 February 1940, sec. 2(i).

21 LAC, RG 18, vol. 8139, file "Patrols and Mileage of St Roch Detachment," vol. 3, Adj. F. A. Blake to O. C. "G" Div., 20 August 1940.

22 Ibid., O. C. "G" Div. To O. C. Aklavik, 8 March 1941.

23 Ibid., 899–900. See also Larsen, *The Big Ship*, 181.

24 Larsen, *The Big Ship*, 145.

25 Sgt. F. S. Farrar, "Arctic Assignment: The Story of the St. Roch," in *Great Stories of Canada* Series, ed. B. Bonnezen (Toronto: Macmillan, 1955), 21, 24, 34, 36.

26 LAC, RG 18, vol. 8139, file "Patrols and Mileage of St Roch Detachment," Larsen to O. C. "G" Div., 12 November 1940.

27 A feature of the long winter confinements was a series of lengthy patrols by members of the nine-man crew to neighbouring territories, including Banks Island, Princess Royal Islands, Victoria Island, King William Island, Boothia Peninsula, Somerset Island, and Simpson Peninsula. "The Voyage of the St. Roch through the North-West Passage, 1940–42," *Polar Record* 4, no. 27 (January 1944): 115–18. For personal accounts of this voyage, see Larsen, *Big Ship*, 140–79, and *The North-West Passage 1940–1942 and 1944* (Ottawa: Queen's Printer, 1958).

28 LAC, RG 18, vol. 8139, file "Patrols and Mileage of St Roch Detachment", Larsen to O. C. "G" Div., 31 December 1941.

29 See also, besides references previously cited, the following: John B. Thompson, *St. Roch: 1944: A Photographic Study*, Department of Indian Affairs

and Northern Development, National Historic Sites Service, Manuscript Report Number 86 (Ottawa, 1972); G. J. Tranter, *Plowing the Arctic* (London: Hodder and Stoughton, 1944); Bruce McLeod, "Nor'west Passage," *Maclean's Magazine* (1 March 1945): 19–24; Sandra Gwyn, "The boat who wouldn't sink," *Maclean's* (Oct. 1974): 86–94; A. Stevenson, "Valiant Viking," *North* 14, no. 5 (Sept.–Oct. 1967): 40–45; C. Wilson, "Arctic Odyssey," *The Beaver* (March 1945): 3–7; J. Lewis Robinson, "Conquest of the Northwest Passage by RCMP Schooner St. Roch," *Canadian Geographical Journal* 30, no. 2 (Feb. 1945): 52–73; *Royal Canadian Mounted Police 1945: Reports and Other Papers Relating to the Two Voyages of the R.C.M. Police Schooner "St. Roch" Through the North West Passage*, by H. A. Larsen and Others (Ottawa: King's Printer, 1945); "East Through the North-west Passage" *Royal Canadian Mounted Police Quarterly* 10, no. 2 (Oct. 1942): 148–61; Sgt. F. S. Farrar, "The *St. Roch* Sails South," *Royal Canadian Mounted Police Quarterly* 16, no. 2 (Oct. 1950): 120–41; H. A. Larsen, *The North-West Passage 1940–1942 and 1944: The Famous Voyages of the Royal Canadian Mounted Police Schooner "St. Roch"* (Ottawa: Queen's Printer, 1958); H. A. Larsen, "Our Return Voyage Through the Northwest Passage," *Royal Canadian Mounted Police Quarterly* 10, no. 4 (April 1945): 298–320, also editorial "Canada's Sovereignty in the Arctic," *Royal Canadian Mounted Police Quarterly* 10, no. 4 (April 1945): 273–74; S. W. Horrall, *The Pictorial History of the Royal Canadian Mounted Police* (Toronto: McGraw-Hill Ryerson, 1973), 220–25.

30 *Editor's note*: I have derived this final paragraph from Smith, "Sovereignty in the North: The Canadian Aspect of an International Problem," in *The Arctic Frontier*, ed. R. St. J. Macdonald (Toronto: University of Toronto Press, 1966), 211–12.

Bibliography

Primary Documents

Archival Collections

Colonial Office, *London, United Kingdom*

Department of External Affairs (now Foreign Affairs and International Trade), *Ottawa*

Hudson's Bay Company Archives, *Winnipeg*
A.92/7/1, Correspondence 5th Thule Expedition
A.102/1962, Rasmussen Expedition (London)
RG2/4/63, Knud Rasmussen (Winnipeg)

Library and Archives Canada, *Ottawa*

Government Departmental Records
RG 2 Privy Council Office
RG 15 Dominion Lands Branch
RG 25 Department of External Affairs
RG 85 Northern Affairs Program
RG 88 Surveys Mapping and Remote Sensing

Personal Papers:
MG 30 B40, Rudolph Martin Anderson
MG 26 H, Robert Laird Borden
MG 30 B 38, Charles Camsell
MG 27-IIA2, Joseph Chamberlain
MG 30 E 44, Loring Cheney Christie
MG 30 C12, Fred Cook Papers
MG 30 B 57, John Davidson Craig
MG 31 C 6, Richard Sterling Finnie
MG 30 E 169, James Bernard Harkin
MG 26 J, William Lyon Mackenzie King
MG 26 G, Wilfrid Laurier
MG 30 B 68, Robert Archibald Logan
MG 30 B33, Albert Peter Low
MG 26 A, John A. Macdonald
MG 261, Arthur Meighen
MG 30 B 81, Vilhjalmur Stefansson

Printed Primary Sources

Alaska Boundary Tribunal. *Memorandum for Counsel, Various Documents Bearing on the Question of the Alaska Boundary.* London: McCorquodale, 1903.

Blanchet, G. H. *Great Slave Lake Area Northwest Territories*, booklet issued by the NWT and Yukon Branch, Department of the Interior. Ottawa: King's Printer, 1926.

Blanchet, G. H. *Keewatin and Northeastern Mackenzie: A General Survey of the Life, Activities, and Natural Resources of this Section of the Northwest Territories, Canada.* Booklets issued by the NWT and Yukon Branch, Department of the Interior. Ottawa: King's Printer, 1930.

Blanchet, G. H. *Preliminary Report on the Aerial Mineral Exploration of Northern Canada.* Booklets issued by the NWT and Yukon Branch, Department of the Interior. Ottawa: King's Printer, 1930.

Blanchet, G. H. *Preliminary Report on the Fort Smith Wood Buffalo Park, Department of the Interior Topographical Survey* mimeographed booklet. Ottawa: King's Printer, 1927.

Burwash, L. T. *The Eskimo, Their Country and Its Resources: Economic Survey of the East Coasts of Hudson Bay and James Bay from Richmond Gulf to Rupert House, Including the Belcher and Other Adjacent Islands 1927.* Mimeographed report issued by the NWT and Yukon Branch, Department of the Interior. Ottawa, 1928.

Canada. Department of the Interior. *Annual Reports for 1890–96.* Ottawa: Queen's Printer, 1891–95.

Canada. Department of the Interior. *Annual Reports 1924–26.* Ottawa: King's Printer, 1924–26.

Canada. Department of Marine. *Nineteenth Annual Report* (1886).

Canada. Department of Mines and Technical Surveys Geographical Branch. *Atlas of Canada.* Ottawa: Queen's Printer, 1957.

Canada. House of Commons *Debates.*

Canada. House of Commons, *Journals.*

Canada. Senate, *Journals.*

Canada. Senate *Debates.*

Canada's Arctic Islands: Log of Canadian Expedition 1922. Pamphlet issued by the NWT and Yukon Branch, Department of the Interior. Ottawa: King's Printer, 1923.

Canada's Western Arctic: Report on Investigations in 1925–1926, 1928–29, and 1930. Booklet issued by the NWT and Yukon Branch, Department of the Interior. Ottawa: King's Printer, 1931.

Chambers, Captain Ernest J., ed. *Canada's Fertile Northland: Evidence Heard Before a Select Committee of the Senate of Canada During the Parliamentary Session of 1906–7, and the Report Based Thereon.* Ottawa: Government Printing Bureau, 1908.

Dawson, G. M. *Report on an Exploration in the Yukon District, N.W.T., and Adjacent Northern Portion of British Columbia 1887, Report B in Geological and Natural History Survey of Canada Annual Report 1887–88.* Montreal: Dawson Bros., 1888.

Documents on Canadian External Relations, Vol. 1 (1909–1918). Ottawa: Department of External Affairs, 1967.

Eastern Arctic Patrol S. S. "Ungava" 1932. Pamphlet issued by the NWT and Yukon Branch, Department of the Interior. Ottawa: King's Printer, 1932.

Great Britain. *British and Foreign State Papers* (1818–1898).

Great Britain. *British Colonial Office Papers.*

Great Britain. Parliamentary *Debates.*

Great Britain. *Parliamentary Papers*, Correspondence Respecting the Alaska Boundary, 1877. London: His Majesty's Stationery Office, 1904.

Greely, Adolphus W. *Report on the Proceedings of the United States Expedition to Lady Franklin Bay, Grinnell Land.* Washington, DC: Government Printing Office, 1888.

Hadley, John. *Hadley's Narrative of the Wreck of the "Karluk,"* unpublished typewritten manuscript, and also photostat copy of original, in the Aboriginal Affairs and Northern Development Library, Gatineau, Quebec.

International Boundary Commission. *Joint Report upon the Survey and Demarcation of the International Boundary between the United States and Canada along the 141st Meridian from the Arctic Ocean to Mount St. Elias.* Ottawa, 1918.

King, W. F. *Report upon the* Tide *of Canada to the Islands North of the Mainland of Canada.* Ottawa: Government Printing Bureau, 1905.

Local Conditions in the Mackenzie District 1922. Pamphlet issued by the NWT and Yukon Branch, Department of the Interior. Ottawa: King's Printer, 1923.

Low, A. P. *Report on the Dominion Government Expedition to Hudson Bay and the Arctic Islands on Board the D.G.S. Neptune, 1903–04.* Ottawa: Government Printing Bureau, 1906.

Malloy, W. M., ed. *Treaties, Conventions, International Acts, Protocols and Agreements between the United States of America and Other Powers 1776–1909.* Washington, DC: Government Printing Office, 1910.

McConnell, R. G. *Report of an Exploration in the Yukon and Mackenzie Basins, N.W.T., issued by the Geological and Natural History Survey of Canada.* Montreal: W. F. Brown and Co., 1891.

McLean, N. B. *Report of the Hudson Strait Expedition 1927–28.* Ottawa: King's Printer, 1929.

McLean, N. B. *Report of the Hudson Strait Expedition to December 31, 1927.* Ottawa: King's Printer, 1928.

Millward, Albert E. *Southern Baffin Island.* Ottawa: King's Printer, 1930.

Moore, John Bassett. *A Digest of International Law.* Washington, DC: Government Printing Office, 1906.

Moore, John Bassett. *History and Digest of the International Arbitrations to which the United States had been a Party.* Washington, DC: Government Printing Office, 1898.

Nicholson, Norman L. *The Boundaries of Canada, Its Provinces and Territories, Memoir 2 of Geographical Branch, Department of Mines and Technical Surveys.* Ottawa: Queen's Printer, 1954.

Ray, Patrick H. *Report of the International Polar Expedition to Point Barrow, Alaska.* Washington, DC: Government Printing Office, 1885.

Raymond, C. W. *Report of a Reconnaissance of the Yukon River, Alaska Territory, July to September, 1869.* Washington, DC: Government Printing Office, 1871.

Report of Investigations Affecting Eskimo and Wild Life District of Mackenzie 1924–1925–1926. Pamphlet issued by the NWT and Yukon Branch, Department of the Interior. Ottawa, n.d.

Soper, J. D. *A Faunal Investigation of Southern Baffin Island, National Museum of Canada Bulletin no. 53.* Ottawa: King's Printer, 1928.

Stumbles, W. W. et al. *The Arctic Expedition 1910.* Ottawa: Department of Marine and Fisheries, n.d.

Wakeham, William. *Report of the Expedition to Hudson Bay and Cumberland Gulf in the Steamship "Diana."* Ottawa: Queen's Printer, 1898.

Books

Adney, Tappan. *The Klondike Stampede of 1897–1898*. New York and London: Harper and Bros., 1900.

Allen, Everett S. *Arctic Odyssey: The Life of Rear Admiral Donald B. MacMillan*. New York: Dodd, Mead and Co., 1962.

Amundsen, Roald. *My Life as an Explorer*. London: W. Heinemann, 1927.

———. *The North West Passage*. London: Constable and Co., 1908.

Andrews, Clarence L. *The Story of Alaska*. Caldwell, ID: Caxton Printers, 1947.

Armstrong, Terence E. *Russian Settlement in the North*. Cambridge: Cambridge University Press, 1965.

Bancroft, Hubert H. *History of Alaska*. Volume 33 of *The Works of Hubert Howe Bancroft*. San Francisco: A. L. Bancroft and Co., 1886.

Bartlett, Robert A. *The Log of Bob Bartlett: The True Story of Forty Years of Seafaring and Exploration*. New York: Putnam's Sons, 1928.

Bartlett, Robert A., and Ralph T. Hale. *The Last Voyage of the Karluk*. Boston: Small, Maynard and Co., 1916.

Beriault, Yvon. *Les Problemes politiques du Nord canadien*. Doctoral thesis, University of Ottawa, 1942.

Bernier, Joseph E. *Master Mariner and Arctic Explorer*. Ottawa: Le Droit, 1939.

Bishop, Joseph B. *Theodore Roosevelt and His Time Shown in His Own Letters*. New York: Scribner's Sons, 1920.

Black, Mrs. G. *My Seventy Years*. London: T. Nelson and Sons, 1938.

Berton, Pierre. *The Golden Trail: The Story of the Klondike Rush*. Toronto: Macmillan, 1954.

———. *The Klondike Fever: The Life and Death of the Last Great Gold Rush*. New York: A. A. Knopf, 1959.

Brainard, David L. *The Outpost of the Lost*. Indianapolis: Bobbs-Merrill, 1929.

Burpee, Lawrence. *An Historical Atlas of Canada*. Toronto: T. Nelson and Sons, 1927.

Chatterton, E. Keble. *Whalers and Whaling*. London: P. Allan and Co., 1925.

Clark, Henry W. *History of Alaska*. New York: Macmillan, 1930.

Classen, H. George. *Thrust and Counterthrust: The Genesis of the Canada-United States Boundary*. Don Mills: Longmans Canada, 1965.

Commager Henry S., ed. *Documents of American History*. 8th ed. New York: Appleton-Century-Crofts, 1968.

Cook, Frederick A. *My Attainment of the Pole*. New York: M. Kennerley, 1912.

———. *Return from the Pole*. Edited by F. J. Pohl. New York: Pellegrini and Cudahy, 1951.

Copland, D. *Livingstone of the Arctic*. Ottawa: D. Copland, 1967.

Corbett, Percy E. *The Settlement of Canadian-American Disputes: A Critical Study of Methods and Results*. New Haven, CT: Yale University Press, 1937.

Coxe, William. *Account of the Russian Discoveries between Asia and America*. London: T. Cadell, 1787.

Croft, Andrew. *Polar Exploration*. London: A. and C. Black, 1939.

Crouse, Nellis M. *The Search for the North Pole*. New York: R. R. Smith, 1947.

Dafoe, J. W. *Clifford Sifton in Relation to His Times*. Toronto: Macmillan, 1931.

Dawson, George M. *Report on an Exploration in the Yukon District, N.W.T., and Adjacent Northern Portion of British Columbia 1887, issued by the Geological and Natural History Survey of Canada*. Montreal: Dawson Bros., 1888.

Dawson, Samuel E. *The Line of Demarcation of Pope Alexander VI, in A. D. 1493 and that of the Treaty of Tordesillas in A. D. 1494*. Toronto: Copp Clark, 1899.

DeLong, Emma W. *Explorer's Wife*. New York: Dodd, Mead and Co., 1938.

DeLong, George W. *The Voyage of the Jeannette*. Boston: Houghton, Mifflin, 1884.

Dennett, Tyler. *John Hay: From Poetry to Politics*. Port Washington, NY: Kennikat Press, 1963.

Ewart, John S. *The Kingdom of Canada, Imperial Federation, The Colonial Conferences, The Alaska Boundary, and Other Essays*. Toronto: Morang and Co., 1908.

Fairley, T. C. *Sverdrup's Arctic Adventures*. London: Longmans, 1959.

Fairley, T. C., and Charles E. Israel. *The True North: The Story of Captain Joseph Bernier*. Toronto: Macmillan, 1957.

Finnie, Richard S. *Canada Moves North*. New York: Macmillan, 1942.

Fram Expedition. *Report of the Second Norwegian Arctic Expedition in the "Fram," 1898–1902*. Kristiania: Videnskals-Selskabet, 1904–1930.

Galbraith, John S. *The Hudson's Bay Company as an Imperial Factor 1821–1869*. Toronto: University of Toronto Press, 1957.

Gilder, William H. *Schwatka's Search*. New York: Scribner's Sons, 1881.

Golder, Frank A., *Bering's Voyages, American Geographical Society Research Series* 1 and 2. Edited by W.L.G. Joerg. New York: American Geographical Society, 1922, 1925.

———. *Russian Expansion on the Pacific 1641–1850*. Cleveland: A. H. Clark, 1914.

Graham, Roger. *Arthur Meighen, Vol. 2: And Fortune Fled*. Toronto: Clarke, Irwin, 1963.

Greely, Adolphus W. *A Handbook of Polar Discoveries*. 3rd ed. Boston: Little, Brown, 1907.

———. *The Polar Regions in the Twentieth Century*. London: Harrap and Co., 1929.

———. *Three Years of Arctic Service*. New York: Scribner's Sons, 1886.

Green, Fitzhugh. *Peary: The Man Who Refused to Fail*. New York: Putnam's Sons, 1926.

Grenfell, Sir Wilfred. *Forty Years for Labrador*. Boston: Houghton Mifflin, 1919, 1932.

———. *A Labrador Doctor: The Autobiography of Wilfred Thomason Grenfell*. London: Hodder and Stoughton, 1920, 1940.

Gruening, Ernest. *The State of Alaska*. New York: Random House, 1954.

Hamilton, Walter R. *The Yukon Story*. Vancouver: Mitchell Press, 1964.

Hanson, Earl P. *Stefansson: Prophet of the North*. New York: Harper and Bros., 1941.

Hare, Lloyd C. M. *Salted Tories: The Story of the Whaling Fleets of San Francisco*. Mystic, CT: Marine Historical Association, 1960.

Haskell, William B. *Two Years in the Klondyke and Alaskan Gold-Fields*. Hartford: Hartford Publishing, 1898.

Hayes, J. Gordon. *Robert Edwin Peary*. London: Richards and Toulmin, 1929.

Henson, Matthew A. *A Negro Explorer at the North Pole*. New York: F. A. Stokes, 1912.

Hobbs, William H. *Peary*. New York: Macmillan, 1936.

Howay, Frederic W., Walter N. Sage, and H. F. Angus. *British Columbia and the United States: The North Pacific Slope from Fur Trade to Aviation*. Toronto: Ryerson Press, 1942.

Howgate, Henry W. *Polar Colonization*. Washington, DC: Beresford, 1879.

James, Bessie R. , ed. *Six Came Back: The Arctic Adventure of David L. Brainard*. Indianapolis: Bobbs-Merrill, 1940.

Jenness, Diamond. *Eskimo Administration II: Canada*. Montreal: Arctic Institute of North America, 1964.

Jessup, Philip C. *Elihu Root*. New York: Dodd, Mead and Co., 1938.

Karsheninnikov, Stepan P. *The History of Kamtschatka And the Kurilski Islands, with the Countries Adjacent*. Translated by James Grieve. St. Petersburg, 1754; London, 1764; Chicago: Quadrangle Books, 1962.

Keenleyside, Hugh L. *Canada and the United States: Some Aspects of Their Historical Relations*. Revised ed. New York: A. A. Knopf, 1952.

Keller, Arthur S., Oliver J. Lissitzyn, and Frederick J. Mann. *Creation of Rights of Sovereignty through Symbolics Acts 1400–1800*. New York: Columbia University Press, 1938.

Kerr, J. Lennox. *Wilfred Grenfell: His Life and Work*. Toronto: Ryerson Press, 1959.

Kirwan, Laurence P. *The White Road: A Survey of Polar Exploration*. London: Hollis and Carter, 1959.

Lanman, Charles. *Farthest North: The Life and Explorations of Lieutenant James Booth Lockwood*. New York: Appleton and Co., 1885.

LeBourdais, D. M. *Northward on the New Frontier*. Ottawa: Graphic Publishers, 1931.

———. *Stefansson: Ambassador of the North*. Montreal: Harvest House, 1963.

Lindley, M. F. *The Acquisition and Government of Backward Territory in International Law*. London: Longmans, Green, 1926.

Lingard, Cecil C. *Territorial Government in Canada: The Autonomy Question in the Old North-West Territories*. Toronto: University of Toronto Press, 1946.

Lomon, C J. *Fifty Years in Alaska*. New York: D. McKay, 1954.

Lubbock, Basil. *The Arctic Whalers*. Glasgow: Brown, Son, and Ferguson, 1955.

Lynch, Jeremiah. *Three Years in the Klondike*. Edited by Dale L. Morgan. Chicago: Lakeside Press, 1967.

MacMillan, D. B. *Four Years in the White North*. New York: Harper and Bros., 1918.

Markham, Clements R., ed. *The Voyages of William Baffin 1612–1622*. London: The Hakluyt Society, 1881.

Markham, M. E., and F. A. Markham. *The Life of Sir Albert Hastings Markham*. Cambridge: Cambridge University Press, 1927.

Miller, M. *The Great Trek*. New York: Doubleday, Doran and Co., 1935.

Morton, A. S. *A History of the Canadian West to 1870–71*. London: T. Nelson and Sons, 1939.

Muir, John. *The Cruise of the Corwin*. Boston: Houghton Mifflin, 1917.

Muller, Gerhard F. *Voyages from Asia to America*. Translated by T. Jefferys. London: T. Jefferys, 1764.

Murphy, Charles J. V. *Struggle: The Life and Exploits of Commander Richard E. Byrd*. New York: F. A. Stokes, 1928.

Nevins, Allan. *Henry White: Thirty Years of American Diplomacy*. New York: Harper and Bros., 1930.

Ogilvie, William. *Early Days on the Yukon*. London: John Lane, The Bodley Head, 1913.

Okun, Semen B. *The Russian-American Company*. Edited by B. D. Grekov. Translated by Carl Ginsburg. Cambridge, MA: Harvard University Press, 1951.

Palmer, Frederick. *In the Klondyke*. New York: Scribner's Sons, 1899.

Payer, Julius. *New Lands within the Arctic* Circle. New York: Appleton and Co., 1877.

Peary, Josephine D. *My Arctic Journal*. New York: Contemporary Publishing, 1897.

Peary, Robert E. *Northward over the "Great Ice."* London: Methuen and Co., 1898.

———. *Nearest the Pole*. London: Hutchinson and Co., 1907.

———. *The North Pole*. London: Hodder and Stoughton, 1910.

Penlington, N. *The Alaska Boundary Dispute: A Critical Reappraisal*. Toronto: McGraw-Hill Ryerson, 1972.

Plischke, Elmer. *Jurisdiction in the Polar Regions*. PhD dissertation, Clark University, 1943.

Pope, Maurice, ed. *Public Servant: The Memoirs of Sir Joseph Pope*. Toronto: Oxford University Press, 1960.

Porsild, A. E. *Reindeer Grazing in Northwest Canada, report issued by the Northwest Territories and Yukon Branch, Department of the Interior.* Ottawa: King's Printer, 1929.

Powell, Theodore. *The Long Rescue*. New York: Doubleday and Co., 1960.

Putnam, David Binney. *David Goes to Baffin Land*. New York: G. P. Putnam's Sons, 1927.

Putnam, George P. *Mariner of the North: The Life of Captain Bob Bartlett*. New York: Duell, Sloan and Pearce, 1947.

Rae, John. *Narrative of an Expedition to the Shores of the Arctic Sea in 1846 and 1847.* London: T. and W. Boone, 1850.

Rich, Edwin E. *The History of the Hudson's Bay Company 1670–1870*. London: The Hudson's Bay Record Society, 1958–1959.

———. *Copy-book of Letters Outward 1679–1694*." London: Hudson's Bay Record Society, 1948.

Rich, Edwin E., ed. *Minutes of the Hudson's Bay Company 1671–1674. The Hudson's Bay Record Society Publications* 5. London: The Champlain Society for The Hudson's Bay Record Society, 1942.

Schley, Winfield S., and James R. Soley. *The Rescue of the Greely*. London: Low et al., n.d.

Schwatka, Frederick. *Along Alaska's Great River*. New York: Cassell and Co., 1885.

Scoresby, Captain W. *The Northern Whale-Fishery*. London: Religious Tract Society, n.d.

Seemann, Berthold. *Narrative of the Voyage of H.M.S. Herald*. Vol. 2. London: Reeve and Co., 1853.

Skelton, O. D. *Life and Letters of Sir Wilfrid Laurier*. Toronto: Oxford University Press, 1921.

Smalley, George W. *Anglo-American Memories*. London: Duckworth and Co., 1911.

Smedal, Cf. Gustav. *Skrifter om Svalbard og Ishavet*. Translated by C. Meyer as *Acquisition of Sovereignty over Polar Areas*. Oslo: J. Dybwad, 1931.

Starbuck, Alexander. *History of the American Whale Fishery from its Earliest Inception to the Year 1876*. New York: Argosy-Antiquarian, 1964.

Stefansson, Vilhjalmur. *The Adventure of Wrangel Island*. New York: Macmillan, 1925.

———. *Discovery: The Autobiography of Vilhjalmur Stefansson*. New York: McGraw-Hill, 1964.

———. *The Friendly Arctic: The Story of Five Years in Polar Regions*. Revised ed. New York: Macmillan, 1943.

———. *Hunters of the Great North*. London: G. G. Harrap and Co., 1923.

———. *My Life with the Eskimos*. New York: Macmillan, 1927.

———. *The Northward Course of Empire*. New York: Macmillan, 1924.

———. *The Problem of Meighen Island*. Limited edition privately printed for Mr. Joseph Robinson. New York, 1939.

Summary of Reports of Commander Otto Sverdrup's Explorations in 1898–1902. Oslo: Wittusen and Jensen, 1928.

Svarlien, Oscar. *The Eastern Greenland Case in Historical Perspective*. Gainesville: University of Florida Press, 1964.

Sverdrup, Otto. *New Land: Four Years in the Arctic Regions*. London: Longmans, Green, 1904.

Tansill, Charles C. *Canadian-American Relations, 1875–1911*. New Haven, CT: Yale University Press, 1943.

Taracouzio,T. A. *Soviets in the Arctic*. New York: Macmillan, 1938.

Thayer, William R. *The Life and Letters of John Hay*. Boston: Houghton Mifflin, 1915.

Thomas, Lewis H. *The Struggle for Responsible Government in the North-West Territories 1870–97*. Toronto: University of Toronto Press, 1956.

Todd, Alden L. *Abandoned: The Story of the Greely Arctic Expedition 1880–1884*. New York: McGraw-Hill, 1961.

Tyrrell, James W. *Across the Sub-Arctics of Canada*. 3rd ed. Toronto: Wm. Briggs, 1908.

Tyson, George E. *The Cruise of the Florence*. Edited by Captain Henry W. Howgate. Washington, DC: J. J. Chapman, 1879.

Vancouver, Capt. George. *A Voyage of Discovery to the North Pacific Ocean and Round the World*. London: Robinson and Edwards, 1798.

Verrill, A. Hyatt. *The Real Story of the Whaler*. New York: Appleton and Co., 1931.

Von Wrangel, Ferdinand. *Narrative of an Expedition to the Polar Sea in the Years 1820, 1821, 1822, and 1823*. Translated and edited by Edward and Mrs. Sabine. London: J. Madden and Co., 1840, 1844.

Wade, Frederick Coate. *Treaties Affecting the North Pacific Coast*. Vancouver: Saturday Sunset Presses, 1914.

Walden, Arthur T. *A Dog-Puncher on the Yukon*. Boston: Houghton Mifflin, 1928.

Whymper, Frederick. *Travel and Adventure in the Territory of Alaska*. New York: Harper and Bros., 1871.

Winslow, Kathryn. *Big Pan-Out*. New York: Norton and Co., 1951.

Zaslow, Morris. *The Opening of the Canadian North, 1870–1914*. Toronto: McClelland and Stewart, 1971.

Zaslow, Morris, ed. *A Century of Canada's Arctic Islands 1880–1890*. Ottawa: Royal Society of Canada, 1981.

Articles and Book Chapters

Abrahamson, Gunther. "Canada's Reindeer." *Canadian Geographical Journal* 66, no. 6 (June 1963): 188–93.

Balch, Thomas W. "Is Hudson Bay a Closed or an Open Sea?" *American Journal of International Law* 6 (Pt. 1, 1912): 409–59

Banting, F. G. "With the Arctic Patrol." *Canadian Geographical Journal* 1, no. 1 (May 1930): 19–30.

Blanchet, G. H. "Searching the Arctic by Aeroplane." *Canadian Geographical Journal* 1, no. 8 (December 1930): 641–62.

Boas, Franz. "The Central Eskimo." In *Smithsonian Institution Bureau of Ethnology Sixth Annual Report 1884–1885*, edited by J. W. Powell, 409–658. Washington, DC: Government Printing Office, 1888.

Burwash, L. T. "The Franklin Search." *Canadian Geographical Journal* 1, no. 7 (November 1930): 587–603.

Byrd, Richard E. "Flying over the Arctic." *The National Geographic Magazine* 48, no. 5 (November 1925): 477–532.

Dall, William H. "The Discovery and Exploration of Alaska." In *Alaska*, edited by C. Hart Merriam. London: J. Murray, 1902.

———. "Travels on the Yukon and in the Yukon Territory in 1866–1868." In *The Yukon Territory*, edited by F. Mortimer Trimmer, 1–242. London: Downey and Co., 1898.

Dathan, Wendy. *The Reindeer Botanist: Alf Erling Porsild, 1901–1977*. Calgary: University of Calgary Press, 2012.

Dinwoodie, D. H. "Arctic Controversy: the 1925 Byrd-MacMillan Expedition Example." *Canadian Historical Review* 53, no. 1 (March 1972): 51–65.

Diubaldo, Richard J. "Wrangling over Wrangel Island." *Canadian Historical Review* 48, no. 3 (September 1967): 201–26.

Editorial Comment. "The Fur Seal Question." *American Journal of International Law* 1 (Pt. 2 1907): 742–48.

Ellis, F. H. "First Flights over Hudson Strait." *The Beaver*, Outfit 274 (March 1944): 15–19.

Finnie, O. S. "Reindeer for the Canadian Eskimo." *Natural History* 31, no. 4 (1931): 409–16.

Finnie, Richard. "First Short-Wave in the Arctic II." *The Beaver* (March 1951): 23.

Finnie, Richard S. "Stefansson as I Knew Him." *NorthlNord* 25, no. 3 (May/June 1978): 36–43 and 25, no. 4 (July/August 1978): 12–19.

———. "Farewell Voyages: Bernier and the 'Arctic.'" *Beaver* 54, no. 1 (Summer 1974): 44–54.

———. "Stefansson's Unsolved Mystery." *North/ Nord* 25, no. 6 (November/December 1978): 2–7.

Head, Ivan L. "Canadian Claims to Territorial Sovereignty in the Arctic Regions," *McGill Law Journal* 9 (1963): 200–226.

Hearne, S. *A Journey from Prince of Wales's Fort in Hudson's Bay to the Northern Ocean in the Years 1769, 1770, 1771, and 1772.* Toronto: Champlain Society, 1911.

Hill, R. M. "The Canadian Reindeer Project." *Polar Record* 14, no. 88 (January 1968): 21–24.

Jenness, Diamond. "The Friendly Arctic." *Science* 56, no. 2436 (7 July 1922): 8–12.

Johnston, V. Kenneth. "Canada's Title to the Arctic Islands." *Canadian Historical Review* 14, no. 1 (March 1933): 24–41.

Lakhtine, W. "Rights over the Arctic." *American Journal of International Law* 24, no. 4 (October 1930): 705, 710.

Larmour, W. T. "Symbol of Sovereignty." *Canadian Geographical Journal* 49, no. 2 (August 1954): 82–86

LeNourdais, Donat Marc. "Vilhjalmur Stefansson." *Canadian Geographical Journal* 61, no. 2 (August 1960): 62–67.

MacBrien, J. H. "The Mounties in the Arctic." *Canadian Geographical Journal* 10, no. 4 (April 1935): 156–66.

Manning, V. "The Hudson Strait Expedition 1927–8." *Canadian Geographical Journal* 62, no. 2 (February 1961): 40–53.

McDonald, Eugene F. "First Short-Wave in the Arctic." *The Beaver* (December 1950): 57.

McKeand, D. L. "The Annual Eastern Arctic Patrol." *Canadian Geographical Journal* 17, no. 1 (July 1938): 36–39.

McKitterick, T.E.M. "The Validity of Territorial and Other Claims in Polar Regions." *Journal of Comparative Legislation and International Law* 21 (Pt. 1 1939): 89–97.

Miller, David H. "Political Rights in the Polar Regions." In *Problems of Polar Research*, edited by W.L.G. Joerg. New York: American Geographical Society, 1928.

Moore, J. "Alaska's First American Century: The View Ahead." *Polar Record* 14, no. 88 (January 1968): 3–13.

Munro, J. A. "The Alaska Boundary Dispute." In *Issues in Canadian History Series*, edited by J. L. Granatstein. Toronto: Copp Clark, 1970.

Peary, Robert E. "Four Years' Arctic Exploration, 1898–1902." *Geographical Journal* 22, no. 1 (July 1903): 646–72.

———. "Report of R. E. Peary, C. E., U.S.N., on Work Done in the Arctic in 1898–1902." *Bulletin of the American Geographical Society* 35, no. 5 (1903): 496–534.

Preuss, Lawrence. "The Dispute Between Denmark and Norway over the Sovereignty of East Greenland," *American Journal of International Law* 26, no. 3 (1932): 469–87.

Rich, E. E. *Copy-book of Letters Outward 1679–1694*." London: Hudson's Bay Record Society, 1948.

Schei, P. "Summary of Geographical Results." *Geographical Journal* 22, no. 1 (July 1903): 56–65.

Skelton, O. D. "The Day of Sir Wilfrid Laurier." In *Chronicles of Canada*, edited by George M. Wrong and H. H. Langton. Toronto: Glasgow, Brook, and Co., 1922.

Smith, F.C.G. "The Canadian Hydrographical Survey of the Hudson Bay Route." *Geographical Journal* 87, no. 2 (February 1936): 127–40.

Smith, Gordon W. "Sovereignty in the North: The Canadian Aspect of an International Problem." In *The Arctic Frontier*, edited by R. St. J. Macdonald, 194–255. Toronto: University of Toronto Press, 1966.

Soper, J. D. "Adventuring in Baffin Island." *Canadian Geographical Journal* 1, no. 3 (July 1930): 191–206.

———. "Discovery of the Breeding Grounds of the Blue Goose." *Canadian Field-Naturalist* 44, no. 1 (January 1930): 1–11.

Stefansson, Vilhjalmur. "The Activities of the Canadian Arctic Expedition from October, 1916 to April, 1918." *Geographical Review* (October 1918): 354–69

———. "The Canadian Arctic Expedition of 1913 to 1918." *Geographical Journal* 62, no. 4 (October 1921): 283–305.

———. "Wrangel Island Wrangle." *North* 13, no. 3 (September–October 1966): 20–29.

Svarlien, Oscar. "The Legal Status of the Arctic." *Proceedings of the American Society of International Law* 52 (1958): 136–44.

Sverdrup, Otto. "The Second Norwegian Polar Expedition in the 'Fram,' 1898–1902." *Geographical Journal* 22, no. 1 (July 1903): 38–55.

Taubenfeld, Howard J. "A Treaty for Antarctica." *International Conciliation* 531. New York: Carnegie Endowment for International Peace, January 1961: 253–54.

Treude, E. "The Development of Reindeer Husbandry in Canada." *Polar Record* 14, no. 88 (January 1968): 15–19.

Von der Heydte, Friedrich A. F. "Discovery, Symbolic Annexation and Virtual Effectiveness in International Law." *American Journal of International Law* 29 no. 3 (July 1935): 448–71.

Waultrin, Rene. "Le problème de la souveraineté des poles." *Revue Générale de Droit International Public* 16 (1909): 649–60.

White, James. "Boundary disputes and treaties." In *Canada and Its Provinces, vol. 8*, edited by A. Shortt and A. G. Doughty. Toronto, 1914.

Additional Readings

Anghie, Antony. *Imperialism, Sovereignty, and the Making of International Law.* Cambridge: Cambridge University Press, 2004.

Bankes, Nigel D. "Forty Years of Canadian Sovereignty Assertion in the Arctic, 1947–87." *Arctic* 40, no. 4 (December 1987): 285–91.

Barr, William. *Back from the Brink: The Road to Muskox Conservation in the Northwest Territories.* Calgary: Arctic Institute of North America, 1991.

———. "The career and disappearance of Hans K.E. Krüger, Arctic geologist, 1886–1930." *Polar Record* 29 (1993): 277–304.

———. *Red Serge and Polar Bear Pants: The Biography of Harry Stallworthy, RCMP.* Edmonton: University of Alberta Press, 2004.

———. *The Expeditions of the First International Polar Year, 1882–83.* 2nd ed. Calgary: Arctic Institute of North America, 2008.

Bartlett, Bob. *The Log of Bob Bartlett: The True Story of Forty Years of Seafaring and Exploration.* St. John's: Flanker Press, 2006.

Billman, Christine W. "Jack Craig and the Alaska Boundary Survey." *Beaver* 51, no. 2 (Autumn 1971): 44–49.

Bockstoce, J. R. *Whales, Ice and Men: The History of Whaling in the Western Arctic.* Seattle: University of Washington Press, 1986.

Bothwell, Robert. *Loring Christie: The Failure of Bureaucratic Imperialism.* New York and London: Garland, 1988.

Brested, Jens. "Danish Accession to the Thule District, 1937." *Nordic Journal of International Law* 57 (1988): 259–65.

Brown, Stephen. *The Last Viking: The Life of Roald Amundsen.* Vancouver: Douglas & McIntyre, 2012.

Bryant, John H., and Harold N. Cones. *Dangerous Crossings: The First Modern Polar Expedition, 1925.* Annapolis, MD: Naval Institute Press, 2000.

Castellino, Joshua, and Steve Allen. *Title to Territory in International Law: A Temporal Analysis.* Aldershot, UK: Ashgate, 2003.

Cavell, Janice. "The Second Frontier: The North in English-Canadian Historical Writing." *Canadian Historical Review* 83, no. 3 (September 2002): 364–89.

———. "Arctic Exploration in Canadian Print Culture, 1890–1930," *Papers of the Bibliographical Society of Canada* 44, no. 2 (2006): 7–44.

———. "'A little more latitude': Explorers, Politicians, and Canadian Arctic Policy during the Laurier Era." *Polar Record* 47, no. 4 (2010): 289–309.

———. "'As far as 90 north': Joseph Elzéar Bernier's 1907 and 1909 sovereignty claims." *Polar Record* 46, no. 239 (2010): 372–76.

———. "Historical Evidence and the Eastern Greenland Case." *Arctic* 61, no. 4 (December 2008): 433–41.

Cavell, Janice, and Jeff Noakes. "Explorer without a country: the question of Vilhjalmur Stefansson's citizenship." *Polar Record* 45, no. 234 (2009): 237–41.

———. "The origins of Canada's first Eastern Arctic Patrol, 1919–1922." *Polar Record* 45, no. 233 (2009): 97–112.

Coates, Ken. *Best Left as Indians: Native-White Relations and the Yukon Territory.* Montreal: McGill-Queen's University Press, 1991.

———. "Controlling the Periphery: The Territorial Administrations of the Yukon and Alaska, 1867–1959." *Pacific Northwest Quarterly* 78, no. 4 (October 1987).

Coates, Ken, and William R. Morrison. *Land of the Midnight Sun: A History of the Yukon Territory.* 2nd ed. Montreal: McGill-Queen's University Press, 2005.

———. *The Sinking of the Princess Sophia: Taking the North Down With Her.* Toronto: Oxford University Press, 1990.

———. "'To Make These Tribes Understand': The Trial of Alikomiak and Tatamigana." *Arctic* 51, no. 3 (September 1998).

———, eds. *An Apostle of the North: Memoirs of the Right Reverend William Carpenter Bompas.* Edmonton: University of Alberta Press, 2002.

———, eds. *Interpreting Canada's North: Selected Readings.* Toronto: Copp Clark Pitman, 1989.

Coates, Ken, Whitney Lackenbauer, Bill Morrison, and Greg Poelzer. *Arctic Front: Defending Canada in the Far North.* Toronto: Thomas Allen & Son, 2008.

Dathan, Wendy. *The Reindeer Botanist: Alf Erling Porsild, 1901–1977.* Calgary: University of Calgary Press, 2012.

Dick, Lyle. *Muskox Land: Ellesmere Island in the Age of Contact.* Calgary: University of Calgary Press, 2001.

———. "Robert Peary's North Polar Narratives and the Making of an American Icon." *American Studies* 45, no. 2 (2004): 5–34.

Dinwoodie, D. H. "Arctic Controversy: The 1925 Byrd-MacMillan Expedition Example." *Canadian Historical Review* 53, no. 1 (March 1972): 51–65.

Diubaldo, Richard. *Stefansson and the Canadian Arctic.* Montreal: McGill-Queen's University Press, 1978.

Dorion-Robitaille, Yolande. *Captain J. E. Bernier's Contribution to Canadian Sovereignty in the Arctic.* Ottawa: Department of Indian and Northern Affairs, 1978.

Eber, Dorothy Harley. *When the Whalers Were Up North: Inuit Memories from the Eastern Arctic.* Kingston: McGill-Queen's University Press, 1989.

Fogelson, Nancy. *Arctic Exploration and International Relations, 1900–1932.* Fairbanks: University of Alaska Press, 1992.

Francis, Daniel. *Arctic Chase. A History of Whaling in Canada's North.* St. John's: Breakwater Books, 1984.

Geller, Peter. *Northern Exposures: Photographing and Filming the Canadian North, 1920–45.* Vancouver: UBC Press, 2004.

Gilberg, Rolf. "Inughuit, Knud Rasmussen, and Thule." *Etudes/Inuit/Studies* 12, nos. 1–2 (1988): 45–55.

Granatstein, J. L. "A Fit of Absence of Mind: Canada's National Interest in the North to 1968." In *The Arctic in Question*, edited by E. J. Dosnan, 13–33. Toronto: Oxford University Press, 1976.

Grant, Shelagh. *Arctic Justice: On Trial for Murder, Pond Inlet, 1923.* Montreal and Kingston: McGill-Queen's University Press, 2002.

———. *Polar Imperative: A History of Sovereignty in North America.* Vancouver: Douglas & McIntyre, 2010.

———. *Sovereignty or Security? Government Policy in the Canadian North, 1936–1950.* Vancouver: University of British Columbia Press, 1988.

Guttridge, Leonard F. *Ghosts of Cape Sabine: The Harrowing True Story of the Greely Expedition.* New York: Putnam, 2000.

Herbert, Wally. *The Noose of Laurels: Robert E. Peary and the Race to the North Pole.* New York: Athenaeum, 1989.

Hilliker, John. *Canada's Department of External Affairs, Volume 1: The Early Years, 1909–1946.* Montreal and Kingston: McGill-Queen's University Press, 1990.

Hunt, William R. *Stef: A Biography of Vilhjalmur Stefansson, Canadian Arctic Explorer.* Vancouver: UBC Press, 1986.

Huntford, Roland. *Shackleton.* London: Hodder and Stoughton, 1985.

Jenness, Stuart E. *The Making of an Explorer: George Hubert Wilkins and the Canadian Arctic Expedition, 1913–1916.* Montreal & Kingston: McGill-Queen's University Press, 2004.

———. *Stefansson, Dr. Anderson and the Canadian Arctic Expedition, 1913–1918: A Story of Exploration, Science and Sovereignty.* Gatineau: Canadian Museum of Civilization, 2011.

Jessup, David Eric. "J. E. Bernier and the Assertion of Canadian Sovereignty in the Arctic." *American Review of Canadian Studies* 38, no. 4 (2008): 409–29.

Kenney, Gerard. *Ships of Wood and Men of Iron: A Norwegian-Canadian Saga of Exploration in the High Arctic.* Toronto: Dundurn, 2005.

Levere, Trevor H. "Vilhjalmur Stefansson, the Continental Shelf, and a New Arctic Continent." *British Journal for the History of Science* 12, no. 2 (June 1988): 233–47.

———. *Science and the Canadian Arctic: A Century of Exploration, 1818–1918.* Cambridge: Cambridge University Press, 1993.

Lloyd, Trevor. "Knud Rasmussen and the Arctic Islands Preserve." *Musk-Ox* 25 (1979): 85–90.

MacEachern, Alan. "J. E. Bernier's Claims to Fame." *Scientia Canadensis* 33, no. 2 (2010): 43–73.

Mackay, Daniel S. C. "James White: Canada's Chief Geographer, 1899–1909." *Cartographica* 19, no. 1 (Spring 1982): 51–61.

Mackinnon, C. S. "Canada's Eastern Arctic Patrol 1922–68." *Polar Record* 27, no. 161 (April 1991): 93–101.

McGoogan, Kenneth. *Race to the Polar Sea: The Heroic Adventures and Romantic Obsessions of Elisha Kent Kane.* Toronto: HarperCollins, 2008.

Mimeault, Mario. "A Dundee Ship in Canada's Arctic: SS *Diana* and William Wakeham's Expedition of 1897." *Northern Mariner* 8, no. 3 (1998): 51–61.

Morrison, David R. *The Politics of the Yukon Territory, 1898–1909.* Toronto: University of Toronto Press, 1968.

Morrison, William R. "Canadian Sovereignty and the Inuit of the Central and Eastern Arctic." *Etudes/Inuit/Studies* 10, nos. 1–2 (1986): 245–59.

———. "Eagle Over the Arctic: Americans in the Canadian North, 1867–1985." *Canadian Review of American Studies* (Spring 1987): 61–85.

———. *Showing the Flag: The Mounted Police and Canadian Sovereignty in the North, 1894–1925.* Vancouver: UBC Press, 1985.

———. *True North: The Yukon and Northwest Territories.* Toronto: Oxford University Press, 1998.

Niven, Jennifer. *Ada Blackjack: A True Story of Survival in the Arctic.* New York: Hyperion, 2003.

North, Dick. *The Lost Patrol.* Anchorage, Alaska: Northwest Publishing, 1978.

———. *The Mad Trapper of Rat River.* Toronto: Macmillan, 1972.

Osborn, Season L. "Closing the Front Door of the Arctic: Capt. Joseph E. Bernier's Role in Canadian Arctic Sovereignty." Unpublished M.A. thesis, Carleton University, 2003.

Palsson, Gish. *Travelling Passions: The Hidden Life of Vilhjalmur Stefansson.* Winnipeg: University of Manitoba Press, 2003.

Park, Robert W., and Douglas R. Stenton, "A Hans Krüger Arctic Expedition Cache on Axel Heiberg Island, Nunavut." *Arctic* 60, no. 1 (Mar. 2007): 1–6.

Pharand, Donat. *Canada's Arctic Waters in International Law.* Cambridge: Cambridge University Press, 1988.

Robinson, Michael F. *The Coldest Crucible: Arctic Exploration and American Culture.* Chicago: University of Chicago Press, 2006.

Ross, W. Gillies, *Whaling and Eskimos: Hudson Bay 1860–1915.* Ottawa: National Museums of Canada, 1975.

———, ed. *Arctic Whalers, Icy Seas: Narratives of the Davis Strait Whale Fishery.* Toronto: Irwin Publishing, 1985.

———, ed. *An Arctic Whaling Diary: The Journal of Captain George Comer in Hudson Bay, 1903–1905.* Toronto: University of Toronto Press, 1984.

Rothwell, Donald. *The Polar Regions and the Development of International Law.* Cambridge: Cambridge University Press, 1996.

Rowley, Graham. *Cold Comfort: My Love Affair with the Arctic*, 2nd ed. Montreal: McGill-Queen's University Press, 2007.

Saint-Pierre, Marjolaine. *Joseph-Elzéar Bernier: Capitaine et coureur des mers.* Sillery, Quebec: Septentrion, 2004.

Sandlos, John. *Hunters at the Margin: Native People and Wildlife Conservation in the Northwest Territories.* Vancouver: UBC Press, 2007.

Stone, Thomas. "Flux and Authority in a Subarctic Society: The Yukon Miners in the Nineteenth Century." *Ethnohistory* 30, no. 4 (1983): 203–16.

———. "Whalers and Missionaries at Herschel Island." *Ethnohistory* 28, no. 2 (1981): 101–24.

Thorleifsson, Thorleif Tobias. "Norway 'Must Really Drop Their Absurd Claims Such as That to the Otto Sverdrup Islands': Bi-Polar International Diplomacy – The Sverdrup Islands Question, 1902–1930." Unpublished M.A. thesis, Simon Fraser University, 2006.

Vaughan, Richard. *Northwest Greenland: A History.* Orono: University of Maine Press, 1991.

Waiser, William. "Canada Ox, Ovibos, Woolox ... Anything but Musk-Ox." In *For Purposes of Dominion: Essays in Honour of Morris Zaslow*, edited by Kenneth Coates and William R. Morrison, 189–200. Toronto: Captus Press, 1989.

Webb, Melody. "Arctic Saga: Vilhjalmur Stefansson's Attempt to Colonize Wrangel Island." *Pacific Historical Review* 61, no. 2 (May 1992): 215–39.

Zaslow, Morris. *The Northward Expansion of Canada, 1914–1967.* Toronto: McClelland & Stewart, 1988.

Index

A

B

C

G

H

I

J

K

L

M

N

O

P

T

U

V

W

Y

Z